WORLD POLITICS

Trend and Transformation

2014–2015 Edition

Charles William Kegley
Carnegie Council for Ethics in International Affairs
and
Shannon Lindsey Blanton
The University of Memphis

CENGAGE
Learning·

Australia · Brazil · Japan · Korea · Mexico · Singapore · Spain · United Kingdom · United States

CENGAGE
Learning

World Politics: Trend and Transformation, 2014–2015 Edition

Charles William Kegley, Shannon Lindsey Blanton

Product Director: Suzanne Jeans

Product Team Manager: Carolyn Merrill

Content Developer: Rebecca Green

Content Coordinator: Jessica Wang

Product Assistant: Abigail Hess

Senior Media Developer: Laura Hildebrand

Marketing Manager: Valerie Hartman

Senior Content Project Managers: Joshua Allen and Jessica Rasile

Senior Art Director: Linda May

Print Buyer: Fola Orekoya

Senior Rights Acquisitions Manager: Jennifer Meyer Dare

Production Service: Integra

Interior Designer: Pier 1 Design

Cover Designer: Pier 1 Design

Cover Images: YadvigaGr/Shutterstock

For product information and technology assistance, contact us at
Cengage Learning Customer & Sales Support, 1-800-354-9706

For permission to use material from this text or product, submit all requests online at **www.cengage.com/permissions**. Further permissions questions can be emailed to **permissionrequest@cengage.com**.

Library of Congress Control Number: 2013956463

Student Edition:

ISBN-13: 978-1-285-43727-9

ISBN-10: 1-285-43727-6

Wadsworth
20 Channel Center Street
Boston, MA 02210
USA

Cengage Learning is a leading provider of customized learning solutions with office locations around the globe, including Singapore, the United Kingdom, Australia, Mexico, Brazil and Japan. Locate your local office at **international.cengage.com/region**

Cengage Learning products are represented in Canada by Nelson Education, Ltd.

For your course and learning solutions, visit **www.cengage.com.**

Purchase any of our products at your local college store or at our preferred online store **www.CengageBrain.com.**

Instructors: Please visit **login.cengage.com** and log in to access instructor-specific resources.

Printed in Canada
1 2 3 4 5 6 7 16 15 14

Brief Contents

CONTENTS

CHAPTER 3

CHAPTER 4

CHAPTER 5

CHAPTER 6

PART 3: Confronting Armed Conflict   189

CHAPTER 7

THE THREAT OF ARMED CONFLICT TO THE WORLD   190

CHAPTER 8

THE PURSUIT OF POWER THROUGH ARMS AND ALLIANCES   227

CHAPTER 9

PART 4: Human Security, Prosperity, and Responsibility   309

CHAPTER 10

CHAPTER 11

INTERNATIONAL TRADE IN THE GLOBAL MARKETPLACE   **339**

CHAPTER 12

THE DEMOGRAPHIC AND CULTURAL DIMENSIONS OF GLOBALIZATION   **374**

CHAPTER 13

THE PROMOTION OF HUMAN DEVELOPMENT AND HUMAN RIGHTS

CHAPTER 14

GLOBAL RESPONSIBILITY FOR THE PRESERVATION OF THE ENVIRONMENT

Preface

Understanding twenty-first-century world politics requires up-to-date information, analysis, and interpretation. In a world undergoing constant and rapid change, it is imperative to accurately describe, explain, and predict the key events and issues unfolding in international affairs. These intellectual tasks must be performed well so that world citizens and policy makers can harness this knowledge and ground their decisions on the most pragmatic approaches to global problems available. Only informed interpretations of world conditions and trend trajectories, as well as cogent explanations of why they exist and how they are unfolding, can provide the tools necessary for understanding and improving the world. By presenting the leading ideas and the latest information available, *World Politics: Trend and Transformation* provides the tools necessary for understanding world affairs in our present period of history, for anticipating probable developments, and for thinking critically about the potential long-term impact of those developments on countries and individuals across the globe.

World Politics: Trend and Transformation aims to put both changes and continuities into perspective. It provides a picture of the evolving relations among all transnational actors, the historical developments that affect those actors' relationships, and the salient contemporary global trends that those interactions produce. The major theories scholars use to explain the dynamics underlying international relations—realism, liberalism, and constructivism, as well as feminist and Marxist interpretations—frame the investigation. That said, this book resists the temptation to oversimplify world politics with a superficial treatment that would mask complexities and distort realities. Moreover, the text refuses to substitute mere subjective opinion for evidence-based assessments and intentionally presents contending views so that students have a chance to critically evaluate the opposed positions and construct their own judgments about key issues. It fosters critical thinking by repeatedly asking students to assess the possibilities for the global future and its potential impact on their own lives.

OVERVIEW OF THE BOOK

To facilitate student learning and provide the tools and information for analyzing the complexities of world politics, this book is organized into five parts. Part 1 introduces the concepts central to understanding world politics, global trends, and their meaning. It introduces the leading theories used to interpret international relations and considers the processes and procedures by which transnational actors make decisions. Part 2 examines the globe's transnational actors—the great powers, the less developed countries of the "Global South," intergovernmental organizations (IGOs), and nongovernmental organizations (NGOs)—and looks at relations and interactions between them. Part 3 examines armed threats to world security, and places emphasis on contending ideas and theoretical perspectives about how to best confront armed conflict. Part 4 explores the ways in which human security and prosperity are truly global issues, and looks at the economic, demographic, and environmental dimensions of the global human condition. The book concludes with Part 5, which considers scenarios about the likely future of world politics and poses six questions raised by prevailing trends in order to stimulate further thinking about the global future.

CHANGES IN THE 2014–2015 EDITION

In order to keep you abreast of the latest developments, *World Politics* has always changed in response to unfolding events around our world. Since the publication of the 2013–2014 update edition in January 2013, numerous changes have taken place in international relations. To provide students the most current information, the entire text of this 2014–2015 edition has been revised to incorporate the latest global events and scholarly research.

Changes to Design, Presentation, and Pedagogical Aids

This 2014–2015 edition of *World Politics* features an attractive new interior design while retaining comprehensive and timely coverage of world politics and highly praised features from the prior edition. To enhance the flow of the book, there are five parts and fifteen chapters, with chapters focusing on armed conflict and the military preceding those on economics, human security, demographics, and the environment. A rich array of teaching and learning tools are integrated throughout this edition, including the "Controversy" boxes, "A Closer Look" boxes, numerous maps and illustrations, key glossary terms in the margins, online exercises, and listings at the end of chapters of "Suggested Readings." With this revised fifteenth edition, changes have further strengthened the structure and presentation of the material and provide additional pedagogical aids. Changes in this edition include:

New "Questions to Consider" section. This brand-new feature, provided at the beginning of every chapter, highlights the key questions that the particular chapter seeks to address. It provides a framework to guide student inquiry and, upon finishing the chapter, students should be equipped with the knowledge necessary to formulate their own answers to the questions. This feature can be used to foster class discussion and to assess understanding of the material.

A video resources program, provided in partnership with the Carnegie Council for Ethics in International Affairs (CCEIA), that highlights current international trends and issues. Through a partnership with the Carnegie Council for Ethics in International Affairs, *World Politics* provides an enhanced video resource program that is directly linked to the concepts and issues discussed in this book. Indicated by a CourseMate: Carnegie Council icon, videos can be access through links on the book's CourseMate site (students can access CourseMate through **www.cengagebrain.com**) or directly through the Carnegie Council's site at **www.ir101.org/kb**. There, you can see top international relations thinkers and practitioners apply *World Politics'* key terms and concepts in real-world applications. At the end of each chapter, you'll also be directed to Carnegie Council readings and video resources for more in-depth topics. The Carnegie Council is a nonpartisan, nonprofit educational institution whose mission is to be the voice for ethics in international affairs and to explore a key question: "How do you choose?" More information about the organization can be found at **www.carnegiecouncil.org**.

CARNEGIE COUNCIL *for Ethics in International Affairs*

ABOUT   PROGRAMS   STUDIO   PUBLICATIONS   EDUCATION   EVENTS   NEWS   SUPPORT

Contests and Activities » | World Politics Textbook | Concepts » | Course Ideas » | Bibliography » | **Books and Book Notes »**

Chapter 6: Nonstate Actors and the Quest for Global Community

This is Carnegie Council's companion guide of glossary terms and video resources to *World Politics: Trend and Transformation*, by Charles W. Kegley, Jr. and Shannon L. Blanton.

- Responsible Sovereignty
- Nongovernmental Organizations (NGOs)
- European Union
- Political Integration
- Nonstate Nations
- Ethnic Groups
- Indigenous Peoples
- Theocracy
- Militant Religious Movements
- Secession (Separative Revolt)
- Terrorism
- Civil Society

A Closer Look — Ethics and Humanitarian Intervention

Terrorism
PHILIP BOBBITT | OCTOBER 4, 2011

Philip Bobbitt Columbia University

Open Pop-up Player | Right-click to download

CourseMate

Carnegie Council Video:
Terrorism

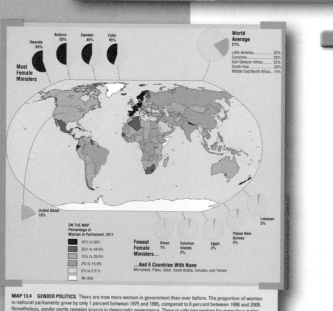

CONTROVERSY

HOW MIGHT COUNTRIES RESPOND TO A ZOMBIE OUTBREAK?

Zombies are a "popular figure in pop culture/entertainment and they are usually portrayed as being brought about through an outbreak or epidemic," as noted by researchers at Carleton University and the University of Ottawa (Munz et al., 2009, p. 133), who mathematically modeled the spread of a zombie infestation. Modeling the spread of a zombie outbreak, and assessing the relative effectiveness of various strategies within the lens of international relations theories, offers a fun way to think about how states might behave in wildly improbable (we hope) situations. But examining how countries might respond to a zombie outbreak allows students to explore whether and how the assumptions underlying the theories used to explain state, and individual, behavior hold up.

Consider these questions in reference to a zombie outbreak. What predictions would different systemic, state, and individual level theories make, and would it be of little consequence, or would some theories offer better guidance than others?

- **Structural realism.** Due to its emphasis on state actors, structural realism anticipates that some countries could misperceive the actions and intentions of others, and power politics could come into play, thereby complicating a global response to the global spread of a zombie outbreak. As its emphasis on relative gains suggests, "states could fail to cooperate with one another, and go so far as to squelch irredentist moves by the zombies" (Drezner, 2007).
- **Liberal institutionalism.** In contrast, liberal theories might view a zombie outbreak as a problem to be tackled for the betterment of the international community writ large. This perspective would anticipate that countries could coordinate efforts to combat the menace, perhaps drawing on international regimes and institutions that could foster collaboration in containing and directing the humanitarian response, much as international institutions could be helpful in combating the spread of a disease outbreak (such as a zombie outbreak (see Chapter 12)).
- **Social constructivism.** Emphasizing the importance of ideas and norms, social constructivism envisions a different response. It anticipates that the distinction between humans and zombies could give rise to an "us versus them—we aren't killed" norm. Alternatively, constructivists note the potential for a broader "that bands together all human beings (in recognition that they share the same state" (Drezner, 2007). Here again, we see the potential importance of group identity, where the boundaries of identity could hinge on whether one is opposed to zombies, or not.

WHAT DO YOU THINK?

- If you were the leader of a country, what international relations theory might best help you address the zombie menace?
- Reflect upon the "realist" and "liberal" predictions about state responses to global warming to the potential spread of a zombie epidemic. Which would have the greatest impact upon international efforts to contain the threat and mobilize a deal with these threats?
- Should a country worry about the relative, or absolute, gains of others? Draw on realism, liberalism, and constructivism to explain.

A Closer Look

THE UNITED NATIONS AND THE SYRIAN CIVIL WAR

Inspired in part by the Arab Spring, hostilities between Syrian rebels and forces loyal to Syria's president Bashar al-Assad began in March 2011 as demonstrators took to the streets in peaceful protest of the imprisonment and torture of a number of young students for anti-government graffiti. After troops fired on the rioting crowds, however, the protests turned into armed conflict over the legitimacy of al-Assad's rule. Fighting continued between the Syrian army and various opposition forces, and as of May 2013, UN General Assembly president Vuk Jeremic estimated that at "least 80,000 have perished since the start of the hostilities, with most of those casualties believed to be civilians" (Nichols, 2013). The UN additionally estimates that at least 4 million Syrians have been displaced by the violence (Abedine et al, 2013).

Despite considerable international concern over the conflict in Syria, there has been division within the United Nations, particularly among the Security Council members, over the extent to which it should intervene. The United States and many other Western governments have condemned the Syrian government's brutal response to the protests, and called for al-Assad to step down from power. They have supported a stronger role for the UN in addressing the violent conflict. Many supporters see UN intervention as supported by the UN Charter, which envisions the protection of human rights as the responsibility of global society. Unanimously adopted by UN members in 2005, the *Responsibility to Protect* doctrine also calls for intervention by the international community if a state fails to protect its citizens from war, ethnic cleansing, genocide, and crimes against humanity.

However, critics of intervention argue that action motivated by nonhumanitarian reasons is in contradiction to the UN Charter, which rests on the principle of sovereignty and prohibits forceful intervention that violates the political independence and territorial integrity of any state. China and Russia have opposed UN actions that they see as constituting intervention into the internal concerns of a sovereign state. Although they have joined the United States and others in calling for a peace process that would bring an end to the civil war, they repeatedly have used their veto rights as members of the UN Security Council to block decisive UN action beyond the supervision mission already in place (UN, 2012). Russia has explicitly criticized UN resolutions, such as the one passed by the UN Human Rights Council in May 2013 that condemned the intervention of foreign combatants on the government's side, as, according to Russian Foreign Minister Sergey Lavrov, "odious and one-sided."

This gridlock, and the United Nation's inability to stop the violence in Syria, raises questions about the efficacy of the organization. It also highlights the tension between a state's sovereign authority over its territory, its responsibility to protect and provide for the compelling needs of its own people, and the grounds for intervention by the international community.

WATCH THE VIDEO:

Carnegie Council Video:
"Ethics and Humanitarian Intervention"

ON THE MAP
Percentage of
Women in Parliament, 2011

MAP 13.4 GENDER POLITICS There are now more women in government than ever before. The proportion of women in national parliaments grew by only 1 percent between 1975 and 1995, compared to 8 percent between 1998 and 2008. Nonetheless, gender parity remains scarce in democratic governance. There is only one woman for every four males in legislatures around the world, and in mid-2013 only 17 heads of state were female. According to the United Nations, "countries with 'first past the post' electoral systems without any type of quota arrangements will not reach the 40 percent threshold of women in public office until near to the end of this century" (UNIFEM, 2013).

☐ **New and revised "A Closer Look" and "Controversy" boxes that highlight real-world events and feature essential debates.** First introduced in the fourteenth edition and revised for this subsequent edition, "A Closer Look" boxes stimulate student application of concepts and theories to their understanding of real-world events. This pedagogical feature examines newsworthy issues, includes a short thematically relevant video segment prepared by the Carnegie Council, and poses "You Decide" questions to further develop critical thinking skills and prompt students to apply the main ideas to current global affairs issues and events. The long-praised "Controversy" boxes each focus on a major issue on which there are opposing positions and conclude with "What Do You Think?" questions. This pedagogical aid encourages students to consider rival viewpoints and formulate their own perspective. Several brand-new "A Closer Look" and "Controversy" boxes are included in this edition, and are excellent starting points for class discussions or research papers.

☐ **Revised, up-to-date map and illustration program.** One of the most popular pedagogical features of the text, the illustration program, has been revised to broaden the book's coverage, provoke interest, and enable students to visualize the central developments and most recently available data. Students today are often woefully uninformed about world geography, and the extensive map program helps remedy this problem. This 2014–2015 edition of *World Politics* includes 19 brand-new maps, figures, and tables—in addition to revisions that update 24 other maps and 19 other figures—to introduce the timeliest of topics and incorporate the latest data available.

There are 28 brand-new photos, along with detailed captions explaining their relevance to the larger issues discussed in the text.

A revised glossary of key term definitions. This reference tool appears at the end of the text, so students can easily access terms they may not remember from previous chapters. New terms have been added to keep students up to date with key concepts in the study of world politics. The glossary also indicates the chapter in which the term first appears.

Enhanced end-of-chapter coverage. In this edition, revised listings of "Suggested Readings" are included at the end of each chapter to bring attention to the most recent and authoritative scholarship on discussed topics. Also at the end of each chapter, there is an alphabetical listing of the "Key Terms" introduced, as well as a listing of video resources in addition to those prompted by the icons placed throughout the chapter. There is a link provided at the conclusion of each chapter encouraging students to use a host of online materials to further enhance and assess their knowledge and understanding of the presented material. These include an interactive quiz, flashcards, and simulations, as well as other pedagogical aids to facilitate teaching and learning.

STUDY. APPLY. ANALYZE.

Changes to Content by Chapter

This text continues to take pride in identifying and reporting the most recent developments in international affairs and in providing the latest data on the most significant related trends. The 2014–2015 edition covers the most important issues on the global agenda, from the spread of nuclear capabilities to the continued oppression of people around the globe, from instability and the outbreak of armed conflict to the volatility of global finance and worldwide poverty, from risks posed by global warming to the implications of technological innovation.

As always, this leading text incorporates many thematic shifts in emphasis that capture the latest changes in the understanding of key issues and problems in our world. Kegley and Blanton have revisited every passage and the entire text has been revised to reflect the most current information available since the 2013–2014 edition was released. The authors integrate clear explanations of theoretical arguments and concepts with thorough and engaging coverage of substantive issues, all supported with references to prevailing scholarly literature and policy positions. The result is a comprehensive and compelling presentation and analysis of global trends and transformations.

Without identifying every revision in this new edition, the following descriptions pinpoint the most important updates in each chapter in the 2014–2015 edition:

Chapter 1, "Exploring World Politics," succinctly presents the book's approach and organization, with a new introduction incorporating recently available information on current events. Revised discussion of the United States' relationship with Cuba is presented in the "A Closer Look" box, and this chapter includes updated coverage of the conflict in Syria as well as a the prospect of a rising China as a transformative phenomenon in world politics.

Chapter 2, "Theories of World Politics," contains a revised discussion of theories and the explanation of change. The chapter takes a close look at variants of realism and liberalism, and compares the two. It also expands discussion of constructivism and feminism, and the manner in which these perspectives enhance understanding of world politics. Additionally, coverage of theories with a Marxist perspective has been revised and expanded.

Chapter 3, "Theories of International Decision Making," rounds out Part 1 of *World Politics* with a survey of decision-making theories. The discussion of the "three-part framework" that influences decision making has been reorganized and revised, with discussion of individual and internal sources of international decision making preceding that on global factors. Enhanced discussion and a brand-new figure provide insights into the role of personality attributes and facilitate understanding of leaders' motivations and behavior.

Chapter 4, "Rivalries and Relations among the Great Powers," contains updated discussion of the military and economic power of the major powers, with revised data on military expenditures and global prosperity. There is enhanced discussion about the prospect of the relative decline of the United States, and a new "A Closer Look" box examines the issue of whether China poses a serious challenge to U.S. hegemony. Leadership changes in several major powers are noted, and there is updated discussion about the nature and status of Russo–U.S. and Sino–U.S. relations.

Chapter 5, "The Global South in a World of Powers," is revised to reflect changes in the challenges facing Global South countries and the possibilities for narrowing the divide between wealthy and poor countries. Using the most recently available data, updates have been included on population growth in the Global South, varied levels of development around the world, the continuing digital divide, and the challenge of corruption. The chapter also examines money flows to the Global South—including foreign aid, remittances, trade, and foreign direct investment. Tables, figures, and maps have been thoroughly revised to reflect these changes.

Chapter 6, "Nonstate Actors and the Quest for Global Community," includes revised discussion of the many intergovernmental and nongovernmental organizations that play a role in world politics. Revised discussion focuses on the United Nations (UN), and an all-new graph highlights the budgetary challenges it faces. There is enhanced discussion of the World Bank under the leadership of Jim Yong Kim, the prospects for reducing global poverty, expansion and change within the European Union, and activities of IGOs, NGOs, and other nonstate actors around the world. A brand-new "A Closer Look" box examines the role of the United Nations in the conflict in Syria.

Chapter 7, "The Threat of Armed Conflict to the World," begins Part 3 of *World Politics* with updated discussion on armed conflicts and failed states, as well as the prospects for democratic peace, economic peace, third-party arbitration, and the nature of a credible commitment. Also covered are the implications of the youth bulge, poverty, regime type, education, and the treatment of women for conflict, as well as discussion of continued uprisings across the Arab world. Revised maps include those of failed states around the world as well as levels of global peace, and the most recent data are incorporated into discussion of intrastate conflict and coup attempts.

Chapter 8, "The Pursuit of Power through Arms and Alliances," introduces the core premises and policy prescriptions underlying realist approaches to war and peace. The latest international trends in military readiness are captured in updated data on military expenditures, military technology, and the proliferation of nuclear and chemical weapons. A new map about the possession and use of ballistic missiles around the world is presented, as well as a brand-new controversy box that considers the pros and cons of the use of drones in warfare. The chapter also includes enhanced discussion of military intervention and alliances.

Chapter 9, "The Quest for Peace through International Law and Collective Security," focuses on liberal and constructivist paths to peace. Enhanced coverage focuses on the current role and future prospects of the United Nations as a global peacekeeper. There is updated discussion of various treaties and agreements, nuclear capabilities, and the prevalence of landmines around the world. In this edition, coverage of the global judicial framework, including the International Criminal Court, has been revised to reflect changes in both purpose and membership.

Chapter 10, "The Globalization of International Finance," contains enhanced discussion of globalization and its implications for international finance. The discussion of the 2008 Global Economic Crisis and its consequences in countries around the world has been updated to include the latest information and expert analysis. Discussion on foreign direct investment, balance of trade, and inflation has been revised with the latest figures and trends. There is also revised coverage of women in business and government, as well as the activities of the IMF and G-20.

Chapter 11, "International Trade in the Global Marketplace," continues coverage of the international political economy. There is revised discussion of the globalization of trade and labor, with updated coverage of global exports and foreign direct investment. The chapter proceeds with a revised discussion of the World Trade Organization and the handling of disputes, the effectiveness of sanctions and subsidies as policy tools, the state of economic freedom around the world, and the influence of multinational corporations. A brand-new map illustrates the extent of regional trade agreements, and there is expanded discussion of the importance of plurilateral agreements, supply chains, and "nearsourcing" for global trade.

Chapter 12, "The Demographic and Cultural Dimensions of Globalization," examines trends in global population changes and the challenges they pose. There is revised discussion of the demographic divide between the Global North and Global South, as well as issues related to global migration, the challenges faced by global refugees, and a revised figure that reflects the latest trend toward greater urbanization and the proliferation of megacities. Updated coverage addresses the threat of disease faced by people around the world and the implications of the diffusion of communications technology for freedom and social movements. Also included is an all-new map and revised figure that address the issue of aging populations around the world.

Chapter 13, "The Promotion of Human Development and Human Rights," includes revised discussion of the divide in human development between the Global North and Global South, with updated data on poverty, education, democracy, and life expectancy. There is enhanced discussion and a brand-new map of the use of a death penalty in countries across the world as punishment for infractions against the laws and norms of a society. Coverage of the status of women includes updated information on gender inequalities, the vast number of female refugees, and the role of women in public office. Discussion of children's human rights is revised, especially their vulnerability to violence in conflict zones.

Chapter 14, "Global Responsibility for the Preservation of the Environment," puts into perspective an entire range of global ecological issues, including revised discussions of climate change and global warming, drought, desertification, and deforestation. There is enhanced discussion of ecopolitics addressing the planet's carrying capacity, the status of the Montreal Protocol, and the potential benefits and risks associated with various forms of alternative energy. The discussion of man-made climate change and extreme weather events has been revised and expanded, with an all-new graph depicting the trend in average global temperature for more than a century. Also included in this chapter is enhanced discussion of food crises and riots around the world.

Chapter 15, "Looking Ahead at Global Trends and Transformations." The chapter continues to inventory insights from philosophers and policy makers about the interpretation of the global condition. It introduces six leading debates about the global future, with this edition considering the challenges posed by the increasing use of drones for surveillance and warfare, the extent to which the world has a responsibility to respond to global atrocities, the promise of advancements in communication and access to information around the world, the possibility of space as a growing frontier in international relations, and the potential of technological developments to shape the future of energy. The chapter concludes with a challenge to students to formulate their own ideas about the possibilities for humanity's common future.

SUPPLEMENTS

The publisher proudly offers the following state-of-the-art supplements prepared specifically for *World Politics: Trend and Transformation.*

INSTRUCTORS...

Access your *World Politics* resources via www.cengage.com/login.

Log in using your Cengage Learning single sign-on user name and password, or create a new instructor account by clicking on "New Faculty User" and following the instructions.

STUDENTS...

Access your *World Politics* resources via www.cengagebrain.com/shop/ISBN/9781285437279

If you purchased CourseMate access with your book, enter your access code and click "Register." You can also purchase CourseMate access here separately through the "Study Tools" tab or access the free companion website through the "Free Materials" tab.

International Relations CourseMate
PAC ISBN: 9781285450339 | IAC ISBN: 9781285450353

CourseMate brings course concepts to life with interactive learning, study, and exam preparation tools that support the printed textbook. Interactive quizzes, audio summaries, and flashcards help students master key concepts and prepare for their exams. Video activities, case studies, animated learning modules, simulations, and timelines bring concepts to life. The Carnegie Council videos referenced in the text can be accessed through CourseMate. The International Relations NewsWatch is a real-time news and information resource, updated daily, that includes interactive maps, videos, podcasts, and hundreds of articles from leading journals, magazines, and newspapers from the United States and the world. It's a great resource for current events based assignments. Also included is the KnowNow! International Relations Blog, which highlights three current events stories per week and consists of a succinct analysis of the story, multimedia, and discussion-starter questions. Instructors can use CourseMate's Engagement Tracker to assess student preparation and engagement in the course, and watch student comprehension soar as their class works with the textbook-specific website.

Included within CourseMate is MindTap Reader, Cengage Learning's re-imagination of the traditional eBook, specifically designed for how students assimilate content and media assets in a fully online—and often mobile—reading environment. MindTap Reader combines thoughtful navigation ergonomics, advanced student annotation support and a high level of instructor driven personalization through the placement of inline documents and media assets. These features create an engaging student reading experience further enhanced through tightly integrated web apps (e.g., social media, note-taking, and utilities) that ultimately deliver a holistic learning tool driving immediacy, relevancy, and engagement for today's learners.

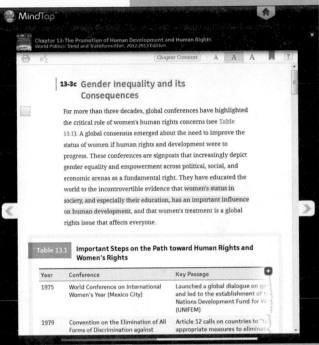

Look for CourseMate icons in the margins of the text for activity suggestions to complement your reading. Instructors can access their course via **www.cengage.com/login**. CourseMate for students can come packaged with the text (see the access card that comes with the book for registration details) or optionally purchased through **www.cengagebrain.com.**

Simulation:
Realism v. Liberalism

Free Companion Website
ISBN: 9781285437354

A free companion website for *World Politics: Trend and Transformation* accessible through **www.cengagebrain.com** allows access to chapter-specific interactive learning tools including flashcards, quizzes, glossaries, and more.

Online PowerLecture with Cognero®
ISBN: 9781285775456

PowerLecture is an all-in-one multimedia online resource for instructors' class preparation, presentation, and testing. Accessible through **www.cengage.com/login** with your faculty account, you will find available for download: book-specific Microsoft® PowerPoint® presentations; a Test Bank in both Microsoft® Word® and Cognero® formats; an Instructor Manual; Microsoft® PowerPoint® Image Slides; and a JPEG Image Library.

The Test Bank, offered in Microsoft Word® and Cognero® formats, contains learning objective–specific multiple-choice and essay questions for each chapter. Cognero® is a flexible, online system that allows you to author, edit, and manage test bank content for Kegley/Blanton's *World Politics: Trend and Transformation, 2014–2015*. Create multiple test versions instantly and deliver through your LMS from your classroom, or wherever you may be, with no special installs or downloads required. This edition's Test Bank is authored by Kristina Mitchell of Texas Tech University.

The Instructor's Manual contains chapter-specific learning objectives, an outline, key terms with definitions, and a chapter summary. Additionally, the Instructor's Manual features a critical thinking question, lecture launching suggestion, and an in-class activity for each learning objective. This edition's Instructor's Manual is authored by Lucas McMillan of Lander University.

The Microsoft PowerPoint® presentations are ready-to-use, visual outlines of each chapter. These presentations are easily customized for your lectures and offered along with chapter-specific Microsoft PowerPoint® Image Slides and JPEG Image Libraries.

Access your Online PowerLecture at **www.cengage.com/login**.

CourseReader 0-30: International Relations
PAC ISBN: 9781111480608 | IAC ISBN: 9781111480592

CourseReader: International Relations allows instructors to create a customized reader in just minutes. This affordable, fully customizable online reader provides access to thousands of permissions-cleared readings, articles, primary sources, and audio and video selections from the regularly updated Gale research library database. Each selection opens with a descriptive introduction to provide context, and concludes with critical-thinking and multiple-choice questions to reinforce key points. CourseReader is loaded with convenient tools like highlighting, printing, note-taking, and downloadable PDFs and MP3 audio files for each reading. It can be bundled with your current textbook, sold alone, or integrated into your learning management system. CourseReader 0–30 allows access to up to 30 selections in the reader. Please contact your Cengage sales representative for details.

ACKNOWLEDGMENTS

Many people—in fact, too many to identify and thank individually—have contributed to the development of this leading textbook in international relations, including Eugene R. Wittkopf, who served as coauthor of the first six editions. We are thankful for the constructive comments, advice, and data provided by an array of scholars and colleagues. These include:

The reviewers for this edition:

Duane Adamson, Brigham Young University – Idaho

Daniel Allen, Anderson University

Christopher R. Cook, University of Pittsburgh at Johnstown

Rebecca Cruise, University of Oklahoma

Agber Dimah, Chicago State University

John Freeman, University of Minnesota–Minneapolis

Todd Myers, Grossmont College

Jeff Ringer, Brigham Young University

Seth Weinberger, University of Puget Sound

Past reviewers and other contributors to this text:

Ruchi Anand, American Graduate School of International Relations and Diplomacy in Paris

Osmo Apunen, University of Tampere

Bossman Asare, Graceland University

Chad Atkinson, University of Illinois

Andrew J. Bacevich, Boston University

Yan Bai, Grand Rapids Community College

George Belzer, Johnson County Community College

John Boehrer, University of Washington

Pamela Blackmon, Penn State Altoona

Robert Blanton, The University of Memphis

Linda P. Brady, University of North Carolina at Greensboro

Leann Brown, University of Florida

Dan Caldwell, Pepperdine University

John H. Calhoun, Palm Beach Atlantic University

John Candido, La Trobe University

Colin S. Cavell, Bluefield State College

Roger A. Coate, Georgia College & State University

Jonathan E. Colby, Carlyle Group in Washington, D.C.

Phyllis D. Collins, Keswick Management Inc. in New York City

Reverend George Crow, Northeast Presbyterian Church

Jonathan Davidson, European Commission

Philippe Dennery, J-Net Ecology Communication Company in Paris

Drew Dickson, Atlantic Council of the United States

Agber Dimah, Chicago State University

Gregory Domin, Mercer University

Thomas Donaldson, Wharton School of the University of Pennsylvania

Nicole Detraz, The University of Memphis

Zach Dorfman, Carnegie Council for Ethics in International Affairs

Ayman I. El-Dessouki and Kemel El-Menoufi, Cairo University

Sid Ellington, University of Oklahoma

Robert Fatton, University of Virginia

Matthias Finger, Columbia University

Eytan Gilboa, Bar-Ilan University in Israel

Giovanna Gismondi, University of Oklahoma

Srajan Gligorijevic, Defense and Security Studies Centre of the G-17 Plus Institute in Belgrade Serbia

Richard F. Grimmett, Congressional Research Office

Ted Robert Gurr, University of Maryland

Aref N. Hassan, St. Cloud State University

Russell Hardin, New York University

James E. Harf, Maryville University in St. Louis

Cristian A. Harris, North Georgia College and State University

Charles Hermann, Texas A&M University

Margaret G. Hermann, Syracuse University

Stephen D. Hibbard, Shearman & Sterling LLP

Steven W. Hook, Kent State University

Jack Hurd, Nature Conservatory

Lisa Huffstetler, The University of Memphis

Patrick James, University of Southern California

Loch Johnson, University of Georgia

Christopher M. Jones, Northern Illinois University

Christopher Joyner, Georgetown University

Boris Khan, American Military University

Michael D. Kanner, University of Colorado

Mahmoud Karem, Egyptian Foreign Service

Deborah J. Kegley, Kegley International, Inc.

Mary V. Kegley, Kegley Books in Wytheville, Virginia

Susan Kegley, University of California-Berkeley

Julia Kennedy, Carnegie Council for Ethics in International Affairs

Lidija Kos-Stanišic, University of Zagreb in Croatia

Matthias Kranke, University of Tier

Barbara Kyker, The University of Memphis

Imtiaz T. Ladak, Projects International in Washington, D.C.

Jack Levy, Rutgers University

Carol Li, Taipei Economic and Cultural Office, New York

Urs Luterbacher, Graduate Institute of International and Development Studies in Geneva

Gen. Jeffrey D. McCausland, U.S. Army War College in Carlisle, Pennsylvania

James McCormick, Iowa University

Kelly A. McCready, Maria College, Albany, New York

Karen Ann Mingst, University of Kentucky

James A. Mitchell, California State University

Mahmood Monshipouri, San Francisco State University

Robert Morin, Western Nevada Community College

Donald Munton, University of Northern British Columbia

Ahmad Noor, Youth Parliament Pakistan

Evan O'Neil, Carnegie Council for Ethics in International Affairs

Anthony Perry, Henry Ford Community College

Jeffrey Pickering, Kansas State University

Desley Sant Parker, United States Information Agency

Albert C. Pierce, U.S. Naval Academy

Alex Platt, Carnegie Council for Ethics in International Affairs

Ignacio de la Rasilla, Université de Genève

James Ray, Vanderbilt University

Gregory A. Raymond, Boise State University

Andreas Rekdal, Carnegie Council for Ethics in International Affairs

Neil R. Richardson, University of Wisconsin

Peter Riddick, Berkhamsted Collegiate

James N. Rosenau, George Washington University

Joel Rosenthal, Carnegie Council for Ethics in International Affairs

Tapani Ruokanen, Suomen Kuvalehti, Finland

Alpo M. Rusi, Finnish Ambassador to Switzerland

Jan Aart Scholte, University of Warwick, UK

Rebecca R. Sharitz, International Association for Ecology

Shalendra D. Sharma, University of San Francisco

Richard H. Shultz, Fletcher School of Law and Diplomacy, Tufts University

Dragan R. Simic', Centre for the Studies of the USA in Belgrade, Serbia

Michael J. Siler, University of California

Christopher Sprecher, Texas A&M University

Jelena Subotic, Georgia State University

Bengt Sundelius, National Defense College in Stockholm

David Sylvan, Graduate Institute of International

and Development Studies in Geneva

William R. Thompson, Indiana University

Clayton L. Thyne, University of Kentucky

Rodney Tomlinson, U.S. Naval Academy

Deborah Tompsett-Makin, Riverside Community College, Norco Campus

John Tuman, University of Nevada, Las Vegas

Denise Vaughan, Bellevue Community College

Rob Verhofstad, Radmoud University in Nijmegen, the Netherlands

William C. Vocke, Jr., Carnegie Council for Ethics in International Affairs

Robert Weiner, University of Massachusetts/Boston

Jonathan Wilkenfeld, University of Maryland

Alex Woodson, Carnegie Council for Ethics in International Affairs

Samuel A. Worthington, InterAction

Also helpful was the input provided by graduate students William Wagstaff and Ashley Huddleston at The University of Memphis, who provided invaluable research assistance. The always helpful and accommodating project manager Indumathy Gunasekaran with Integra and Photo Researcher Aiswarya Narayanan with PreMediaGlobal made valuable contributions to this book. In addition, also deserving of special gratitude are our highly skilled, dedicated, and helpful editors at Cengage: Product Team Manager Carolyn Merrill and Content Developer Rebecca Green, who exercised extraordinary professionalism in guiding the process that brought this edition into print, assisted by the project management of Joshua Allen and Jessica Rasile. Gratitude is also expressed to the always instructive advice of Valerie Hartman, Cengage's skilled Political Science Marketing Manager.

Charles William Kegley
Shannon Lindsey Blanton

Kegley & Blanton, Cengage Learning, 2015

CHARLES WILLIAM KEGLEY is currently serving on the board of trustees of the Carnegie Council for Ethics in International Affairs. A past president of the International Studies Association, Kegley holds the title of Pearce Distinguished Professor of International Relations Emeritus at the University of South Carolina. A graduate of the American University (B.A.) and Syracuse University (Ph.D.) and a Pew Faculty Fellow at Harvard University, Kegley previously served on the faculty at Georgetown University, and has held visiting professorships at the University of Texas, Rutgers University, the People's University of China, and the Institute Universitaire de Hautes Études Internationales Et du Développement in Geneva Switzerland. He is also a recipient of the *Distinguished Scholar Award* of the Foreign Policy Analysis Section of the International Studies Association. A founding partner of Kegley International, Inc. (a publishing, research, and consulting foundation), Kegley has authored more than 50 scholarly books (and over 100 articles in journals), including coauthorship with Gregory A. Raymond for Cengage of five editions of *The Global Future*, as well as with Eugene R. Wittkopf seven editions of *American Foreign Policy: Pattern and Process.*

SHANNON LINDSEY BLANTON is Professor of Political Science at The University of Memphis, where she is also the vice provost for undergraduate programs. She oversees all undergraduate programs and provides leadership for curriculum development, general education, retention programming, the Center for International Programs and Services, the Honors Program, Learning

Communities, and academic advising services. She is a past department chair and undergraduate coordinator, and has served nationally as a facilitator for leadership development in higher education. A graduate of Georgia College (B.A.), the University of Georgia (M.A.), and the University of South Carolina (Ph.D.), she has received numerous research awards and was named in 2007 as the recipient of The University of Memphis' esteemed *Alumni Association Distinguished Research in the Social Sciences and Business Award*. She has served on a number of editorial boards, including those for four of the discipline's foremost journals, *International Studies Quarterly*, *Foreign Policy Analysis*, *International Interactions*, and *International Studies Perspectives*.

Professors Kegley and Blanton have individually published extensively in leading scholarly journals, including *Alternatives*, *American Journal of Political Science*, *Armed Forces and Society*, *Asian Forum*, *The Brown Journal of International Affairs*, *Business and Society*, *Comparative Political Studies*, *Conflict Management and Peace Science*, *Conflict Quarterly*, *Cooperation and Conflict*, *Ethics and International Affairs*, *The Fletcher Forum of World Affairs*, *Foreign Policy Analysis*, *Futures Research Quarterly*, *Harvard International Review*, *International Interactions*, *International Organization*, *International Politics*, *International Studies Quarterly*, *The Jerusalem Journal of International Relations*, *The Journal of Conflict Resolution*, *The Journal of Peace Research*, *The Journal of Politics*, *Journal of Political and Military Sociology*, *Journal of Third World Studies*, *The Korean Journal of International Studies*, *Leadership*, *Orbis*, *Social Science Journal*, and *Western Political Quarterly*.

Together Kegley and Blanton have coauthored publications appearing in *The Brown Journal of World Affairs*, *Futures Research Quarterly*, *Mediterranean Quarterly*, and *Rethinking the Cold War*, as well as multiple editions of *World Politics* (since the twelfth edition's 2009–2010 update).

DEDICATION

To my loving wife Debbie and the Carnegie Council for Ethics in International
Affairs, in appreciation for its invaluable contribution to building through education a
more just and secure world
– Charles William Kegley

To my husband Rob and our sons Austin and Cullen, in appreciation
of their love and support
– Shannon Lindsey Blanton

PART 1

NASA Images

TREND AND TRANSFORMATION IN WORLD POLITICS

THESE ARE TURBULENT TIMES, INSPIRING BOTH ANXIETY AND HOPE. What lies ahead for the world? What are we to think about the global future? Part 1 of this book introduces you to the study of world politics in a period of rapid change. It opens a window on the many unfolding trends, some of them moving in contrary directions. Chapter 1 explains our perceptions of global events and realities can lead to distorted understandings,

A WORLD WITHOUT BORDERS

As viewed from outer space, planet Earth looks as if it has continents without borders. Reflecting on his space shuttle experience, astronaut Sultan bin Salman Al-Saud

"The world is at a critical juncture, and so are you ... Go ahead and make your plans ... and don't stop learning. But be open to the detours that lead to new discoveries."

—*Kofi Annan, former UN secretary-general*

CHAPTER 1
Exploring World Politics

AP Photos/Aleppo Media Center AMC

WHAT FUTURE FOR HUMANKIND?
Many global trends are sweeping across a transforming planet. Among those are popular movements calling for greater political representation and improved human security for some of the world's 7 billion people. Pictured here during a demonstration in Aleppo, Syria on June 28, 2013, protestors holding Syrian revolution flags call for the end of the repressive Ba'ath Party government.

QUESTIONS TO CONSIDER

- *What challenges does investigating international relations pose?*
- *How do perceptions influence our images of global realities?*
- *How do we conceptualize and discuss world politics?*
- *Who are the primary transnational actors?*
- *What are levels of analysis?*

Imagine yourself returning home from a two-week vacation on a tropical island where you had no access to the news. The trip gave you a well-deserved break before starting a new school term, but now you are curious about what has happened while you were away. As you glance at a newspaper, the headlines catch your eye. Death and destruction rage across the Middle East and North Africa. Although fighting and heavy casualties persist in Syria as insurgents seek regime change, Russia supports the incumbent government and opposes direct international intervention to stop the rebellion. Violent conflict in South Sudan continues, which is also beset with food shortages and widespread corruption. The elected Egyptian leader Mohamed Morsi was ousted by a military coup and the legacy of the Arab Spring in Egypt, as elsewhere, remains uncertain. Other countries in North Africa, such as Tunisia and Mali, face the scourge of ethnic and religiously motivated sectarian violence. Libya's new government faces serious challenges to its authority from rebellious militias. Violence persists in Iraq and Afghanistan as the United States withdraws its troops after more than a decade of war and seeks to set up an effective security force in those countries.

As you ride home from the airport, you hear a radio broadcast about economic conditions around the world. China's economic growth is slowing, although estimates by the International Monetary Fund (IMF) still anticipate a healthy 7.7 percent growth in 2014. Far less hopeful, the situation in Greece is dire as it faces austerity measures to address rampant debt and poor public finance. Although financial conditions across Europe are tumultuous, there are signs that some European countries, such as Great Britain, Germany, and France, may be slowly emerging from the recession. Likewise, it appears that the economic decline in the United States is leveling off, although there are concerns that rapid cuts in government spending may reverse these gains. You hope that conditions improve before you graduate and enter the job market.

Shortly after arriving home, you connect to the Internet and read about the poor health of the anti-apartheid revolutionary and former president of South Africa, Nelson Mandela. You also learn that ninety-five people died, and over a thousand were injured, in two earthquakes in northwestern China. Additionally, the former U.S. National Security Agency contractor Edward Snowden, who gave journalists secret documents that described extensive digital surveillance activities, seeks political asylum to avoid prosecution by the U.S. government on charges of espionage.

Finally, while listening to CNN later that evening, you hear several other reports: There are concerns over efforts by Pakistan, India, and Iran to enhance their nuclear capabilities and fears of further nuclear tests by North Korea. In France, protests have erupted by Muslims opposing the fine imposed by the government on a woman who dressed in a burka in defiance of the ban on such concealing clothing. In addition, there is coverage of the violence by drug cartels in Mexico, and you worry about whether this will affect your plans for a study abroad tour over the winter break.

The scenario just described is not hypothetical. The events identified record what actually occurred during the month of July 2013. Undoubtedly, many individuals experienced fear and confusion during this period. But it is, uncomfortably, not so different from other eras. Putting this information about unfolding events together, you cannot help but be reminded that international affairs matter and events around the world powerfully affect your circumstances and future. The "news" you received is not really new, because it echoes many old stories from the past about the growing sea of turmoil sweeping the contemporary world. Nevertheless, the temptation to wish that this depressing, chaotic world would just go away is overwhelming. If only the unstable world would stand still long enough for a sense of predictability and order to prevail.... Alas, that does not appear likely. You cannot escape the world or control its turbulence, and you cannot single-handedly alter its character.

We are all a part of this world. If we are to live adaptively amid the fierce winds of global change, then we must face the challenge of discovering the dynamic properties of *world politics*. Because world events increasingly influence every person, all can benefit from investigating how the global system works and how changes are remaking our political and economic lives. Only through learning how our own decisions and behavior, as well as those of powerful state governments and nonstate transnational actors, contribute to the global condition, and how all people and groups in turn are heavily conditioned by changes in world politics, can we address what former U.S. President Bill Clinton defined as "the question of our time—whether we can make change our friend and not our enemy."

world politics

The study of how global actors' activities entail the exercise of influence to achieve and defend their goals and ideals, and how it affects the world at large.

Carnegie Council Video: World Politics

Education either functions as an instrument which is used to facilitate integration of the younger generation into the logic of the present system and bring about conformity or it becomes the practice of freedom, the means by which men and women deal critically and creatively with reality and discover how to participate in the transformation of their world.

—Richard Shaull, American theologian

THE CHALLENGE OF INVESTIGATING INTERNATIONAL RELATIONS

It is critical that we perceive our times accurately in order to best understand the political convulsions that confront the globe's 7 billion people. Yet interpreting the world in which we now live and anticipating what lies ahead for the globe's future—and yours—presents formidable challenges. Indeed, it could be the most difficult task you will ever face. Why? In part because the study of international relations requires taking into account every factor that influences human behavior. This is a task that, as seminal scientist Albert Einstein believed, is extremely challenging. He once hinted at how big the challenge of explaining world politics was when he was asked, "Why is it that when the mind of man has stretched so far as to discover the structure of the atom we have been unable to devise the political means to keep the atom from destroying us?" He replied, "This is simple, my friend; it is because politics is more difficult than physics."

Another part of the challenge stems from our constant bombardment with a bewildering amount of new information and new developments, and the tendency of people to resist new information and ideas that undermine their habitual ways of thinking about world affairs. We know from repeated studies that people do not want to accept ideas that do not conform to their prior beliefs. A purpose of this book is to help you question your preexisting beliefs about world affairs and about the world stage's many actors. To that end, we will ask you to evaluate rival perspectives on global issues, even if they differ from your current images. Indeed, we will expose you to prevailing schools of thought that you may find unconvincing, and possibly offensive.

Why are they included? Because many other people make these views the bedrock of their interpretations of the world around them, and these viewpoints accordingly enjoy a popular following. For this reason, the text describes some visions of world politics with which even your authors may not agree so that you may weigh the wisdom or foolishness of contending perspectives. The interpretive challenge, then, is to observe unfolding global realities objectively, in order to describe and explain them accurately.

To appreciate how our images of reality shape our expectations, we begin with a brief introduction to the role that subjective images play in understanding world politics. This will be followed by a set of analytic tools that this book uses to help you overcome perceptual obstacles to understanding world politics and to empower you to more capably interpret the forces of change and continuity that affect our world.

HOW DO PERCEPTIONS INFLUENCE IMAGES OF GLOBAL REALITY?

Although you may not have attempted to explicitly define your perceptions about the world in your subconscious, we all hold mental images of world politics. Whatever our levels of self-awareness, however, these images perform the same function: they simplify "reality" by exaggerating some features of the real world while ignoring others. Thus, we live in a world defined by our images.

Many of our images of the world's political realities may be built on illusions and misconceptions. They cannot fully capture the complexity and configurations of even physical objects, such as the globe itself (see "Controversy: Should We Believe What We See?"). Even images that are now accurate can easily become outdated if we fail to recognize changes in the world. Indeed, the world's future will be determined not only by changes in the "objective" facts of world politics but also by the meaning that people ascribe to those facts, the assumptions on which they base their interpretations, and the actions that flow from these assumptions and interpretations—however accurate or inaccurate they might be.

The Nature and Sources of Images

The effort to simplify one's view of the world is inevitable and even necessary. Just as cartographers' projections simplify complex geophysical space so that we can better understand the world, each of us inevitably creates a "mental map"—a habitual way of organizing information—to make sense of a confusing abundance of information. These mental maps are neither inherently right nor wrong, and they are important because we tend to react according to the way the world appears to us rather than the way it is.

How we view the world (not what it is really like) determines our attitudes, our beliefs, and our behavior. Most of us—political leaders included—look for information that reinforces

CONTROVERSY

SHOULD WE BELIEVE WHAT WE SEE?

Without questioning whether the ways they have organized their perceptions are accurate, many people simply assume seeing is believing. But is there more to seeing than meets the eye? Students of perceptual psychology think so. They maintain that seeing is not a strictly passive act: What we observe is partially influenced by our preexisting values and expectations (and by the visual habits reinforced by the constructions society has inculcated in us about how to view objects). Students of perception argue that what you see is what you get, and that two observers looking at the same object might easily see different realities.

This principle has great importance for investigation of international relations, where, depending on one's perspective, people can vary greatly on how they will view international events, actors, and issues. Intense disagreements often arise from competing images.

To appreciate the controversies that can result when different people (with different perspectives) see different realities, even though they are looking at the same thing, consider something as basic as objectively viewing the location and size of the world's continents. All maps of the globe are distorted because it is impossible to perfectly represent the three-dimensional globe on a two-dimensional piece of paper. The difficulty cartographers face can be appreciated by trying to flatten an orange peel. You can only flatten it by separating pieces of the peel that were joined when it was spherical.

Cartographers who try to flatten the globe on paper, without ripping it into separate pieces, face the same problem. Although there are a variety of ways to represent the three-dimensional object on paper, all of them involve some kind of distortion. Thus, cartographers must choose among the imperfect ways of representing the globe by selecting those aspects of the world's geography they consider most important to describe accurately, while making adjustments to other parts.

There exists a longstanding controversy among cartographers about the "right" way to map the globe, that is, how to make an accurate projection. Cartographers' ideas of what is most important in world geography have varied according to their own global perspectives. In turn, the accuracy of their rival maps matters politically because they shape how people view what is important.

Consider these four maps (Maps 1.1, 1.2, 1.3, and 1.4). Each depicts the distribution of the Earth's land surfaces and territory but portrays a different image. Each is a model of reality, an abstraction that highlights some features of the globe while ignoring others.

WHAT DO YOU THINK?

- *What are some of the policy implications associated with the image of the world as depicted in each of the respective projections?*

- *Why are some features of the map distorted? Consider the role that politics, history, culture, and racism, among others, might play. Can you think of any ways modern cartographers might modify any of these world projections?*

- *In thinking about images and the important role they play in foreign policy, should a consensus be made as to the world projection that is "least" distorted? Would it be better for everyone to use one map or to use many different types of projections? Why?*

(Continued)

SHOULD WE BELIEVE WHAT WE SEE? (Continued)

MAP 1.1 MERCATOR PROJECTION
This Mercator projection, named for the Flemish cartographer Gerard Mercator, was popular in sixteenth-century Europe and presents a classic Eurocentric view of the world. It mapped the Earth without distorting direction, making it useful for navigators. However, distances were deceptive, placing Europe at the center of the world and exaggerating the continent's importance relative to other landmasses.

MAP 1.2 PETER'S PROJECTION In the Peter's projection, each landmass appears in correct proportion in relation to all others, but it distorts the shape and position of the Earth's landmasses. In contrast with most geographic representations, it draws attention to the less developed countries of the Global South, where more than three-quarters of the world's population lives today.

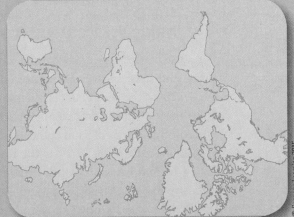

MAP 1.3 ORTHOGRAPHIC PROJECTION The orthographic projection, centering on the mid-Atlantic, conveys some sense of the curvature of the Earth by using rounded edges. The sizes and shapes of continents toward the outer edges of the circle are distorted to give a sense of spherical perspective.

MAP 1.4 "UPSIDE-DOWN" PROJECTION This projection gives a different perspective on the world by depicting it upside down, with the Global South positioned above the Global North. The map challenges the modern "Eurocentric" conceptualization of the positions of the globe's countries and peoples by putting the Global South "on top."

our preexisting beliefs about the world, assimilate new data into familiar images, mistakenly equate what we believe with what we know, and ignore information that contradicts our expectations. We also rely on our intuitions without thinking and emotionally make snap judgments (Ariely, 2012; Walker et al., 2011). Reflecting upon this tendency, political scientist Richard Ned Lebow (1981, p. 277) warns that, just like the rest of us, "Policymakers are prone to distort reality in accord with their needs even in situations that appear … relatively unambiguous."

In addition, we rely on learned habits for viewing new information and making judgments, because these "schema" guide our perceptions and help us organize information. Research in cognitive psychology shows that human beings are "categorizers," who match what they see with images in their memories of prototypical events and people when attempting to understand the world by *schematic reasoning*. The absentminded professor, the shady lawyer, and the kindly grandmother are examples of "stock" images that many of us have created about certain types of people. Although the professors, lawyers, and grandmothers that we meet may bear only a superficial resemblance to these stereotypical images, when we know little about someone, our expectations will be shaped by presumed similarities to these characters.

Many factors shape our images, including how we were socialized as children, traumatic events we experience that shape our personalities and psychological needs, exposure to the ideas of people whose expertise we respect, and the opinions about world affairs expressed by our frequent associates such as close friends and coworkers. Once we have acquired an image, it seems self-evident. Accordingly, we try to keep that image consistent with other beliefs and, through a psychological process known as *cognitive dissonance*, reject information that contradicts that image of the world. In short, our minds select, screen, and filter information; consequently, our perceptions depend not only on what happens in daily life but also on how we interpret and internalize those events.

The Impact of Perceptions on World Politics

We must be careful not to assume automatically that what applies to individuals applies to entire countries, and we should not equate the beliefs of leaders, such as heads of states, with the beliefs of the people under their authority. Still, leaders have extraordinary influence, and their images of historical circumstances often predispose them to behave in particular ways toward others, regardless of "objective" facts. For instance, the loss of 26 million Soviet lives in the "Great Patriotic War" (as the Russians refer to World War II) reinforced a longstanding fear of foreign invasion, which caused a generation of Soviet policy makers to perceive U.S. defensive moves with suspicion and often alarm.

Similarly, the founders of the United States viewed eighteenth-century European power politics and its repetitive wars as corrupt, contributing to two seemingly contradictory tendencies later evident in U.S. foreign policy. The first is America's impulse to isolate itself (its disposition to withdraw from world affairs), and the other is its determination to reform the world in its own image whenever global circumstances become highly threatening. The former led the country to reject membership in the League of Nations after World War I; the latter gave rise to the U.S. globalist foreign policy since World War II, which committed the country

schematic reasoning

The process of reasoning by which new information is interpreted according to a memory structure, a schema, which contains a network of generic scripts, metaphors, and simplified characterizations of observed objects and phenomena.

cognitive dissonance

The general psychological tendency to deny discrepancies between one's preexisting beliefs (cognitions) and new information.

to active involvement nearly everywhere on nearly every issue. Most Americans, thinking of their country as virtuous, have difficulty understanding why others sometimes regard such far-reaching international activism as arrogant or threatening; instead, they see only good intentions in active U.S. interventionism.

Because leaders and citizens are prone to ignore or reinterpret information that runs counter to their beliefs and values, mutual misperceptions often fuel discord in world politics, especially when relations between countries are hostile (see "A Closer Look: Perceptions, Freedom, and Equality"). Distrust and suspicion arise as conflicting parties view each other in the same negative light—that is, as *mirror images* develop. This occurred in Moscow and Washington during the Cold War. Each side saw its own actions as constructive but its adversary's responses as hostile, and both sides erroneously assumed that their counterparts would clearly interpret the intentions of their own policy initiatives. When psychologist Urie Bronfenbrenner (1961) traveled to Moscow, for example, he was amazed to hear Russians describing the United States in terms that were strikingly similar to the way Americans described the Soviet Union: Each side saw itself as virtuous and peace-loving, whereas the other was seen as untrustworthy, aggressive, and ruled by a corrupt government.

Mirror-imaging is a property of nearly all *enduring rivalries*—long-lasting contests between opposing groups. For example, in rivalries such as Christianity's with Islam during the Crusades in the Middle Ages, Israel's and Palestine's since the birth of the sovereign state of Israel in 1948, and the United States' with Al Qaeda today, both sides demonize the image of their adversary while perceiving themselves as virtuous. Self-righteousness often leads one party to view its own actions as constructive but its adversary's responses as negative and hostile.

When this occurs, conflict resolution is extraordinarily difficult. Not only do the opposing sides have different preferences for certain outcomes over others, but they do not see the underlying issues in the same light. Further complicating matters, the mirror images held by rivals tend to be self-confirming. When one side expects the other to be hostile, it may treat its opponent in a manner that leads the opponent to take counteractions that confirm the original expectation, therein creating a vicious circle of deepening hostilities that reduce the prospects for peace (Sen, 2006). Clearing up mutual misperceptions can facilitate negotiations between the parties, but fostering peace is not simply a matter of expanding trade and other forms of transnational contact, or even of bringing political leaders together in international summits. Rather, it is a matter of changing deeply entrenched beliefs.

Although our constructed images of world politics are resistant to change, change is possible. Overcoming old thinking habits sometimes occurs when we experience punishment or discomfort as a result of clinging to false assumptions. As Benjamin Franklin once observed, "The things that hurt, instruct." Dramatic events in particular can alter international images, sometimes drastically. The Vietnam War caused many Americans to reject their previous images about using military force in world politics. The defeat of the Third Reich and revelations of Nazi atrocities committed before and during World War II caused the German people to confront their past as they prepared for a democratic future imposed by the victorious Allies. More recently, the human and financial costs of the prolonged U.S. war in Iraq led many

mirror images

The tendency of states and people in competitive interaction to perceive each other similarly—to see others the same hostile way others see them.

enduring rivalries

Prolonged competition fueled by deep-seated mutual hatred that leads opposed actors to feud and fight over a long period of time without resolution of their conflict.

Carnegie Council Video:
Enduring Rivalries

**Video:
Determining
Foreign Policy**

A Closer Look

PERCEPTIONS, FREEDOM, AND EQUALITY

In 1959, Fidel Castro led a revolution that resulted in the overthrow of the authoritarian dictator Fulgencio Batista and the establishment of communist government. In the aftermath of the revolution, relations between Cuba and the United States deteriorated rapidly and both countries came to view the other with suspicion.

The United States' image of the Castro regime is one of a repressive communist dictatorship that is aggressive, expansionistic, and hostile to U.S. interests. This perception of Cuba is not without basis. With his ascent to power, Castro's government "seized private land, nationalized hundreds of private companies—including several local subsidiaries of U.S. corporations—and taxed American products so heavily that U.S. exports were halved in just two years" (Suddath, 2009). According to some accounts, Castro's regime nationalized as much as $25 billion in private property, of which $1 billion was American (Lazo, 1970). Eliciting further U.S. ire, Cuba aligned with the Soviet Union in the 1960s and allowed the Soviets to place missiles on its territory (resulting in the subsequent Cuban Missile Crisis; see Chapter 9). Cuba also participated in a number of "anti-imperialist" wars in countries such as Angola and Ethiopia. Domestically, the Cuban government has been accused by organizations such as Human Rights Watch of comprehensively crushing political dissent and enforcing "political conformity using short-term detentions, beatings, public acts of repudiation, travel restrictions, and forced exile" (HRW, 2013). Vast numbers of Cubans have sought refuge in the United States; the U.S. Census Bureau (2011) reports that as of 2010, 1.8 million people of Cuban origin resided in the United States.

For its part, Cuba similarly holds an image of the United States' government as aggressive, expansionistic, and hostile to Cuban interests. The United States responded to Castro's nationalization of private property by imposing trade restrictions on all goods except medical supplies and food, and in 1962 President John Kennedy made these economic sanctions permanent. When Cuba expanded its trade with the Soviet Union, the United States severed diplomatic ties. Cubans attribute their continuing poor economic situation, in part, to the U.S. embargo, which the UN General Assembly has denounced as a violation of international law every year since 1992. The Castro regime also portrays the United States as an imperialist power that, over time, has aggressively sought to expand its territory and power across the Americas, pointing not only to the U.S. notion of Manifest Destiny and its repeated interventions in Latin America, but also efforts by the CIA to overthrow and assassinate Castro (Frasquieri, 2011).

February 2, 2012, marked the fiftieth anniversary of the U.S. embargo of Cuba. Many have noted its ineffectiveness and, in the words of Republican Senator Richard Lugar, have called for the United States "to reevaluate a complex relationship marked by misunderstanding, suspicion, and open hostility" (Fetini, 2009). Yet while even "supporters of the policy acknowledge that many American strategic concerns from the 1960s are now in the past, such as curbing Soviet influence and keeping Fidel Castro from exporting revolution throughout Latin America" (NYT, 2012, p. A8), old images and perceptions remain entrenched and make change in relations between the two countries difficult to achieve.

(Continued)

policy makers and political commentators to reexamine their assumptions about the meaning of "victory" and the potential implications as U.S. engagement moved beyond initial combat to address issues of governance and stability.

Often, such jolting experiences encourage us to construct new mental maps, perceptual filters, and criteria through which we interpret later events and define situations. As we shape and reshape our images of world politics and its future, we need to think critically about the foundations on which our perceptions rest. Are they accurate? Are they informed? Should they be modified to gain greater understanding of others? Questioning our images is one of the major challenges we all face in confronting contemporary world politics.

KEY CONCEPTS AND TERMS FOR UNDERSTANDING WORLD POLITICS

If we exaggerate the accuracy of our perceptions and seek information that confirms what we believe, how can we escape the biases created by our preconceptions? How can we avoid overlooking or dismissing evidence that runs counter to our intuition?

There are no sure-fire solutions to ensure accurate observations, no ways to guarantee that we have constructed an impartial view of international relations. However, there are a number of tools available that can improve our ability to interpret world politics. As you undertake an intellectual journey of discovery, a set of intellectual roadmaps will provide guidance for your interpretation and understanding of past, present, and future world politics. To arm you for your quest, *World Politics: Trend and Transformation* advances four keys to aid you in your inquiry.

> *The belief that one's own view of reality is the only reality is the most dangerous of all delusions.*
>
> **—Paul Watzlawick, Austrian psychologist**

Introducing Terminology

A primary goal of this text is to introduce you to the vocabulary used by scholars, policy makers, and the "attentive public" who routinely look at international developments. You will need to be literate and informed about the shared meaning of common words used worldwide to discuss and debate world politics and foreign policy. Some of this language has been in use since antiquity, and some of it has only recently become part of the terminology employed in diplomatic circles, scholarly research, and the media—television, newspapers, and the Internet. These words are the kind of vocabulary you are likely to encounter long after your formal collegiate education (and the course in which you are reading *World Politics*) has ended. It is also the terminology your future employers and educated neighbors will expect you to know. Some of these words are already likely to be part of your working vocabulary, but others may look new, esoteric, pedantic, and overly sophisticated. Nonetheless, you need to know their meaning in order to engage in effective analysis and well-informed debate with other scholars, practitioners, and attentive observers of world affairs. So take advantage of this "high definition" feature of *World Politics*. Learn these words and use them for the rest of your life—not to impress others, but to understand and communicate intelligently.

To guide you in identifying these terms, as you may already have noticed, certain words are printed in **boldface** in the text, and a broad definition is provided in the margin. In cases when a word is used again in a different chapter, it will be highlighted at least once in *italics,* although the marginal definition will not be repeated. In all cases, the primary definition will appear in the Glossary at the end of book.

Distinguishing the Primary Transnational Actors

actor

An individual, group, state, or organization that plays a major role in world politics.

Carnegie Council Video:
Actor

The globe is a stage, and in the drama there are many players. It is important to identify and classify the major categories of actors (sometimes called agents) who take part in international engagements. The actions of each transnational *actor*—individually, collectively, and with various degrees of influence—shape the trends that are transforming world politics. But how do scholars conventionally break the types of actors into categories and structure thinking about them as players in international affairs?

The essential building-block units, of course, are individual people—all 7 billion of us. Every day, whether each of us chooses to litter, light a cigarette, or parent a child, we affect some small measure of how trends in the world will unfold. People, however, also join and participate in various groups. All of these groups combine people and their choices in various collectivities and thereby aggregate the *power* of each group. Such groups often compete with one another because they frequently have divergent interests and goals.

For most periods of world history, the prime actors were groupings of religions, tribes whose members shared ethnic origins, and empires or expansionist centers of power. When they came into contact, they sometimes collaborated with each other for mutual benefit; more often they competed for and fought over valued resources. The more than 8000 years of recorded international relations history between and among these groups provided the precedent for the formation of today's system of interactions.

As a network of relationships among independent territorial units, the modern state system was not born until the Peace of Westphalia in 1648, which ended the Thirty Years' War (1618–1648) in Europe. Thereafter, rulers refused to recognize the secular authority of the Roman Catholic Church, replacing the system of papal governance in the Middle Ages with geographically and politically separate states that recognized no superior authority. The newly independent states all gave to rulers the same legal rights: territory under their sole control, unrestricted control of their domestic affairs, and the freedom to conduct foreign relations and negotiate treaties with other states. The concept of *state sovereignty*—that no other actor is above the state—still captures these legal rights and identifies the state as the primary actor today.

The Westphalian system continues to color every dimension of world politics and provides the terminology used to describe the primary units in international affairs. Although the term nation-state is often used interchangeably with state and nation, technically the three are different. A *state* is a legal entity that enjoys a permanent population, a well-defined territory, and a government capable of exercising sovereignty. A *nation* is a collection of people who, on the basis of ethnic, linguistic, or cultural commonality, so construct their reality as to primarily perceive themselves to be members of the same group, which defines their identity. Thus, the term *nation-state* implies a convergence between territorial states and the psychological identification of people within them (Steward, Gvosdev, and Andelman, 2008).

However, in employing this familiar terminology, we should exercise caution because this condition is relatively rare; there are few independent states comprising a single nationality. Most states today are populated by many nations, and some nations are not states. These "nonstate nations" are *ethnic groups*—such as Native Americans in the United States, Sikhs in India, Basques in Spain, or Kurds in Iraq, Turkey, Iran, and Syria—composed of people without sovereign power over the territory in which they live.

The history of world politics since 1648 has largely been a chronicle of interactions among states, which remain the dominant political organizations in the world. However, the supremacy of the state has been severely challenged in recent years by nonstate actors. Increasingly, global affairs are influenced by intergovernmental organizations (IGOs) and nongovernmental organizations (NGOs).

Intergovernmental organizations, which transcend national boundaries and whose members are states, carry out independent foreign policies and therefore can be considered

power

The factors that enable one actor to change another actor's behavior against its preferences.

Carnegie Council Video:
Power

state sovereignty

A state's supreme authority to manage internal affairs and foreign relations.

state

An independent legal entity with a government exercising exclusive control over the territory and population it governs.

Carnegie Council Video:
State

nation

A collectivity whose people see themselves as members of the same group because they share the same ethnicity, culture, or language.

ethnic groups

People whose identity is primarily defined by their sense of sharing a common ancestral nationality, language, cultural heritage, and kinship.

global actors in their own right. Purposively created by states to solve shared problems, IGOs include global organizations such as the United Nations (UN) and the North Atlantic Treaty Organization (NATO), and derive their authority from the will of their membership. IGOs are characterized by permanence and institutional organization, and vary widely in their size and purpose.

Nongovernmental organizations (NGOs), whose members are private individuals and groups, are another principal type of nonstate actor. NGOs are diverse in scope and purpose, and seek to push their own agendas and exert global influence on an array of issues, such as environmental protection, disarmament, and human rights. For example, Amnesty International, the World Wildlife Federation, and Doctors Without Borders are all NGOs that work to bring about change in the world and influence interna-tional decision making. Yet although many NGOs are seen in a positive light, others, such as terrorist groups and international drug cartels, are seen as ominous nonstate actors.

In thinking about world politics and its future, we shall probe all of these "units" or categories of actors. The emphasis and coverage will vary, depending on the topics under examination in each chapter. But you should keep in mind that all actors (individuals, states, and nonstate organizations) are simultaneously active today, and their importance and power depend on the trend or issue under consideration. So continuously ask yourself the question, now and in the future: which actors are most active, most influential, on which issues, and under what conditions? Doing so will help you think like an international relations scholar.

Distinguishing Levels of Analysis

When we describe international phenomena, we answer a "what" question. What is happen-ing? What is changing? When we move from description to explanation, we face the more difficult task of answering a "why" question. Why did a particular event occur? Why is global warming happening? Why is the gap between rich and poor widening?

One useful key for addressing such puzzles is to visualize an event or trend as part of the end result of some unknown process. This encourages us to think about the causes that might have produced the phenomenon we are trying to explain. Most events and developments in world politics are undoubtedly influenced simultaneously by many determinants, each connected to the rest in a complex web of causal linkages.

World Politics provides an analytic set of categories to help make interpretive sense of the multiple causes that explain why international events and circumstances occur. This analytic distinction conforms to a widespread scholarly consensus that international events or devel-opments can best be analyzed and understood by first separating the multiple pieces of the puzzle into different categories or levels. Most conventionally, investigators focus on one (or more) of three levels. Known as *levels of analysis*, as shown in Figure 1.1, this classification distinguishes individual influences, state or internal influences, and global influences for the system as a whole.

To predict which forces will dominate the future, we also must recognize that many influences are operating at the same time. No trend or trouble stands alone; all interact simultaneously. The future is influenced by many determinants, each connected to the rest in a complex web of linkages. Collectively, these may produce stability by limiting the impact of any single disruptive force. If interacting forces converge, however, their combined effects can accelerate the pace of change in world politics, moving it in directions otherwise not possible.

The *individual level of analysis* refers to the personal characteristics of human beings, including those responsible for making important decisions on behalf of state and nonstate actors, as well as ordinary citizens whose behavior has important political consequences. At this level, for example, we may properly locate the impact of individuals' perceptions on their political attitudes, beliefs, and behavior. We may also explore the questions of why each person is a crucial part of the global drama and why the study of world politics is relevant to our lives and future.

The *state level of analysis* consists of the authoritative decision-making units that govern states' foreign policy processes and the internal attributes of those states (e.g., their type of government, level of economic and military power, and number of nationality groups), which both shape and constrain leaders' foreign policy choices. The processes by which states make decisions regarding war and peace and their capabilities for carrying out those decisions, for instance, fall within the state level of analysis.

The *global level of analysis* refers to the interactions of states and nonstate actors on the global stage whose behaviors ultimately shape the international political system and

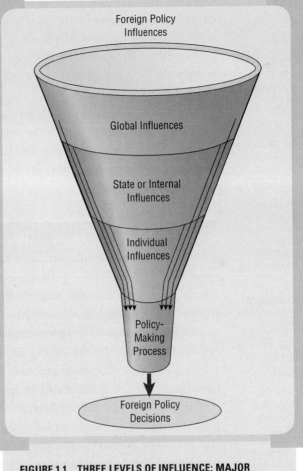

© Kegley and Blanton/Cengage Learning 2015

FIGURE 1.1   THREE LEVELS OF INFLUENCE: MAJOR FACTORS SHAPING FOREIGN POLICY DECISIONS AND INTERNATIONAL RELATIONS The factors that affect states' foreign policies and the decisions of all other global actors can be categorized at three basic levels. At the global level are those structural features of the international system such as the prevalence of civil wars and the extent of trade interdependence. At the state level are internal or domestic influences such as the state's type of government or the opinions of its citizens. At the individual level are the characteristics of leaders—their personal beliefs, values, and personality. All three levels simultaneously affect decisions, but their relative weight usually depends on the issues and circumstances at the time of decision.

the levels of conflict and cooperation that characterize world politics. The capacity of rich states to dictate the choices of poor states falls properly within the global level of analysis. So does the capacity (or incapacity) of the UN to maintain peace.

Examples abound of the diverse ways in which global trends and issues are the product of influences at each level of analysis. Protectionist trade policies by an importing

individual level of analysis

An analytical approach that emphasizes the psychological and perceptual variables motivating people, such as those who make foreign policy decisions on behalf of states and other global actors.

state level of analysis

An analytical approach that emphasizes how the internal attributes of states influence their foreign policy behaviors.

global level of analysis

An analytical approach that emphasizes the impact of worldwide conditions on foreign policy behavior and human welfare.

country increase the costs to consumers of clothing and cars and reduce the standard of living of citizens in the manufacturing states. Such policies are initiated by a state government (national level), but they diminish the quality of life of people living both within the protectionist country and those living abroad (individual level) and reduce the level of global trade while threatening to precipitate retaliatory trade wars (global level).

Of course, for some developments and issues, factors and forces emanating primarily from one or two particular levels provide more analytical leverage than do those from the other level(s). Accordingly, as we confront specific global issues in subsequent chapters, we emphasize those levels of analysis that provide the most informative lens for viewing them.

Distinguishing Change, Continuities, and Cycles

After having identified factors from different levels of analysis that may combine to produce some outcome, it is then useful to place them in a chronological sequence. Anyone who owns a combination lock knows that the correct numbers must be entered in their proper order to open the lock. Similarly, to explain why something happened in world politics, we must determine how various factors at the individual, state, and global system levels fit together in a configuration that unfolds over time.

One key to anticipating probable human destiny is to look beyond the confines of our immediate time. It is important to appreciate the impact of previous ideas and events on current realities. As philosopher George Santayana cautioned, "Those who cannot remember the past are condemned to repeat it." Similarly, former British Prime Minister Winston Churchill advised, "The farther backward you look, the farther forward you are likely to see." Thus, to understand the dramatic changes in world politics today and to predict how they will shape the future, it is important to view them in the context of a long-term perspective that examines how transnational patterns of interaction have changed and how some of their fundamental characteristics have resisted change.

What do evolving diplomatic practices suggest about the current state of world politics? Are the episodic shock waves throughout the world clearing the way for a truly new twenty-first-century world order? Or will many of today's dramatic disruptions ultimately prove temporary, mere spikes on the seismograph of history? We invite you to explore these questions with us. To begin our search, we discuss how the differences between continuities, changes, and cycles in world history can help you orient your interpretation.

Every historical period is marked to some extent by change. Now, however, the pace of change seems more rapid and its consequences more profound than ever. To many observers, the cascade of events today implies a revolutionary restructuring of world politics. Numerous integrative trends point to that possibility. The countries of the world are drawing closer together in communications and trade, producing a globalized market. Yet at the same time, disintegrative trends paint a less promising picture. Weapons proliferation, global environmental deterioration, and the resurgence of ethnic conflict all portend a restructuring fraught with disorder.

To predict which forces will dominate the future, we must recognize that no trend stands alone, and that different trends may produce stability by limiting the impact of any one disruptive force. It is also possible for converging trends to accelerate the pace of change, moving world politics in directions not possible otherwise.

It appears that world politics is now going through a transition period. The opposing forces of integration and disintegration point toward the probable advent on the horizon of a *transformation*, but distinguishing true historical watersheds from temporary change is difficult. The moment of transformation from one system to another is not immediately obvious. Nevertheless, another useful key for students of world history is to recognize that certain times are especially likely candidates.

In the past, major turning points in world politics usually have occurred at the conclusion of wars with many participants, which typically disrupt or destroy preexisting international arrangements. In the twentieth century, World Wars I and II and the Cold War caused fundamental breaks with the past and set in motion major transformations, providing countries with incentives to rethink the premises underlying their interests, purposes, and priorities. Similarly, many people concluded that the terrorist attacks on September 11, 2001 (9/11) produced a fundamental transformation in world affairs. Indeed, 9/11 seemed to change everything: in former U.S. President George W. Bush's words, "Night fell on a different world."

Yet it is equally important to look also for the possibility of continuity amidst apparent transformation. Consider how, despite all that may appear radically different since the 9/11 terrorist attacks, much also may remain the same. As journalist William Dobson (2006) wrote on the eve of the fifth anniversary of 9/11, "what is remarkable is how little the world has changed." Similarly, historian Juan Cole notes that "The massive forces of international trade and globalization were largely unaffected by the attacks" (2006, p. 26). Decades-old flash points also persist, including the conflicts between India and Pakistan, North Korea and the United States, and Israel and militants in southern Lebanon and the Palestinian territories. "For all their visibility and drama," concludes Cole (2006, p. 26), "the 9/11 attacks left untouched many of the underlying forces and persistent tensions that shape international politics."

We often expect the future to bring changes automatically, and later are surprised to discover that certain patterns from the past have reappeared. Headlines are not trend lines, and a trend does not necessarily signal transformation. Given the enduring continuities that persist even alongside rapid changes, it is dangerous to assume that a major transformation in world politics is under way.

So, what criteria can help determine when an existing pattern of relationships gives way to a completely new global system? Stanley Hoffmann (1961) argues that we can identify a new *global system* when we have a new answer to one of the following three questions. Following this line of argument, we might conclude that a new system has now emerged.

■ **What are the system's basic units for global governance**? Although states remain a fixture of the international system, supranational institutions and nongovernmental actors are becoming increasingly prominent. New trade partnerships have been

transformation

A change in the characteristic pattern of interaction among the most active participants in world politics of such magnitude that it appears that one "global system" has replaced another.

Case Studies:
The End of History or the Clash of Civilizations? and Terrorism

global system

The predominant patterns of behaviors and beliefs that prevail internationally to define the major worldwide conditions that heavily influence human and national activities.

Carnegie Council Video:
Global System

forged in Europe, the cone of South America, North America, and the Pacific Rim, and these trading blocs may behave as unitary, or independent, nonstate actors as they compete with one another. Moreover, international organizations such as the European Union (EU) now flex their political muscles in contests with individual states, and transnational religious movements such as Islamic extremist groups challenge the global system itself.

■ **What are the predominant foreign policy goals that these units seek with respect to one another**? Territorial conquest is no longer states' predominant foreign policy goal. Instead, their emphasis has shifted from traditionally military methods of exercising influence to economic means. Meanwhile, the ideological contest between democratic capitalism and the Marxist-Leninist communism of the Cold War era no longer constitutes the primary cleavage in international politics, and a major new axis has yet to become clear.

■ **What can these units do to one another with their military and economic capabilities**? The proliferation of weapons technology has profoundly altered the damage enemies can inflict on one another. *Great powers* alone no longer control the world's most lethal weapons. Increasingly, however, the great powers' prosperity depends on economic circumstances throughout the globe, reducing their ability to engineer growth.

great powers

The most powerful countries, militarily and economically, in the global system.

Carnegie Council Video:
Great Powers

anarchy

A condition in which the units in the global system are subjected to few, if any, overarching institutions to regulate their conduct.

Carnegie Council Video:
Anarchy

cycles

The periodic reemergence of conditions similar to those that existed previously.

The profound changes in recent years of the types of actors (units), goals, and capabilities have dramatically altered the hierarchical power ranking of states, but the hierarchies themselves endure. The economic hierarchy that divides the rich from the poor, the political hierarchy that separates the rulers from the ruled, the resource hierarchy that makes some suppliers and others dependents, and the military asymmetries that pit the strong against the weak—all still shape the relations among states, as they have in the past. Similarly, the perpetuation of international *anarchy*, in the absence of institutions to govern the globe, and continuing national insecurity still encourage preparations for war and the use of force without international mandate. Thus, change and continuity coexist, with both forces simultaneously shaping contemporary world politics.

The interaction of constancy and change will determine future relations among global actors. This perhaps explains why *cycles*, periodic sequences of events that resemble patterns in earlier periods, so often appear to characterize world politics: because the emergent global system shares many characteristics with earlier periods, historically minded observers may experience déjà vu—the illusion of having already experienced something actually being experienced for the first time.

Preparing for Your Intellectual Journey

Because world politics is complex and our images of it are often dissimilar, scholars differ in their approaches to understanding world politics. Some view the world through a macro-political lens, meaning they look at world politics from a "bird's eye view" and explain the behavior of world actors based on their relative position within the global system. Other scholars adopt a micro-political perspective that looks at world politics from the "ground up," meaning the individual is the unit of analysis from which aggregate behavior is extrapolated.

Both approaches make important contributions to understanding world politics: the former reveals how the global environment sets limits on political choice; the latter draws attention to how every transnational actor's preferences, capabilities, and strategic calculations influence global conditions. By looking at world politics from a macro-political perspective, we can see why actors that are similarly situated within the system may behave alike, despite their internal differences. By taking a micro-political perspective, we can appreciate why some actors are very different or behave differently, despite their similar placement within the global system (see Waltz, 2000).

From this analytic point of departure, *World Politics* will accordingly inspect (1) the major macro trends in world politics that set the boundaries for action; (2) the values, interests, and capabilities of the individual actors affected by these global trends; and (3) the ways these actors interact in their individual and collective

WAS 9/11 A GLOBAL TRANSFORMING EVENT? The terrorist attack on the World Trade Center's Twin Towers on 9/11 is widely regarded as a revolutionary date in world history, producing a sea of change in world politics. Time will tell whether this event will rank alongside the birth of the nuclear age on August 6, 1945, when the United States bombed Hiroshima, or the November 1989 dismantling of the Berlin Wall, which signaled the end of the Cold War, as events that truly changed the world. Alternatively, a rising China may pose a new challenge that will displace 9/11 as a transformative phenomenon in world politics.

efforts to modify existing global circumstances and how these interactions shape the ultimate trajectories of global trends. This analytic approach looks at the dynamic interplay of actors and their environment as well as how the actors respond and seek to influence each others' behavior.

The approach outlined here can open a window for you not only to understand contemporary world politics but also to predict the likely global future. The approach has the advantage of taking into account the interplay of proximate and remote explanatory factors at the individual, state, and global levels of analysis while avoiding dwelling on particular countries, individuals, or transitory events whose long-term significance is likely to decrease. Instead, *World Politics* attempts to identify behaviors that cohere into general patterns that measurably affect global living conditions. Thus, you will explore the nature of world politics from a perspective that places historical and contemporary events into a larger, lasting theoretical

Shannon Blanton

IT'S A SMALL WORLD As you begin your journey of discovery to extend your knowledge of world politics, it is important to be aware of the images that you hold and be open to new experiences and interpretations of the world around you. Take full advantage of all of your opportunities to study and learn about the global community. Shown here in March 2013 are U.S. students from the University of Memphis enjoying their study abroad program in South Africa.

context, to provide you with the conceptual tools that will enable you to interpret subsequent developments later in your lifetime.

> *The ability to learn how to learn will be the only security you have.*
>
> **—Thomas L. Friedman, political journalist**

STUDY. APPLY. ANALYZE.

Key Terms

actor	global level of analysis	mirror images	state level of analysis
anarchy	global system	nation	state sovereignty
cognitive dissonance	great powers	nongovernmental organizations	transformation
cycles	individual level of analysis	power	world politics
enduring rivalries	intergovernmental organizations	schematic reasoning	
ethnic groups	levels of analysis	state	

Suggested Readings

Ellis, David C. (2009) "On the Possibility of 'International Community,'" *The International Studies Review* 11 (March):1–26.

Friedman, George. (2011) *The Next Decade: Where We've Been … and Where We're Going.* New York: Doubleday, Random House.

Fukuyama, Francis. (2011) *The Origins of Political Order: From Prehuman Times to the French Revolution.* New York: Farar, Straus and Giroux.

Holsti, K. J. (2004) *Taming the Sovereigns: International Change in International Politics.* New York: Cambridge University Press.

Jervis, Robert. (2008) "Unipolarity: A Structural Perspective," *World Politics* 61:188–213.

Puchala, Donald. (1994) "The History of the Future of International Relations," *Ethics & International Affairs* 8: 177–202.

Rosenau, James N. (1992) "Normative Challenges in a Turbulent World," *Ethics & International Affairs* 6:1–19.

Shapiro, Robert J. (2008) *Futurecast: How Superpowers, Populations, and Globalization Will Change the Way You Live and Work.* New York: St. Martin's Press.

Stewart, Devin T., Nikolas K. Glosdev, and David Andelman. (2008) "Roundtable: The Nation-State," www.carnegiecouncil.org.

Suggested Videos

CourseMate

Carnegie Council Video

Kupchan, Charles. "How Enemies Become Friends: The Sources of Stable Peace."

CourseMate

Log in to CourseMate to access the following study tools for this chapter:

- Interactive Quiz
- eBook
- Flashcards & Key Term Crossword Puzzle
- Chapter Audio Summary
- Carnegie Council Videos
- Video Activities

- Simulation
- Animated Learning Module
- Case Study
- International Relations NewsWatch

"He who loves practice without theory is like the sailor who boards ship without a rudder and compass and never knows where he may cast."

—*Leonardo da Vinci, artist*

CHAPTER 2
Theories of World Politics

THEORETICAL CHALLENGES *We live in a world of ever-changing conditions. Many trends are unfolding, some in contrary directions, and obstacles exist to understanding world politics accurately. As you begin your study of trends and transformations in world politics, your challenge is to interpret theoretically the meaning of a changing world.*

SuperStock

QUESTIONS TO CONSIDER

- *Why is theory important?*
- *What is realism?*
- *What is liberalism?*
- *What is constructivism?*
- *What are some alternative perspectives on international relations?*
- *What are the strengths and limitations of these theories for understanding world politics?*

Imagine yourself the newly elected president of the United States. You are scheduled to deliver the State of the Union address on your views of the current global situation and your foreign policy to deal with it. You face the task of both defining the aspects of international affairs most worthy of attention and explaining the reasons for their priority. To convince citizens that these issues are important, you must present them as part of a larger picture of the world. Therefore, based on your perceptions of world politics, you must think theoretically. You must be careful, because your interpretations will necessarily depend on your assumptions about international realities that your citizens might find questionable. The effort to explain the world, predict new global problems, and sell others on a policy to deal with them is bound to result in controversy because even reasonable people often see reality differently.

When leaders face these kinds of intellectual challenges, they can benefit from drawing on various theories of world politics. A *theory* is a set of conclusions derived from assumptions and evidence about some phenomenon, including its character, causes, probable consequences, and ethical implications. Theories provide a map, or frame of reference, that makes the complex, puzzling world around us intelligible.

THEORIES AND CHANGE IN WORLD POLITICS

Theories of international relations specify the conditions under which relationships between two or more factors exist, and explain the reasons for such linkages. As political scientists Bruce Jentleson and Ely Ratner (2011, p. 9) explain, "Theory deepens understanding of patterns of causality within any particular case by penetrating beyond the situational and particularistic to get at factors with broader applicability." Choosing which theory to use is an important task, because each one rests on different assumptions about the nature of international politics, advances different claims about causes, and offers a different set of foreign policy recommendations.

Indeed, the menu of theories from which to choose is large. Rival theories of world politics abound, and there is no agreement about which one is most useful (Snyder, 2004; Walt, 1998). The reason is primarily that the world is constantly changing, and no single theory has proven capable of making international events understandable for every global circumstance. So there are fads and fashions in the popularity of international theories; they rise and fall over time in popularity and perceived usefulness, depending on the global conditions that prevail in any historical period.

The history of the world is the history of changes in the theoretical interpretation of international relations. In any given era, a *paradigm*, or dominant way of looking at a particular subject such as international relations, influences judgments regarding which characteristics of the subject are most important, what puzzles need to be solved, and what analytical criteria should govern investigation. Over time, paradigms are modified or abandoned as their assertions fail to mirror the prevailing patterns of international behavior. These paradigms, or "fundamental assumptions scholars make about the world they are studying" (Vasquez, 1997), tend eventually to be revised in order to explain new developments.

theory

A set of hypotheses postulating the relationship between variables or conditions advanced to describe, explain, or predict phenomena and make prescriptions about how to pursue particular goals and follow ethical principles.

paradigm

Derived from the Greek paradeigma, meaning an example, a model, or an essential pattern; a paradigm structures thought about an area of inquiry.

Yet theories are not merely passive agents for explaining historical events. As they inform the worldviews of policy leaders, theoretical perspectives can play a key role in influencing policy choices. For policy makers, theory has three important applications (Jentleson and Ratner, 2011):

- **Diagnostic value.** Helps policy makers assess issues they face by facilitating their ability to discern patterns and focus on important causal factors.

- **Prescriptive value.** Provides a framework for conceptualizing strategies and policy responses.

- **Lesson-drawing value.** Facilitates critical assessment so that policy makers reach accurate conclusions about the successes and failures of a policy.

For example, the insights of realist theory (discussed later in this chapter), particularly the importance of balance of power, drove U.S. President Nixon's decision to establish diplomatic relations with China in 1971. Along realist lines, Nixon overlooked his profound ideological differences with their government and sought to establish relations based on common strategic interests, particularly, countering the power of the Soviet Union. More recently, liberal ideas about the spread of democracy, combined with a realist emphasis on military power and disdain for international institutions, shaped the *neoconservative* approach to foreign policy and were pivotal in the U.S. decision to go to war against Iraq in 2003.

As British economist John Maynard Keynes (1936, p. 241) famously argued, "The ideas of economists and political philosophers, both when they are right and when they are wrong, are more powerful than is commonly understood. Indeed, the world is ruled by little else. Practical men, who believe themselves to be quite exempt from any intellectual influences, are usually the slaves of some defunct economist."

Simply put, the relationship between theory and historical events is interactive—theories both influence, and are influenced by, events and behaviors in world politics. The purpose of this chapter is to compare the assumptions, causal claims, and policy prescriptions of realism, liberalism, and constructivism—the most common theoretical perspectives policy makers and scholars use to interpret international relations. Moreover, the chapter broadens coverage of the range of contemporary international theorizing by also introducing you to the feminist and socialist critiques of world politics and the theoretical lens that each provide for understanding international interactions.

> *Critical reflection on practice is a requirement of the relationship between theory and practice. Otherwise theory becomes simply "blah, blah, blah," and practice, pure activism.*
>
> **—Paulo Freire, Brazilian pedagogical theorist**

REALISM

Realism is the oldest of the prevailing schools of thought and has a long and distinguished history dating back to Thucydides' writings about the Peloponnesian War in ancient Greece. Other influential figures who contributed to realist thought include sixteenth-century Italian

neoconservative

A political movement in the United States calling for the use of military and economic power in foreign policy to bring freedom and democracy to other countries.

realism

A paradigm based on the premise that world politics is essentially and unchangeably a struggle among self-interested states for power and position under anarchy, with each competing state pursuing its own national interests.

philosopher Niccolò Machiavelli and seventeenth-century English philosopher Thomas Hobbes. Realism deserves careful examination because its worldview continues to guide much understanding of international politics.

What is the Realist Worldview?

Realism, as applied to contemporary international politics, views the state as the most important actor on the world stage because it answers to no higher political authority. States are sovereign: they have supreme *power* over their territory and populace, and no other actor stands above them to wield legitimacy and coercive capability and govern the global system. Emphasizing the absence of a higher authority to which states can turn for protection and resolve disputes, realists depict world politics as a ceaseless, repetitive struggle for power where the strong dominate the weak. Because each state is ultimately responsible for its own survival and feels uncertain about its neighbors' intentions, realism claims that prudent political leaders build strong armies and allies to enhance national security. In other words, international anarchy leads even well-intentioned leaders to practice *self-help*, increase their own military strength, and opportunistically align with others to deter potential enemies.

Realist theory, however, does not preclude the possibility that rival powers will cooperate on arms control or on other security issues of common interest. Rather, it simply asserts cooperation will be rare because states worry about the unequal distribution of *relative gains*, or the unequal distribution of benefits from cooperation, and the possibility that the other side will cheat on agreements. Leaders should never entrust the task of self-protection to international security organizations or international law, and should resist efforts to regulate international behavior through global governance.

At the risk of oversimplification, realism's message can be summarized by the following assumptions and related propositions:

- People are by nature selfish and are driven to compete with others for domination and self-advantage. "The focus on gain and greed is one reason why morality cannot be expected to play a role in relations among states" (Rathbun, 2012, p. 611) or people. Machiavelli captures the realist view of human nature in his work *The Prince*, arguing that people in general "are ungrateful, fickle, and deceitful, eager to avoid dangers, and avid for gain, and while you are useful to them they are all with you, offering you their blood, their property, and their sons so long as danger is remote, but when it approaches they turn on you."

- By extension, the primary obligation of every state—the goal to which all other national objectives should be subordinated—is to acquire power in order to promote the *national interest*. Power is the "most important currency in international politics both to take from others and to prevent the inevitable effort by others to steal" (Rathbun, 2012, p. 622). "Might makes right," and a state's philosophical or ethical preferences are neither good nor bad. What matters is whether they serve its self-interest. As Thucydides put it, "The standard of justice depends on the equality of power to compel … the strong do what they have the power to do and the weak accept what they have to accept."

self-help

The principle that, because in international anarchy all global actors are independent, they must rely on themselves to provide for their security and well-being.

relative gains

Conditions in which some participants in cooperative interactions benefit more than others.

national interest

The goals that states pursue to maximize what they perceive to be selfishly best for their country.

■ World politics is a struggle for *power*—in the words of Thomas Hobbes, "a war of all against all"—and the possibility of eradicating the instinct for power is a hopeless utopian aspiration. In the pursuit of power, states must acquire sufficient military capabilities to deter attack by potential enemies and to exercise influence over others; hence states "prepare for war to keep peace." Economic growth is important primarily as a means of acquiring and expanding state power and prestige and is less relevant to national security than is military might.

■ International anarchy and a lack of trust perpetuate the principle of self-help and can give rise to the *security dilemma*. As a state builds up its power to protect itself, others inevitably become threatened and are likely to respond in kind. An arms race is commonly seen as a manifestation of the security dilemma, for even if a state is truly arming only for defensive purposes, it is rational in a self-help system for opponents to assume the worst and keep pace in any arms buildup.

■ If all states seek to maximize power, stability is maintained with a *balance of power*, facilitated by shifts in alliances that counter another state's growing power or expansionist behavior. Thus, allies might be sought to increase a state's ability to defend itself, but their loyalty and reliability should not be assumed, and commitments to allies should be repudiated if it is no longer in a state's national interests to honor them (see Chapter 8 for further discussion).

With their emphasis on the ruthless nature of international life, realists often question letting ethical considerations enter foreign policy deliberations. As they see it, some policies are driven by strategic imperatives that may require national leaders to disregard moral norms. Embedded in this "philosophy of necessity" is a distinction between private morality, which guides the behavior of ordinary people in their daily lives, and raison d'état (reason of state), which governs the conduct of leaders responsible for the security and survival of the state. Actions that are dictated by national interest must be carried out no matter how repugnant in the light of private morality. Reflecting upon his decision in 2009 to send additional U.S. troops to Afghanistan, in his acceptance speech for the Nobel Peace Prize President Obama noted that "I face the world as it is, and cannot stand idle in the face of threats to the American people."

The Evolution of Realism

We have seen how the intellectual roots of realism reach back to ancient Greece. They also extend beyond the Western world to India and China. Discussions of "power politics" abound in the *Arthashastra*, an Indian treatise on statecraft written during the fourth century BCE by Kautilya, as well as in works written by Han Fei and Shang Yang in ancient China.

Modern realism emerged on the eve of World War II, when the prevailing belief in a natural harmony of interests among states came under attack. Just a decade earlier, this belief had led numerous countries to sign the 1928 *Kellogg-Briand Pact*, which renounced war as an instrument of national policy. Now, with Nazi Germany, fascist Italy, and Imperial Japan all violating the treaty, British historian and diplomat E. H. Carr (1939) complained that the assumption of a universal interest in peace had allowed too many people to "evade the unpalatable fact of

security dilemma

The tendency of states to view the defensive arming of adversaries as threatening, causing them to arm in response so that all states' security declines.

balance of power

The theory that peace and stability are most likely to be maintained when military power is distributed to prevent a single superpower hegemon or bloc from controlling the world.

Kellogg-Briand Pact

A multilateral treaty negotiated in 1928 that outlawed war as a method for settling interstate conflicts.

REALIST PIONEERS OF POWER POLITICS In *The Prince* (1532) and *The Leviathan* (1651), Niccolò Machiavelli (left) and Thomas Hobbes (right), respectively, argued for basing international decisions on self-interest, prudence, power, and expediency above all other considerations. This formed the foundation of what became a growing body of modern realist thinking that accepts the drive for power over others as necessary and wise statecraft.

a fundamental divergence of interest between nations desirous of maintaining the status quo and nations desirous of changing it."

In an effort to counter what they saw as a utopian, legalistic approach to foreign affairs, Reinhold Niebuhr (1947), Hans J. Morgenthau (1948), and other realists painted a pessimistic view of human nature. Echoing seventeenth-century philosopher Baruch Spinoza, many of them pointed to an innate conflict between passion and reason; furthermore, in the tradition of St. Augustine, they stressed that material appetites enabled passion to overwhelm reason. For them, the human condition was such that the forces of light and darkness would perpetually combat for control.

The realists' picture of international life appeared particularly persuasive after World War II. The onset of rivalry between the United States and the Soviet Union, the expansion of the Cold War into a wider struggle between East and West, and the periodic crises that threatened to erupt into global violence all supported the realists' emphasis on the inevitability of conflict, the poor prospects for cooperation, and the divergence of national interests among incorrigibly selfish, power-seeking states.

Whereas these so-called classical realists sought to explain state behavior by examining assumptions about peoples' motives at the individual level of analysis, the next wave of realist theorizing emphasized the global level of analysis. *Neorealism* (often called "structural realism") understands human identity, motivation, and behavior as being driven by the environment in which actors are situated. In other words, it is "based on a belief in the shaping power of conditions over *agency*" (Harknett and Yalcin 2012, p. 500).

As Kenneth Waltz (2013; 1979), the leading proponent of neorealism, proposed that international anarchy—not some allegedly evil side of human nature—explained why states were locked in fierce competition with one another. The absence of a central arbiter was the defining structural feature of international politics. Vulnerable and insecure, states behaved defensively by forming alliances against looming threats. According to Waltz, balances of power form automatically in anarchic environments. Even when they are disrupted, they are soon restored.

neorealism

A theoretical account of states' behavior that explains it as determined by differences in their relative power within the global hierarchy, defined primarily by the distribution of military power, instead of by other factors such as their values, types of government, or domestic circumstances.

agency

The capacity of an actor to make choices and achieve objectives.

Although there are common themes throughout realist thought, different variants of realism emphasize certain features. As shown in Table 2.1, classical realism focuses primarily on "the sources and uses of national power ... and the problems that leaders encounter in conducting foreign policy" (Taliaferro et al., 2009, p. 16). Structural realism, as envisioned by Kenneth Waltz, is often referred to as defensive realism to distinguish it from the more recent variant, offensive realism. Although both are structural realist theories, the two perspectives differ with regard to the underlying motivation for state behavior and conflict. *Defensive realism* sees states as focused on maintaining security by balancing others and essentially preserving the status quo, whereas *offensive realism* sees states as seeking to ensure security by aggressively maximizing their power. According to offensive realism, states are locked in perpetual struggle and must be "primed for offense, because they can never be sure how much military capacity they will need in order to survive over the long run" (Kaplan, 2012; Mearsheimer, 2001). Neoclassical realism draws on both classical realism and structural realism to emphasize "how systemic-level variables are 'translated through unit-level intervening variables such as decision-makers' perceptions and domestic state structure'" (Rynning and Ringsmose, 2008, p. 27).

defensive realism

A variant of realist theory that emphasizes the preservation of power, as opposed to the expansion of power, as an actor's primary security objective.

The Limitations of Realist Thought

offensive realism

A variant of realist theory that stresses that, in an anarchical international system, states should always look for opportunities to gain more power.

However persuasive the realists' image of the essential properties of international politics, their policy recommendations suffered from a lack of precision in the way they used such key terms as *power* and *national interest*. Thus, once analysis moved beyond the assertion that national leaders should acquire power to serve the national interest, important questions remained: What were the key elements of national power? What uses of power best served the national interest? Did arms furnish protection or provoke costly arms races? Did alliances enhance one's defenses or encourage threatening counter-alliances?

From the perspective of realism's critics, seeking security by amassing power was self-defeating. The quest for absolute security by one state would be perceived as creating absolute insecurity for other members of the system, with the result that everyone would become locked in an upward spiral of countermeasures jeopardizing the security of all (Glaser, 2011).

TABLE 2.1	Comparing Various Strands of Realist Theory			
Variant	**View of International System**	**Systemic Pressure**	**Primary State Objective**	**Rational State Preference**
Defensive realism	Very important	Power buildup to deter potential aggressors	Survival	Status quo
Offensive realism	Very important	Emphasis on extensive accumulation of power	Survival	Revisionist (hegemons excepted)
Classical realism	Somewhat important	Either defensive or offensive	Varies (e.g., security, power, or glory)	Status quo or revisionist
Neoclassical realism	Important	Either defensive or offensive	Varies (e.g., security, power, or glory)	Status quo or revisionist

Source: *Based on Taliaferro et al., 2009; Rynning and Ringsmose, 2008.*

Realism offered no criteria for determining what historical data were significant in evaluating its claims and what epistemological rules to follow when interpreting relevant information (Vasquez and Elman, 2003). Even the policy recommendations that purportedly flowed from its logic were often conflicting. Realists themselves, for example, were sharply divided as to whether U.S. intervention in Vietnam served American national interests and whether nuclear weapons contributed to international security. Similarly, although some observers used realism to explain the rationale for the 2003 U.S. invasion of Iraq (Gvosdev, 2005), others drew on realist arguments to criticize the invasion (Mansfield and Snyder, 2005a; Mearsheimer and Walt, 2003).

A growing number of critics also pointed out that realism did not account for significant new developments in world politics. For instance, it could not explain the creation of new commercial and political institutions in Western Europe in the 1950s and 1960s, where the cooperative pursuit of mutual advantage led Europeans away from the unbridled power politics that had brought them incessant warfare since the birth of the nation-state some three centuries earlier. Other critics began to worry about realism's tendency to disregard ethical principles and the material and social costs some of its policy prescriptions imposed, such as hindered economic growth resulting from unrestrained military expenditures.

Despite realism's shortcomings, many people continue to think about world politics in the language constructed by realists, especially in times of global tension. This can be seen in Israel's Prime Minister Benjamin Netanyahu's declaration in March 2013 that Israel has "both the right and the capability" to defend itself (Yellin and Cohen, 2013). Placing great emphasis on military security and national self-interest, his statement comes amid speculation about the possibility of a unilateral Israeli military strike in response to Iran's continuing pursuit of a nuclear program.

**Case Study:
Realism**

LIBERALISM

Liberalism has been called the "strongest contemporary challenge to realism" (Caporaso, 1993, p. 465). Like realism, it has a distinguished pedigree, with philosophical roots extending back to the political thought of John Locke, Immanuel Kant, and Adam Smith. Liberalism warrants our attention because it speaks to issues realism disregards, including the impact of domestic politics on state behavior, the implications of economic interdependence, and the role of global norms and institutions in promoting international cooperation.

What Is Liberalism's Worldview?

There are several distinct schools of thought within the liberal tradition, and drawing broad conclusions from such a diverse body of theory runs the risk of misrepresenting the position of any single author. Nevertheless, there are sufficient commonalities to abstract some general themes.

Liberals differ from realists in several important ways. At the core of liberalism is a belief in reason and the possibility of progress. Liberals view the individual as the seat of moral value and assert that human beings should be treated as ends rather than means. Whereas realists counsel

liberalism

A paradigm predicated on the hope that the application of reason and universal ethics to international relations can lead to a more orderly, just, and cooperative world; liberalism assumes that anarchy and war can be policed by institutional reforms that empower international organization and law.

Carnegie Council Video:
Liberalism

decision makers to seek the lesser evil rather than the absolute good, liberals emphasize ethical principle over the pursuit of power, and institutions over military capabilities (see Ikenberry, 2011; Wilkinson, 2011). While realism anticipates competition and conflict over power and resources, liberalism expects "increasing or potentially greater cooperation and progress in international affairs, generally defined in terms of increased peace and prosperity" (Rathbun, 2012, p. 612). Politics at the global level, then, becomes more a struggle for consensus and mutual gain than a struggle for power and prestige.

Several corollary ideas give definition to liberal theory. These include:

- An emphasis on the unity of humankind rather than parochial national loyalties to independent sovereign states.

- The importance of individuals—their essential dignity and fundamental equality—and the analogous need to place the protection and promotion of human rights and freedom ahead of national interests and state autonomy.

- The use of the power of ideas through education to arouse world public opinion against warfare.

- The conditions under which people live, rather than an inherent lust for power, as an underlying source of international conflict. Reforming those conditions, liberals argue, will enhance the prospects for peace.

Additionally, an element common to various strands of liberal thought is an emphasis on undertaking political reforms to establish stable democracies. Based on tolerance, compromise, and civil liberties, democratic political cultures are said to shun lethal force as a means of settling disagreements. Woodrow Wilson, for example, proclaimed that "democratic government will make wars less likely." Franklin Roosevelt later agreed, asserting "the continued maintenance and improvement of democracy constitute the most important guarantee of international peace."

In place of force, *diplomacy* provides a means for achieving mutually acceptable solutions to a common problem, and enables leaders to negotiate and compromise with each other in a peaceful manner. Politics is not seen as a *zero-sum* game as the use of persuasion rather than coercion, and a reliance on judicial methods to settle rival claims, is the primary means of dealing with conflict.

According to liberal theory, conflict-resolution practices used at home can also be used when dealing with international disputes. Leaders socialized within democratic cultures share a common outlook. Viewing international politics as an extension of domestic politics, they generalize about the applicability of norms to regulate international competition. Disputes between democratic governments rarely escalate to war because each side accepts the other's legitimacy and expects it to rely on peaceful means of conflict resolution. These expectations are reinforced by the transparent nature of democracies. The inner workings of open polities can be scrutinized by anyone; hence, it is difficult to demonize democratically ruled states as scheming adversaries.

A second command strand in liberal theorizing is an emphasis on free trade. The idea that commerce can reduce conflict has roots in the work of Immanuel Kant, Charles de Secondat

diplomacy

Communication and negotiation between global actors that is not dependent upon the use of force and seeks a cooperative solution.

Carnegie Council Video:
Diplomacy

zero-sum

An exchange in a purely conflictual relationship in which what is gained by one competitor is lost by the other.

Carnegie Council Video:
Zero-sum

Montesquieu, Adam Smith, Jean-Jacque Rousseau, and various Enlightenment thinkers. "Nothing is more favourable to the rise of politeness and learning," noted liberal philosopher David Hume (1817), "than a number of neighboring and independent states, connected by commerce." This view was later embraced by the Manchester School of political economy and formed the basis for Norman Angell's (1910) famous rebuttal of the assertion that military conquest produces economic prosperity.

Today, some studies contend that economic interconnectedness is an even more important factor than democracy in fostering peace (Mousseau, 2013). The doctrine that unfettered trade helps prevent disputes from escalating to wars rests on several propositions. First, commercial intercourse creates a material incentive to resolve disputes peacefully: war reduces profits by interrupting vital economic exchanges. Second, cosmopolitan business elites who benefit most from these exchanges comprise a powerful transnational interest group with a stake in promoting amicable solutions to festering disagreements. Finally, the web of trade between countries increases communication, erodes national selfishness, and encourages both sides to avoid ruinous clashes. In the words of Richard Cobden, an opponent of the protectionist Corn Laws that once regulated British international grain trade: "Free Trade! What is it? Why, breaking down the barriers that separate nations; those barriers, behind which nestle the feelings of pride, revenge, hatred, and jealousy, which every now and then burst their bounds, and deluge whole countries with blood."

Finally, the third commonality in liberalism is an advocacy of global institutions. Liberals recommend replacing cutthroat, balance-of-power politics with organizations based on the

Christie's Images/Corbis

The Granger Collection

PIONEERS IN THE LIBERAL QUEST FOR WORLD ORDER A product of the Enlightenment, Scottish philosopher David Hume (left) tried to temper his realist concern that reason is a "slave of the passions" by embracing the liberal faith in wealth-generating free markets and free trade that could cohesively bind people together to create a peaceful civil society. Influenced by David Hume and Jean-Jacques Rousseau, Immanuel Kant (right) in *Perpetual Peace* (1795) helped to redefine modern liberal theory by advocating global (not state) citizenship, free trade, and a federation of democracies as a means to peace.

principle that a threat to peace anywhere is a common threat to everyone. They see foreign policy as unfolding in a nascent global society populated by actors who recognize the cost of conflict, share significant interests, and can realize those interests by using institutions to mediate disputes whenever misconceptions, wounded sensibilities, or aroused national passions threaten peaceful relations. Realists counter, however, that "neither globalization nor international institutions impose genuine constraints on great powers, simply because states have sufficient power to interpret sovereignty" (Ziegler, 2012, p. 402) and participate in global institutions only to the extent that it suits their own national interest.

The Evolution of Liberalism

In the wake of World War I, contemporary liberal theory rose to prominence. Not only had the war involved more participants over a wider geographic area than any previous war, but modern science and technology made it a war of machinery. Old weapons were improved and produced in greater quantities; new and far more deadly weapons were rapidly developed and deployed. By the time the carnage was over, nearly 20 million people were dead.

For liberals such as U.S. President Woodrow Wilson, World War I was "the war to end all wars." Believing that another horrific war would erupt if states resumed practicing power politics, liberals set out to reform the global system. These "idealists," as they were sometimes called by realists, generally fell into one of three groups (Herz, 1951). The first group advocated creating global institutions to contain the raw struggle for power between self-serving, mutually suspicious states. The League of Nations was the embodiment of this strain of liberal thought. Its founders hoped to prevent future wars by organizing a system of *collective security* that would mobilize the entire international community against would-be aggressors. The League's founders declared that peace was indivisible: an attack on one member of the League would be considered an attack on all. Because no state was more powerful than the combination of all other states, aggressors would be deterred and war averted.

A second group called for the use of legal procedures to adjudicate disputes before they escalated to armed conflict. Adjudication is a judicial procedure for resolving conflicts by referring them to a standing court for a binding decision. Immediately after the war, several governments drafted a statute to establish a Permanent Court of International Justice (PCIJ). Hailed by Bernard C. J. Loder, the court's first president, as the harbinger of a new era of civilization, the PCIJ held its inaugural public meeting in early 1922 and rendered its first judgment on a contentious case the following year. Liberal champions of the court insisted that the PCIJ would replace military retaliation with a judicial body capable of bringing the facts of a dispute to light and issuing a just verdict.

A third group of liberal thinkers followed the biblical ideal that states should beat their swords into plowshares and sought disarmament as a means of avoiding war. Their efforts were illustrated between 1921 and 1922 by the Washington Naval Conference, which tried to curtail maritime competition among the United States, Great Britain, Japan, France, and Italy by placing limits on battleships. The ultimate goal of this group was to reduce international tensions by promoting general disarmament, which led them to convene the 1932 Geneva Disarmament Conference.

collective security

A security regime agreed to by the great powers that sets rules for keeping peace, guided by the principle that an act of aggression by any state will be met by a collective response from the rest.

Carnegie Council Video:
Collective Security

Although a tone of idealism dominated policy rhetoric and academic discussions during the interwar period, little of the liberal reform program was ever seriously attempted, and even less of it was achieved. The League of Nations failed to prevent the Japanese invasion of Manchuria (1931) or the Italian invasion of Ethiopia (1935); major disputes were rarely submitted to the PCIJ, and the 1932 Geneva Disarmament Conference ended in failure. When the threat of war began gathering over Europe and Asia in the late 1930s, enthusiasm for liberal idealism receded.

The next surge in liberal theorizing arose decades later in response to realism's neglect of *transnational relations* (see Keohane and Nye, 1971). Although realists continued to focus on the state, the events surrounding the 1973 oil crisis revealed that nonstate actors could affect the course of international events and occasionally compete with states. This insight led to the realization that *complex interdependence* (Keohane and Nye, 1977; 2013) sometimes offered a better description of world politics than realism, especially on international economic and environmental matters.

Rather than contacts between countries being limited to high-level governmental officials, multiple communication channels connect societies. Instead of security dominating foreign policy considerations, issues on national agendas do not always have a fixed priority, and although military force often serves as the primary instrument of statecraft, other means frequently are more effective when bargaining occurs between economically interconnected countries. In short, the realist preoccupation with government-to-government relations ignored the complex network of public and private exchanges crisscrossing state boundaries. States were becoming increasingly interdependent, that is, mutually dependent on, sensitive about, and vulnerable to one another in ways that were not captured by realist theory.

Although interdependence was not new, its growth during the last quarter of the twentieth century led many liberal theorists to challenge the realist conception of anarchy. Although they agreed that the global system was anarchic, they also argued that it was more properly conceptualized as an "ordered" anarchy because most states followed commonly acknowledged normative standards, even in the absence of hierarchical enforcement. When a body of norms fosters shared expectations that guide a regularized pattern of cooperation on a specific issue, we call it an *international regime*. Various types of regimes have been devised to govern behavior in trade and monetary affairs, as well as to manage access to common resources such as fisheries and river water. By the turn of the century, as pressing economic and environmental issues crowded national agendas, a large body of liberal "institutionalist" scholarship explored how regimes developed and what led states to comply with their injunctions.

Fueled by the recent history that suggested that international relations can change and that increased interdependence can lead to higher levels of cooperation, *neoliberalism* emerged in the last decade of the twentieth century to challenge realism and neorealism. This new departure goes by several labels, including "neoliberal institutionalism" (Grieco, 1995), "neoidealism" (Kegley, 1993), and "neo-Wilsonian idealism" (Fukuyama, 1992a).

Like realism and neorealism, neoliberalism does not represent a consistent intellectual movement or school of thought. Whatever the differences that divide them, however, all neoliberals share an interest in probing the conditions under which the convergent and overlapping interests among otherwise independent transnational actors may result in cooperation.

transnational relations

Interactions across state boundaries that involve at least one actor that is not the agent of a government or intergovernmental organization.

complex interdependence

A model of world politics based on the assumptions that states are not the only important actors, security is not the dominant national goal, and military force is not the only significant instrument of foreign policy; this theory stresses crosscutting ways in which the growing ties among transnational actors make them vulnerable to each other's actions and sensitive to each other's needs.

international regime

Embodies the norms, principles, rules, and institutions around which global expectations unite regarding a specific international problem.

neoliberalism

The "new" liberal theoretical perspective that accounts for the way international institutions promote global change, cooperation, peace, and prosperity through collective programs for reforms.

Neoliberalism departs from neorealism on many assumptions. In particular, neoliberalism focuses on the ways in which influences such as democratic governance, liberal commercial enterprise, international law and organization, collective security, and ethically inspired statecraft can improve life on our planet. Because they perceive change in global conditions as progressing over time through cooperative efforts, neoliberal theorists maintain that the ideas and ideals of the liberal legacy could describe, explain, predict, and prescribe international conduct in ways that they could not during the conflict-ridden Cold War.

The Limitations of Liberalism

Liberal theorists share an interest in probing the conditions under which similar interests among actors may lead to cooperation. Taking heart in the international prohibition, through community consensus, of such previously entrenched practices as slavery, piracy, dueling, and colonialism, they emphasize the prospects for progress through institutional reform. Studies of European integration during the 1950s and 1960s paved the way for the liberal institutionalist theories that emerged in the 1990s. The expansion of trade, communication, information, technology, and migrant labor led Europeans to sacrifice portions of their sovereign independence to create a new political and economic union out of previously separate units. These developments were outside of realism's worldview, creating conditions that made the call for a theory grounded in the liberal tradition more convincing. In the words of former U.S. President Bill Clinton, "In a world where freedom, not tyranny, is on the march, the cynical calculus of pure power politics simply does not compute. It is ill-suited to the new era."

Yet, as compelling as contemporary liberal institutionalism may seem at the onset of the twenty-first century, many realists complain that it has not transcended its idealist heritage. They charge that just like the League of Nations and the PCIJ, institutions today exert minimal influence on state behavior. International organizations cannot stop states from behaving according to balance-of-power logic, calculating how each strategic move affects their relative position in a world of relentless competition.

Critics of liberalism further contend that most studies supportive of international institutions appear in the arena of commercial, financial, and environmental affairs, not in the arena of national defense. Although it may be difficult to draw a clear line between economic and security issues, some scholars note that "different institutional arrangements" exist in each realm, with the prospects for cooperation among self-interested states greater in the former than the latter (Lipson, 1984). National survival hinges on the effective management of security issues, realists insist. Collective security organizations naïvely assume that all members perceive threats in the same way and that they are willing to run the same risks and pay the same costs of countering those threats. Because power-lusting states are unlikely to always see their vital interests in this light, global institutions cannot provide timely, muscular responses to aggression. On security issues, conclude realists, states will trust in their own power, not in the promises of supranational institutions.

A final complaint lodged against liberalism is an alleged tendency to turn foreign policy into a moral crusade. Whereas realists claim that heads of state are driven by strategic necessities, many liberals believe moral imperatives can guide and constrain leaders. Consider the 1999 war in Kosovo, which pitted the North Atlantic Treaty Organization (NATO) against the Federal Republic of Yugoslavia. Pointing to Yugoslav leader Slobodan Milosevic's repression of ethnic Albanians living in the province of Kosovo, NATO Secretary General Javier Solana, British Prime Minister Tony Blair, and U.S. President Bill Clinton all argued that humanitarian intervention was a moral necessity. Although nonintervention into the internal affairs of other states has long been a cardinal principle of international law, they saw military action against Yugoslavia as a duty because human rights are an international entitlement and governments that violate them forfeit the protection of international law.

Sovereignty, according to many liberal thinkers, is not sacrosanct. The international community has a *responsibility to protect* (RtoP) vulnerable populations and an obligation to use armed force to stop flagrant violations of human rights. In accounting for U.S. military intervention in Libya in March 2011, these sentiments were reflected in President Barack Obama's declaration that the United States had a responsibility and moral obligation to respond to the violence perpetuated by Muammar al-Qaddafi's troops. "Some nations may be able to turn a blind eye to atrocities in other countries," proclaimed Obama. "The United States of America is different. And as President, I refused to wait for the images of slaughter and mass graves before taking action."

To sum up, realists remain skeptical about liberal claims of moral necessity and contend that "internal abuses by states—including the slaughter of civilians—do not automatically qualify as 'international' threats" (Doyle, 2011). On the one hand, they deny the universal applicability of any single moral standard in a culturally pluralist world. On the other hand, they worry that adopting such a standard will breed a self-righteous, messianic foreign policy. Realists embrace *consequentialism*. If there are no universal standards covering the many situations in which moral choice must occur, then policy decisions can be judged only in terms of their consequences in particular circumstances. Prudent leaders recognize that competing moral values may be at stake in any given situation, and they must weigh the trade-offs among these values, as well as how pursuing them might impinge on national security and other important interests. As former U.S. diplomat and celebrated realist scholar George Kennan (1985) once put it, the primary obligation of government "is to the interests of the national society it represents, not to the moral impulses that individual elements of that society may experience."

> *It's important that we take a hard clear look ... not at some simple world, either of universal goodwill or universal hostility, but the complex, changing, and sometimes dangerous world that really exists.*
>
> **—Jimmy Carter, U.S. president**

CONSTRUCTIVISM

Constructivism is rapidly growing in influence as an approach for studying world politics. With intellectual roots in the twentieth-century Frankfurt School of critical social theory, contemporary scholars who have influenced the theoretical development of this perspective

responsibility to protect

Unanimously adopted in a resolution by the UN General Assembly in 2005, this principle holds that the international community must help protect populations from war crimes, ethnic cleansing, genocide, and crimes against humanity.

Simulation:
Theories of International Relations: Realism v. Liberalism

Animated Learning Module:
Realism v. Liberalism

consequentialism

An approach to evaluating moral choices on the basis of the results of the action taken.

constructivism

A paradigm based on the premise that world politics is a function of the ways that states construct and then accept images of reality and later respond to the meanings given to power politics; as consensual definitions change, it is possible for either conflictual or cooperative practices to evolve.

include Alexander Wendt, Friedrich Kratochwil, and Nicholas Onuf. Constructivism merits careful consideration because awareness of how our understandings of the world are individually and socially constructed, and of how prevailing ideas mold our beliefs about what is unchangeable and what can be reformed, allows us to see international relations in a new and critical light.

What is the Constructivist Worldview?

Sometimes described as a philosophically informed perspective rather than a full-fledged general theory, constructivism posits that world politics is best understood through the prism of intersubjective human action and the socially constructed nature of political life (DeBardeleben, 2012; Rathbun, 2012). Along these lines, a complete understanding of international relations requires knowledge of the social context underlying these relations—the identities of the actors, their norms of behavior, and their social interactions within the international system.

As discussed in the previous chapter, our images and understandings of the world define and shape reality. Though constructivists do not limit their analysis to the individual level, they view ideas, norms, and individual speech acts as shaping the global structure (Simão, 2012) and stress the intersubjective quality of images—how prevailing attitudes shape perception. For constructivists, this underscores the potential for *agency* as actors can reflect on their environment and seek change. Ideas define identities, which in turn impart meaning to material capabilities and behavior.

In the years following the Cold War, new norms about sovereignty emerged, particularly with regard to the acceptability of intervention in cases of gross human rights violations. Constructivism, like liberalism, recognizes the evolution of shared ideas as underpinning the growing legitimacy of the *responsibility to protect* concept, even though in practice it entails a violation of Westphalian sovereignty. From a constructivist perspective, this illustrates that "key elements of sovereignty, including territory, national identity and authority are not constants, but will change and evolve depending on society" (Ziegler 2012, p. 404).

Similarly, the meaning of a concept such as "anarchy" depends on underlying shared knowledge. As Wendt (1992, p. 395) expressed, "anarchy is what states make of it." Anarchy among allies, for instance, holds a different meaning than anarchy among bitter rivals. Thus, British nuclear weapons are less threatening to the United States than the same weapons in North Korean hands, because shared Anglo-American expectations about one another differ from those between Washington and Pyongyang. The nature of an anarchic international system, therefore, is not a given. Anarchy and other socially constructed concepts, such as "sovereignty" and "power," are simply what we make of them (Wendt, 2013).

Moreover, because the social structure underlying these relationships is malleable, the ideas and interests of actors may change as the nature of their interactions, and the way they understand the other actors, changes. Thus states with a history of rivalry can change the fundamental nature of their relationships if they are able to establish patterns of peaceful interactions and cooperation over time. A prominent example of this is the European Union, which is made up of many states that fought against each other in both World War I and World War II but subsequently have been able to develop a common identity, or "we-feeling," in the latter half of the twentieth century. Key concepts of international relations, such as the institutions of war and slavery, may likewise change over time as the normative consensus surrounding them evolves.

Table 2.2 shows how constructivists differ from realists and liberals. As opposed to realism and liberalism, which assume that the fundamental structures of world politics are material and emphasize how objective factors such as military power and economic wealth affect international relations, constructivism sees the fundamental structures as social. Whereas realism and liberalism assume that an actor's preferences are given and fixed—with realism focusing on power, and liberalism on peace and prosperity—constructivism rejects rationalism and asserts that social structures shape behavior, as well as an actor's identity and interests. In other words, realism and liberalism "portray a world occupied by undifferentiated rational actors (i.e., self-interested states), whose relations are structured by the balance of material power. In contrast, constructivism ... locate(s) actors in a social structure that both constitutes those actors and is constituted by their interaction" (Farrell, 2002, p. 50). Realism and liberalism take interests and identities as given, whereas these concepts are the central concern for constructivism.

The Evolution of Constructivist Thought

The unraveling of the Warsaw Pact, the subsequent disintegration of the Soviet Union, the rise of religious fundamentalism, and the growth of micro-nationalism through the 1990s stimulated scholarly interest in constructivist interpretations of world politics. As political scientist Barry Buzan (2004, p. 1) observed, "after a long period of neglect, the social (or societal) dimension of the international system is being brought back into fashion within International Relations by

TABLE 2.2	A Comparison of Realist, Liberal, and Constructivist Theories		
Feature	**Realism**	**Liberalism**	**Constructivism**
Core concern	War and security: how vulnerable, self-interested states survive in an environment where they are uncertain about the intentions and capabilities of others	Institutionalized peace and prosperity: how self-serving actors learn to see benefits to coordinating behavior through rules and organizations in order to achieve collective gains	Social groups' shared meanings and images: how ideas, images, and identities develop, change, and shape world politics
Key actors	States	States, international institutions, global corporations	Individuals, nongovernmental organizations, transnational networks
Central concepts	Anarchy, self-help, national interest, relative gains, balance of power	Collective security, reciprocity, international regimes, complex interdependence, transnational relations	Ideas, images, shared knowledge, identities, discourses, and persuasion leading to new understandings and normative change
Approach to peace	Protect sovereign autonomy and deter rivals through military preparedness and alliances	Institutional reform through democratization, open markets, and international law and organization	Activists who promote progressive ideas and encourage states to adhere to norms for appropriate behavior
Global outlook	Pessimistic: great powers locked in relentless security competition	Optimistic: cooperative view of human nature and a belief in progress	Agnostic: global prospect hinges on the content of prevailing ideas and values

the upsurge of interest in constructivism." Neither realism nor liberalism foresaw the peaceful end to the Cold War, and both theories had difficulty explaining why it occurred when it did (see Table 4.2 in Chapter 4). Constructivists attributed this to the material and individualist orientation of realism and liberalism, and argued that an explanation addressing the role of changing ideas and identities provided superior explanations for this systemic change.

Like realism and liberalism, within the constructivist perspective there are several strands of thought. One of the most prominent is *social constructivism*, which emphasizes collective identity formation. Alexander Wendt, who is widely credited with the contemporary application of social constructivism to world politics, challenges the material and individualist foundations of realism and liberalism. For social constructivists, ideational construction of the self and the other are crucial: "It is through reciprocal interaction ... that we create and instantiate the relatively enduring social structures in terms of which we define our identities and our interests" (Wendt, 2013). They see the structure of the international system in terms of the distribution of shared ideas, whereas neorealists view systemic structure within the context of the distribution of material capabilities and neoliberals see it as the distribution of capabilities within an institutional superstructure (see "Controversy: How Might Countries Respond to a Zombie Outbreak?"). According to social constructivism, all of us are influenced by collective conceptions of world politics that are reinforced by social pressures from the reference groups to which we belong.

There is, however, concern that social constructivism overemphasizes the role of social structures at the expense of the purposeful agents—such as a state's or organizations' political leaders—whose practices help create and change these structures. Social constructivism tends to reify states by picturing them like individuals whose decisions become the authors of international life, and constructivism says little about the "practices that produce states as producers" (Weber, 2005, p. 76). A second strand of constructivism, *agent-oriented constructivism*, addresses this weakness with its emphasis on individual influences on identities.

According to agent-oriented constructivism, independent actors in world politics may differ in their internal ideas or identities. Thus, domestic or internal identities "are crucial for their perceptions of one another in the international arena" (Risse-Kappen, 1996, p. 367). An actor can hold both domestic and international identities, which are shaped by respective dialogue at home and within the international community. Whereas social constructivists attribute the development of these identities to repeated social practices and view most identity as a shared or collective understanding, agent-oriented constructivists suggest identities need not be universally shared and allow for individual or autonomous identity within the collectivity. They credit the development of ideas in part to individual actors with the capacity for independent and critical thinking, making it far easier for new ideas to (re)construct and change the international system.

Accordingly, agent-oriented constructivists point to the challenge that Mikhail Gorbachev's "new thinking" posed to traditional Russian ideas about national security. Shifting from belief in irreconcilable conflict between capitalism and communism to the possibility of a foreign policy rooted in shared moral and ethical principles, Gorbachev's new thinking was reflected in a greater emphasis on political influence, diplomatic relations, and economic cooperation rather than intimidation and posturing through military power. Agent-oriented constructivism

social constructivism

A variant of constructivism that emphasizes the role of social discourse in the development of ideas and identities.

Carnegie Council Video: Social Constructivism

agent-oriented constructivism

A variant of constructivism that sees ideas and identities as influenced in part by independent actors.

CONTROVERSY

HOW MIGHT COUNTRIES RESPOND TO A ZOMBIE OUTBREAK?

Zombies are a "popular figure in pop culture/entertainment and they are usually portrayed as being brought about through an outbreak or epidemic," as noted by researchers at Carleton University and the University of Ottawa (Munz et al., 2009, p. 133), who mathematically modeled the spread of the lethal infection. Viewing a zombie outbreak as a strategic threat, and assessing the relative usefulness and applicability of different international relations theories, offers a fun way to learn about theories by applying them to clearly hypothetical (we hope) situations. But there are real insights to be gained through such an exercise, which allows students to explore the extent to which various international relations theories are able to explain state, and individual, responses to a cataclysmic systemic change (Blanton, 2012).

Consider these questions: In a world suffering from a zombie outbreak, what effects would different systemic international relations theories predict? Would the outcomes be of little consequence, or would they result in the demise of human society as we know it?

- **Structural realism.** Due to an uneven distribution of capabilities, structural realism anticipates that some countries are better able than others to ward off zombies. Balance-of-power politics could ensue, with human states aligning with other human states to counter the global spread of zombieism. Or, as political analyst Daniel Drezner (2010b, p. 37) suggests, "states could also exploit the threat from the living dead to acquire new territory, squelch irredentist movements, settle old scores, or subdue enduring rivals."
- **Liberal institutionalism.** As a strand of liberalism, liberal institutionalism sees a zombie outbreak as a problem that transcends national borders and threatens the global community writ large. Therefore, prudent states seek to cooperate with one another and coordinate efforts to contain and squash the zombie threat. Both global and regional regimes and institutions could serve as important means for facilitating communication and directing the human response. For example, a World Zombie Organization (WZO) could be helpful in codifying international rules and procedures for responding to the zombie outbreak (see Drezner, 2011).
- **Social constructivism.** With its emphasis on the development of norms and ideas, social constructivism envisions a number of different scenarios. On one hand, relations between humans and zombies might best be reflected by the Hobbesian "kill or be killed" norm. Alternatively, a Kantian pluralistic antizombie community could emerge "that bands together and breaks down nationalist divides in an effort to establish a world state" (Drezner, 2009). Hostilities between humans and zombies might also strengthen group identity, where humans who have not been infected identify with one another as opposed to zombies, who seem to recognize each other as fellow "brain-eaters."

WHAT DO YOU THINK?

- *If you were the leader of your country, which theoretical orientation do you think would best help you address a zombie outbreak? Why?*
- *Reflect upon the "real" global challenges facing us today, from the threat of terrorism to global warming to the worldwide economic downturn. Which concerns have the greatest impact upon our security, and how do realism, liberalism, and constructivism deal with these threats?*
- *Should a country work toward international cooperation or international dominance? Draw on realism, liberalism, or constructivism to frame your response.*

suggests that Gorbachev's new thinking led to the rise of new *norms* governing the relations between Moscow and Washington.

Shared conceptions of moral and legal norms can also change the world through the capacity of some activist transnational nongovernmental organizations, such as Human Rights Watch or Greenpeace, to promote global change by convincing people to accept their ideas about political liberties and environmental protection. Consensual understandings of interests, self-identities, and images of the world—how people think of themselves, who they are, and what others in the world are like—demonstrably can alter the world when these constructions of international realities change (Finnemore, 2013; Barnett, 2005).

The Limitations of Constructivism

Although constructivists have offered "path-breaking perspectives in the study of international politics" (Palan, 2000, p. 576) that share certain distinctive themes, some argue that constructivism is not a theory as such, but rather a general social scientific framework or "meta-approach." Whereas theoretical paradigms embrace a set of assumptions about how politics work, "constructivism is a set of assumptions about how to study politics," and hence is compatible with a variety of paradigms (Barkin, 2003, p. 338; Rathbun, 2012). Along this line of argument, constructivism supplements rather than supplants realism and liberalism.

Realists criticize constructivism for its emphasis on norms and values, and suggest that norms are simply manifestations of state or individual interests and can be superficially adopted for strategic reasons. Liberals, likewise, challenge that although many constructivists point to norms and values in explaining world politics, constructivism is agnostic and does not provide core notions about what should be right or ethical in international affairs (see Hoffmann, 2009). Although constructivism seeks to explain change, critics charge that constructivists remain unclear about what factors cause particular ideas to become dominant while others fall by the wayside. "What is crucial," asserts Robert Jervis (2005, p. 18), "is not people's thinking, but the factors that drive it." Constructivists, he continues, have excessive faith in the ability of ideas that seem self-evident today to replicate and sustain themselves; however, future generations who live under different circumstances and who may think differently could easily reject these ideas.

Although constructivism has often been portrayed as the opposite of realism due to differences in terms of realism's objective material emphasis and constructivism's intersubjective ideational focus—and the liberal normative disposition of many constructivist scholars—it is now more commonly thought that realism and constructivism are not implacably opposed (Jackson, 2004; Nexon, 2011). Although constructivists recognize that shared ideas are not predetermined and can change over time, they claim a blending of constructivism with the realist and liberal paradigms could lead to greater understanding of change in the international system. Realist constructivism, for example, could look at the manner in which power structures shape patterns of normative change (Barkin, 2003).

Although the constructivist approach is increasingly viewed as a vital perspective for understanding world politics, it is still criticized for its limited attention to methodological issues. According to Amir Lupovici (2009, p. 197), "scholars have tended to neglect the methodological dimension, providing little guidance on how to conduct a constructivist study." In an effort to address this deficiency, scholars have begun to call for a more systematic and unified framework

---

norms

Generalized standards of behavior that, once accepted, shape collective expectations about appropriate conduct.

CourseMate

Carnegie Council Video:
Norms

PIONEERING INFLUENCES ON CONSTRUCTIVIST THOUGHT Many constructivists have been influenced by critical theory, especially as it was developed by Max Horkheimer (1947), left, and Jurgen Habermas (1984), right. Rather than viewing the world as a set of neutral, objective "facts" that could be perceived apart from the situation in which observation occurred, critical theorists saw all phenomena as being embedded within a specific socio-historical context ascribing normative meaning to information.

that combines a number of existing methods so as to enable us to "examine the mutual influences of constitutive effects upon causal effects and vice versa" (Lupovici, 2009, p. 200; Pouliot, 2007). In other words, such a pluralistic methodology would help us to consider both the material and ideational factors that shape world politics.

Despite these criticisms, constructivism is a very popular theoretical approach in world politics. By highlighting the influence that socially constructed images of the world have on your interpretations of international events, and by making you aware of their inherent subjectivity, constructivism can remind you of the contingent nature of all knowledge and the inability of any theory of world politics to fully capture global complexities.

> *When I was working in Washington and helping formulate American foreign policies, I found myself borrowing from all three types of thinking: realism, liberalism, and constructivism. I found them all helpful, though in different ways and in different circumstances.*

—**Joseph S. Nye, international relations scholar and U.S. policy maker**

OTHER THEORETICAL PERSPECTIVES: FEMINIST AND MARXIST CRITIQUES

Although realism, liberalism, and constructivism dominate thinking about international relations in today's academic and policy communities, these schools of thought have been challenged. Although there are many different challengers, two of the most significant are feminism and Marxism.

The Feminist Critique

Beginning in the late 1980s, feminism began challenging conventional international relations theory. Cast as a "critical theory," contemporary feminist scholars called for a "shift from mechanistic causal explanations to a greater interest in historically contingent interpretive theories" (Tickner, 2010, p. 37). In particular, feminist theory was concerned with the gender bias inherent in both mainstream theory and the practice of international affairs, and sought to demonstrate how gendered perspectives pervade world politics. As *feminist theory* evolved over time, it moved away from focusing on a history of discrimination and began to explore how gender identity shapes foreign policy decision making and how gendered hierarchies reinforce practices that perpetuate inequalities between men and women (see Ackerly and True, 2008; Bolzendahl, 2009; Enloe, 2004; Peterson and Runyan, 2009; Tickner, 2013).

feminist theory

Body of scholarship that emphasizes gender in the study of world politics.

According to the feminist critique, the mainstream literature on world politics dismisses the plight and contributions of women and treats differences in men's and women's status, beliefs, and behaviors as unimportant. Similar to social constructivism, the feminist critique emphasizes the role of identity in the construction of knowledge—but focuses specifically on gender identity and contends that the study of international relations draws heavily on male experiences to explain international affairs, largely dismissing the feminine dimension.

For example, as feminist scholar J. Ann Tickner contends, "While realists claim that their theories are 'objective' and of universal validity, the assumptions they use when analyzing states and explaining their behavior in the international system are heavily dependent on characteristics that we, in the West, have come to associate with masculinity . . . it is therefore a worldview that offers us only a partial view of reality. . . ." (Tickner, 2013, p. 280). This can be seen in Morgenthau's classical realist depiction of states in an anarchical environment engaged in a persistent pursuit of power to further their own self-interest (Hutchings, 2008). Feminism challenges the heavy reliance on such assumptions and posits that characteristics dismissed due to their "feminine" quality play an important role in international affairs as well.

Feminism challenges the fundamentals of traditional international relations theory in four primary ways:

- **Fundamental gender bias.** Feminism notes that the basic assumptions of the mainstream theoretical literature, as well as the practice of foreign policy, are heavily colored by a masculine tradition of thought. Rationality, independence, strength, protector, and public are characteristics that are considered to be masculine in nature, whereas emotionality, relational, weakness, protected, and private are associated with femininity (Tickner and Sjoberg, 2006). Whether characterizing individuals or states, these traits are seen as unequal. "To be a soldier is to be a man, not a woman; more than any other social institution, the military separates men from women. Soldiering is a role into which boys are socialized in school and on the playing fields. A soldier must be a protector; he must show courage, strength, and responsibility and repress feelings of fear, vulnerability, and compassion. Such feelings are womanly traits, which are liabilities in time of war" (Tickner, 2013, p. 283; also see Tickner and Sjoberg, 2007).

■ **Reformulation of core concepts.** Feminists call for a closer examination of key concepts in world politics—such as state, power, interest, and security—and ask whether a "masculine" conceptualization of these ideas shapes the conduct of foreign policy. Realism, for instance, attributes to the state masculine characteristics of sovereignty that emphasize a hierarchical leader, the capacity to wage war, desirability of wealth and reputation, and the conduct of international affairs as separate from the domestic concerns of its populace. Feminist scholars such as Cynthia Enloe (2007), however, argue that power relations are influenced by gender in ways that shape practices of war and diplomacy, and that alternative formulations of key concepts allow for the relevance of a wide range of other issues and structures, including social and economic ones, in world politics.

■ **Incorporation of the female perspective.** Historically, the role of women has been marginalized in most societies. In order to understand how unequal gender relations have excluded women from foreign policy, perpetuated injustice and oppression, and shaped state interests and behavior, it is critical to purposively examine the female experience. Christine Sylvester's (2002) examination of women's cooperatives in Zimbabwe and women's peace activism at Greenham Common reflects a feminist commitment to a more flexible understanding of security that expands upon the traditional state-centric conceptualization as protection from external aggressors to include threats to economic and family concerns as well.

■ **The scientific study of world politics.** As we have previously discussed, traditional international relations theory—particularly neorealism—has influenced the scientific study of world politics, which attempts to explain the behavior of states in the international system by universal, objective laws. Yet feminism questions the true objectivity of these approaches. Spike Petersen, a prominent feminist theorist, notes that there was an explicit masculine bias in the scientific revolution of the seventeenth century, with science/reasoning attributed as a "male" trait and emotion/intuition as a "female" one. Feminism does not embrace a sole methodological approach, and the "idea that theorizing is 'objective'" is rejected by many feminists in favor "of a perspectival approach, which links the possibility of insight to specific standpoints and political agendas" (Hutchings, 2008, p. 100; see also Tickner, 2005).

Some critics of feminism are skeptical of the historical and interpretative approach to investigating research questions. They argue that there is a greater need for feminist scholars to develop scientifically testable hypotheses (Keohane, 1998); this would make it easier to assess competing claims and increase the validity of feminist research. Other critics argue that feminism has an inherent normative bias and active political agenda, and are skeptical about objectivity in feminist scholarship. As feminist scholar J. Ann Tickner (1997, p. 622) observes, the linkage between feminist insights and political action is "unsettling to proponents of scientific methodologies who frequently label such knowledge claims as relativist and lacking in objectivity." Still others charge that feminism errs when it treats women as a homogenous category (Mohanty, 1988). Not all women are the same or share similar life

AP Photo/David Caulkin

PROTESTING FOR PEACE Between 1981 and 2000, tens of thousands of British women mobilized to protest against nuclear proliferation and the stationing of U.S. nuclear air missiles at the Greenham Common Airbase in Berkshire, England. They saw peace as a feminist issue, and asserted their power by holding hands and creating a 14-mile chain around the airbase with their bodies. Not only did they see nuclear weapons as a direct threat to themselves and their children, they protested that trillions were being spent on weapons of mass destruction while so many around the world suffered from a lack of food and water, inadequate healthcare, and underfunded schools. Their nearly two-decade demonstration attracted worldwide media attention and generated the support of millions throughout the world.

experiences, and important differences may exist that are conditioned by factors such as social class, race, and culture.

Although all feminists stress the importance of gender in studying international relations and are interested in gender emancipation, there are numerous theoretical perspectives within feminism. *Liberal feminism* is a prominent category of feminist theory and draws on liberalism's emphasis on liberty and equality. Liberal feminists object to the marginalization and exclusion of women in international affairs. They argue that women are just as skilled and competent as men, and they should have an equal opportunity to participate in world politics. Furthermore, whether in positions of political, economic, or military leadership, excluding women squanders talent and means that state and organizational capabilities fall short of their full potential. Liberal feminists call for the removal of legal and societal barriers that prevent women from full participation, and hence see the state and the international community as a possible ally (or in some cases, opponent) for overcoming the oppression of women. Unlike some other variants of feminist theory, liberal feminism calls for greater participation of women within the existing structures and does not think that inclusion of women in positions of leadership would fundamentally change the practice of world politics or the nature of the international system.

liberal feminism

A category of feminist theory that sees men and women as equal in skills and capabilities, and promotes the equal participation of women under existing political, legal and social institutions and practices.

Standpoint feminism argues that real differences exist between men and women. Whether biological or cultural in origin, the lives and roles of women in most societies across the world are very different from those of men, and therefore women have a unique standpoint or perspective. For instance, women are thought to have a greater aptitude in nurturing and social interactions, and so may also have greater skill in community building and conflict resolution. This strand of feminism urges us to examine events from the personal perspectives of the countless women who have been involved in international affairs as caregivers, grassroots activists, or participants in the informal labor force. Standpoint feminism, however, focuses particularly on the subordination of women and how this condition shapes the feminine perspective (Dietz, 2003). Women's experiences—as citizens in countries where they have no political rights or voice, or as victims of human trafficking where they face a life of prostitution or slave labor, or as cheap and easily exploited workers in factories across the globe—provide insights that paint a very different picture of global relations than portrayed from a masculine point of view.

A third variant, *post-structural feminism*, argues that "our reality is mediated through our use of language" (Tickner and Sjoberg, 2006, p. 191). This category of feminism focuses on the ways in which gendered language and action pervade world politics (Steans, 2006). Consider, for example, the phallic nature of military weapons and the use of force—the "potency" of weapons, "penetration" of targets, and the masculine "warrior"—that invokes imagery of male virility and female submissiveness. Similarly, dichotomist constructions such

standpoint feminism

A category of feminism that sees women as experiencing a very different reality from that of men, and consequently holding a different perspective on international affairs.

post-structural feminism

A category of feminist theory that focuses on the implications of gendered language for world politics.

Martin Bernetti/AFP/Getty Images

GIRL POWER Although still far outnumbered by men, women are increasingly seeking prominent political leadership positions. Although unsuccessful in her bid for the U.S. presidency, Hillary Clinton inspired many with her remarks that "although we weren't able to shatter that highest, hardest glass ceiling this time, thanks to you, it's got about 18 million cracks in it." Pictured here are three female heads of state that, as liberal feminism encourages, are participants within the existing political structures: from left are Brazilian President Dilma Rousseff, German Chancellor Angela Merkel, and Argentinian President Cristina Fernandez de Kirchner in Santiago, Chile on January 26, 2013 at the opening of the first Summit of the Community of Latin American and Caribbean States (CELAC) and the European Union (EU).

postcolonial feminism

A category of feminist theory that looks at differences in the experiences of women, and argues there is no universal feminine perspective or approach.

as rational/emotional, strong/weak, protector/protected convey a preference for the masculine. Post-structural feminists are critical of these linguistic constructions and believe they have real consequences in world politics. They are also concerned that those who construct such meaning and determine legitimate knowledge (generally males) gain power (Hooper, 2001). Post-structuralist feminists contend that women have typically been marginalized as both generators of knowledge and as subjects of knowledge, but that the spoken meaning of gender can be changed.

Postcolonial feminism argues that not only are there differences between men and women, but there are differences between women from different parts of the world. Postcolonial feminists argue that factors such as culture, ethnicity, and geographic location are important for understanding the marginalization and oppression of women, and that "women's experiences in the developing world are significantly dissimilar to those of privileged white women in the western/developed world" (Kaufmann and Williams, 2007, p. 11). Thus, there is not a universal approach to understanding and overcoming the subordination of women.

It is important to keep in mind that the various types of feminist theory are not mutually exclusive. Rather, "endless mixing is the rule, not the exception, so assuming lenses constitute discrete 'boxes' misrepresents the diversity, the range, and especially the extensive overlap among many perspectives" (Peterson and Runyan, 2010, p. 80). Yet regardless of the position taken on the issue of gender differences, feminist scholars are critical of traditional theoretical perspectives that ignore the ways in which gender shapes international relations.

The feminist critique continues to expand across a range of issues, from foreign policy to humanitarian intervention to terrorism, and a variety of actors, from states to nongovernmental organizations. "Women have never been absent in world politics," writes Franke Wilmer (2000). They have, for the most part, remained "invisible within the discourse conducted by men." To counter this marginalization of women, "We must search deeper to find ways in which gender hierarchies serve to reinforce these socially constructed boundaries which perpetuate inequalities between women and men" (Tickner, 2010, p. 38).

The Marxist Critique

For much of the twentieth century, socialism was the primary radical alternative to mainstream international relations theorizing. Although there are many strands of socialist thought, most are influenced by Karl Marx's argument that explaining events in world affairs requires understanding the detrimental effects of capitalism on the world stage. Whereas realists emphasize state security, liberals accentuate individual freedom, and constructivists highlight ideas and identities, socialists focus on class conflict and the material interests of each class.

"The history of all hitherto existing society," proclaimed Marx and his coauthor Friedrich Engels (1820–1895), in the *Communist Manifesto*, "is the history of class struggles." Capitalism, they argued, has given rise to two antagonistic classes: a ruling class (bourgeoisie) that owns the means of production and a subordinate class (proletariat) that sells its labor for only a token compensation. The working class is estranged from, and lacks authority over, the products of their labor. Instead, the ruling class controls and benefits disproportionately from the fruits of the subordinate class's labor.

This antagonistic relationship, in turn, plays a key role in determining the characteristics of international relations. In Marxism, human nature per se is not treated as a given or as a primary determinant of international relations, but is rather seen as "shaped by interaction with others and with the environment" (Brown, 2012, p. 650). This interaction creates a predatory international system with the core states benefiting from the subjugation of peripheral states. According to Marx and Engels, "The need of a constantly expanding market for its products chases the bourgeoisie over the whole surface of the globe." By expanding worldwide, the bourgeoisie give "a cosmopolitan character to production and consumption in every country."

Building on these ideas, Vladimir Ilyich Lenin (1870–1924) in the Soviet Union extended Marx's analysis to the study of *imperialism*, which he interpreted as a stage in the development of capitalism when monopolies overtake free-market competition. Drawing from the work of British economist John Hobson (1858–1940), Lenin maintained that advanced capitalist states eventually face the twin problems of overproduction and underconsumption. They respond by waging wars to divide the world into spheres of influence, forcing these new foreign markets to consume the surplus goods and capital. Although his assertions have been heavily

INTERFOTO/Alamy

KARL MARX CHALLENGES INTERNATIONAL THEORETICAL ORTHODOXY Pictured here is the German philosopher Karl Marx (1818–1883). His revolutionary theory of the economic determinants of world history inspired the spread of communism to overcome the class struggles so pronounced in most countries. The target of his critique was the compulsion of the wealthy great powers to subjugate foreign people by military force and to create colonies for purposes of financial exploitation. Imperial conquest of colonial peoples could only be prevented, Marx warned, by humanity's shift from a capitalist to a socialist economy and society.

criticized on conceptual and empirical grounds, the socialist attention on social classes and uneven development stimulated several new waves of theorizing about capitalism as a global phenomenon.

One prominent example is *dependency theory*. As expressed in the writings of André Gunder Frank (1969), Amir Samin (1976), and others (Dos Santos 1970; see Chapter 4), dependency theorists claimed that much of the poverty in Asia, Africa, and Latin America stemmed from the exploitative capitalist world economy. As they saw it, the economies of less developed countries had become dependent on exporting inexpensive raw materials and agricultural commodities to advanced industrial states, while simultaneously importing expensive manufactured goods from them. Theotonio Dos Santos (1971, p. 158), a

imperialism

The policy of expanding state power through the conquest and/or military domination of foreign territory.

prominent dependency scholar, described dependency as a "historical condition which shapes a certain structure of the world economy such that it favors some countries to the detriment of others." Dependency theory was criticized for recommending withdrawal from the world economy (Shannon, 1989), and eventually theoretical efforts arose to trace the economic ascent and decline of individual countries as part of long-term, systemwide change (Clark, 2008).

World-system theory, which was influenced by both Marxist and dependency theorists, represents the most recent effort to interpret world politics in terms of an integrated capitalist division of labor (Wallerstein, 1988, 2005). The capitalist world economy, which emerged in sixteenth-century Europe and ultimately expanded to encompass the entire globe, is viewed as containing three structural positions: a core (strong, well-integrated states whose economic activities are diversified and centered on possession and use of capital), a periphery (areas lacking strong state machinery and engaged in producing relatively few unfinished goods by unskilled, low-wage labor), and a semiperiphery (states embodying elements of both core and peripheral production). Within the core, a state may gain economic primacy by achieving productive, commercial, and financial superiority over its rivals. Primacy is difficult to sustain, however. The diffusion of technological innovations and the flow of capital to competitors, plus the massive costs of maintaining global order, all erode the dominant state's economic advantage. Thus, in addition to underscoring the exploitation of the periphery by the core, world-system theory calls attention to the cyclical rise and fall of hegemonic superpowers at the top of the core hierarchy.

These various radical challenges to mainstream theorizing enhance our understanding of world politics by highlighting the roles played by corporations, transnational religious movements, and other nonstate actors. Furthermore, they help to push mainstream theorists to identify, question, and clarify their own assumptions and theoretical propensities. Yet they overemphasize economic interpretations of international events and consequently omit other potentially important explanatory factors. Some critics of Marxism have also accused it of partaking in the theoretical simplification that it had sought to overcome and leaving key political ideas, such as revolutionary social change, ambiguous. In fact, international relations scholar Andrew Davenport (2013) goes so far as to suggest that this is one of the major deficiencies of Marxist theorizing today.

INTERNATIONAL THEORY AND THE GLOBAL FUTURE

To understand our changing world and to make reasonable prognoses about the future, we must begin by arming ourselves with an array of information and conceptual tools, entertain rival interpretations of world politics in the global marketplace of ideas, and question the assumptions on which these contending worldviews rest. Because there are a great (and growing) number of alternative, and sometimes incompatible, ways of organizing theoretical inquiry about world politics, the challenge of capturing the world's political problems cannot be reduced to any one simple, yet compelling account (Chernoff, 2008). Each paradigmatic

A Closer Look

VALUES AND INTERESTS

One of the major flash points in the ongoing dispute between Israel and the Palestinians is the continued Israeli settlement of land that was captured during the Six-Day War. Much of the international community views the land as occupied territory and sees settlement construction as a breach of international law, a violation of Palestinian human rights, and an obstacle to the peace process. Palestinians argue that such activity is an effort to preempt or undermine any agreement that provides for Palestinian sovereignty and that the presence of Jewish settlements hinders the possibility of having a viable and contiguous state. Israel disagrees with these views and argues that most of the settlements are both legal and necessary for Israel's security (Balmer, 2012).

As Israel's staunchest ally, the United States often finds itself in a position where there is tension between its pursuit of strategic interest and its normative values and preferences. In June 2009, President Barack Obama criticized Israel, saying that "The United States does not accept the legitimacy of continued Israeli settlements." This led to an outcry by Israel, lamenting that U.S.–Israeli relations had suffered, in the words of Israeli ambassador to the U.S. Michael Oren, a "tectonic rift" and were at their lowest point in thirty-five years.

Yet, despite its disapproval of continued Israeli settlement, in January 2011 the United States actively opposed a campaign to bring the issue to the United Nations (UN) Security Council. Reaffirming its long-term stance that there should be a negotiated resolution to the Palestinian-Israeli dispute, then-Secretary of State Hillary Clinton said, "We continue to believe strongly that New York [site of UN headquarters] is not the place to resolve the long-standing conflict." Critics suggested that the U.S. position was largely motivated by a desire to preserve its ability to strategically influence key Middle East peace issues.

WATCH THE VIDEO:

Carnegie Council Video:
Interests or Values: The
West and Israel

YOU DECIDE:

1. Are there always trade-offs between values and interests in any given policy?
2. Is it possible to bridge the gap so that values and interests are consistent?
3. How do you think this conundrum is reflected in relations between Western countries, particularly the United States, and Israel?
4. How do the theories introduced in this chapter inform your thinking?

effort to do so in the past has ultimately lost advocates as developments in world affairs eroded its continuing relevance.

As you seek to understand changing global conditions, it is important to be humble in recognizing the limitations of our understandings of world politics and, at the same time, inquisitive about its character. The task of interpretation is complicated because the world is complex. Donald Puchala framed the challenge in 2008 by observing:

> Conceptually speaking, world affairs today can be likened to a disassembled jigsaw puzzle scattered on a table before us. Each piece shows a fragment of a broad picture that as yet remains indiscernible. Some pieces depict resurgent nationalism; others show spreading democracy; some picture genocide; others portray prosperity through trade and investment; some picture nuclear disarmament; others picture nuclear proliferation; some indicate a reinvigorated United Nations; others show the UN still enfeebled and ineffective; some describe cultural globalization; others predict clashing civilizations.
>
> How do these pieces fit together, and what picture do they exhibit when they are appropriately fitted?

All theories are maps of possible futures. Theories can guide us in fitting the pieces together to form an accurate picture. However, in evaluating the usefulness of any theory to interpret global conditions, the historical overview in this chapter suggests that it would be wrong to oversimplify or to assume that a particular theory will remain useful in the future. Nonetheless, as American poet Robert Frost observed, any belief we cling to long enough is likely to be true again someday because "most of the change we think we see in life is due to truths being in and out of favor." So in our theoretical exploration of world politics, we must critically assess the accuracy of our impressions, avoiding the temptation to embrace one worldview and abandon another without any assurance that their relative worth is permanently fixed.

Although realism, liberalism, and constructivism are the dominant ways of thinking about world politics today, none of these theories is completely satisfactory. Recall that realism is frequently criticized for relying on ambiguous concepts, liberalism is often derided for making naïve policy recommendations based on idealistic assumptions, and constructivism is charged with being a social scientific framework rather than a "real" theory. Moreover, as the challenges mounted by feminism and the Marxist critique suggest, these three mainstream theories overlook seemingly important aspects of world politics, which limits their explanatory power. Despite these drawbacks, each has strengths for interpreting certain kinds of international events and foreign policy behaviors.

Because we lack a single overarching theory able to account for all facets of world politics, we will draw on realist, liberal, and constructivist thought in subsequent chapters. Moreover, we will supplement them with insights from feminism and the Marxist critique, where these theoretical traditions can best help to interpret the topic covered.

If you tell people the world is complicated, you're not doing your job as a social scientist. They already know it's complicated. Your job is to distill it, simplify it, and give them a sense of what is the single [cause], or what are the couple of powerful causes that explain this powerful phenomenon.

—Samuel Huntington, political scientist

STUDY. APPLY. ANALYZE.

Key Terms

agency
agent-oriented constructivism
balance of power
collective security
complex interdependence
consequentialism
constructivism
defensive realism

dependency theory
diplomacy
feminist theory
imperialism
international regime
Kellogg-Briand Pact
liberal feminism
liberalism

national interest
neoconservative
neoliberalism
neorealism
norms
offensive realism
paradigm
postcolonial feminism

post-structural
feminism
realism
relative gains
responsibility to
protect
security dilemma
self-help

social constructivism
standpoint feminism
theory
transnational relations
world-system theory
zero-sum

Suggested Readings

Drezner, Daniel W. (2011) *Theories of International Politics and Zombies.* Princeton, NJ: Princeton University Press.

Lobell, Steven E., Norrin M. Ripsman, and Jeffrey W. Taliaferro. (2009) *Neoclassical Realism, the State, and Foreign Policy.* New York: Cambridge University Press.

Puchala, Donald J. (2003) *Theory and History in International Relations.* New York: Routledge.

Smith, Martin A. (2012) *Power in the Changing Global Order: The US, Russia and China.* Cambridge: Polity Press.

Tickner, J. Ann and Laura Sjoberg (Eds.). (2011) *Conversations in Feminist*

International Relations: Past, Present and Future? New York: Routledge.

Waltz, Kenneth. (2001) *Man, the State, and War.* New York: Columbia University Press. Revised ed.

Wendt, Alexander. (1999) *Social Theory of International Politics.* Cambridge: Cambridge University Press.

Suggested Videos

Betts, Richard. "The World Ahead: Conflict or Cooperation?"

Nye, Joseph, Jr. "The Future of Power."

Kegley, Charles, Jr. "East Asian Security and Democracy: The Place of Taiwan."

Slaughter, Anne-Marie and Joanne Myers. "The Crisis of American

Foreign Policy: Wilsonianism in the Twenty-First Century."

Wright, Robin. "Dreams and Shadows: The Future of the Middle East."

CourseMate

Log in to CourseMate to access the following study tools for this chapter:

- Interactive Quiz
- eBook
- Flashcards & Key Term Crossword Puzzle
- Chapter Audio Summary
- Carnegie Council Videos

- Video Activities
- Simulation
- Animated Learning Module
- Case Study
- International Relations NewsWatch

"Decisions and actions in the international arena can be understood, predicted, and manipulated only insofar as the factors influencing the decision can be identified and isolated."

— *Arnold Wolfers, political scientist*

CHAPTER 3
Theories of International Decision Making

CHOICE AND CONSEQUENCE The choices that leaders make, and the decisions that they reach, can have far-reaching consequences—both purposeful and unintended—on their country and the world around them. Pictured here, outside Parliament in Athens, are protestors who are part of a public backlash against austerity measures called for by international lenders and approved by Greek policy makers in response to the Greek financial crisis.

AP Photo/Thanassis Stavrakis

QUESTIONS TO CONSIDER

- *How can a level-of-analysis framework account for foreign policy decision making?*
- *What factors shape decision making by individual leaders?*
- *What are the internal sources of foreign policy making?*
- *What are the global sources of foreign policy making?*

Y ou have completed your higher education degrees in international studies and have now embarked on your career. Your employment allows you to apply your acquired knowledge to help make the world a better place. As a result of your wise and efficient use of your analytic capabilities in your work with the World Health Organization (WHO), you now find that you have earned a very important appointment: to head and lead an established nongovernmental organization (NGO) in your area of expertise. In that role, you are expected to construct your NGO's *foreign policy*. Your challenge is to make decisions, based on your organization's values, about the foreign policy goals your NGO should pursue as well as the means by which those international goals might best be realized.

Congratulations! You have decision-making power. Now your task is to make critical choices that are destined to determine whether or not your foreign policies will succeed. How will you, as a governing authority of a transnational *actor* on the world stage, make decisions that will best serve your organization's interest and the world at large?

As an international decision maker, your approach will partly depend on your preferences and priorities, but there is no sure path as to how to make foreign policy decisions that are workable, moral, and successful. You will face many obstacles and constraints on your ability to make informed choices. As former U.S. Secretary of State Henry Kissinger warns, foreign policy decisions are rarely made by people who have all the facts; the policy maker "has to act in the fog of incomplete knowledge without the information that will be available later to the analyst." What is more, any choice you might make is certain to carry with costs that compromise some values you hold dear and undermine some of the other goals you would like to pursue. So, you now face the kind of challenge that has befuddled every decision maker who has had the power to make foreign policy decisions on behalf of the transnational actor he or she led.

CourseMate

**Case Study:
Foreign Policy**

FOREIGN POLICY MAKING IN INTERNATIONAL AFFAIRS

The purpose of this chapter is to introduce you to the lessons that history provides about the patterns, pitfalls, and payoffs surrounding alternative approaches for making international decisions. This introduction opens a window to rival ways of describing the processes by which transnational actors make foreign policy decisions.

Transnational Actors and Decision Processes

This chapter, which is based on historical experience and theories of international relations, looks at patterns of international decision making by all transnational actors—the individuals, groups, states, and organizations that play a role in world politics. Thus, it will not only cover the decision-making practices of countries but also those of international organizations such as the United Nations; nongovernmental organizations (NGOs) such as Amnesty International; multinational corporations such as Exxon; indigenous nationalities such as Kurds in Iran, Iraq, and Turkey; and terrorist networks such as Al Qaeda.

In addition, it is important to reflect on how each and every one of us—all individual people—are part of the equation. We are all, in a sense, transnational actors capable of making free choices that contribute to the direction of trends in world politics. When mobilized and inspired by a sense of purpose, individuals can make a difference in the course of world history; indeed, the decisions that we make every day and the groups that we join are reflections of our own personal "foreign policies," whether or not we are aware of the consequences of our daily choices. Every person matters. As American anthropologist Margaret Mead advised, "Never doubt that a small group of thoughtful, committed citizens can change the world. Indeed, it is the only thing that ever has."

To stimulate your thinking about international decision making by all types of transnational actors, *World Politics* provides a framework for analyzing and explaining the processes by which foreign policies are made.

Influences on the Making of Foreign Policy Decisions

To structure theoretical thinking about international decision making, it is useful to think in terms of the factors or causes that influence the ways in which all transnational actors make foreign policy decisions. What variables or causal influences impact foreign policy decision making?

For starters, it is important to recognize that no single category of causation can fully explain foreign policy decisions; rather, a number of influences converge to codetermine the decisions that produce foreign policy "outputs." Speaking on the making of American foreign policy decisions, former U.S. Secretary of State Henry Kissinger pointed out, "One of the most unsettling things for foreigners is the impression that our foreign policy can be changed by any new president on the basis of the president's personal preference." Yet, although a president's personal inclinations may influence policy decisions, all leaders are constrained by various circumstances that restrict free choice. As former U.S. presidential adviser Joseph A. Califano observed, "a president is a prisoner of historical forces that will demand his attention whatever his preference in policy objectives." Thus, to get to the essence of how international decision making takes place, we must go beyond a single-factor explanation and think in terms of multiple causes.

For that, it is useful to identify the various clusters of variables that affect the choices all types of transnational actors make when they formulate a foreign policy. Similar to the *level-of-analysis* distinction introduced in Chapter 1 (see Figure 1.1), we can construct an framework of the determinants of decision making in the foreign-policy-making process by reference to three major sets of causal variables at the individual, internal, and global levels of analyses:

■ **Individual decision makers**. The personal characteristics of the leaders heading international actors assume great importance in the making of international decisions as their individual values, personalities, beliefs, intelligence, and prior experiences predispose them to take certain kinds of positions on global issues. As political scientist Arnold Wolfers (1962, p. 50) explained, leaders are influential because:

> factors external to the actor can become determinants only as they affect the mind, the heart, and the will of the decision maker. A human decision to act in a specific way necessarily represents the last link in the chain of antecedents of any act of policy. A geographical set of conditions, for instance, can affect the behavior of a nation only as specific persons perceive and interpret these conditions.

Although changes in global conditions and actors' collective internal characteristics may influence the costs and benefits of particular foreign policy options and stimulate the need for choice, these are mediated by leaders' perceptions. As *constructivist theory* argues, ideas and expectations within the heads of leaders are the intellectual filters through which objective realities are interpreted. Therefore, in any explanation of why any international decision is made, it is imperative to take into account how leaders' ideas and images influence the choices taken.

- **Internal influences**. Every actor on the global stage is defined by its own attributes, which also act to determine the actor's foreign policy choices. As important as the individual decision maker is, it would be a mistake to think foreign policy leaders alone are the sole source driving international decision making. Internal characteristics—such as wealth, military might, and public opinion—of the transnational actor making the decision heavily shape the range of choices open to the individual decision maker.

  All international actors organized to take action abroad are composed of a collection of individuals. How these group actors are governed, and the processes and procedures they follow to reach foreign policy decisions, are forces of their own that structure and determine the decisions that are reached. The size of the organization, its power relative to the other actors with which it interacts, the financial resources, and the distribution of opinion within the actor all affect its capacity to make foreign policy choices in response to changes in global circumstances.

- **Global factors**. Global conditions provide constraints and opportunities for international decision making and color the degree to which both an actor's internal attributes and individual leader preferences can account for the choices made. The changing state of the world—everything that occurs beyond the actor—affects the decisions of international actors. The prevailing global circumstances define the decisional situation, provoking the need to make decisions and restricting policy options available to the actor. As John Quincy Adams noted while U.S. secretary of state, "I know of no change in policy, only of circumstances."

  Take any global trend highlighted in *World Politics,* and we can easily visualize how changes in the state of the world condition the issues on the global agenda: global warming, nuclear proliferation, international trade, international terrorism, and civil unrest—you name it. All shifts in global circumstances have an important impact upon decisions by international actors. The view that changes of global circumstances serve as a catalyst for international decision making was captured by U.S. President Richard Nixon when he declared, "The world has changed. Our foreign policy must change with it."

This three-part framework encourages you to think in causal terms about categories of phenomena that explain why particular decisions are made. Each category encompasses a large number of factors, which, together with the influences grouped in the other two categories, tell you what to observe when you construct an explanation as to why a particular decision by a particular international actor was made. Factors in the three categories serve as "inputs" that shape the policy-making process. They ultimately lead to foreign policy decisions and outcomes, or foreign policy "outputs," which in turn provide "feedback" that may subsequently affect the inputs themselves (see Figure 3.1).

This organization for interpretation is explanatory. The framework provides clues as to where to look when asking "why" a foreign policy decision has been reached. Each policy decision can be

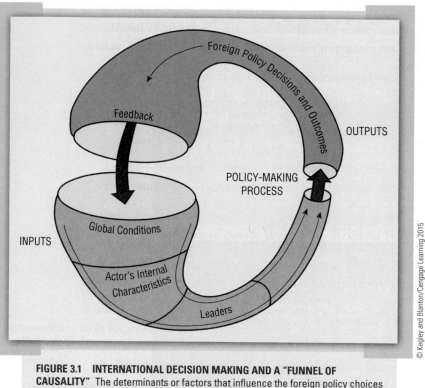

Foreign Policy Decisions and Outcomes

Feedback

OUTPUTS

POLICY-MAKING
PROCESS

Global Conditions

INPUTS

Actor's Internal
Characteristics

Leaders

© Kegley and Blanton/Cengage Learning 2015

FIGURE 3.1   INTERNATIONAL DECISION MAKING AND A "FUNNEL OF CAUSALITY" The determinants or factors that influence the foreign policy choices of transnational actors are shown here as a "funnel of causality." This construction classifies three categories of influence in the foreign-policy-making process, whereby policy "inputs" shape the decisions that produce policy "outputs."

viewed as the result of the multiple prior causal events taking place in the funnel. Thus, the model stipulates the conditions that precede and promote policy decisions (bearing in mind that it is frequently difficult to distinguish decision making itself from its prior conditions).

Observe as well that our framework implies a temporal or time sequence in the transition from inputs to outputs in the foreign-policy-making process. That is, changes in the determinants of foreign policy occurring at time t produce decisions at a later time $(t + 1)$, which lead to policy outcomes that affect all of the causal factors at a still later time $(t + 2)$. Moreover, these policy outcomes have consequences for the input factors themselves at a later time $(t + 3)$ because they exert "feedback" on these causal factors as the foreign policy decisions alter the conditions that influence subsequent $(t + 4)$ decisions. For example, a cluster of factors at some point in time (t) led the United States to make the decision in March 2003 $(t + 1)$ to invade Iraq $(t + 2)$. This decision, furthermore, exerted a painfully negative "feedback" influence on public opinion within America and abroad when that invasion increased the level of international terrorism it was originally designed to end. This reaction, in turn, later $(t + 3)$ transformed global conditions as well as attitudes within American society, which began to galvanize revisions $(t + 4)$ of the original policy decision.

Thus, the model advanced here is dynamic. It can be used to account for past policy decisions and behaviors as well as for the effects of those outcomes on later policy decisions. This way of tracing the determinants and consequences of international decisions provides you, the analyst, with a lens through which to view and explain the foreign policy of transnational actors in historical perspective, because the model is not tied analytically to any one time period or actor.

In the episodic and visual comprehension of our foreign policy, there is serious danger that the larger significance of developments will be lost in a kaleidoscope of unrelated events. Continuities will be obscured, causal factors unidentified.

—**George W. Ball, former U.S. under secretary of state**

THREE MODELS OF DECISION MAKING BY TRANSNATIONAL ACTORS

With the "funnel of causality" framework in mind, you are armed intellectually to probe international decision making in greater depth. To better inform your analyses of the causes of international decision making, let us inspect three models of decision making formulated by scholars of this topic: rational choice, bureaucratic politics, and the political psychology of leaders and leadership.

Decision Making as Rational Choice

Realism assumes that foreign policy making consists primarily of an international actor adjusting to the pressures of an anarchical global system whose essential properties do not vary. Accordingly, it presumes that all decision makers are essentially alike in their approach to foreign policy making:

> If they follow the [decision] rules, we need know nothing more about them. In essence, if the decision maker behaves rationally, the observer, knowing the rules of rationality, can rehearse the decisional process in his own mind, and, if he knows the decision maker's goals, can both predict the decision and understand why that particular decision was made (Verba, 1969, p. 225).

Because realists believe that every leader's goals and corresponding approach to making foreign policy choices are the same, the decision-making processes of each actor can be studied as though each were a *unitary actor*—a homogeneous or monolithic unit with few or no important internal differences that affect its choices. From this assumption can be derived the expectation that international actors can and do make decisions by rational calculations of the costs and benefits of different choices. We define rationality, or *rational choice*, as purposeful, goal-directed behavior exhibited when "the individual responding to an international event … uses the best information available and chooses from the universe of possible responses most likely to maximize his [or her] goals" (Verba, 1969). Scholars describe rationality as a sequence of decision-making activities involving the following intellectual steps:

- **Problem recognition and definition**. The need to decide begins when policy makers perceive an external problem and attempt to define objectively its distinguishing characteristics. Objectivity requires full information about the actions, motivations, and capabilities of other actors as well as the character of the global environment and trends within it. Ideally, the search for information will be exhaustive, and all the facts relevant to the problem will be gathered.

- **Goal selection**. Next, those responsible for making foreign policy choices must determine what they want to accomplish. This disarmingly simple requirement is often difficult. It requires the identification and ranking of *all* values (such as security and economic prosperity) in a hierarchy from most to least preferred.

unitary actor

A transnational actor (usually a sovereign state) assumed to be internally united, so that changes in its domestic opinion do not influence its foreign policy as much as do the decisions that actor's leaders make to cope with changes in its global environment.

rational choice

Decision-making procedures guided by careful definition of situations, weighing of goals, consideration of all alternatives, and selection of the options most likely to achieve the highest goals.

Carnegie Council Video: Rational Choice

■ **Identification of alternatives**. Rationality also requires the compilation of an exhaustive list of *all* available policy options and an estimate of the costs associated with each alternative.

■ **Choice**. Finally, rationality requires selecting the single alternative with the best chance of achieving the desired goal(s). For this purpose, policy makers must conduct a rigorous cost–benefit analysis guided by an accurate prediction of the probable success of each option.

Policy makers often describe their own behavior as resulting from a rational decision-making process designed to reach the "best" decision possible, which employs the logic of *consequentialism* to estimate the results that can be expected from the decision taken.

The quest for rational decision making was illuminated, for example, in the debate about what level of involvement the United States should maintain in Afghanistan following the death of Osama bin Laden on May 2, 2011. Those who advocated for a withdrawal of U.S. troops and a clear exit strategy argued that bin Laden's death should force a reevaluation of the war, in part because the terrorist leader was found by a small special operations force in Pakistan and not by the 100,000 ground troops in Afghanistan, thus bringing into question whether the large commitment of U.S. resources, with the risk to the lives of American soldiers, was the most effective way to combat the terrorist threat. Furthermore, according to critics, with bin Laden's death the Afghans themselves should be able to take more responsibility for their own security. As Richard Lugar, a former chair of the Senate Foreign Relations Committee, argued, "it is exceedingly difficult to conclude that our vast expenditures in Afghanistan represent a rational allocation of our military and financial assets." The message reflected the language of deliberate rational choice to convince skeptics that the costs and benefits of all options had been carefully weighed.

"HOW ARE FOREIGN POLICY DECISIONS REACHED?" That was the question put to former U.S. Secretary of State Henry A. Kissinger in an interview with one of your text's authors, Charles Kegley. Kissinger has observed that "Much of the anguish of foreign policy results from the need to establish priorities among competing, sometimes conflicting, necessities."

Charles Kegley, Jr.

However, like beauty, rationality often lies in the eye of the beholder, and reasonable, clear-thinking people can and often do disagree about the facts and wisdom of foreign policy goals. House Speaker John Boehner reproached calls from fellow Republican legislators for the reduction of U.S. involvement in Afghanistan, instead viewing the killing of bin Laden as evidence that the country should recommit to the U.S. counterinsurgency strategy in Afghanistan and continue to press its advantage (Fahrenthold and Kane, 2011). "This war on terrorism is critical to the safety and security of the American people," said Boehner. "We still face a complex and dangerous terrorist threat. And it's important that we remain vigilant."

This debate demonstrated that although rationality is a decision-making goal to which all transnational actors aspire, it is difficult to determine when the criteria for rational choice have been met or what those rational choices look like in practice. This raises the question: what are the barriers to rationality?

> *It is doubtful that decision makers hear arguments on the merits and weigh them judiciously before choosing a course of action.*
>
> **—Daniel Kahneman and Jonathan Renshon, decision-making theorists**

Impediments to Rational Choice   Despite the apparent application of rationality in these crises, rational choice is often more an idealized standard than an accurate description of real-world behavior. Theodore Sorenson—one of President Kennedy's closest advisers and a participant in the Cuban Missile Crisis deliberations—has written not only about the steps that policy makers in the Kennedy administration followed as they tried to adhere to rational choice but also about how actual decision making often departed from it. He described an eight-step process for policy making that is consistent with the rational model we have described: (1) agreeing on the facts, (2) agreeing on the overall policy objective, (3) precisely defining the problems, (4) canvassing all possible solutions, (5) listing the consequences that flow from each solution, (6) recommending one option, (7) communicating the option selected, and (8) providing for its execution. But he explained how difficult it is to follow these steps, because:

> each step cannot be taken in order. The facts may be in doubt or dispute. Several policies, all good, may conflict. Several means, all bad, may be all that are open. Value judgments may differ. Stated goals may be imprecise. There may be many interpretations of what is right, what is possible, and what is in the national interest (Sorensen 1963, pp. 19–20).

Despite the virtues rational choice promises, the impediments to its realization in foreign policy making are substantial. In fact, *bounded rationality* is more common, as decision makers typically only approximate rational decision making due to the many constraints that arise (Kahneman, 2011; Simon, 1997).

Some of the barriers that make errors in foreign policy decisions so common are human, deriving from deficiencies in the intelligence, capability, and psychological needs and aspirations of foreign policy decision makers. Others are organizational, because most decisions require group agreement about the actor's best interests and the wisest course of action. Reaching agreement is not easy, however, because reasonable people with different values often disagree about goals, preferences, and the probable results of alternative options. Thus, the impediments to rational policy making are not to be underestimated.

Scrutiny of the actual process of decision making reveals other hindrances. Available information is often insufficient to recognize emergent problems accurately, resulting in decisions made on the basis of partial information and vague memories. As the U.S. commander in the Iraq and Afghanistan wars, General David Petraeus, quoted Charles W. Kegley and Eugene Wittkopf (1982) in his 1987 Princeton University Ph.D. dissertation, "Faced with incomplete information about the immediate problem at hand, it is not surprising that decision makers turn to the past for guidance" and rely on historical analogies. Moreover, the available

bounded rationality

The concept that decision maker's capacity to choose the best option is often constrained by many human and organizational obstacles.

AP Photos/Pool Reuters/Kevin Lamarque

ROAD-TRIP DIPLOMACY President Barack Obama has emphasized a willingness to engage in dialogue with leaders of all nations as a key component of his commitment to diplomacy, with a pledge to "personally lead a new chapter of American engagement." Pictured here (from left) at a meeting of Transatlantic Trade and Investment Partnership members at the G8 Summit in Northern Ireland on June 17, 2013, he converses with British prime minister David Cameron, German chancellor Angela Merkel, and others.

information is often inaccurate because the bureaucratic organizations that political leaders depend upon for advice often screen, sort, and rearrange it.

Compounding the problem is decision makers' susceptibility to *cognitive dissonance*—they are psychologically prone to block out dissonant, or inconsistent, information and perceptions about their preferred choice and to look instead for information that conforms to their preexisting beliefs to justify their choice. On top of that, they are prone to make decisions on the basis of "first impressions, or intuition, or that amorphous blending of 'what is' with 'what could be' that we call imagination [even though] there is a great body of data suggesting that formal statistical analysis is a much better way of predicting everything … than the intuition even of experts" (Brooks, 2005, but see also Gladwell, 2001, who argues that snap judgments and "rapid cognition can be as good as decisions made cautiously and deliberately"). Those who see themselves as "political experts" are habitually mistaken in their judgments and forecasts (Tetlock, 2006), and leaders are prone to place faith in their prior prejudices, to draw false analogies with prior events (Brunk, 2008), and to make decisions based on emotion (McDermott, 2013). As so-called "behavioral international relations" research on decision making and *game theory* shows (Mintz, 2007), leaders are limited in their capacity to process information and avoid biases; preoccupied with preventing losses, leaders are also prone to "wishful

game theory

Mathematical model of strategic interaction where outcomes are determined not only by a single actor's preferences but also by the choices of all actors involved.

thinking" and "shooting from the hip," which frequently results in irrational decisions. These intellectual propensities explain why policy makers sometimes pay little heed to warnings, overlook information about dangers, and repeat their past intellectual mistakes.

To better capture the way most leaders make policy decisions, Robert Putnam coined the phrase *two-level games*. Challenging the assumptions of realism, he asserted that leaders should formulate policies simultaneously in both the international and domestic arenas and should make those choices in accordance with the rules dictated by the "game":

> At the national level, domestic groups pursue their interests by pressuring the government to adopt favorable policies, and politicians seek power by constructing coalitions among these groups. At the international level, national governments seek to maximize their own ability to satisfy domestic pressures, while minimizing the adverse consequences of foreign developments. Neither of the two games can be ignored by central decision makers so long as their countries remain interdependent, yet sovereign (Putnam, 1988, p. 434).

Most leaders must meet the often incompatible demands of internal politics and external diplomacy, and it is seldom possible to make policy decisions that respond rationally to both sets of goals. Policies at home often have many consequences abroad. Foreign activities commonly heavily influence an actor's internal condition. This is why many leaders are likely to fuse the two sectors when contemplating policy decisions.

Yet critics suggest that the two-level game model does not go far enough and could be improved by incorporating insights from *constructivism*. These critics argue that two-level games still rely too heavily on rationalism in assuming "that international negotiators have clear self-interests, represent certain domestic and state interests, and seek to maximize these interests; how these interests are constituted is left unexplored" (Deets, 2009, p. 39). "Are domestic divisions—those based on ideology, on competing interests, on the struggle for power across political institutions—so serious as to make rational decision making impossible?" (Kanet, 2010, p. 127).

States are administered by individuals with varying beliefs, values, preferences, and psychological needs, and such differences generate disagreements about goals and alternatives that are seldom resolved through orderly, rational processes. Moreover, these individuals are greatly shaped by the socially accepted shared understandings within their own policy-making community and culture (O'Reilly, 2013). In order to more fully understand international decision making, it is important to consider not only domestic interests and identities, but also the "interactive processes among domestic and international actors through which interests and identities are created and changed" (Deets, 2009, p. 39).

Yet there seldom exists a confident basis for making foreign policy decisions. Decision making often revolves around the difficult task of choosing among values, so that the choice of one option means the sacrifice of others. Indeed, many decisions tend to produce unintended consequences—what economists call *externalities*. Especially in the realm of foreign policy, where risk is high and there is much uncertainty, decision makers' inability to rapidly gather and digest large quantities of information constrains their capacity to make informed choices.

Because policy makers work with an overloaded *policy agenda* and short deadlines, the search for policy options is seldom exhaustive. "There is little time for leaders to reflect," observed Henry Kissinger (1979). "They are locked in an endless battle in which the urgent

two-level games

A concept referring to the growing need for national policy makers to make decisions that will meet both domestic and foreign goals.

externalities

The unintended side effects resulting from choices, such as inflation from runaway government spending, that are not taken into account at the time of the decision.

Carnegie Council Video:
Externalities

policy agenda

The changing list of problems or issues to which governments pay special attention at any given moment.

Carnegie Council Video:
Policy Agenda

constantly gains on the important. The public life of every political figure is a continual struggle to rescue an element of choice from the pressure of circumstance." In the choice phase, then, decision makers rarely make value-maximizing decisions.

Rooted in the experiments of Amos Tversky and Daniel Kahneman, who won the 2002 Nobel Prize in economics, prospect theory similarly challenges the idea that decision makers behave rationally. *Prospect theory* looks at how people perceive and misperceive risks when making choices under conditions of uncertainty, and posits that there are consistent and predictable biases in the way that people depart from rational decision making. People perceive alternatives in terms of their sense of potential gains and losses—"those faced with gains tend to be risk averse, while those confronting losses become much more risk seeking" (McDermott et al., 2008, p. 335). Indeed, "evidence suggests that individuals value losses twice as much as they value gains" (Elms, 2008, p. 245).

One implication for decision making is that people tend to gravitate toward the "status quo" (Grunwald, 2009). Like people everywhere, leaders tend to overvalue certainty and "peace of mind," even to their detriment. They do not calculate the consequence of choices and are more concerned with the potential losses that may result from a change than with the potential gains. This problematic outcome is compounded by another common decision-making error—the tendency to myopically frame decisions by focusing on short-term choices rather than long-term ones (Elms, 2008). U.S. leaders, for example, are often more concerned with the loss of sovereignty and power that would result from greater authority of international organizations such as the United Nations or the International Criminal Court than they are with the gains that could be had from greater global integration and shared governance.

Another implication of prospect theory is that when leaders take risks to initiate bold new foreign policy directions, they will have great difficulty admitting and correcting those choices if they later prove mistaken. As critics lament of George W. Bush's refusal to acknowledge decision-making failures regarding the Iraq War (Draper, 2008; Goldsmith, 2008), leaders are prone to cling to failed policies long after their deficiencies have become apparent. Similar criticisms were also made regarding both the Johnson and Nixon administrations' decisions to keep the United States mired in the unpopular war in Vietnam (Polsky, 2010).

The dilemma that prospect theory presents, of course, is that "if people can't be trusted to make the right choices for themselves, how can they possibly be trusted to make the right decisions for the rest of us?" (Kolbert, 2008). Yet while decision making that departs from rationality can be problematic, irrationality can still produce "good" decisions. Along these lines, experimental literature indicates that people tend to incorporate a sense of fairness into their decision making even if it is contrary to their own rational self-interest. As economic behaviorist Dan Ariely's (2008) work demonstrates, "People, it turns out, want to be generous and they want to retain their dignity—even when it doesn't really make sense" (Kolbert, 2008, p. 79).

Despite the image that policy makers seek to project, often the degree of rationality "bears little relationship to the world in which officials conduct their deliberations" (Rosenau, 1980). Yet although rational foreign policy making is more an ideal than a reality, we can still assume that policy makers aspire to rational decision-making behavior, which they may occasionally approximate. Indeed, as a working proposition, it is useful to accept rationality as a picture of how the decision process *should* work as well as a description of key elements of how it *does* work (see Table 3.1).

prospect theory

A social-psychological theory explaining decision making under conditions of uncertainty and risk that looks at the relationship between individual risk propensity and the perceived prospects for avoiding losses and realizing big gains.

**Video:
Determining
Foreign Policy**

TABLE 3.1	Foreign Policy Decision Making in Theory and Practice
Ideal Rational Process	**Actual Common Practice**
Accurate, comprehensive information	Distorted, incomplete information
Clear definition of national interests	Personal motivations and organizational interests shape choices about national goals
Exhaustive analysis of all options	Limited number of options considered; none thoroughly analyzed
Selection of optimal course of action for producing desired results	Courses of action selected by political bargaining and compromise
Effective statement of decision and its rationale to mobilize domestic support	Confusing and contradictory statements of decision, often framed for media consumption
Careful monitoring of the decision's implementation by foreign affairs bureaucracies	Neglect of the tedious task of managing the decision's implementation by foreign affairs bureaucracies
Instantaneous evaluation of consequences followed by correction of errors	Superficial policy evaluation, uncertain responsibility, poor follow-through, and delayed correction

The Leverage and Impact of Leaders

The course of history is determined by the decisions of political elites. Leaders and the style of leadership they employ shape the way in which foreign policies are made and the resulting behavior of the actors in world politics. "There is properly no history, only biography" is how Ralph Waldo Emerson encapsulated the view that individual leaders move history.

Leaders as Movers of World History   This *history-making individuals model* of policy decision making perceives world leaders as the people who create global changes. History abounds with examples of the seminal importance of political leaders who emerge in different times and places and under different circumstances to play critical roles in shaping world history. Mikhail Gorbachev dramatically illustrates an individual's capacity to change the course of history. Many experts believe that the Cold War could not have been brought to an end, nor Communist Party rule in Moscow terminated and the Soviet state set on a path toward democracy and free enterprise, had it not been for Gorbachev's vision, courage, and commitment to engineering these revolutionary, system-transforming changes.

We expect leaders to lead, and we assume new leaders will make a difference. We reinforce this image when we routinely attach the names of leaders to policies—as though the leaders were synonymous with major international developments—as well as when we ascribe most successes and failures in foreign affairs to the leaders in charge at the time they occurred. The equation of U.S. foreign policy with the *Bush Doctrine* in the 2000s is a recent example.

Citizens are not alone in thinking that leaders are the decisive determinants of states' foreign policies and, by extension, world history. Leaders themselves seek to create impressions of their own self-importance while attributing extraordinary powers to other leaders. The assumptions they make about the personalities of their counterparts, consciously or unconsciously, in turn influence their own behavior.

Moreover, leaders react differently to the positions they occupy. All are influenced by the *roles* or expectations that by law and tradition steer the decision maker to behave in conformity

history-making individuals model

An interpretation of world politics that sees foreign policy decisions that affect the course of history as products of strong-willed leaders acting on their personal convictions.

Bush Doctrine

The unilateral policies of the George W. Bush Administration proclaiming that the United States will make decisions to meet America's perceived national interests, not to concede to other countries' complaints or to gain their acceptance.

Carnegie Council Video:
Bush Doctrine

with prevailing expectations about how the role is to be performed. Most people submissively act in accordance with the customary rules that define the positions they hold, behaving as their predecessors tended to behave when they held the same position. Others, however, are by personality or preference more bold and ambitious, and they seek to decisively escape the confines of their new role by redefining how it will be performed.

In seeking a more rigorous understanding of the role of personality, there is an emerging consensus that personality traits can be grouped in five broad categories: extraversion, agreeableness, conscientiousness, emotional stability, and openness. While subsuming thousands of individual personality attributes, the categories in what is known as the Big Five Model (see Figure 3.2) are consistent across gender, culture, ethnicity, and time. They provide insights into leader's motivations and can be used to predict behavior (Gallagher and Allen, 2013; Mondak and Halperin, 2008).

In world politics, "all leaders face decision making under uncertainty. The personality of a particular leader can tell us a great deal about how he or she will choose to deal with that uncertainty" (Gallagher and Allen, 2013, p. 7). For instance, it has been shown that high levels of extraversion and openness, and low levels of conscientiousness, are associated with a greater likelihood of risk-acceptance (Kam and Simas, 2010). This has implications for understanding the sources of conflict as leaders who are risk-acceptant are more likely to engage in brinksmanship and the use of force.

One of the challenges illuminated by leader-driven explanations of international decision making is that history's movers and shakers often pursue decidedly irrational policies. Personality likely plays a role as it affects a rational actor's optimization process by influencing the options seen as acceptable in a particular situation. For example, "while risk-acceptant leaders may perceive the use of force as an alternative option for carrying out their foreign policies, leaders who are risk-averse will not seriously consider such actions" (Gallagher and Allen, 2013, p. 2). A classic example is Adolf Hitler, whose ruthless determination to seek military conquest of the entire European continent proved disastrous for Germany.

How do we square this kind of behavior with the logic of realism? Realism discounts leaders by assuming that "individual leaders remain significantly constrained in ways that assure that regardless of whether individual differences might exist, political outcomes will emerge indistinguishable precisely because environmental pressures exert decisive influence" (McDermott, 2013, p. 1). Realism says that

roles

The constraints written into law or custom that predispose decision makers in a particular governmental position to act in a manner and style that is consistent with expectations about how the role is normally performed.

Carnegie Council Video:
Roles

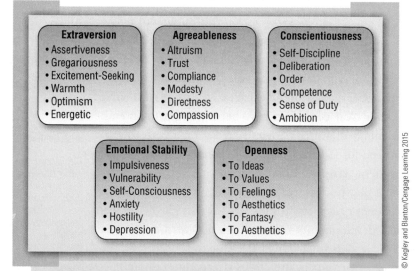

FIGURE 3.2   THE BIG FIVE PERSONALITY MARKERS The Big Five personality factors represent broad dimensions that encompass a number of facets as depicted above. People who are highly extraverted are outgoing and enjoy the company of others. Those who are very conscientious have a preference for planned behavior, and high levels of openness reflect creativity and intellectual curiosity. Emotional stability is linked to one's tolerance for stress and ability to regulate emotions. Those who score high on the agreeableness factor tend to be cooperative and empathetic (see Gallagher and Allen, 2013; McCrae and Costa, 2003).

survival is the paramount goal of all states and that all leaders engage in rational calculations to advance their countries' self-advantage. But realism cannot account for the times when leaders' choices ultimately prove counterproductive. Even defects in states' foreign-policy-making processes cannot easily explain such wide divergences between the decisions leaders sometimes make and what cold cost–benefit calculations would predict.

Constraints on Individual Leadership   Having said that the history-making individuals model may be compelling, we must be cautious and remember that leaders are not all-powerful determinants of states' foreign policy behavior. Emmet John Hughes (1972), an adviser to President Dwight D. Eisenhower, concluded that "all of [America's presidents] from the most venturesome to the most reticent have shared one disconcerting experience: the discovery of the limits and restraints—decreed by law, by history, and by circumstances—that sometimes can blur their clearest designs or dull their sharpest purposes."

Personal influence varies with the context, and often the context is more influential than the leader (see "Controversy: Do Leaders Make a Difference?"). The "great person" versus *zeitgeist* ("spirit of the times") debate is pertinent here, as constructivist theorists like to observe. At the core of this enduring controversy is the question of whether certain times are conducive to the emergence of leaders or whether famous leaders would have an impact whenever and wherever they lived. That question may be unanswerable, but at least it reminds us that multiple factors affect states' foreign policy decisions. The history-making individuals model alone appears too simple an explanation of how transnational actors react to external challenges.

The question is not whether political elites lead or whether they can make a difference. They clearly do both, but leaders are not in complete control, and their influence is severely constrained. "Although leaders are quick to take credit for foreign policy successes and the public is often quick to blame them for failures, leaders rarely make foreign policy alone" (Breuning, 2007, p. 9). As former Secretary of State Henry Kissinger cautioned, we must not place too much reliance on personalities and personal political preferences:

> [There is] a profound American temptation to believe that foreign policy is a subdivision of psychiatry and that relations among nations are like relations among people. But the problem [of easing protracted conflicts] is not so simple. Tensions … must have some objective causes, and unless we can remove these causes, no personal relationship can possibly deal with them. We are [not] doing … ourselves a favor by reducing the issues to a contest of personalities (University of South Carolina Commencement Address, 1985).

The relevant question, then, is not whether leaders' personal characteristics make a difference, but rather under what conditions their characteristics are influential. As Margaret G. Hermann has observed, the impact of leaders is modified by at least six factors:

> (1) what their world view is, (2) what their political style is like, (3) what motivates them to have the position they do, (4) whether they are interested in and have any training in foreign affairs, (5) what the foreign policy climate was like when the leader was starting out his or her political career, and (6) how the leader was socialized into his or her present position. World view, political style, and motivation tell us something about the leader's personality; the other characteristics give information about the leader's previous experiences and background (Hermann, 1988, p. 268).

zeitgeist

The "spirit of the times," or the dominant cultural norms assumed to influence the behavior of people living in particular periods.

CONTROVERSY

DO LEADERS MAKE A DIFFERENCE?

Some theorists, such as proponents of realism, embrace the assumption of rationality and assume that any leader will respond to a choice in the same way: the situation structures the reaction to the existing costs and benefits of any choice. But does this assumption square with the facts? What do we know about the impact of people's perceptions and values on the way they view choices? Political psychology and constructivism tell us that the same option is likely to have different value to different leaders. Does this mean that different leaders would respond differently to similar situations?

Consider the example of Richard Nixon. In 1971, Americans took to the streets outside the White House to protest the immorality of Nixon's massive bombing of Vietnam. His reaction to this perceived threat was to shield himself from the voice of the people, without success, as it happened. Nixon complained that "nobody can know what it means for a president to be sitting in that White House working late at night and to have hundreds of thousands of demonstrators charging through the streets. Not even earplugs could block the noise."

Earlier, on a rainy afternoon in 1962, John F. Kennedy faced a similar citizen protest. Americans had gathered in front of the White House for a "Ban the Bomb" demonstration. His response was to send out urns of coffee and doughnuts and invite the leaders of the protest to come inside to state their case, believing that a democracy should encourage dissent and debate.

Nixon saw protesters as a threat; Kennedy saw them as an opportunity. This comparison suggests that the type of leader can make a difference in determining the kinds of choices likely to be made in response to similar situations (see Gallagher and Allen, 2013). More important than each president's treatment of the protesters, however, was whether he actually changed his policy decisions based on the protests. Although Kennedy was hospitable to protesters, he did not ban nuclear weapons; in fact, military spending under Kennedy grew to consume half of the federal budget. Many would protest that Kennedy alone could not be expected to eliminate nuclear weapons—that the zeitgeist was dominated by fear of the Soviet Union and intense concern for national security. The protesters in 1971, however, were more in keeping with the spirit of the times. Although they alone may not have persuaded Nixon to alter his policies in Vietnam, widespread protest and discontentment with the war, as well as America's inability to win, eventually prompted Nixon to order the gradual withdrawal of U.S. troops, ending American participation in the Vietnam War. These outcomes suggest that leaders are captive to zeitgeist, or larger forces that drive international relations in their times.

WHAT DO YOU THINK?

- *Did Kennedy and Nixon choose courses of action that reflected who they were as individuals? Or would any president in their respective eras have made similar choices?*

- *How would rational choice theorists understand the behavior of Nixon? Of Kennedy? What are limitations of the rational choice approach for explaining their decisions?*

- *Thinking ahead, what are some other factors, domestic or international, that could have affected Kennedy's and Nixon's decisions regarding their respective military engagements, beyond zeitgeist?*

The impact of leaders' personal characteristics on foreign policy decisions generally increases when their authority and legitimacy are widely accepted or when leaders are protected from broad public criticism. Moreover, certain circumstances enhance individuals' potential influence. Among them are new situations that free leaders from conventional approaches to defining the situation, complex situations involving many different factors, and situations without social sanctions, which permit freedom of choice because norms defining the range of permissible options are unclear (DiRenzo, 1974).

A leader's *political efficacy* or self-image—that person's belief in his or her own ability to control political events—combined with the citizenry's relative desire for leadership, will also influence the degree to which personal values and psychological needs govern decision making. For example, when public opinion strongly favors a powerful leader, and when the head of state has an exceptional need for admiration, foreign policy will more likely reflect that leader's inner needs. Thus, Kaiser Wilhelm II's narcissistic personality allegedly met the German people's desire for a symbolically powerful leader, and German public preferences in turn influenced the foreign policy that Germany pursued during Wilhelm's reign, which ended in World War I (Baron and Pletsch, 1985).

Leaders' gender may also influence their decision making. *Feminism* suggests that men and women tend to see issues such as war, peace, security, and the use of military force in different ways, and this may influence the way in which they make decisions and interact with the world around them. Similarly, *social constructivism* considers the existence of different values and views between women and men as a product of distinct socialization experiences. "Because women tend to define themselves more through their relationships than do men, their actions and rhetoric … may be more oriented toward maintaining and protecting these relationships. In contrast, men tend to focus on end gains, making the achievement of personal preferences and goals" central to their decision making (Boyer et al., 2009, p. 27). It is likely, therefore, that gender influences the decision-making process, even if it does not make a difference in terms of the final decision outcome.

Other factors undoubtedly influence how much leaders can shape their states' choices. For instance, when leaders believe that their own interests and welfare are at stake, they tend to respond in terms of their private needs and psychological drives. When circumstances are stable, however, and when leaders' egos are not entangled with policy outcomes, the influence of their personal characteristics is less apparent. The timing of a leader's assumption of power is also significant. When an individual first assumes a leadership position, the formal requirements of that role are least likely to restrict what he or she can do. That is especially true during the "honeymoon" period routinely afforded to newly elected leaders, during which time they are relatively free of criticism and excessive pressure. Moreover, when a leader assumes office following a dramatic event (a landslide election, for example, or the assassination of a predecessor), he or she can institute policies almost with a free hand, as "constituency criticism is held in abeyance during this time" (Hermann, 1976).

A national crisis is a potent circumstance that increases a leader's control over foreign policy making. Crisis decision making is typically centralized and handled exclusively by the top leadership. Crucial information is often unavailable, and leaders see themselves as responsible for outcomes. Not surprisingly, great leaders (e.g., Napoleon Bonaparte, Winston Churchill, and Franklin D. Roosevelt) customarily emerge during periods of extreme tumult. A crisis can

political efficacy

The extent to which policy makers' self-confidence instills in them the belief that they can effectively make rational choices.

Carnegie Council Video:
Political Efficacy

liberate a leader from the constraints that normally would inhibit his or her capacity to control events or engineer foreign policy change.

> *Nothing comes to my desk that is perfectly solvable. Any given decision you make you'll wind up with a 30 to 40 percent chance that it isn't going to work. You have to own that and feel comfortable with the way you made the decision.*

> **—Barack Obama, U.S. president**

The Bureaucratic Politics of Foreign Policy Decision Making

multiple advocacy

The concept that better and more rational choices are made when decisions are reached in a group context, which allows advocates of differing alternatives to be heard so that the feasibility of rival options receives critical evaluation.

Carnegie Council Video:
Multiple Advocacy

bureaucracy

The agencies and departments that conduct the functions of a central government or of a nonstate transnational actor.

bureaucratic politics model

A description of decision making that sees foreign policy choices as based on bargaining and compromises among competing government agencies.

To make the right choices, leaders must seek information and advice, and must see that the actions their decisions generate are carried out properly. Who can assist in these tasks?

In today's world, leaders must depend on large-scale organizations for information and advice as they face critical foreign policy choices: "Institutions and individuals matter in the making and implementation of foreign policy" (Kanet, 2010, p. 127). Even transnational actors without large budgets and complex foreign policy bureaucracies seldom make decisions without the advice and assistance of many individuals and administrative agencies to cope with changing global circumstances.

Bureaucratic Efficiency and Rationality   Bureaucracies, according to the theoretical work of the German social scientist Max Weber, are widely believed to increase efficiency and rationality by assigning responsibility for different tasks to different people. They define rules and standard operating procedures that specify how tasks are to be performed; they rely on record systems to gather and store information; they divide authority among different organizations to avoid duplication of effort; they often lead to meritocracies by hiring and promoting the most capable individuals.

Bureaucracies also permit the luxury of engaging in forward planning to determine long-term needs and the means to attain them. Unlike leaders, whose roles require attention to the crisis of the moment, bureaucrats are able to consider the future as well as the present. The presence of several organizations also can result in *multiple advocacy* of rival choices (George, 1972), thus improving the chance that all possible policy options will be considered.

The Limits of Bureaucratic Organization   What emerges from our description of *bureaucracy* is another idealized picture of the policy-making process. Before jumping to the conclusion that bureaucratic decision making is a modern blessing, however, we should emphasize that the foregoing propositions tell us how bureaucratic decision making *should* occur; they do not tell us how it *does* occur. The actual practice and the foreign policy choices that result show that bureaucracy produce burdens as well as benefits.

Consider the 1962 Cuban Missile Crisis, arguably the single most threatening crisis in the post–World War II era. The method that U.S. policy makers used in orchestrating a response is often viewed as having nearly approximated the ideal of rational choice. From another decision-making perspective, however, the missile crisis reveals how decision making by and within organizational contexts sometimes compromises rather than facilitates rational choice.

In Graham Allison's well-known book on the missile crisis, *Essence of Decision* (1971), he advanced what is widely known as the *bureaucratic politics model* (see also Allison and Zelikow, 1999). This model of decision making highlights the constraints that organizations in *policy networks* place on decision makers' choices and the "pulling and hauling" that occurs among the key participants and *caucuses* of aligned bureaucracies in the decision process.

The bureaucratic politics model emphasizes how large-scale bureaucratic organizations contribute to the policy-making process by devising *standard operating procedures (SOPs)*—established methods to be followed in the performance of designated tasks. Not surprisingly, participants in the deliberations that lead to policy choices also often define issues and favor policy alternatives that serve their organization's needs. "Where you stand depends on where you sit" is a favorite aphorism reflecting these bureaucratic imperatives. Consider why professional diplomats typically favor diplomatic approaches to policy problems, whereas military officers routinely favor military solutions.

The consequence is that "different groups pulling in different directions produce a result, or better a resultant—a mixture of conflicting preferences and unequal power of various individuals—distinct from what any person or group intended" (Allison, 1971). Rather than being a value-maximizing process, then, policy making is itself an intensely competitive game of *politics*. Rather than presupposing the existence of a *unitary actor*, "bureaucratic politics" shows why "it is necessary to identify the games and players, to display the coalitions, bargains, and compromises, and to convey some feel for the confusion" (Allison, 1971).

Fighting among insiders and the formation of factions to carry on battles over the direction of foreign policy decisions are chronic in nearly every transnational actor's administration (but especially in democratic actors' accepting of participation by many people in the policy-making process). Consider the United States. Splits among key advisers over important foreign policy choices have been frequent. For example, under Presidents Nixon and Ford, Secretary of State Henry Kissinger fought often with James Schlesinger and Donald Rumsfeld, who headed the Department of Defense, over strategy regarding the Vietnam War; Jimmy Carter's national security adviser, Zbigniew Brzezinski, repeatedly engaged in conflicts with Secretary of State Cyrus Vance over the Iran hostage crisis; and under Ronald Reagan, Caspar Weinberger at Defense and George Shultz at State were famous for butting heads on most policy issues.

Such conflicts are not necessarily bad because they force each side to better explain its viewpoint, and this allows heads of state the opportunity to weigh their competing advice before making decisions. However, battles among advisers can lead to paralysis or to rash decisions that produce poor results. That possibility became evident in the fall of 2002, when serious divisions within George W. Bush's administration developed over the "how and why" surrounding the president's goal to wage war against Saddam Hussein in Iraq. Fissures became apparent as key officials publicly debated the wisdom of diplomacy versus invasion, and then how best to conduct the invasion. Similarly, such tension is evident in former U.S. Under Secretary of State George W. Ball's warning that the nature of the institutional machinery produced the decisions that led to America's failed war in Vietnam: "The process was the author of the policy."

In addition to their influence on the policy choices of political leaders, bureaucratic organizations possess several other characteristics that affect decision making. One view proposes that bureaucratic agencies are parochial and that every administrative unit within an international actor's foreign-policy-making bureaucracy seeks to promote its own purposes and power. Organizational needs, such as large staffs and budgets, come before the actor's needs, sometimes encouraging the sacrifice of the actor's interests to bureaucratic interests.

policy networks

Leaders and organized interests (such as lobbies) that form temporary alliances to influence a particular foreign policy decision.

Carnegie Council Video:
Policy Networks

caucuses

Informal groups that individuals in governments and other groups join to promote their common interests.

standard operating procedures (SOPs)

Rules for reaching decisions about particular types of situations.

Characteristically, bureaucratic agencies are driven to enlarge their prerogatives and expand the conception of their mission, seeking to take on other units' responsibilities and powers. Far from being neutral or impartial managers, desiring only to carry out orders from the leaders, bureaucratic organizations frequently take policy positions designed to increase their own influence relative to that of other agencies. Moreover, in contrast to rational choice theory, which sees decisions made by a unitary actor, bureaucratic agencies and their staff may not agree with the leader's values and priorities. As former National Security Adviser Zbigniew Brzenski (2010, p. 18) cautions, an actor's foreign policy priorities may become diluted or delayed by unsympathetic bureaucrats, as "officials who are not in sympathy with advocated policies rarely make good executors."

The tragic surprise terrorist attack on September 11, 2001, provides a telling example of these ascribed characteristics of bureaucratic politics. Many regarded the attacks on 9/11 as the worst intelligence failure since Pearl Harbor. Alarmed U.S. citizens asked why, with an enormous army of agencies gathering intelligence, weren't the multitude of messages and warnings about the attack on the World Trade Center and the Pentagon translated in time to prevent the disaster? Why weren't those dots connected? Why were the warnings ignored?

The answer at first accepted by most analysts was that America's chaotic system of intelligence was paralyzed by the morass of cross-cutting bureaucracies. They engaged in turf battles with one another and did not share the vital information that arguably could have identified and prevented the Al Qaeda plot. The problem was miscommunication and noncommunication; the signals about the attack were not forwarded to the executive branch in time. Why? Morton Abramowitz (2002), a former assistant secretary of state in the Reagan administration, voiced his explanation when he wrote, "Three features pervade the making of foreign policy in Washington today: massive overload, internal warfare, and the short term driving out the long term." These problems exist in every administration, but are particularly problematic when intense ideological perspectives are in play.

As the horror of 9/11 persisted, so did interest and concern about who did what to disrupt the Al Qaeda terrorist network operation prior to September 11, 2001. A bipartisan congressional commission was created to investigate what had gone wrong, in order to make needed corrections in the way the U.S. government makes decisions for national security and counterterrorism. The 9/11 Commission (2004) produced a new set of explanations for why so many opportunities to head off the 9/11 disaster were missed.

The Commission did not center blame on the inadequacies and infighting of the country's "alphabet soup" intelligence agencies, such as the Central Intelligence Agency (CIA) and Federal Bureau of Investigation (FBI). Instead, the Commission pointed its criticism at the growing complaints (Mann, 2004; Woodward, 2004) about the White House's inaction and pre-9/11 downplaying or ignoring of the loud and clear warnings submitted by U.S. intelligence bureaucracies of the true, imminent dangers of a likely terrorist attack. In this case, the failure of the U.S. government to protect its citizens might have been more due to the unwillingness of American leadership to listen to the warnings of its national security bureaucracies than to the crippling effects of bureaucratic struggles.

Still, consider the problems faced by every U.S. president who must seek to manage hundreds of competing agencies and subagencies, each of which is habitually loath to share

CourseMate

Simulation:
Explaining U.S.
Intervention in Iraq

information with one another for fear of compromising "sources and methods." Each agency competes with its rivals and engages in finger-pointing and scapegoating as a blood sport. Moreover, as FBI Special Agent Coleen Rowley testified, "There's a mutual-protection pact in bureaucracies. Mid-level managers avoid decisions out of fear a mistake will sidetrack their careers while a rigid hierarchy discourages agents from challenging superiors. There is a saying: 'Big cases, big problems; little cases, little problems; no cases, no problems.' The idea that inaction is the key to success manifests itself repeatedly" (Toner, 2002).

We can discern still another property of bureaucratic politics: the natural inclination of professionals who work in large organizations is to adapt their outlook and beliefs to those prevailing where they work. As constructivist theory explains, every bureaucracy develops a shared mind-set, or dominant way of looking at reality, akin to the *groupthink* characteristic that small groups often manifest (Janis, 1982). Scholars often cite groupthink as a process governing policy decision making that leads to riskier choices. This, in turn, leads to more extreme policies (that ultimately fail miserably) than likely would have been made by individuals without the pressures in peer groups. An institutional mind-set, or socially constructed consensus, also discourages creativity, dissent, and independent thinking: it encourages reliance on standard operating procedures and deference to precedent rather than the exploration of new options to meet new challenges. This results in policy decisions that rarely deviate from conventional preferences.

Yet research shows that debate and criticism stimulate, rather than inhibit, ideas. "There's this Pollyannaish notion that the most important thing to do when working together is stay positive and get along, to not hurt anyone's feelings," explains psychology professor Charlan Nemeth.

groupthink

The propensity for members of a group to accept and agree with the group's prevailing attitudes, rather than speaking out for what they believe.

COLLECTIVE DECISION MAKING Policy decisions are often made in small groups. Pictured here in a meeting with members of his cabinet and advisors on February 7, 2013, U.S. President Barack Obama listens to Secretary of State John Kerry discuss immigration issues.

"Well, that's just wrong. Maybe debate is going to be less pleasant, but it will always be more productive" (Lehrer, 2012, p. 24).

In your future employment, you are likely to directly observe the efforts of your employer to make rational decisions. You also are bound to notice firsthand within your organization both the advantages of bureaucratic administration and its liabilities. Many students, before they entered the workforce, found that the payoffs of rational choice and the pitfalls of bureaucratic politics surrounding actual practice described here were *not* figments of scholars' imagination. Rather, these properties and propensities of decision making speak to the real experiences of professionals who have entered into policy-making positions. (Many a student reader of previous editions of *World Politics* have later reported that these interpretations prepared them well for what they encountered later in their careers and helped them overcome some naïve expectations that governments, as well as nonstate actors, stand united, when most of the effort *within* them centers on debate and dispute among participating factions within their decision-making unit.) And keep in mind that Harvard University's John F. Kennedy School of Government bases its entire curriculum on the conviction that the essence of national and international service requires awareness of interagency bureaucratic bargaining and the contributions and impediments that competition makes to rational decision making.

In classifying the determinants of international actors' foreign policies, the levels-of-analysis framework introduced in Chapter 1 (see Figure 1.1) helps to describe the multiple influences on the decision-making process. Recall that in addition to the level of the individual decision maker, the internal and global levels of analysis also influence foreign policy decisions. To place decision making into proper perspective, this chapter will next consider insights from the comparative study of foreign policy to help us better appreciate how foreign policy decision making by states is shaped.

THE DOMESTIC DETERMINANTS OF FOREIGN POLICY DECISIONS

Internal or "domestic" influences are those that exist at the level of the international actor, not the global system. While nonstate actors have internal attributes that shape their policy decisions, here we focus on states as they are the most powerful player on the world stage, their foreign policy decisions are the most consequential, and the factors that influence their capacity to make decisions are arguably different from many of those that influence other international actors' decisions. To illustrate the impact of internal factors, consider how variations in states' attributes—such as differences in military capabilities, level of economic development, and type of government—may influence different countries' foreign policy choices.

Military Capabilities   The realist proposition that states' internal capabilities shape their foreign policy priorities is supported by the fact that states' preparations for war strongly influence their later use of force (Levy, 2001). Thus, although most states may seek similar goals, their ability to realize them will vary according to their military capabilities.

Because military capabilities limit a state's range of prudent policy choices, they act as a mediating factor on leaders' national security decisions. For instance, in the 1980s, Libyan leader Muammar Qaddafi repeatedly provoked the United States through anti-American and anti-Israeli rhetoric and by supporting various terrorist activities. Qaddafi was able to act as he did largely because neither bureaucratic organizations nor a mobilized public existed in Libya to constrain his personal whims. However, Qaddafi was doubtlessly more highly constrained by the outside world than were the leaders in the more militarily capable countries toward whom he directed his anger. Limited military muscle compared with the United States precluded the kinds of belligerent behaviors he threatened to use.

Conversely, Saddam Hussein made strenuous efforts to build Iraq's military might and by 1990 had built the world's fourth-largest army. Thus, invading Kuwait to seize its oil fields became a feasible foreign policy option. In the end, however, even Iraq's impressive military power proved ineffective against a vastly superior coalition of military forces, headed by the United States. The 1991 Persian Gulf War forced Saddam Hussein to capitulate and withdraw from the conquered territory. Twelve years later, the United States invaded Iraq and finally ousted Saddam Hussein from office. The lesson: what states believe about their own military capabilities and those of their adversaries (and their enemies' intentions) guide their decisions about war and peace.

Economic Conditions   The level of economic and industrial development a state enjoys also affects the foreign policy goals it can pursue. Generally, the more economically developed a state, the more likely it is to play an activist role in the global political economy. Rich states have interests that extend far beyond their borders and typically possess the means to pursue and protect them. Not coincidentally, states that enjoy industrial capabilities and extensive involvement in international trade also tend to be militarily powerful—in part because a robust economy is, generally speaking, a prerequisite for military might.

Although economically advanced states are more active globally, this does not mean that their privileged circumstances dictate adventuresome policies. Rich states are often "satisfied" states that have much to lose from revolutionary change and global instability (Wolfers, 1962). As a result, they usually perceive the status quo as serving their interests and often forge international economic policies to protect and expand their envied position at the pinnacle of the global hierarchy.

Levels of productivity and prosperity also affect the foreign policies of the poor states at the bottom of the global hierarchy. Some economically weak states respond to their situation by complying subserviently with the wishes of the rich on whom they depend. Others rebel defiantly, sometimes succeeding (despite their disadvantaged bargaining position) in resisting the efforts by great powers and powerful international organizations to control their behavior.

Thus, generalizations about the economic foundations of states' international political behavior often prove inaccurate. Although levels of economic development vary widely among states in the global system, they alone do not determine foreign policies. Instead, leaders' perceptions of the opportunities and constraints that their states' economic resources provide may have a larger influence on their foreign policy choices.

Type of Government   A third important attribute affecting states' international behavior is their type of political system. Although realism predicts that all states will act similarly to protect their interests, a state's type of government demonstrably constrains important choices, including whether threats to use military force are carried out. Here the important distinction is between *constitutional democracy* (representative government), at one end of the spectrum, and *autocratic rule* (authoritarian or totalitarian) at the other.

---

constitutional democracy

Government processes that allow people, through their elected representatives, to exercise power and influence the state's policies.

---

autocratic rule

A system of authoritarian or totalitarian government in which unlimited power is concentrated in a single leader.

Carnegie Council Video:
Autocratic Rule

**diversionary
theory of war**

*The hypothesis
that leaders
sometimes initiate
conflict abroad as
a way of increasing
national cohesion
at home by divert-
ing national public
attention away
from controversial
domestic issues
and internal
problems.*

In neither democratic (sometimes called "open") nor autocratic ("closed") political systems can political leaders survive long without the support of organized domestic political interests, and sometimes the mass citizenry. But in democratic systems, those interests are likely to spread beyond the government itself. Public opinion, interest groups, and the mass media are a more visible part of the policy-making process in democratic systems. Similarly, the electoral processes in democratic societies more meaningfully frame choices than the processes in authoritarian regimes, where the real choices are made by a few elites behind closed doors. In a democracy, public opinion and preferences may matter, and therefore differences in who is allowed to participate and how much they exercise their right to participate are critical determinants of foreign policy choices.

The proposition that domestic stimuli, and not simply international events, are a source of foreign policy is not novel. In ancient Greece, for instance, the realist historian Thucydides observed that what happened within the Greek city-states often did more to shape their external behavior than did the interactions between the states. He added that Greek leaders frequently concentrated their efforts on influencing the political climate within their own polities. Similarly, leaders today sometimes make foreign policy decisions for domestic political purposes—as, for example, when bold or aggressive acts abroad are intended to divert public attention from economic woes, improve public opinion of their leader's policymaking, or influence election outcomes at home. This is sometimes called the "scapegoat" phenomenon or the *diversionary theory of war* (DeRouen and Sprecher, 2006; Gallagher and Allen, 2013).

THE BURDEN OF FOREIGN POLICY CHOICE FOR GLOBAL LEADERSHIP The United States is called upon to provide visionary leadership for the world, and this entails a careful assessment of priorities and strategies. Barack Obama declared that "I will strengthen our common security by investing in our common humanity. Our global engagement cannot be defined by what we are against; it must be guided by a clear sense of what we stand for. We have a significant stake in ensuring that those who live in fear and want today can live with dignity and opportunity tomorrow."

Some see the intrusion of domestic politics into foreign policy making as a disadvantage of democratic political systems that undermines their ability to deal decisively with crises or to bargain effectively with less democratic adversaries and allies (see "A Closer Look: Democratic Governance—A Foreign Policy Handicap?"). Democracies are subject to inertia. They move slowly on issues, because so many disparate elements are involved in decision making. Furthermore, officials in democracies are accountable to public opinion and must respond to pressure from a variety of domestic interest groups (groups mobilized to exercise influence over the future direction of their country's foreign policies, especially on issues highly important to them).

A crisis sufficient to rouse the attention and activity of a large proportion of the population may need to erupt in order for large changes in policy to come about. As French political sociologist Alexis de Tocqueville

A Closer Look

DEMOCRATIC GOVERNANCE—A FOREIGN POLICY HANDICAP?

Realism anticipates that in order to protect their national interests, states should ideally conduct their foreign policies free of ideological and domestic political constraints. Along those lines, democracies may be seen as comparatively "weak" in that they rely on public support and their political power is less centralized. Liberal theorists counter that these very constraints may be conducive to peace, as they hinder leaders from making impulsive foreign policy choices.

This tension between democratic governance and effective foreign policy making was seen within the United States in the aftermath of the U.S.-led assault on Libya on March 19, 2011. As part of a coalition effort that was authorized by the United Nations (UN) Security Council, U.S. military forces participated in a series of air strikes against Libyan air defenses and government forces. Though confronting the threat to peace and security posed by Libyan leader Muammar Qadhafi's regime was endorsed by many in the U.S. Congress—indeed on March 1 the Senate unanimously approved a resolution that called for the UN to impose a no-fly zone over Libya—U.S. president Barack Obama faced a firestorm of criticism from members of both political parties who expressed outrage that Obama did not first seek congressional approval before committing U.S. military forces to the mission. They argued that Obama had exceeded his constitutional authority, and that "the merits of the operation" are "separate from the domestic legal question of whom—the president or Congress—has the authority to decide whether the United States will take part in combat" (Savage, 2011, p. A14).

For his part, Obama countered that not only were his actions in the national interest but, as chief executive and commander in chief of the U.S. military, he had the power to authorize the strikes. Obama's decision was among the latest in a long line of presidential authorizations of military action without prior congressional approval, which include Harry Truman's entrance into the Korean War and Bill Clinton's bombing of Kosovo in 1999. Nonetheless, Obama later sought a resolution of support from Congress for continued U.S. military involvement in Libya, saying that "it has always been my view that it is better to take military action ... with congressional engagement, consultation and support."

WATCH THE VIDEO:

Carnegie Council Video:
Democracy and Waging
War

YOU DECIDE:

1. Does the nature of democratic rule help or hinder those governments' capacity to achieve their foreign policy goals?

2. What arguments and evidence can you provide to support your general conclusion?

3. Do you think that authoritarian governments are better able to conduct effective foreign policy? Why or why not?

argued in 1835, democracies may be inclined to "impulse rather than prudence" because they overreact to perceived external dangers once they recognize them. "There are two things that a democratic people will always find difficult," de Tocqueville mused, "to start a war and to end it."

In contrast, authoritarian governments can "make decisions more rapidly, ensure domestic compliance with their decisions, and perhaps be more consistent in their foreign policy" (Jensen, 1982). But there is a cost: non-democracies "often are less effective in developing an innovative foreign policy because of subordinates' pervasive fear of raising questions." In short, the concentration of power and the suppression of public opposition can be both advantageous and disadvantageous.

GLOBAL INFLUENCES ON FOREIGN POLICY

States' internal attributes influence their foreign policies. However, the global environment within which states operate also shapes opportunities for action, setting an ecological context that limits some foreign policy choices but facilitates others (Sprout and Sprout, 1965; Starr and Most, 1978). Global or "external" influences on foreign policy include all activities occurring beyond a state's borders that affect the choices its officials and the people they govern make. Such factors as military alliances and levels of international trade sometime profoundly affect the choices of decision makers. To recognize the influence of external factors, here we comment briefly on how two other aspects of the international environment—the global distribution of power and geostrategic position—affect international decision making.

Global Distribution of Power

Power can be distributed in many ways. It can be concentrated in the hands of a single state, as in the ancient Mediterranean world at the zenith of the Roman Empire, or it may be diffused among several rival states, as it was at the birth of the state system in 1648 following the Thirty Years' War, when a handful of great power rivals possessed approximately equal strength. Scholars use the term *polarity* to describe the distribution of power among members of the global system. As will be explained further in Chapter 4, unipolar systems have one dominant power center, bipolar systems contain two centers of power, and multipolar systems possess three or more such centers.

Closely related to the distribution of power is the pattern of alignments among states. *Polarization* refers to the degree to which states cluster around the powerful. For instance, a highly bipolarized system is one in which small and medium-sized states form alliances with one of the two dominant powers. The network of alliances around the United States and Soviet Union during the Cold War exemplified such a system. Today, the "nature of the international system … will have to be rethought as new powers rise, old ones continue to fade, and attention shifts from the Atlantic to the Pacific" (Mead, 2010, p. 64). The growing prominence of China as an active player in world politics, and the United States' attentiveness to developments in Asia, reflects a shift in political power across the globe.

Polarity and alliance polarization influence foreign policy by affecting the decision latitude possessed by states. For example, as discussed in Chapters 4 and 8, when power is concentrated in the hands of a single state in a unipolar system, it can more easily choose to use military force

polarity

The degree to which military and economic capabilities are concentrated in the global system that determines the number of centers of power, or "poles."

polarization

The formation of competing coalitions or blocs composed of allies that align with one of the major competing poles, or centers, of power.

and intervene in the affairs of others than it would in a system characterized by a distribution of shared power, where rivals might obstruct its actions. However, when alliances are tight military blocs, the small state members of each alliance will feel compelled to conform to the dictates of the alliance's leader.

Conversely, when alliances are loosely shifting with fluid membership, smaller states can more readily choose to craft foreign policies that are independent of the wishes of the powerful. Of course, you could think of other examples to show how the structural properties of the global system affect decision latitude. What they would show is that the foreign policy impact of polarity and polarization hinges on the geostrategic position of a given state.

Geopolitical Factors

Some of the most important influences on a state's foreign policy behavior stem from its location vis-à-vis other states in the international system, and the geostrategic advantages that this conveys. The presence of natural frontiers, for example, may profoundly guide policy makers' choices (see Map 3.1). Consider the United States, which was secure throughout most of its early history because vast oceans separated it from potential threats in Europe and Asia. The advantage of having oceans as barriers to foreign intervention, combined with the absence of militarily powerful neighbors, permitted the United States to develop into an industrial giant and to safely practice an isolationist foreign policy for more than 150 years. Consider also mountainous Switzerland, whose easily defended topography has made neutrality a viable foreign policy option.

Similarly, maintaining autonomy from continental politics has been an enduring theme in the foreign policy of Great Britain, an island country whose physical detachment from Europe long served as a buffer separating it from entanglement in major power disputes on the Continent. Preserving this protective shield has long been a priority for Britain, and it helps to explain why London has been so hesitant in the past twenty years to accept full integration in the European Union (EU).

Most countries are not insular, however; they have many states on their borders, denying them the option of noninvolvement in world affairs. Germany, which sits in the geographic center of Europe, historically has found its domestic political system and foreign policy preferences shaped by its geostrategic position. In the twentieth century, for example, Germany struggled through no less than six major radical changes in governing institutions, each of which pursued very different foreign policies: (1) the empire of Kaiser Wilhelm II; (2) the Weimar Republic; (3) Adolf Hitler's dictatorship; its two post–World War II successors, (4) the capitalist Federal Republic in West Germany and (5) the communist German Democratic Republic in East Germany; and, finally, (6) a reunited Germany after the end of the Cold War, now committed to liberal democracy and full integration in the EU. Each of these governments was preoccupied with its relations with neighbors but responded to the opportunities and challenges presented by Germany's position in the middle of the European continent with very different foreign policy goals. In no case, however, was isolationistic withdrawal from involvement in continental affairs a practical geostrategic option.

History is replete with other examples of geography's influence on states' foreign policy goals. This is why geopolitical theories are valuable. The *geopolitics* school of realist thought, and political geography generally, stresses the influence of geographic factors on state power

geopolitics

The theoretical postulate that states' foreign policies are determined by their location, natural resources, and physical environment.

Carnegie Council Video:
Geopolitics

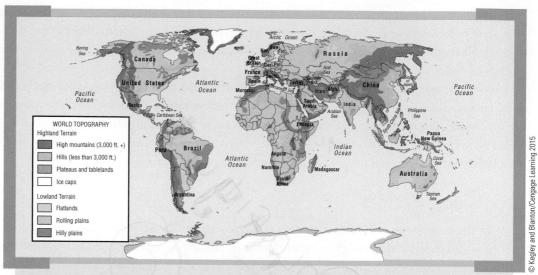

MAP 3.1 GEOGRAPHIC INFLUENCES ON FOREIGN POLICY The number of neighboring states and the protection afforded by natural barriers shape how countries interact with one another. This map suggests how, until recently, the separation of the United States from Eurasia encouraged an isolationist policy during many periods in U.S. history. Also note how topography, location, and other geopolitical factors may have influenced the foreign policy priorities of Great Britain, Germany, China, Finland, and states in South America—hypotheses advanced by the geopolitics approach to international politics.

and international conduct (Cohen, 2003). Illustrative of early geopolitical thinking is Alfred Thayer Mahan's *The Influence of Sea Power in History* (1890), which maintains that control of the seas shaped national power and foreign policy. States with extensive coastlines and ports enjoyed a competitive advantage. Later geopoliticians, such as Sir Halford Mackinder (1919) and Nicholas Spykman (1944), argued that topography, size (territory and population), climate, and distance between states, in addition to location, are powerful determinants of individual countries' foreign policies. The underlying principle behind the geopolitical perspective is self-evident: leaders' perceptions of available foreign policy options are influenced by the geopolitical circumstances that define their states' place on the world stage.

Can global actors, whether state or nonstate, respond to the demands that external challenges and internal politics simultaneously place on their leaders? The trends and transformations currently unfolding in world politics are the products of countless decisions made daily throughout the world. Some decisions are more momentous than others, and how actors respond to one another has profound consequences for the entire drama of world politics. To better understand this, Part 2 begins in Chapter 4 by examining the dynamics of great power rivalry on the world stage. Countries of the Global South are investigated in Chapter 5, followed by examination of nonstate actors in Chapter 6.

STUDY. APPLY. ANALYZE.

Key Terms

autocratic rule
bounded rationality
bureaucracy
bureaucratic politics model
Bush Doctrine
caucuses
constitutional democracy

diversionary theory of war
externalities
game theory
geopolitics
groupthink
history-making individuals
model

multiple advocacy
polarity
polarization
policy agenda
policy networks
political efficacy
prospect theory

rational choice
roles
standard operating procedures (SOPs)
two-level games
unitary actor
zeitgeist

Suggested Readings

Hermann, Margaret G., ed. (2007) *Comparative Foreign Policy Analysis: Theories and Methods*. Upper Saddle River, NJ: Prentice Hall.

Hudson, Valerie M. (2007) *Foreign Policy Analysis: Classic and Contemporary Theory*. Lanham, MD: Rowman & Littlefield Publishers.

Kahneman, Daniel. (2011) *Thinking, Fast and Slow*. New York: Farrar, Straus, and Giroux.

Gallagher, Maryann E. and Susan H. Allen. (2013) "Presidential Personality: Not Just a Nuisance," *Foreign Policy Analysis* (Feb): 1–21.

McCausland, Jeffrey D. (2008, March 6) "Developing Strategic Leaders for the 21st Century," http://www.carnegiecouncil.org/resources/articles_papers_reports/0004.html.

Renshon, Jonathan, and Stanley A. Renshon. (2008) "The Theory and Practice of Foreign Policy Decision Making," *Political Psychology* 29: 509–536.

Rosenthal, Joel H. (2009, July 20) "Leadership as Practical Ethics," *The Essence of Ethics*, http://www.carnegiecouncil.org/education/001/ethics/0003.html.

Wittkopf, Eugene R., Christopher Jones, and Charles W. Kegley, Jr. (2007) *American Foreign Policy: Pattern and Process*, 7th ed. Belmont, CA: Thomson Wadsworth.

Suggested Videos

Dallek, Robert. "The Lost Peace: Leadership in a Time of Horror and Hope, 1945–1953."

Freedman, Sir Lawrence. "A Choice of Enemies: America Confronts the Middle East."

Goldstein, Gordon M. "Lessons in Leadership from JFK and LBJ for America's Next Commander-in-Chief."

Nye, Jr., Joseph S. "The Power to Lead."

Vocke, William. "Secrecy in Foreign Policy."

Vocke, William. "Tunisia: The Jasmine Revolution and Western Foreign Policy."

CourseMate

Log in to CourseMate to access the following study tools for this chapter:

- Interactive Quiz
- eBook
- Flashcards & Key Term Crossword Puzzle
- Chapter Audio Summary
- Carnegie Council Videos

- Video Activities
- Simulation
- Animated Learning Module
- Case Study
- International Relations NewsWatch

PART 2

THE GLOBE'S ACTORS AND THEIR RELATIONSHIPS

Shakespeare wrote that "all the world's a stage and all the men and women merely players." When it comes to world politics, not just people but also organizations, groups, and countries have a variety of roles to play on the global stage. Part 2 identifies the major actors in world politics today and describes the roles they perform, the policies they pursue, and the predicaments they face.

MARCHING FOR CHANGE

People, like states and international

organizations, are transnational actors.

Mobilized publics often use demonstrations

to express their dissent and to draw global

"Great powers fear each other. They regard each other with suspicion, and they worry that war may be in the offing. They anticipate danger. There is little room for trust.... From the perspective of any one great power, all other great powers are potential enemies.... The basis of this fear is that in a world where great powers have the capability to attack each other and might have the motive to do so, any state bent on survival must be at least suspicious of other states and reluctant to trust them."

—*John Mearsheimer, realist political theorist*

CHAPTER 4

Rivalries and Relations among the Great Powers

Popperfoto/Getty Images

THE PATH NOT TAKEN? After the close of World War II, the United States and the Soviet Union stood at a crossroads. The decisions that were made, and the actions that were taken, determined whether they would be allies or rivals. Indeed, the thermonuclear standoff that became the Cold War might not have occurred had the two made other choices: "The Cold War was not predetermined," argues Melvyn Leffler (2007). "These leaders made choices." Shown here are Harry Truman (left) and Joseph Stalin (right).

QUESTIONS TO CONSIDER

- *How might transitions in power follow a cyclical pattern?*
- *What were the causes and consequences of World War I?*
- *What were the causes and consequences of World War II?*
- *What were the causes, and phases, of the Cold War?*
- *What has been the nature of international relations in the Post–Cold War Era?*
- *What does the future look like for the great powers?*

Who's number one? Who's gaining on the leader? What does it mean for the future if the strongest is seriously challenged for the predominant position? These are the kinds of questions sports fans often ask when the rankings of the top teams are adjusted after the preceding week's competition. World leaders also adopt what former U.S. Secretary of State Dean Rusk called a "football stadium approach to diplomacy." And many people throughout the world habitually make comparisons of countries, asking which states are the biggest, strongest, wealthiest, and most militarily powerful and evaluating which states are rising and which are falling relative to one another.

When making such rankings, both groups are looking at world politics through the lens of realism. They see an international system of competitors, with winners and losers in an ancient contest for supremacy. And they look most closely at the shifting rankings at the very top of the international hierarchy of power—at the rivalry and struggle among the "great powers." Moreover, they picture this conflict as perpetual. As Arnold J. Toynbee's (1954) famous cyclical theory of history explains: "The most emphatic punctuation in a uniform series of events recurring in one repetitive cycle after another is the outbreak of a great war in which one power that has forged ahead of all its rivals makes so formidable a bid for world domination that it evokes an opposing coalition of all the other powers."

Toynbee's conclusion lies at the center of realism. The starting point for understanding world politics, as a leading post–World War II realist theorist Hans J. Morgenthau (1985) elaborates, is to recognize that "all history shows that nations active in international politics are continuously preparing for, actively involved in, or recovering from organized violence in the form of war." Cycles of war and peace colored twentieth-century world politics, with three global wars breaking out. World Wars I and II were fought with fire and blood; the Cold War was fought without the same magnitude of destruction but with equal intensity. Each of these wars triggered major transformations in world politics.

This chapter explores the causes and consequences of great power rivalries. By understanding the origins and impact of these three struggles over world leadership, you will be better positioned to anticipate whether the great powers will be able to avoid yet another global war in the twenty-first century.

Mankind must put an end to war or war will put an end to mankind.

—**John F. Kennedy, U.S. president**

THE QUEST FOR WORLD LEADERSHIP

Rivalry between great powers has long characterized world politics. As Toynbee suggested, there is a strong probability that this historical pattern is cyclical. *Long-cycle theory* elaborates on this understanding of world politics and provides a framework for our analysis of evolving great power rivalries. According to long-cycle theory (see Chapter 7 for further discussion), transitions in world leadership unfold through a series of distinct phases where periods of global war are followed by relatively stable periods of international rule making and institution building (see Table 4.1). Shifts in the cycle have occurred alongside changes in the major states' relative power, changing their relations with one another (see Chase-Dunn and

long-cycle theory

A theory that focuses on the rise and fall of the leading global power as the central political process of the modern world system.

TABLE 4.1	The Evolution of Great Power Rivalry for World Leadership, 1495–2025		
Dates	Preponderant State(s) Seeking Hegemony	Other Powers Resisting Domination	Global War	New Order after Global War
1495–1540	Portugal	Spain, Valois, France, Burgundy, England	War of Italy and the Indian Ocean, 1494–1517	Treaty of Tordesillas, 1517
1560–1609	Spain	The Netherlands, France, England	Spanish-Dutch Wars, 1580–1608	Truce of 1608; Evangelical Union and the Catholic League formed
1610–1648	Holy Roman Empire (Hapsburg dynasty in Spain and Austria-Hungary)	Shifting ad hoc coalitions of mostly Protestant states (Sweden, Holland) and German principalities as well as Catholic France against remnants of papal rule	Thirty Years' War, 1618–1648	Peace of Westphalia, 1648
1650–1713	France (Louis XIV)	The United Provinces, England, the Hapsburg Empire, Spain, major German states, Russia	War of the Grand Alliance, 1688–1713	Treaty of Utrecht, 1713
1792–1815	France (Napoleon)	Great Britain, Prussia, Austria, Russia	Napoleonic Wars, 1792–1815	Congress of Vienna and Concert of Europe, 1815
1871–1914	Germany, Turkey, Austria-Hungary	Great Britain, France, Russia, United States	World War I, 1914–1918	Treaty of Versailles creating the League of Nations, 1919
1933–1945	Germany, Japan, Italy	Great Britain, France, Soviet Union, United States	World War II, 1939–1945	Bretton Woods, 1944; United Nations, Potsdam, 1945
1945–1991	United States, Soviet Union	Great Britain, France, China, Japan	Cold War, 1945–1991	NATO/Partnerships for Peace, 1995; World Trade Organization, 1995
1991–2025?	United States	China, European Union, Japan, Russia, India	A cold peace or hegemonic war, 2015–2025?	A new security regime to preserve world order?

hegemon

A preponderant state capable of dominating the conduct of international political and economic relations.

Carnegie Council Video: Hegemon

Anderson, 2005). Over the past five centuries, each global war has led to the emergence of a *hegemon*. With its unrivaled power, the hegemon has reshaped the rules and institutions of the global system to preserve its preeminent position.

Hegemony always imposes an extraordinary burden on the world leader. "By virtue of the great resources they command, Great Powers, and, even more, superpowers, have special rights and special responsibilities," notes political scientist Robert Jervis (2012, p. 623), "even though their great power may tempt them to overreach and neglect their duties." A hegemon must bear the costs of maintaining political and economic order while protecting its position and upholding its dominion. Over time, as the weight of global engagement takes its toll, every previous hegemon has overextended itself. As challengers have arisen, the security agreements so carefully crafted after the last global war have come under attack. Historically, this struggle for power has set the stage for another global war, the demise of one hegemon and the ascent

MIGHT MAKES FRIGHT Shown here is one example of resistance to U.S. global preeminence: Pakistanis burn a U.S. flag in an anti-American rally in protest of drone attacks in Pakistan's tribal regions. U.S. Director of Central Intelligence John Brennan defended drone attacks in Pakistan, claiming that airstrikes for targeted killings protect lives and prevent potential terror attacks. Pakistani demonstrators, however, charge that many civilians are killed, including innocent children.

of another. Table 4.1 summarizes 500 years of the cyclical rise and fall of great powers, their global wars, and their subsequent efforts to restore order.

Critics note that long-cycle theorists disagree on whether economic, military, or domestic factors produce these cycles. They also take issue with the deterministic tone of the theory, which to them implies that global destiny is beyond any policy maker's control. Must great powers rise and fall as if by the law of gravity—what goes up must come down?

Still, long-cycle theory suggests you should consider how shifts in the relative strength of great powers affect world politics. It draws attention to hegemonic transitions, the rise and fall of leading states in the global system, and in so doing provokes questions about whether this long cycle can be broken. To underscore the importance of struggles over world leadership and their impact on trends and transformations in world politics, this chapter accordingly asks you to inspect the three great power wars of the twentieth century, as well as the lessons these clashes suggest for the twenty-first century.

WORLD WAR I

World War I erupted when a Serbian nationalist seeking to free his ethnic group from Austrian rule assassinated Archduke Ferdinand, heir to the Hapsburg throne of the Austrian-Hungarian Empire, at Sarajevo in June 1914. This assassination sparked a series of great power actions and reactions in the five weeks that followed, shattering world peace.

By the time the first major European war of the twentieth century had ended, nearly 10 million people had died, three empires had crumbled, new states had been born, seven decades of communist rule in Russia had begun, and the world geopolitical map had been redrawn in ways that paved the way for the rise of Adolf Hitler in Nazi Germany.

The Causes of World War I

How can such a catastrophic war be explained? Multiple answers are possible. Most popular are structural realist explanations, which hold that World War I was inadvertent, not the result of any master plan. Neorealists believe that it was a war bred by circumstances beyond the control of those involved, one that people neither wanted nor expected. Revisionist historians, however, have argued that the war was the result of deliberate choices—"a tragic and unnecessary conflict … because the train of events that led to its outbreak might have been broken at any point during the five weeks of crisis that preceded the first clash of arms, had prudence or common goodwill found a voice" (Keegan, 1999, p. 3).

structuralism

The neorealist proposition that states' behavior is shaped primarily by changes in the properties of the global system, such as shifts in the balance of power, instead of by individual heads of states or by changes in states' internal characteristics.

Structuralism   Framed at the *global level of analysis*, *structuralism* postulates that the changing distribution of power within the anarchical global system is the primary factor that determines state behavior. Looking at the circumstances on the eve of World War I, many historians hypothesize that the way in which the great powers were aligned against one another created an environment conducive to an armed conflict. The great powers' prior rearmament efforts, as well as their alliances and resulting counteralliances, created a momentum that, along with the pressures created by the mobilization of armies and arms races, dragged European statesmen toward war (Tuchman, 1962).

This structural explanation concentrates attention on the nineteenth century, when Britain dominated world politics. Britain was an island country isolated from continental affairs by temperament, tradition, and geography. Britain's sea power gave it command of the world's shipping lanes and control over a vast empire stretching from the Mediterranean to Southeast Asia. This dominance helped to deter aggression. Germany, however, presented a challenge to British power.

Carnegie Council Video: Structuralism

After becoming a unified country in 1871, Germany prospered and used its growing wealth to create a formidable army and navy. This strength resulted in greater ambition and resentment of British preeminence. As the predominant military and industrial power on the European continent, Germany sought to compete for international position and status. As Kaiser Wilhelm II proclaimed in 1898, Germany had "great tasks outside the narrow boundaries of old Europe." Germany's rising power and global aspirations altered the European geopolitical landscape.

Furthermore, Germany was not the only new emergent power at the turn of the century. Russia was also expanding and becoming a threat to Germany. The decline of the Austrian-Hungarian Empire, Germany's only ally, heightened Germany's fear of Russia, which can be seen in Germany's strong reaction to the assassination of Archduke Ferdinand. Fearing that a long war might result in an unfavorable shift in the *balance of power*, Germany sought a short localized war with a more favorable outcome. Germany thus supported Austria-Hungary's unrestrained assault on Serbia.

Although the logic behind Germany's calculation was clear—a victorious war would bolster Austria-Hungary and hamper Russian influence—it turned out to be a serious miscalculation. France and Russia joined forces to defend Serbia, and were soon joined by Britain in an effort to oppose Germany and defend Belgian neutrality. In April 1917, the war became truly global in scope when the United States, reacting to German submarine warfare, entered the conflict.

Here we observe, again at the global level of analysis, the dynamics of shifts in the *balance of power* as a causal factor: the historic tendency for opposed coalitions to form so that the distribution of military power is "balanced" to prevent any single power or bloc from seriously threatening others. And that is what happened in the decade prior to Archduke Ferdinand's assassination. European military alignments had become polarized, pitting the Triple Alliance of Germany, Austria-Hungary, and the Ottoman Empire against the Triple Entente of Britain, France, and Russia. According to this structural interpretation, after Russia mobilized its armies in response to Austria's attack on Serbia, cross-cutting alliance commitments pulled one European great power after another into the war.

Nationalism   As an alternative interpretation of the origins of World War I at the *state level of analysis*, many historians view the growth of *nationalism*, especially in southeastern Europe, as having created a climate of opinion that made war likely. Groups that glorified the distinctiveness of their national heritage began championing their own country above all others (Woodwell, 2008). Long-suppressed ethnic prejudices soon emerged, even among leaders. Russian foreign minister Sergei Sazonov, for example, claimed to "despise" Austria, and Kaiser Wilhelm II of Germany proclaimed "I hate the Slavs" (Tuchman, 1962).

Domestic unrest inflamed these passions, making it hard to see things from another point of view. Believing that they were upholding their national honor, the Austrians could not comprehend why Russians labeled them the aggressors. German insensitivity to others' feelings prevented them from understanding "the strength of the Russians' pride, their fear of humiliation if they allowed the Germans and Austrians to destroy their little protégé, Serbia, and the intensity of Russian anger" (White, 1990). With each side belittling the national character and ethnic attributes of the other, diplomatic alternatives to war become untenable.

nationalism

A mind-set glorifying a particular state and the nationality group living in it, which sees the state's interest as a supreme value.

Carnegie Council Video: Nationalism

Rational Choice   At the *individual level of analysis, rational choice theory* offers a third interpretation of the causes of World War I. From this perspective—which emphasizes that leaders make decisions based upon careful evaluation of the relative usefulness of alternative options for realizing the best interests of themselves and their states (see Chapter 3)—the war's outbreak was a result of the German elites' preference for a war with France and Russia in order to consolidate Germany's position on the continent, confirm its status as a world power, and divert domestic attention from its internal troubles (Kaiser, 1990). Under this interpretation, the people gathered at the Imperial Palace in Berlin pushed Europe over the brink.

The rational choice model of decision making suggests that World War I is best seen as a consequence of the purposive goal of rival great powers to compete against one another for global power. This is a drive that realists believe is an "iron law of history." It resulted from "an attempt by Germany to secure its position before an increasingly powerful Russia had achieved a position of equality with Germany (which the latter expected to happen by 1917)" (Levy, 1998b).

As these rival interpretations suggest, the causes of World War I remain in dispute. Structural explanations emphasize the global distribution of power, domestic interpretations look at causal factors *within* states, and rational choice explanations direct attention to the calculations and goals of particular leaders. All partially help us to understand the sequences that produced the world's first truly global war.

The Consequences of World War I

World War I changed the face of Europe (see Map 4.1). In its wake, three multi-ethnic empires—the Austrian-Hungarian, Russian, and Ottoman (Turkish)—collapsed, and the independent states of Poland, Czechoslovakia, and Yugoslavia emerged in their place. In addition, the countries of Finland, Estonia, Latvia, and Lithuania were born. The war also contributed to the independence of the Republic of Ireland from Britain in 1920 and the overthrow of the Russian czar in 1917 by the Bolsheviks. The emergence of communism under the leadership of Vladimir Lenin produced a change in government and ideology that would have geopolitical consequences for another 70 years.

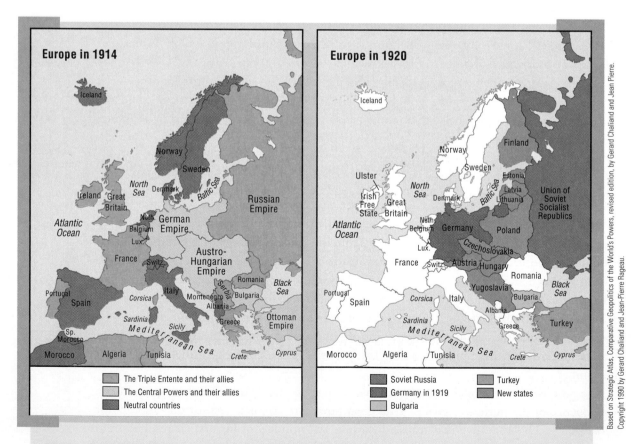

Based on Strategic Atlas, Comparative Geopolitics of the World's Powers, revised edition, by Gerard Chaliand and Jean Pierre. Copyright 1990 by Gerard Chaliand and Jean-Pierre Rageau.

MAP 4.1   TERRITORIAL CHANGES IN EUROPE FOLLOWING WORLD WAR I The map on the left shows state boundaries on the eve of war in 1914, as well as the members of the two major opposing coalitions that formed. The map on the right shows the new borders in 1920, with the nine new states that emerged from the war.

Despite its costs, the coalition consisting of Britain, France, Russia, and (later) the United States and Italy defeated the threat of domination posed by the Central powers (Germany, Austria-Hungary, Turkey, and their allies). Moreover, the war set the stage for a determined effort to build a new global system that could prevent another war:

> For most Europeans, the Great War had been a source of disillusionment.... When it was all over, few remained to be convinced that such a war must never happen again. Among vast populations there was a strong conviction that this time the parties had to plan a peace that could not just terminate a war, but a peace that could change attitudes and build a new type of international order....
>
> For the first time in history, broad publics and the peacemakers shared a conviction that war was a central problem in international relations. Previously, hegemony, the aggressive activities of a particular state, or revolution had been the problem. In 1648, 1713, and 1815, the peacemakers had tried to resolve issues of the past and to construct orders that would preclude their reappearance. But in 1919 expectations ran higher. The sources of war were less important than the war itself. There was a necessity to look more to the future than to the past. The problem was not just to build a peace, but to construct a peaceful international order that would successfully manage all international conflicts of the future (K. Holsti, 1991, pp. 175–176, 208–209).

A consequence of World War I was a pronounced distaste for war and theories of *realism* that justified great power competition, armaments, secret alliances, and *balance-of-power* politics. The staggering human and material costs of the previous four years led many of the delegates to the 1919 peace conference convened at Versailles, outside Paris, to reevaluate their convictions about statecraft. The time was ripe for a new approach to building world order. Disillusioned with realism, many turned to *liberalism* for guidance on how to manage the global future.

The decade following World War I was the high point of liberal idealism. Woodrow Wilson's ideas about world order, as expressed in his January 1917 "Fourteen Points" speech, were anchored in a belief that by reordering the global system according to liberal principles, the "Great War" (as World War I was then called) would be "the war to end all wars." Wilson's chief proposal was to construct a League of Nations that allegedly would guarantee the independence and territorial integrity of all states. His other recommendations included strengthening international law, settling territorial claims on the basis of self-determination, and promoting democracy, disarmament, and free trade.

However, once the peace conference began, parochial national interest resurfaced and undermined Wilson's proposals as many European leaders had been offended by the pontificating American president. "God was content with Ten Commandments," growled Georges Clemenceau, the cynical realist French prime minister. "Wilson must have fourteen."

As negotiations at the conference proceeded, hard-boiled power politics prevailed. Ultimately, the delegates were only willing to support those elements in the Fourteen Points that served their national interests. After considerable wrangling, Wilson's League of Nations was written into the peace treaty with Germany as the first of 440 articles. The rest of the treaty was punitive, aimed at stripping the country of its great power status. Similar treaties were later forced on Austria-Hungary and Germany's other wartime allies.

The Treaty of Versailles grew out of a desire for retribution. In brief, Germany's military was drastically cut; it was forbidden to possess heavy artillery, military aircraft, or submarines,

CourseMate

**Case Study:
Liberal Idealism**

and its forces were banned from the Rhineland. Germany also lost territory in the west to France and Belgium, in the south to the new state of Czechoslovakia, and in the east to the new states of Poland and Lithuania. Overseas, Germany lost all of its colonies. Finally, in the most humiliating clause of the treaty, Germany was assigned responsibility for the war and charged with paying heavy financial reparations for the damages. On learning of the treaty's harsh provisions, the exiled German kaiser is said to have declared "the war to end wars has resulted in a peace to end peace."

WORLD WAR II

Germany's defeat in World War I and its humiliation under the Treaty of Versailles did not extinguish its hegemonic aspirations. On the contrary, they intensified. Thus, conditions were ripe for the second great power war of the twentieth century, which pitted the Axis trio of Germany, Japan, and Italy against an unlikely "grand alliance" of four great powers, who united despite their incompatible ideologies—communism in the case of the Soviet Union and democratic capitalism in the case of Britain, France, and the United States.

The world's fate depended upon the outcome of this massive effort to defeat the Axis threat. The Allied powers achieved success, but at a terrible cost: 23,000 lives were lost each day, and at least 53 million people died during six years of fighting. To understand the origins of this devastating conflict, we will once again examine causal factors operating at different *levels of analysis*.

The Causes of World War II

Following Germany's capitulation in 1918, a democratic constitution was drafted by a constituent assembly meeting in the city of Weimar. Many Germans had little enthusiasm for the Weimar Republic. Not only was the new government linked in their minds to the humiliating Versailles Treaty, but it also suffered from the 1923 French occupation of the industrial Ruhr district, various political rebellions, and the ruinous economic collapse of 1929. By the parliamentary elections of 1932, over half of the electorate supported extremist parties that disdained democratic governance. The largest of these was the Nazi, or National Socialist German Workers, Party. Thus began the long and tragic path toward World War II.

Proximate Causes on the Road to War On January 30, 1933, the Nazi leader, Adolf Hitler, was appointed chancellor of Germany. Less than a month later, the Reichstag (Parliament) building burned down under mysterious circumstances. Hitler used the fire to justify an emergency edict allowing him to suspend civil liberties and repress communists and other political adversaries. Once all meaningful parliamentary opposition had been eliminated, Nazi legislators passed an enabling act that suspended the constitution and granted Hitler dictatorial power.

In his 1924 book *Mein Kampf* ("My Struggle"), Hitler urged Germany to recover territories taken by the Treaty of Versailles, absorb Germans living in neighboring lands, and colonize Eastern Europe. During his first year in power, however, he cultivated a pacifist image, signing a nonaggression pact with Poland in 1934. The following year, the goals originally outlined in *Mein Kampf* climbed to the top of Hitler's foreign policy agenda. He thoroughly ignored the *Kellogg-Briand Pact*, which prohibited the use of military force as a means for resolving interstate conflicts. In 1935, he repudiated the military clauses of the Versailles Treaty; in 1936, he ordered troops into the demilitarized Rhineland; in March 1938, he annexed Austria; and in September 1938, he demanded control over the Sudetenland, a region of Czechoslovakia containing ethnic Germans. To address the Sudeten German question, a conference was convened in Munich. Hitler, British prime minister Neville Chamberlain, and leaders of France and Italy (ironically, Czechoslovakia was not invited) all attended. Convinced that *appeasement* would halt further German expansionism, Chamberlain and the others agreed to Hitler's demands.

appeasement

A strategy of making concessions to another state in the hope that, satisfied, it will not make additional claims.

Rather than satisfying Germany, appeasement whetted its appetite and that of the newly formed fascist coalition of Germany, Italy, and Japan, which aimed to overthrow the international status quo. In the Eastern Hemisphere, Japan had grown disillusioned with Western liberalism and the Paris settlements, and it was suffering from the economic devastation of the Great Depression. Like Germany, Japan embraced militarism as key to its global expansion. In the might-makes-right climate that Germany's imperialistic quest for national aggrandizement helped create, Japanese nationalists led their country on the path to imperialism and *colonialism*. Japan's invasions of Manchuria in 1931 and further forays into China in 1937 were paralleled by Italy's absorption of Abyssinia (modern-day Ethiopia) in 1935 and Albania in 1939. Further, both Germany and Italy intervened in the 1936–1939 Spanish civil war on the side of the fascists, headed by General Francisco Franco, whereas the Soviet Union supported antifascist forces.

colonialism

The rule of a region by an external sovereign power.

After Germany occupied the rest of Czechoslovakia in March 1939, Britain and France formed an alliance to protect the next likely victim, Poland. They also opened negotiations with Moscow in hopes of enticing the Soviet Union to join the alliance, but the negotiations failed. Then, on August 23, 1939, Hitler, a fascist, and the Soviet dictator, Joseph Stalin, a communist, stunned the world with the news that they had signed a nonaggression pact, promising not to attack one another. Now confident that Britain and France would not intervene, Hitler invaded Poland. However, Britain and France honored their pledge to defend Poland, and two days later declared war on Germany. World War II had begun.

The war expanded rapidly. Hitler next turned his forces to the Balkans, North Africa, and westward, as the mechanized German troops invaded Norway and marched through Denmark, Belgium, Luxembourg, and the Netherlands. The German army swept around the Maginot line, the defensive barrier on the eastern frontier that France boasted could not be breached. The quick and nearly bloodless German victory forced the British to evacuate a nearly 340,000-strong expeditionary force from the French beaches at Dunkirk. Paris itself fell in June 1940. Within six weeks France surrendered, even though Germany's forces were numerically inferior to those of France and its allies. In the months that followed, the German air force, the Luftwaffe, pounded Britain in an attempt to force it into submission as well. Instead of invading Britain, however, the Nazi troops launched a surprise attack on the Soviet Union, Hitler's supposed ally, in June 1941. Such a move would later prove to be a great strategic blunder.

isolationism

A policy of withdrawing from active participation with other actors in world affairs and instead concentrating state efforts on managing internal affairs.

multipolarity

The distribution of global power into three or more great power centers, with most other states allied with one of the rivals.

Carnegie Council Video: Multipolarity

political economy

A field of study that focuses on the intersection of politics and economics in international relations.

irredentism

A movement by an ethnic national group to recover control of lost territory by force so that the new state boundaries will no longer divide the group.

fascism

A far-right ideology that promotes extreme nationalism and the establishment of an authoritarian society built around a single party with dictatorial leadership.

Meanwhile, in the East, tensions were growing. The United States, Great Britain, and France viewed Japan's imperial expansion as a threat to their own interests in the region. In an effort to hamper Japan's ability to carry out its global ambitions, the United States embargoed the sale of strategic raw materials, such as scrap iron, steel, and oil.

Poor in natural resources, Japan saw the United States as a serious threat to its national security. In September 1940 Japan forged the Tripartite Pact with Germany and Italy that pledged the three Axis powers to come to one another's aid if attacked by another great power, such as the United States. Japan continued its aggressive expansion, and in July 1941 moved into southern Indochina (region in Southeast Asia that encompasses the present-day countries of Laos, Vietnam, and Cambodia). In response, the United States froze Japanese assets in the United States and issued demands for Japanese withdrawal. Deciding that the eviction of the United States from the Pacific was critical to its national interest, on December 7th of that same year, Japan launched a surprise assault on the United States at Pearl Harbor. Following this attack, Germany quickly declared war on the United States. The Japanese assault and the German challenge ended U.S. aloofness and *isolationism*, enabling President Franklin Roosevelt to forge a coalition with Britain and the Soviet Union to oppose the fascists.

Underlying Causes at Three Analytic Levels   Structural realism emphasizes *polarity* as a defining feature of the international system and, at the global level of analysis, regards the reemergence of *multipolarity* in global power distribution as a key factor in the onset of World War II. The post–World War I global system was precarious because the number of sovereign states increased at the same time the number of great powers declined. In 1914, Europe had only 22 key states, but by 1921 the number had nearly doubled. When combined with resentment over the Versailles treaty, the Russian Revolution, and the rise of fascism, the increased number of states and the resurgence of nationalistic revolts and crises made "the interwar years the most violent period in international relations since the Thirty Years' War and the wars of the French Revolution and Napoleon" (K. Holsti 1991, p. 216).

The 1930s collapse of the global economic system also contributed to the war. Great Britain found itself unequal to the leadership and regulatory roles it had performed in the world *political economy* before World War I. Although the United States was the logical successor, its refusal to exercise leadership hastened the war. The 1929–1931 depression was followed in 1933 "by a world Monetary and Economic Conference whose failures—engineered by the United States—deepened the gloom, accelerated protectionist barriers to foreign trade such as tariffs and quotas, and spawned revolution" (Calvocoressi, Wint, and Pritchard, 1989, p. 6). In this depressed global environment, heightened by deteriorating economic circumstances at home, Germany and Japan sought solutions abroad through *imperialism*.

At the state level of analysis, collective psychological forces also led to World War II. These included "the domination of civilian discourse by military propaganda that primed the world for war," the "great wave of hypernationalism [that] swept over Europe [as] each state taught itself a mythical history while denigrating that of others," and the demise of democratic governance (Van Evera, 1990–1991, pp. 18, 23). During the Nuremberg Trials after World War II, when Nazi officials were prosecuted for war crimes committed during the Holocaust, senior Nazi Hermann Goering reflected on the Nazi propaganda success. "Why of course the people don't want war," he said, but "it is always a simple matter to drag the people along, whether it is a democracy, or a fascist dictatorship, or a parliament, or a communist dictatorship…. All you have to do is to tell them they are being attacked, and denounce the pacifists for lack of patriotism and exposing the country to danger."

Domestically, German nationalism inflamed latent *irredentism* and rationalized the expansion of German borders both to regain provinces previously lost in wars to others and to absorb Germans living in Austria, Czechoslovakia, and Poland. The rise of *fascism*—the Nazi regime's *ideology* championing the flag, the fatherland, nationalism, imperialism, and anti-Semitism—animated this renewed imperialistic push and preached an extreme version of realism that stressed power politics to justify the forceful expansion of the German state and other Axis powers that were aligned with Germany. "Everything for the state, nothing outside the state, nothing above the state" was the way Italy's dictator, Benito Mussolini, constructed his understanding of the fascist political philosophy, in a definition that embraced the extreme realist proposition that the state was entitled to rule every dimension of human life by force.

The importance of leaders at the individual level of analysis stands out. The war would not have been possible without Adolf Hitler and his plans to conquer the world. World War II arose primarily from German aggression. Professing the superiority of Germans as a "master race" along with virulent anti-Semitism and anticommunism, Hitler chose to wage war to create an empire that he believed could resolve once and for all the historic competition and precarious coexistence of the great powers in Europe by eliminating Germany's rivals:

> The broad vision of the Thousand-Year Reich was … of a vastly expanded—and continually expanding—German core, extending deep into Russia, with a number of vassal states and regions, including France, the Low Countries, Scandinavia, central Europe, and the Balkans, that would provide resources and labor for the core. There was to be no civilizing mission in German

ideology

A set of core philosophical principles that leaders and citizens collectively construct about politics, the interests of political actors, and the ways people ought to behave.

The Print Collector/Alamy

THE RISE OF HITLER AND GERMAN NATIONALISM Consistent with the realist view that states have an inherent right to expand, Adolf Hitler persuaded the German people of the need to persecute the Jews and expand German borders through armament and aggression. He constructed and cultivated a widespread perception in Germany that, in his words, "an evil exists that threatens every man, woman and child of this great nation. We must take steps to ensure our domestic security and protect our homeland." Pictured here on April 20, 1941, Hitler (far right) confers with senior Nazi leaders.

Yalta Conference

The 1945 summit meeting of the Allied victors to resolve postwar territorial issues and voting procedures in the United Nations to collectively manage world order.

imperialism. On the contrary, the lesser peoples were to be taught only to do menial labor or, as Hitler once joked, educated sufficiently to read the road signs so they wouldn't get run over by German automobile traffic. The lowest of the low, the Poles and Jews, were to be exterminated.... To Hitler ... the purpose of policy was to destroy the system and to reconstitute it on racial lines, with a vastly expanded Germany running a distinctly hierarchical and exploitative order. Vestiges of sovereignty might remain, but they would be fig leaves covering a monolithic order. German occupation policies during the war, whereby conquered nations were reduced to satellites, satrapies, and reservoirs of slave labor, were the practical application of Hitler's conception of the new world order. They were not improvised or planned for reasons of military necessity (Holsti 1991, pp. 224–225).

The Consequences of World War II

Having faced ruinous losses in Russia and a massive Allied bombing campaign at home, Germany's Thousand-Year Reich lay in ruins by May 1945. By August of that same year, the U.S. atomic bombing of Hiroshima and Nagasaki forced Japan to end its war of conquest.

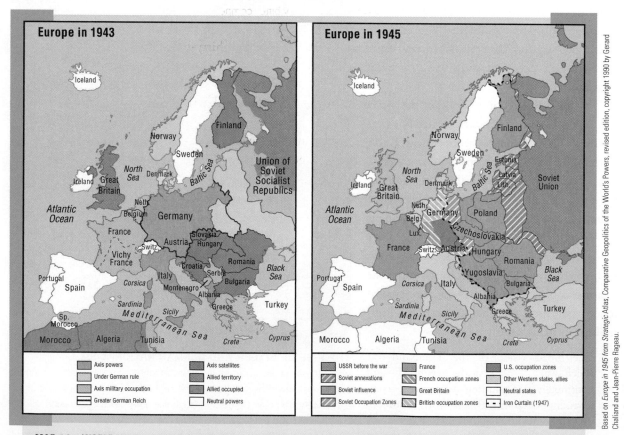

Based on *Europe in 1945* from *Strategic Atlas, Comparative Geopolitics of the World's Powers*, revised edition, copyright 1990 by Gerard Chaliand and Jean-Pierre Rageau.

MAP 4.2   WORLD WAR II REDRAWS THE MAP OF EUROPE The map on the left shows the height of German expansion in 1943, when it occupied Europe from the Atlantic Ocean and the Baltic Sea to the gates of Moscow in the Soviet Union. The map on the right shows the new configuration of Europe after the "Grand Coalition" of Allied forces—Great Britain, the United States, and the Soviet Union—defeated the Axis's bid for supremacy.

The Allied victory over the Axis redistributed power and reordered borders, resulting in a new geopolitical terrain.

The Soviet Union absorbed nearly 600,000 square kilometers of territory from the Baltic states of Estonia, Latvia, and Lithuania, and from Finland, Czechoslovakia, Poland, and Romania—recovering what Russia had lost in the 1918 Treaty of Brest-Litovsk after World War I. Poland, a victim of Soviet expansionism, was compensated with land taken from Germany. Germany itself was divided into occupation zones that eventually provided the basis for its partition into Cold War–era East and West Germany. Finally, pro-Soviet regimes assumed power throughout Eastern Europe (see Map 4.2). In the Far East, the Soviet Union took the four Kurile Islands from Japan—or the "Northern Territories," as Japan calls them—and Korea was divided into Soviet and U.S. occupation zones at the Thirty-Eighth Parallel.

ALLIES OR NEW RIVALS? The "Big Three" (Winston Churchill, Franklin Roosevelt, and Joseph Stalin) meet at Yalta as victorious great power allies to establish rules for all states to follow in the post–World War II global order, but that cooperation would soon be replaced by bitter competition.

With the defeat of the Axis, one global system ended, but the defining characteristics of the new system had not yet become clear. Although the United Nations was created to replace the old, discredited League of Nations, the management of world affairs still rested in the hands of the victors. Yet victory only magnified their distrust of one another.

The "Big Three" leaders—Winston Churchill, Franklin Roosevelt, and Joseph Stalin—met at the *Yalta Conference* in February 1945 to design a new world order. But the vague compromises they reached concealed the differences percolating below the surface. Following Germany's unconditional surrender in May, the Big Three (with the United States now represented by Harry Truman) met again in July 1945 at Potsdam. The meeting ended without agreement, and the facade of Allied unity began to disintegrate.

In the aftermath of the war, the United States and the Soviet Union were the only two great powers that were still strong and had the capacity to impose their will. The other major-power victors, especially Great Britain, had exhausted themselves and slipped from the apex of the world-power hierarchy. The vanquished axis powers also fell from the great power ranks. Thus, as Alexis de Tocqueville had foreseen in 1835, the Americans and Russians now held in their hands the destinies of half of humankind. In comparison, all other states were dwarfs.

In this atmosphere, ideological debate arose about whether the twentieth century would become "the American century" or "the Russian century." Thus, perhaps the most important product of World War II was the *transformation* it caused, after a short interlude, in the distribution of global power from *multipolarity* to **bipolarity**. In what, after 1949, became known as the *Cold War*, Washington and Moscow used the fledgling United Nations to pursue their competition with each other rather than to keep the peace. As the third and last hegemonic

bipolarity

A condition in which power is concentrated in two competing centers so that the rest of the states define their allegiances in terms of their relationships with both rival great power superstates, or "poles."

Carnegie Council Video: Bipolarity

Cold War

The 44-year (1947–1991) rivalry between the United States and the Soviet Union, as well as their competing coalitions, which sought to contain each other's expansion and win worldwide predominance.

CourseMate

Carnegie Council Video: Cold War

struggle of the twentieth century, the Cold War and its lessons still cast dark shadows over today's geostrategic landscape.

> *The United States should take the lead in running the world in the way that the world ought to be run.*
>
> **—Harry S Truman, U.S. president**

THE COLD WAR

The second great war of the twentieth century, without parallel in the number of participants and destruction, brought about a global system dominated by two superpowers whose nuclear weapons radically changed the role that threats of warfare would play in world politics. The competition between the United States and the Soviet Union for hegemonic leadership grew out of these circumstances.

The Causes and Evolutionary Course of the Cold War

The origins of the twentieth century's third hegemonic battle for domination are debated because the historical evidence lends itself to different interpretations (see Leffler and Westad, 2009). Several postulated causes stand out. At the global level of analysis, the first is advanced by realism: the Cold War resulted from a transition in power and leadership that propelled the United States and the Soviet Union to the top of the international hierarchy and made their rivalry inescapable. "As both sides searched beyond their core alliances for strategic advantage, the Cold War began to affect the trajectories of states and political movements across the globe" (Freedman, 2010, p. 137). Circumstances gave each superpower reasons to fear and struggle against the other's potential global leadership, and encouraged both competitors to carve out and establish wide *sphere of influence*, or specified areas of the globe.

sphere of influence

A region of the globe dominated by a great power.

A second interpretation, at the state level of analysis, holds that the Cold War was simply an extension of the superpowers' mutual disdain for each other's professed beliefs about politics and economics. U.S. animosity toward the Soviet Union was stimulated by the 1917 Bolshevik Revolution, which brought to power a government that embraced the radical Marxist critique of capitalistic imperialism (see Chapter 2). American fears of Marxism stimulated the emergence of anticommunism as an opposing ideology. Accordingly, the United States embarked on a missionary crusade of its own to contain and ultimately remove the atheistic communist menace from the face of the Earth.

Similarly, Soviet policy was fueled by the belief that capitalism could not coexist with communism. The purpose of Soviet policy, therefore, was to push the pace of the historical process in which communism eventually would prevail. However, Soviet planners did not believe that this historical outcome was guaranteed. They felt that the capitalist states, led by the United States, sought to encircle the Soviet Union and smother communism in its cradle, and that resistance by the Soviets was obligatory. As a result, ideological incompatibility may have ruled out compromise as an option (see "Controversy: Was Ideology the Primary Source of East–West Conflict?").

CONTROVERSY

WAS IDEOLOGY THE PRIMARY SOURCE OF EAST–WEST CONFLICT?

Cold War America was gripped by a "great fear" not simply of the Soviet Union but also of communism. Senator Joseph McCarthy led the most infamous hunt for communist sympathizers in government, Hollywood production companies blacklisted supposed communist sympathizers, and average American citizens were often required to take loyalty oaths at their offices. Everywhere, communism became synonymous with treasonous, un-American activity. As the nuclear arms race escalated and the U.S. government took military action to contain the Soviet Union, its justification was almost always expressed in terms of ideology. The threat, as the population learned to perceive it, was that of an atheistic, communistic system that challenged the fundamental American principles of democratic capitalism. Also, according to the *domino theory*, which suggested that communism was inherently driven to knock over one country after another, Soviet communism was inherently expansionistic. The communist regime also couched its Cold War rhetoric in terms of ideology, objecting to the imperialistic, capitalist system that the Soviets said America planned to impose on the whole world.

Some would argue that fear of the Soviet's world dominance may have been more important in the Cold War than pure ideology. Both the American and the Soviet governments may have entered the Cold War to secure their relative power in the world order as much as to protect pure principles. After all, the United States and the Soviet Union had managed to transcend differing ideologies when they acted as allies in World War II. After World War II, however, a power vacuum created by the demise of Europe's traditional great powers drew them into conflict with each other, and as they competed, ideological justifications surfaced.

Liberalism, communism, socialism, and capitalism are examples of ideologies of international politics. Ideologies help us to interpret life and its meaning and are for that reason indispensable for organizing thought and values. As social constructivism suggests, ideology provides meaning within a social context and enables a society to use its domestic values and norms to frame its interests and convictions. But commitment to an ideology may at times cause hatred and hostility. Institutional proponents of particular ideologies are prone to perceive other ideologies competitively—as challenges to the truth of their own ideology's core beliefs. When this happens, ideology can also become an excuse for armed violence. Communist theoretician Vladimir Lenin described the predicament that he perceived as the fundamental cause of the Cold War. He predicted—prophetically, it turned out—that "As long as capitalism and socialism exist, we cannot live in peace; in the end, either one or the other will triumph—a funeral dirge will be sung either over the Soviet Republic or over world capitalism." Although scholars are still debating the causes of the Cold War, we need to ask whether it was, in fact, an ideological contest over ideas, or a more general contest for power.

domino theory

A metaphor popular during the Cold War that predicted that if one state fell to communism, its neighbors would also fall in a chain reaction, like a row of falling dominoes.

WHAT DO YOU THINK?

- *Was the Cold War really an ideological contest between international communism and the free-market capitalism espoused by the liberal democracies, or were there other, deeper conflicts of interest involved?*

- *Did the end of the Cold War signify the triumph of Western values over communist ones? What is the potential for ideological differences to reemerge and fuel conflict between the two countries?*

- *Can you think of other examples in more recent years where ideological differences have appeared to play a role in shaping conflict between countries? In particular, think of the implications associated with the rise of China.*

A third explanation, rooted in decision making at the individual level of analysis, sees the Cold War as being fueled by the superpowers' misperceptions of each other's motives. From this constructivist perspective, conflicting interests were secondary to misunderstandings and ideologies. Mistrustful actors are prone to see only virtue in their own actions and only malice in those of their adversaries. This tendency to see one's opponent as the complete opposite, or *mirror image*, of oneself makes hostility virtually inevitable. Moreover, when perceptions of an adversary's evil intentions are socially constructed and become accepted as truth, a self-fulfilling prophecy can develop and the future can be affected by the way it is anticipated. Thus, viewing each other suspiciously, each rival giant acted in hostile ways that encouraged the very behavior that was suspected.

Additional factors, beyond those rooted in divergent interests, ideologies, and images, undoubtedly combined to produce this explosive Soviet–American hegemonic rivalry. To sort out the relative causal influence of the various factors, we must evaluate how, once it erupted after the 1945–1948 gestation period, the Cold War changed over its 44-year duration. The character of the Cold War shifted in three phases over its long history (see Figure 4.1), and several distinct patterns emerged that not only provide insights into the impetus behind the Cold War but also illustrate the properties of other great power rivalries.

Confrontation, 1947–1962   Though a brief period of wary Soviet–American cordiality prevailed in the immediate aftermath of World War II, this goodwill rapidly vanished as the two giants' vital interests collided. At this critical juncture, George F. Kennan, then a diplomat in the American embassy in Moscow, sent Washington his famous "long telegram" assessing the sources of Soviet conduct. Published in 1947 by the influential *Foreign Affairs* journal, and signed as "X" to conceal his identity, Kennan argued that Soviet leaders would forever feel insecure about their political ability to maintain power against forces both within Soviet society and in the outside world. Their insecurity would lead to an active—and perhaps aggressive—Soviet foreign policy. However, the United States had the power to increase the strains under which the Soviet leadership would have to operate, which could lead to a gradual mellowing or final end of Soviet power. Kennan concluded: "In these circumstances it is clear that the main element of any United States policy toward the Soviet Union must be that of a long-term, patient but firm and vigilant containment of Russian expansive tendencies" (Kennan, 1947).

Soon thereafter, President Harry S Truman made Kennan's assessment the cornerstone of American postwar foreign policy. Provoked in part by violence in Turkey and Greece, which Truman and others believed to be communist inspired, Truman declared that he believed "it must be the policy of the United States to support free peoples who are resisting attempted subjugation by armed minorities or by outside pressures." Eventually known as the *Truman Doctrine*, this statement defined the strategy that the United States would pursue for the next 40 years, over Kennan's objections. This strategy, called *containment*, sought to prevent the expansion of Soviet influence by encircling the Soviet Union and intimidating it with the threat of a military attack.

A seemingly endless series of Cold War crises soon followed. They included the communist coup d'état in Czechoslovakia in 1948, the Soviet blockade of West Berlin in June of that year, the communist rise to power on the Chinese mainland in 1949, the outbreak of the Korean War in 1950, the Chinese invasion of Tibet in 1950, and the on-again, off-again Taiwan Strait

---

Truman Doctrine

The declaration by President Harry S Truman that U.S. foreign policy would use intervention to support peoples who allied with the United States against communist external subjugation.

Carnegie Council Video:
Truman Doctrine

containment

A strategy of confronting attempts of a power rival to expand its sphere of influence, with either force or the threat of force, thereby preventing it from altering the balance of power.

Carnegie Council Video:
Containment

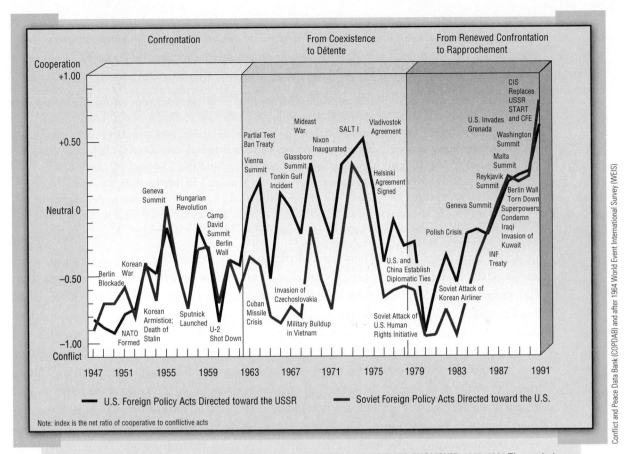

FIGURE 4.1   KEY EVENTS IN THE COLD WAR EVOLUTION OF THE U.S.–SOVIET RELATIONSHIP, 1947–1991 The evolution of U.S.–Soviet relations during the Cold War displays a series of shifts between periods of conflict and cooperation. As this figure shows, each superpower's behavior toward the other tended to be reciprocal, and, for most periods before 1983, confrontation prevailed over cooperation.

crises. The Soviets finally broke the U.S. atomic monopoly in 1949. Thereafter, the risks of massive destruction necessitated restraint and changed the terms of the great powers' rivalry.

Because the Soviet Union remained strategically inferior to the United States, Nikita Khrushchev (who, upon Stalin's death in 1953, succeeded him) pursued a policy of *peaceful coexistence* with capitalism. Even so, the Soviet Union sought, however cautiously, to increase its power in places where opportunities appeared to exist. As a result, the period following Stalin's death saw many Cold War confrontations, with Hungary, Cuba, Egypt, and Berlin serving as flash points.

In 1962, the surreptitious placement of Soviet missiles in Cuba set the stage for the greatest test of the superpowers' capacity to manage their disputes—the Cuban Missile Crisis. The superpowers stood eyeball to eyeball. Fortunately, one (the Soviet Union) blinked, and the crisis ended. This painful learning experience both reduced enthusiasm for waging the Cold War by military means and expanded awareness of the suicidal consequences of a nuclear war.

peaceful coexistence

Soviet leader Nikita Krushchev's 1956 doctrine that war between capitalist and communist states is not inevitable and that inter-bloc competition could be peaceful.

Case Study: The Cold War

From Coexistence to Détente, 1963–1978　The growing threat of mutual destruction, in conjunction with the approaching parity of American and Soviet military capabilities, made coexistence or nonexistence appear to be the only alternatives. At the American University commencement exercises in 1963, U.S. President John F. Kennedy warned that

> should total war ever break out again—no matter how—our two countries would become the primary targets. It is an ironical but accurate fact that the two strongest powers are the two in the most danger of devastation…. We are both caught up in a vicious and dangerous cycle in which suspicion on one side breeds suspicion on the other and new weapons beget counter-weapons. In short, both the United States and its allies, and the Soviet Union and its allies, have a mutually deep interest in a just and genuine peace and in halting the arms race….
>
> So let us not be blind to our differences, but let us also direct attention to our common interests and to the means by which those differences can be resolved. And if we cannot end now our differences, at least we can help make the world safe for diversity.

Kennedy signaled a shift in how the United States hoped thereafter to bargain with its adversary, and the Soviet Union reciprocally expressed its interest in more cooperative relations. That movement took another step forward following Richard Nixon's election in 1968. Coached by his national security adviser, Henry A. Kissinger, President Nixon initiated a new approach to Soviet relations that in 1969 he officially labeled *détente*. As Kissinger explained, détente was a foreign policy strategy that sought to create "an environment in which competitors can regulate and restrain their differences and ultimately move from competition to cooperation." Along these lines, the objective of the U.S. *linkage strategy* was to shape superpower relations and lessen incentives for war through the continuation of mutually rewarding exchanges. Cooperative interaction became more commonplace than hostile relations (see Figure 4.1). Visits, cultural exchanges, trade agreements, arms control talks, and joint technological ventures replaced threats, warnings, and confrontations.

détente

In general, a strategy of seeking to relax tensions between adversaries to reduce the possibility of war.

linkage strategy

A set of assertions claiming that leaders should take into account another country's overall behavior when deciding whether to reach agreement on any one specific issue so as to link cooperation to rewards.

From Renewed Confrontation to Rapprochement, 1979–1991　Despite the careful nurturing of détente, its spirit did not endure. When the Soviet invasion of Afghanistan in 1979 led to détente's demise, President Jimmy Carter defined the situation as "the most serious strategic challenge since the Cold War began." In retaliation, he declared America's willingness to use military force to protect its access to oil supplies from the Persian Gulf, suspended U.S. grain exports to the Soviet Union, and attempted to organize a worldwide boycott of the 1980 Moscow Olympics.

Relations deteriorated dramatically thereafter. President Ronald Reagan and his Soviet counterparts (first Yuri Andropov and then Konstantin Chernenko) exchanged a barrage of confrontational rhetoric. Reagan asserted that the Soviet Union "underlies all the unrest that is going on" and described the Soviet Union as "the focus of evil in the modern world." The atmosphere was punctuated by Reagan policy adviser Richard Pipes's bold challenge in 1981 that the Soviets would have to choose between "peacefully changing their communist system … or going to war." Soviet rhetoric was equally unrestrained and alarmist.

As talk of war increased, preparations for it escalated. The arms race resumed feverishly, often at the expense of addressing domestic economic problems. The superpowers also extended the confrontation to new territory, such as Central America, and renewed their public diplomacy (propaganda) efforts to extol the virtues of their respective systems throughout the world. Reagan pledged U.S. support for anticommunist insurgents who sought to overthrow Soviet-supported governments in Afghanistan, Angola, and Nicaragua. In addition, American leaders spoke loosely about the "winability" of a nuclear war through a "prevailing" military strategy that included the threat of a "first use" of nuclear weapons in the event of conventional war. Relations deteriorated as these moves and countermoves took their toll. The new Soviet leader, Mikhail Gorbachev summarized the alarming state of superpower relations in 1985 by fretting that "The situation is very complex, very tense. I would even go so far as to say it is explosive."

EASING TENSIONS: U.S.–SOVIET DÉTENTE Pictured here, President Richard Nixon, one of the architects of the U.S. linkage strategy along with Secretary of State Henry Kissinger, toasts Soviet General Secretary Leonid Brezhnev and fellow dignitaries at their meeting to discuss approaches to relaxing tensions between the superpowers.

However, the situation did not explode. Instead, prospects for a more constructive phase improved greatly following Gorbachev's advocacy of "new thinking" in order to achieve a *rapprochement*, or reconciliation, of the rival states' interests. He sought to settle the Soviet Union's differences with the capitalist West in order to halt the deterioration of his country's economic and international position.

rapprochement

In diplomacy, a policy seeking to reestablish normal cordial relations between enemies.

As cornerstones of this new thinking, Gorbachev promoted "glasnost" and "perestroika." The former signifies greater openness and individual freedom, and the latter refers to the restructuring of political and economic systems. Embracing these principles, Gorbachev embarked on domestic reforms to promote democratization and the transition to a market economy, and proclaimed his desire to end the Cold War contest. "We realize that we are divided by profound historical, ideological, socioeconomic, and cultural differences," he noted during his first visit in 1987 to the United States. "But the wisdom of politics today lies in not using those differences as a pretext for confrontation, enmity, and the arms race." Soviet spokesperson Georgi Arbatov elaborated, informing the United States that "we are going to do a terrible thing to you—we are going to deprive you of an enemy."

Surprisingly, to many adherents of realism who see great power contests for supremacy as inevitable and strategic surrender or acceptance of defeat as impossible, the Soviets did what they promised: they began to act like an ally instead of an enemy. The Soviet Union agreed to end its aid to and support of the Castro regime in Cuba, withdrew from Afghanistan, and announced unilateral reductions in military spending. Gorbachev also agreed to two new disarmament agreements: the START (Strategic Arms Reduction Treaty) treaty for deep cuts in strategic arsenals and the Conventional Forces in Europe (CFE) treaty to reduce the Soviet presence in Europe.

In 1989, the Berlin Wall came down, and by 1991 the Cold War had truly ended when the Soviet Union dissolved, accepted capitalist free-market principles, and initiated democratic reforms. To nearly everyone's astonishment, the Soviet Union acquiesced in the defeat of communism, the reunification of Germany, and the disintegration of its east European bloc of allies, the Warsaw Pact. The conclusion of the enduring rivalry between East and West, and with it the end of the 70-year ideological dispute, was a history-transforming event. "Liberalism seemed to have triumphed—not merely capitalism but democracy and the rule of law, as represented in the West, and particularly in the United States" (Keohane and Nye, 2001a).

The collapse of the Cold War suggested something quite different from the lesson of the twentieth century's two world wars, which had implied that great power rivalries are necessarily doomed to end in armed conflict. Indeed, the unanticipated outcome undermined confidence in the adequacy of conventional realist theories that argued that no great power would ever accept the loss of position to another hegemonic rival without a fight. The Cold War was different; it came to an end peacefully, as a combination of factors contributed at various stages in the Cold War's evolution to transform a global rivalry into a stable, even cooperative, relationship (see Table 4.2). This suggests that it is sometimes possible for great power rivals to reconcile their competitive differences without warfare.

The Consequences of the Cold War

Although they were locked in a geostrategic rivalry made worse by antagonistic ideologies and mutual misperceptions, the United States and the Soviet Union avoided a fatal showdown. In accepting the decay of their empire, Russian leaders made perhaps the most dramatic peaceful retreat from power in history. The end of the Cold War altered the face of world affairs in profound and diverse ways. With the dissolution of the Soviet Union in 1991, no immediate great power challenger confronted American hegemonic leadership. However, a host of new security threats emerged, ranging from aspiring nuclear powers such as North Korea and Iran to terrorist networks such as Al Qaeda. As the turbulent twentieth century wound down, the simple Cold War world of clearly defined adversaries gave way to a shadowy world of elusive foes.

THE POST–COLD WAR ERA

Rapid, unanticipated changes in world politics create uncertainty about the global future. To optimists, the swift transformations following the collapse of communism "ushered in a generation of relative political stability" (Zakaria, 2009) and signaled "the universalization of Western liberal democracy as the final form of government" (Fukuyama, 1989). To pessimists, these sea changes suggested not history's end but the resumption of contests for hegemonic domination and opposition over contested ideas and ideologies.

unipolarity

A condition in which the global system has a single dominant power or hegemon

Both groups recognized that, in the years immediately following the end of the Cold War, bipolarity was superseded by *unipolarity*—a hegemonic configuration of power with only one predominant superstate. As time passed, however, other great powers began to vie for increased influence and visibility in world politics. This renewed contest has fueled debate as to whether *multipolarity* better describes the emerging distribution of power today. Of interest is what this

TABLE 4.2	Contending Interpretations of the Causes of the Cold War's End		
Level of Analysis	**Theoretical Perspective**		
	Realism	**Liberalism**	**Constructivism**
Individual	**Power Politics**	**Leaders as Movers of History**	**External Influences on Leadership**
	"The people who argued for nuclear deterrence and serious military capabilities contributed mightily to the position of strength that eventually led the Soviet leadership to choose a less bellicose, less menacing approach to international politics."—Richard Perle, U.S. presidential adviser	"[The end of the Cold War was possible] primarily because of one man—Mikhail Gorbachev. The transformations … would not have begun were it not for him."—James A. Baker III, U.S. secretary of state	"Reagan's 'tough' policy and intensified arms race [did not persuade] communists to 'give up.' [This is] sheer nonsense. Quite the contrary, this policy made the life for reformers, for all who yearned for democratic changes in their life, much more difficult…. The [communist hard-line] conservatives and reactionaries were given predominant influence…."—Georgi Arbatov, director of the USSR's Institute for the USA and Canada Studies
State	**Economic Mismanagement**	**Grassroots Movements**	**Ideas and Ideals**
	"Soviet militarism, in harness with communism, destroyed the Soviet economy and thus hastened the self-destruction of the Soviet empire."—Fred Charles Iklé, U.S. deputy secretary of defense	"It was man who ended the Cold War in case you didn't notice. It wasn't weaponry, or technology, or armies or campaigns. It was just man. Not even Western man either, as it happened, but our sworn enemy in the East, who went into the streets, faced the bullets and the batons and said: we've had enough."—John Le Carré, author	"The root of the conflict was a clash of social systems and of ideological preferences for ordering the world. Mutual security in those circumstances was largely unachievable. A true end to the Cold War was impossible until fundamental changes occurred in Soviet foreign policy."—Robert Jervis, political scientist
Global	**Containment**	**International Public Opinion**	**Cross-Border Contagion Effects**
	"The strategy of containment that won the Cold War was the brainchild of realists…. Containment focused first and foremost on preventing Moscow from seizing the key centers of industrial power that lay near its borders, while eschewing attempts to 'roll back' Communism with military force."—Stephan Walt, political scientist	"The changes wrought by thousands of people serving in the trenches [throughout the world] were at least partially responsible [for ending the Cold War]."—David Cortright, political scientist	"The acute phase of the fall of communism started outside of the Soviet Union and spread to the Soviet Union itself. By 1987, Gorbachev made it clear that he would not interfere with internal experiments in Soviet bloc countries…. Once communism fell in Eastern Europe, the alternative in the Soviet Union became civil war or dissolution."—Daniel Klenbort, political journalist

might mean for relations among the great powers in meeting the new and difficult challenges in world politics in the post–Cold War era.

America's "Unipolar Moment"

Unipolarity refers to the concentration of power in a single preponderant state. With the end of the Cold War, in a historical "moment" in world history (Krauthammer, 2003), the United States stood alone at the summit of the international hierarchy. It remains the only country with the military, economic, and cultural assets to be a decisive player in any part of the world it chooses. Its military is not just stronger than anybody else's; it

soft power

The capacity to co-opt through such intangible factors as the popularity of a state's values and institutions, as opposed to the "hard power" to coerce through military might.

Carnegie Council Video:
Soft Power

unilateralism

An approach to foreign policy that relies on independent, self-help strategies in foreign policy.

selective engagement

A great power grand strategy using economic and military power to influence only important particular situations, countries, or global issues by striking a balance between a highly interventionist "global policeman" and an uninvolved isolationist.

imperial overstretch

The historic tendency for hegemons to sap their own strength through costly imperial pursuits and military spending that weaken their economies in relation to the economies of their rivals.

is stronger than everybody else's, with defense expenditures in 2013 larger than those of nearly all other countries combined.

Complementing America's military might is its awesome economic strength. With less than 5 percent of the global population, the United States accounts for a fifth of global income and two-fifths of the entire world's combined spending on research and development. Further, America continues to wield enormous *soft power* because it is the hub of global communications and popular culture, through which its values spread all over the world (Nye, 2008). In the words of former French Foreign Minister Hubart Vedrine, the United States is not simply a superpower; it is a "hyperpower."

This rare confluence of military, economic, and cultural power gives the United States what might appear to be an extraordinary ability to shape the global future to its will. This is why America's unique superpower position atop the global pyramid of power seemingly allows it to act independently without worries about resistance from weaker powers. Rather than working in concert with others, a strong and dominant hegemon can address international problems without reliance on global organizations and can "go it alone," even in the face of strident foreign criticism.

Such *unilateralism* derives from the desire for control over the flexible conduct of a great power's foreign relations, independent of control by or pressure from other great powers. Unilateralism can involve isolationism, an attempt to exert hegemonic leadership, a strategy of *selective engagement* that concentrates external involvements on vital national interests, or an effort to play the role of a "balancer" that skillfully backs one side or another in a great power dispute (but only when necessary to maintain a military equilibrium between the other great power disputants).

Unilateralism has its costs, however. Acting alone may appear expedient, but it erodes international support on issues such as combating terrorism, on which the United States is in strong need of cooperation from others. At the extreme, unilateralism can lead the global leader to play the role of international bully, seeking to run the world. And overwhelming power, observes Henry Kissinger, "evokes nearly automatically a quest by other societies to achieve a greater voice … and to reduce the relative position of the strongest." Characterizing U.S. foreign policy at the start of the century, the emphasis of the *Bush Doctrine* on self-interested unilateralism led to a surge of anti-Americanism between 2003 and 2008:

Anti-Americanism has seemed to be the reaction, more than to controversial foreign policy decisions, to their unchecked elaboration and unilateral implementation. For world public opinion, the legitimacy of the foreign policy-making process counts more than the latter's outcomes (Fabbrini, 2010, p. 557).

The status of being a superpower, the single "pole" or center of power, without a real challenger, has fated the United States with heavy and grave responsibilities. Although the United States may hold an unrivaled position in the world today, in the long run, unipolarity is very unlikely to endure. Indeed, every previous leading great power has been vulnerable to *imperial overstretch*, the gap between internal resources and external commitments (Kennedy, 1987). Throughout history, hegemons repeatedly have defined their security interests more broadly than other states, only to slip from the pinnacle of power by reaching beyond their grasp.

From Unipolarity to Multipolarity: The Rise of the Rest?

Excessive costs to preserve America's empire by military means could prove to burst "the bubble of American supremacy" (Sanger, 2005; Soros, 2003). A recent report (Bilmes, 2013) concludes that the wars in Iraq will eventually cost the United States between four and six billion dollars. This figure includes the most obvious costs of conflict, such as military operations, base security, reconstruction, foreign aid, embassy costs, and other programs related to the battle against terrorism. What will end up costing the most, however, is the long-term medical care that veterans of the conflict will end up requiring.

Overall, defense spending by the United States has more than doubled since the terrorist attacks on September 11, 2001 and, when adjusted for inflation, remains at the highest level since World War II. Former U.S. Defense Secretary Robert Gates expressed concerns that the U.S. force structure is likely out of scale to existing threats. "Does the number of warships we have and are building really put America at risk when the U.S. battle fleet is larger than the next thirteen navies combined, eleven of which belong to allies and partners? Is it a dire threat that by 2020 the United States will have only twenty times more advanced stealth fighters than China?"

Trade-offs posed by allocating enormous national resources to military preparedness are reflected in former U.S. President Dwight Eisenhower's warning that "the problem in defense spending is to figure out how far you should go without destroying from within what you are trying to defend from without." Yet it is not only the financial cost of expansive military commitments itself that has some worried about America's ability to sustain its predominant position in the international system; The United States' predominance in the world has been further eroded by the financial crisis of 2008, which originated in the United States and spread throughout the global financial system.

Although the United States continues to rank at the top in terms of the size of its military, other indicators signal a relative decline. For example, in 2000 the United States made up 31 percent of the world economy, but that figure dropped to 23.5 percent in 2010 and is projected to decrease further to 16 percent in 2020 (Debusmann, 2012). Following years of mounting deficits, the United States is now the world's largest debtor nation and owes more than $5.7 trillion to other countries, a third of which is held by China and Japan (U.S. Treasury Department, 2013). Because of this indebtedness, economists Steven Cohen and J. Bradford DeLong (see Thomson, 2011, p. 14) argue that "America has followed an all-too-familiar pattern for once powerful but slowly declining nations by borrowing unwisely—and much too often—against the future." They conclude that the United States is slowly eroding the foundation of its superpower status.

Foreseeing a world characterized by the "rise of the rest," realist political journalist Fareed Zakaria attributes transformative significance to the economic growth experienced by countries throughout the globe during the post–Cold War period, and the subsequent economic challenges posed by what many perceive as the worst downturn since the Great Depression:

> The rise of the rest is at heart an economic phenomenon, but the transition we are witnessing is not just a matter of dollars and cents. It has political, military, and cultural consequences. As countries become stronger and richer, and as the United States struggles to earn back the world's faith, we're likely to see more challenges and greater assertiveness from rising nations (Zakaria, 2009, p. xxiii).

There is growing recognition that the distribution of power in the international system is shifting to what political scientist Samuel Huntington (2005) has described as *uni-multipolar*. According to this perspective, although the United States continues to be the only superpower,

Simulation:
Explaining U.S.
Intervention in Iraq

uni-multipolar

A global system where there is a single dominant power, but the settlement of key international issues always requires action by the dominant power in combination with that of other great powers.

A RESURGENT RUSSIA Following a period of post–Cold War decline, in recent years Russia has gone to great lengths to project its image "not only as the most important regional power in the Commonwealth of Independent States (CIS) region and a very important one in Europe and Asia, but also a global power enmeshed in a contest with the United States over global issues" (Nygren, 2012, p. 520). Shown here, Russian President Vladimir Putin enters the Kremlin on May 7, 2012, for his third inauguration as president.

other states are not easily dominated. The potential for great power rivalry is increased as other countries—particularly those in Europe and Asia—begin to resist and challenge U.S. hegemony (see "A Closer Look: Is China a Serious Challenge to United States' Hegemony?"). Although U.S. involvement remains critical in addressing key international issues, resolution of transnational problems also requires action by some combination of other major states. Such limitations of a unipolar system in addressing multifaceted security threats were revealed by the terrorist attacks of 9/11 and the subsequent global war on terror:

> The vulnerability of the United States to non-Westphalian threats demanded a rethinking of how security was conceptualized and rendered operational. Even if the United States was still by far the most important military power, a unilateral drive visible during the early period of the G.W. Bush administration was quickly replaced by coalitions of the willing and a growing reliance on the international community to contribute to sustained long-term peace in remote areas such as Afghanistan and Iraq (Simão, 2012, p. 487).

There are growing limits on American domination, and the "shift in economic and political power has important implications for the world order. A weaker United States is less willing and able to play a leading role in sorting out the world's economic and political crises" (Drezner, Rachman, and Kagan, 2012). If some combination of U.S. imperial overstretch alongside rising economic and political influence by America's chief challengers transforms the current distribution of global power, many scholars and policy makers predict that a multipolar global system with more than two dominant centers of power will emerge.

LOOKING AHEAD: WHAT DOES THE FUTURE LOOK LIKE FOR THE GREAT POWERS?

There is a deepening sense that shifts in the global distribution of power are under way. Of current debate is the extent to which the United States will continue to hold its position as the principal global leader. Leslie Gelb, a renowned foreign policy expert, rejects the idea that we are moving into a period where the United States will be no more significant than the other great powers. He shares the view that the United States will remain an indispensable leader for years to come:

> The shape of global power is decidedly pyramidal—with the United States alone at the top, a second tier of major countries (China, Japan, India, Russia, the United Kingdom, France, Germany, and Brazil), and several tiers descending below. Even the smallest countries now occupy a piece of the international pyramid and have, particularly, enough power to resist the strong. But among all nations, only the United States is a true global power with global reach (Gelb, 2009, p. xv).

A Closer Look

IS CHINA A SERIOUS CHALLENGE TO UNITED STATES' HEGEMONY?

There is widespread consensus that we currently live in a world "in which no single country or bloc of countries has the political and economic leverage—or the will—to drive a truly international agenda" (Bremmer and Roubini, 2011, p. 2). Yet perspectives vary as to what the prospects are for continued U.S. predominance in the international system. Arguably, the past seven decades of American assertiveness abroad made the world more peaceful and prosperous, and the United States "willed, and paid for, an imperial role in the modern world" (Ajami, 2010, p. 195). Even with a dispersion of global power and innovation, the United States continues to have the largest military and one of the most dynamic economies in the world, and its international leadership remains indispensable (Gelb, 2009; Von Drehle, 2011).

Today, however, many see growing economic constraints on American power and question whether the United States has the resources to continue to be the primary provider of international security and other global public goods (Bremmer and Roubini, 2011; Mandelbaum, 2010). At the same time, with China's meteoric rise on the international stage, many wonder about the future of China's role in the international system. "The United States is still the sole reigning superpower, but it is being challenged by the rising power of China, just as ancient Rome was challenged by Carthage, and Britain was challenged by Germany in the years before World War I" (Feldman, 2013). Is China a serious contender to replace the United States as the preeminent global power?

Some, such as Juan Cardenal and Heriberto Araújo (2013) suggest that the world will eventually fall under China's leadership. Pointing to China's increased economic ties to the Global South, they foresee a possible "future conquest of western markets and, eventually, a new world order controlled by Beijing" (as quoted in Anderlini, 2013). China's continued military growth, coupled with its expanding economy, also signal global aspirations. Others, however, believe that China will only remain a "partial power" because, even though China has a large international presence, it lacks the capacity to influence international events (Shambaugh, 2013).

What is certain, though, is that China as a global power is not likely to fade away any time soon. So what does this mean for U.S.–China relations? Will the two countries face off in a hostile geopolitical confrontation reminiscent of the Cold War? Or will they continue to engage each other while seeking to manage peacefully the strategic threat posed by the other?

Perhaps the United States and China will follow a path different from that of past global power struggles. Particularly if "it is not governing, but rather economic institutions that account for the peace among nations" (Mousseau 2013, p. 1194), it may be that relations between the two will be characterized by an "economic peace." As Harvard law professor Noah Feldman notes, "The world's major power and its leading challenger are economically interdependent to an unprecedented degree. China needs the United States to continue buying its products. The United States needs China to continue lending it money. Their economic fates are, for the foreseeable future, tied together."

(Continued)

IS CHINA A SERIOUS CHALLENGE TO UNITED STATES' HEGEMONY? (Continued)

WATCH THE VIDEO:

CourseMate

Carnegie Council Video:
The U.S.: Shedding Hegemony with Grace

YOU DECIDE:

1. How important is it that the United States continues to play a central role in international politics?

2. If not, should the United States more narrowly define its interests and what should those interests include?

3. Do you think that China poses a serious challenge to the United States' hegemony? If so, does this pose a problem for the United States?

4. Is movement to a multipolar system a reflection of declining American power, or rather a result of the rise of the rest? Alternatively, do you think that we are seeing a shift towards a bipolar system dominated by the United States and China?

Others see the world from a somewhat different perspective, perceiving a great transformation marked by the ascendance of other great powers in what has been coined a "post-American" world, where many other state and nonstate actors help to define and direct how we respond to global challenges. "At the politico-military level, we remain in a single-superpower world. But in every other dimension—industrial, financial, educational, social, cultural—the distribution of power is shifting, moving away from American dominance" (Zakaria, 2009, p. 4). As Map 4.3 shows, when we take into account multiple dimensions of what it means to be prosperous, the United States remains in the top tier with many of its Western allies—though it is no longer the single most prosperous country in the world.

Predicting what cleavages and partnerships will develop among the great powers in the future will be difficult because it will be hard to foresee what will become the next major axis of conflict. After years of decline following the Cold War, Russia seeks to restore what it sees as its rightful place as a global leader among the great powers. Although it is not particularly interested in directly challenging the West (Mankoff, 2009), relations with the United States have oscillated from warm to cool. Collaboration has been evident in the global war on terror, further reductions in nuclear weapons, and Russia entry into the World Trade Organization. However, tensions also erupted over the Arab Spring, the overthrow of Libya's dictator Muammar al-Qaddafi, and what the United States saw as the nondemocratic election that returned Vladimir Putin to the presidency.

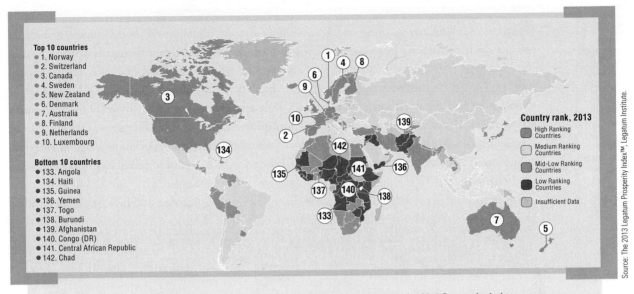

Source: The 2013 Legatum Prosperity Index™, Legatum Institute.

MAP 4.3   GLOBAL PROSPERITY Based on 89 measures of wealth and well-being, the 2013 Prosperity Index assesses performance in various areas: the economy, entrepreneurship and opportunity, education, health, governance, safety and security, social capital, and personal freedom. Despite the worst financial crisis in modern times and citizen uprisings in protest of autocratic regimes around the world, global prosperity has increased across all regions of the world over the last 5 years. The United States ranks 11th in overall prosperity out of 142 countries; Norway, Switzerland, and Canada enjoy the highest levels of prosperity.

Nonetheless, the United States and Russia continue to engage in dialogue about key global issues. For instance, despite the clash caused by Russia's opposition to international intervention to remove undesirable governments from power and calls for the United States to act more forcefully in Syria, Russia's foreign minister Sergey Lavrov and U.S. Secretary of State John Kerry met in May 2013 and discussed the prospect for a negotiated settlement to the civil war in Syria (Meyers and Herszenhorn, 2013). "The world has changed," says Mikhail Margelov, chairman of the Foreign Affairs Committee of the upper chamber of the Russian Parliament. "It's not a bipolar world anymore. We are facing many threats, and many of the same threats. We are made to cooperate."

China's status as an economic powerhouse has led some to predict that global power is shifting from the United States to China. As Kissinger (2012a, p. 546) reminds us, "China does not see itself as a rising but as a returning power… It does not view the prospect of a strong China exercising influence in economic, cultural, political, and military affairs as an unnatural challenge to world order—but rather as a return to a normal state of affairs." By some estimates, the Chinese economy will reach $123 trillion by 2040, which will be nearly triple the size of the economic output of the entire world in 2000. Per capita income in China will reach $85,000, twice the predicted income for people living in the European Union and even more than that for those living in India and Japan. Although it will not surpass the United States in per capita wealth, China's 40 percent share of global gross domestic product (GDP) will eclipse that of the United States (14 percent) and the European Union (5 percent), leading to speculation that we are entering the "Asian Century" (Fogel, 2010).

TABLE 4.3	Transitions in Wealth and Economic Power?					
2012 GDP Rank, at PPP	**Country**	**GDP at PPP**	**Projected 2050 GDP Rank, at PPP**	**Country**	**Projected GDP at PPP**
1	United States	$14,991	1	China	$59,475
2	China	$11,290	2	India	$43,180
3	India	$4,532	3	United States	$37,876
4	Japan	$4,303	4	Brazil	$9,762
5	Germany	$3,227	5	Japan	$7,664
6	Russia	$3,134	6	Russia	$7,559
7	France	$2,306	7	Mexico	$6,682
8	Brazil	$2,289	8	Indonesia	$6,205
9	United Kingdom	$2,234	9	Germany	$5,707
10	Italy	$1,984	10	United Kingdom	$5,628

Dollar amounts in billions.

Source: "The World in 2050," 2011, London: PwC; World Bank, 2013.

"With Western, and especially American, economic and political pre-eminence challenged in ways it has not been before, the downturn could end up redistributing power and influence" (Bradsher, 2009, p. 1). Using purchasing power parities (PPPs) to remove differences in countries' price levels, Table 4.3 indicates the probable size of the largest economies in 2050. The projections show that the rank order of the largest economic powerhouses by 2050 will be substantially different from today's.

However, although Asia is indeed increasing its economic footprint in the world, "it still lags far behind the United States in military might, political and diplomatic influence, and even most measures of economic stability." Notes Joshua Kurlantzick (2010), a senior fellow at the Council of Foreign Relations, "Asia's growth, the source of its current strength, also has significant limits—rising inequality, disastrous demographics, and growing unrest that could scupper development."

Pervasive hostilities could emerge between any pair of great powers, for example, between the globe's two major contenders for supremacy, the United States and China, if their competition escalates and the United States practices containment to try to prevent China's rise (see "A Closer Look: Is China a Serious Challenge to United States' Hegemony?"). However, this kind of armed rivalry need not develop; cooperation could increase instead (Kissinger, 2012b). Quite different political types of great power relations could emerge in the economic and military spheres. There is the probability of economic rivalry growing as global trade expands the integration of states' economies in an ever-tightening web of interdependence. However, the likelihood of security cooperation for many of these same relationships is also high. Under these circumstances, the danger of *polarization* could be managed if the great powers develop international rules and institutions to manage their fluid, mixed-motive relationships. Such potential for collaboration is reflected in former Chinese Minister of Defense Liang Guanglie's assertion that:

A NEW GLOBAL HEGEMON? According to Chris Patten, a former British governor of Hong Kong, China was the world's leading economic power for 18 of the past 20 centuries. "To the West, the notion of a world in which the center of global economic gravity lies in Asia may seem unimaginable. But, economist Robert Fogel (2010, p. 75) reminds us, "it wouldn't be the first time." Shown here, U.S. Secretary of State John Kerry meets with Chinese Foreign Minister Wang Yi on April 13, 2013. Kerry outlined a vision for the "Pacific Dream" in which "Asian nations could grow more closely together with each other and the U.S. than ever before on economic and security issues during the decades to come" (Taylor, 2013).

China's participation in world security cooperation is by no means enlargement of a sphere of influence or territorial expansion….The Chinese military's outreach for international security cooperation is not intended to impair the international system, but to become a player and builder of the system, providing additional public goods to the international community so that the benefit of security can be truly shared by all.

Today the paradox prevails that many pairs of great powers that are the most active trade partners are also the greatest military rivals, but the key question is whether economic cooperation will help to reduce the potential for military competition in the future. The opportunities and challenges that we face in the world today call for a multilateral approach, with all of the great powers working cooperatively to achieve global solutions.

One possibility along these lines is the development of a *concert*, or a cooperative agreement, among the great powers to manage the global system jointly and to prevent international disputes from escalating to war. The Concert of Europe, at its apex between 1815 and 1822, is the epitome of previous great power efforts to pursue this path to peace. The effort to build a great power coalition to wage a war against global terrorism following 9/11 is a more recent

concert

A cooperative agreement among great powers to jointly manage the global system.

multilateralism

Cooperative approaches to managing shared problems through collective and coordinated action.

Carnegie Council Video: Multilateralism

example of *multilateralism* to construct a concert through collective action. Some policy makers also recommend that today's great powers unite with the lesser powers in constructing a true system of *collective security*. The formation of the League of Nations in 1919 is the best example of this multilateral approach to peace under conditions of *multipolarity*, and despite Russia's invasion of neighboring Georgia in 2008, some believe Russia's pledge to cooperate with NATO is representative of a collective security quest to maintain peace through an alliance of powerful countries.

> *Challenge and opportunity always come together—under certain conditions one could be transformed into the other.*
>
> **—Hu Jintao, former Chinese president**

Of course, we have no way of knowing what the future holds. Patterns and practices can change, and it is possible for policy makers to learn from previous mistakes and avoid repeating them. What is crucial is how the great powers react to the eventual emergence of a new global system where power and responsibility are more widely distributed. It is clear that the choices the great powers make about war and peace will determine the fate of the world. In Chapter 5, we turn your attention from the rich, powerful, and commercially active great powers at the center of the world system to the poorer, weaker, and economically dependent states in the Global South and the emerging powers in the Global East.

STUDY. APPLY. ANALYZE.

Key Terms

appeasement	fascism	long-cycle theory	soft power
bipolarity	hegemon	multilateralism	sphere of influence
Cold War	ideology	multipolarity	structuralism
colonialism	imperial	nationalism	Truman Doctrine
concert	overstretch	peaceful coexistence	unilateralism
containment	irredentism	political economy	uni-multipolar
détente	isolationism	rapprochement	unipolarity
domino theory	linkage strategy	selective engagement	Yalta Conference

Suggested Readings

Cohen, Steven, and J. Bradford DeLong. (2010) *The End of Influence: What Happens When Other Countries Have the Money.* New York: Basic Books.

Gelb, Leslie H. (2009) *Power Rules: How Common Sense Can Rescue American Foreign Policy.* New York: HarperCollins.

Kissinger, Henry. (2012b) "The Future of U.S.-Chinese Relations: Conflict Is a Choice, Not a Necessity," *Foreign Affairs* 91(2):44–55.

Mandelbaum, Michael. (2010) *The Frugal Superpower: America's Global Leadership in a Cash-Strapped Era.* Philadelphia, PA: Public Affairs.

Mankoff, Jeffrey. (2009) *Russian Foreign Policy: The Return of Great Power Politics.* New York: Rowman and Littlefield.

Morris, Ian. (2010) *Why the West Rules—for Now: The Patterns of History, and What They Reveal about the Future.* New York: Farrar, Straus, and Giroux.

Shambaugh, David. (2013) *China Goes Global: The Partial Power.* Oxford, UK: Oxford University Press.

Speedie, David C. (April 15, 2010) "Rise of the Rest," http://www.carnegiecouncil.org/resources/articles_papers_reports/0049.html.

Zakaria, Fareed. (2009) *The Post—American World.* New York: W.W. Norton.

Suggested Videos

Gelb, Leslie. "Power Rules: How Common Sense Can Rescue American Foreign Policy."

Matlock, Jack F. "Superpower Illusions: How Myths and False Ideologies Led

America Astray—and How to Return to Reality."

Vocke, William. "The U.S.: Shedding Hegemony with Grace."

Zelizer, Julian E. "Arsenal of Democracy: The Politics of National Security—from World War II to the War on Terrorism."

CourseMate

Log in to CourseMate to access the following study tools for this chapter:

- Interactive Quiz
- eBook
- Flashcards & Key Term Crossword Puzzle
- Chapter Audio Summary
- Carnegie Council Videos

- Video Activities
- Simulation
- Animated Learning Module
- Case Study
- International Relations NewsWatch

"A global human society based on poverty for many and prosperity for a few, characterized by islands of wealth surrounded by a sea of poverty, is unsustainable."

—*Thabo Mbeki, former president of South Africa*

CHAPTER 5
The Global South in a World of Powers

Jake Lyell/Alamy

MAKING NEW FRIENDS The fortunes of small powers are increasingly integrated with those of major powers. According to the IMF, Chinese investment has led to economic growth in sub-Saharan Africa—with estimates of 5.5 percent growth in 2013—and China is currently Africa's largest business partner with over $166 billion in trade (IMF, 2013; *The Economist*, 2013). "Through significant investment in a continent known for its political and social risks, China has helped many African countries develop their nascent oil sectors while benefiting from that oil through advantageous trade deals" (Alessi and Hanson, 2012). Shown here, patients leave a Chinese-operated hospital in Dar es Salaam in Tanzania.

QUESTIONS TO CONSIDER

- *Why did great powers colonize the Global South?*
- *What is the legacy of colonialism?*
- *How different are the Global North and Global South?*
- *What are the sources of underdevelopment in the Global South?*
- *What are the prospects for closing the gap between the Global South and Global North?*
- *What does the future hold for the Global South?*

Earth is divided into two hemispheres, north and south, at the equator. This artificial line of demarcation is, of course, meaningless except for use by cartographers to chart distance and location on maps. This divide also represents a popular way of describing the inequalities that separate rich and poor states. By and large, these two groups are located on either side of the equator (see Map 5.1).

Life for most people in the Northern Hemisphere is very different from that in the Southern Hemisphere. The disparities are profound and in many places appear to be growing. The division in power and wealth characterizing the *Global North* and *Global South* pose both moral and security problems. As the philosopher Plato in fifth-century BCE Greece counseled, "There should exist neither extreme poverty nor excessive wealth, for both are productive of great evil." Although poverty and inequality have existed throughout recorded history, today the levels have reached extremes. The poor countries find themselves marginalized, in a subordinate position in the global hierarchy. What are the causes and consequences of the pronounced inequalities between the great powers and the disadvantaged countries trapped in poverty? That is the central question that you will consider in this chapter.

Global North

A term used to refer to the world's wealthy, industrialized countries located primarily in the Northern Hemisphere.

Global South

A term now often used instead of "Third World" to designate the less developed countries located primarily in the Southern Hemisphere.

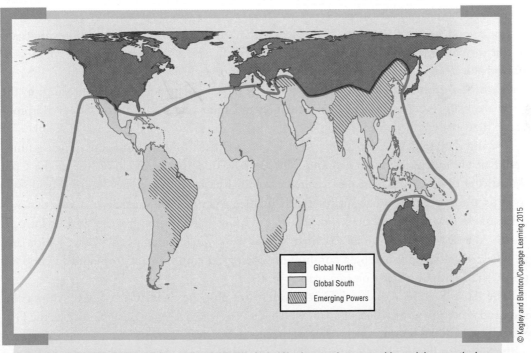

© Kegley and Blanton/Cengage Learning 2015

MAP 5.1 THE GLOBAL NORTH AND GLOBAL SOUTH Global North countries are wealthy and democratic. In contrast, according to the World Bank, the Global South countries are home to 83.7 percent of the world's population, but the impoverished people living there possess only 46.4 percent of the world's gross domestic product (WDI, 2013). Yet there is considerable variation within the Global South, with some countries enjoying higher levels of prosperity and global influence than others. These "emerging powers" have arisen from the former Global South and now challenge the Global North by seeking a greater role in global governance and institutions.

COLONIAL ORIGINS AND CONSEQUENCES

Carnegie Council Video:
Second World

Many analysts trace the roots of today's inequalities among states at the *global level of analysis* because they believe the global system has properties built into it that account for most poor countries' inability to close the gap with the wealthy countries. Taking their hypothesis that prevailing worldwide conditions are part of a much longer historical pattern, they note that the rules governing international politics today were constructed in the 1648 Peace of Westphalia following Europe's Thirty Years' War. These rules were crafted by the most powerful actors on the world stage—the great powers at the time—to serve their parochial self-interests by preserving their predominant positions in the international system and preventing less-powerful states from joining them (see Kegley and Raymond, 2002a).

The origins and persistence of the inequalities of states stem in part from the fact that today's modern global system was initially, and remains, a socially constructed reality by, of, and for the most powerful states. The powerful did not design a global system for equals; the great powers followed the prescription of realist thought to always seek self-advantage. Accordingly, they did not build the global system with an eye to preventing the victimization of the weak and the disadvantaged.

So, a good starting place is to begin your inquiry by taking into consideration the legacy of this system today. Many analysts see the history of *colonialism*, the European conquest of *indigenous peoples* and the seizure of their territory for exclusively European gain, as the root source of the problem. They note that almost all of the independent sovereign states in the Southern Hemisphere were at one time colonies and argue that today's inequalities are a product of that past colonization.

During the Cold War, the term *Third World* was used to distinguish the growing number of newly independent but economically less developed states on either side of the Cold War divide that, for the most part, shared a colonial past. However, the "Third World" was soon used to refer to those countries that had failed to grow economically in a way that was comparable to countries of the *First World*, the industrialized great powers such as Europe, North America, and Japan. The so-called *Second World*, consisting of the Soviet Union and its allies, was distinguished by a communist ideological commitment to planned economic policies rather than reliance on free-market forces.

The terms Second World and Third World carry obsolete Cold War baggage. More common today are the terms Global North, which refers to what was previously known as the First World, and Global South, which refers to the less developed countries that are mostly located in the Southern Hemisphere. Additionally, these contemporary terms largely correspond to the distinction between *great powers* and *small powers* (Kassimeris, 2009). Among the countries of the Global South, a distinction is also made that recognizes the *emerging powers* as those that seek a more assertive role in international affairs, possess enough resources to potentially realize their goals, and are experiencing increasing influence in world politics—particularly with regard to the global economy.

The placement of particular states within these categories is not easy. Although journalists, policy makers, and scholars frequently generalize about the Global South, considerable diversity exists within this grouping of states. For example, it includes low-income countries such as Ghana and Haiti, where a majority of the population tries to survive through subsistence agriculture; middle-income countries such as Brazil and Malaysia, which produce manufactured goods; and some countries such as Kuwait and Qatar, whose petroleum exports have generated incomes rivaling those of Global North.

Global South countries are different in other ways as well. Their ranks include both Indonesia—an archipelago nation of more than 17,500 islands scattered across an oceanic expanse larger than the United States—and Timor-Leste, an island state roughly the same size as Connecticut. This category also includes Nigeria, with 148 million inhabitants, and Guinea-Bassau, with just one and a half million people. In addition to these geographic and demographic differences, Global South countries also vary politically and culturally, ranging from democratic Costa Rica to autocratic Myanmar.

The emergence of the Global South as an identifiable group of states is a distinctly contemporary phenomenon. Although most Latin American countries were independent before World War II, not until afterward did other countries of the Global South gain that status. In 1947, Great Britain granted independence to India and Pakistan, after which *decolonization*—the freeing of colonial peoples from their dependent status—gathered speed. Since then, a diverse array of new sovereign states has joined the global community, nearly all carved from the British, Spanish, Portuguese, Dutch, and French empires built under colonialism four hundred years ago.

Today, few colonies exist and the decolonization process is almost complete. However, the effects persist. Most of the ethnic national conflicts that are now so prevalent have colonial roots, as the imperial powers drew borders within and between their domains with little regard for the national identities of the indigenous peoples. Similarly, the disparity in wealth between the rich Global North and the poor Global South is attributed in part to unequal and exploitative relations during the colonial period, as is a legacy of mistrust and insecurity that persists not only across this global divide but also within the former colonial countries themselves (see Map 5.2).

The Congo is but one example of how the colonial experience eroded the strength of a former medieval great power (Gebrekidan, 2010). Four centuries of the slave trade by the Portuguese claimed more than 13 million lives. This was followed in 1885 by decades of further exploitation under the rule of King Leopold II of Belgium, who was, at least indirectly, responsible for 10 million deaths as he turned the country into a virtual labor camp and amassed a personal fortune through the harvest of wild rubber (Haskin, 2005). Although independence was achieved in 1960, peace and prosperity did not follow. Instead, colonial rule was replaced with violent internal divisions. Rising to power in 1965, Mobutu Sese Seko established an authoritarian state and controlled the people through fear and repression until his overthrow in 1997. Over the course of his reign, Mobutu perpetuated the colonial legacy of exploitation. According to Transparency International, he embezzled over $5 billion from his country, ranking him as the most corrupt African leader over the past two decades.

The First Wave of European Imperialism

The first wave of European empire building began in the late fifteenth century, as the Dutch, English, French, Portuguese, and Spanish used their naval power to conquer territories for commercial gain. Scientific innovations made the European explorers' adventures possible, and merchants followed in their wake, "quickly seizing upon opportunities to increase their business and profits. In turn, Europe's governments perceived the possibilities for increasing their own power and wealth. Commercial companies were chartered and financed, with military and naval expeditions frequently sent out after them to ensure political control of overseas territories" (Cohen, 1973, p. 20).

The economic strategy underlying the relationship between colonies and colonizers during this era of "classical imperialism" is known as *mercantilism*—an economic philosophy advocating government regulation of economic life to increase state power.

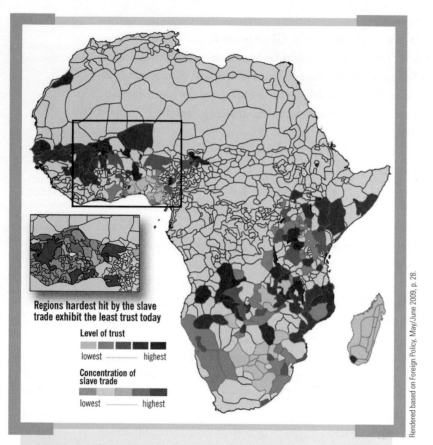

Rendered based on Foreign Policy, May/June 2009, p. 28.

Regions hardest hit by the slave trade exhibit the least trust today

Level of trust

lowest ——— highest

Concentration of slave trade

lowest ——— highest

MAP 5.2 A LEGACY OF MISTRUST Spurred by the quest for labor in the New World (Africans proved much more resistant than the indigenous peoples to the diseases brought by Europeans), the expanding colonial powers eagerly participated in transatlantic slave trade from the mid-1500s through the late 1700s. Harvard economist Nathan Nunn attributes the stalled economic development of much of Africa to the trauma of this colonial legacy, arguing that major shocks can "change people's behavior in ways that seem pretty permanent." Indeed, in "regions of Africa where the slave trade was most concentrated, people today extend less trust to other individuals: not only to foreigners, but also to relatives and neighbors" (Keating, 2009, p. 28).

mercantilism

A government trade strategy for accumulating state wealth and power by encouraging exports and discouraging imports.

Carnegie Council Video: Mercantilism

European rulers believed that power flowed from the possession of national wealth measured in gold and silver, and that cultivating mining and industry to attain a favorable balance of trade (exporting more than they imported) was the best way to become rich.

> Colonies were desirable in this respect because they afforded an opportunity to shut out commercial competition; they guaranteed exclusive access to untapped markets and sources of cheap materials (as well as, in some instances, direct sources of the precious metals themselves). Each state was determined to monopolize as many of these overseas mercantile opportunities as possible (Cohen, 1973, p. 21).

States adhering to realist justifications of the competitive drive for global power saw the imperial conquest of foreign territory by war as a natural by-product of active government management of the economy.

By the end of the eighteenth century, the European powers had spread themselves, albeit thinly, throughout virtually the entire world. But the colonial empires they had built began to crumble. Britain's 13 North American colonies declared their independence in 1776, and most of Spain's possessions in South America won their freedom in the early nineteenth century. Nearly 100 colonial relationships worldwide ended in the half-century ending in 1825 (Bergesen and Schoenberg, 1980).

As Europe's colonial empires dissolved, belief in the mercantilist philosophy also waned. As liberal political economist Adam Smith argued in his 1776 treatise, *The Wealth of Nations*, national wealth grew not through the accumulation of precious metals but rather from the capital and goods they could buy. Smith's ideas about the benefits of the "invisible hand" of the unregulated marketplace laid much of the intellectual foundation for *classical liberal economic theory*. Following Smith and other liberal free-trade theorists, faith in the precepts of *laissez-faire economics* (minimal government interference in the market) gained widespread acceptance (see also Chapter 12). Henceforth, European powers continued to seek colonies, but the rationale for their imperial policies began to change.

> *I hate imperialism. I detest colonialism. And I fear the consequences of their last bitter struggle for life. We are determined, that our nation, and the world as a whole, shall not be the play thing of one small corner of the world.*
>
> **—Sukarno, former president of Indonesia**

The Second Wave of European Imperialism

A second wave of imperialism washed over the world, as Europe—joined later by the United States and Japan— aggressively colonized new territories from the 1870s until the outbreak of World War I. Europeans controlled one-third of the globe in 1800, two-thirds by 1878, and four-fifths by 1914 (Fieldhouse, 1973). As illustrated in Map 5.3, in the last 20 years of the nineteenth century, Africa fell under the control of seven European powers (Belgium, Britain, France, Germany, Italy, Portugal, and Spain), and in all of the Far East and the Pacific, only China, Japan, and Siam (Thailand) were not completely conquered. However, the foreign great powers carved China into separate zones of commerce, which they each individually controlled and exploited for profit. Japan itself also invaded and occupied Korea and Formosa (now Taiwan).

Elsewhere, the United States expanded across its continent, acquired Puerto Rico and the Philippines in the 1898 Spanish-American War, extended its colonial reach west to Hawaii, leased the Panama Canal Zone "in perpetuity" from the new state of Panama (an American creation), and exercised considerable control over several Caribbean islands, notably Cuba. The preeminent imperial power, Great Britain, created an empire that covered one-fifth of the Earth's land area and comprised around one-fourth of its population (Cohen, 1973). As British imperialists proudly proclaimed: The sun never set on the British Empire.

So why did most of the great powers—and those that aspired to great power status—engage in this expensive and often vicious competition to control other peoples and territories? What explains this new imperialism?

classical liberal economic theory

A body of thought based on Adam Smith's ideas about the forces of supply and demand in the marketplace, emphasizing the social and economic benefits when individuals pursue their own self-interest.

Carnegie Council Video: Classic Liberal Economic Theory

laissez-faire economics

The philosophical principle of free markets and free trade to give people free choices with little government regulation.

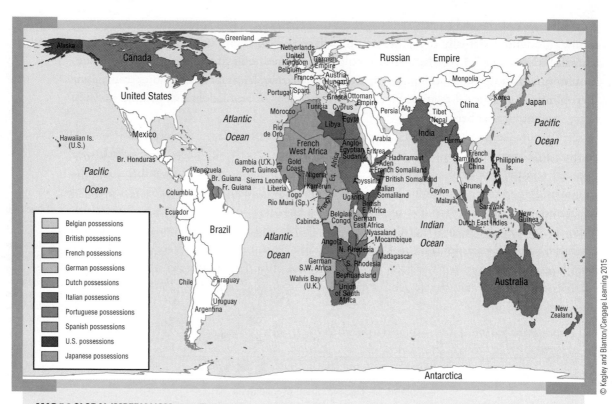

MAP 5.3 GLOBAL IMPERIALISM 1914 The ten major imperial powers competed for colonies throughout the globe in the present-day Global South, and on the eve of World War I, their combined territories covered most of the world.

communism

The Marxist ideology maintaining that if society is organized so that every person produces according to his or her ability and consumes according to his or her needs, a community without class distinctions will emerge, sovereign states will no longer be needed, and imperial wars of colonial conquest will vanish from history.

One answer lies in the nature of the global economy. With the Industrial Revolution, capitalism grew—emphasizing the free market, private ownership of the means of production, and the accumulation of wealth. Radical theorists following Karl Marx and Vladimir Lenin, who called themselves adherents of *communism*, saw imperialism's aggressive competition as caused by a capitalist need for profitable overseas outlets for surplus production. Sharing a critical perspective of the capitalist world economy, *world-system theory* saw a world division of labor where the (industrial) "core" areas exploit the (nonindustrial) "periphery," and colonization provided a means for imperial control over foreign lands. Liberal economists, by contrast, regarded the new imperialism not as a product of capitalism but, rather, as a response to certain maladjustments that could be corrected. Despite these differences, the three perspectives shared the belief that economics explained the new imperialism: Imperialism was rooted in the material needs of advanced capitalist societies for cheap raw materials and additional markets to consume growing production (see Chapter 2).

Another explanation emphasizes purely political factors as the source of the second wave of imperialism. As liberal British economist J. A. Hobson argued in his seminal 1902 book *Imperialism*, jockeying for power and prestige between competitive empires had always characterized the great powers' behavior in the European balance-of-power system. Hobson believed that imperialism through overseas expansion was simply a global extension of this inter-European competition for dominance inspired by the *realpolitik* premise that all states have an unquenchable thirst for more and more power.

By the 1800s, Britain emerged from Europe's perpetual conflict as the world's leading power. By 1870, however, British hegemony began to decline. Germany emerged as a powerful industrial state, as did the United States. Understandably, Britain tried to protect its privileged global position in the face of growing competition from the newly emerging core states. Its efforts to maintain the status quo help to explain the second wave of imperial expansion, especially in Africa, where partition served the imperial powers' purposes to the detriment of the local populations.

Self-Determination and Decolonization in the Twentieth Century

The climate of opinion turned decidedly against imperialism when the 1919 Versailles peace settlement that ended World War I embraced *liberalism*—the body of theoretical thought that stresses the importance of ideas, ideals, and institutions to generate progress, prosperity, and peace. Part of that reform program was the principle of national *self-determination* that U.S. President Woodrow Wilson championed. Self-determination advocated giving indigenous nationalities the moral right to decide which authority would rule them.

Wilson and other *liberal theorists* (see Chapter 2) reasoned that freedom would lead to the creation of states and governments that were content with their territorial boundaries and, therefore, less inclined to make war. In practice, however, the attempt to redraw states' borders to separate nationality groups was applied almost exclusively to war-torn Europe, where six new states were created from the territory of the former Austrian-Hungarian Empire (Austria, Czechoslovakia, Hungary, Poland, Romania, and the ethnically divided Yugoslavia). Other territorial adjustments were also made in Europe, but the proposition that self-determination should be extended to Europe's overseas empires did not receive serious support.

Still, the colonial territories of the powers defeated in World War I were not simply parceled out among the victorious allies, as had typically happened in the past. Instead, the territories controlled by Germany and the Ottoman Empire were transferred, under League of Nations auspices, to countries that would govern them as "mandates" until their eventual self-rule. Many of these territorial decisions gave rise to subsequent conflicts across the globe. For example, the League of Nations called for the eventual creation of a Jewish national homeland in Palestine and arranged for the transfer of control over Southwest Africa (called Namibia) to what would become the white minority regime of South Africa.

The principle implicit in the League of Nations mandate system gave birth to the idea that "colonies were a trust rather than simply a property to be exploited and treated as if its peoples had no rights of their own" (Easton, 1964, p. 124). This set an important precedent so that after World War II the defeated powers' territories placed under the United Nations (UN) trusteeship system were not absorbed by others but were promised eventual self-rule. Thus, support for self-determination gained momentum.

The decolonization process accelerated in 1947, when the British consented to the independence of India and Pakistan. War eventually erupted between these newly independent states as

realpolitik

The theoretical outlook prescribing that countries should increase their power and wealth in order to compete with and dominate other countries.

self-determination

The liberal doctrine that people should be able to determine the government that will rule them.

Carnegie Council Video: Self Determination

FREEDOM AND SELF-DETERMINATION When World War I broke out, only 62 independent countries existed. With secession from Sudan in July 2011, the emergence of South Sudan as the world's newest nation brought the count to 195, according to the U.S. Department of State. Pictured here, Sudan's President Omar al-Bashir (left) and South Sudan's President Salva Kiir (right) listen to South Sudan's national anthem. al-Bashir visited Juba, South Sudan, on Friday, April 12, 2013 for the first time since South Sudan's independence.

each sought to gain control over disputed territory in Kashmir in 1965, in 1971, and again as the nuclear-armed states clashed in 2002. Violence also broke out in Vietnam and Algeria in the 1950s and early 1960s when the French sought to regain control over their pre–World War II colonial territories. Similarly, bloodshed followed closely on the heels of independence in the Congo when the Belgians granted their African colony independence in 1960, and it dogged the unsuccessful efforts of Portugal to battle the winds of decolonization that swept over Africa as the 1960s wore on.

Despite these political convulsions, decolonization was for the most part not only extraordinarily rapid but also remarkably peaceful. This may be explained by the fact that World War II sapped the economic and military vitality of many of the colonial powers. World-system analysts contend that a growing appreciation of the costs of empire also eroded support for colonial empires (Strang, 1991). Whatever the underlying cause, colonialism became less acceptable. In a world increasingly dominated by rivalry between East and West, Cold War competition for political allies gave both superpower rivals incentive to lobby for the liberation of overseas empires. Decolonization "triumphed," as Inis Claude (1967, p. 55) explains, in part "because the West [gave] priority to the containment of communism over the perpetuation of colonialism."

As the old order crumbled—and as the leaders in the newly emancipated territories discovered that freedom did not translate automatically into autonomy, economic independence, or domestic prosperity—the conflict between the rich Global North and the emerging states of the Global South began.

NORTH AND SOUTH TODAY: WORLDS APART

The Global South is sometimes described today as a "zone of turmoil" or an "axis of upheaval," in large measure because, in contrast with the peaceful and democratic Global North, most of the people in the Global South face chronic poverty amidst war, tyranny, and anarchy. In the poorest countries of the Global South where dictatorships and dismal financial prospects persist, the odds increase that these countries will experience civil wars and armed conflicts with each other (Collier, 2005; Ferguson, 2009). Indeed, more than 90 percent of the inter- and intrastate conflicts and 90 percent of the casualties in the past 60 years occurred within the Global South (see Chapter 7).

Democracy has spread rapidly and widely since the 1980s, becoming the preferred mode of governance throughout much of the Global South as a means of promoting both economic development and peace. Because the Global North's history suggests that "economic and technological development bring a coherent set of social, cultural, and political changes … and they also bring growing mass demands for democratic institutions and for more responsive behavior on the part of elites" (Inglehart and Welzel, 2009, p. 39), the continuing expansion of Global South market economies under capitalism appears likely to hasten democratization.

Even so, the continued spread of the liberal democratic community is not guaranteed, with some seeing democracy as failing even while elections become more commonplace. In many places, democratization is only "skin deep." As Oxford economist Paul Collier (2009, p. 149) points out:

> In the average election held among the bottom billion poorest of the world's population, despite the fact that voters usually have many grounds for complaint, the incumbent "wins" a healthy 74 percent of the vote. In elections with particularly weak restraints, it is an even healthier 88 percent. Somehow or other, incumbents in these societies are very good at winning elections.

Furthermore, many Global South countries lack well-developed domestic market economies based on entrepreneurship and private enterprise. Indeed, the global financial crisis has exacerbated the disappointment of some in the Global South with "the failure of free-market policies to bring significant economic growth and reduce the region's yawning inequality" (Schmidt and Malkin, 2009, p. 5), and has generated a renewed interest in the radical ideas of Karl Marx, who would likely have seen the crisis as the natural by-product of "the 'contradictions' inherent in a world comprised of competitive markets, commodity production and financial speculation" (Panitch, 2009, p. 140).

The fact that 83.7 percent of the world's population is poor is both a reflection and cause of these unequally distributed resources. To measure the disparities, the World Bank differentiates the "low-income" and "low- and middle-income" economies in *developing countries*, whose *gross national income (GNI)* is an average of $256 billion, from the "high-income" *developed countries*, which average $624 billion for each (WDI, 2013).

Numbers paint pictures and construct images, and the data on the division between the Global North and Global South point to brutal disparities and inequalities. When we compare the differences on some key indicators differentiating low- and middle-income countries from high-income countries, we discover huge gaps. As Table 5.1 shows, where people live on Earth influences how they live. The situation is much more favorable—and the quality of life is relatively advantageous—in the developed countries of the Global North than it is in the Southern Hemisphere, where nearly all the Global South countries are located.

This picture darkens even more when the focus shifts to the plight of the poorest in the low-income developing countries. More than 816.8 million people (11.7 percent of

developing countries

A category used by the World Bank to identify low-income Global South countries with an annual GNI per capita at or below $1,025 and middle-income countries with an annual GNI per capita of more than $1,026 but less than $$12,476 (WDI, 2013).

gross national income (GNI)

A measure of the production of goods and services within a given time period, which is used to delimit the geographic scope of production. GNI measures production by a state's citizens or companies, regardless of where the production occurs.

developed countries

A category used by the World Bank to identify Global North countries with an annual GNI per capita of $12,476 or more (WDI, 2013).

TABLE 5.1	Two Worlds of Development: An International Class Divide	
Characteristic	Developing Global South	Developed Global North
Number of countries/economies	146	80
Population (millions)	5,839.2	1,135
Average annual population growth rate, 2010–2020	13%	0.7%
Population density (people for each sq km)	61	33
Women in parliaments (% of total seats)	20%	24%
Land area (thousands of km²)	95,718.5	33,991.4
Gross national income per capita (PPP)	$6,451	$38,471
Average annual % growth of GDP, 2010–2011	6.3%	1.5%
Net foreign direct investment inflows (% of GDP)	2.8%	2.1%
Exports—Goods and Services ($ billions)	$7,009.4	$15,509.8
Imports—Goods and Services ($ billions)	$7,031.0	$15,306.3
Workers' remittances received (in millions)	$358,394	$120,853
Refugees by country of origin (thousands)	10,032.6	77.5
Access to improved sanitation (% of population)	56%	100%
Prevalence of undernourishment (% of population)	14%	5%
Health expenditure (% of GDP)	5.8%	12.3%
Internet users for each 100 people	24	76
Life expectancy at birth (years)	68	80
Population living in cities (% of total population)	47%	80%
Number of passenger cars for each 1,000 people	63	626
Electric power consumption per person (kWh)	1,661	9,415
Armed forces (thousands)	22,402	5,618

Source: WDI, 2013.

least developed of the less developed countries (LLDCs)

The most impoverished countries in the Global South.

humanity) live in one of the thirty-six countries at the bottom of the global hierarchy, the *least developed of the less developed countries (LLDCs)*, where barter of one agricultural good for another (rather than money) typically is used for economic exchanges (WDI, 2013). Sometimes described as the "Third World's Third World," these countries are the very poorest, with little economic growth and rapid population growth that is increasingly straining their overburdened society and environment. These countries are not emerging or reemerging to break the chains of their destitution; they are falling behind the other Global South countries.

The daunting scale of misery and marginalization is thus evident across the Global South, from which only a fraction of its countries have begun to escape. For most Global South countries, the future is bleak, and the opportunities and choices most basic to freedom from fear and poverty are unavailable. When we consider that nearly all the population growth in the twenty-first century will occur in the Global South, the poorest countries cut off from circulation in the globalized marketplace, it is hard to imagine how the gap can close and how the soil of poverty can be prevented from producing terrorism and civil war.

This tragic portrayal of unspeakable despair for so many Global South states raises the basic theoretical question: Why does the Global South, at this historical juncture, suffer from such dismal destitution?

WHY DO SUCH DIFFERENCES PERSIST?

Why has the Global South lagged far behind the Global North in its comparative level of well-being and *development*? Furthermore, why have the developmental experiences even within the Global South differed so widely?

The diversity evident in the Global South invites the conclusion that underdevelopment is explained by a combination of factors. Some theorists explain the underdevelopment of most developing economies by looking primarily at *internal* causes within states. Other theorists focus on *international* causes such as the position of developing countries within the global political economy. We will take a brief look at each of these schools of thought.

Internal Sources of Underdevelopment

Liberal economic development theories of *modernization* first emerged in the years immediately following World War II. They argued that major barriers to development were posed by the Global South countries' own internal characteristics. To overcome these barriers, most classical theorists recommended that the wealthy countries supply various "missing components" of development, such as investment capital through foreign aid or private foreign direct investment.

Once sufficient capital was accumulated to promote economic growth, these liberal theorists predicted that its benefits would eventually "trickle down" to broad segments of society. Everyone, not just a privileged few, would begin to enjoy rising affluence. Walt W. Rostow, an economic historian and U.S. policy maker, formalized this theory in *The Stages of Economic Growth* (1960). He predicted that traditional societies beginning the path to development would inevitably pass through various stages by means of the free market and would eventually "take off" and eventually become similar to the mass-consumption societies of the capitalist Global North. Even though the rich are likely to get richer, it was argued, as incomes in the world as a whole grow, the odds increase that a preindustrialized economy will grow faster and eventually reduce the gap between it and richer countries.

The countries of the Global South rejected that prognosis and the premises on which it was based. Leaders there did not accept the classical liberal argument that the countries of the Global North became prosperous because they concentrated on hard work, innovative inventions of new products, and investments in schooling. Furthermore, by the mid-1970s, it was apparent that assistance from the rich countries of the Global North had not brought about the expected prosperity or democracy in the Global South. The Global South countries were instead persuaded by a rival theory that attributed their lack of development to the international links between developing countries and the Global North's leadership in the global political economy.

development

The processes, economic and political, through which a country develops to increase its capacity to meet its citizens' basic human needs and raise their standard of living.

Carnegie Council Video: Development

modernization

A view of development popular in the Global North's liberal democracies that wealth is created through efficient production, free enterprise, and free trade, and that countries' relative wealth depends on technological innovation and education more than on natural endowments such as climate and resources.

Carnegie Council Video: Modernization

International Sources of Underdevelopment

import-substitution industrialization

A strategy for economic development that centers on providing investors at home incentives to produce goods so that previously imported products from abroad will decline.

Whereas classical theory attributes the causes of most developing countries' underdevelopment to internal conditions within states, *dependency theory* emphasizes international factors, specifically the Global South's dependence on the dominant great powers. As noted in Chapter 2, dependency theory builds on Vladimir Lenin's Marxist critique of imperialism, but it goes beyond it to account for changes that have occurred in recent decades. Its central proposition is that the structure of the capitalist world economy is based on a division of labor between a dominant core and a subordinate periphery. As a result of colonialism, the Global South countries that make up the periphery have been forced into an economic role whereby they export raw materials and import finished goods. Whereas classical liberal theorists submit that specialization in production according to comparative advantage will increase income in an unfettered market and thereby help close the gap between the world's haves and have-nots, dependency theorists maintain that global inequalities cannot be reduced so long as developing countries continue to specialize in producing primary products for which there are often numerous competing suppliers and limited demand.

export-led industrialization

A growth strategy that concentrates on developing domestic export industries capable of competing in overseas markets.

Breaking out of their dependent status and pursuing their own industrial development remains the greatest foreign policy priority for countries in the Global South. To this end, some countries (particularly those in Latin America) have pursued development through an *import-substitution industrialization* strategy designed to encourage domestic entrepreneurs to manufacture products traditionally imported from abroad. Governments (often dictatorships) became heavily involved in managing their economies, and in some cases became the owners and operators of industry.

multinational corporations (MNCs)

Business enterprises headquartered in one state that invest and operate extensively in many other states.

Import-substitution industrialization eventually fell from favor, in part because manufacturers often found that they still had to rely on Global North technology to produce goods for their domestic markets. The preference now is for *export-led industrialization*, based on the realization that "what had enriched the rich was not their insulation from imports (rich countries do, in fact, import all sorts of goods) but their success in manufactured exports, where higher prices could be commanded than for [Global South] raw materials" (Sklair, 1991).

dualism

The separation of a country into two sectors, the first modern and prosperous centered in major cities, and the second at the margin, neglected and poor.

Dependency theorists also argue that countries in the Global South are vulnerable to cultural penetration by *multinational corporations (MNCs)* and other outside forces, which saturate them with values alien to their societies. Once such penetration has occurred, the inherently unequal exchanges that bind the exploiters and the exploited are sustained by elites within the penetrated societies who sacrifice their country's welfare for personal gain. The argument that a privileged few benefit from dependency at the expense of their societies underscores the dual nature of many developing countries.

Dualism refers to the existence of two separate economic and social sectors operating side by side. Dual societies typically have a rural, impoverished, and neglected sector operating alongside an urban, developing, or advanced sector—but with little interaction between the two. Multinational corporations contribute to dualism by favoring a minority of well-compensated employees over the rest, which increases gaps in pay, and widens differences between rural and urban economic opportunities.

newly industrialized countries (NICs)

The most prosperous members of the Global South, which have become important exporters of manufactured goods as well as important markets for the major industrialized countries that export capital goods.

Although dependency theory has great appeal within the Global South, it cannot easily explain the rapid economic development of what many people refer to as the *newly industrialized countries (NICs)*. Today, the NICs are among the largest exporters of manufactured goods and are leaders in the information processing industry. Neither does it do a good job of explaining the lack of sustained development of countries such as Cuba, Myanmar, and North Korea that focused their economic growth efforts inwardly and have had little involvement in global trade. Recently, however, there has been a reincarnation of modernization theory that once again looks at how internal characteristics, such as social and cultural conditions, may shape political and economic development (see "Controversy: Theories of Development—A Return to Modernization?").

A NEW FACE OF GLOBAL SOUTH SOCIALISM Though disappointingly little has been done thus far to alleviate poverty and repression, there are indications of what social constructivists would see as significant transitions in economic thought in Cuba. Raul Castro, who succeeded his brother Fidel as president in 2008, has spoken of the necessity of ending a system where the state pays for everything, arguing that socialism "means social justice and equality, but equality of rights, of opportunities, not of income. Equality is not the same as egalitarianism. Egalitarianism is in itself a form of exploitation: exploitation of the good workers by those who are less productive and lazy."

CLOSING THE GAP? THE GLOBAL SOUTH'S PROSPECTS IN A WORLD OF GREAT POWERS

The vast political, economic, and social differences separating the Global North and the Global South suggest that the remaining countries in the Global South are increasingly vulnerable, insecure, and defenseless, and that these conditions are products of both internal and international factors. Given the multiple problems standing in the way of the Global South's security and prosperity, ask yourself, were you to become a head of state of a Global South country, how you would approach these immense challenges. Your choices would undoubtedly benefit by considering the different approaches Global South countries have taken to pursue their objectives, particularly in their relationships with the Global North.

Technology and Global Communications

The Global North and the Global South have long differed in terms of their technological capabilities:

> Twenty years ago North America, Europe and Japan produced almost all of the world's science. They were the aristocrats of technical knowledge, presiding over a centuries-old regime. They spent the most, published the most and patented the most. And what they produced fed back into their industrial, military and medical complexes to push forward innovation, productivity, power, health and prosperity (*The Economist*, 2010b, p. 95).

CONTROVERSY

THEORIES OF DEVELOPMENT—A RETURN TO MODERNIZATION?

Over time, the perceived effectiveness and credibility of development theories have waxed and waned depending, at least in part, upon their ability to explain and predict current world events. During its heyday in the 1960s, classical theory prescribed that countries should emulate the path of industrial democracies in order to develop. However, it was apparent by the 1970s that such efforts had not resulted in widespread prosperity or democracy. For example, many countries in Latin America suffered from authoritarian rule and abject poverty. Dependency theory grew in popularity at this time, with its focus on the global capitalist system—rather than the internal problems of the Global South countries—as the reason for persistent underdevelopment. Yet the relevance of this theoretical explanation came to be questioned as well, particularly in light of the success of countries that experienced meaningful growth by participating in the global market and pursuing export-oriented strategies.

As both perspectives fell out of vogue, critics suggested that modernization theory was dead. However, since the end of the Cold War, a nuanced version of modernization theory has emerged and is gaining credibility. Responding to changes in the world such as the demise of communism and the economic success of East Asian countries, its core premise is that producing for the world market enables economic growth; investing the returns in human capital and upgrading the work force to produce high-tech goods brings higher returns and enlarges the educated middle class; once the middle class becomes large and articulate enough, it presses for liberal democracy—the most effective political system for advanced industrial societies (Inglehart and Welzel, 2009, p. 36).

Like earlier incarnations of modernization theory, this more recent version similarly sees economic development as eliciting important and predictable changes in politics, culture, and society. Yet it provides a more complex understanding in a number of ways (Inglehart and Welzel, 2009):

- **History Matters**. A society's beliefs, values, and traditions shape its larger worldview and its engagement with the forces of modernization.
- **Modernization Is Not Westernization**. The success of industrialization in the Global East challenges earlier ethnocentric assumptions.
- **Modernization Is Not Democratization**. Increases in per capita GDP do not automatically result in democracy.
- **Modernization Is Not Linear**. There are multiple inflection points, as individual phases of modernization tend to be associated with particular changes in society.

WHAT DO YOU THINK?

- *How are liberalism, constructivism, and Marxist perspectives reflected in the various versions of modernization theory?*

- *What are the implications of the new modernization theory for the rise of gender equality? For political reform and democratization? For international organizations as instruments of development?*

- *New modernization theory suggests that the rise of the middle class is critical for a country's development into a democracy. How might this be an important policy perspective for decision makers, both domestically and internationally?*

Typically, Global South countries have been unable to develop indigenous technology appropriate to their own resources and have been dependent on powerful Global North multinational corporations (see Chapter 6) to transfer technical know-how. This means that research and development expenditures are devoted to solving the Global North's problems, with technological advances seldom meeting the needs of the Global South. However, though the Global North was responsible for more than 95 percent of global research and development in 1990, by 2009 this figure had declined to 72.9 percent (UNESCO, 2013).

Countries in the Global South are making strides in their own technological innovation (see Figure 5.1). Emerging multinationals in the Global South have made advances and are "spooking the rich world's established multinationals with innovative products and bold acquisitions" (*The Economist*, 2009i, p. 20). Nonetheless, technology has not been distributed equally geographically: the lowest density of computer connections to the Internet is in the Global South (see Map 5.4).

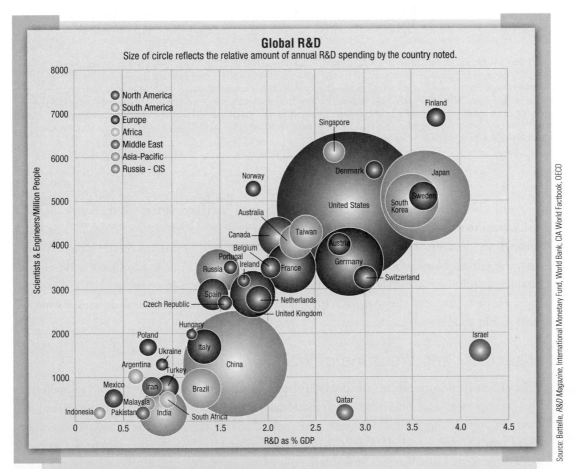

Source: Battelle, *R&D Magazine*, International Monetary Fund, World Bank, CIA World Factbook, OECD

FIGURE 5.1   GLOBAL RESEARCH AND DEVELOPMENT The amount of money that a country spends on scientific research and development is one indicator of its global scientific standing. Comparing the gross domestic expenditure on research and development (GERD) as a percentage of a country's total GDP, this figure shows that Israel spent the largest portion—4.2 percent of its GDP—on scientific discovery in 2013. While the United States and the European Union continued to invest in scientific development, a number of emerging powers in the Global South increased their scientific expenditures, further signaling what some see as the "rise of the rest."

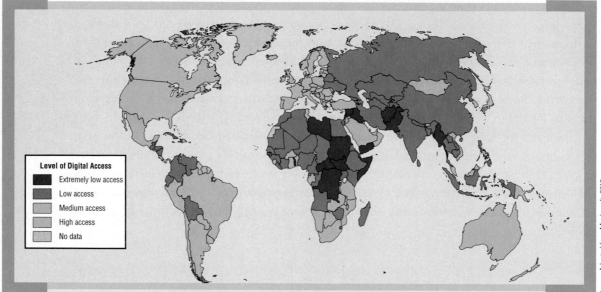

Level of Digital Access

- Extremely low access
- Low access
- Medium access
- High access
- No data

Source: Adapted from Maplecroft, 2013

MAP 5.4 THE DIGITAL DIVIDE IN INFORMATION AND COMMUNICATION TECHNOLOGIES Information and communication technology (ICT) has spread rapidly in recent years. However, the level of penetration varies both among and within countries; a digital divide has emerged in which some countries have high levels of access and others have limited access. Based on the Digital Inclusion Risk Index 2013, which takes into account access to personal computers, Internet and broadband, and mobile telephones and fixed-line telephones, the map above depicts relative levels of access to ICT across the globe. Countries are grouped into four categories that range from high to low ICT access. As shown, the United States enjoys high access, whereas countries on Africa's west coast have limited access.

digital divide

The division between the Internet-technology rich Global North and the Global South in the proportion of Internet users and hosts.

communications technology

The technological means through which information and communications are transferred.

Carnegie Council Video: Communications Technology

With the expanding importance of the Internet to global commerce and communication, critics fear that the *digital divide* in access to *communications technology* is not closing quick enough and that small entrepreneurs in the Global South will be put at a disadvantage. At present, the Global North (and particularly the United States, where the Internet was developed) remains predominant and the primary beneficiary of the *information technology (IT)* revolution. However, most of the growth in the media and telecommunications industries is expected to occur in the Global South.

Insecurity and Weapons of War

Global South countries must face the fateful question of whether they dare to call for help from the great powers and dominating international organizations when violence, terrorism, and anarchy prevail. The cry for assistance poses risks, because where there is outside involvement, there tends to be outside influence, some of which may be unwelcome. There is a fine line between external involvement and interference. On top of this concern is another: the threat of great power indifference or inability to agree about when, where, why, and how they should collectively become involved within Global South borders where violence, ethnic cleansing, and terrorism occur.

Faced with seemingly endless conflict at home or abroad, and a desire to address military insecurity on their own terms, it is not surprising that the Global South countries have joined the rest of the world's quest to acquire modern weapons of war—including nuclear weapons, as in the cases of China, India, North Korea, and Pakistan. As a result, the burden of military spending (measured by the ratio of military expenditures to GNP) is highest among those least able to bear it (SIPRI, 2013). In the Global South, military spending typically exceeds expenditures on health and education; impoverished states facing ethnic, religious, or tribal strife at home are quite prepared to sacrifice economic development in order to acquire weapons.

Few Global South states produce their own weapons. Instead, most Global South countries have increased their military spending to purchase arms produced in the Global North (SIPRI, 2013). Thus, in responding to a world of powers, the Global South appears to be increasing its dependence for arms purchases on the very same rich states whose military and economic domination they historically have most feared and resented.

Reform of the Economic Order

Although some Global South countries benefit from global economic integration and prosper, others seem unable to take advantage of the alleged benefits of globalization and are especially vulnerable to recessions in the global economy. How to cope with dominance and dependence thus remains a key concern in the Global South.

The emerging Global South countries were born into a political-economic order with rules they had no voice in creating. In order to gain control over their economic futures, they began coordinating their efforts within the United Nations, where their growing numbers and voting power gave them greater influence than they could otherwise command. In the 1960s, they formed a coalition, the *Group of 77 (G-77)*, and used their voting power to convene the UN Conference on Trade and Development (UNCTAD). UNCTAD later became a permanent UN organization through which the Global South would express its interests concerning development issues. A decade later, the G–77 (then numbering more than 120 countries) again used its numerical majority in the UN to push for a *New International Economic Order (NIEO)* to replace the international economic regime championed by the United States and the other capitalist powers since World War II. Motivated by the oil-exporting countries' rising bargaining power, the Global South sought to compel the Global North to abandon practices perceived as perpetuating the Global South's dependence.

Not surprisingly, the Global North rebuffed many of the South's proposals, although some of the issues that were raised (such as debt relief) remain on the global agenda. At the 2003 World Trade Organization meeting in Cancún, Mexico, for example, the poor countries demanded major concessions from the wealthy countries, especially with regard to foreign subsidies. In 2008, another step was taken when "Banco del Sur" (Bank of the South) was launched by Brazil and Argentina to compete directly with the World Bank by funding big infrastructure projects through the region's new oil wealth without Global North interference. Today, disputes about the appropriate intersection between global governance and national sovereignty persist, with the Global North wanting the International Monetary Fund to assume a more overt surveillance responsibility over its member states' macroeconomic policies, whereas the Global South opposes a larger role (Patrick, 2010).

FROM RAGS TO RICHES A number of formerly poor Global South countries have catapulted to affluence, either through free markets and aggressive trade or by capitalizing on abundant natural resources. Dubai (shown left) and Kuwait (shown right) are prime examples, as rising oil prices have created a boom that is transforming both of these Arab kingdoms into zones of prosperity. In Dubai, the construction of one of the world's largest shopping malls, with the world's largest aquarium and a five-story underwater hotel, demonstrate its wealth. Kuwait enjoys similar good fortunes, with construction projects in 2013 valued at $250.6 billion (*Kuwait Times*, 2013).

Foreign Aid and Remittances

foreign aid

Economic assistance in the form of loans and grants provided by a donor country to a recipient country for a variety of purposes.

Carnegie Council Video:
Foreign Aid

bilateral

Interactions between two transnational actors.

official development assistance (ODA)

Grants or loans to countries from donor countries, now usually channeled through multilateral aid institutions such as the World Bank for the primary purpose of promoting economic development and welfare.

One approach for closing the gap between the Global South and the Global North is the distribution of foreign assistance. Urging the wealthy countries to help the poorest, Chinese president Hu Jintao declared in February 2009 that "developed countries should assume their responsibilities and obligations, continue to deliver their aid, [keep their] debt relief commitments, maintain and increase assistance to developing countries and effectively help them maintain financial stability and economic growth."

Some *foreign aid* consists of outright grants of money, some of loans at concessional rates, and some of shared technical expertise. Although most foreign aid is *bilateral* and is termed *official development assistance (ODA)*—meaning the money flows directly from one country to another—an increasing portion is now channeled through global intergovernmental institutions such as the World Bank, and hence is known as "multilateral aid" (see Chapter 6).

The purposes of aid are as varied as its forms. Commonly stated foreign aid goals include not only the reduction of poverty through economic development but also human development, environmental protection, reduced military spending, enhanced economic management, the development of private enterprise, increased women's rights, the promotion of democratic governance and human rights, and humanitarian disaster relief and assistance to refugees (Barrett, 2007; Dimiral-Pegg and Moskowitz, 2009; Woods, 2008). Security objectives have also figured prominently in motives of both economic and military assistance. For example, the United States continues to target Israel and Egypt as major recipients to symbolize friendship, maintain a balance of power, and tilt the scales toward peace in the Middle East. Also, security was the primary motive behind the doubling of the U.S. foreign assistance budget following 911 to provide funds for allies' use in the global war on terrorism.

The assumption that development will support other goals, such as fostering solidarity among allies and promoting commercial advantage, free markets, or democratization, still underpins most donors' assistance programs. With the Millennium Challenge Account (MCA), the United States committed to provide from 2006 onward at least $5 billion each year in aid to 17 eligible countries that "govern justly, invest in their people, and encourage economic freedom." This represented the largest increase in U.S. development assistance since the Marshall Plan in 1948.

The general global trend in the overall amount of foreign aid allocations since 1970 has been toward gradual increases. However, foreign aid as a percentage of a donor country's total gross national income has remained stagnant (OECD, 2013). Many donor countries have not met their targeted ODA levels due, in part, to the global economic downturn (see Figure 5.2).

Many aid donors have become frustrated with the slow growth rates of numerous Global South recipients and have grown doubtful of the effectiveness of their aid programs, despite strong evidence that foreign aid has had a positive influence (Easterbrook, 2002). Critics particularly resent what they perceive to be an entrenched state of mind in many Global South cultures that stands in the way of development, which—while bemoaning poverty—condemns

Video:
Embarrassing the Rich
to Help the Poor

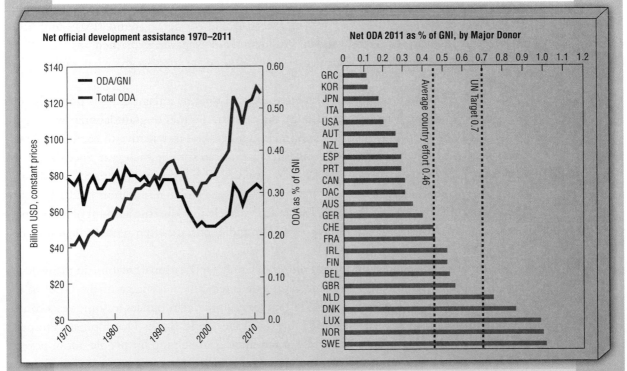

FIGURE 5.2   BROKEN PROMISES With UN Resolution 2626, the wealthy countries of the Global North agreed in 1970 to allocate 0.7 percent of their GNP as aid for the long-term development of the poorer countries of the Global South. While official development assistance in real terms has increased between 1970 and 2011, the same is not true of giving as a percentage of gross national income (shown left). In fact, the global average for ODA as a percentage of GNI in 2011 was less than half of 1 percent (0.46). In absolute dollars, the United States, Germany, Britain, and France were the biggest donors; however, in terms of giving relative to the size of the national economy, Luxembourg, Sweden, and Norway were the most generous (shown right).

the profit motive, competition, and consumerism that lie at the heart of capitalism. Donors are especially resentful that the countries seeking aid do not value the core Western values of hard work, economic competition, and entrepreneurial creativity believed to be crucial for progress and prosperity.

In response to this viewpoint, donors have grown increasingly insistent on "conditionality," or demands that aid recipients must meet to receive continued assistance. Donors also persist in "tying" development assistance to the donors for their benefit, such as requiring purchases from the donors, even though the World Bank estimates this practice reduces the value of aid by 15 to 30 percent, decreases its efficiency, and violates the same free-market principles that the Global North claims to promote.

On top of this, Global South countries complain that the Global North donors have been promising for the past 40 years to allocate 0.7 percent of their gross national product (GNP) to foreign aid, but only a few have kept the promise or even come close (see Figure 5.2). This is true despite the evidence that more assistance does indeed contribute to development when it is designed properly and delivered in a sustained way to countries with records of improving democratic governance (Sachs, 2005). Recently, however, many Global South leaders have joined Global North critics of foreign aid, interpreting it as an instrument of neocolonialism and neoimperialism and resenting the conditionality criteria for receiving aid imposed by the International Monetary Fund (IMF) and other multilateral institutions. As Rwandan President Paul Kagame explained in May 2009, "We appreciate support from the outside, but it should be support for what we intend to achieve ourselves."

remittances

The money earned by immigrants working in rich countries (which almost always exceeds the income they could earn working in their home country) that they send to their families in their home country.

Much more money—more than double the global total in foreign aid—is primarily funneled into Global South economies through the *remittances* that migrant laborers working in the Global North faithfully send home to their families. Not as sensitive to economic downturns as private-capital flows, global remittances have risen steadily each year since the 1970s. They have quadrupled over the past 12 years, from $132 billion in 2000 to $529 billion in 2012. The World Bank estimates that $401 billion of total global remittances in 2012 went to developing countries (World Bank, 2013a), and it is likely that the true amount of remittances is much larger than the official figures as money and goods are often sent through informal networks (see Map 5.5 and Figure 5.3).

The money received is an important source of family (and national) income in many developing economies, representing in some cases a very relevant percentage of the GDP of the receiving countries. In Lebanon and Tajikistan, for example, remittances in some years constitute more than a fifth of their GDP. As Director of the World Bank's Development Prospects Group Hans Timmer explains, "The role of remittances in helping lift people out of poverty has always been known, but there is also abundant evidence that migration and remittances are helping countries achieve progress towards … access to education, safe water, sanitation and healthcare."

Carnegie Council Video:
Remittances

Trade and Foreign Direct Investment

The developing countries have long pleaded for "trade, not aid" to improve their global position, turning to the NIC's and the Global East experience to support the view that access to

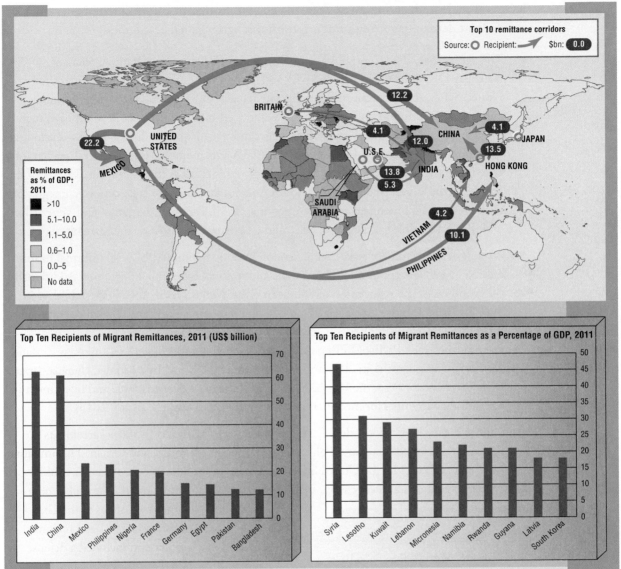

MAP 5.5 AND FIGURE 5.3   SENDING MONEY BACK HOME The billions of dollars that migrant workers send home each year are vital to developing countries. Having remained stable relative to other resource flows during the global economic crisis of recent years, remittances are expected to increase by 8.8 percent annually, reaching $515 billion in 2015 (World Bank, 2013b). India and China are among the largest recipients of migrant remittances, though low-income countries such as Tajikistan and Liberia are among the top recipients of remittances as a share of GDP (shown bottom).

Source: World Bank estimates based on the International Monetary Fund's Balance of Payments Statistics Database.

the Global North's markets is critical to Global South economic growth. And those requests for greater trade through reduced barriers have generally been successful: The number of free-trade agreements in force between and among the Global South and Global North countries has ballooned to more than 350 agreements in 2012 (World Bank, 2013c). Indeed, many countries of the Global South have benefited from a "virtuous cycle" (Blanton and Blanton, 2008), wherein increased trade leads to improved domestic conditions that in turn facilitate trade. Consider some recent developments to promote growth through regional economic agreements:

- **The Americas**. The Central America-Dominican Republic Free Trade Agreement (CAFTA-DR) aims to emulate NAFTA and create a free-trade zone that includes the United States, the Dominican Republic, Guatemala, El Salvador, Nicaragua, Honduras, and Costa Rica. Intent on liberalizing U.S. and Central American markets, the agreement is the first major "subregional" agreement between very unequal trading partners—excluding the United States, the combined GDP of CAFTA-DR members is just above 1 percent of U.S. GDP (WDI, 2013). Mercosur, commonly referred to as the "Common Market of the South," is the largest trading bloc in South America and aims for full economic integration of the region. Full members include Argentina, Brazil, Paraguay, Uruguay, and Venezuela, with Bolivia, Colombia, Ecuador, Peru, and Chile holding associate membership status.

- **Asia**. The association of Asia-Pacific Economic Cooperation (APEC), an informal forum created in 1989, is committed to free trade and regional economic integration. Additionally, the members of the Association of Southeast Asian Nations (ASEAN), first established in 1967 by Brunei, Indonesia, Malaysia, the Philippines, Singapore, and Thailand, and now including Vietnam, Cambodia, Laos, and Myanmar, agreed to set up a free-trade area. More recently, the Trans-Pacific (TPP) partnership—Brunei, Chile, Singapore, and New Zealand were original signatories in 2005 and were subsequently joined by Australia, Canada, Japan, Malaysia, Mexico, Peru, the United States, and Vietnam—deepens trade and investment in a region that accounts for more than 40 percent of global trade (Kaneko, 2013).

- **Middle East**. The U.S.-Middle East Free Trade Area (MEFTA) includes agreements between the United States and Bahrain, Israel, Jordan, Morocco, and Oman. This initiative was begun in 2003 by the United States, and there are still many countries that could become member-states very soon, such as Algeria, Kuwait, and Yemen. The Gulf Cooperation Council for the Arab States of the Gulf (GCC) was established in 1981 as a regional common market that also included a defense council. It includes countries with similar political systems rooted in Islamic beliefs, and the founding members included Bahrain, Kuwait, Oman, Qatar, Saudi Arabia, and the United Arab Emirates.

EMERGING MARKET GIANTS Launched in March 2009, the Tata Nano is the world's cheapest car and is the innovation of an emerging multinational in Mumbai, India. With low-cost production models based on inexpensive local labor and growing domestic markets, companies in the Global South are competing with the rich-country multinationals in the Global North.

Face to Face/UPPA/Photoshot, Inc.

- **Sub-Saharan Africa**. The Southern African Development Community (SADC) is the largest of twelve regional free-trade areas in the region. With a membership of 15 southern African states, its objective is to facilitate socio-economic cooperation. In the western region of Africa, the Economic Community of West African States (ECOWAS) was established in 1975 as a regional economic and trade union.

Will the lofty expectations of these regional politico-economic groups be realized? In the past, political will and shared visions have proven to be indispensable elements in successful regional trade regimes that set rules for members' collaboration. Economic complementarity is another essential component, as the goal is to stimulate greater trade among the members of the free-trade area, not simply between it and other regions.

In an effort to shore up the global economy, global leaders pledged to finance trade, resist protectionist measures, and assist the Global South. These efforts met with success, as seen in the recovery of global trade volumes by the start of 2010 following their sharp decline in 2008 (Gregory et al., 2010). However, as evidenced by the shift at the 2010 G-20 summit meeting in Toronto from an emphasis on spending programs to debt reduction as a response to the global economic crisis, there is a potential for the developed and emerging market economy countries to reduce spending, enact protectionist measures, and focus on their own economic problems—an approach that could disrupt the fragile recovery of the worldwide economy and disadvantage the Global South.

The "North-South gap has not narrowed so far during the most recent globalization era" (Reuveny and Thompson, 2008, p. 8). Many Global South countries have not improved their lot: market access remains difficult because domestic pressure groups in these low-growth Global South countries have lobbied their governments to reduce the imports of other countries' products that compete with their own industries. Moreover, some continue to suffer from the negative effects of trade deficits—among the least-developed countries the average trade deficit is more than 15 percent of GDP—and such imbalances can inhibit economic growth and encourage dependency in the South (WDI, 2013). Trade may be preferred to aid, but political barriers often interfere with free trade.

In the Global South, another important tactic for escaping destitution and stagnant economic growth has been to attract a greater share of *foreign direct investment (FDI)*. Indeed, "FDI into the Global South has increased more rapidly than trade and surpassed foreign aid as the leading source of capital in developing countries" (Blanton and Blanton, 2012a, p.1), and it is attractive to potential host countries in the Global South as it contributes to capital formation, enhances access to international marketing networks, and provides for the transfer of production technology, skills and organizational practices between countries (Blanton and Blanton, 2009).

Yet this strategy for economic growth has always been the target of critics who question whether the investment of capital by MNCs (and, to a lesser extent, private investors) into local or domestic business ventures is really a financial remedy. The strategy has always been controversial, because there are many hidden costs, or *externalities*, associated with permitting corporations controlled from abroad to set up business within the host state for the purpose of making a profit. Who is to be the ultimate beneficiary, the foreign investor or the states in which the investments are made? Do ordinary people within the Global South benefit or are they exploited by corporations and the elite? Such policies entail considerable risks and trade-offs, and they can create conflict between those with competing values and goals.

The primary danger with this strategy is the potential for foreign investments to lead to foreign control and the erosion of the sovereign governments' capacities to regulate the economy within their borders. An additional danger is that the multinational foreign investors might not invest their profits locally but channel them abroad for new investments or disburse them as dividends for their wealthy

foreign direct investment (FDI)

A cross-border investment through which a person or corporation based in one country purchases or constructs an asset such as a factory or bank in another country so that a long-term relationship and control of an enterprise by non-residents results.

CourseMate

Carnegie Council Video:
Foreign Direct
Investment

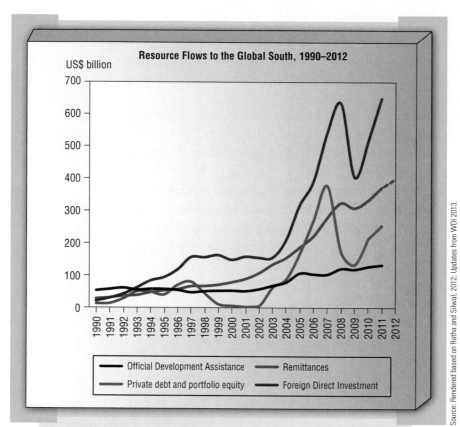

Resource Flows to the Global South, 1990–2012

US$ billion

Source: Rendered based on Ratha and Silwal, 2012; Updates from WDI 2013.

— Official Development Assistance   — Remittances
— Private debt and portfolio equity   — Foreign Direct Investment

FIGURE 5.4   THE RISE AND FALL OF THE GLOBAL ECONOMY Over the past decade, foreign capital has been a primary source for growth in the Global South. However, the recent global economic downturn challenged future growth. Private equity, portfolio investment, and FDI experienced great volatility between 2007 and 2009, although remittances and ODA were more stable. Since then, capital flows to the Global South have increased.

Global North shareholders. Furthermore, there have long been fears that a "race to the bottom" may occur whereby governments restrict labor rights and human rights in order to enhance a country's attractiveness to foreign investors (Blanton and Blanton, 2012a, 2012b).

However, despite the risks, many developing countries have relaxed restrictions in order to attract foreign investors, with less emphasis placed on liberalizing investment restrictions and encouraging open domestic economic competition than on offering tax and cash enticements and opportunities for joint ventures. This has stimulated a recent surge in the flow of capital investments to the Global South (see Figure 5.4).

The impact of this new infusion of foreign investments in developing countries has been substantial, given the Global South's relatively small economies. It has paved the way for emerging markets to expand their rates of economic development—despite the resistance of local industries that are threatened by the new competition and the critics who complain about the increasing income inequalities that the investments are causing. Such fears and consequences notwithstanding, developing countries are intensifying their competition for foreign investment capital in order to liberate themselves from dependence and destitution. And foreign direct investment is the leading cause of the shift from farm work to service jobs in Global South urban areas (now 47 percent of the developing countries' population) that is lifting millions of people out of poverty while at the same time outsourcing skilled jobs from the Global North (WDI, 2011, p. 168; WDI, 2013).

Debt Management and Governmental Corruption

The prospects for foreign aid, trade, or foreign direct investments to contribute to the future development of, and relief of poverty in, the Global South will depend on a number of other factors. Foremost is the extent to which the staggering level of debt facing many Global South countries can be managed. The World Bank estimates that Global South debt in 2009 exceeded

$4,076 billion and that the debt-service payments of these countries were equivalent to 21 percent of their gross national income (WDI, 2012). This is unsustainable and threatens their economic health and future growth.

But national debt is not the only drain on a country's economic and political resources; corruption also undermines essential institutional structures and foments a culture of fear and distrust. The abuse of entrusted power for private gain poses enormous costs on four dimensions (Transparency International, 2013):

- **Political.** Corruption is a barrier to democratic governance and the rule of law. When public officials use their offices for personal gain, they undermine the government's legitimacy and the expectation of accountability.

- **Economic.** National wealth is depleted through corrupt practices. Often, public resources are funneled away from the development of infrastructure in areas such as education and health care. Widespread corruption also compromises market structures and discourages investment.

- **Social.** The violation of public trust that results from widespread corruption weakens civil society. Pervasive apathy and disengagement of ordinary citizens enhances the opportunity for public officials to use their position and national assets for personal gain. Bribery becomes a norm.

- **Environmental.** Environmental regulations are often ignored, and environmental projects are often easy to exploit for private gain. As a result, corruption frequently leads to pronounced environmental degradation within a country.

The Global North is not immune to public corruption, but it is a pervasive problem in many countries throughout the Global South (see Map 5.6). In the aftermath of the Jasmine Revolution in Tunisia in 2011, the breadth and scope of the corrupt practices by the ruling Ben Ali family came to light. According to a report by the watchdog group Global Financial Integrity, the "amount of illegal money lost from Tunisia due to corruption, bribery, kickbacks, trade mispricing and criminal activity between 2000 and 2008 was, on average, over one billion dollars a year" (*The Economist*, 2011h, p. 32). For a country with a GNP that only reaches $80 billion in a single year, this amount was staggering.

THE GLOBAL SOUTH'S FUTURE

It is useful to remember the historical trends underlying the emergence of the Global South as an actor on the global stage. Many of the countries share similar characteristics: Most were colonized by people of another race, experience varying degrees of poverty and hunger, and feel powerless in a world system dominated by the affluent countries that once controlled them and perhaps still do. Considerable change occurred among the newly emergent states as post–World War II decolonization took place, but much also remained the same.

The relationships between the world's great and small powers will no doubt continue to change—exactly how remains uncertain (see "A Closer Look: Democracy and Foreign Aid"). However, the future of Global South development is certain to depend in part on the activities

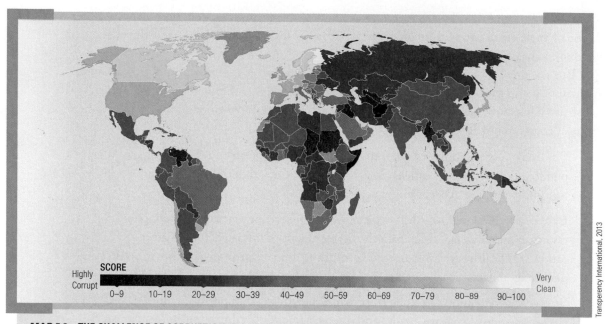

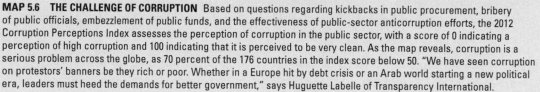

SCORE

Highly Corrupt — Very Clean

0–9 10–19 20–29 30–39 40–49 50–59 60–69 70–79 80–89 90–100

Transparency International, 2013

MAP 5.6   THE CHALLENGE OF CORRUPTION Based on questions regarding kickbacks in public procurement, bribery of public officials, embezzlement of public funds, and the effectiveness of public-sector anticorruption efforts, the 2012 Corruption Perceptions Index assesses the perception of corruption in the public sector, with a score of 0 indicating a perception of high corruption and 100 indicating that it is perceived to be very clean. As the map reveals, corruption is a serious problem across the globe, as 70 percent of the 176 countries in the index score below 50. "We have seen corruption on protestors' banners be they rich or poor. Whether in a Europe hit by debt crisis or an Arab world starting a new political era, leaders must heed the demands for better government," says Huguette Labelle of Transparency International.

of the Global North. A turn inward toward isolationist foreign policies in the Global North could lead to a posture of "benign neglect" of the Global South. Conversely, a new era of North–South–East cooperation could begin, dedicated to finding solutions to common problems ranging from commercial to environmental and security concerns. Elements of both approaches are already evident.

Relations between the Global South and the Global North remain dominated by the great powers. That domination is funneled in part through powerful international organizations, such as the United Nations and the World Bank, which the great powers have created. At the same time, intergovernmental organizations (IGOs) provide an opportunity for the small powers of the Global South to exert influence on world politics. To understand world politics and the roots of changes in international affairs, it is important to understand the impact of these influential IGOs as actors in the global arena. To complete the picture, you also need to inspect the thousands of nongovernmental organizations (NGOs), whose presence and pressure as nonstate actors are also transforming international politics, for both the Global North and the Global South. We turn to both of these transnational actors in Chapter 6.

A multipolar world cannot exist without recognizing the status and participation of developing countries.

—Li Peng, former Chinese premier

A Closer Look

DEMOCRACY AND FOREIGN AID

The Arab Spring of 2011 ushered in a wave of revolutionary protests and demonstrations. From revolutions in Tunisia and Egypt to civil war in Libya to civil unrest in Algeria, Syria, Yemen, and Bahrain, ordinary people spoke out en masse against corrupt dictators. As dramatically illustrated in the immolation of twenty-six-year-old Mohamed Bouazizi, a college-educated Tunisian fruit-seller who set himself on fire to protest the demands for bribes and the abuse he suffered from the police, it was a movement that called for justice and equity as much as it did democracy. In societies with "youthful populations, high unemployment, grotesque inequality, abusive police, reviled leaders, and authoritarian systems that stifle free expression" (Coll, 2011, p. 21), this show of people power revealed widespread frustration and a fundamental instability of existing regimes.

So what role should the Global North play in response to these developments? "The movements are also profoundly suspicious of foreign interference," notes former United Nations under-secretary general for peacekeeping operations Jean-Marie Guehenno, "and Western nations, which for many years have had a cozy relationship with dictators and profiteers, will be utilized, but they are unlikely to be trusted or to serve as models as they were in 1989," when the communist system was dismantled. It is critical that the Global North strike a balance between engagement and restraint that offers support of emerging democracies and respects the development of domestic political processes.

Despite long-time U.S. support of authoritarian regimes in the region, on May 19, 2011, President Obama hailed the benefits of democracy and respect for human rights, and signaled U.S. support for the uprisings. He announced a foreign aid commitment that will result in billions of dollars being allocated to Tunisia, Egypt, and other countries that embrace democracy. The United States drew foreign policy parallels between this effort and the aid provided to former communist countries after the fall of the Berlin Wall in 1989 (MacAskil, 2011).

WATCH THE VIDEO:

Carnegie Council Video:
Assisting Political Parties
in the Middle East

YOU DECIDE:

1. What role should the Global North, and the United States in particular, play in promoting democracy in the Middle East and North Africa?
2. What might the consequences be if the Global North does not offer its financial and political support?
3. Should aid donors work with anti-democratic or politically extremist domestic groups?
4. Or should they place constraints on their financial assistance that exclude such groups from the political process?

STUDY. APPLY. ANALYZE.

Key Terms

bilateral
classical liberal economic
    theory
communications
    technology
communism
decolonization
developed countries
developing countries
development
digital divide
dualism
emerging powers

export-led
    industrialization
First World
foreign aid
foreign direct
    investment (FDI)
Global North
Global South
gross national income
    (GNI)
Group of 77 (G-77)
import-substitution
    industrialization

indigenous peoples
information technology
    (IT)
laissez-faire economics
least developed of the less
    developed countries
    (LLDCs)
mercantilism
modernization
multinational
    corporations (MNCs)

New International
    Economic Order
    (NIEO)
newly industrialized
    countries (NICs)
official development
    assistance (ODA)
realpolitik
remittances
Second World
self-determination
small powers
Third World

Suggested Readings

Barry, Christian. (2003)
"Privatization and GATS: A Threat
to Development?" (September 9)
http://www .carnegiecouncil.
org/resources/articles_papers_
reports/1016.html.

Chant, Sylvia, and Cathy
McIlwaine. (2009) *Geographies of
Development in the 21st Century:
An Introduction to the Global
South.* New York: Edward Elgar
Publishing.

Halperin, Sandra. (2013)
*Re-Envisioning Global
Development: A Horizontal
Perspective.* New York: Taylor
and Francis.

Mahbubani, Kishore. (2009)
*The New Asian Hemisphere: The
Irresistible Shift of Global Power to the
East.* New York: Basic Civitas Books.

Palley, Thomas I. (2003)
"Sovereign Debt Restructuring
Proposals: A Comparative Look,"
Ethics & International Affairs 17,
no. 2 (Fall):26–33.

Pettifor, Ann. (2003) "Resolving
International Debt Crises Fairly,"
Ethics & International Affairs 17
no.2 (Fall):2–9.

Prashad, Vijay. (2013) *The Poorer
Nations: A Possible History of the
Global South.* London, UK: Verso.

Reuveny, Rafael, and William R.
Thompson, eds. (2008) *North
and South in the World Political
Economy.* Malden, MA: Blackwell.

Williams, Glyn, Paula Meth,
and Katie Willis. (2009) *New
Geographies of the Global South:
Developing Areas in a Changing
World.* New York: Taylor & Francis.

Woodward, Susan L. (2009)
"Shifts in Global Security Policies:
Why They Matter for the South,"
IDS Bulletin 40:121–128.

World Bank. (2011) *Atlas of
Global Development,* 3rd edition.
Washington, DC: World Bank.

Suggested Videos

Collier, Paul. "The Bottom Billion: Why the Poorest Countries Are Failing and What Can Be Done About It."

Myers, Jeanne J. "The New Asian Hemisphere: The Irresistible Shift of Global Power to the East."

Moyo, Dambisa, "Dead Aid: Why Aid Is Not Working and How There Is a Better Way for Africa."

Vocke, William. "Development Aid."

Vocke, William. "International Aid: Does Help Hurt?"

CourseMate

Log in to CourseMate to access the following study tools for this chapter:

- Interactive Quiz
- eBook
- Flashcards & Key Term Crossword Puzzle
- Chapter Audio Summary
- Carnegie Council Videos

- Video Activities
- Simulation
- Animated Learning Module
- Case Study
- International Relations NewsWatch

"A novel redistribution of power among states, markets, and civil society is underway, ending the steady accumulation of power in the hands of states that began with the Peace of Westphalia in 1648."

—*Jessica T. Mathews, international relations scholar*

CHAPTER 6

Nonstate Actors and the Quest for Global Community

PEOPLE POWER Shown here are members of the Red Cross, an international humanitarian organization, working in a spirit of global community to provide relief to the people of Syria. Since the start of the uprising against President Bashar al-Assad, the International Committee of the Red Cross has delivered food and medicine to civilians. As the only international aid agency with aid workers in Syria, the ICRC delivers care during breaks in the fighting. It's a "humanitarian situation that's deteriorating constantly," said ICRC spokesman Bihan Farnoudi, adding that "basic goods are lacking, and even when supplies are available, people don't have access to them because they're afraid to leave their homes" (Epatko, 2012).

QUESTIONS TO CONSIDER

☐ *What are the different types of nonstate actors?*
☐ *What are the most important intergovernmental organizations and what do they do?*
☐ *What are the basic characteristics of regional intergovernmental organizations?*
☐ *What are some prominent types of nongovernmental organizations and what do they do?*
☐ *What are some malevolent nonstate actors and what role do they play in international relations?*
☐ *Are nonstate actors becoming more or less important in world politics?*

Y̶ou are a member of the human race, and your future will be determined to a large degree by the capacity of humanity to work together to manage the many common problems confronting the entire world. But how does the world respond to this challenge?

The answer for centuries has primarily relied upon sovereign territorial states. As realism posits, countries remain the most influential actors on the world stage. States' foreign policy decisions and interactions, more than any other factor, give rise to trends and transformations in world politics. Today, however, as liberal theory posits, the extraordinary power of states over global destiny is eroding as our world becomes increasingly complex and interdependent, and as nonstate actors continue to multiply and seek greater influence in the global community. Moreover, a new concept of *responsible sovereignty*, a principle that requires states to protect not only their own people but also to cooperate across borders to protect global resources and address transnational threats, is gaining traction among global leaders—it is a principle that "entails obligations and duties to one's own citizens and other states" and provides for a greater role by IGOs and NGOs as it "differs from the traditional interpretation of sovereignty (sometimes called Westphalian sovereignty) as noninterference in the internal affairs of states" (Jones, Pascual, and Stedman 2009, p. 9).

A critical question to consider, then, is whether or not the predicted decline of states' sovereign authority will ultimately prove to be a cure for global problems. Conversely, will reducing an individual state's ability to rely on *self-help* measures to address problems unilaterally prove to be a curse?

This chapter provides information and insight to help you evaluate this question. More specifically, it will enable you to confront and assess the theoretical hypothesis advanced by world leader Jean-Francois Rischard, former World Bank vice president for Europe, who argues, "One thing is sure: global complexity [is creating a] global governance crisis that will have to be solved through new ways of working together globally, and bold departures from old, trusted concepts."

Global problems often require global solutions. Impressive numbers of nonstate actors on the world stage are increasingly flexing their political muscle in an effort to engineer global changes. This chapter will explore two broad types of nonstate actors—international organizations that carry out independent foreign policies as transnational actors and NGOs made up of individual people who band together in coalitions of private citizens to exercise international influence. To introduce this discussion, we begin with a look at the general characteristics of both types of nonstate actors.

> *The quest for international security involves the unconditional surrender by every nation, in a certain measure, of its liberty of action, its sovereignty that is to say, and it is clear beyond all doubt that no other road can lead to such security.*
>
> **—Albert Einstein, Nobel Prize–winning physicist**

responsible sovereignty

A principle that requires states to protect not only their own people but to cooperate across borders to protect global resources and address transnational threats.

CourseMate

Carnegie Council Video: Responsible Sovereignty

NONSTATE ACTORS IN WORLD POLITICS

There are two main types of international nonstate actors, *intergovernmental organizations (IGOs)* and *nongovernmental organizations (NGOs)*. What distinguishes the two is that intergovernmental organizations are international organizations whose members are states, whereas nongovernmental organizations are associations composed of private individuals. Both types experienced a sharp increase in their numbers during the twentieth century: In 1909 there were 37 IGOs and 176 NGOs; by 1960 the numbers had risen to 154 IGOs and 1255 NGOs; and at the start of 2012, the numbers had escalated to 262 conventional IGOs and 8382 conventional NGOs (see Figure 6.1). This does not include the 707 unconventional IGOs and 4566 unconventional NGOs (organizations such as international funds and foundations) that are recorded by the Yearbook of International Organizations (2012/2013, vol. 5, p. 25).

Intergovernmental Organizations (IGOs)

IGOs are purposely created by states to solve problems. IGOs are generally regarded as more important than NGOs, in part because IGOs members are powerful state governments and tend to be more permanent. IGOs meet at regular intervals, and they have established rules for making decisions and a permanent secretariat or headquarters staff.

IGOs vary widely in size and purpose. Only thirty-four IGOs qualify as "intercontinental organizations," and only 36 are, like the United Nations (UN), "universal membership" IGOs. The rest, accounting for more than 73 percent of the total, are limited in their scope and confined to particular regions. The variation among the organizations in each subcategory is great, particularly with single-purpose, limited-membership IGOs. The North Atlantic Treaty Organization (NATO), for example, is primarily a military alliance, whereas others, such as the Organization of American States (OAS), promote both economic development and democratic reforms. Still, most IGOs concentrate their activities on specific economic or social issues of special concern to them, such as the management of trade or transportation.

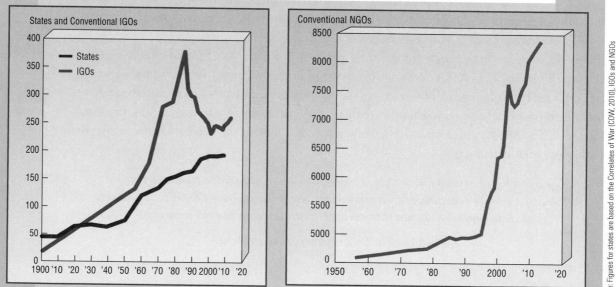

Source: Figures for states are based on the Correlates of War (COW, 2010), IGOs and NGOs are from the Yearbook of International Organizations (2012/2013, p. 25), and moving averages are from prior volumes.

FIGURE 6.1   TRENDS IN THE NUMBER OF IGOS, NGOS, AND STATES SINCE 1900   Since 1900, the number of independent states has increased dramatically, with growth accelerating after World War II when the decolonization movement began. But note that the number of NGOs has grown even more rapidly in this period, declining only since the late 1980s when a number of formerly independent IGOs began to merge with one another. The number of NGOs has grown even more rapidly, with more than 8000 conventional NGOs worldwide.

The expansion of IGOs has created a complex network of overlapping international organizations that cooperate with one another to deal with a wide range of global issues. They support one another on issues as varied as trade, defense, disarmament, economic development, agriculture, health, culture, human rights, the arts, illegal drugs, tourism, labor, gender inequality, education, debt, the environment, crime, humanitarian aid, civilian crisis relief, telecommunications, science, globalization, immigration, and refugees.

Nongovernmental Organizations (NGOs)

The term *NGO* can be applied to *all* nonstate and nonprofit organizations that operate as intermediaries to build transnational bridges between those with resources and a targeted group. Thus, it is also customary to think of NGOs as intersocietal organizations that contribute to negotiations between and among states in the hope of reaching agreements for global governance on nearly every issue of international public policy. NGOs link the global society by forming "transnational advocacy networks" working for policy changes (Keck and Sikkink, 2008). According to a constructivist perspective, they are inspired to action by their interests and values.

Like IGOs, NGOs differ widely in their characteristics. For example, some are small with membership in the hundreds; others are huge, with one of the largest being Amnesty International, which in 2013 included three million members spread across more than 150 countries and regions. In 2013, the Union of International Associations categorized the major "conventional" NGOs as split, with almost 6 percent as "universal," more than 15 percent as "intercontinental," and the vast majority, almost 79 percent, as "regionally oriented." Functionally, NGOs span virtually every facet of political, social, and economic activity in an increasingly borderless globalized world, ranging from earth sciences to ethnic unity, health care, language, history, culture, education, theology, law, ethics, security, and defense.

> Nongovernmental organizations are not a homogeneous group. The long list of acronyms that has accumulated around NGOs can be used to illustrate this. People speak of NGOs, INGOs (International NGOs), BINGOs (Business International NGOs), RINGOs (Religious International NGOs), ENGOs (Environmental NGOs), QUANGOs (Quasi-Non-Governmental Organizations—i.e., those that are at least partially created or supported by states), and many others. Indeed, all these types of NGOs and more are among those having consultative status at the UN. Among the NGOs … are the Academic Council on the UN System, the All India Women's Conference, the Canadian Chemical Producers Association, CARE International, the World Young Women's Christian Association, the World Wide Fund for Nature International, the Union of Arab Banks, the Women's International League for Peace and Freedom, the World Energy Council, the World Federation of Trade Unions, and the World Veterans Association. Thus, it is difficult to generalize about NGOs at the UN (Stephenson, 2000, p. 271).

In general, the socially constructed image of NGOs widely accepted throughout the world is very positive—most pursue objectives that are held by large segments of society and, therefore, do not provoke much opposition. This perspective is reflected in the World Bank's definition of NGOs as "private organizations that pursue activities to relieve suffering, promote the interests of the poor, protect the environment, provide basic social services, or undertake community development" (World Bank, 2013m). For example, NGOs such as Amnesty

International, the International Chamber of Commerce, the International Red Cross, Save the Children, and the World Wildlife Federation enjoy widespread popular support. Others, however, are more controversial because they unite people for collective action in ways that can harm others, as in the case of terrorist groups, international drug rings, or transnational pirates.

Many NGOs interact formally with IGOs. For instance, more than 3000 NGOs actively consult with various agencies of the extensive UN system, maintain offices in hundreds of cities, and hold parallel conferences with IGO meetings to which states send representatives. Such partnerships between NGOs and IGOs enable both types to work (and lobby) together in pursuit of common policies and programs. As IGOs and NGOs rise in numbers and influence, a key question to contemplate is whether a "global society" will materialize to override the traditional state-centric global system and, if so, whether this structural transformation will democratize or disrupt global governance.

PROMINENT INTERGOVERNMENTAL ORGANIZATIONS

Let us continue our analysis of nonstate actors in world affairs by examining the most prominent and representative IGOs: the United Nations, the European Union, and various other regional organizations. As we do so, ask yourself whether IGOs' activities are adequate for dealing with the pressing threats to human welfare, whether these IGOs are undermining states' continuing autonomy, and if so, whether an erosion of state power will prove helpful or harmful.

The United Nations

The United Nations (UN) is the best-known global organization. What distinguishes it from most other IGOs is its nearly universal membership, today including 193 independent member states from across the Global North and Global South. The UN's nearly fourfold growth from the 51 states that joined it at the UN's birth in 1945 has been spectacular, but the admission process has from the start been governed by political conflicts. These conflicts show the extent to which the organization reflects the relationships of the five great powers that created it and govern it through veto authority in the Security Council. In principle, any sovereign state that accepts the UN's goals and regulations can join, but the great powers have often let the realist belief that countries should put their own national interest above concern for the global community guide their admissions decision making. This was especially true during the Cold War, when both the United States and the Soviet Union prevented countries aligned with their adversaries from joining.

The UN's Agenda   Peace and security figured prominently in the thinking of the great powers responsible for creating the UN and its predecessor, the League of Nations. These institutional forms were inspired by the liberal conviction that both war and the management of other global problems are best controlled by managing global *anarchy*—the absence of supranational authority to regulate relations between states—on the international scene. The League of Nations sought to prevent a recurrence of the catastrophic World War I by replacing the balance-of-power system with one based on the construction of a *collective security* regime made up of rules for keeping peace, guided by the principle that an act of aggression by any state would be met by a collective retaliatory response from the rest. When the League failed to restrain expansionistic aggression by Germany, Japan, and Italy during the 1930s, it collapsed.

During World War II, the U.S., British, and Russian allies began planning for a new international organization, the United Nations, to preserve the postwar peace because it was believed that peace could not be maintained unilaterally by any one great power acting alone. Article 1 of the UN Charter defines the UN's objectives as centered on:

■ Maintaining international peace and security

■ Developing friendly relations among states based on respect for the principle of equal rights and the self-determination of peoples

■ Achieving international cooperation in solving international problems of an economic, social, cultural, or humanitarian character and in promoting and encouraging respect for human rights and for fundamental freedoms for all

■ Functioning as a center for harmonizing the actions of countries to attain these common ends

The history of the UN reflects the fact that countries from both the Global North and the Global South have successfully used the organization to promote their own foreign policy goals. This record has led to the ratification of more than three hundred treaties and conventions consistent with the UN's "six fundamental values": international freedom, equality, solidarity, tolerance, respect for nature, and a sense of shared responsibility. Although faith in the UN's ability eroded when it became paralyzed by the unforeseen Cold War between the United States and the Soviet Union, in the post–Cold War era it was freed from paralysis and returned to its original mission.

The UN now manages an expanding agenda of urgent military and nonmilitary problems, and in response to these global demands has evolved over time into a vast administrative machinery (see Map 6.1). To assess the capacity of the United Nations to fulfill its growing responsibilities, let us consider how it is organized.

Organizational Structure   The UN's limitations are perhaps rooted in the ways it is organized for its wide-ranging purposes. According to the Charter, the UN structure contains the following six major organs:

■ **General Assembly**. Established as the main deliberative body of the United Nations, all members are equally represented according to a one-state/one-vote formula. Decisions are reached by a simple majority vote, except on so-called important questions, which require a two-thirds majority. The resolutions it passes, however, are only recommendations.

■ **Security Council**. Given primary responsibility by the charter for dealing with threats to international peace and security, the Security Council consists of five permanent members with the power to veto substantive decisions (the United States, the United

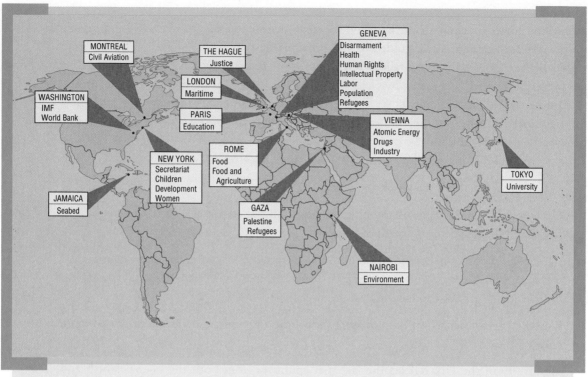

MAP 6.1   THE UN'S HEADQUARTERS AND GLOBAL NETWORK To reduce the gap between aspiration and accomplishment, the UN has spread its administrative arm to every corner of the globe in order to fulfill its primary purpose of spearheading international cooperation. "Although best known for peacekeeping, peace building, conflict prevention, and humanitarian assistance, there are many other ways the United Nations and its System (specialized agencies, funds, and programmes) affect our lives and make the world a better place. The Organization works on a broad range of fundamental issues, from sustainable development, environment and refugees' protection, disaster relief, counter terrorism, disarmament and non-proliferation to promoting democracy, human rights, governance, economic and social development and international health, clearing land mines, expanding food production, and more, in order to achieve its goals and coordinate efforts for a safer world for this and future generations" (United Nations, May 8, 2013).

Kingdom, France, Russia, and the People's Republic of China), and 10 nonpermanent members elected by the General Assembly for staggered two-year terms.

▨ **Economic and Social Council.** Responsible for coordinating the UN's social and economic programs, functional commissions, and specialized agencies, its 54 members are elected by the General Assembly for staggered three-year terms. This body has been particularly active in addressing economic development and human rights issues.

▨ **Trusteeship Council.** Charged with supervising the administration of territories that had not achieved self-rule, the Trusteeship Council suspended operation in 1994, when the last remaining trust territory gained independence.

▨ **International Court of Justice.** The principal judicial organ of the United Nations, the International Court of Justice is composed of 15 independent judges who are elected for nine-year terms by the General Assembly and Security Council (see Chapter 9). The competence of the court is restricted to disputes between states, and its jurisdiction is based on the consent of the disputants. The court may also give nonbinding advisory opinions on legal questions raised by the General Assembly, Security Council, or other UN agencies.

■ **Secretariat**. Led by the secretary-general, the Secretariat contains the international civil servants who perform the administrative and secretarial functions of the UN.

The founders of the UN expected the Security Council to become the organization's primary body, because it was designed to maintain peace and its permanent members were the victorious allied great powers during World War II. It is exclusively permitted by the UN Charter to initiate actions, especially the use of force. The General Assembly, however, can only make recommendations.

Despite the intentions of the founders of the UN, the General Assembly has assumed wider responsibilities as countries in the Global South—seizing advantage of their growing numbers under the one-state/one-vote rules of the General Assembly—have guided UN involvement in directions of particular concern to them. Today, a coalition of Global South countries constituting three-fourths of the UN membership seeks to resist domination by the Global North. This coalition pushes the UN to address economic and social needs and protests when it fails to respect the Global South's special interests.

The growth of the General Assembly's power may not be sufficient to ensure the Global South's control of the agenda, however, as the original five great powers in the Security Council continue to run the show—with the U.S. *hegemon* in a preeminent position. The United States resisted the 2005 proposal to expand the Security Council to 24 members because it

BAN KI-MOON, 2007–PRESENT
With a global reputation as someone who will do the right thing, he is one of the most popular leaders of the world.

KOFI ANNAN, 1996–2006
He had a quiet charisma, but the Iraq war and the oil-for-food scandal marred his second term.

BOUTROS BOUTROS-GHALI, 1992–1996 The United States dumped the acerbic and undiplomatic Egyptian after one turbulent term.

JAVIER PEREZ DE CUELLAR, 1982–1991 He quietly guided the organization out of Cold War paralysis and back into business.

KURT WALDHEIM, 1972–1981
An effective bureaucrat, Waldheim is now remembered mainly for his Nazi past.

U THANT, 1961–1971
The placid Thant had a low profile but got flak for pulling UN peacekeepers from Sinai.

DAG HAMMARSKJOLD, 1953–1961 The UN's most effective leader. Hammarskjold died on a peacekeeping mission to Congo.

TRYGVE LIE, 1946–1952
The gruff politician helped create the organization but accomplished little in office.

would dilute American power, and it announced that it would not support extension of the veto power held by the big five permanent members to other members. In a similar move to maintain power within the UN, China surprised many with its refusal to support an Indian bid for a permanent seat in 2008.

Budget Controversy   Differences between the Global North and the Global South over perceived priorities are most clearly exhibited in the heated debate over the UN's budget. This controversy centers on how members should interpret the organization's Charter, which states that "expenses of the Organization shall be borne by the members as apportioned by the General Assembly."

The UN budget consists of three distinct elements: the core budget, the peacekeeping budget, and the budget for voluntary programs. States contribute to the voluntary programs and some of the peacekeeping activities as they see fit. The core budget and other peacekeeping activities are subject to assessments (see Figure 6.2).

The precise mechanism by which assessments have been determined is complicated, but, historically, assessments have been allocated according to states' capacity to pay. Thus, the United States, which has the greatest resources, is assessed 22 percent of the UN's regular budget, for a net contribution in 2013 of over $618 million. Yet, the poorest 17 percent of the UN's members, or a total of 33 member states, pay the minimum (0.001 percent), each contributing only $28,113 annually and altogether less than 1 percent of the UN's 2013 budget. In comparison, the richest 20 percent of states were assessed to pay almost 95 percent of the UN's 2013 budget. Although this formula is under attack in many wealthy states, it still governs.

Resistance to this budgetary formula for funding UN activities has always existed. It has grown progressively worse in large part because when the General Assembly apportions expenses, it does so according to majority rule. The problem is that those with the most votes (the less developed countries) do not have the money, and the most prosperous countries do not have the votes.

Wide disparities have grown—the largest contributors command only 10 votes but pay 65 percent of the cost, while the other members pay only 35 percent of the UN budget but command 183 votes. Even with, and perhaps because of, the 8.7 percent budget increase in 2013, the wealthy members charge that the existing budget procedures institutionalize a system of taxation without fair representation. The critics counter with the argument that, for fairness and justice, the great power members should bear financial responsibilities commensurate with their wealth and influence.

At issue, of course, is not simply money, which is paltry. "The United Nations and all its agencies and funds spend about $30 billion each year, or about $4 for each of the world's inhabitants. This is a very small sum compared to most government budgets and it is less than 3 percent of the world's military spending." By way of comparison, at the start of 2013, world military spending was $1.76 trillion—which amounts to an average global per capita spending of $249 (SIPRI, 2013). A difference in opinion about what is important and which states should have political influence are the real issues. Poor states argue that need should determine expenditure levels rather than rich countries' interests, while major contributors do not want to pay for programs they oppose. At the start of 2013, 22 members were in arrears and in danger of losing their ability to vote in the General Assembly (UN, 2013).

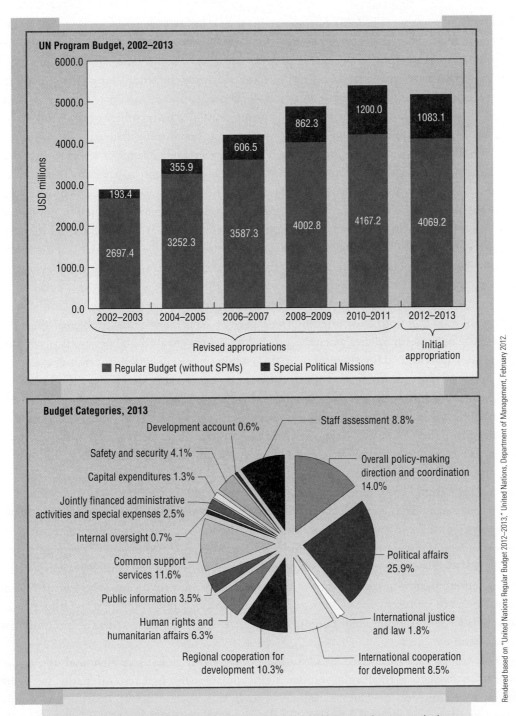

Rendered based on "United Nations Regular Budget 2012–2013." United Nations, Department of Management, February 2012.

FIGURE 6.2   UN BUDGET PRIORITIES   The UN General Assembly approved a program budget of $5.15 billion for the 2012–2013 fiscal year (shown top). Although it reflects an overall budget decline from the prior year, the amount allocated to special political missions has grown to 21 percent of the budget from just 6.7 percent a decade earlier. Among the various budget categories (shown bottom), political affairs is the largest with an allocation of 25.9 percent of the program budget.

Future Challenges The UN's future remains uncertain, and its persistent financial troubles leave it without the resources to combat global problems and carry out the responsibilities assigned to it. However, given the UN's successful history of organizational adaptation to challenges, supporters have reasons to be optimistic about the organization's long-term prospects to live up to its creators' bold mandate to attack world problems (see "A Closer Look: The United Nations and the Syrian Civil War"). Despite some resistance by members of the Global South that feared that Secretary-General Ban Ki-moon might bend to big-donor pressure and compromise the interests of small powers, the UN has undertaken a series of reforms since 2006 to change its management procedures and bring its recruitment, contracting, and training responsibilities into line with its vast new responsibilities. These reforms include protection for "whistleblowers" who report scandals, an antifraud and anticorruption policy, a unified standard of conduct for peacekeepers to prevent sexual abuse, and expanded financial disclosure requirements for senior officials. These massive reforms also cut the Secretariat's administrative costs by one-third, from 38 percent of the core budget to 25 percent, and put the savings into a development fund for poor countries.

The UN will likely remain an arena for heated jockeying among member states and hemispheric blocs, a fact bound to undermine its capacity to solve new global problems. The UN is frequently blamed for failures when the real failure belongs to its members, particularly those of the Global North. "Those powers are seldom willing to give it sufficient resources, attention and boots on the ground to accomplish the ambitious mandates they set for it" (Fukuyama, 2008, p. 14). Moreover, the UN is often faced with very difficult tasks that individual states have been unable to solve. As former Secretary-General U Thant observed, "Great problems usually come to the United Nations because governments have been unable to think of anything else to do about them. The United Nations is a last-ditch, last resort affair, and it is not surprising that the organization should often be blamed for failing to solve problems that have already been found to be insoluble by governments."

In the final analysis, the UN can be no more than the mandates and power that the member states give to it. Yet as supporters point out, the UN remains "the forum of choice for regime negotiation and norm promotion for contested contemporary challenges" (Thakur and Weiss, 2009, p. 18). From a *constructivist* perspective, the legitimacy of the United Nations is based on its representation of the common will of states, and "in certain cases, the United Nations even claims to represent the collective will of humanity" (Ellis, 2009, p. 4)—although constructivists recognize that identifying just what that will is can be a dynamic and hotly contested issue.

The UN is well positioned to formulate policies with global relevance and application, as seen in its success in shaming human rights violators through resolutions in the United Nations Commission on Human Rights (Lebovic and Voeten, 2009), its efforts to combat global pandemics such as HIV/AIDS (Thakur and Weiss, 2009), and its role in promoting confidence-building measures that do more than prevent conflict but have actually encouraged members to proactively discuss and work through their grievances (Shannon, 2009). Although much maligned, the UN is very much needed. "Only a global organization is capable of meeting global challenges," observed former UN Secretary-General Kofi-Annan. "When we act together, we are stronger and less vulnerable to individual calamity."

CourseMate

Case Study:
The United Nations

A Closer Look

THE UNITED NATIONS AND THE SYRIAN CIVIL WAR

Inspired in part by the Arab Spring, hostilities between Syrian rebels and forces loyal to Syria's president Bashar al-Assad began in March 2011 as demonstrators took to the streets in peaceful protest of the imprisonment and torture of a number of young students for anti-government graffiti. After troops fired on the rioting crowds, however, the protests turned into armed conflict over the legitimacy of al-Assad's rule. Fighting continued between the Syrian army and various opposition forces, and as of May 2013, UN General Assembly president Vuk Jeremic estimated that at "least 80,000 have perished since the start of the hostilities, with most of those casualties believed to be civilians" (Nichols, 2013). The UN additionally estimates that at least 4 million Syrians have been displaced by the violence (Abedine et al., 2013).

Despite considerable international concern over the conflict in Syria, there has been division within the United Nations, particularly among the Security Council members, over the extent to which it should intervene. The United States and many other Western governments have condemned the Syrian government's brutal response to the protests, and called for al-Assad to step down from power. They have supported a stronger role for the UN in addressing the violent conflict. Many supporters see UN intervention as supported by the UN Charter, which envisions the protection of human rights as the responsibility of global society. Unanimously adopted by UN members in 2005, the *Responsibility to Protect* doctrine also calls for intervention by the international community if a state fails to protect its citizens from war crimes, ethnic cleansing, genocide, and crimes against humanity.

However, critics of intervention argue that action motivated by nonhumanitarian reasons is in contradiction to the UN Charter, which rests on the principle of sovereignty and prohibits forceful intervention that violates the political independence and territorial integrity of any state. China and Russia have opposed UN actions that they see as constituting intervention into the internal concerns of a sovereign state. Although they have joined the United States and others in calling for a peace process that would bring an end to the civil war, they repeatedly have used their veto rights as members of the UN Security Council to block decisive UN action beyond the supervision mission already in place (UN, 2012). Russia has explicitly criticized UN resolutions, such as the one passed by the UN Human Rights Council in May 2013 that condemned the intervention of foreign combatants on the government's side, as, according to Russian Foreign Minister Sergey Lavrov, "odious and one-sided."

This gridlock, and the United Nation's inability to stop the violence in Syria, raises questions about the efficacy of the organization. It also highlights the tension between a state's sovereign authority over its territory, its responsibility to protect and provide for the compelling needs of its own people, and the grounds for intervention by the international community.

WATCH THE VIDEO:

Carnegie Council Video:
Ethics and Humanitarian
Intervention

(Continued)

THE UNITED NATIONS AND THE SYRIAN CIVIL WAR (Continued)

YOU DECIDE:

1. In humanitarian crises, should the principle of sovereignty be superseded by a responsibility to protect? If so, who should intervene?

2. Do you think that the structure of the Security Council reflects the current power distribution in the world? Should it be changed? Does the UN Security Council have the authority and legitimacy to make these decisions, especially in light of the potential for gridlock?

3. Do you think that the United Nations should intervene in Syria?

Other Prominent Global IGOs

Beyond the UN, literally hundreds of other IGOs are active internationally. We look briefly at three of the most prominent of these other IGOs, all of which are specialized in their focus on the international political economy: the World Trade Organization (WTO), the World Bank, and the International Monetary Fund (IMF).

Note that each of these IGOs was created by the great powers in response to the great powers' need for a stable international economic order even though it required the voluntary sacrifice of sovereignty. Why, one may ask, would states give up some of their autonomy, when that surrender reduces some of their control over their destiny? The primary reason is that multilateral cooperation enables those cooperating states to receive benefits that they would not otherwise receive. The creation of international *regimes*, as well as authoritative IGO institutions for global governance, can pay dividends. Shared problems often cannot be managed without multilateral cooperation. Unilateral measures on many issues by even the most powerful great power acting independently simply will not work.

regimes

Norms, rules, and procedures for interaction agreed to by a set of states.

The World Trade Organization   Remembering the hardships caused by the Great Depression of 1929, after World War II the United States sought to create international economic institutions that would prevent another depression by promoting world trade. One proposed institution was the International Trade Organization (ITO), first conceived as a specialized agency within the overall framework of the UN. While negotiations for the anticipated ITO were dragging on, many people urged immediate action. These calls led to a meeting in 1947 in Geneva where 23 states agreed to a number of bilateral tariff concessions between two states. These treaties were written into a final act called the General Agreement on Tariffs and Trade (GATT), which was originally thought of as a temporary arrangement until the ITO came into operation.

When a final agreement on the ITO proved elusive, GATT provided a mechanism for continued multilateral negotiations on reducing tariffs and other barriers to trade. Over the next several decades, eight rounds of negotiations were held to liberalize trade. Under the principle of nondiscrimination, GATT members were to give the same treatment to each other as they gave to their "most favored" trading partner.

On January 1, 1995, GATT was superseded by the World Trade Organization (WTO). Although it was not exactly what the ITO envisaged immediately following World War II, it nevertheless represents the most ambitious tariff-reduction institution yet. Unlike GATT, the WTO is a full-fledged IGO with formal decision-making procedures. Mandated to manage disputes arising from its trading partners, the WTO has been given authority to enforce trading rules and to adjudicate trade disputes.

The WTO now seeks to transcend the existing matrix of free-trade agreements between pairs of countries and within particular regions or free-trade blocs and replace them with an integrated and comprehensive worldwide system of liberal or free trade. This liberal agenda poses a threat to some states. At the heart of their complaint is that the WTO undermines the traditional rule of law that prohibits interfering in sovereign states' domestic affairs, including management of economic practices within the states' territorial jurisdiction. However, it should be kept in mind that the WTO developed as a result of voluntary agreements states reached to surrender some of their sovereign decision-making freedom, under the conviction that this pooling of sovereignty would produce more gains than losses. Nonetheless, the WTO is criticized because "there is little evidence of democracy within the WTO operations" (Smith and Moran, 2001). Just as with the United Nations, many of its policies are orchestrated by its most powerful members, often during informal meetings that do not include the full WTO membership.

The World Bank   In July 1944 at the United Nations Monetary and Financial Conference held in Bretton Woods, New Hampshire, 44 countries created the World Bank (or International Bank for Reconstruction and Development), which was originally established to support reconstruction efforts in Europe after World War II. Over the next decade, the bank shifted its attention from reconstruction to developmental assistance. Because Global South countries often have difficulty borrowing money to finance projects aimed at promoting economic growth, the bank offers them loans with lower interest rates and longer repayment plans than they could typically obtain from commercial banks. Most recently, the World Bank has set a goal to end extreme poverty throughout the world by 2030. It seeks "to reduce extreme poverty to 3 percent globally and targets the bottom 40 percent of people living in each country in the developing world" (Wroughton, 2013). Thus far, this ambitious goal has met with praise from the donor countries.

Administratively, ultimate decision-making authority in the World Bank is vested in a board of governors, consisting of a governor and an alternate appointed by each of the Bank's 188 member countries. A governor customarily is a member country's minister of finance or an equivalent official. The board meets annually in the Bank's Washington, DC, headquarters to set policy directions and delegate responsibility for the routine operations of the Bank to the 24 directors of its executive board. The five countries with the largest number of shares in the World Bank's capital stock (the United States, Germany, Japan, France, and the United Kingdom) appoint their own executive directors, and the remaining executive directors are either appointed (Saudi Arabia), elected by their states (China, Russia, and Switzerland), or elected by groups of countries. This weighted voting system recognizes the differences among members' holdings systems and protects the interests of the great powers that make more substantial contributions to the World Bank's resources. If a country's economic situation changes over time, its quota is adjusted and its allocation of shares and votes changes accordingly.

Over the years, both the self-image and operations of the World Bank have changed—from a strictly financial IGO to now assisting states' development planning and training. Jim Yong Kim, who became the World Bank president in July 2012, declared his commitment to seeing that the World Bank "delivers more powerful results to support sustained growth; prioritizes evidence-based solutions over ideology; amplifies the voices of developing countries; and draws on the expertise and experience of the people" served by the World Bank (Lowrey, 2012, p. B3).

The World Bank's success in addressing poverty has been attributed in part to the introduction of Poverty Reduction Strategy (PRS) programs that include input from the poor themselves (Blackmon, 2008). Now, with a poverty reduction target date of 2030, the World Bank is aggressively pursuing innovative ways to address such a pressing issue. Recently, Jim Yong Kim praised a new portable ATM program in India to better dispense wages, saying "On a larger scale we've got to think about how we can integrate this technology into a massive effort to scale up access to financial services" (World Bank, 2013d). The World Bank also has participated increasingly in consortium arrangements for financing private lending institutions while insisting that democratic reforms are made a condition for economic assistance. Additionally, with charges of bribery, kickbacks, and embezzlement being leveled against World Bank projects, from road building in Kenya to dam construction in Lesotho, the last three bank presidents (James Wolfensohn, Paul Wolfowitz, and Robert Zoellick) have insisted on anticorruption reforms as well.

Yet the World Bank is not able to meet all of the financial assistance needs for developing states. The deficiencies of the World Bank, however, have been partly offset by the International Monetary Fund, another lending IGO.

RAGE AGAINST INSTITUTIONAL SYMBOLS OF GLOBALIZATION
In the recent past, protesters targeted the high-profile meetings of two powerful IGOs—the World Bank and International Monetary Fund. Seen here is one such outburst, when the meeting of the WTO mobilized a broad-based coalition of NGOs to criticize the impact of economic globalization. In recent years, however, the number of demonstrations has declined. Political scientist Daniel Drezner (2010c) speculates that this may be due to the controversial role of global finance (as opposed to trade) in the 2008 financial crisis and the subsequent global recession, as well as the WTO's inability to further liberalization measures first introduced in 2001 at the Fourth Ministerial Conference held in Doha, Qatar.

The International Monetary Fund
Before World War II, the international community lacked institutional mechanisms to manage the exchange of money across borders. At the 1944 Bretton Woods Conference, the United States was a prime mover in creating the International Monetary Fund (IMF), a truly global IGO designed to

maintain currency exchange stability by promoting international monetary cooperation and orderly exchange arrangements. Further, the IMF sometimes functions as a lender of last resort for countries experiencing financial crises.

The IMF is now one of the sixteen specialized agencies within the UN system. Each IMF member is represented on its governing board, which meets annually to fix general policy. Day-to-day business is conducted by a 24-member executive board chaired by a managing director, who is also the administrative head of a staff of approximately 2000 employees.

The IMF derives its operating funds from its 188 member states. Contributions are based on a quota system set according to a state's national income, monetary reserves, and other factors affecting each member's ability to contribute. In this way, the IMF operates like a credit union that requires each participant to contribute to a common pool of funds from which it can borrow when the need arises. The IMF's voting is weighted according to a state's monetary contribution, giving a larger voice to the wealthier states.

The IMF attaches strict conditions to its loans (See "Controversy: The IMF, World Bank, and Structural Adjustment Policies—Is the 'Cure' Worse Than the 'Disease'?" in Chapter 10), which has led to considerable criticism, as IMF loan programs have been linked to slower economic growth (Vreeland, 2003) as well as increased human rights violations (Abouharb and Cingranelli, 2007). Joseph Stiglitz, a Nobel laureate in economics and former chief economist of the World Bank, complains that the policies produce disappointing results because they are anchored in a free-market dogma that ignores the unique sociocultural contexts of the countries where they are applied. Given the diversity of the Global South, development strategies for the future should avoid grandiose claims of universality and one-size-fits-all policies. What works in one country may be impractical or undesirable in another.

REGIONAL INTERGOVERNMENTAL ORGANIZATIONS

The tug of war between individual states and groups of states within the UN, the WTO, the World Bank, and the IMF are reminders of an underlying principle that IGOs are run by the states that join them. This severely inhibits the IGOs' ability to rise above interstate competition and independently pursue their organizational purposes. For this reason, universal IGOs are often viewed from a *realist* perspective as instruments of their members' foreign policies and arenas for debate than as independent nonstate actors. When states dominate universal international organizations like the UN, the prospects for international cooperation can decline because, as realism emphasizes, states are fearful of multilateral organizations that compromise their vital national interests. This limits a given IGO's ability to foster multilateral decision making to engineer global change.

A rival hypothesis—that cooperation among powerful states is possible and international organizations help produce it—emerges from *liberal* theory. From this perspective, the "reality of a world of interconnected and transnational threats is a simple one: You have to cooperate with others to get them to cooperate with you" (Jones et al., 2009, p. 5). This viewpoint is widely applicable to regional intergovernmental organizations, most notably the *European Union (EU)*. The EU

Animated Learning Module:
International Organizations and Transnational Actors

European Union (EU)

A regional organization created by the merger of the European Coal and Steel Community, the European Atomic Energy Community, and the European Economic Community (called the European Community until 1993) that has since expanded geographically and in its authority.

Carnegie Council Video:
European Union

security community

A group of states whose high level of institutionalized or customary collaboration results in the settlement of disputes by compromise rather than by military force.

serves as a model for other regional IGOs to emulate as the globe's most successful example of peaceful cross-border cooperation that has produced an integrated *security community* with a single economy. In addition, the EU's dedication to liberal democratic governance and capitalist free markets, as well as its emphasis on searching for a *Third Way* to alleviate human suffering, is paving an approach that other regional IGOs are pursuing.

The European Union

The EU is not, strictly speaking, a freestanding supranational organization for the collective management of European domestic and foreign affairs. The EU coexists with a large number of other European IGOs in which it is nested and with which it jointly makes decisions. Of these, the Organization for Security and Cooperation in Europe (OSCE) and the Council of Europe stand as regional institutions of equal European partners, free of dividing lines, designed to manage regional security and promote the human rights of minorities through democratization. Even within this overlapping network of European IGOs, the EU stands out as the example of how a powerful organization has transformed itself from a single- to a multiple-purpose nonstate actor.

Third Way

An approach to governance advocated primarily by many European leaders who, although recognizing few alternatives to liberal capitalism, seek to soften the cruel social impact of free-market individualism by allowing government intervention in order to preserve social justice and prevent the deprivations caused by disruptions in the global economy.

EU Expansion and Political Integration As *constructivism* argues, ideas have consequences. Big ideas often come from painful experiences and crises, such as devastating wars. That is what happened after World War II—European leaders conceived of a bold plan to eradicate the curse of war by removing the incentives for war. Their reform program aimed at the *political integration* of Europe to build a new supranational institution that transcended individual European states—to seek nothing less than the *transformation* of international relations from instruments of states to institutions over them.

European integration began with the European Coal and Steel Community (ECSC) in 1951, the European Atomic Energy Community (Euratom) in 1957, and the European Economic Community (EEC) in 1957. These initiatives centered on trade development. Since the late 1960s, the three have shared a common organization and, through successive steps, have enlarged the EU's mission, becoming "the European Community." The EU's membership grew, and its geographical scope broadened as it expanded in a series of waves to encompass 15 countries by 1997: Belgium, France, Germany, Italy, Luxembourg, and the Netherlands (the original "six"); Denmark, Ireland, and the United Kingdom (which joined in 1973); Greece (1981); Portugal and Spain (1986); and Austria, Finland, and Sweden (1995). In 2004, the EU reached a new milestone in its path toward enlargement when it formally admitted 10 new members (the Czech Republic, Slovakia, Estonia, Hungary, Latvia, Lithuania, Malta, Poland, Slovenia, and the Greek-controlled part of Cyprus). This bold enlargement added 75 million people to create the globe's biggest free-trade bloc and transformed the face of Europe by ending the continent's division. That enlargement process continued when Bulgaria and Romania joined in 2007 and Croatia in 2013, to bring the EU to 28 members (see Map 6.2).

political integration

The processes and activities by which the populations of many or all states transfer their loyalties to a merged political and economic unit.

Carnegie Council Video:
Political Integration

Further expansion is also conceivable because the admission procedures for possible new membership are currently under way for eight additional countries. Turkey began accession talks in 2005, and could be admitted between 2015 and 2020. Other countries in the western Balkans—Albania, Serbia, Montenegro, Kosovo, the former Yugoslav Republic of Macedonia, and Bosnia and Herzegovina—are also lobbying for future membership. In 2009, Iceland, a

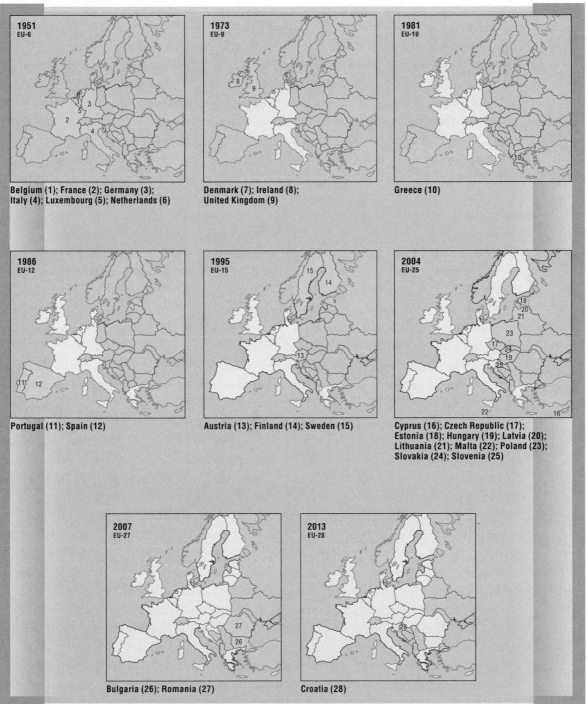

1951
EU-6

Belgium (1); France (2); Germany (3);
Italy (4); Luxembourg (5); Netherlands (6)

1973
EU-9

Denmark (7); Ireland (8);
United Kingdom (9)

1981
EU-10

Greece (10)

1986
EU-12

Portugal (11); Spain (12)

1995
EU-15

Austria (13); Finland (14); Sweden (15)

2004
EU-25

Cyprus (16); Czech Republic (17);
Estonia (18); Hungary (19); Latvia (20);
Lithuania (21); Malta (22); Poland (23);
Slovakia (24); Slovenia (25)

2007
EU-27

Bulgaria (26); Romania (27)

2013
EU-28

Croatia (28)

Based on "Few to Many: The Expansion of the European Union, 1951-2005," Wall St. Journal Europe, May 3, 2004, p. A6.

MAP 6.2   FROM FEW TO MANY: THE EXPANSION OF THE EUROPEAN UNION, 1951–2014 The European Union is the premier example of the formation and integrative growth of a supranational regional IGO. It has grown in seven expansions from six members in 1951 to 27 in 2007, as shown here, and eight other countries, such as Croatia and Turkey, as waiting in the wings. Expansion has enabled the EU to position itself to become a true superpower (see Chapter 4).

state that would give increased access to the resource-rich Artic, applied for membership with a targeted date of 2011 for acceptance into the block. However, accession talks stalled due to dispute over mackerel fishing and the sensitive issue of financial reform.

EU expansion is not simply a procedure for enlarging membership; it has become a foreign policy in that the process seeks to transform external applicants into member states. As Christophe Hellion (2010, p. 6), a professor of European law, notes, the expansion procedure has allowed the European Union "to exercise its normative power, and to organize the continent in its own image." Having such a transformative effect, it is hardly surprising that even EU expansion does not escape controversy. Nationalism has crept into the process in recent years, with legal and political hurdles that call into question the sincerity and credibility of EU commitments to states that aspire to membership. "It may also compromise the integrity of the Treaty provisions and conflict with fundamental principles of EU law, not least the very goal of European (re)unification reaffirmed by the Treaty of Lisbon" (Hellion, 2010, p. 6).

There are numerous challenges to continued expansion and integration. For one, the prospect of a populous Muslim Turkey joining the EU raises fundamental questions about Europe's identity. As constructivist theorists point out, identities shape how agents envision their interests and, in turn, how they act. The possible entry of Turkey and, perhaps, more remote and culturally different countries would have major implications for the way many people, especially within the six Western founders of the EU, conceive of Europe.

These nationalistic inclinations were further reflected in calls for revision of the Schengen rules as thousands of North Africans sought refuge during the protests and violence of the "Arab spring" in 2011—as well as Syrian refugees seeking safety in Europe since then. The migration crisis threatened the viability of the Schengen borderless zone, which is seen as one of the great unification projects as it allows freedom of movement within the EU. Italy, France, and Belgium, have called for the rules to be "revised so that national governments can more easily reimpose border controls" under exceptional circumstances (*The Economist*, 2011a, p. 57), as each sought to control the flow of North African illegal migrants between their countries.

EU enlargement through eastward expansion is further challenged by the fact that the twelve newest members, whose combined economies are less than 10 percent of that of the entire EU, have poorer economies and smaller populations than the previous 15 EU members. As a result, these new members have different needs and interests that can make reaching agreements on policy decisions increasingly difficult. This was dramatically evident in 2010 as Greece negotiated with the EU and the IMF for a three-year economic bailout package—the first for a Eurozone state—in exchange for austerity measures. This deal sparked the first deadly violent protests in Greece in 20 years.

There are also concerns about weak economic conditions and rising government deficits in some countries, and the burden this may place on other members of the EU. Anti-euro feelings are on the rise in a number of member countries in northern Europe, where resistance to tax-payer-funded bailout for crisis-hit eurozone countries is growing (Ward, 2011). At the beginning of 2013, the Eurobarometer, a public opinion survey of Europeans, indicated that only 30 percent of European approve of the EU. This number has fallen from the 52 percent approval rating just five years earlier (Spiegel, 2013). If Germany, France, and other northern European countries join together to oppose the smaller, less developed new members, a "club within a club" could split the EU into two opposed coalitions. Nevertheless, the idea of a single, integrated Europe is compelling for those who are haunted by the specter of European nationalities and states that have been fighting each other ever since the Pax Romana collapsed 1800 years ago.

EU Organization and Management   As the EU has grown and expanded its authority, its principal institutions for governance have changed. As shown in Figure 6.3, the EU organization includes a Council of Ministers, the European Commission, a European Parliament, and a Court of Justice.

The EU's central administrative unit, the Council of Ministers, represents the governments of the EU's member states and retains final authority over policy-making decisions. The Council sets general policy guidelines for the *European Commission*, which consists of 32 commissioners (two each from Britain, France, Germany, Italy, and Spain, and one each from the other member states). Commissioners are nominated by EU member governments and must be approved by the European Parliament. Headquartered in Brussels, the primary functions of the European Commission are to propose new laws for the EU, oversee the negotiation

European Commission

The executive organ administratively responsible for the European Union.

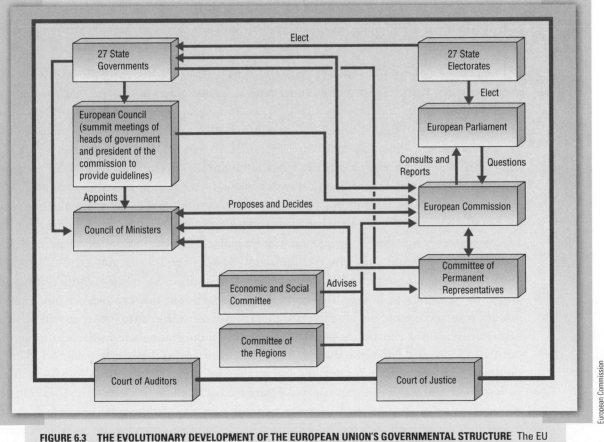

FIGURE 6.3   THE EVOLUTIONARY DEVELOPMENT OF THE EUROPEAN UNION'S GOVERNMENTAL STRUCTURE The EU is a complex organization, with different responsibilities performed by various units. The figure illustrates the principal institutions and the relationships among them that collectively lead to EU decisions and policies.

European Commission

of EU treaties, execute the European Council's decrees, and manage the EU's budget (which, in contrast with those of most international organizations, derives part of its revenues from sources not under the control of member states).

The European Parliament represents the political parties and public opinion within Europe. It has existed since the beginning of Europe's journey toward political unification, although it was initially appointed rather than elected and had little power. That is no longer the case. The citizens of the EU's member states now choose the European Parliament in a direct election. Its more than 600 deputies debate issues at the monumental glass headquarters in Brussels and at its lavish Strasbourg palace in the same way that democratic national legislative bodies do. The European Parliament shares authority with the Council of Ministers, but the Parliament's influence has increased over time. The elected deputies pass laws with the council, approve the EU's budget, and oversee the European Commission, whose decisions the Parliament can overturn.

The European Court of Justice in Luxembourg has also grown to prominence and power as European integration has developed. The court was founded to adjudicate claims and conflicts among EU governments as well as between those governments and the new institutions the EU created. The court interprets EU law for national courts, rules on legal questions that arise within the EU's institutions, and decides cases concerning individual citizens. The fact that its decisions are binding distinguishes the European Court of Justice from most other international tribunals.

EU Decision-Making Challenges

Disagreement persists over the extent to which the EU should become a single, truly united superstate, a "United States of Europe." Debate continues also over how far and how fast such a process toward *pooled sovereignty* should proceed, and several efforts to further integrate the countries of Europe have met with resistance—the Danes rejected the Maastricht Treaty in 1992, the Irish rejected the Nice Treaty in 2001, and the French and Dutch rejected the EU Constitution in 2005. The leaders of the 27 member states agreed to a final draft of the most recent initiative, the Lisbon Treaty, in October 2007. It was presented as an institutional treaty that would streamline the decision-making process for the EU by creating a full-time president and a single foreign policy chief to represent the EU governments as a whole. It would also discard national vetoes in a number of areas, change members' voting weights, and give the European Parliament additional powers.

While proponents of the Lisbon Treaty argued that institutional reform is critical if expansion is to continue and Europe is to be a unified global power that can balance other major powers, resistance within the EU indicated that many were satisfied with the status quo. These detractors remained reluctant to pursue deeper political integration and further constrain the pursuit of individual national self-interest, and concerned about the extent to which EU decision making is democratic. Ratification was required by all 27 member states for the treaty to go into force and was initially anticipated before the end of 2008. However, the Irish initially rejected the treaty in a national referendum, leading to speculation that there was not sufficient popular support for a federal Europe. This decision was reversed during a subsequent referendum in October 2009, and with the final ratification by the Czech Republic, the Lisbon Treaty became law on December 1, 2009. Belgian Herman Van Rompuy became the EU's first full-time president and began his first official working day on January 4, 2010.

pooled sovereignty

Legal authority granted to an IGO by its members to make collective decisions regarding specified aspects of public policy heretofore made exclusively by each sovereign government.

These issues will be debated in the future, and only time will tell how they will be resolved. That said, the EU represents a remarkable success story in international history. Who would have expected that the competitive states that had spent most of their national experiences waging war against one another would put their clashing ideological and territorial ambitions aside and construct a "European-ness" identity built on unity and confederated decision making?

Other Regional IGOs

Since Europe's initial steps toward integration in the 1950s, more than a dozen regional IGOs have been created in other parts of the world, notably among states in Global South. Most seek to stimulate regional economic growth, but many have expanded from that original single purpose to pursue multiple political and military purposes as well. The major regional organizations include:

- **The Asia Pacific Economic Cooperation (APEC) forum**. Created in 1989 as a gathering of twelve states without a defined goal, APEC's membership has grown to twenty-one countries (including the United States). In October 2013 in Bali, Indonesia, APEC held its meeting of economic leaders to further discuss how to promote regional economic integration, achieve shared development and common prosperity, secure inclusive sustainable growth, and cultivate the enormous potential that Asia-Pacific partnerships hold for companies and workers in the region.

- **The Association of Southeast Asian Nations (ASEAN)**. This organization was established in 1967 by five founding members to promote regional economic, social, and cultural cooperation. In 1999, it created a free-trade zone among its ten Southeast Asian members as a counterweight outside the orbit of Japan, China, the United States, and other great powers so that ASEAN could compete as a bloc in international trade.

- **The Council of Arab Economic Unity (CAEU)**. This organization was established in 1964 from a 1957 accord to promote trade and economic integration among its 18 North African and Middle Eastern members.

- **The Caribbean Community (CARICOM)**. This organization was established in 1973 as a common market to promote economic development and integration among its 15 country and territory members.

- **The Economic Community of West African States (ECOWAS)**. This organization was established in 1975 to promote regional economic cooperation among its fifteen members, it has a much larger agenda today. On June 7, 2011, the president of ECOWAS, H. E. James Victor Gbeho, reaffirmed the organization's commitment "to scale up and to strengthen institutions, reform the security system to make it more responsive to democratic control and human rights; and ensure greater separation of powers, adherence to the rule of law and anti-corruption principles."

- **The Latin American Integration Association (LAIA)**. Also known as Asociación Latinoamericana de Integración (ALADI), this organization was established in 1980 to promote and regulate reciprocal trade among its 14 members.

■ **The North Atlantic Treaty Organization (NATO).** This is a military alliance created in 1949 primarily to deter the Soviet Union's activities in Western Europe. The security IGO has expanded its membership to 28 countries and broadened its mission to promote democratization and to police civil wars and terrorism outside its traditional territory within Europe. The United States and Canada are also members.

■ **The Southern African Development Community (SADC).** This organization was established in 1992 to promote regional economic development and integration and to alleviate poverty among its 14 members.

As these examples illustrate, most IGOs are organized on a regional rather than global basis. The governments that create them usually concentrate on one or two major goals (such as liberalizing trade or promoting peace within the region) instead of attempting to address the complete range of issues that they face in common all at once.

The substantial difficulty most regions have experienced in pursuing the EU's level of institutional integration suggests the enormity of the obstacles to creating new political communities out of previously divided ones. The particular reasons why many regional IGOs sometimes fail and are often ineffective vary. It is not enough that two or more countries choose to interact cooperatively. Chances of political integration wane in the absence of geographical proximity, steady economic growth, similar political systems, supportive public opinion led by enthusiastic leaders, cultural homogeneity, internal political stability, similar experiences in historical and internal social development, compatible economic systems with supportive business interests, a shared perception of a common external threat, bureaucratic compatibilities, and previous collaborative efforts (Deutsch, 1957).

At the root of the barriers is one bottom line: all IGOs are limited by national leaders' reluctance to make politically costly choices that would undermine their personal popularity at home and their governments' sovereignty. Nonetheless, regional ventures in cooperation demonstrate that many states accept the fact that they cannot individually manage many of the problems that confront them collectively. IGOs' expanding webs of interdependence are infringing on the power of states and changing the ways in which they network on the global stage. Because the state is clearly failing to manage many transnational policy problems, collective problem solving through IGOs is likely to continue.

IGOs are not, however, the only nonstate actors leading the potential transformation of world politics. Another set of agents is nongovernmental organizations (NGOs). They include transnational humanitarian organizations, multinational corporations, transnational religions and ethnic groups, and global terrorist and criminal networks. Such NGOs are growing in number and roaring with voices too loud to ignore, making them increasingly influential in world politics. Next we will evaluate their behavior and global impact.

The world's 190-plus states now co-exist with a larger number of powerful non-sovereign and at least partly (and often largely) independent actors, ranging from corporations to non-government organizations (NGOs), from terrorist groups to drug cartels ... The near monopoly of power once enjoyed by sovereign entities is being eroded.

—Richard N. Haass, the Foreign Relations Council president

PROMINENT TYPES OF NONGOVERNMENTAL ORGANIZATIONS

Increasing numbers of people have found that through joining nongovernmental organizations (NGOs), they can influence international decision-making. They have chosen to become international decision makers themselves by electing to join one or more NGOs. These tens of thousands of "transitional activists" are influencing the policies of state governments and intergovernmental organizations (IGOs) through a variety of strategies. As a result, NGO activism is transcending the traditional distinctions between what is local and what is global (Tarrow, 2006).

Today, a small subset of increasingly active and self-assertive NGOs receives the most attention and provokes the most controversy. To evaluate if and how NGOs are contributing to global changes, *World Politics* will ask you to examine only four of the most visibly active NGO nonstate actors: *nonstate nations* that include ethnic nationalities and indigenous peoples, transnational religious movements, multinational corporations, and issue-advocacy groups.

Nonstate Nations: Ethnic Groups and Indigenous Peoples

Realists often ask us to picture the all-powerful state as an autonomous ruler of a unified nation, that is, as a *unitary actor*. But, in truth, that construction can be misleading. Most states are divided internally and are highly penetrated from abroad, and few states are tightly unified and capable of acting as a single body with a common purpose.

Although the state unquestionably remains the most visible global actor, as constructivism emphasizes, *ethnic nationalism* (people's loyalty to and identification with a particular ethnic nationality group) reduces the relevance of theories that assume a unitary state. Many states are divided, multiethnic and multicultural societies made up of a variety of politically active groups that seek, if not outright independence, a greater level of regional autonomy and a greater voice in the domestic and foreign policies of the state. Individuals who think nationalistically are very likely to pledge their primary allegiance not to the state and the government that rules them but, rather, to a politically active *ethnic group* whose members identify with one another because they perceive themselves as bound together by kinship, language, and a common culture.

Ethnicity is socially constructed in that members of an ethnic or racial group learn to see themselves as members of that group and thereby perceive their identity as determined by their inherited membership at birth. That perception is likely to be strongly reinforced when recognized by other ethnic groups. Hence, ethnicity is in the eye of the beholder—a constructed identity. "Identity or, more accurately, *identities* are generated in response to the specific historical and social context in which a group or individual is located. These identities, even in the plural, are usually very easily negotiated by their owners and are context-specific. Still there is an aspect of identity that is permanent and enduring regardless of the situation and which identity is most prevalent at any particular time" (Townsend-Bell, 2007).

Three-fourths of the world's larger countries are estimated to contain politically significant minorities, and since 1998, 283 minority groups, comprising 18.5 percent (over one-sixth) of

nonstate nations

National or ethnic groups struggling to obtain power and/or statehood.

Carnegie Council Video:
Nonstate Nations

ethnic nationalism

Devotion to a cultural, ethnic, or linguistic community.

ethnic group

People whose identity is primarily defined by their sense of sharing a common ancestral nationality, language, cultural heritage, and kinship.

Carnegie Council Video:
Ethnic Group

ethnicity

Perceptions of likeness among members of a particular racial grouping leading them to prejudicially view other nationality groups as outsiders.

the world population, have been classified as "at risk" from persecution by the state in which they reside and have mobilized for collective defense against the governments they perceive as perpetuating organized discriminatory treatment (Minorities At Risk, 2013). China came under intense international criticism for its crackdown on ethnic Tibetan groups following rioting in Lhasa, the Tibetan capital. Representing Tibetan interests, the Dalai Lama sought renewed talks with China in "the interest of stability, unity and harmony of all nationalities in the People's Republic of China." The Chinese, however, see him as a "splittist," after the spiritual leader fled Tibet in 1959 following a failed armed uprising against Chinese communist rule (Freeman, 2010). Ethnic divisions such as these challenge the realist "billiard ball" conception of international relations as homogeneous interactions between unified states.

Indigenous peoples are ethnic and cultural groups that are native populations to a particular area. In most cases, indigenous people were at one time politically sovereign and economically self-sufficient, but are now controlled by a state government. Today an estimated 370 million indigenous people, or about 5.2 percent of the world's population, are scattered in more than seventy countries (International Work Group for Indigenous Affairs, 2013).

The number of distinct nonstate nations is usually measured by the number of known spoken languages because each language provides an ethnic and cultural identity (see Map 6.3). As

indigenous peoples

The native ethnic and cultural inhabitant populations within countries ruled by a government controlled by others.

Carnegie Council Video: Indigenous Peoples

Case Study: International Law and Organization: Indigenous Peoples

YASUYOSHI CHIBA/AFP/Getty Images

PROTECTING INDIGENOUS PEOPLES Indigenous groups have frequently found their rights and welfare to fall victim to a larger national interest in progress and development as determined by the state government. Pictured here, representatives of local indigenous communities demonstrate in May 2013 in Sao Paulo, Brazil, against the construction of the Belo Monte dam at the Xingu River in the Brazilian Amazon. Concerned about the impact on their lands and livelihoods, "frustrated at the lack of consultation and angry at the assault on their rights, Brazil's indigenous people have resorted to direct action storming congress, occupying dam sites, blockading railway lines, reclaiming sacred land, mounting hungers strikes, and committing suicide" (Watson, 2013).

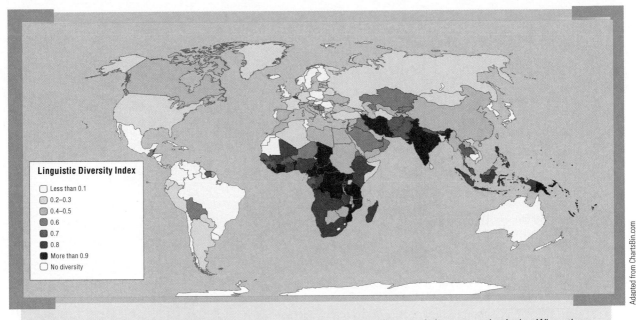

Linguistic Diversity Index

☐ Less than 0.1
☐ 0.2–0.3
☐ 0.4–0.5
☐ 0.6
☐ 0.7
☐ 0.8
☐ More than 0.9
☐ No diversity

MAP 6.3 **ETHNOLINGUISTIC DIVISIONS** Differences in language often reflect differences in interests and attitudes. Where there is great diversity, state governments face a formidable challenge to reconcile these differences and generate common identity and goals—and "empirical cross-country studies suggest that linguistic fractionalization hurts economic performance" and quality of government (WDR, 2009, p. 104). As shown here, the diversity of ethnic language groups in Africa and South Asia is very high.

Edward Sapir and Benjamin Lee Whorf hypothesized in the 1930s, different languages reflect different views of the world that predispose their speakers toward different ways of thought. By this index, indigenous cultures are disappearing. "Some experts maintain that 90 percent of the world's languages will vanish or be replaced by dominant languages by the end of this century" (*Vital Signs, 2006–2007*, p. 112). What this means is that indigenous peoples are at risk, with high percentages nearing extinction.

Although indigenous peoples are located *within* many of the globe's pluralistic states, they also have a transnational dimension because they are geographically spread *across* existing state boundaries. This dispersion has increased as indigenous peoples have migrated across borders from their ancestral homelands. For example, indigenous peoples such as the sizable Kurdish minorities of Turkey, Iraq, Iran, and Syria have members living in more than one of the globe's existing independent states, but as yet there is no single sovereign country the Kurds can call their home.

As a result of these divisions, as many as 11 separate transnational cultural identities, or "civilizations," can be identified across the globe (see Map 6.4). The consequences are not certain, but some possibilities for world politics are alarming. Samuel P. Huntington (1996, 2001a) pessimistically predicts the most troubling outcome: that a *clash of civilizations* is likely between some of these civilization identities, especially between the West and Islam.

That prediction proved rather prophetic on September 11, 2001, when the Al Qaeda terrorist network attacked the United States to vent the anger of its extremist Islamic members against the West. "What recent events demonstrate is that ethnicity, and race [and cultural conflict] are issues that are not disappearing and becoming less important.... Recent processes of global change, often glossed under the term globalization, are rapidly changing the contexts

clash of civilizations

Political scientist Samuel Huntington's controversial thesis that in the twenty-first century the globe's major civilizations will conflict with one another, leading to anarchy and warfare similar to that resulting from conflicts between states over the past 500 years.

Case Study:
The End of History or the Clash of Civilizations?

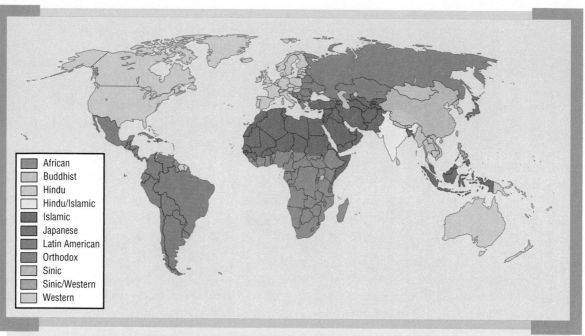

Huntington 1999b, p. 17.

MAP 6.4   THE WORLD'S MAJOR CIVILIZATIONS: WILL THEIR CLASH CREATE GLOBAL DISORDER?   This map shows the location of the world's major civilizations according to the much-debated thesis of Samuel P. Huntington, who predicts that future global war is likely to result from a "clash of civilizations." Critics of this thesis point out that no "civilization" is homogeneous in language or beliefs, that the characteristics of any civilization fail to predict how individual people identified with it will act, and that even identity groups such as distinct cultures have often learned to speak to one another across their differences and to coexist peacefully (Appiah, 2006; Huntington, 1999b; Sen, 2006).

under which ethnic [and cultural] conflict arises [which] are no longer, if they ever were, entirely local" (T. Hall, 2004, p. 150). For that reason, we now turn from ethnic group NGOs to an examination of the ways religious movements may operate as NGOs as well.

Transnational Religious Movements

Ideally, religion would seem a natural worldwide force for global unity and harmony. Yet millions have died in the name of religion. The Crusades, which took place between the eleventh and fourteenth centuries, originally were justified by Pope Urban II in 1095 to combat Muslim aggression, but the fighting left millions of Christians and Muslims dead and, "in terms of atrocities, the two sides were about even [as both religions embraced] an ideology in which fighting was an act of self-sanctification" (Riley-Smith, 1995). Similarly, the religious conflicts during the Thirty Years' War (1618–1648) between Catholics and Protestants killed nearly one-fourth of all Europeans.

Most of the world's more than 7 billion people are affiliated at some level with *transnational religious movements*. At the most abstract level, a religion is a system of thought shared by a group that provides its members with an object of devotion and a code of behavior by which they can ethically judge their actions. This definition points to commonalities across the great diversity of organized religions in the world, but the world's principal religions also vary greatly in the theological doctrines and beliefs they embrace. They also differ widely in the size of their followings (see Figure 6.4), the geographical locations where they are most prevalent (see Map 6.5), and the extent to which they engage in political efforts to direct international affairs.

transnational religious movements

A set of beliefs, practices, and ideas administered politically by religious organizations to promote the worship of their conception of a transcendent deity and its principles for conduct.

These differences make it risky to generalize about the impact of religious movements on world affairs (Haynes, 2004). Those who study religious movements comparatively note that a system of belief provides religious followers with their main source of identity, and that this identification with and devotion to their religion springs from the natural human need to find a set of values with which to determine the meaning of life and the consequences of choices. This human need sometimes leads believers to perceive the values of their own religion as superior to those of others, which, sadly, often results in intolerance.

The proponents of most organized religious movements believe their religion should be universal—that is, accepted by everyone throughout the world. To confirm their faith in their religious movement's natural superiority, many organized religions actively proselytize to convert nonbelievers to their faith, engaging in evangelical campaigns to win over nonbelievers and followers of other religions. Conversion is usually achieved through missionary activities. But conversion has, at times, been achieved though the sword, which has tarnished the reputations of some international religious movements (see "Controversy: Are Religious Movements Causes of War or Sources of Transnational Harmony?").

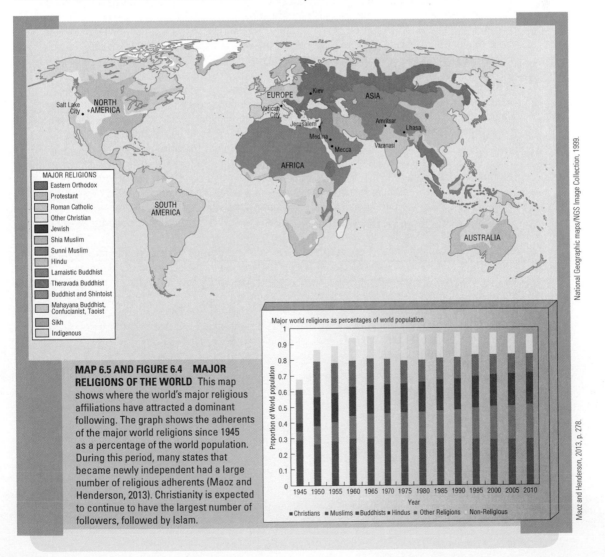

MAJOR RELIGIONS
- Eastern Orthodox
- Protestant
- Roman Catholic
- Other Christian
- Jewish
- Shia Muslim
- Sunni Muslim
- Hindu
- Lamaistic Buddhist
- Theravada Buddhist
- Buddhist and Shintoist
- Mahayana Buddhist, Confucianist, Taoist
- Sikh
- Indigenous

Major world religions as percentages of world population

MAP 6.5 AND FIGURE 6.4   MAJOR RELIGIONS OF THE WORLD This map shows where the world's major religious affiliations have attracted a dominant following. The graph shows the adherents of the major world religions since 1945 as a percentage of the world population. During this period, many states that became newly independent had a large number of religious adherents (Maoz and Henderson, 2013). Christianity is expected to continue to have the largest number of followers, followed by Islam.

National Geographic maps/NGS Image Collection, 1999.

Maoz and Henderson, 2013, p. 278.

ARE RELIGIOUS MOVEMENTS CAUSES OF WAR OR SOURCES OF TRANSNATIONAL HARMONY?

After 9/11, the debate about the impact of religion on international conflict intensified because of the role the Islamic Al Qaeda global terrorist network played in organizing the attack. As a result, the "religious roots of terrorism" (Juergensmeyer, 2003) and religious opposition to democracy in the Global South (Shah, 2004) have received much attention, as have religions and religious bodies acting as NGO global actors more generally (Haynes, 2004).

"To do harm, to promote violence and conflict in the name of religion," said Pope John Paul II in Egypt after fighting between Christians and Muslims led to bloodshed in 2000, "is a terrible contradiction and a great offense against God. But past and present history give us many examples of such misuse of religion." Yet it is difficult to understand the religious origins of violence because most people equate religion with peace, compassion, and forgiveness, not hatred or intolerance. The world's major religious movements voice respect and reverence for the sanctity of life and accept people as equal creations of a deity, regardless of race or color. These are noble ideals.

However, in an age of religious conflict and political violence, the role of religious NGOs in international affairs is controversial. Some hold the view that religious hostility results from the fact that universalistic religions are managed by organizations that often adopt a particularistic and dogmatic outlook (Juergensmeyer, 2003). The virtues that religions uphold can ironically become weapons against those who do not hold such views. In an effort to believe in unshakable doctrines, believers reject the attempt to separate what they wish to be true from what they or other religions think to be true. This constructed reality inspires an ethic that justifies violence, plunder, and conquest. In part, they tend to see outsiders as threatening rivals whose loyalty and allegiance to other deities represents a challenge to their own religion's universal claims. In a word, religious movements often practice intolerance—disrespect for diversity and disregard for the right of people to freely embrace another religion's beliefs.

Yet it is dangerous to accept stereotypes of religious groups as responsible for relentless barrages of terrorism. Paganistic and atheistic societies recognizing no higher deity have equally long histories of waging violent wars against external enemies and their own people. Meanwhile, many religions ably perform the mission of peacemaking, and in fact most religious bodies have historically coexisted peacefully for centuries. Thus, it is important for you to objectively weigh the evidence about the impact of religious NGOs on world affairs.

WHAT DO YOU THINK?

- *If all the world's great religious movements espouse universalistic ideals, why are those same religions increasingly criticized as sources of international conflict—of exclusivism, hatred, terror, and war?*

- *Given that many wars have been fought in the name of religion, how might realism view the impact of religious movements on world politics?*

- *Which global actors are better suited to address the challenges posed to the global community by violent NGOs? Can states respond more effectively, or IGOs? Why?*

In evaluating the impact of religious movements on international affairs, it is important to carefully distinguish between the high ideals of doctrines from the activities of the people who head these religious bodies. The two realms are not the same, and each can be judged fairly only against the standards they set for themselves. To condemn what large-scale religious movements sometimes do administratively when they abuse their own religion's principles does not mean that the principles themselves deserve condemnation. Consider the Hindu ideology of tolerance of different religions, which teaches that there are many paths to truth and accepts pluralism among diverse populations. Similarly, Buddhism preaches pacifism, as did early Christianity, which prohibited Christians from serving in the armies of the Roman Empire (later, by the fourth century, when church and state became allies, only Christians were allowed to join Roman military units).

The relationship between transnational religions and states' governments is a major issue in the global community. In some countries, the two realms are politically separate, with legal protection for freedom of religion and little or no state support for a particular established religion. In many other countries, however, religion and state are tightly linked and almost indistinguishable. In such a country, that is, in a *theocracy*, religious institutions submissively subordinate their religion to state control in order to survive, grow, receive state subsidies, and cement political influence. In these countries, crown and church protect and preserve each other through an alliance.

Most troublesome, however, are radical religious movements that are enraged, militant, and fanatically dedicated to promote their cause globally through violence and terror (Kifner, 2005). The leaders of extreme *militant religious movements* are convinced that those who do not share their convictions must be punished and that compromise is unacceptable. Underlying this perspective, radical religious movements hold some common beliefs and perceptions:

- They view existing government authority as corrupt and illegitimate because it is secular and not sufficiently rigorous in upholding religious authority or religiously sanctioned social and moral values.

- They attack the inability of government to address the domestic ills of society. In many cases, the religious movement substitutes itself for the government at the local level, involving itself in education, health, and other social welfare programs.

- They subscribe to a particular set of behaviors and opinions that they believe political authority must reflect, promote, and protect in all governmental and social activities. This generally means that the government and all of its domestic and foreign activities must be in the hands of believers or subject to their close oversight.

- They are universalists that, unlike ethnic movements, tend to see their views as part of the inheritance of every believer. This tends to give them a trans-state motivation, a factor that then translates their views on legitimacy of political authority into a larger context for action. In some cases, this means that international boundaries are not recognized as barriers to the propagation of the faith, even if this means they must resort to violence.

- They are exclusionists in that they relegate all conflicting opinions on appropriate political and social order to the margins—if they do not exclude them altogether. This translates as second-class citizenship for any nonbeliever in any society where such a view dominates social and political thought (Shultz and Olson, 1994, pp. 9–10).

theocracy

A country whose government is organized around a religious dogma.

CourseMate

Carnegie Council Video:
Theocracy

militant religious movements

Politically active organizations based on strong religious convictions, whose members are fanatically devoted to the global promotion of their religious beliefs.

CourseMate

Carnegie Council Video:
Militant Religious Movements

Militant religious movements tend to stimulate five specific types of international activities. The first is *irredentism*—the attempt by a dominant religion (or ethnic group) to reclaim previously possessed territory in an adjacent region from a foreign state that now controls it, often through the use of force. The second is *secession*, or *separatist revolts*—the attempt by a religious (or ethnic) minority to revolt and break away from an internationally recognized state. Third, militant religions tend to cause migration, the departure of religious minorities from their countries of origin to escape persecution. Whether they move by force or by choice, the result, and the fourth consequence of militant religion, is the same: the emigrants create *diasporas*, or communities that live abroad in host countries but maintain economic, political, and emotional ties with their homelands (Sheffer, 2003). Finally, as we shall see later in this chapter, the fifth effect of militant religions is international terrorism as networks grow to support radical coreligionists abroad (Homer-Dixon, 2005; Sageman, 2004).

In sum, transnational religious movements not only bring people together but also divide them. Through globalization, religions are transforming social forces that create transnational communities of believers with "dual loyalties" to more than one country; immigration by adherents to religion brings more faiths into direct contact with one another and forges global networks that transcend borders (Levitt, 2007). This consequence notwithstanding, transnational religions compete with one another, which tends to divide humanity and breed separatist efforts that can tear countries apart.

PAPAL DIPLOMACY Religious groups are undeniably important nonstate actors on the global stage. Pictured here, on April 9, 2013, Pope Francis meets with UN Secretary-General Ban Ki-moon at the Vatican. Noting the common concerns discussed during his audience with the pope, Ki-moon remarked that the pope "speaks loudly of his commitment to the poor, he has a deep sense of humility, his passion and compassion to improve the human condition."

Multinational Corporations

Multinational corporations (MNCs)—business enterprises organized in one society with activities in others growing out of direct investment abroad—are a third major type of NGO. MNCs have grown dramatically in scope and influence with the globalization of the world political economy since World War II (see Chapters 10 and 11). As a result of their immense resources and power, MNCs have provoked both acceptance and animosity. As advocates of liberal free trade and active contributors to the globalization of world politics, MNCs receive both credit for the positive aspects of free trade and globalization and blame for their costs. This has made them highly controversial nonstate actors, especially in the Global South, where people frequently see MNCs as the cause of exploitation and poverty.

In the past, MNCs were headquartered almost exclusively in the United States, Europe, and Japan, and their common practice was to make short-term investments in the Global South's plants, sales corporations, and mining operations. At the start of the twenty-first century, about 80 percent of all MNCs' employees worked in developing countries, where wages were lower, which helped to bolster corporate profits at the parent headquarters in the Global North—but no longer. "More and more multinationals will shift the operation and control of key business functions away from their home office.... A growing number of companies are setting up regional headquarters or relocating specific headquarter functions elsewhere" (Hindle, 2004, pp. 97–98).

Such *outsourcing* to locations where wages and costs are lower but skills are substantial is likely to continue, accelerating the consolidation of the global economy into a seamless, integrated web. Outsourcing and corporate restructuring are heralded as critical to facilitating business without borders, enhancing corporate growth and profitability, and better using skilled staff in both the Global North and the Global South. However, there is widespread controversy regarding the threat that the offshore transfer of labor poses to workers in the Global North, as "even highly educated tech and service professionals ... compete against legions of hungry college grads in India, China, and the Philippines willing to work twice as hard for one-fifth the pay" (Engardio, Arndt, and Foust, 2006).

The recent global recession has accelerated this structural shift in the economy. Former U.S. Secretary of Labor Robert Reich (2010) recently noted that:

> Companies have used the downturn to aggressively trim payrolls, making cuts they've been reluctant to make before. Outsourcing abroad has increased dramatically. Companies have discovered that new software and computer technologies have made many workers in Asia and Latin America almost as productive as Americans and that the Internet allows far more work to be efficiently moved to another country without loss of control.

This outsourcing is now eagerly welcomed by the Global South's developing countries as a means to economic growth, where once MNC domination was resisted. Nonetheless, wealth and power remain highly concentrated; the big seem to get bigger and bigger. The assets controlled by the one hundred largest MNCs from the Global South are 20 percent of the amount controlled by the one hundred largest MNCs from the Global North (Oatley, 2012, p. 164).

MNCs are increasingly influential NGOs because the world's giant producing, trading, and servicing corporations have become the primary agents of the globalization of production.

outsourcing

The transfer of jobs by a corporation usually headquartered in a Global North country to a Global South country able to supply trained workers at lower wages.

Carnegie Council Video: Outsourcing

Table 6.1 captures their importance in world politics, ranking firms by annual sales and states by GNI. The profile shows that of the world's top 35 economic entities, multinationals account for only five, but in the next 35 they account for 12. Altogether, MNCs comprise almost a quarter of the top seventy economic entities, illustrating that MNCs' financial clout rivals or exceeds that of most countries.

In part due to their global reach and economic power, MNCs' involvement in the domestic political affairs of local or host countries is controversial. In some instances this concern has extended to MNCs' involvement in the domestic politics of their home countries, where they actively lobby their governments for more liberal trade and investment policies to enhance the profitability of their businesses. In turn, both host and home governments have sometimes used MNCs as instruments in their foreign policy strategies.

Perhaps the most notorious instance of an MNC's intervention in the politics of a host state occurred in Chile in the early 1970s when International Telephone and Telegraph (ITT) tried to protect its interests in the profitable Chiltelco telephone company by seeking to prevent the election of Marxist-oriented Salvador Allende as president and, once Allende was elected, pressured the U.S. government to disrupt the Chilean economy. Eventually Allende was overthrown by a military dictatorship. More recently, the huge profits and activities of corporate giant Halliburton to rebuild the infrastructure of Iraq after the 2003 U.S. invasion provoked widespread complaints that this MNC was exploiting the circumstances to line its pockets—at U.S. taxpayers' expense. Further, and as a sign of the times, in 2007 Halliburton moved its headquarters from Texas to Dubai.

This global penetration positions the biggest MNCs to propel changes in relations between countries and within them, as well as in the global marketplace. For example, the MNCs have recently taken steps toward engineering a "social responsibility revolution" by "making products and delivering services that generate profits and also help the world address challenges such as climate change, energy security, healthcare, and poverty. It's not just about public relations any more. Firms see big profits in green solutions" (Piasecki, 2007). Consider Wal-Mart, with annual sales of more than $469 billion (more than the GDPs of all but 24 countries) and over 2 million employees (Rothkopf, 2012), which has developed its "Sustainability 360" initiative to sell environmentally friendly products in order to increase the one hundred million customers throughout the world Wal-Mart currently attracts every week.

In the interest of corporate social responsibility, MNCs in many sectors are also increasingly sensitive to human rights conditions in potential host countries, as well as the impact MNCs themselves may have upon human rights. Developing business partnerships with countries in the Global South where there is greater respect for human rights tends to translate into reduced political risk and a more productive work force for investors (Blanton and Blanton, 2009). Moreover, due to increased oversight by activist NGOs that monitor and publicize corporate involvement in human rights violations, multinational corporations are aware that associating too closely with human rights abusers may result in damage to corporate image—and potentially share values as well (Spar, 1999).

The blurring of the boundaries between internal and external affairs adds potency to the political role that MNCs unavoidably play as nonstate actors at the intersection of foreign and domestic policy. Because multinationals often make decisions over which leaders of states have little control (such as investments), MNCs' growing influence appears to contribute to the

TABLE 6.1   Countries and Corporations: A Ranking by Size of Economy and Revenues

Rank	Country/Corporation	GNI/Revenues (billions of dollars)
1	United States	15,211.3
2	China	7,305.4
3	Japan	6,041.6
4	Germany	3,667.9
5	France	2,825.3
6	United Kingdom	2,469.9
7	Brazil	2,429.9
8	Italy	2,177.3
9	India	1,856.8
10	Russia	1,797.6
11	Canada	1,705.5
12	Spain	1,447.1
13	Australia	1,323.3
14	Mexico	1,162.5
15	Republic of Korea	1,119.3
16	Netherlands	843.3
17	Indonesia	822.7
18	Turkey	767.2
19	Switzerland	676.1
20	Saudi Arabia	587.2
21	Sweden	549.2
22	Belgium	519.3
23	Poland	494.4
24	Norway	494.3
25	Wal-Mart	469.2
26	Royal Dutch Shell	467.2
27	Argentina	435.2
28	Exxon Mobil	420.7
29	Austria	416.2
30	Sinopec-China Petroleum	411.7
31	South Africa	399.1
32	BP	370.9
33	United Arab Emirates	360.2
34	Denmark	341.7
35	Thailand	334.4
36	Iran	328.6
37	Colombia	317.6
38	PetroChina	308.9

(Continued)

TABLE 6.1	Countries and Corporations: A Ranking by Size of Economy and Revenues (Continued)	
Rank	Country/Corporation	GNI/Revenues (billions of dollars)
39	Venezuela	308.8
40	Greece	281.2
41	Malaysia	280.8
42	Finland	264.4
43	Hong Kong	257.4
44	Volkswagen Group	254.0
45	Total	240.5
46	Israel	236.7
47	Chile	234.6
48	Singapore	234.5
49	Portugal	228.6
50	Philippines	226.1
51	Toyota Motor	224.5
52	Egypt	223.5
53	Chevron	222.6
54	Nigeria	221.0
55	Pakistan	219.8
56	Glencore International	214.4
57	Czech Republic	201.8
58	Samsung Electronics	187.8
59	Romania	187.3
60	Algeria	181.2
61	Ireland	178.2
62	E.ON	174.2
63	Qatar	169.3
64	Phillips 66	166.1
65	Apple	164.7
66	ENI	163.7
67	Peru	163.2
68	Berkshire Hathaway	162.5
69	ENI	143.2
70	Samsung Electronics	142.4

Source: Gross National Income (GNI), World Bank, 2013 World Development Indicators; MNC revenues, *Forbes* (accessed June 3, 2013).

erosion of the global system's major organizing principle—that the state alone should be sovereign. MNCs' awesome financial resources are much greater than the official statistics suggest, and this is why many states fear that MNCs, which insist on freedom to compete internationally, are stripping away their sovereignty. And in fact, in some respects states *are* losing control of their national economies as MNCs merge with one another and, in the process, cease to remain tied to any one parent state or region.

"Who owns whom?" can no longer be answered. This is because many MNCs are now *globally integrated enterprises* that produce the same goods in different countries so that their horizontal organization no longer ties them to any single country. Consider this: "Half of Xerox's employees work on foreign soil, and less than half of Sony's employees are Japanese. More than 50 percent of IBM's revenues originate overseas; the same is true for Citigroup, ExxonMobil, DuPont, Procter & Gamble, and many other corporate giants. Joint ventures are no longer merely a domestic decision. Corning obtains one-half of its profits from foreign joint ventures with Samsung in Korea, Asahi Glass in Japan, and Ciba-Geigy in Switzerland" (Weidenbaum, 2004, pp. 26–27). Business organizations today are better thought of as "global" than as "multinational."

Controlling the webs of corporate interrelationships, joint ventures, and shared ownership for any particular state purpose is nearly impossible. Between 1988 and 2008, the number of MNCs grew to more than 82,000 parent firms that control 810,000 foreign affiliates spanning every continent in the world (Oatley, 2012). This further undermines states' ability to identify the MNCs they seek to control, and contributes to the perception that MNCs are becoming "stateless." Thus, how can any single state manage such multinational giants when no country can claim that an MNC is "one of ours"?

"In just over forty years, the number of firms engaged in international production has increased about elevenfold" (Oatley, 2012, p. 161), and MNCs are playing a correspondingly larger and larger role in world politics. This is forcing sovereign states to confront many challenges. How will they respond? Assessing the future requires a theoretical examination of contemporary thinking regarding MNCs and other types of NGOs.

Issue-Advocacy Groups

As citizens increasingly participate in NGOs in order to gain a voice in and influence over the institutions that shape the conditions in which they live, issue-advocacy group activity on the global stage has risen to unprecedented levels. "In its simplest form, issue advocacy is about three things: defining a problem (e.g., social, environmental, economic, etc.), identifying and advocating a specific solution, and motivating action" (Hannah, 2009). Greenpeace, Amnesty International, and Doctors Without Borders are just a few examples of nongovernmental issue-advocacy groups that actively seek to influence and change global conditions.

Many people now see NGOs as a vehicle empowering individuals to engineer transformations in international affairs. What is clear is that networks of transnational activists have formed NGOs at an accelerating rate, and through their leverage, have performed an educational service that has demonstrably contributed to the emergence of a global *civil society*. The growth of transnational activism by NGOs "is leading to a diffusion of power away from central governments" (Nye, 2007), and these networks of transnational social movements are altering international culture by reshaping values about international conduct (Heins, 2008; Keck and Sikkink, 1998).

A growing trend is for celebrities who want to effect change to establish issue—advocacy organizations that promote their issue of interest. Sean Penn founded J/P Haitian Relief Organization to provide temporary housing and medical care, Alicia Keys cofounded Keep a Child

globally integrated enterprises

MNCs organized horizontally, with management and production located in plants in numerous states for the same products they market.

civil society

A community that embraces shared norms and ethical standards to collectively manage problems without coercion and through peaceful and democratic procedures for decision making aimed at improving human welfare.

Scripps Howard Photo Service/Newscom

THE POWER OF FAME George Clooney has been involved in Sudan for over six years in efforts to combat genocide, and has worked to help the people of South Sudan peacefully achieve independence. Says Clooney, "Celebrity can help focus news media where they have abdicated their responsibility. We can't make policy, but we can 'encourage' politicians more than ever before." Pictured here, he speaks with people in a remote village in southern Sudan.

Alive to provide medical support for AIDS orphans in Africa, and Don Cheadle, along with George Clooney, Matt Damon, Brad Pitt, David Pressman, and Jerry Weintraub, created the anti-genocide advocacy group Not on Our Watch. Celebrities are also serving as "celebrity statesmen [who] function like freelance diplomats, adopting issue experts and studying policy" (Avlon, 2011, p. 17). In 2012 George Clooney played a role in focusing attention on the political violence and independence efforts in South Sudan (*The Economist*, 2012c), and Angelina Jolie visited the Democratic Republic of Congo and Rwanda in March 2013 as a special envoy of the United Nations in an effort to bring attention to the atrocities being committed (Blas, 2013). As journalist Nicholas Kristof observed, "the truth is that the spotlight of public attention is lifesaving—whether it's a genocide, disease, or hunger... . Stars can generate attention and then generate the political will to do something about a problem."

That said, studies of the impact of NGO pressure on global policy making suggest some conclusions that temper confidence in the expectation that NGO pressure can lead to far-reaching transformational reforms in the conduct of international relations:

- Interest group activity operates as an ever-present, if limited, constraint on global policy making. Single-issue NGO interest groups have more influence than large, general-purpose organizations. However, the impact varies with the issue.

- As a general rule, issue-advocacy groups are relatively weak in the arena of military security because states remain in control of defense policy and are relatively unaffected by external NGO pressures.

- Conversely, the clout of issue-advocacy groups is highest with respect to other transnational issues such as protecting endangered species or combating climate change, which are of concern to great and small powers alike.

- The influence between state governments and NGOs is reciprocal, but it is more probable that government officials manipulate transnational interest groups than that NGOs exercise influence over governments' foreign policies.

- Issue-advocacy groups sometimes seek inaction from governments and maintenance of the status quo; such efforts are generally more successful than efforts to bring about major changes in international relations. For this reason NGOs are often generally seen as agents of policy continuities rather than policy transformation.

The characteristics of NGO efforts to redirect global policy depicted above suggest that the mere presence of such groups, and the mere fact they are organized to persuade, does not guarantee their penetration of the global policy-making process. On the whole, NGOs have participation without real power and involvement without real influence, given that the ability of any *one* to exert influence is offset by the tendency for other, countervailing powers to oppose that influence. That is, when any coalition of interest groups seeks vigorously to push policy in one direction, other nonstate actors—aroused that their established interests are being disturbed—tend to push policy in the opposite direction. Global policy making consequently resembles a taffy pull: Every nonstate actor attempts to pull policy in its own direction while resisting the pulls of others.

The result is often that the quest for consensus proves elusive, the capacity of a network to push history forward rapidly in a particular direction is constrained, and the international community's posture toward many global problems fails to move in any single direction. The result is usually a continuous battleground over the primary global issues from which no permanent resolution of the struggle materializes. The debate and contests between those wishing to make environmental protection a global priority and those placing economic growth ahead of environmental preservation provide one example among many.

> *Even the weak become strong when they are united.*
>
> —Friedrich Schiller, German philosopher

MALEVOLENT NONSTATE ACTORS

Are transnational terrorist organizations and global crime organizations correctly seen as a particular category of nonstate actors—as NGOs—on the global stage? Taking a broad conceptualization of NGOs as transnational nongovernmental associations of people, these groups can be seen as a virulent type of NGO. However, others argue that these organizations do not meet expectations for NGOs given their illegal activities and use of violence. No matter how we categorize these groups, they are clearly nonstate actors whose behaviors transcend national boundaries and pose a threat to global well-being.

Transnational Terrorist Groups

Terrorism has plagued world politics for centuries and, according to historian Max Boot (2013), such irregular warfare is far older than conventional warfare. Some place the beginnings of terrorism in the first century BCE with the Sicarii Zealots, who violently targeted Jewish high priests whom they saw as collaborating with the Romans in violation of Jewish religious law. Yet terrorism today is arguably much different than in the past. Terrorism now is seen as:

■ Global, in the sense that with new technology redefining limitations of distance, borders no longer serve as barriers to terrorism

■ Lethal, because now terrorists have shifted their tactics from theatrical violent acts seeking to gain media attention to purposeful destruction of a target's civilian

terrorism

Premeditated violence perpetrated against noncombatant targets by subnational, transnational groups, or clandestine agents, usually intended to influence an audience.

Carnegie Council Video:
Terrorism

postmodern terrorism

To Walter Laqueur, the terrorism practiced by an expanding set of diverse actors with new weapons "to sow panic in a society, to weaken or even overthrow the incumbents, and to bring about political change."

information age

The era in which the rapid creation and global transfer of information through mass communication contribute to the globalization of knowledge.

A TERRORIST MASTERMIND
Osama Bin Laden, the head of Al Qaeda who was behind the September 11, 2001 terrorist attacks on the United States, was killed by U.S. forces on May 1, 2011. A decade after those atrocious attacks, Americans celebrated as President Obama declared "justice is done." Roughly a year later, in June 2012, Al Qaeda's deputy leader Abu Yahya al-Libi was killed by a CIA drone strike in Mir Ali, Pakistan.

noncombatants, to kill as many as possible for the purpose of instilling fear in as many people as possible

▪ Waged by civilians without state sanction in ways and by means that erase the classic boundaries between terrorism and a declared war between states

▪ Reliant on the most advanced technology of modern civilization, despite viewing sophisticated technological, modern societies as a threat to the terrorists' sacred traditions

▪ Orchestrated by transnational nonstate organizations through global conspiratorial networks of terrorist cells located in many countries, involving unprecedented levels of communication and coordination (Sageman, 2004)

Renowned historian and terrorism expert Walter Laqueur sees a future of *postmodern terrorism* that poses great threat to technologically advanced societies, where terrorists tend to be less ideological, more likely to hold ethnic grievances, and increasingly difficult to distinguish from other criminals. So-called postmodern terrorism is likely to expand because the globalized international environment, without meaningful barriers separating countries, allows terrorists to practice their ancient trade by new rules and methods. The *information age* facilitates transnational networking among terrorists and has made available a variety of new methods, such as electronic "cyberterrorism" and "netwar" strategies.

Moreover, this new global environment encourages the rapid spread of new weapons and technology across borders, which provides unprecedented opportunities for terrorists to commit atrocities and to change their tactics in response to successful counterterror operations. The growing difficulty of detecting and deterring the attacks of disciplined globalized terrorist networks is further exacerbated by their ties to international organized crime (IOC) syndicates and internationally linked networks of thousands of gangs, which facilitate their profit in the narcotics trade and provide resources to support terrorist activities.

The activities of nonstate terrorist organizations are likely to remain a troubling feature of world politics also because every spectacular terrorist act generates a powerful shock effect and gains worldwide publicity through the global news media. In an effort to diminish the capacity of terrorists to garner such worldwide attention, U.S. Senator Joe Lieberman called on Google and others to remove Internet video content that was produced by terrorist organizations: "Islamist terrorist organizations use YouTube to disseminate their propaganda, enlist followers, and provide weapons training ... (and) YouTube also, unwittingly, permits Islamist terrorist groups to maintain an active, pervasive, and amplified voice, despite military setbacks."

Table 6.2 identifies some of the known terrorist NGOs. As you can see, the primary goals of the various groups are diverse. Some, such as FARC and ETA, focus on secular nonreligious objectives such as ethnic self-determination or overthrow of a government. Others, most notably Al Qaeda, are driven by religious convictions and have more sweeping

TABLE 6.2	Some Terrorist NGOs: Primary Location and Goals	
Name	**Primary Location**	**Goal**
Al Qaeda	A global network with cells in a number of countries and tied to Sunni extremist networks. Despite bin Laden's death, top associates are still suspected to reside in Afghanistan, the border region in Pakistan, and Somalia, and Yemen.	To establish pan-Islamic rule throughout the world by working with allied Islamic extremist groups to overthrow regimes it deems "non-Islamic" and expel Westerners and non-Muslims from Muslim countries.
Revolutionary Armed Forces of Colombia (FARC)	Colombia, with some activities (e.g., extortion, kidnapping, logistics) in Venezuela, Panama, and Ecuador.	To replace the current government with a Marxist regime.
Hezbollah (Party of God), a.k.a. Islamic Jihad, Revolutionary Justice Organization, Organization of the Oppressed on Earth, and Islamic Jihad for the Liberation of Palestine	In the Bekaa Valley, the southern suburbs of Beirut, and southern Lebanon. Has established cells in Europe, Africa, South America, North America, and Asia.	To increase its political power in Lebanon, and opposing Israel and the Middle East peace negotiations.
Hamas (Islamic Resistance Movement)	Primarily the occupied territories, Israel.	To establish an Islamic Palestinian state in place of Israel and gain international acceptance of its rule in Gaza.
Basque Fatherland and Liberty (ETA), a.k.a. Euzkadi Ta Askatasuna	Primarily in the Basque autonomous regions of northern Spain and southwestern France.	To establish an independent homeland based on Marxist principles in the Basque autonomous regions.
Al-Gama'a al-Islamiyya	Primarily southern Egypt, but has a worldwide presence, including Afghanistan, Yemen, Sudan, Austria, and the United Kingdom.	To overthrow the Egyptian government and replace it with an Islamic state; to attack United States and Israeli interests in Egypt and abroad.
Liberation Tigers of Tamil Eelam	Sri Lanka.	To establish an independent Tamil state. On May 19, 2009, the Sri Lankan government declared an end to the 25-year civil war and a defeat of what had been characterized as the fiercest terrorist force in the world.
Aum Supreme Truth (Aum), a.k.a. Aum Shinrikyo, Aleph	Principal membership is located only in Japan, but a residual branch comprising an unknown number of followers has surfaced in Russia.	To take over Japan and then the world.
Sendero Luminoso (Shining Path)	Peru.	To destroy existing Peruvian institutions and replace them with a communist peasant revolutionary regime.
New People's Army (NPA)	Philippines.	To overthrow the government of the Philippines.

Source: Adapted from the Center for Defense Information (accessed June 17, 2011).

goals. There is also variation in the manner in which their organizations are structured, with some having a hierarchical structure and newer groups tending to favor networked insulated cells dispersed across the globe.

Though terrorists are popularly portrayed as "madmen" bent on death and destruction, terrorist expert Robert Pape has noted that even "suicide terrorism follows a strategic logic. Even if many suicide attackers are irrational or fanatical, the leadership groups that recruit and direct them are not" (2003, p. 344). Take care to consider how your value judgments can affect your interpretation of the identity and purpose of any group you may believe belongs in this menacing category of nonstate actors. The cliché "one person's terrorist is another person's freedom fighter" springs from the hold of prior and subjective perceptions on many people's definitions of objective realities.

Transnational Crime Organizations

Like terrorists, transnational crime groups pose a serious challenge to global security in the twenty-first century and are expected to continue to proliferate because, as Director of the Terrorism, Transnational Crime and Corruption Center Louise Shelly explains, "these crime groups are major beneficiaries of globalization. They take advantage of increased travel, trade, rapid money movements, telecommunications and computer links, and are well positioned for growth." Spanning multiple countries, they use systematic violence and corruption to carry out their illicit activities, which commonly include cybercrime, money laundering, intellectual property theft, maritime piracy, and the trafficking of humans, drugs, weapons, body parts, endangered species, environmental resources, or nuclear material (see Figure 6.5). Because

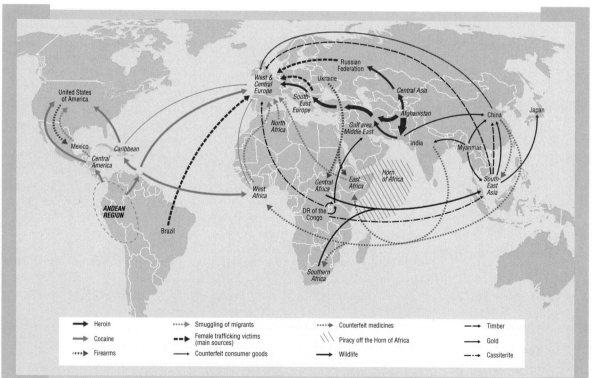

FIGURE 6.5   MAJOR GLOBAL CRIME FLOWS   The specific markets of transnational crime organizations are in constant fluctuation. Drug epidemics rise and fall; trafficking in humans and firearms expands rapidly in areas of conflict and subsides in times of peace. According to the UN Office on Drugs and Crime (2010, p. 3), "Future trends are likely to be affected by global shifts in demographics, migration, urbanization, conflict and economics." It is therefore critical that the international community better understand the way that transnational crime relates to broader social changes.

terrorists require significant resources to function, there is frequently an overlap between terrorist organizations and transnational crime organizations, as terrorists are often involved in an array of domestic and transnational crime.

One well-known crime network includes the Russian mafia, which includes 200 Russian groups operating in almost 60 countries. Another is La Cosa Nostra, otherwise known as the Italian mafia. Between 1920 and 1990 this organization was the most prominent international organized crime group in the world. Targeted law enforcement in the United States greatly reduced the organization's activities in that country, although it remains active in Italy and elsewhere. Japan's Yakuza is yet another organized crime group that is heavily involved in global human trafficking.

International criminal activity poses a threat to economic growth in legitimate business activities, particularly in emerging states that are vulnerable to internationally organized crime. Internationally organized crime groups also take a toll on domestic state institutions (Zartner, 2010). According to the U.S. government's National Institute of Justice (2012):

> Transnational crime ring activities weaken economies and financial systems and undermine democracy. These networks often prey on governments that are not powerful enough to oppose them, prospering on illegal activities, such as drug trafficking, that bring them immense profits. In carrying out illegal activities, they upset the peace and stability of nations worldwide, often using bribery, violence, or terror to achieve their goals.

As Yuriy A. Voronin, a criminal law professor, notes "transnational criminal rings are becoming more and more powerful and universal, and their mobility is growing. The means and resources of any state are not enough to seriously harm them." In order to stop the international activity of transnational organized crime groups, it is necessary to integrate national responses into regional and international strategies:

- **Collaboration between states**. Traditionally states have taken a realist approach to sovereignty, and carefully guarded their own territory. However, as Director Antonio Maria Costa of the UN Office on Drugs and Crime cautions, "If police stop at borders while criminals cross them freely, sovereignty is already breached." To combat this, states must engage in law-enforcement collaboration and trans-border intelligence sharing.

- **Disruption of criminal markets**. Displacing international criminal groups is not sufficient, as new groups will simply fill the void. It is necessary to disrupt the markets that drive organized crime.

- **Strengthening of the rule of law**. Criminal groups flourish in areas where there is rampant corruption, instability, and a lack of development. Strengthening laws not only provides a more solid foundation from which to combat crime groups, but also makes an area less conducive to transnational crime activity in the first place.

- **Oversight and integrity of financial practices**. Transnational crime groups are motivated by money. To disrupt cash flows, it is important for governments and financial institutions to work together to regulate and stop informal money transfers, recycling through real estate, offshore banking, and banking privacy practices that protect criminal profits.

As the world grows more interdependent and transactions across state borders increase through the movement of people, information, and traded products, it is likely that world politics will be increasingly affected by the activities of both IGO and NGO nonstate actors. Many work to improve the human condition, though nonstate actors such as terrorists and transnational crime organizations prey on the vulnerabilities and misfortunes of others. Global cooperation is necessary if we are to successfully counter this "dark side" of globalization. Otherwise, the efforts by states and other organizations to fight terrorism and international crime will result in merely displacing the problem from one country to another.

NONSTATE ACTORS AND THE FUTURE OF WORLD POLITICS

The growth and rising importance of nonstate actors is likely to challenge the iron grip sovereign states have exercised in determining the global system's architecture and rules since the 1648 Peace of Westphalia:

> The idea of sovereign equality reflected a conscious decision governments made 60 years ago that they would be better off if they repudiated the right to meddle in the internal affairs of others. That choice no longer makes sense. In an era of rapid globalization, internal developments in distant states affect our own well-being, even our security. That is what Sept. 11 taught us. Today respect for state sovereignty should be conditional on how states behave at home, not just abroad. Sovereignty carries with it a responsibility to protect citizens against mass violence and a duty to prevent internal developments that threaten others. We need to build an international order that reflects how states organize themselves internally (Daalder and Lindsay, 2004).

Are transnational nonstate actors truly capable of flexing their muscles in ways that can directly challenge states' sovereign control over both their foreign and domestic policies? If so, are the pillars of the Westphalian state system beginning to crumble, as some predict (Falk and Strauss, 2001; Kegley and Raymond, 2002a)?

As you contemplate these questions, keep in mind one clear lesson: It is misleading to think that politics is only about territorial states in interaction with each other, exercising supreme authority within their own borders. The outlines of a future type of dual global system may be coming into view, driven simultaneously by the continuing importance of relations between states and by the growing impact of multiple cross-border transactions and channels of communication among nonstate actors.

Are the *liberal* and *constructivist* perspectives on the processes by which trends in world politics are set in motion correct? As nonstate actors "multiply the channels of access to the international system," are they "blurring the boundaries between a state's relations with its own nationals and the recourse both citizens and states have to the international system" (Keck and Sikkink, 2008, p. 222), and thus paving the path for a possible *transformation* of world politics? This change would lead to a hybrid or two-tiered world in which the clout and authority of the governments that rule countries decline while the relative power of nonstate actors rise.

That said, skeptics counter that nonstate actors have failed to become "a serious rival to the power and processes of the state"—their goals of transforming the dominant processes of policy making and corporate capitalism have not met with success (Price, 2003, p. 591). Indeed, it has been argued that IGOs and NGOs "have helped states retain—and in some instances even increase—their internal and external control, autonomy and legitimacy" (Weir, 2007). Seen through *realist theory*, the critical choices that direct global destiny are ultimately made by the most powerful states.

These speculations by no means resolve the question of whether the era of state dominance is coming to an end as nonstate actors increase their clout. Relations between global actors, as well as broader developments in world politics, are the consequence of innumerable decisions made by states, transnational organizations, and individuals. In Part 3, we will look more closely at issues that arise in confronting armed aggression. In Chapter 7, you will have an opportunity to examine the global character and consequences of violent threats to security. In Chapters 8 and 9, we will weigh the rival ideas presented by the realist road to security and the liberal path to peace. You will also be invited to consider the insights that alternative constructivist, Marxist, and feminist theories provide in grappling with the challenge of finding solutions to the grave threat of armed conflict.

STUDY. APPLY. ANALYZE.

Key Terms

civil society
clash of civilizations
diasporas
ethnicity
ethnic groups
ethnic nationalism
European Commission
European Union (EU)

globally integrated
  enterprises
indigenous peoples
information age
militant religious
  movements
nonstate nations
outsourcing

political integration
pooled sovereignty
postmodern terrorism
regimes
responsible sovereignty
secession, or separatist
  revolts
security community

terrorism
theocracy
Third Way
transnational religious
  movements

Suggested Readings

Boehmer, Charles, and Timothy Nordstrom. (2008) "Intergovernmental Organization Memberships: Examining Political Community and the Attributes of International Organizations," *International Interactions* 34:282–309.

Buchanan, Allen, and Robert O.Keohane.2006 "The Legitimacy of Global Governance Institutions," *Ethics & International Affairs* 20, no. 4 (Winter):405–437.

Jones, Bruce, Carlos Pascual, and Stephen John Stedman. (2009) *Power & Responsibility: Building*

International Order in an Era of Transnational Threats. Washington, DC: Brookings.

Milner, Helen V., and Andrew Moravcsik. (2009) *Power, Interdependence, and Nonstate Actors in World Politics.* Princeton, NJ: Princeton University Press.

Rothkopf, David. (2012) *Power, Inc: The Epic Rivalry between Big Business and Government—and the Reckoning that Lies Ahead.* New York: Farrar, Straus, and Giroux.

Stephenson, Max, and Laura Zanotti. (2012) *Peacebuilding Through Community-Based NGOs: Paradoxes and Possibilities.* Boulder, CO: Kumarian Press.

Thakur, Ramesh, and Thomas G. Weiss, eds. (2009) *The United Nations and Global Governance: An Unfinished Journey.* Bloomington: Indiana University Press.

Zoellick, Robert B. (2012) "Why We Still Need the World Bank: Looking Beyond Aid," *Foreign Affairs* 91, no. 2:66–78.

Suggested Videos

Carnegie Council Video

Bosco, David L. *"Five to Rule Them All: The UN Security Council and the Making of the Modern World."*

Brown, Mark Malloch. *"The Unfinished Global Revolution: The Pursuit of a New International Politics."*

Shanbaum, Elena. *"International Humanitarian Law and Non-State Actors."*

Sorensen, Gillian, van Puyenbroeck, Robin. *"Facing the Crises of Our Time: The United Nations and the*

United States in the 21st Century."

Vocke, William. *"The EU and Serbia."*

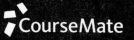CourseMate

Log in to CourseMate to access the following study tools for this chapter:

- Interactive Quiz
- eBook
- Flashcards & Key Term Crossword Puzzle
- Chapter Audio Summary
- Carnegie Council Videos

- Video Activities
- Simulation
- Case Study
- Animated Learning Module
- International Relations NewsWatch

PART 3

Roger Ressmeyer/Historical/Corbis

CONFRONTING ARMED CONFLICT

WHEN YOU THINK ABOUT WORLD POLITICS, WHAT IS THE FIRST IMAGE THAT RACES TO YOUR MIND? For many people, world politics is about arms, alliances, and the exercise of military force over rivals and other actors on the global stage. Indeed, many people equate world politics with war and its threat to their country, city, and the world at large. This preoccupation is as old as recorded history itself. And for understandable reasons: An attack by an enemy is the most dangerous direct threat to survival, and preventing such death and destruction is a precondition for attaining all other important values, such as food, water, freedom, and the possession of a territory on which to live safely. Yet war is a problem, and changes are required in the practices of states toward one another if we are to control armed conflict and reduce its frequency and destructiveness.

In Part 3 of *World Politics*, you will have the opportunity to explore the many contending ideas and theoretical perspectives about how to best ameliorate armed conflict. Chapter 7 looks at the military threats to international security posed by wars between states, wars within states, and international terrorism. In Chapter 8, the pursuit of national interest defined in terms of military power is examined through the lens of realist approaches to national and international security, with consideration of trends in weapons of war, alternative military methods, and alliances. In Chapter 9, you will consider liberal ideas for negotiating at the bargaining table rather than fighting on the battlefield to settle international disputes, as well as the role of international law, disarmament, economic sanctions, and empowering international organizations for maintaining the collective security of all countries.

NUCLEAR TESTING

Pictured here is a French atomic test in the South Pacific of a nuclear bomb smaller than the U.S. hydrogen bomb that, in 1952, created a 3-mile fireball 1000 times more powerful than each of the bombs the United States dropped on Hiroshima and Nagasaki. More than 2000 nuclear weapons tests have occurred since 1945.

"There is no instance of a nation benefiting from prolonged warfare."

—*Sun Tzu, ancient Chinese philosopher and strategist*

CHAPTER 7

The Threat of Armed Conflict to the World

AP Photo/Shaam News Network via AP video

THE GLOBALIZATION OF ARMED CONFLICT Over the past two decades, external actors have directly intervened with military force in more than a fourth of all internal armed conflicts. Yet attempts to influence the outcomes of such conflicts are often more subtle, such as providing weapons, signaling intent to do so, or generating international support for a given side. Pictured here, the Syrian government drops a bomb near Damascus on May 20, 2013, as the Syrian conflict continues. As external actors, Russia opposed UN intervention and supplied the Syrian government with weaponry while the United States voiced support for opposition forces and called for UN resolutions that would sanction the Syrian government for its use of force.

QUESTIONS TO CONSIDER

- *What causes armed conflict?*
- *What are the different types of conflict and how often do they occur?*
- *What are the most important characteristics of conflict within states?*
- *What distinguishes terrorism from other forms of conflict?*
- *What is the future of armed conflict?*

In the calm summer of 2001, complacency had taken hold in the generally peaceful Global North, where many thoughtful observers, noting the disappearance of interstate war among the economic giants, began to ask if war had become obsolete. That mood was shattered shortly thereafter on September 11, 2001, when international terrorists destroyed New York's World Trade Center. The 9/11 attack and the U.S. war in Afghanistan; terrorist attacks elsewhere around the world, such as in Madrid in 2004, London in 2005, and Moscow in 2011; the U.S.-led military struggle in Iraq; the 2006 Israeli-Hezbollah War in Lebanon; and a wave of civil wars dashed all prior hopes for sustained peace. Although the 2011 popular protests and demonstrations across much of the Arab world raised hopes that democratization might take place, the violent clashes with state authorities and counterdemonstrators put such reforms in jeopardy and raise concerns about the ubiquity of violence.

Based on even these few events, it becomes understandable why so many people think that armed conflict is the essence of world politics. In *On War*, Prussian strategist Karl von Clausewitz advanced his famous dictum that war is merely an extension of diplomacy by other means, albeit an extreme form. This insight underscores the realist belief that *war* is a policy instrument that transnational actors use to resolve their conflicts. War, however, is the deadliest instrument of conflict resolution, and its onset usually means that persuasion and negotiations have failed.

In international relations, *conflict* regularly occurs when actors interact and disputes over incompatible interests arise. In and of itself, conflict is not necessarily threatening, because war and conflict are different. Conflict may be seen as inevitable and occurs whenever two parties perceive differences between themselves and seek to resolve those differences to their own satisfaction. Some conflict results whenever people interact and may be generated by religious, ideological, ethnic, economic, political, or territorial issues; therefore, it should not be regarded as abnormal. Nor should we regard conflict as necessarily destructive. Conflict can promote social solidarity, creative thinking, learning, and communication—all factors critical to the resolution of disputes and the durability of cooperation. However, the costs of conflict do become threatening when the parties take up arms to settle perceived irreconcilable differences or to settle old scores. When that happens, violence occurs, and we enter the sphere of warfare.

This chapter presents information and ideas so you can explore the nature of *armed conflict* in your world—its causes, changing characteristics, and frequency. You will be forced to confront the ethical dilemmas that these military threats create—about when it is moral or immoral to take up arms. *World Politics* spotlights the three most frequent forms of armed conflict today: wars between states, wars within states, and terrorism. You will have the opportunity to review the leading theories that seek to explain the causes of these three types of armed conflict in world politics.

war

A condition arising within states (civil war) or between states (interstate war) when actors use violent means to destroy their opponents or coerce them into submission.

Carnegie Council Video:
War

conflict

Discord often arising in international relations over perceived incompatibilities of interest.

Carnegie Council Video:
Conflict

armed conflict

Combat between the military forces of two or more states or groups.

Carnegie Council Video:
Armed Conflict

Only the dead have seen the end of war.

—**George Santayana, Spanish-American philosopher**

WHAT CAUSES ARMED CONFLICT?

**Video:
A Long-Term Decision**

**Animated Learning
Module:
Threats**

Throughout history, efforts have been made to explain why people engage in organized violence. Inventories of war's origins (see Bennett and Stam, 2004; Cashman and Robinson, 2007; Vasquez, Justino, and Bruck, 2009) generally agree that hostilities are rooted in multiple sources found at various *levels of analysis* (recall Chapter 1 and 3). Some causes directly influence the odds of war; others are remote and indirect, creating the context in which any one of a number of more proximate factors may trigger violence. The most commonly cited causes of armed conflict are customarily classified by three broad categories: aggressive traits tied to human nature and individual human behavior, detrimental national attributes that make some states likely to engage in armed conflict, and volatile conditions within the global system that encourage disputes to become militarized.

The First Level of Analysis: Individuals' Human Nature

**intraspecific
aggression**

*Killing members of
one's own species.*

**interspecific
aggression**

*Killing others that
are not members
of one's own
species.*

pacifism

*The liberal idealist
school of ethical
thought that
recognizes no
conditions that
justify the taking
of another human's
life, even when
authorized by a
head of state.*

**survival of the
fittest**

*A realist concept
derived from
Charles Darwin's
theory of evolution
that advises that
ruthless competition
is ethically accept-
able to survive, even
if the actions violate
moral commands
not to kill.*

"At a fundamental level, conflict originates from individuals' behavior and their repeated interactions with their surroundings" (Verwimp, Justino, and Bruck, 2009, p. 307). In a sense, all wars originate from the decisions of the leaders of states or transnational nonstate actors such as terrorist organizations. Leaders' choices, and even their emotions, ultimately determine whether armed conflict will occur (McDermott, 2013; see also Chapter 3). So a good starting point for explaining why warfare occurs is to consider the relationship of armed conflict to the choices of individual leaders. For this level of analysis, questions about human nature are central.

The repeated outbreak of war has led some, such as psychiatrist Sigmund Freud, to conclude that aggression is an instinctive part of human nature that stems from humanity's genetic psychological programming. Identifying *Homo sapiens* as the deadliest species, ethologists (those who study animal behavior) such as Konrad Lorenz (1963) similarly argue that humans are one of the few species that practice *intraspecific aggression* (routine killing of their own kind), in comparison with most other species that practice *interspecific aggression* (killing only other species, except in the most unusual circumstances—cannibalism in certain tropical fish being one exception). Realist theorists likewise believe that all humans are born with an innate drive for power that they cannot avoid and that this instinct leads to competition and war. They, therefore, accept the sociological premise suggested by Charles Darwin's theories of evolution and natural selection. Life entails a struggle for survival of the fittest, and natural selection eliminates the traits that interfere with successful competition. To realists, *pacifism* is counterproductive because it is contrary to basic human nature, which they see as aggressive, greedy, and power-seeking. Additionally, by ruling out military action, pacifism rejects the primary realist policy instrument for ensuring state security.

Many question these theories on both empirical and logical grounds. If aggression is truly an inevitable impulse deriving from human nature, then why do not all humans exhibit this genetically determined behavior? Most people, at least outwardly, reject killing as evil based on certain ethical principles. In fact, at some fundamental genetic level, human beings are wired to seek consensus, not conflict. Or so certain international theorists, such as Francis Fukuyama (1999a) argue: "people feel intensely uncomfortable if they live in a society that doesn't have moral rules."

Liberal theory and behavioral social science research suggest that genetics fails to explain why individuals may be belligerent only at certain times. Social Darwinism's interpretation of the biological influences on human behavior can be countered by examining why people cooperate and act morally. As James Q. Wilson (1993, p. 23) argues, Darwinian *survival of the fittest* realist theory overlooks the fact that "the moral sense must have adaptive value; if it did not, natural selection would have worked against people who had such useless traits as sympathy, self-control, or a desire for fairness in favor of those with the opposite tendencies."

Although the *nature-versus-nurture* debate regarding the biological bases of aggression has not been resolved (Kluger, 2007; McDermott, 2013; Ridley, 2003), most social scientists now strongly disagree with the realist premise that because humans are essentially selfish, they are also aggressive—which then leads them to murder and kill. Instead, they interpret war as a learned cultural habit. Aggression is a propensity acquired early in life as a result of *socialization*. Therefore, aggression is a learned rather than a biologically determined behavior, and "violent human nature is a myth" (Murithi, 2004).

Individuals' willingness to sacrifice their lives in war out of a sense of duty to their leaders and country is one of history's puzzles. It appears as though this self-sacrifice stems from learned beliefs that some convictions are worth dying for, such as loyalty to one's own country. "It has been widely observed that soldiers fight—and noncombatants assent to war—not out of aggressiveness but obedience" (Caspary, 1993). But this does not make human nature a cause of war, even if learned habits of obedience taught in military training are grounds for participation in aggression authorized by others, and even if at times the mass public's chauvinistic enthusiasm for aggression against foreign adversaries encourages leaders to start wars.

This suggests that factors other than *national character* (the inborn collective traits of particular peoples) may be better suited to explain why certain countries tend to engage in organized violence. Rather, armed conflict occurs most often as a result of the choices leaders make, and not because of the popular preferences of their entire societies. As English statesman Saint Thomas More (1478–1535) remarked, "The common people do not go to war of their own accord, but are driven to it by the madness of kings." Similarly, U.S. diplomat Ralph Bunche argued before the United Nations (UN): "there are no warlike people—just warlike leaders."

This idea introduces an important analytic problem. Can the characteristics of cultures and populations within countries in the aggregate, the sum of the parts, predict the behaviors of the individuals within those groups? No. To generalize from the whole to the part is to commit what demographers and statisticians call a logical *ecological fallacy*. Why? Because, unless all members of the group are exactly alike, the characteristics of the collectivity (the entire state or culture, for example) cannot reliably predict the beliefs and behaviors of the individuals in that group.

Do all Americans think alike? All Muslims? All Chinese? Hardly. Such racial and cultural stereotyping is misleading. Rarely can we safely generalize from groups to individuals. However, the opposite, what logicians call the *individualistic fallacy*, is also a mental error. We cannot generalize safely about the beliefs or behavior of individual leaders (Angela Merkel of Germany, Xi Jinping of China, Barack Obama of the United States, David Cameron of Great Britain, or Vladimir Putin of Russia) and ascribe them to the prevailing preferences of the collective cultures and states that each of them heads.

nature-versus-nurture

The controversy over whether human behavior is determined more by the biological basis of "human nature" than it is nurtured by the environmental conditions that humans experience.

socialization

The processes by which people learn to accept the beliefs, values, and behaviors that prevail in a given society's culture.

CourseMate

Carnegie Council Video:
Socialization

national character

The collective characteristics ascribed to the people within a state.

Carnegie Council Video:
National Character

ecological fallacy

The error of assuming that the attributes of an entire population—a culture, a country, or a civilization—are the same attributes and attitudes of each person within it.

individualistic fallacy

The logical error of assuming that an individual leader, who has legal authority to govern, represents the people and opinions of the population governed, so that all citizens are necessarily accountable for the vices and virtues (to be given blame or credit) of the leaders authorized to speak for them.

civil wars

Wars between opposing groups within the same country or by rebels against the government.

What should be obvious is that leaders do make some immoral foreign policy decisions. Moreover, many of those decisions by countries' leaders are the outcome of flawed decision-making processes; they fail to conform to the *rational choice* model of foreign policy decision making, which assumes that decision makers make choices through cool-headed cost–benefit calculations in order to select the option with the best chance of accomplishing preferred goals. In addition, even intelligent and moral leaders are sometimes prone to make unnecessarily high-risk decisions to wage war because they are pressured through *groupthink* by influential advisers rather than acting on what they personally believe to be the most rational choice.

This observation about the determinants of leaders' choices about war and peace directs attention to the domestic factors that encourage some states to engage in foreign aggression. These internal factors create the context that constrains or enables the policy decisions leaders can make.

The Second Level of Analysis: States' Internal Characteristics

We next examine some theories about the internal characteristics of states that influence leaders' choices regarding the use of force. Implicit in this approach to explaining armed conflict at the *state level of analysis* is the assumption that differences in the types or categories of states determine whether they will engage in war. Arguing that the prospects for war are influenced most heavily by national attributes challenges the *structural realism* premise that war is inevitable and that global circumstances, not internal factors, are the most important determinants of warfare.

Geopolitical Factors and Length of Independence   Of all the issues that spark conflict, territorial disputes are the most likely to escalate to war (Vasquez, 2009; Wiegand, 2011). The setting and location of states—including key geographic circumstances, such as low supplies of cropland, fresh water, and treasured natural resources such as oil and gas reserves—and their distances from one another influence the likelihood of disputes and war (Gibler, 2007; Starr, 2006). The amount of resources and the market price of those particular resources even influence the intensity of the conflict (van der Ploeg, 2012) "When valuable natural resources are discovered in a particular region of a country, the people living in such localities suddenly have an economic incentive to succeed violently if necessary … conflict is also more likely in countries that depend heavily on natural resources for their export earnings, in part because rebel groups can extort the gains from this trade to finance their operations" (Collier, 2003, p. 41).

Duration of independence also influences the likelihood of armed conflict and disputes over territory. Newly independent countries usually go through a period of political unrest following their acquisition of independence as sovereign members in the international community of states. They then are likely to seek to resolve longstanding internal grievances and take up arms over contested territories with their neighbors (Rasler and Thompson, 2006). Such foreign disputes frequently expand into larger wars because throughout history they have frequently provoked great power *intervention*, or external interference by other states or non-state IGOs into the opposed countries' internal affairs. The high levels of *civil wars* and wars between neighboring states throughout the Global South may be explained by the fact that nearly all of these less developed countries have recently gained independence, many through violent revolutions.

Nationalism and Cultural Traditions   A country's behavior is strongly influenced by the cultural and ethical traditions of its peoples. In the state system, governed by the rules championed by realism, moral constraints on the use of force do not command wide acceptance (Hensel, 2007). Instead, most governments encourage their populations to glorify the state and accept whatever decisions their leaders proclaim as necessary for national security, including warfare against adversaries. Advocates of the cultural origins of war argue that most people in most societies are disengaged, or "numb," to what is going on around them and this prevents them from opposing their leaders' decisions to wage war. The modern state thus organizes its society to accept war and "builds a culture that affirms death" and accepts senseless carnage (Caspary, 1993).

As a natural extension of unerring loyalty to a nation, *nationalism* is widely believed to be the cauldron from which wars often spring (Van Evera, 1994). Nationalism began as a serious force in Europe 350 years ago when monarchical rulers such as Ferdinand and Isabella of Spain engaged in "state building" by fomenting nationalism to mobilize and manage the population, which bred religious and political intolerance, the repression of minorities, and, ultimately, war (Marx, 2003). English essayist Aldous Huxley saw nationalism as "the religion of the twentieth century"—when history's most destructive interstate wars were fought—and the linkage between nationalism and war has since grown over time (Woodwell, 2008). Today nationalism plays a role in fomenting hostilities in East Asia, particularly between China and Japan over the disputed South China Sea (Dittmer, 2013).

"The tendency of the vast majority of people to center their supreme loyalties on the nation-state," Jack Levy explains, is a powerful catalyst to war. When people "acquire an intense commitment to the power and prosperity of the state [and] this commitment is strengthened by national myths emphasizing the moral, physical, and political strength of the state and by individuals' feelings of powerlessness and their consequent tendency to seek their identity and fulfillment through the state, ... nationalism contributes to war" (Levy, 1989a, p. 271). This leads many to critique nationalism, although many defend it as a virtue that creates unity and solidarity within a country. Whatever its consequences, nationalism is widely seen as potentially the most powerful political force in today's world, an idea and *ideology* that animates the constructed images of many around the world.

Additionally, critics operating from the perspective of feminist theories of international relations argue that the foundation of war worldwide, alongside cultural numbing, is rooted in the masculine ethos of realism, which prepares people to accept war and to respect the warrior as a hero (see Enloe, 2000, 2004; Tickner, 2002). Feminist theory contends that gender roles, supported by realist values, contribute to the prevalence of militarism and warfare. To feminists and other constructivist theorists who embrace a cultural interpretation, the penchant for warfare does not evolve in a vacuum but is produced by the ways in which societies shape their populations' beliefs and norms. Many governments, through the educational programs they fund in schools and other institutions, indoctrinate militaristic values in their political culture that, taken to the extreme, condone war. Ironically, in a world of diverse national cultures,

CourseMate

**Case Study:
Hitler's Rise to Power
and Its Lessons**

NATIONALISM'S DARK AND DEADLY PAST Under the fascist dictatorship of Adolf Hitler (left), the Nazi government glorified the state and claimed that the German people were a superior race. What followed from this extreme form of nationalism was a ruthless German world war and campaign of genocide that exterminated six million Jews and other ethnic minorities. U.S. troops under the command of General George Patton (right) liberated the concentration camp at Buchenwald in May 1945, but not in time to save the lives of the prisoners whom the Nazi guards had put to death in the gas chambers.

cultural conditioning

The impact of national traditions and societal values on the behavior of states, under the assumption that culture affects national decision making about issues such as the acceptability of aggression.

the messages of obedience and of duty to make sacrifices to the state through such *cultural conditioning* are common. States often disseminate the belief that their right to make war should not be questioned and that the ethical principles of religious and secular philosophies prohibiting violence should be disregarded. Consequently, critics highlight the existence of powerful institutions that prepare individuals to subconsciously accept warfare as necessary and legitimate.

Feminist theory extends this explanation of armed aggression. It accounts for the fact that the probability of violence increases in cultures in which gender discrimination, inequality, and violence toward women are an accepted way of life (Hudson, 2012). Where cultural norms condone the mistreatment of women and deny them opportunities for education and employment, the outbreak of civil war is high (Caprioli, 2005; Melander, 2005).

Poverty, Relative Deprivation, and Demographic Stress   A country's level of economic development affects the probability of its involvement in war and armed revolution. Indeed, "underdevelopment is a statistically significant predictor of war" (Lemke, 2003, p. 58), and discontent with globalization and foreign economic liberalization can result in violent protest and civil war (Bussmann and Schneider, 2007).

relative deprivation

Inequality between the wealth and status of individuals and groups, and the outrage of those at the bottom about their perceived exploitation by those at the top.

Armed conflict, often an angry response to frustration, is a product of *relative deprivation*—people's perception that they are unfairly deprived of the wealth and status that they believe they deserve in comparison with more advantaged others. Violence erupts so frequently because hundreds of millions "belong to groups that face some form of cultural exclusion and are disadvantaged or discriminated against relative to others in their country," the UN observes. The same is true for national images of relative deprivation between countries. This is partially why the probability of armed conflict is the highest in the Global South, where people's expectations of what they deserve are rising more rapidly than their material rewards, and the existing gap in the distribution of wealth and opportunities is widening.

Popular support is critical to the success of armed rebellions, and poverty is a great motivator for allegiance to armed groups that promise security and an improved standard of living. Families "in conflict areas draw on local armed groups to protect their economic status when anticipating violence and … the poorer the household is at the start of the conflict, the higher is the probability of the household participating and supporting an armed group" (Justino, 2009, p. 315). Indeed, as poverty reduces the "mobilization costs" associated with any social movement, there are fewer disincentives to fight (Kuhn and Weidmann, 2013).

This relationship between poverty and armed conflict is all the more pronounced in countries where there is a *youth bulge*, where a large portion of the population is young and cannot secure jobs, provide for families, and achieve economic security. "Young men—out of school, out of work, and charged with hatred—are the lifeblood of deadly conflict. Countries with a high proportion of adults under thirty have two and a half times the probability of experiencing a new outbreak of civil conflict as do those more mature age structures relative to population size" (Cincotta and Engleman, 2004, p. 18).

youth bulge

A burgeoning youth population, thought to make countries more prone to civil conflicts.

AP Photo/Hani Mohammed

NOTHING TO SHOW Shown here, pro-democracy demonstrators march in Sanaa, Yemen on January 27, 2013, to demand a trial of former president Ali Abdullah Saleh. The discontent that led to Saleh stepping down from power was fueled in large part by the lack of jobs and resources, and the perception of corruption and discrimination. In Yemen, 74 percent of the population is less than 30 years old and almost half are neither in school nor employed. Said Yemen journalist Nadia Al-Sakkaf, "If you're a young Yemini, you don't have any reason for hope. There's no reason to think your life will be better than [that of] your parents" (Ghosh, 2011, p. 49).

So the near future faces an increasing threat—"a clash of generations"—as youth bulges increase the risk of internal armed conflict and political violence (Urdal, 2011). This is pointed to as one, among many, of the factors that will continue to contribute to unrest in the Middle East as the youth unemployment rate continues to hover around 25 percent. Among the highest in the world, this level of joblessness is a primary source of the anger that sparked the Arab Spring (Schuman, 2012).

Yet government policy and changing demographic trends have the potential to alter the outlook in the longer term. The risk of political violence can be reduced to some extent by providing education and concomitant employment opportunities. Furthermore, the "importance of youth bulges in causing violence is expected to fade in most parts of the world over the next decades because of declining fertility" (Urdal, 2011, p. 9).

Before concluding that poverty always breeds armed conflict, note that the *most* impoverished countries have been the least prone to start wars. The poorest countries cannot vent their frustrations aggressively because they lack the military or economic resources to do so. This does not mean that the poorest countries are always peaceful. If the past is a guide to the future, then the impoverished countries that develop economically will be the most likely to acquire arms and engage in future external wars. In particular, states are likely to initiate foreign wars *after* sustained periods of economic growth—that is, during periods of rising prosperity, when they can afford them (Cashman and Robinson, 2007). This signals looming dangers if the most rapidly growing Global South economies direct their growing resources toward armaments rather than investing in sustainable development.

Militarization   "If you want peace, prepare for war," realism counsels. It is questionable whether the acquisition of military power leads to peace or to war, but most Global South countries agree with the realists' thesis that weapons contribute to their security. They have been among the biggest customers in the robust global arms trade and have built huge armies to guard against their neighboring states' potential aggression as well as to control their own citizens (Blanton and Nelson, 2012; and see Chapter 8).

As Global South countries continue to equip their militaries, many worry that war will become more frequent. In other words, militarization has *not* led to peace in the Global South. Will the curse of violence someday be broken there?

One clue comes from an examination of the relationship between changes in military capabilities and war that occurred over centuries in Europe. During the period leading to the peak of the region's development, the world's most frequent and deadly wars occurred in Europe. The major European states armed themselves heavily and were engaged in warfare about 65 percent of the time during the sixteenth and seventeenth centuries (Wright, 1942). Between 1816 and 1945, three-fifths of all interstate wars took place in Europe, with one erupting roughly every other year (Singer, 1991). Not coincidentally, this happened when the developing states of Europe were most energetically building their militaries in competition with one another. Perhaps as a consequence, the great powers—those with the largest armed forces—were the most involved in, and most often initiated, war. Since 1945, however, with the exception of war among the now-independent states of the former Yugoslavia and between Russia and Georgia, interstate war has not occurred in Europe. As the European countries moved up the ladder of economic and political development, they moved away from war with one another.

In contrast, the developing countries now resemble Europe before 1945. If, in the immediate future, the Global South follows the model of Europe before 1945, we are likely to see an ocean of Global South violence surrounding a European (and Global North) island of peace and prosperity.

Economic System   Does the character of states' economic systems influence the frequency of warfare? The question has provoked controversy for centuries. Particularly since Marxism took root in Russia following the Bolshevik Revolution in 1917, communist theoreticians claimed that capitalism was the primary cause of imperialistic wars and colonialism. They were fond of quoting Vladimir Lenin's 1916 explanation of World War I as a war caused by imperialistic capitalists' efforts "to divert the attention of the laboring masses from the domestic political crisis" of collapsing incomes under capitalism.

According to the *communist theory of imperialism*, capitalism is mired in excess production. The need to export this excess provokes wars to capture and protect foreign markets. Thus, *laissez-faire economics*—based on the philosophical principle of free markets with little governmental regulation of the marketplace—rationalized militarism and imperialism for economic gain. Citing the demonstrable frequency with which wealthy capitalist societies militarily intervened on foreign soil for capital gain, Marxists believed, and generally still believe, that the best way to end international war was to end capitalism.

Contrary to Marxist theory, *commercial liberalism* contends that free-market systems promote peace, not war. Defenders of capitalism have long believed that free-market countries that practice free trade abroad are more pacific. They cite many reasons, but they center on the premise that commercial enterprises are natural lobbyists for an *economic peace* because their profits depend on it (Mousseau, 2013). War interferes with trade, blocks profit, destroys property, causes inflation, consumes scarce resources, and necessitates big government, counterproductive regulation of business activity, and high taxes. Conflict within a country similarly reduces its international trade (Magee and Massoud, 2011). By extension, this reasoning continues, as government regulation of internal markets declines, prosperity increases and fewer wars will occur.

The evidence for these rival theories is, not surprisingly, mixed. Conclusions depend in part on perceptions regarding economic influences on international behavior because alternative perspectives focus on different dimensions of the linkage. This controversy was at the heart of the ideological debate between the East and the West during the Cold War, when the relative virtues and vices of two radically different economic systems—communism and capitalism—were uppermost in people's minds.

The end of the Cold War did not end the historic debate about the link between economics and war. This basic theoretical question commands increasing interest, especially given the "shift in the relevance and usefulness of different power resources, with military power declining and economic power increasing in importance" (Huntington, 1991b, p. 5).

Regime Type   Realist theories discount the importance of government type as an influence on war and peace. Not so with liberalism. As noted in Chapter 2, *liberal theory* assigns great weight to the kinds of political institutions that states create to make policy decisions, and it predicts that the spread of "free" democratically ruled governments will promote peaceful interstate relations.

communist theory of imperialism

The Marxist-Leninist economic interpretation of imperialist wars of conquest as driven by capitalism's need for foreign markets to generate capital.

commercial liberalism

An economic theory advocating free markets and the removal of barriers to the flow of trade and capital as a locomotive for prosperity.

Carnegie Council Video: Commercial Liberalism

economic peace

The premise that economic institutions associated with a contract-intensive economy are the source of peace between countries.

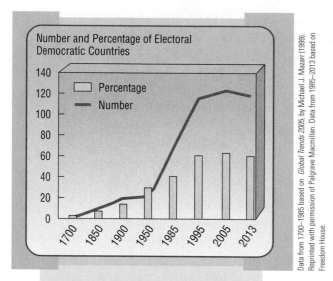

Number and Percentage of Electoral Democratic Countries

Data from 1700–1985 based on *Global Trends 2005*, by Michael J. Mazarr (1999). Reprinted with permission of Palgrave Macmillan. Data from 1985–2013 based on Freedom House.

FIGURE 7.1   THE ADVANCE OF ELECTORAL DEMOCRACY, 1700–2013 For 250 years since 1700, most choices about war were made by monarchs, despots, dictators, and autocrats. As this figure shows, that has changed with the growth of "electoral democracy" worldwide, with competitive and regular multiparty elections conducted openly without massive voting fraud. In 1974 only one in four countries was an electoral democracy. By the start of 2013, the number had grown to 118 countries, or approximately 61 percent (Freedom House, 2013). Whether this long-term transformation will produce peace is being tested.

As Immanuel Kant in 1795 argued in *Perpetual Peace*, when citizens are given basic human rights such as choosing their leaders through ballots as well as civil liberties such as free speech and a free press, these democracies would be far less likely to initiate wars than would countries ruled by dictators and kings. This is because a government accountable to the people would be constrained from waging war by public opinion. Other liberal reformers have since agreed with Kant, such as Thomas Jefferson, James Madison, and Woodrow Wilson. They all believed that an "empire of liberty" (as Madison pictured a growing community of liberal democracies) would be one freed of the curse of war, and that if democratic institutions spread throughout the world, the entire past pattern of belligerent international relations would be replaced by a new pacific pattern.

The impact of government type on propensity for armed conflict has taken on great significance following the rapid conversion of many dictatorships to democratic rule. These liberal government conversions have occurred in three successive "waves" since the 1800s (Huntington, 1991a). The first wave occurred between 1878 and 1926, and the second between 1943 and 1962. The third wave began in the 1970s when a large number of nondemocratic countries began to convert their governments to democratic rule. In a remarkable global *transformation* from past world history, the once radical idea that democracy is the ideal form of decision making has triumphed. According to Freedom House, almost two-thirds of the world's countries are now fully or partially democratic (see Figure 7.1).

Much research demonstrates that democracies resolve their differences with one another at the bargaining table rather than the battlefield, and that they are more likely to win wars than are nondemocracies. This pattern provides the cornerstone for the *democratic peace* proposition:

democratic peace

The theory that although democratic states sometimes wage wars against non-democratic states, they do not fight one another.

Democracies are unlikely to engage in any kind of militarized disputes with each other or to let any such disputes escalate into war. They rarely even skirmish. Pairs of democratic states have been only one-eighth as likely as other kinds of states to threaten to use force against each other, and only one-tenth as likely actually to do so…. Democracies are more likely to employ "democratic" means of peaceful conflict resolution. They are readier to reciprocate each other's behavior, to accept third-party *mediation* or *good offices* in settling disputes, and to accept binding third-party *arbitration* and *adjudication* (Russett, 2001a, p.235; see also Russett, 2005).

A considerable body of empirical evidence supports the proposition that democracies do not wage war against each other (Dafoe, Oneal, and Russett, 2013; Rasler and Thompson, 2005). Although there is debate about the specific causal mechanisms, it appears that the type of government, specifically multiparty elections, strongly influences foreign policy goals (Ungerer, 2012). Others point to an "us versus them" mentality that leads democracies to band together in the face of a common threat from autocracies (Gartzke and Weisiger, 2013). The democratic peace has also been attributed to a democratic state's "greater ability to more credibly reveal information" than other regime types (Lektzian and Souva, 2009, p. 35).

The growing recognition that ballots serve as a barrier against the use of bullets and bombs by one democracy against another has been inspired by the growth of democratic governance over the past three centuries (see Figure 7.1). Yet there is no certainty that liberal democracy will become universal or that the continued democratic reforms will automatically produce a peaceful world order. Emerging democracies are, in fact, prone to fight wars (Mansfield and Snyder, 2005a). The fact that leaders in elective democracies are accountable to public approval and electoral rejection does not guarantee that they will not use force to settle disputes with other democracies.

The fragility of democratic institutions was vividly illustrated by the sham reelection of President Mahmoud Ahmadinejad in Iran in 2009. Although analysts had predicted a close race, the official result claimed a margin of 63 percent for the incumbent. Most Iranians believe that electoral fraud occurred on an enormous scale, and three days after the election,

DISILLUSIONMENT AND CIVIL UNREST In reaction to the disputed outcome of the presidential election in Iran in 2009, the country witnessed the largest street demonstrations since the Islamic Revolution in 1979. Shown here are protestors at a mass rally in Azadi (Freedom) Square in Tehran. Said one Iranian citizen at the time, "People are depressed, and they feel they have been lied to, robbed of their rights and now are being insulted … It is not just a lie; it's a huge one" (Fathi, 2009, p. A6). The victory of centrist candidate Hassan Rouhani in the presidential election in 2013 gave many Iranians hope for a more moderate regime with greater respect for individual liberties.

mediation

A conflict-resolution procedure in which a third party proposes a nonbinding solution to the disputants.

good offices

Third-party provision of a place for negotiation among disputants; but the third party does not serve as a mediator in the actual negotiations.

arbitration

A conflict-resolution procedure in which a third party makes a binding decision between disputants through a temporary ruling board created for that ruling.

adjudication

A conflict-resolution procedure in which a third party makes a binding decision about a dispute in an institutional tribunal.

hundreds of thousands of Iranians took to the street in protest. The pillars of the Islamic Republic's pretensions of democracy were shaken as the government responded with a vicious crackdown that crushed dissent and restricted the opposition.

However, in the election in June 2013, Hassan Rouhani won the Iranian presidency. A centrist who appealed to both traditional conservatives and reform-minded voters, he promised to support greater personal freedoms, an improved economy with more job opportunities, and reduction in global tensions regarding Iran's nuclear program. Offering hope for moderation, reform, and respect for democracy, he proclaimed that "the sun of rationality and moderation is shining over Iran again to send the voice of unity and cohesion of this nation to the world."

This discussion of the characteristics of states that influence their proclivity for war does not exhaust the subject. Many other potential causes internal to the state exist. Yet, however important domestic influences might be as a source of war, many believe that the nature of the *global system* is even more critical. In the next section we will learn about the global context within which actors decide whether or not to wage armed conflict.

Case Study: Democracy and Peace

The Third Level of Analysis: The Global System

Realism emphasizes that the roots of armed conflict rest in human nature. In contrast, structural realism, or *neorealism*, sees war springing from changes at the global level of analysis, that is, as a product of the decentralized character of the global system that requires sovereign states to rely on *self-help* for their security:

> Although different realist theories often generate conflicting predictions, they share a core of common assumptions: The key actors in world politics are sovereign states that act rationally to advance their security, power, and wealth in a conflictual international system that lacks a legitimate governmental authority to regulate conflicts or enforce agreements.
>
> For realists, wars can occur not only because some states prefer war to peace, but also because of unintended consequences of actions by those who prefer peace to war and are more interested in preserving their position than in enhancing it. Even defensively motivated efforts by states to provide for their own security through armaments, alliances, and deterrent threats are often perceived as threatening and lead to counteractions and conflict spirals that are difficult to reverse. This is the *security dilemma*—the possibility that a state's actions to provide for its security may result in a decrease in the security of all states, including itself (Levy, 1998b, p. 145).

International *anarchy*, or the absence of institutions for global governance, may promote an outbreak of war. However, anarchy fails to provide a complete explanation of changes in the levels of war and peace over time or why particular wars are fought. To capture the many global determinants of armed conflict, also consider how and why global systems change. This requires exploring the impact of such global factors as the distribution of military capabilities, balances (and imbalances) of power, the number of alliances and international organizations, and the rules of international law. At issue is how the system's characteristics and institutions combine to influence changes in war's frequency. You can examine many of these factors in Chapters 8 and 9. Here we focus on cycles of war and peace at the global level.

Does Violence Breed Violence? Many interpreters of world history have noted that the seeds of future wars are often found in past wars (see Walter, 2004). Renaissance moral philosopher Erasmus of Rotterdam once asked, "What can war beget except war? But good will begets goodwill, equity, equity." Similarly, in his acceptance speech of the 2002 Nobel Peace Prize, former U.S. President Jimmy Carter sadly observed that "violence only begets conditions that beget future violence." For example, World War II was an outgrowth of World War I, the U.S. attack of Iraq in 2003 was an extension of the 1990 Persian Gulf War, and the successive waves of violent protest and brutal state retaliation in the Middle East that began in 2011 were seen by many as a domino effect, with each armed conflict stimulated by its predecessor.

Because the frequency of past wars is correlated with the incidence of wars in later periods, war appears to be contagious and its future outbreaks inevitable. If so, then something within the dynamics of global politics—its anarchical nature, its weak legal system, its uneven distribution of power, the inevitable destabilizing changes in the principal actors' relative power, or some combination of structural attributes—makes the global system that is centered on states a "war system."

However, it is not safe to infer that past wars *cause* later wars. The fact that a war precedes a later one does not mean that it caused the one that followed. Thus, many scholars reject the deterministic view that history is destiny, with outcomes caused by previous events. Instead, they embrace the *bargaining model of war*, which sees war as a product of a rational choice that weighs anticipated costs against benefits. The decision to engage in warfare—as well as the decision to conclude it—is part of a cost–benefit analysis and bargaining process that occurs between adversaries to settle disputes and disagreements "over scarce goods, such as the placement of a border, the composition of a national government, or control over national resources" (Reiter, 2003, p. 27; see also Reiter, 2009).

War's recurrence throughout history does not necessarily mean we will always have it. War is not a universal institution; some societies have never known war and others have been immune to it for prolonged periods. Moreover, since 1945 the outbreak of armed aggression *between* states has greatly declined, despite the large increase in the number of independent countries. This indicates that armed conflict is not necessarily inevitable and that historical forces do not control people's freedom of choice or experiences.

Power Transitions   These trends notwithstanding, when changes have occurred in the major states' military capabilities, war has often resulted. Although not inevitable, war has been likely whenever competitive states' power ratios (the differentials between their capabilities) have narrowed. As Monica Toft (2007, pp. 244–246) concludes, "Peace is clearly a value most states share, but not always, and not always above all other values.... Shifts in the distribution of power go a long way toward explaining the likelihood of violence."

This hypothesis is known as the *power transition theory*. This theoretical explanation of armed conflict is a central tenant of structural realism—the neorealist theory that emphasizes that change in the great powers' military capabilities relative to those of their closest rivals is a key determinant of the behavior of states within the global system and of the probability of warfare (Palmer and Morgan, 2007). As Michelle Benson (2007) explains, "this theory has proven itself to be the most successful structural theory of war [suggesting] that three simple conditions—power transition, relative power parity, and a dissimilarity of preferences for the status quo—are necessary for great power war."

bargaining model of war

An interpretation of war's onset as a choice by the initiator to bargain through aggression with an enemy in order to win on an issue or to obtain things of value, such as territory or oil.

power transition theory

The theory that war is likely when a dominant great power is threatened by the rapid growth of a rival's capabilities, which reduces the difference in their relative power.

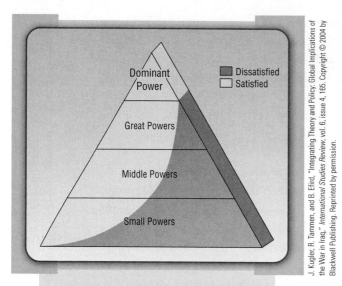

J. Kugler, R. Tammen, and B. Efird, "Integrating Theory and Policy: Global Implications of the War in Iraq," *International Studies Review*, vol. 6, issue 4, 165. Copyright © 2004 by Blackwell Publishing. Reprinted by permission.

FIGURE 7.2 A POWER TRANSITION IN THE GLOBAL HIERARCHY Where countries sit in the world pyramid of power predicts their posture toward global change. As this figure suggests, the more favorable a country's position is in the world hierarchy, the more satisfied it is with the international status quo; conversely, states lower in the hierarchy are more dissatisfied and therefore promote change. The power transition theory provides leverage for "anticipating when and where great power and regional wars most likely will occur. With a warning well ahead of time comes the opportunity to construct current policies that can manage the events that lead to future disputes" (Kugler, Tammen, and Efird, 2004).

During the transition from developing to developed status, emergent challengers can use force to achieve the recognition that their newly formed military muscles allow them. Conversely, established powers ruled by risk-acceptant leaders are often willing to employ force to put the brakes on their relative decline. Thus, when advancing and retreating states seek to cope with the changes in their relative power, war between the rising challenger(s) and the declining power(s) becomes especially likely (see Figure 7.2). For example, the rapid changes in the power and status that produced the division of Europe among seven great powers nearly equal in military strength are often (along with the alliances they nurtured) interpreted as the tinderbox from which World War I ignited.

Rapid shifts in the global distribution of military power *have* often preceded outbursts of aggression, especially when the new distribution nears approximate equality and thereby tempts the rivals to wage war against their hegemonic challengers. According to the power transition theory, periods in which rivals' military capabilities are nearly balanced create "the necessary conditions for global war, while gross inequality assures peace or, in the worst case, an asymmetric, limited war" (Kugler, 2001). Moreover, transitions in states' relative capabilities can potentially lead the weaker party to start a war in order to either overtake its rival or protect itself from domination. Presumably, the uncertainty created by a rough equilibrium prompts the challenger's effort to wage war against a stronger opponent. Though the challenger tends to be unsuccessful in its bid for victory, there are notable exceptions where the initiator has advantages (such as the Vietnam, the Six-Day, Bangladesh, Yom Kippur/Ramadan, Falklands, and Persian Gulf wars).

Today, there is much speculation that a power transition is under way that will witness the decline of the United States and the ascendance of emerging non-Western powers, most notably China (Kastner and Saunders, 2012; Kissinger, 2012). Along with this, there is concern that there may also be a transition in the ideas and principles that underlie the existing global order—with commitment to democracy, free markets, and the acceptability of U.S. military power replaced by alternative illiberal constructions that present an authoritarian capitalist alternative. However, John Ikenberry (2011, p. 57) presents a more nuanced perspective, arguing:

> This panicked narrative misses a deeper reality: although the United States' position in the global system is changing, the liberal international order is alive and well. The struggle over international order today is not about fundamental principles. China and other emerging great powers do not want to contest the basic rules and principles of the liberal international order; they wish to gain more authority and leadership within it.

While a global diffusion of wealth and power is occurring, emerging powers are benefitting from the rules and institutions that have been largely shaped by the United States. And, to date, no viable alternatives have emerged to challenge the current construction of the existing international order.

Cyclical Theories   If war is recurrent but not necessarily inevitable, are there other global factors besides power transitions that might also explain changes over time in the outbreak of armed conflict? The absence of a clear trend in war's frequency since the late fifteenth century, and its periodic outbreak after intermittent stretches of peace, suggests that world history seesaws between long cycles of war and peace. This provides a third global explanation of war's onset.

Long-cycle theory seeks to explain the peaks and valleys in the frequency with which major wars have erupted periodically throughout modern history. As noted in Chapter 4, its advocates argue that cycles of world leadership and global war have existed over the past five centuries, with a "general war" erupting approximately once every century, although at irregular intervals (Ferguson, 2010; Modelski and Thompson, 1996; Wallerstein, 2005).

Long-cycle theory draws its insights from the observation that a great power has risen to a hegemonic position about every 80 to 100 years. Using as a measure of dominance the possession of disproportionate sea power, we observe the rise of a single hegemon regularly appearing after particular hegemonic wars (see Figure 7.3). Portugal and the Netherlands rose at the beginning of the sixteenth and seventeenth centuries, respectively; Britain climbed to dominance at the beginning of both the eighteenth and nineteenth centuries; and the United States became a world leader at the end of World War II and regained its position of global

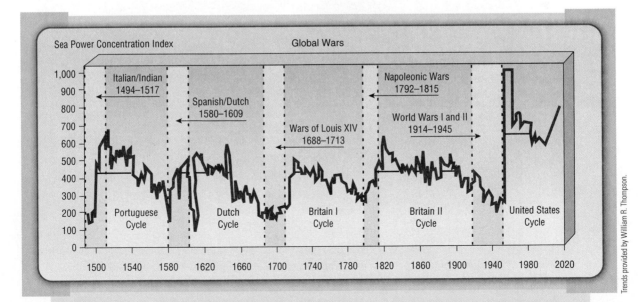

FIGURE 7.3　THE LONG CYCLE OF GLOBAL LEADERSHIP AND GLOBAL WAR, 1494–2020 Over the past 500 years, five great powers have risen to control the global system, but in time each former hegemonic leader's top status eventually slipped and a new rival surfaced and waged a global war in an effort to become the next global leader. The troubling question is whether this long cycle of war can be broken in the future when U.S. leadership is eventually challenged by a rising military rival such as China.

supremacy after the Cold War ended in 1991. Now the question remains as to whether or not China's rise is sustainable and, if so, whether or not it signals a transition in yet another cycle of hegemonic dominance (Doran, 2012).

During their reigns, these hegemonic powers monopolized military power and trade and determined the system's rules. *Hegemonic stability theory* expects that a stable world order requires sustained global leadership by a single great power. By exercising its preponderance of power, the hegemon establishes the conditions necessary for order in the international system, and discourages aggressors who would challenge the global status quo.

Yet no previous hegemonic power has retained its top-dog position perpetually (see Table 4.1 in Chapter 4). "The best instituted governments," observed British political philosopher Henry St. John in 1738, "carry in them the seeds of their destruction: and, though they grow and improve for a time, they will soon tend visibly to their dissolution. Every hour they live is an hour the less that they have to live." In each cycle, over-commitments, the costs of empire, and ultimately the appearance of rivals have led to the delegitimation of the hegemon's authority and to the deconcentration of power globally. As challengers to the hegemon's rule grew in strength, a "global war" has erupted after a long period of peace in each century since 1400. At the conclusion of each previous general war, a new world leader emerged, and the cyclical process began anew. As Brock Tessman and Steve Chan summarize and explain:

hegemonic stability theory

A body of theory that maintains that the establishment of hegemony for global dominance by a single great power is a necessary condition for global order in commercial transactions and international military security.

Paul Conroy/Alamy

STATE SOVEREIGNTY AND THE USE OF FORCE The principle of nonintervention posits that states should not intervene into the internal affairs of other sovereign states. Increasingly, however, this principle is challenged as more powerful states have militarily intervened into smaller states for a variety of humanitarian and strategic reasons. In 2011, NATO forces supported rebels in Libya seeking to overthrow the authoritarian regime of Libyan leader Muammar Gaddafi. Pictured here, a 500-pound bomb strikes a rebel-held position in the village of Ras Lanouf.

The theory of power cycles contends that the growth and decline of national power holds the key to understanding the occurrence of extensive wars. Certain critical points in a state's power trajectory are especially dangerous occasions for such armed clashes [from which we can] derive expectations about the risk propensity of states during different periods in their power cycle.... Critical points tend to incline states to initiate deterrence confrontations and escalate them to war.... Changes in national power tend to follow a regular pattern of ascendance, maturation, and decline and ... these trajectories reflect the major states' relative competitiveness in the international system. When these states encounter an unexpected reversal in the direction or rate of change in their power trajectory, they are subject to various psychological impulses or judgmental challenges that increase the danger of extensive wars (Tessman and Chan, 2004, p. 131).

Such deterministic theories have intuitive appeal. It seems plausible, for instance, that just as long-term downswings and recoveries in business cycles profoundly affect subsequent behaviors and conditions, wars produce after-effects that may last for generations. The idea that a country at war will become exhausted and lose its enthusiasm for another war, but only for a time, is known as the *war weariness hypothesis* (Pickering, 2002). Italian historian Luigi da Porto expresses one version: "Peace brings riches; riches bring pride; pride brings anger; anger brings war; war brings poverty; poverty brings humanity; humanity brings peace; peace, as I have said, brings riches, and so the world's affairs go round." Because it takes time to move through these stages, alternating periods of enthusiasm for war and weariness of war appear to be influenced by learning and forgetting over time.

war weariness hypothesis

The proposition that fighting a major war is costly in terms of lost lives and income, and these costs greatly reduce a country's tolerance for undertaking another war until enough time passes to lose memory of those costs.

FREQUENCY AND TYPES OF ARMED CONFLICT

You have now considered some of the major contending hypotheses and theories about the sources of armed conflict. In a world of seemingly constant change, a grim continuity stands out: violence—or, in the words of former UN Secretary-General Boutros Boutros-Ghali, a "culture of death."

Since 1900, at least 750 armed conflicts have been waged, killing millions, creating hordes of refugees, and costing trillions of dollars, as well as untold human misery. The belief that "only the dead will see the end of war" is based on the fact that warfare has been an ugly, almost constant factor in a changing world. In the past 3400 years, "humans have been entirely at peace for 268 of them, or just 8 percent of recorded history" (Hedges, 2003).

Scientists who study war quantitatively through the scientific methodologies of *behavioralism* have attempted to estimate the frequency of armed conflicts and to measure trends and cycles in the global system's level of violent conflicts. Different definitions and indicators produce somewhat different pictures of variations over time (as *constructivism* emphasizes they will; see Gleditsch, 2004). Nonetheless, various measures converge on the basic trends and patterns, from different periods of measurement. In the long term (over the past 600 years), armed conflict has been continual, with a general trend toward rising incidence. In the relative short term (since 1950), however, the pattern has shown fewer, but more deadly, armed conflicts. These inventories report in different ways what the mass media tell us—that violence and global insecurity are inherent in world politics. Armed conflict in 2013 in Syria, Sudan,

South Sudan, Lebanon, and elsewhere—as well as the tension surrounding the South China Sea dispute—cast a dark shadow.

In the past, when people thought about armed conflicts, they thought primarily about wars *between* states and secondarily about civil wars *within* existing sovereign states. Both types of wars were frequently under way at similar rates each year between 1816 and World War II. However, since then, internal wars have increasingly defined the global landscape.

Figure 7.4 records the changes in both the number of conflicts over the past half-century as well as the type of conflict. This new pattern of civil wars and armed conflicts that do not involve government forces on at least one side has become especially prevalent since 1990. Indeed, between 1989 and 2012, only 9 of all 141 active armed conflicts worldwide, or 6 percent, were interstate wars between countries. The conflicts between Eritrea–Ethiopia (1998–2000) and India–Pakistan (1997–2003) concerned territory, whereas the war between Iraq and the United States and its allies (2003) was fought over governmental power. In 2012, all but one of the thirty-two armed conflicts were waged within states. Eight of the major intrastate armed conflicts were internationalized, where troops from states that were not primary parties to the conflict aided the side of the government. These included the conflict between the United States and Al Qaeda, as well as those involving Afghanistan, Somalia, Rwanda, Yemen, Azerbaijan, Central African Republic, and the Democratic Republic of the Congo. Over the past seven years, external involvement in conflicts has been on the rise, and 25 percent of conflicts were characterized by this phenomenon in 2012 (Themnér and Wallensteen, 2013).

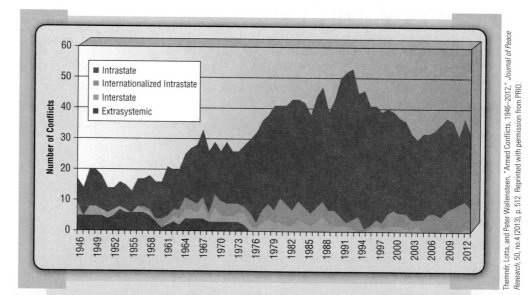

Themnér, Lotta, and Peter Wallensteen, "Armed Conflicts, 1946–2012," *Journal of Peace Research*, 50, no.4 (2013), p. 512. Reprinted with permission from PRIO.

FIGURE 7.4   CHANGING FREQUENCY AND TYPE OF ACTS OF ARMED CONFLICT
Measuring the frequency of armed conflicts each year since 1946, the figure depicts a gradual increase in the frequency of conflicts until the peak in 1992, after which a decline transpired that lasted roughly a decade before, in 2003, the number of conflicts again began to rise. Throughout this period, the type of conflict has changed, with extra-systemic armed aggression becoming, it is hoped, extinct and interstate conflict between countries becoming very rare. At the same time, however, the occurrence of armed conflict within states has grown, as has the number of internal conflicts where there is intervention from third-party states on one side or the other.

Until 911, most security analysts expected civil wars to remain the most common type of global violence. However, they have had to revise their strategies and thinking to accommodate changing realities. Today, military planners face two unprecedented security challenges. As described by Henry Kissinger, these challenges are "terror caused by acts until recently considered a matter for internal police forces rather than international policy, and scientific advances and proliferation that allow the survival of countries to be threatened by developments entirely within another state's territory." This suggests an increased risk of further armed aggression, fought by irregular militia and private or semiprivate forces (such as terrorist networks) against the armies of states, or by "shadow warriors" commissioned by states as "outsourced" mercenaries or paid militia.

The characteristics of contemporary warfare appear to be undergoing a major transformation, even though many of the traditional characteristics of armed conflict continue. The general trends show the following:

- The proportion of countries throughout the globe engaged in wars has declined.

- Most wars now occur in the Global South, which is home to the highest number of states, with the largest populations, the least income, and the least stable governments.

- The goal of waging war to conquer foreign territory is no longer a motive.

THE CHANGING NATURE OF WAR The asymmetric struggle in Afghanistan between the world's most powerful military and insurgents raised questions about the conventional understanding of war—in particular, how it is conducted and what constitutes "victory." As the longest U.S. war to date, U.S. forces are to withdraw from a combat role by the end of 2014, with only minimal troops remaining behind to train Afghan forces and pursue a counter-terrorism mission. "We're transitioning, not leaving," explained U.S. Secretary of Defense Chuck Hagel in June 2013. "We intend to be [in Afghanistan] for the long haul." Pictured here U.S. soldiers conduct a patrol in Chorah, Afghanistan, on February 23, 2013.

■ Wars between the great powers are becoming obsolete; since 1945 the globe has experienced a *long peace*—the most prolonged period in modern history (since 1500) in which no wars have occurred between the most powerful countries.

Although in the long term, armed conflict *between* states may disappear, the frequency of armed conflict *inside* established states is growing. Next we examine the characteristics of armed conflict *within* states.

ARMED CONFLICT WITHIN STATES

Large-scale civil strife is bred by the failure of state governments to effectively govern within their territorial borders. Mismanagement by governments lacking authority and unable to meet the basic human needs of their citizens is a global trend. This incompetence has led to an epidemic of *failed states* throughout the globe. Today as many as 70 state governments are under stress and vulnerable to civil war (see Map 7.1). Sometimes the armed conflict is confined to local regions that seek secession and independence, and other times failing states are victims of widespread but episodic fighting by insurgents and warlords. The citizens of failing states pay the heaviest price for the internal conflict, political violence, and humanitarian catastrophe that commonly befall states that cannot discharge basic functions. The proliferation of failing states is also a growing global danger, because "violent conflict, refugee flow, arms trafficking, and disease are rarely contained within national borders" (Patrick, 2011, p. 55).

There are many causes of state failure and civil disintegration, but failed states share some key characteristics that make them vulnerable to disintegration, civil war, and terrorism. In general, studies of this global trend suggest the following (Collier, 2007; Acemoglu and Robinson, 2012; Piazza, 2008):

■ A strong predictor of state failure is poverty, but extreme income and gender inequality within countries are even better warning signs.

■ The failing states most vulnerable to internal rebellion are ruled by corrupt governments widely regarded as illegitimate and ineffective.

■ Democracy, particularly with a strong parliament, generally lowers the risk of state failure; autocracy increases it.

■ Poor or young democracies, however, are more unstable than either wealthy or established democracies or poor nondemocracies, and poor democracies that do not improve living standards are exceptionally vulnerable.

■ Population pressures, exacerbated by internally displaced people, refugees, and food scarcity, contribute to state failure and civil unrest.

■ Governments that do not protect human rights are especially prone to fail.

■ So-called petrostates relying on oil and gas for income are shaky, especially if the governing authority is weak and permissive of huge gaps in the distribution of political power and wealth.

■ States with governments that do not protect freedom of religion are especially likely to fail.

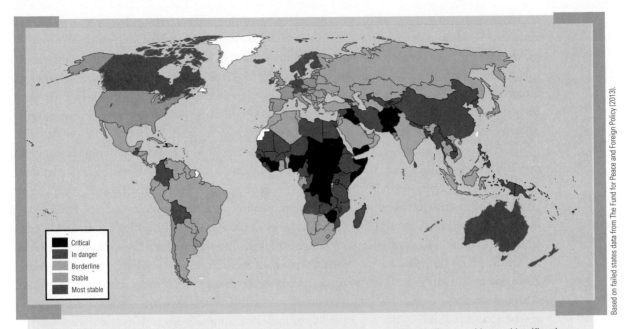

Based on failed states data from The Fund for Peace and Foreign Policy (2013).

MAP 7.1   THE THREAT OF FAILED STATES   Based upon 12 social, economic, and political indicators, this map identifies the world's 16 most vulnerable countries whose governments are most critically in danger of failing and most likely to collapse in civil war and anarchy. Also identified are an additional 54 countries that are "in danger," where some significant elements of their societies and institutions are vulnerable to failure. These potential "failed states" threaten the progress and stability of surrounding countries. State failure and civil war are particularly evident in the high-risk, weak, and impoverished states in Africa. In a ranking of state failure among 178 countries in 2013, Somalia topped the list for the sixth year in a row, followed closely by the Democratic Republic of the Congo.

- States that have strong rules protecting free international trade gain stability; states with high inflation are prone to fail.

- The existence of a youth bulge increases the risk of state failure through war because large pools of underemployed youths are easily mobilized into military action.

The globe is speckled with many dangerous flash points where countries are highly vulnerable to dissolution as a result of state failure, mismanagement, civil revolt, and violent government takeovers. Inasmuch as most of the sovereign states in the world have one or more of these attributes, it is likely that the prevalence of failed states is a growing problem in the globalized twenty-first century.

Intrastate Conflict

Armed conflicts within states have erupted far more frequently than have armed conflicts between states. Between 1989 and 2014, internal armed conflict over government or territory has by far been the most common. For example, of the thirty-two armed conflicts active in 26 locations around the world in 2012, all but one were intrastate conflicts involving a government fighting with, in some cases, more than one opposition group at a time (Themnér and Wallensteen, 2013).

Civil war, where the intensity of internal armed conflict reached at least 1000 battle related deaths per year, occurred 155 times between 1816 and the start of 2013. Their outbreak has been somewhat irregular, with over 60 percent erupting after 1946 and with the frequency steadily climbing each decade (see Table 7.1). However, this accelerating trend is, in part, a product of the increased number of independent states in the global system, which makes the incidence of civil war statistically more probable. In 2012, however, the number of internal armed conflicts (where at least twenty-five battle-related deaths occurred) declined by 5 from the prior year, and the number of civil wars with more than 1000 battle-related deaths, though comparatively modest, remained at six (Themnér and Wallensteen, 2013).

Civil wars dominate the global terrain because they start and re-ignite at a higher rate than they end, and they last longer (Hironaka, 2005). There is a tendency for countries that have experienced one civil war to undergo two or more subsequent civil wars (Quinn, Mason, and Gurses, 2007), and this pattern is even more pronounced for conflicts characterized by an *enduring internal rivalry (EIR)*. Empirical evidence shows that "76% of all civil war years from 1946 to 2004 took place in the context of EIRs," and that such civil wars were more likely to recur and to be followed by shorter periods of relative peace (DeRouen and Bercovitch, 2008, p. 55). Moreover, the average duration of civil wars once they erupt has increased; one study estimates that 130 civil wars fought worldwide since World War II lasted an average of 11 years (Stark, 2007). Consider examples of long-lasting and resumed civil wars in Afghanistan, Burundi, Chad, Colombia, Congo, Indonesia, Iran, Iraq, Ivory Coast, Lebanon, Liberia, Myanmar, Peru, the Philippines, Rwanda, Somalia, Sri Lanka, Sudan, Syria, Turkey, and Uganda.

Another noteworthy characteristic of intrastate armed conflicts is their severity. The number of lives lost in civil violence has always been very high, and casualties from civil wars since World War II have increased at alarming rates, especially among children who have been both innocent victims and major participants. Given that the most lethal civil wars in history have erupted recently, the cliché that "the most savage conflicts occur in the home" captures the ugly reality, as genocide and mass slaughter aimed at depopulating entire regions have become commonplace in recent civil wars (see A Closer Look: Sudan and the Human Cost of War).

enduring internal rivalry (EIR)

Protracted violent conflicts between governments and insurgent groups within a state.

TABLE 7.1	Civil Wars, 1816–2012		
Period	Key System Characteristics	System Size (average number of states)	Number of Civil Wars Begun
1816–1848	Monarchies in Concert of Europe suppress democratic revolutions	28	12
1849–1881	Rising nationalism and civil wars	39	20
1882–1914	Imperialism and colonialization	40	18
1915–1945	World wars and economic collapse	59	14
1946–1988	Decolonialization and independence for emerging Global South countries during Cold War	117	65
1989–2012	Age of failed states and civil wars	198	26
1816–2012			155

Source: Data for 1816–1945 courtesy of the Correlates of War project under the direction of J. David Singer and Melvin Small; data from 1946 to 2012 for intrastate armed conflicts with 1000 or more battle-related deaths drawn from the Uppsala Conflict Data Program Dyadic Dataset v.1-2013. (see Themnér and Wallensteen, 2013).

A **Closer** Look

SUDAN AND THE HUMAN COST OF WAR

Sudan provides a horrifying example of the mass slaughter of civilians that occurs when government seeks to keep power by destroying minority opposition groups. Since the outbreak of civil war in 1955, Sudan has been in an almost continuous state of violent internal conflict. The first phase of civil war erupted when the Arab-led Khartoum government broke its promises to southerners to create a federal system to ensure their representation and regional autonomy in the newly independent state. Compounded by deep cultural and religious differences, violent aggression raged, eventually claiming the lives of more than a half million people—of which only 20 percent were armed combatants—and displacing hundreds of thousands more. With mediation from religious NGOs, in 1972 the Addis Ababa Agreement was reached, which established a single southern administrative region and brought an end to armed hostilities.

However, the cease-fire proved to be only a fleeting peace. Due to perceived transgression by the north, unrest in the south grew. In 1983, civil war broke out again, fueled by racial and religious tensions, competition over oil resources, and struggles for political power. The Arab-controlled Sudanese government and government-backed Janjaweed militia suspended democracy in 1989 and undertook a divide-and-destroy campaign of *state-sponsored terrorism* against those living in the south.

The historical north-south conflict began to move toward resolution, and eventually a peace agreement was signed in 2005 that called for sharing wealth and power, and included mutual security arrangements. Yet attacks on non-Arab civilians in the extremely marginalized district of Darfur escalated. In July 2005, U.S. President George W. Bush characterized the situation in Darfur as "clearly genocide." By February 2010, when the Sudanese government signed a cease-fire agreement with the JEM, the largest rebel group in Darfur, UN estimates put the death toll at roughly 300,000 people, with another 2.5 million having fled their homes.

Though a mostly peaceful process for secession of South Sudan took place in 2011, another fault line erupted in 2012 when vicious armed conflict sprung up along the border between the two countries over control of the oil-rich regions that lie largely in South Sudan. Additionally, fierce fighting continued in the Nuba Mountains of central Sudan, with the northern Sudanese Army waging an aggressive campaign to crush rebel fighters. The bloodbath throughout Sudan and South Sudan has made this tragic place of death the worst since World War II, and raises questions about the prospects for lasting peace.

state-sponsored terrorism

Formal assistance, training, and arming of foreign terrorists by a state in order to achieve foreign policy goals.

WATCH THE VIDEO:

CourseMate

Carnegie Council Video:
Southern Sudan: Would
You Declare War?

(Continued)

SUDAN AND THE HUMAN COST OF WAR (Continued)

YOU DECIDE:

1. At what point is war no longer rational? How well does the rational actor model explain the persistence of armed conflict? What insights do other theoretical traditions provide?

2. Given the history of endemic violence in Sudan, under what conditions can a lasting peace be reached?

3. Why have so many noncombatants been targeted, and what responsibility does the international community have to protect them?

Another salient characteristic of internal armed conflicts is the resistance to negotiated settlement. Making peace between rival factions that are struggling for power, driven by hatred, and poisoned by the inertia of prolonged killing is difficult. Few domestic enemies fighting in a civil war have succeeded in ending the combat through negotiated compromise. The reoccurrence of civil war is often due to commitment problems and uncertainties about the military capabilities of the opponent. Typically, a civil war settlement requires insurgents to lay down

Eye Ubiquitous/SuperStock

WARFARE AND CHILDREN Children have often been the major victims of civil strife and even active participants as child soldiers. They join for many reasons—some are kidnapped and forced to join; others are lured by promises of money; others have lost loved ones and seek vengeance. After putting down arms, says Philippe Houdard, the founder of Developing Minds Foundation, the "biggest challenge is making them emotionally whole again ... to get them from being killing machines to normal human beings" (Drost, 2009, p. 8). Here we see young children in Angola armed for combat.

their arms. This shifts the balance of power in favor of the government, which may be tempted to press its advantage and exploit the cease-fire. "Because the rebels know about the government's incentive to renege on the deal, they are less likely to be willing to sign and maintain a peace agreement" (Mattes and Savun, 2010, p. 512). Therefore, commitment problems arise when the government is not able to credibly obligate itself to a peaceful resolution of the conflict (Hartzell and Hoddie, 2007).

For this reason, states may choose to bind themselves to an international agreement, or make a "credible commitment," by joining institutions such as the International Criminal Court (Simmons and Danner, 2010). Further evidence shows that the concerns of insurgents can be addressed through third-party guarantees, the adoption of institutional safeguards that promote the sharing of power between domestic groups, and transparent information-sharing regarding military capabilities and resolve. "Carefully designed peace agreements can guard against renewed civil war by calling for international monitoring, making the belligerents submit military information to third parties, and providing for verification of this information" (Mattes and Savun, 2010, p. 511). Third-party arbitration, however, can also lead to prolonged violence if, for example, multiple countries with conflicting interests are involved in the negotiations (Aydin and Regan, 2012). This can be seen in the international negotiations—and the opposing perspectives of the United States and Russia—regarding the Syrian civil war. It is to the international dynamics of internal conflict that we now turn.

The International Dimensions of Internal Conflict

The rise of failing states and their frequent fall into intrastate conflict may make it tempting to think of armed conflict within states as stemming exclusively from conditions within those countries. However, "states do not exist in a vacuum but are influenced by external actors" (Thyne, 2006, p. 937). As George Modelski (1964, p. 41) explained, "war has two faces…. Internal wars affect the international system [and] the international system affects internal wars."

Take, for example, the consequences of violent government takeover through a *coup d'etat*. Historically, successful coups tended to result in authoritarian regimes seizing power, such as Pinochet in Chile or Suharto in Indonesia. Between 1950 and 2013, there were 475 coup attempts in 96 countries around the world (see Map 7.2). The highest frequency of coup attempts occurred in the 1960s, followed by peaks in the 1970s and early 1990s (Powell and Thyne, 2011). Although coups continue to occur—on May 1, 2013, a suspected rebel group attempted and failed to overthrow the president of Chad, Idriss Deby—since the end of the Cold War, the frequency of coups has declined by almost half, and the resulting governments have generally permitted competitive elections within five years. Political scientists Hein Goemans and Nikolay Marinov attribute this changed pattern, in part, to an external factor: "Since the end of Cold War rivalry for spheres of influence, Western powers have become less willing to tolerate dictatorships—and more likely to make aid contingent upon holding elections" (Keating, 2009b, p. 28).

Because the great powers have global interests, they have played roles "behind the scenes," not only in the occurrence of coup d'etats, but also militarily in intrastate conflict to support friendly governments and to overthrow unfriendly ones. Intergovernmental relations influence

coup d'etat

A sudden, forcible takeover of government by a small group within that country, typically carried out by violent or illegal means with the goal of installing their own leadership in power.

CourseMate

Carnegie Council Video:
Coup D'etat

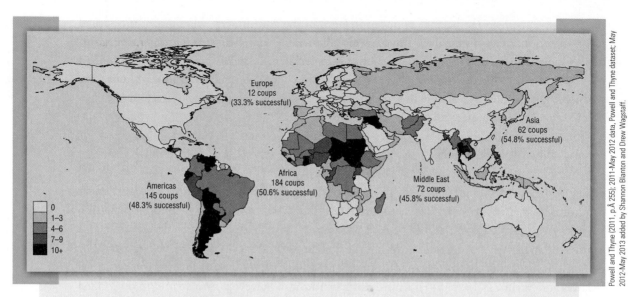

Powell and Thyne (2011, p. Å 255); 2011–May 2012 data. Powell and Thyne dataset; May 2012–May 2013 added by Shannon Blanton and Drew Wagstaff.

MAP 7.2 COUPS ATTEMPTS, 1950–2013 Of the 476 coup attempts between 1950 and 2013, about 49 percent (233) were successful. Coups are most common in the Global South, with Africa and Latin America experiencing the greatest number. In July 2013, a successful military coup occurred in Egypt that ousted Mohamed Morsi, who is considered by many to be Egypt's first democratically-elected president.

the onset and conduct of internal armed conflict "because they signal information about an outside actor's likelihood of aiding either the government or the opposition if a civil war were to begin" (Thyne, 2006, p. 939; see also Thyne, 2009). Neighboring states may also intervene within another country in an effort to thwart the diffusion of war across shared boundaries (Kathman, 2010). Outside intervention in intrastate conflict has been fairly common, and has occurred in over a fourth of all intrastate armed conflicts since 1989 (Themnér and Wallensteen, 2012).

In the aftermath of external intrusions, the targets' domestic societies have been transformed. At times, external actors (states and IGOs) have sent armed forces into failed states to contain and control the civil conflict causing violence and attempt to reestablish governing authority. A recent exception to the usual tendency for intrastate wars to become internationalized by foreign intervention is the U.S.-led invasion of Iraq: "In a reversal of the classic spillover of conflict from intra- to interstate, developments in Iraq during 2004 raised the prospect of an international conflict creating a fully-fledged civil war" rather than restoring peace (SIPRI, 2009).

There is another dimension to the internationalization of intrastate conflict. Many analysts believe that domestic insurrections become internationalized when leaders faced with internal opposition intentionally provoke an international *crisis*, hoping their citizens will become less rebellious if their attention is diverted to the threat of foreign aggression. This proposition has become known as the *diversionary theory of war*. This theory draws a direct connection between civil strife and foreign aggression. It maintains that when leaders sense their country is suffering from conflict at home, they are prone to attempt to contain that domestic strife by waging a war against foreigners—hoping that the international danger will take citizens' attention away from their dissatisfaction with their home leadership.

It is logical for leaders to assume that national unity will rise when a foreign rivalry exists. This creates strong temptations for them to seek to manage domestic unrest by initiating foreign adventures and demonstrating their competence. To put it cynically, "when domestic unrest threatens a loss of political support from groups that are politically important to the leadership … we expect leaders to try and rally their support through heightened international conflict" (Nicholls, Huth, and Appel, 2010, p. 915; see also Münster and Staal, 2011).

Indeed, many political advisers have counseled this strategy, as realist theorist Niccolò Machiavelli did in 1513 when he advised leaders to undertake foreign wars whenever turmoil within their state became too great. John Foster Dulles echoed him in 1939 when he recommended before he became U.S. secretary of state that "the easiest and quickest cure of internal dissension is to portray danger from abroad." This strategy was suspected in Ugandan President Idi Amin's invasion of Tanzania in 1978 as an effort, in part, to counter growing domestic dissent and cover up an army mutiny in the southwestern region of his own country.

Whether leaders actually start wars to offset domestic conflict and heighten public approval remains a subject of debate. We cannot demonstrate that many leaders intentionally undertake diversionary actions to defend themselves against domestic opposition, even in democracies during bad economic times, or to influence legislative outcomes (Oneal and Tir, 2006). Unpopular leaders may instead be highly motivated to exercise caution in foreign affairs and to avoid the use of force overseas in order to cultivate a reputation as a peacemaker. It may be better for leaders facing opposition to avoid further criticism that they are intentionally manipulative by addressing domestic problems rather than engaging in reckless wars

THE PAINFUL LEGACY OF ARMED CONFLICT Armed struggles within countries occur more frequently than those between states, though many intrastate conflicts still have repercussions for world politics more broadly. Pictured here are residents of the Pakistani district of Dir fleeing the fighting between Taliban militants and government.

overseas—especially unpopular wars that trigger protest demonstrations and reduce leaders' public opinion approval ratings.

On the other hand, recent scholarship has pointed to the increased probability to engage in violent conflict if leaders are approaching their term limit (Zeigler, Pierskalla, and Mazumder, 2013). This may be due to the fact that leaders in their final term are not constrained by the drive for reelection (Williams, 2013). Another potential explanation involves a leader's "conceptual complexity," or the degree to which leaders display awareness of nuanced international relations concepts. A recent study (Foster and Keller, 2013) found that those leaders with low "conceptual complexity" had a greater tendency to use diversionary tactics than those with high "conceptual complexity." This is particularly true if the leader is inclined to view the use of force as a legitimate and effective foreign policy tool.

In sum, intrastate conflicts can become internationalized through both the tendency for them to invite external intervention as well as the propensity for leaders of failing governments to wage wars abroad as a means of preventing rebellion at home. These two trends are making for the globalization of armed conflict. That globalization of conflict is evident in yet another type of armed aggression that characterizes violence in world politics: the threat of global terrorism that knows no borders and that is spreading worldwide.

TERRORISM

Since the birth of the modern state system some three and a half centuries ago, national leaders have prepared for wars against other countries. Throughout this period, war has been conceived as large-scale organized violence between the regular armies of sovereign states. Although leaders today still ready their countries for such clashes, they are increasingly faced with the prospect of *asymmetric warfare*—armed conflict between terrorist networks and conventional military forces.

asymmetric warfare

Armed conflict between belligerents of vastly unequal military strength, in which the weaker side is often a nonstate actor that relies on unconventional tactics.

As you learned in Chapter 6, terrorist groups are a type of transnational nonstate actor distinguished by the fact that they use violence as their primary method of exercising influence. Terrorism was well known even in ancient times, as evident in the assassination campaigns conducted by the Sicarii (named after a short dagger, or sica) in Judea during the first century bce. Indeed, as historian Max Boot (2013, p. 100) explains:

> Pundits and the press too often treat terrorism and guerrilla tactics as something new, a departure from old-fashioned ways of war. But nothing could be further from the truth. Throughout most of our species' long and bloody slog, warfare has primarily been carried out by bands of loosely organized, ill-disciplined, and lightly armed volunteers who disdained open battle in favor of stealthy raids and ambushes: the strategies of both tribal warriors and modern guerrillas and terrorists.

Carnegie Council Video:
Asymmetric Warfare

Today terrorism is practiced by a diverse group of movements (see Chapter 6, Table 6.3). As Todd Sandler (2010, p. 205) explains, political terrorism is "the premeditated use or threat to use violence by individuals or subnational groups to obtain a political or social objective through the intimidation of a large audience beyond that of the immediate victims." Because perpetrators of terrorism often strike symbolic targets in a horrific manner, the psychological impact of an attack can exceed the physical damage. A mixture of drama and dread, terrorism is not senseless violence; it is a premeditated political strategy that threatens people with a coming danger that seems ubiquitous, unavoidable, and unpredictable.

Consider estimates of the growing intensity of terrorism's threat. According to the U.S. Department of State's Office of the Coordinator for Counterterrorism, the yearly number of acts of international terrorism increased steadily from 174 in 1968 to a peak of 666 in 1987, but then began to decline just as steadily to 200 acts in 2002. After the United States broadened its definitional criteria to include the deaths of civilian victims in Iraq, the estimates of the number of global terrorist acts rose dramatically (see Map 7.3). Many experts believe that the presence of U.S. soldiers on Islamic soil in Iraq counterproductively ignited a new wave of deadly terrorist activity throughout the world. And even after the killing of Al Qaeda leader Osama Bin Laden by U.S. Special Forces in May 2011, the threat of terrorist attacks remains. Warns terrorism expert Richard Bloom, "the security threat remains consistent. We are still very much at risk."

Terrorism can be used to support or to change the political status quo. Repressive terror, which is wielded to sustain an existing political order, has been utilized by governments as well as by vigilantes. From the Gestapo (secret state police) in Nazi Germany to the "death squads" in various countries, violence perpetrated by the establishment attempts to defend the prevailing political order by eliminating opposition leaders and by intimidating virtually everyone else.

The perpetrators of terrorism are not mindless; they have shown that they have long-term aims and rationally calculate how different operations can accomplish their purposes. Indeed, it is their ability to plan, execute, and learn from these operations that make today's terrorists so dangerous. Moreover, exposure to terrorism can encourage political exclusionism and threaten the principles of democratic governance (Sandler, 2011).

U.S. National Counterterrorism Center (NCTC, 2011).

MAP 7.3   THE PERSISTENT THREAT OF GLOBAL TERRORISM Shown here are the locations of terrorist attacks that occurred from 2005 until the start of 2011, with incidents most heavily concentrated in the Near East, South Asia, and Africa. Reflecting upon initiatives to combat terrorism, UN Secretary-General Ban Ki-moon noted that the "complexity and interdependence of these issues mean that no single country or organization can provide solutions alone. Dialogue and cooperation are critical."

Alongside the heavy losses and fear, terror creates an enormous challenge to the fabric of democratic societies. In many cases, there is a difficult inner tension between the fundamental need to feel secure and the aspiration to sustain democratic values and preserve democratic culture. More specifically, in times of terrorist threat and severe losses, when direct confrontation with the perpetrators of terrorism is either impossible or does not guarantee public safety, rage is frequently aimed at minority groups and their members. This rage can be easily translated into support for nondemocratic practices in dealing with minorities. Hence, one of the key psycho-social-political consequences of terrorism is the development of hostile feelings, attitudes, and behaviors toward minority groups (Canetti-Nisim et al., 2009, p. 364).

Dissidents who use terrorism to change the political status quo vary considerably. Some groups, like the MPLA (Popular Movement for the Liberation of Angola), used terrorism to expel colonial rulers; others, such as ETA (Basque Homeland and Liberty), adopt terrorism as part of an ethnonational separatist struggle; still others, including the Islamic Jihad, the Christian Identity Movement, the Sikh group Babbar Khalsa, and Jewish militants belonging to Kach, use terror in the service of what they see as religious imperatives. Finally, groups such as the Japanese Red Army and Italian Black Order turn to terrorism for left- or right-wing ideological reasons. This dissident terror may be grounded in anticolonialism, separatism, religion, or secular ideology.

To accomplish their objectives, terrorists use a variety of tactics, including bombing, assault, hijacking, and taking hostages (see Figure 7.5). Bombing alone accounts for over one-third of all recorded terrorist incidents. Hijacking and hostage-taking generally involve more complex operations than planting a bomb in a crowded department store or gunning down travelers in a train station. However, such activities do occur and can be seen in the careful planning required by the September 1970 coordinated hijacking of five airliners by Palestinians, which eventually led to one airliner being blown up in Cairo and three others in Jordan.

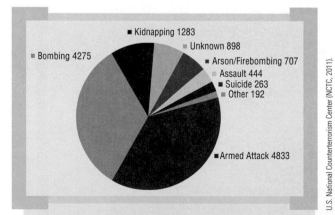

U.S. National Counterterrorism Center (NCTC, 2011).

FIGURE 7.5 TOOLS OF TERRORIST WARFARE
The figure indicates the major methods used by terrorists worldwide in 2010, and the number of attacks associated with each. As the second most frequently used tactic, bombings included all of the 263 suicide attacks committed. Ramadan Shalah of the Palestinian Jihad explained the military logic of suicide tactics through asymmetric warfare by asserting: "Our enemy possesses the most sophisticated weapons in the world. . . . We have nothing . . . except the weapon of martyrdom. It is easy and costs us only our lives."

To be successful, these kinds of seizures require detailed preparation and the capacity to guard captives for long periods of time. Among the payoffs of such efforts is the opportunity to articulate the group's grievances. The Lebanese group behind the 1985 hijacking of TWA Flight 847, for instance, excelled at using U.S. television networks to articulate its grievances to the American public, which reduced the options that the Reagan administration could consider while searching for a solution to the crisis.

Beyond the conventional tactics of bombings, assaults, hijacking, and hostage taking, two other threats—what former U.S. Navy Secretary Richard Danzig called "nonexplosive warfare"—could become part of the terrorist repertoire. First, dissidents may acquire weapons of mass destruction to deliver a mortal blow against their enemies. There is a widespread fear, for instance, that Pakistan's deteriorating internal political conditions may allow nuclear material to fall into the hands of extremist groups (Clarke, 2013). According to Director of the U.S. Central Intelligence Agency John Brennan, "The threat of nuclear terrorism is real, it is serious, it is growing, and it constitutes one of the greatest threats to our national security and, indeed, to global security."

While nuclear armaments may be the ultimate terror weapons, radiological, chemical, and biological weapons also pose extraordinary dangers. Crude radiological weapons can be fabricated by combining ordinary explosives with nuclear waste or radioactive isotopes, stolen from hospitals, industrial facilities, or research laboratories. Rudimentary chemical weapons can be made from herbicides, pesticides, and other toxic substances that are available commercially. Biological weapons based on viral agents are typically more difficult to produce, although the dispersal of anthrax spores through the mail during the fall of 2001 illustrated that low-technology attacks with bacterial agents in powder form are a frightening possibility.

The second tactical innovation on the horizon is cyberterrorism. Not only can the extremists use the Internet as a recruiting tool and a means of coordinating their activities with like-minded groups, they can also hack into a foe's computer system to case potential targets. Viruses and other weapons of *information warfare* could also cause havoc if they disable financial institutions. Cyber-attacks have risen as a heated issue between the United States and China, with the U.S. charging China with responsibility for high-tech spying in 2013 that compromised more than two dozen major U.S. weapons systems. China contends that it too has been subject to extensive hacking from the United States, and that "if the U.S. government wants to keep weapons programs secure, it should not allow them to be accessed online" (Jones, 2013).

Both bioweapons and cyber-attacks challenge our thinking about the future of terrorism and war as they pose a strategic quandary: because they are extraordinarily difficult to trace back to the perpetrator, they defy *deterrence* and elude defenses. "The concept of deterrence depends on the threat of certain retaliation that would cause a rational attacker to think twice. So if the attacker can't be found, then the certainty of retaliation dissolves, and deterrence might not be possible" (Hoffman, 2011, p. 78). Moreover, although we tend to expect warning of an impending attack and a chance for defense, as Nobel Prize laureate Joshua Lederberg warned, it is not likely that a perpetrator "is going to give you that opportunity."

The New Global Terrorism

The events of September 11, 2001, challenged the conventional view of terrorism as a rare and relatively remote threat. The horrors visited on the World Trade Center, the Pentagon, and the crash victims in Pennsylvania forced the world to confront a grim new reality: terrorists were capable of executing catastrophic attacks almost anywhere, even without an arsenal of sophisticated weapons. Not only did groups like Al Qaeda have global reach, but stealth, ingenuity, and meticulous planning could compensate for their lack of firepower. "America is full of fear," proclaimed a jubilant Osama bin Laden. "Nobody in the United States will feel safe."

What arguably made 9/11 a symbolic watershed was that it epitomized a deadly new strain of terrorism. Previously, terrorism was regarded as political theater, a frightening drama where the perpetrators wanted a lot of people watching, not a lot of people dead. Now there seems to be a desire to kill as many people as possible. Driven by searing hatred, annihilating enemies appears more important to global terrorists than winning sympathy for their cause.

information warfare

Attacks on an adversary's tele-communications and computer networks to degrade the technological systems vital to its defense and economic well-being.

Carnegie Council Video:
Information Warfare

deterrence

Preventive strategies designed to dissuade an adversary from doing what it would otherwise do.

Carnegie Council Video:
Deterrence

Other features of this new strain of terrorism are its organizational form and ideological emphasis. Instead of having a hierarchical command structure, for example, Al Qaeda possesses a decentralized horizontal structure. Although the leadership offers ideological inspiration to small, disparate cells scattered around the world, leaders do not directly plan and execute of most of the attacks undertaken in Al Qaeda's name.

What makes the new breed of terrorists who belong to organizations such as Al Qaeda more lethal than previous terrorists is their religious fanaticism, which allows them to envision acts of terror on two levels. At one level, terrorism is a means to change the political status quo by punishing those culpable for perceived wrongs. At another level, terrorism is an end in itself, a sacrament performed for its own sake in an eschatological confrontation between good and evil (Juergensmeyer, 2003). Functioning only on the first level, most secular terrorist groups employ suicide missions less frequently. Operating on both levels, religious terrorist groups see worldly gain as well as transcendent importance in a martyr's death (Bloom, 2005; Pape, 2005a).

Compounding these challenges is the fact that states have often financed, trained, equipped, and provided sanctuary for terrorists whose activities serve their foreign policy goals. In the throes of the terrorist attack on the United States on September 11, 2001, U.S. President George W. Bush described the threat as a network of terrorist groups as well as the rogue states that harbored them. Efforts to combat this threat, he insisted, "will not end until every terrorist group of global reach has been found, stopped, and defeated." In what was subsequently called the *Bush Doctrine*, the president declared that each nation had a choice to make: "Either you are with us, or you are with the terrorists."

Terrorism poses a huge threat to global security. However, disagreement about the character and causes of global terrorism remain pronounced, and without agreement on these basic

TERRORISTS BEHIND MASKS Shown here is the faceless militia that targets armies in uniforms: looking like self-funded criminal gangs with no ranks and uncertain allegiances, many terrorist groups hide their identity and report to no superiors.

characteristics, a consensus on the best response is unlikely. Much like a disease that cannot be treated until it is accurately diagnosed, the plague of new global terrorism cannot be eradicated until its sources are understood. Those persuaded by one image of terrorism are drawn to certain counterterrorism policies, whereas those holding a different image recommend contrary policies. As constructivist theorists remind us, what we see depends on what we expect, what we look at, and what we wish to see.

Consider the diametrically opposed views of whether repression or conciliation is the most effective counterterrorist policy. Those advocating repression see terrorism springing from the cold calculations of extremists who should be neutralized by preemptive surgical strikes. In contrast to this coercive counterterrorist approach, those who see terrorism rooted in frustrations with a lack of civil liberties and human rights (Krueger, 2007) or widespread poverty and poor education (Kavanagh, 2011) urge negotiation and cooperative nonmilitary approaches (Cortright and Lopez, 2008). Rather than condoning military strikes aimed at exterminating the practitioners of terrorism, they endorse conciliatory policies designed to reduce terrorism's appeal.

The debate about how to deal with the new global terrorism has provoked serious concerns about strategies for combating this global threat (see "Controversy: Can the War against Global Terrorism Be Won?"). The debate revolves around a series of interconnected issues: Are repressive counterterrorist policies ethical? Are they compatible with democratic procedures? Do they require multilateral (international) backing to be legal, or can they be conducted unilaterally? Is conciliation more effective than military coercion? What are the relative costs, risks, and benefits of these contending approaches to combat terrorism? Although most experts would agree that it is not possible to wipe terrorism from the face of the globe, "it should be possible to reduce the incidence and effectiveness of terrorism" (Bapat, 2011; Mentan, 2004, p. 364).

CourseMate

Case Study: Terrorism

ARMED CONFLICT AND ITS FUTURE

You have now inspected three trends in the major types of armed conflict in the world: wars between states, wars within states, and global terrorism. Some of these trends, you have noticed, are promising. War between states is disappearing, and this inspires optimists who hope that it will vanish from human interaction altogether. As some security studies experts predict, "Unlike breathing, eating or sex, war is not something that is somehow required by the human condition or by the forces of history. Accordingly, war can shrivel up and disappear, and it seems to be in the process of doing so" (Mueller, 2004, p. 4).

However, that threat remains, and because armed conflict between and within states threatens everyone in the borderless globalized world, all of humanity is at risk. Between 2008 and 2013, the level of peace in the world declined by 5 percent (see Map 7.4), due in large part to "major outbreaks of violence in the Middle East, caused by the Arab spring; a deterioration of security in Afghanistan and Pakistan; civil wars in Libya and Syria; the escalation of the drug war in Central America; continued deteriorations in peace in Somalia, DRC and Rwanda and violent demonstrations associated with the economic downturn in a number of European countries such as Greece" (The Institute for Economics and Peace, 2013, p. 1). And, of course, the specter of international terrorism casts a very dark shadow over the world's future.

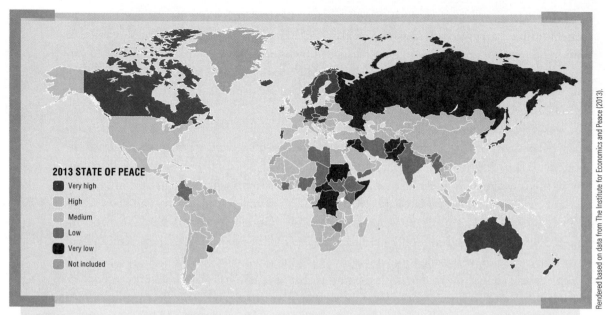

Rendered based on data from The Institute for Economics and Peace (2013).

2013 STATE OF PEACE

- Very high
- High
- Medium
- Low
- Very low
- Not included

MAP 7.4 THE QUEST FOR GLOBAL PEACE Based upon 22 indicators across 162 countries that are home to 99 percent of the globe's population, the 2013 Global Peace Index gauges peacefulness in terms of the extent to which countries are involved in international and intrastate conflicts, their degree of militarization, and the level of safety and security within a state. For 2013, scores dipped most sharply for Syria, Cote D'Ivoire, and Burkina Faso; Europe remains the most peaceful region, despite unrest due to challenging economic conditions in countries such as Greece, Spain, Portugal, and France.

There is no sure guide to what the future will hold. But the sad news is that your life and livelihood are certain to be threatened by the continuing onset of armed conflict. That threat imperils the future and affects *all* other aspects of world politics—which is why much of world history is written about the causes and consequences of armed conflict from the vantage point of all peoples' and professions' perspectives. As British poet Percy B. Shelley framed it:

> War is the statesman's game, the priest's delight,
> The lawyer's jest, the hired assassin's trade,
> And, to those royal murderers, whose mean thrones
> Are brought by crimes of treachery and gore,
> The bread they eat, the staff on which they lean.

Lucius Annaeus Seneca, a Roman statesman and philosopher in the first century ce, wryly noted that "Of war men ask the outcome, not the cause." Yet in order for us to reduce and possibly eliminate the plague of armed conflict in the world, it is necessary for us to first understand what drives violent conflict. The correlates of war speak to the correlates of peace. Thus, in this chapter you also have been given the opportunity to examine the many leading causes of armed conflict that theorists have constructed to explain why political violence in its various forms erupts.

It is the alternative potential paths to peace, security, and world order that you will next consider. In Chapter 8, we examine the vision realism advances about dealing with the threat of war, specifically as it deals with arms, military strategy, alliances, and the balance of power.

Peace cannot be kept by force; it can only be achieved by understanding.

—**Albert Einstein, Nobel Prize–winning physicist**

CONTROVERSY

CAN THE WAR AGAINST GLOBAL TERRORISM BE WON?

In the wake of 9/11, a new conventional wisdom arose—as then-U.S. Secretary of Defense Donald Rumsfeld put it, "if the [United States] learned a single lesson from 9/11, it should be that the only way to defeat terrorists is to attack them. There is no choice. You simply cannot defend in every place at every time against every technique. All the advantage is with the terrorist in that regard, and therefore you have no choice but to go after them where they are."

Others argue that to truly undermine terrorism, we must address the underlying conditions that give it appeal. Efforts to defeat Al Qaeda in Afghanistan must include establishing a government that can meet the needs of the people and jobs that provide an alternative to fighting. Assessing the prospects of winning the war on terror in Afghanistan, Lieutenant Colonel Brett Jenkinson, commander of the U.S. battalion in the Korengal Valley, explains that "What we need is a better recruiting pitch for disaffected youth. You can't build hope with military might. You build it through development and good governance" (Baker and Kolay, 2009, p. 27).

Exactly what approach to take to control the new global terrorism remains controversial. To conduct a worldwide war requires an enduring commitment at high costs. That is why proposals for an effective and just response to the new global terrorism differ, as do recommendations about how the world can most effectively reduce terrorism.

What makes counterterrorism so problematic is that strategists often fail to distinguish different types of terrorist movements and their diverse origins. Therefore, they construct counterterrorist strategies in the abstract—with a single formula—rather than tailoring approaches for dealing with terrorism's alternate modes. As one expert advises, "One lesson learned since 911 is that the expanded war on terrorism has created a lens that tends to distort our vision of the complex political dynamics of countries" (Menkhaus, 2002, p.210).

In evaluating proposed methods to fight the latest wave of global terrorism, you will need to confront a series of incompatible conclusions: "concessions only encourage terrorists' appetite for further terrorism," as opposed to "concessions can redress the grievances that lead to terrorism." Your search for solutions will necessarily spring from assumptions you make about terrorism's nature and sources, and these assumptions will strongly affect your conclusions about the wisdom or futility of contemplated remedies.

Keep in mind that what may appear to be a policy around which an effective counterterrorist program might be constructed could potentially make the problem worse. Counterterrorism is controversial because one person's solution is another person's problem, the answers are often unclear, and the ethical criteria for applying just-war theory to counterterrorism need clarification (Patterson, 2005).

WHAT DO YOU THINK?

- *How does armed aggression, such as terrorism, by nonstate actors change the circumstances of war for policy makers? How does it change the circumstances of intervention for policy makers?*

- *What would you advise governments about the best methods of fighting terrorism? Keep in mind the promises and perils of each possible solution.*

- *How might intergovernmental organizations such as the United Nations complement, or hinder, states' abilities to fight terrorism?*

STUDY. APPLY. ANALYZE.

Key Terms

adjudication
arbitration
armed conflict
asymmetric warfare
bargaining model of war
civil war
commercial liberalism
communist theory of
    imperialism
conflict

coup d'etat
cultural conditioning
democratic peace
deterrence
ecological fallacy
economic peace
enduring internal rivalry
    (EIR)
failed states
good offices

hegemonic stability
    theory
individualistic fallacy
information warfare
interspecific aggression
intraspecific aggression
long peace
mediation
national character
nature versus nurture

pacifism
power transition theory
relative deprivation
socialization
state-sponsored terrorism
survival of the fittest
war
war weariness hypothesis
youth bulge

Suggested Readings

Combs, Cynthia C. (2013) *Terrorism in the Twenty-First Century*, 7th edition. Boston, MA: Pearson.

Levy, Jack, and William R. Thompson. (2010) *Causes of War*. Malden, MA: Wiley-Blackwell.

Kegley, Charles W., ed. (2003) *The New Global Terrorism: Characteristics, Causes, Controls*. Upper Saddle River, NJ: Prentice Hall.

Lemke, Douglas. (2008) "Power Politics and Wars without States," *American Journal of Political Science* 52:774–786.

Sandler, Todd. (2011) "New Frontiers of Terrorism Research: An Introduction," *Journal of Peace Research* 48:279–286.

Thyne, Clayton. (2009) *How International Relations Affect Civil Conflict: Cheap Signals, Costly Consequences*. Lexington, MA: Lexington Books.

Vasquez, John. (2009) *War Puzzle Revisited*. Cambridge: Cambridge University Press.

Wallensteen, Peter. (2011) *Understanding Conflict Resolution: War, Peace, and the Global System*. London: Sage.

Zalman, Amy, and Jonathan Clarke. (2009) "The Global War on Terror: A Narrative in Need of a Rewrite," *Ethics & International Affairs* 23, no. 2:101–113.

Suggested Videos

Carnegie Council Video

Bacevich, Andrew J. "Washington Rules: America's Path to Permanent War."

Betts, Richard K. "The World Ahead: Conflict or Cooperation?"

Reiss, Mitchell B. "Negotiating with Evil: When to Talk to Terrorists."

CourseMate

Log in to CourseMate to access the following study tools for this chapter:

- Interactive Quiz
- eBook
- Flashcards & Key Term Crossword Puzzle
- Chapter Audio Summary
- Carnegie Council Videos
- Video Activities
- Simulation
- Animated Learning Module
- Case Study
- International Relations NewsWatch

"Political power grows out of the barrel of a gun."

—*Mao Zedong, founding father of communist China*

CHAPTER 8
The Pursuit of Power through Arms and Alliances

AP Photo/US Airforce

MISSILES, BOMBS, AND BULLETS, OH MY! Throughout history, countries have used missiles, bombs, and bullets as a means for backing their enemies into surrender. Realists regard the prudent use of armed force as a powerful instrument for maintaining security and stability in world politics. Shown here is one example: the use of air power to compel an adversary without waging a ground war. Amid growing controversy over the circumstances under which they are used, armed unmanned predator drones such as this were used by the United States between 2001 and 2013 for an estimated 425 targeted killings in Pakistan, Yemen and Somalia, with a death toll of at least 3000 people (Lobe, 2013).

QUESTIONS TO CONSIDER

▪ *What perspective does realism offer on war and peace?*

▪ *What is the role of power in world politics?*

▪ *How are military capabilities evolving?*

▪ *What are the different military strategies associated with coercive diplomacy?*

▪ *According to realism, what are the advantages and disadvantages of alliances?*

▪ *What are the key assumptions and claims of balance of power theory?*

Imagine yourself someday becoming the next secretary-general of the United Nations. You would face the awesome responsibility for fulfilling the UN's charter to preserve world peace. But looking at the globe, you would likely see that many countries are engaged in armed conflict and that those wars are destroying life and property. Moreover, you would undoubtedly also be distressed by the countries and possibly some transnational terrorist groups with the new capacity to annihilate their enemies with weapons of mass destruction. And you shudder at the realization that many states are living in constant fear of threats to their security, while at the same time these armed actors are increasing the military power in their arsenals.

As a result of the escalating destructive power of modern weapons, you cannot help but notice that the UN members most feverishly working to increase their capacity to resist threats to their physical survival are the same countries whose *national security*, or psychological freedom from fear of foreign aggression, seems to be declining the most rapidly. Taking a picture of the pregnant fears circulating the globe, you conclude that as a consequence, a true *security dilemma* has been created: the armaments amassed by states for what they claim to be defensive purposes are seen by others as threatening, and this has driven the alarmed competitors to undertake, as countermeasures, additional military buildups—with the result that the arming states' insecurities are increasing even as their military strength increases.

As you watch the jockeying for power and position among the UN members, you also notice that countries tend to forge partnerships, based on converging and clashing interests and values. As realist policy maker Steven Rosen remarked, "It is the existence of an enemy that gives rise to the need for allies, and [it] is for the advantageous conduct of fighting that alliances are formed." And when relationships and conditions change, new alliances form and established alliances dissolve as transnational actors—all obsessed with the power of their rivals—realign.

What course should you counsel the UN's members to pursue in order to escape the dilemma of rising insecurity in which they have imprisoned themselves? Alas, your options are limited and your advice ignored. Why? Because when the topic of war and peace is debated, and in periods when international tensions are high, policy makers (and theorists) turn to realist theory for guidance.

> *The adversaries of the world are not in conflict because they are armed. They are armed because they are in conflict and have not yet learned peaceful ways to resolve their conflicting interests.*
>
> **—Richard M. Nixon, U.S. president**

REALIST APPROACHES TO WAR AND PEACE

Nearly all states continue to believe that the anarchical global system requires them to rely on *self-help* and depend only on themselves for security. They have been schooled in the lessons constructed from *realism*—the school of thought that teaches that the drive for power and the domination of others for self-advantage is a universal and permanent motive throughout world history. For this reason, most states follow the realist roads to national and international

---

national security

A country's psychological freedom from fears that the state will be unable to resist threats to its survival and national values emanating from abroad or at home.

security. This worldview, or *paradigm*, for organizing perceptions pictures the available and practical choices for states primarily among three time-honored options: (1) arming themselves, (2) forming or severing alliances with other countries, or (3) constructing strategies for controlling their destinies through military approaches and *coercive diplomacy*, such as acts of military intervention that target their enemies.

In this chapter, you will explore states' efforts to follow the realist recipes for reducing threats to their national security by creating a favorable balance of power. In the spirit of seventeenth-century English philosopher Thomas Hobbes, who viewed the natural human condition as one of "war of all against all" and advised that successful states are those that hold the "posture of Gladiators; having their weapons pointing, and their eyes fixed on one another," this chapter introduces the acquisition and use of arms, major trends in weaponry, and the role of alliances in ensuring that national security and national interests are served and a balance of power persists among rivals that prevents any one transnational actor from using force against the others.

This discussion begins by underscoring the high importance that realists place on *power*, which they believe has, throughout history, been key in driving world politics. National security is truly a paramount priority for the policy makers responsible for constructing their country's foreign policy agendas. Because the threat of armed conflict persists, realism recommends that war be placed at the very top of a state's concerns and that, to contain dangers, the pursuit of power must be the top priority. As Table 8.1 demonstrates, this emphasis is part and parcel of a much broader range of foreign policy recommendations realists embrace to chart the safest routes to national and international security (see also Chapter 2).

coercive diplomacy

The use of threats or limited armed force to persuade an adversary to alter its foreign and/or domestic policies.

Carnegie Council Video:
Coercive Diplomacy

TABLE 8.1   Realist Roads to Security: Premises and Policy Recommendations
Realist Perspective of the Global Environment
Primary global condition: anarchy; or the absence of authoritative governing institutions
Probability of system change/reform: low, except in response to extraordinary events, such as 9/11
Primary transnational actors: states and especially great powers
Principal actor goals: power over others, self-preservation, and physical security
Predominant pattern of actor interaction: competition and conflict
Pervasive concern: national security
Prevalent state priorities: acquiring military capabilities
Popular state practice: use of armed force for coercive diplomacy
Policy Premises
If you want peace, prepare for war.
No state is to be trusted further than its national interest.
Standards of right and wrong apply to individuals but not states; in world affairs amoral actions are sometimes necessary for security.
Isolationism is not an alternative to active global involvement.
Strive to increase military capabilities and fight rather than submit to subordination.
Do not let any other state or coalition of states become predominant.
Negotiate alliances to maintain a favorable military balance.

POWER IN WORLD POLITICS

Realist theorists since antiquity have based their thinking and policy recommendations on the belief that all people and states seek power. Even texts such as the Bible reflect this assumption, as it observes and warns that people seem born to sin, and the drive for power to dominate others is one of their inalterable compulsions. That said, the abstraction called power, which realists assume to be humanity's primary objective, defies precise definition. Constructivists recognize that in the broadest sense power is usually interpreted as the political capacity of one actor to exercise influence over another actor to the first's benefit.

Most leaders follow *realpolitik* and operate from the traditional construction that conceives of power as a combination of factors that gives states the capability to promote national interests, to win in international bargaining, and to shape the rules governing interaction in the global system. As former Secretary of State Condoleezza Rice observed, "Power is nothing unless you can turn it into influence." However, beyond the semantic definition of power as *politics*—the exercise of influence to control others—power is an ambiguous concept, and difficult to measure. A dictionary definition begs the question: What factors most enable an actor to control or coerce another?

The Elements of State Power

Of all the components of state power, realists see military capability as by far the most important. Realist theory maintains that the ability to coerce militarily is more important than rewarding favors or buying concessions. Thus, realists reject the view of liberal strategic thinkers who maintain that under conditions of *globalization*, which links countries economically, politically, and culturally in webs of interdependence, economic resources are becoming increasingly more critical to national strength and security than are military capabilities (Nye, 2008).

power potential

The capabilities or resources held by a state that are considered necessary to its asserting influence over others.

Following tradition, one way to estimate the ***power potential*** of states is to compare their military expenditures. On this dimension, the United States is the undisputed military powerhouse of the world, with defense spending that leaves all other countries far behind. Figure 8.1 shows the trend in U.S. defense budgets over six decades that has made America unsurpassed in military spending: at $669 billion in 2012, the United States was responsible for 39 percent of all of the world's military expenditures for that year. Of special note is that 2012 saw the first decrease in world military expenditures, which amounted to $1.76 trillion, since 1998 (SIPRI, 2013). Even so, the U.S. Congressional Budget Office further expects that between fiscal years 2012 and 2018, the United States will spend more than $5.54 trillion in defense (Adams and Leatherman, 2011).

Carnegie Council Video:
Power Potential

Power potential also derives from factors other than military expenditures. Among the so-called elements of power, analysts also consider such capabilities as the relative size of a state's economy, its population and territorial size, geographic position, raw materials, technological capacity, political culture and values, efficiency of governmental decision making, volume of trade, educational level, national morale, and internal solidarity. For example, if power potential were measured by territorial size, Russia, which is twice as large as its closest rivals (Canada, China, the United States, Brazil, and Australia, in that order), would be the globe's most

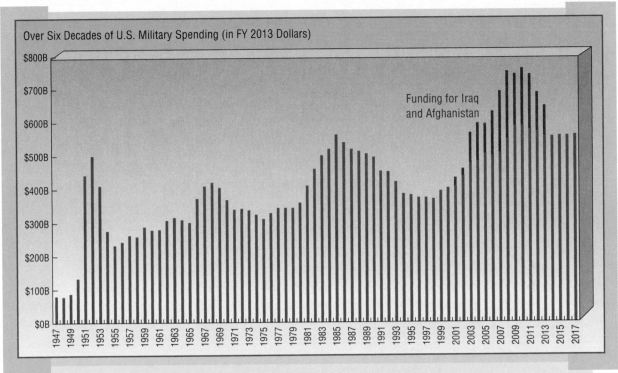

Source: Center for Strategic and Budgetary Assessments.

FIGURE 8.1   OVER SIX DECADES OF U.S. MILITARY SPENDING America's military expenditures spiked during the Korean and Vietnam Wars, expanded in the 1980s under President Ronald Reagan, dipped after the end of the Cold War, and have risen rapidly since 9/11 and the start of its global "war on terror." Due in part to its extensive military capabilities, the United States continues to be regarded as a true hegemonic superpower, without rival. In 2014, U.S. military spending is expected to include $526.6 billion in base budget, which excludes nuclear expenditures, plus $88.5 billion to fight the wars in Afghanistan and Iraq and counterinsurgency in Pakistan. This brings the U.S. defense budget to $615.1billion in 2014 (DOD, 2013).

powerful country. Likewise, if power were measured by the UN's projections for countries' populations by the year 2025, China, India, the United States, Indonesia, Pakistan, Nigeria, and Brazil, in that order, would be the most powerful. In a similar comparison, the rankings of countries' expenditures on research and development (as a percentage of GDP) to fund future economic growth and military strength would rank Israel, Finland, South Korea, Sweden, Japan, Denmark, Switzerland, the United States, Germany, Austria, Iceland, Singapore, and Australia as the countries with the brightest future (WDI, 2013). Clearly, strength is relative. The leading countries in some dimensions of power potential are not leaders in others because power comes in many forms (see Maps 8.1 and 8.2).

Thus, there is little consensus on how best to weigh the various factors that contribute to military capability and national power. Moreover, those with the largest arsenals have not necessarily triumphed in conflicts. In fact, since 1950 weak states have won more than half of all asymmetric wars between belligerents of vastly unequal military strength. This is in part because the weaker party has a greater interest in surviving, and that greater interest, rather than relative military capabilities, is the major deciding factor in wars between the strong and weak (Arreguín-Toft, 2006).

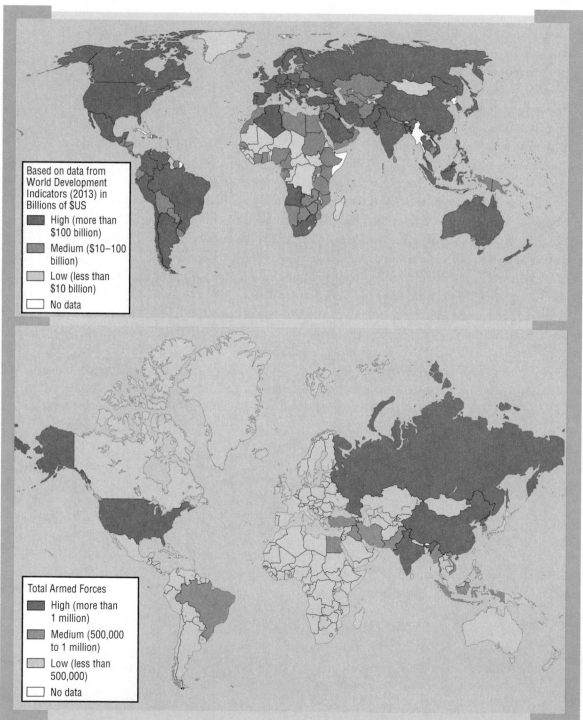

MAPS 8.1 AND 8.2   TWO MEASURES OF POWER POTENTIAL: STATE WEALTH AND SIZE OF NATIONAL ARMIES
The map on top measures gross national income (GNI) across countries to estimate the differences in national wealth that contribute to state power, and the distribution categorizes differences in the size of states' economies that separate the rich from the poor (and the strong from the weak). Another measure of power projection is the number of uniform personnel in states' armies, navies, and air forces. The map on the bottom classifies the varying size of each country's armed forces available for military operations.

There are many cases of weak transnational actors prevailing in armed conflicts with significantly stronger opponents. Although Vietnam was weak in the conventional military sense, it succeeded against a vastly stronger France and, later, the United States. Similarly, the United States' superior military power did not prevent North Korea from seizing the USS *Pueblo* in 1968, Iran from taking American diplomats as hostages a decade later, or the Al Qaeda terrorist network's 9/11 attack. The Soviet Union's inability, prior to its disintegration, to control political events in Afghanistan, Eastern Europe, or even among its own constituent republics (despite awesome military might) shows that the impotence of military power is not particular to the United States.

History is replete with examples of small countries that won wars or defended their independence against much more militarily powerful enemies. Consider the seventeenth century, for example, with Switzerland against the Hapsburg Empire, the Netherlands against Spain, and Greece against the Ottomans. In each case, intangible factors such as the will of the target population to resist a more powerful army and their willingness to die to defend the homeland were key elements in the capacity of each of these weaker countries to defend itself against a much stronger military force. Great Britain reluctantly recognized this in 1781 when it concluded that the price of reclaiming the far weaker American colonies was too great.

Nonetheless, the quest for security through arms and the realist belief in military force remain widespread. Most security analysts believe that this is because military capability is a prerequisite for the successful exercise of *coercive diplomacy* through the threat of limited force. Perhaps this conviction is what inspired former U.S. President George W. Bush to assert that "a dangerous and uncertain world requires America to have a sharpened sword."

The "Cost" of Military Spending

Military power is central in leaders' concepts of national security, and even though the end of the Cold War reduced tensions worldwide and therefore the need for military preparations, world military spending rose to $1.76 trillion in 2012, which represents slightly less than a 1 percent decrease since 2011, and a 55 percent increase since 2000. This staggering number is equal to 2.5 percent of global gross domestic product, or $246.9 for each person in the world (WDI, 2013; SIPRI, 2013). The world is spending $3,329,528 each *minute* for military preparations.

Historically, rich countries have spent the most money on arms acquisitions, and this pattern has continued (see Figure 8.2). As 2013 began, the Global North was spending $1,304 billion for defense, in contrast with the developing Global South's $494 billion. Thus, the high-income developed countries' share of the world total was about 75 percent. However, when measured against other factors, the differences become clearer. The Global North's average military expenditure constituted 2.8 percent of GDP, whereas the Global South spent an average 2.1 percent—at a relatively greater sacrifice of funding to promote human development and economic growth among the poor (WDI, 2013).

In addition, these two groups' military spending levels are converging over time. The Global South's military expenditure in 1961 was about 7 percent of the world total, but by 2013 its share had increased to 25 percent (WDI, 2013). This trend indicates that poor states are copying the past costly military budget habits of the wealthiest states.

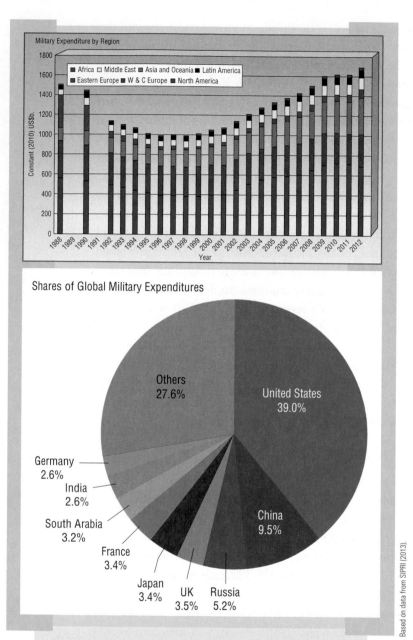

FIGURES 8.2 AND 8.3 RISING GLOBAL MILITARY EXPENDITURES
Global military budgets have fluctuated since 1960, with total
expenditures worldwide peaking in 1987, after which they fell about
a third until the 9/11 terrorist attacks. As shown on top, the military
budget of the Global South's developing countries, particularly in
Asia and Oceania, has grown to command a significant portion of
world military expenditures, amounting to as much as 22 percent of
the world total in 2012. However, as shown on bottom, U.S. military
expenditures far exceed those of any other country, and are four
times more than the expenditures of the next closest country—China
(SIPRI, 2013).

Military expenditures incur *opportunity costs*—when what is gained for one purpose is lost for other purposes—so that any particular choice means the cost of some lost opportunity must be paid. Military spending, for example, retards economic growth and creates fiscal deficits. The substantial costs of defense can erode national welfare—the very thing that policy makers hope to defend with military might. As political scientist Richard Rosecrance notes, "States can afford more 'butter' if they need fewer 'guns'. The two objectives sometimes represent trade-offs: The achievement of one may diminish the realization of the other."

Since 1945, only a handful of states have borne crushing military costs. Figure 8.3 shows that the United States' military spending accounted for 39 percent of the world total in 2012, followed by China with 9.5 percent, Russia with 5.2 percent, and the United Kingdom with 3.5 percent (SIPRI, 2013). Many countries have gained a relative competitive edge by investing in research on the development of goods to export abroad, while conserving resources by relying on allies and global institutions to provide defense against potential threats. The United States is somewhat of an exception: While accounting for 39 percent of world military expenditures in 2012, the United States has also been the dominant investor in research and development funding. Its emphasis, however, has been on military preparation, which accounts "for the majority of U.S. federal R&D spending" (Battelle, 2008, p. 16; SIPRI, 2013).

Some believe that this *military-industrial complex* exercises enormous influence over the U.S. defense budget and arms sales agreements. One symptom of this influence is the ability of defense contractors to charge the Pentagon inflated prices for their products. The U.S. government is estimated to overpay by as much as 20 percent for military goods through the Pentagon's prime vendor procurement program, which greased the sale of a deep fat fryer for $5919, a waffle iron for $1781, and a toaster for $1025 (Borenstein, 2006; Markoe and Borenstein, 2005). It is hardly surprising that arms manufacturers seek to increase their profits, but their corporate greed alarms critics, who worry about the manufacturers' success in lobbying Congress and the Pentagon for high military spending to gain government permission to sell new weapons worldwide.

Of late, the issue of whether or not to decrease military spending, especially in the face of the economic crisis, has become a hotly debated topic. In 2012, global military expenditures began to reflect this economic reality with the first decrease in world military spending since 1998, due to a large extent to the United States' reduced spending as it continued to disengage from its wars in Afghanistan and Iraq (SIPRI, 2013).

Politics requires making hard choices about priorities and about how public funds should be spent. "Guns versus butter"—how to allocate scarce finances for military preparedness as opposed to meeting the human needs of citizens and enabling them to live secure and long lives—is a serious controversy in every country. The former category looks to arms to combat threats and preserve *national security*, and the latter stresses *human security*, which places an emphasis on protecting the well-being of individuals. Neither goal can be pursued without making some sacrifice for the other, and different countries deal with this dilemma in different ways.

That difference is captured by the range in states' willingness to pay a heavy burden for defense—by grouping states according to the share of gross domestic product (GDP) they devote to the military and then juxtaposing this relative burden with their GDP. The *relative burden of military spending*, the ratio of defense spending to GDP, is the customary way to measure the sacrifices required by military spending (see Map 8.3). The global trend shows that the share of resources used for military purposes has increased steadily since 2000, and the military burden now corresponds to 2.5 percent of world GDP (SIPRI, 2013).

Indeed, some comparatively wealthy states (Saudi Arabia, Israel, and Brunei) bear a heavy burden, whereas other states that provide a high average income for their citizens (Japan, Austria, and Luxembourg) have a low defense burden. Likewise, the citizens of some very poor countries (Sierra Leone, Mozambique, and Chad) are heavily burdened, whereas those of others (Bhutan and the Democratic Republic of Congo) are not. It is, therefore, difficult to generalize about the precise relationship between a country's defense burden and its citizens' standard of living, human development, or stage of development. That said, a simple look at this map reveals that the majority of the countries with the highest military burden are also the countries that are experiencing the highest levels of armed conflict, or are located in regions with huge security problems, such as the Middle East and Africa (recall Chapter 7).

How much should a country sacrifice for national security? For many realists, the price is never too high. Others caution, however, that leaders should take heed of U.S. President Dwight Eisenhower's warning: "The world in arms is not spending money alone. It is spending

---

opportunity costs

The sacrifices that result when the decision to select one option means that the opportunity to realize gains from another options is lost.

military-industrial complex

A combination of defense establishments, contractors who supply arms for them, and government agencies that benefit from high military spending, which acts as a lobbying coalition to pressure governments to appropriate large expenditures for military preparedness.

Carnegie Council Video: Military-Industrial Complex

human security

A measure popular in liberal theory of the degree to which the welfare of individuals is protected and promoted, in contrast to realist theory's emphasis on putting the state's interests in military and national security ahead of all other goals.

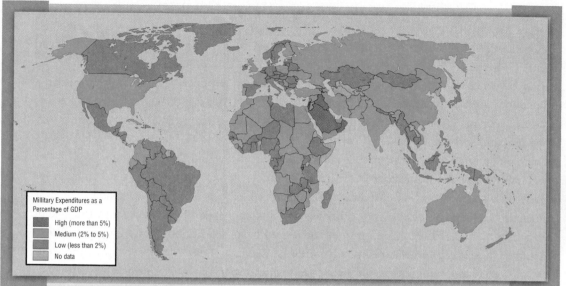

Based on data from the World Development Indicators (2013).

MAP 8.3   MILITARY EXPENDITURES AS A PERCENTAGE OF GDP   As the map shows, wide variations exist in the percentage of a country's gross domestic product that is allocated toward military spending. Many countries allocate a high proportion of their total GDP to defense, and others spend their wealth to enhance human security. In 2011, Saudi Arabia and Israel had the highest relative burden of military spending, followed by the United Arab Emirates, Azerbaijan, and Afghanistan (WDI, 2013).

relative burden of military spending

Measure of the economic burden of military activities calculated by the share of each state's gross domestic product allocated to military expenditures.

the sweat of its children." These skeptics of high military spending believe the high costs can easily reduce the human security found within a particular country. "It is important to remember that every defense dollar spent to over-insure against a remote or diminishing risk," cautioned former U.S. Secretary of Defense Robert Gates, "is a dollar not available to take care of our people, reset the force, win the wars we are in, and improve capabilities in areas where we are underinvested and potentially vulnerable." The consequences for the United States are not encouraging. Consider how, given the U.S. choice to prioritize military spending, the United States ranks on various nonmilitary measures of human security (see Table 8.2).

These rankings raise serious questions about the true costs of national security. The choices in balancing the need for defense against the need to provide for the common welfare are difficult because they entail a necessary trade-off between competing values. For this reason, military-spending decisions are highly controversial everywhere.

How governments allocate their revenues reveals their priorities. Examination of national budgets discloses an unmistakable pattern: although the sources of global political power may be changing, many states continue to seek security by spending substantial portions of their national treasures on arms.

A nation that continues year after year to spend more money on military defense than on programs of social uplift is approaching spiritual doom.

—Martin Luther King, Jr., American civil rights activist

TABLE 8.2	Human Security: How the U.S. Ranks in the World	
Indicator		**Rank**
GNI for each person		9
Unemployment rate (% of labor force)		29
Female economic activity rate (aged 15 and older)		65
Human development (HDI)		3
Gender inequality		42
Life expectancy		42
Carbon dioxide emissions (per capita)		10
Under age 5 mortality rate		47
Primary public education expenditures for each student (% of GDP)		46
Total health expenditure (% of GDP)		3

Based on data from World Development Indicators (2013); Human Development Report (2013).

CHANGES IN MILITARY CAPABILITIES

The growing militarization of the United States, the other great powers, and now mobilized nonstate terrorist groups has altered the global distribution of military capabilities. Part of the reason is that weapons production capabilities are more widespread than ever, with even Global South countries and terrorist organizations participating in the business of manufacturing modern aircraft, tanks, and small arms. Furthermore, a growing trend since the beginning of the Iraq War has been the increased use of *private military services*, which enhances a state's military capabilities by allowing the government to conduct operations with fewer troops than would otherwise be needed.

Trends in the Weapons Trade

During the Cold War, many states sought to increase their security by purchasing arms produced by suppliers eagerly seeking allies as well as profits from exports. In 1961, the world arms trade was valued at $4 billion. Thereafter, the traffic in arms imports climbed rapidly and peaked in 1987 at $82 billion (U.S. ACDA, 1997, pp. 10, 100). The end of the Cold War did not end the arms trade, however. Since 1991 when the Cold War ended, and continuing throughout the era of global terrorism that began on 9/11, the total value of all international arms transfers through 2012 was over $535 billion and the volume of arms transfers each year continues to grow (SIPRI, 2013).

There have been troubling trends in the global arms trade in recent years. From 2002 to 2012 arms imported by the government of Algeria increased by 277 percent. Imports to Nigeria, which has struggled with political violence, have doubled over the past decade. Among the major powers, arms imports to China decreased by 47 percent last year, though this may have resulted more from China's increased indigenous weapons production rather than a shift towards a more pacific foreign policy stance. In fact, China replaced the United Kingdom as the fifth largest exporter of arms in 2012 (SIPRI, 2013).

private military services

The outsourcing of activities of a military-specific nature to private companies, such as armed security, equipment maintenance, IT services, logistics, and intelligence services.

Carnegie Council Video:
Private Military Services

Overall, the major recipients of all global arms shipments remain heavily concentrated in a subset of Global South arms purchasers. Between 2003 and 2012, India, China, South Korea, Pakistan, and Singapore were the top five arms recipients. Of special note, India has replaced China as the largest weapons importer (SIPRI, 2013). The stream of weapons to these insecure and eager buyers with money to spend is not likely to end soon. To promote what it called a "security dialogue" in the Persian Gulf, the United States proposed transferring $63 billion in new arms sales to the Middle East over the next 10 years, though in recent years the majority of U.S. arms exports have gone to Asia, accounting for a total of 45 percent of all U.S. arms exports (Hartung, 2007, p. 8; SIPRI, 2013).

Along with the changing demands of arms importers, changes in the activities of arms suppliers are also important. During the Cold War, the superpowers dominated the arms export market. Between 1975 and 1989, the U.S.-Soviet share of global arms exports varied between one-half and three-fourths, and the United States alone had cornered 40 percent of the world arms export market when the Cold War ended (U.S. ACDA, 1997). In that period, the two superpowers together "supplied an estimated $325 billion worth of arms and ammunition to the Third World" (Klare, 1994, p. 139). In the post-9/11 global war on terrorism, the United States increased its worldwide supply of weapons to countries that agreed to be partners in the "coalition of the willing" in wars in Afghanistan and Iraq. Interestingly, it is still these two superpowers, the United States and Russia, that dominate the arms export market, supplying 30 and 26 percent of all conventional weapons exports, respectively, between 2008 and 2012 (SIPRI, 2013).

Yet although countries themselves are typically identified as global suppliers of arms, in some countries private companies are major producers of weapons and compete in the profitable arms marketplace (see Table 8.3). The 2011 arms sales of Lockheed Martin, an American-based company, were greater than the GDPs of 107 countries. The sales of weapons by the British-based BEA Systems (at 29.1 billion) exceed the baseline budget of the Marine Corps in 2012 by roughly $5 billion.

Another development in the post–Cold War era, which has been likened to modern-day mercenaries, is the growth in companies that provide private military services for hire on the global market. The outsourcing of military-like activities enables governments to maintain their force structure for a lower cost than otherwise possible. However, relying on private contractors in war zones may compromise democratic accountability and the state's monopoly on the use of force, as well as raise issues about legal status (see "A Closer Look: Private Soldiers and the Conduct of War").

The Strategic Consequences of Arms Sales

The transfer of arms across borders has produced some unintended and counterproductive consequences. For example, during the Cold War, the United States and the Soviet Union thought they could maintain peace by spreading arms to strategically important countries. Between 1983 and 1987, the United States provided arms to 59 Global South countries, whereas the Soviet Union supplied arms to 42 (Klare, 1990, p. 12). Yet many of these recipients went to war with their neighbors or experienced internal rebellion. Of the top 20 arms importers in 1988, more than half "had governments noted for the frequent use of violence"

TABLE 8.3	Sellers of Security or Merchants of Death? Top 20 Arms-Producing Companies		
Rank		Arms Sales ($ billions)	
2011	2010	Company (Country)	2011	2010
1	1	Lockheed Martin (USA)	36.3	35.7
2	3	Boeing (USA)	31.8	31.4
3	2	BAE Systems (UK)	29.1	32.9
4	5	General Dynamics (USA)	23.8	23.9
5	6	Raytheon (USA)	22.5	23.0
6	4	Northrop Grumman (USA)	21.4	28.2
7	7	EADS (W. Europe)	16.4	16.4
8	8	Finmeccanica (Italy)	14.6	14.4
9	9	L-3 Communications (USA)	12.5	13.1
10	10	United Technologies (USA)	11.6	11.4
11	11	Thales (France)	9.5	10.0
12	12	SAIC (USA)	7.9	8.2
13	-	Huntington Ingalls (USA)	6.4	-
14	15	Honeywell (USA)	5.3	5.4
15	16	Safran (France)	5.2	4.8
16	14	Computer Sciences Corp. (USA)	4.9	5.9
17	17	Rolls-Royce (UK)	4.7	4.3
18	21	United Aircraft Corp. (Russia)	4.4	3.4
19	13	Oshkosh Truck (USA)	4.4	7.1
20	18	General Electric (USA)	4.1	4.3

Based on data from SIPRI (2013).

(Sivard, 1991, p. 17). The toll in lives from the wars in the Global South since 1945 exceeds tens of millions of people.

Undoubtedly, the import of such huge arsenals of weapons aided this level of destruction. As the arms exporters "peddle death to the poor," they seldom acknowledge how this scouting for customers contradicts other proclaimed foreign policy goals. For example, while seeking to promote democratization, less democratic countries receive the greatest amounts of U.S. arms (Blanton, 2005). Since 2001, less than three-fifths of U.S. arms have been exported to governments classified by Freedom House as "free" (O'Reilly, 2005, p. 11), and now four-fifths of the countries that receive U.S. arms are classified by the U.S. State Department as either being undemocratic or having a poor human rights record (Jackson, 2007, p. A9).

The inability of arms suppliers to control the uses of their military hardware is troubling. Friends can become foes, and supplying weapons can backfire—generating what the CIA calls *blowback* to describe what can happen when foreign activities such as covert shipments of arms are later used in retaliations against the supplier (C. Johnson, 2004a). The United States learned this painful lesson the hard way. The weapons it shipped to Iraq when Saddam Hussein was fighting Iran in the 1980s were later used against U.S. forces in the Persian Gulf War (Timmerman, 1991). This also happened when the Stinger missiles the United States supplied

blowback

The propensity for actions undertaken for national security to have the unintended consequence of provoking retaliatory attacks when relations later sour.

A Closer Look

PRIVATE SOLDIERS AND THE CONDUCT OF WAR

On September 16, 2007, Blackwater private security contractors guarding U.S. diplomats in Iraq opened fire in Nisoor Square, a crowded Baghdad intersection. An angry Iraqi government blamed them for the shooting deaths of 17 civilians and the injuries of 20 others—some of whom were women and children. Although Blackwater said the guards were responding to an ambush by insurgents and were innocent of any crime, others said the shooting was unprovoked and the Blackwater guards fired indiscriminately. The incident inflamed anti-American sentiment in the country (Blackwater renamed itself Xe Services in an effort to distance its brand from the incident) and raised questions about the role and accountability of private military companies in war zones.

Iraq is not the only place where private solders are prevalent; in 2011 Muammar al-Qaddafi's government recruited mercenaries from Guinea and Nigeria, offering up to $2000, to quash the ongoing protests in Libya against his regime. Supporters of private military services point out that private contractors like Blackwater, Triple Canopy, and DynCorp are not of the same ilk as Qaddafi's mercenary forces that come from informal networks of former civil war combatants. Military contractors from reputable companies tend to be professional, efficient, and effective. Hiring private soldiers for a single mission is less expensive than maintaining a standing army, and it has been argued that they may be less likely to maltreat civilians "than public soldiers precisely because their motivation is pecuniary and not ideological or rooted in loyalties to a nation, group, clan or tribe" (Leander, 2005, p. 609). Moreover, "they are bound to follow the laws of the countries where they are based and operate and, in theory, are only hired for noncombat operations like guard duty (though that line is often a thin one in war zones)" (Keating, 2011).

Critics, however, point out that private military companies operate in a legal gray area and that they do not receive adequate monitoring and evaluation. In the Blackwater case, it was unclear whether the employees were subject to Iraqi, U.S., civilian, or military law. And even if employees are found culpable, it is difficult to establish corporate liability unless it can be proven that the company itself intended to break the law. Others worry that private military services have a financial incentive for armed conflicts to persist and that the outsourcing process for lucrative government contracts is not sufficiently competitive, with private military companies effectively establishing a monopoly once they are awarded a long-term contract (Markusen, 2003).

WATCH THE VIDEO:

Carnegie Council Video:
Paying Others to Fight
Our Battles

YOU DECIDE:

1. Does hiring private military services encourage the use of force to resolve conflicts, and make it easier for us to look the other way when it comes to death and destruction in war?
2. Do private military services compromise the states' monopoly on the use of force? Do you think reliance on such services should continue?
3. Are there areas where private contractors could prove particularly useful?

A WORLD AWASH WITH GUNS The sale of arms is a big trans-border business. Part of its growth has occurred because the line between legal and illegal trades is blurred—there is a vibrant black market for the sale of arms to illicit groups, though "almost every firearm on the black market was originally traded legally" (De Soysa, Jackson, and Ormhaug, 2009, p. 88). Shown here is an example of the thriving international trade in weapons: one of the many "arms bazaars" in the global weapons marketplace. There are over 875 million firearms in circulation, and as Nobel Laureate Oscar Arias Sanchez sadly noted, "The greatest percentage of violent deaths occurs from the use of light weapons and small arms."

to Taliban forces resisting the Soviet Union's 1979 invasion in Afghanistan fell into the hands of terrorists who later used them against the United States.

Likewise, in 1982 Great Britain found itself shipping military equipment to Argentina just eight days before Argentina's attack on the British-controlled Falkland Islands; and in 1998 U.S. military technology sold to China was exported to Pakistan, making its nuclear weapons test possible.

Such developments have long-term consequences and are particularly alarming, as in the case of Pakistan, where there is grave concern about the ability of the state to ensure the security of nuclear material. According to Graham Allison, a leading nuclear expert, "The nuclear security of the arsenal is now a lot better than it was. But the unknown variable here is the future of Pakistan itself, because it's not hard to envision a situation in which the state's authority falls apart, and you're not sure who's in control of the weapons, the nuclear labs, the materials" (Sanger, 2009b).

Nuclear Weapons

Technological research and development has radically expanded the destructive power of national arsenals. Albert Einstein, the Nobel Prize–winning physicist whose ideas were the basis for the development of nuclear weapons, was alarmed by the threat they posed. He professed uncertainty about the weapons that would be used in a third world war but was confident that in a fourth world war they would be "sticks and stones." He warned that inasmuch as "the unleashed power of the atom has changed everything save our modes of thinking we thus drift toward unparalleled catastrophe."

The use of nuclear weapons could not only destroy entire cities and countries but also, conceivably, the world's entire population. The largest "blockbuster" bombs of World War II delivered the power of 10 tons of TNT. The atomic bomb that leveled Hiroshima had the power of over 15,000 tons of TNT. Less than 20 years later, the Soviet Union built a nuclear bomb with the explosive force of 57,000,000 tons of TNT.

Since 1945, more than 130,000 nuclear warheads have been built, all but 2 percent by the United States (which has built 55 percent) and the Soviet Union (43 percent). Most have been dismantled since the 1986 peak, but as many as 4000 remained deployed at the start of 2013. The United States possessed 1950 deployed warheads; Russia, 1,740; France, less than 300; and Britain, less than 160. Other countries have warheads, but do not have them deployed such as China (300), India (80–100), Pakistan (90–110), and Israel (about 80). The size of North Korea's nuclear weapons inventory remains uncertain, but is likely less than 10 (The Center for Arms Control and Non-Proliferation, 2013).

In addition, as many as 21 other states (such as Iran and Brazil) or NGO terrorist organizations are widely believed to be seeking to join the nuclear club. The *proliferation* of arms is a serious global concern, because the so-called *Nth country problem* (the addition of new nuclear states) is expected to become increasingly probable. Both *horizontal nuclear proliferation* (the increase in the number of nuclear states) and *vertical nuclear proliferation* (increases in the capabilities of existing nuclear powers) are likely.

Consider India and Pakistan's successful nuclear programs and North Korea's nuclear tests, as well as Iran's and Syria's self-proclaimed aims to acquire nuclear weapons. Nuclear proliferation is likely to continue as states face strong incentives to join the nuclear club and acquire missiles and bombers for their delivery. As long as they do, the threat remains that Argentina, Brazil, Libya, and Taiwan, which once had active nuclear programs, could revive these capabilities to manufacture nuclear weapons.

Likewise, there is widespread international concern regarding the expansion of existing nuclear programs. With the fastest-growing program in the world, Pakistan is aggressively accelerating construction at its Khushab nuclear site and is expected to increase its nuclear weapons arsenal by 100 percent by 2021. "Pakistani officials say the buildup is a response to the threat from India, which is spending $50 billion over the next five years on its military" (Bast, 2011, p. 45) and will likely grow its number of nuclear weapons by 67 percent in the same time frame. In April 2012, within days of each other, Pakistan and India both successfully launched missiles capable of carrying nuclear warheads thousands of kilometers (Abbot, 2012). Most recently, in April 2013, China and Pakistan reached a formal agreement whereby China will help Pakistan build a third nuclear reactor in Chashma. This move is widely seen a undermining any anti-proliferation efforts underway in Pakistan (Gertz, 2013).

"Grounded in the tradition of realist and security-based approaches to nuclear proliferation and nuclear deterrence," the rationale behind the decision to acquire nuclear weapons is clear,

proliferation

The spread of weapon capabilities from a few to many states in a chain reaction, so that increasing numbers of states gain the ability to launch an attack on other states with devastating (e.g., nuclear) weapons.

Carnegie Council Video: Proliferation

Nth country problem

The expansion of additional new nuclear weapon states.

horizontal nuclear proliferation

An increase in the number of states that possess nuclear weapons.

vertical nuclear proliferation

The expansion of the capabilities of existing nuclear powers to inflict increasing destruction with their nuclear weapons.

since "nuclear weapons on average and across a broad variety of indicators enhance the security and diplomatic influence of their possessors" (Gartzke and Kroenig, 2009, p. 152). The complaint of former French President Charles de Gaulle, who argued that without an independent nuclear capability, France could not "command its own destiny," reflects the strong incentive of nonnuclear states to develop weapons similar to those of the existing nuclear club. Similarly, in 1960 Britain's Aneurin Bevan asserted that without the bomb, Britain would go "naked into the council chambers of the world."

This sentiment continues to be reflected today by aspiring nuclear powers. Despite the tightening of sanctions by the UN Security Council in reaction to its nuclear and missile tests conducted in 2009, North Korea resolutely responded that "It has become an absolutely impossible option for (North Korea) to even think about giving up its nuclear weapons" (Fackler, 2009, p. A12). In 2013, North Korea conducted further nuclear tests, with North Korean leader Kim Jong-un's defiant rhetoric adding to global tensions as he challenged other countries, including the United States, with the threat of nuclear annihilation.

Because of the widespread conviction, rooted in realism, that military power confers political stature, many countries, such as Iran and North Korea, regard the *Nuclear Nonproliferation Treaty (NPT)* as hypocritical because it provides a seal of approval to the United States, Russia, China, Britain, and France for possessing nuclear weapons while denying it to all others. The underlying belief that it is acceptable to develop a nuclear capacity for deterrence, political influence, and prestige was expressed in 1999 by Brajesh Mishra, India's national security adviser, when he justified India's nuclear program by asserting that "India should be granted as much respect and deference by the United States and others as is China today."

Although the underlying demand for nuclear weapons is rather straightforward, the supply of nuclear weapons does not appear to make as much sense. Aside from economic motivations, it is less clear why nuclear-capable states themselves have contributed to the global spread of nuclear weapons by providing sensitive nuclear know-how to nonnuclear states. Consider, for example, that Israel built its first nuclear weapon just two years after receiving nuclear assistance from France in the early 1960s. Similarly, after receiving assistance from China in the early 1980s with its nuclear program, Pakistan constructed its first nuclear weapon. Pakistani scientist A.Q. Khan operated a black market nuclear proliferation ring in the late 1990s, and this is thought to have aided Libya, Iran, and North Korea in their efforts to develop nuclear weapons.

Nuclear Nonproliferation Treaty (NPT)

An international agreement that seeks to prevent horizontal proliferation by prohibiting further nuclear weapons sales, acquisitions, or production.

CourseMate

Carnegie Council Video: Nuclear Nonproliferation Treaty

A ROGUE NUCLEAR POWER Shown here, in April 2012, North Korea launched a ballistic missile in defiance of UN Security Council resolutions and an agreement with the United States. According to former U.S. Ambassador to South Korea Donald Gregg, "This is [Kim Jong Un's] way of demonstrating to the people of North Korea he is in charge and his country is capable of high tech things. It is a manifestation of his power." Although the launch ended in failure, it generated international condemnation—as did North Korea's underground nuclear test in 2013.

**nonproliferation
regime**

*Rules to contain
arms races so
that weapons or
technology do not
spread to states
that do not have
them.*

**multiple
independently
targetable
reentry vehicles
(MIRVs)**

*A technological
innovation permit-
ting many weapons
to be delivered
from a single
missile.*

**nonlethal
weapons (NLWs)**

*The wide array of
"soft kill," low-
intensity methods
of incapacitating
an enemy's people,
vehicles, commu-
nications systems,
or entire cities
without killing
either combatants
or noncombatants.*

Focusing on the supply side of nuclear proliferation, political scientist Matthew Kroenig (2009, p. 114) identifies three basic conditions under which states are likely to share sensitive nuclear assistance:

> First, the more powerful a state is relative to a potential nuclear recipient, the less likely it is to provide sensitive nuclear assistance. Second, states are more likely to provide sensitive nuclear assistance to states with which they share a common enemy. Third, states that are less vulnerable to superpower pressure are more likely to provide sensitive nuclear assistance.

These strategic characteristics of the supplier provide some insight into the nuclear proliferation problem, which is also exacerbated by the widespread availability of materials needed to make a nuclear weapon. This is partly because of the widespread use of nuclear technology for generating electricity. Today, almost 437 nuclear-power reactors are in operation in 32 countries throughout the world. The number of new operational nuclear reactors is certain to increase because about 68 new nuclear reactors are now planned or under construction.

In addition to spreading nuclear know-how, states could choose to reprocess the uranium and plutonium, which power plants produce as waste, for clandestine nuclear weapons production. Commercial reprocessing reactors are producing enough plutonium to make as many as 40,000 nuclear weapons. Conversion of peacetime nuclear energy programs to military purposes can occur either overtly or, as in the case of India and Pakistan, covertly. The safeguards built into the *nonproliferation regime* are simply inadequate to detect and prevent secret nuclear weapons development programs.

It is very unlikely that the nuclear threat will disappear (see Figure 8.4). As Matthew Bunn, editor of *Arms Control Today*, explains, "There's not a snowball's chance in hell we'll eliminate all nuclear weapons from the face of the Earth. That genie is long since out of the bottle and there's no chance of ever getting him back in."

The Revolution in Military Technology

Another trend that is increasing the lethality of the weapons of war is the rapidity of technological refinements that increase the capacity of states to send their weapons great distances with ever-greater accuracy. Missiles can now send weapons from as far away as 11,000 miles to within one hundred feet of their targets in less than 30 minutes. One example is the development by the United States and Russia of the ability to equip their ballistic missiles with *multiple independently targetable reentry vehicles (MIRVs)*. This allows these countries to launch many warheads on a single missile toward different targets simultaneously and accurately. One MIRV U.S. MX Peacekeeper missile could carry 10 nuclear warheads—enough to wipe out a city and everything else within a 50-mile radius.

Other technological improvements have led to steady increases in the speed, accuracy, range, and effectiveness of weapons. Laser weapons, nuclear-armed tactical air-to-surface missiles (TASMs), stealth air-launched cruise missiles (ACMs), and antisatellite (ASAT) weapons that can project force and wage war from outer space have become a part of the military landscape.

The global terrain is being transformed by another sea change in the kinds of arms being developed to wage war: the new high-tech *nonlethal weapons (NLWs)* made possible by the

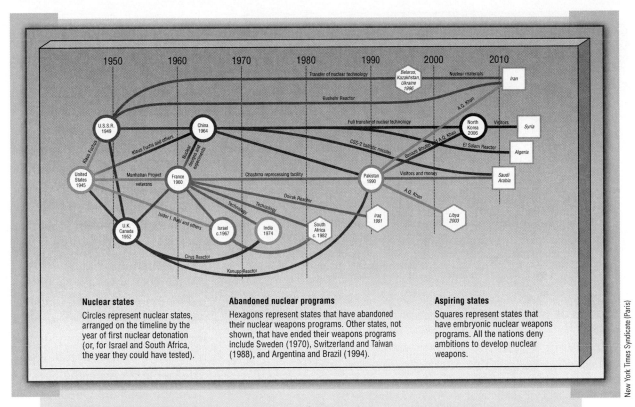

Nuclear states

Circles represent nuclear states, arranged on the timeline by the year of first nuclear detonation (or, for Israel and South Africa, the year they could have tested).

Abandoned nuclear programs

Hexagons represent states that have abandoned their nuclear weapons programs. Other states, not shown, that have ended their weapons programs include Sweden (1970), Switzerland and Taiwan (1988), and Argentina and Brazil (1994).

Aspiring states

Squares represent states that have embryonic nuclear weapons programs. All the nations deny ambitions to develop nuclear weapons.

New York Times Syndicate (Paris)

FIGURE 8.4   A CHAIN REACTION OF PROLIFERATION Since the dawn of the nuclear age, the secrets for making nuclear weapons have spread, either through intentional transfer, leak, or espionage. The connections depicted above indicate the flow of information and technology, through either one-way or two-way transfers. Today there are five official nuclear states (the United States, Russia, the United Kingdom, China, and France) and four additional de facto nuclear states (India, Pakistan, North Korea, and Israel). Many others are poised to join the club of nuclear weapon powers, as this figure shows. Halting nuclear proliferation continues to be seen as one of the most urgent challenges facing the world, the importance of which was unanimously reaffirmed by the 189 members of the Nuclear Non-Proliferation Treaty at their five-year meeting in May 2010.

revolution in military technology (RMT). The new generation includes sounds, shocks, and smells to disperse or incapacitate crowds. For example, the Long Range Acoustic Device (LRAD) blasts sounds at a deafening 150 decibels to incapacitate everyone within 300 meters by giving them an instant and intense headache. Another example is the U.S. Air Force's "active denial technology" that uses electromagnetic radiation to penetrate clothing and cause water molecules to vibrate and burn skin tissue. And it's humorous, but true, that the Pentagon has considered various nonlethal chemical weapons to disrupt enemy discipline and morale, including an aphrodisiac chemical weapon "that would make enemy soldiers sexually irresistible to one another" (Hecht, 2007).

More seriously, NLWs are already deployed in information-warfare squadrons to protect military computer networks from electronic sneak attacks. Other forms of these weapons include energy pulses to knock out or take down enemies without necessarily killing them, biofeedback, beamed electromagnetic and sonic wavelengths that can modify the human behavior of targets (for example, putting people to sleep through electromagnetic heat and

revolution in military technology (RMT)

The sophisticated new weapons technologies that make fighting war without mass armies possible.

Carnegie Council Video:
Revolution in Military Technology

K9 Storm Inc

THE DOGS OF WAR Although technological innovations are transforming military capabilities, some advances get back to the basics. Although there is a long history of canines fighting alongside soldiers, it was not until 1942 that dogs were officially inducted into the U.S. Army. Today they play a key role in U.S. efforts in Afghanistan and Iraq—with 2,800 active-duty dogs deployed in 2010 and plans to add 600 more by 2013 (Frankel, 2011). In addition to fierce loyalty and ability for lethal attack, canines are valuable because their sense of smell is forty times greater than that of a human's and is used to sniff out human targets and bombs. Shown here, U.S. Special Operations Handler and his dog wearing the patented designed K9 Storm Vest jump from 30,100 feet.

magnetic radiation), and ground-penetrating *smart bombs*, which can penetrate a buried bunker at 1000 feet per second and, at the proper millisecond, detonate 500 pounds of explosive to destroy an adversary's inventory of buried chemical and biological weapons.

The precision and power of today's conventional weapons have expanded exponentially, at precisely the moment when the revolution in military technology is leading to "the end of infantry" in the computer age. Countries (and now, terrorist groups) increasingly rely on a variety of new cyberstrategies using innovation in information technology to deter and demobilize enemies (Dombrowski and Gholz, 2007). Examples include such futuristic weapons as the electromagnetic pulse (EMP) bomb, which can be hand-delivered in a suitcase and

---

smart bombs

Precision-guided military technology that enables a bomb to search for its target and detonate at the precise time it can do the most damage.

can immobilize an entire city's computer and communications systems; computer viruses of electronic-seating microbytes that can eliminate a country's telephone system; and logic bombs that can confuse and redirect traffic on the target country's air and rail systems.

Robotic Weaponry

A revolution in robotic military technology is also already under way (see "Controversy: Should Drones Be Used in the Conduct of Warfare?"), with new unmanned systems such as the 42-pound PackBot used in Iraq and Afghanistan to detect improvised explosive devices. "When U.S. forces went into Iraq in 2003, they had zero robotic units on the ground. By the end of 2004, the number was up to 150. By the end of 2005 it was 2,400 and it more than doubled the next year" (Singer, 2009b). By the start of 2013, the U.S. military had more than 12,000 unmanned ground robots (Singer, 2013). Altogether, at least 22 different robot systems are now in use on the ground, with prototypes for a variety of others, from automated machine guns to robotic stretcher bearers to lethal robots the size of insects. Robot soldiers that can think, see, and react like human beings are based on nanotechnology (the science of very small structures) and, predicts Robert Finkelstein, a veteran engineer who leads Robotic Technologies Inc., by "2035 we will have robots as fully capable as human soldiers on the battlefield."

CONTROVERSY

SHOULD DRONES BE USED IN THE CONDUCT OF WARFARE?

A major development in the conduct of warfare has been the widespread use of unmanned aerial vehicles (UAV), commonly referred to as drones. Roughly 70 countries possess such capabilities, with the United States operating the largest number with at least 679 (Rogers, 2012). Drones have extensive surveillance capabilities, as they are able to fly at 17,500 feet and still observe 15 square miles in a single image with enough clarity to identify the kind of cell phone an individual is carrying (Gayle, 2013). While the bulk of drones deployed around the world function as tools for unarmed surveillance, the United States has provoked controversy over its growing use of drones as lethal robots of war both on and off of the battlefield. During the Bush administration, drones were used in roughly 50 "non-battlefield targeted killings," and by 2013 that number had jumped to at least 387 under the Obama administration (Zenko, 2013a).

Such capabilities raise important questions about the limitations that should, or should not, be placed on the use of drones. Addressing the privacy concerns of ordinary civilians, proponents of drones point out that they are operated by trained personnel as part of a security strategy; they are not controlled by voyeuristic amateurs. Furthermore, given their strategic utility for targeted strikes, drones save human lives since they remove the risk that a pilot could be shot down and, due to their accuracy, arguably minimize collateral damage (Shwayder and Mahapatra, 2013). Drones are also cost-effective because they eliminate the need for a fighter pilot to be trained and deployed (Faust and Boyle, 2012).

Detractors paint a very different picture. They question the moral and legal basis for the use of drones—pointing out that the legal parameters concerning their use are vague, government usage is generally shrouded in secrecy, and signature strikes of anonymous military-aged males in targeted-killings fail to meet the legal principal of distinction to engage only valid military targets (Davis et al., 2013, Zenko, 2013b). Using drones to strike targets abroad may also be counterproductive as such attacks anger the populace, which might create more enemies as these people decide to take up arms (Shwayder and Mahapatra, 2013). Moreover, there is growing concern about the extent to which drones are used to observe domestic noncombatants for nonmilitary security purposes. Naomi Gilens of the American Civil Liberties Union cautions that as "drone use becomes more and more common, it is crucial that the government's use of these spying machines be transparent and accountable to the American people … We should not have to guess whether our government is using these eyes in the sky to spy on us." This sentiment may be directed toward a host of entities. In the United States, the Federal Aviation Administration released a list in 2013 that identified 81 U.S. organizations with applications for permission to fly drones, and estimated that by 2018 there may be 10,000 active commercial drones in that country alone (Davis, Litvan, and Stohr, 2013).

WHAT DO YOU THINK?

- *Weighing the pros and cons of drones, are they an effective weapon of war?*
- *Do secret drone programs place too much power in the hands of leaders?*
- *With drone production underway around the world, are they the weapon of the future? To what extent is there a risk that the rights of ordinary people will be violated?*

Note: Prepared with the advice and assistance of William Wagstaff.

AP Photo/Wally Santana

REMOTE-CONTROL WARFARE? The United States is building a new generation of technologically sophisticated weapons. Shown here, U.S. soldiers with land mine detectors wait as another soldier maneuvers a robot into a cave to check for mines, traps, and other weapons that may have been hidden by Taliban or Al Qaeda fugitives in the eastern border town of Qiqay, Afghanistan. The war in Afghanistan is the first time that robots have been used by the U.S. military for combat purposes. They are intended to help prevent U.S. casualties.

The Pentagon is enthusiastic, in part because weapons that are symbols of military might like stealth bombers and nuclear submarines are of little use in today's *asymmetric warfare*, in which individual soldiers equipped with the latest technologies are needed for search-and-destroy missions against guerrilla militias. Moreover, robotic forces are not vulnerable to human frailties. Gordon Johnson, of the Pentagon's Joint Forces Command, notes the appeal of robotic forces, "They're not afraid. They don't forget their orders. They don't care if the guy next to them has just been shot. Will they do a better job than humans? Yes." Technological advances thus may make obsolete current ways of classifying weapons systems and measuring power ratios.

Even though these new weapons have been heralded as a way to accomplish the mission without exposing soldiers to the risks of combat, there are concerns about long-term implications. General Robert E. Lee famously observed, "It is good that we find war so horrible, or else we would become fond of it." Some worry that times are changing, and that war waged by remote control will become too easy and irresistibly tempting as a means to resolve conflicts. Lee "didn't contemplate a time when a pilot could 'go to war' by commuting to work each morning in his Toyota to a cubicle where he could shoot missiles at an enemy thousands of miles away and then make it home in time for his kids' soccer practice" (Singer, 2009a).

Biological and Chemical Weapons

Biological and chemical weapons pose a special and growing threat, particularly in the hands of terrorists aiming for mass destruction rather than influencing public opinion. These unconventional weapons of mass destruction (WMD) are sometimes regarded as a "poor man's atomic bomb" because they can be built at comparatively little cost and cause widespread injury and death. Chemical weapons proliferation is of worldwide concern. In addition to the American hegemon, which led the way in building these weapons, 12 other states have declared past production of chemical weapons, still others are suspected of secret production, and many terrorists claim they intend to acquire and use them. Following the 9/11 terrorist attacks on the United States, for example, there were fears that the spread of anthrax through the U.S. mail system was the first step in an endless series of future biological warfare by terrorist networks.

International law prohibits the use of chemical weapons. The 1925 Geneva Protocol banned the use of chemical weapons in warfare, and the Chemical Weapons Convention, ratified by 188 (96 percent) of the world's countries, requires the destruction of existing stocks. Israel and Myanmar signed the treaty in 1993, but as of May 23, 2013, have yet to ratify it. Only Syria, North Korea, Angola, Egypt, Somalia, and South Sudan have declined to sign or accede to the Chemical Weapons Convention. However, Iran and Iraq's use of gas in their eight-year 1980s war against each other, and Iraq's 1989 use of chemical weapons against its own Kurdish population, demonstrate the weaknesses of this, and similar, legal barriers. In addition, many radical extremists, often beyond the control of weak state governments, see chemical and biological weapons as a cheap and efficient terrorist method.

Pervasive insecurity haunts much of the world because there do not exist real supranational controls over the proliferation of biological and chemical weapons. The twenty-first century has not become the peaceful and prosperous period many people expected. In May 2013, the famous "Doomsday Clock" estimated that the world was only "five minutes" from nuclear Armageddon—two minutes closer than when the clock was originally set in 1947 when the threat of the end of the world loomed large. From an antiwar feminist perspective, which sees war as a gendered identity construct and seeks to change the specific social processes that associate manliness with militarized violence, "State security may sometimes be served by war, but too often human security is not" (Cohn and Ruddick, 2008, p. 459).

The world is *not* a safer place. In response to military dangers, many leaders today still adhere to the realist axiom that "if you want peace prepare for war." Security, realists insist, requires military capabilities. However, because the possession of over-powering military capabilities does not automatically result in their prudent use, realists counsel that what matters greatly in the pursuit of national security are the *methods* on which states rely to use the capabilities they have acquired. How can weapons be most effectively used to promote national interests and exercise international influence? This question underscores the vital importance of choices about the types of military strategies employed.

Military Strategies

The most important event distinguishing pre– from post–World War II politics occurred on August 6, 1945, when the United State dropped the first atomic bomb on Hiroshima, Japan. In the blinding flash of a single weapon and the shadow of its mushroom cloud, the world was transformed from a "balance-of-power" to a "balance-of-terror" system. Since then, policy makers have had to grapple with two central policy questions: (1) whether they should use weapons of mass destruction and (2) how to prevent others from using them.

The search for answers is critical because both the immediate and delayed effects of weapons of mass destruction are terrifying to contemplate. Consider that even a short war using a tiny fraction of any great power's nuclear arsenal would destroy all life as we know it. A *nuclear winter* would result, with devastating consequences that could make the planet uninhabitable. Even a more limited nuclear conflict would greatly affect the atmosphere, with the sun at least partially blocked by large patches of dense smoke that would move around the world (Westin, 2013). It has been estimated that "the missiles on board a single [U.S.] SLBM submarine may be enough to initiate nuclear winter" (Quester, 1992, p. 43)—enough to end human existence.

Since World War II, not only have nuclear arsenals and the number of states that possess nuclear capabilities grown, but many have also come to think of biological, chemical, and radiological weapons as weapons of mass destruction because of their capacity for large-scale devastation and casualties. Rogue states and nonstate actors, such as terrorist organizations, also pose a threat to global security with their potential use of WMDs. Military strategies that respond to changes in technologies, defense needs, capabilities, and global actors and conditions are critical. For analytical convenience, we consider three broad postures: compellence, deterrence, and preemption.

Compellence   Countries that possess military preeminence often think of weapons as instruments in diplomatic bargaining. Military capabilities do not have to be used for them to be instrumental; a country can exercise influence over enemies simply by demonstrating the power of its weapons and signaling its willingness to use them. Through a show of force, or a convincing threat of force, countries can use *compellence* as a strategy to convince others to do what they might not otherwise do.

The United States, the world's first and for many years unchallenged nuclear power, adopted the strategy of compellence when it enjoyed a clear-cut nuclear superiority over the Soviet Union. The United States sought to gain bargaining leverage by giving the impression that it would actually use its nuclear weapons. This posture was especially evident during the Eisenhower administration, when Secretary of State John Foster Dulles practiced *brinkmanship*, deliberately threatening U.S. adversaries with nuclear destruction so that, on the brink of war, they would concede to U.S. demands. Brinkmanship was part of the overall U.S. strategic doctrine known as *massive retaliation*. To contain communism and Soviet expansionism, this doctrine called for aiming U.S. nuclear weapons at what the Soviets valued most—their population and industrial centers.

Massive retaliation heightened fears in the Kremlin that a nuclear exchange would destroy the Soviet Union but permit the survival of the United States. In addition to responding by increasing their nuclear capabilities, Soviet leaders accelerated their space program and successfully launched the world's first space satellite (*Sputnik*). This demonstrated Moscow's ability to deliver nuclear weapons beyond the Eurasian landmass. Thus, the superpowers' strategic competition took a new turn as the United States for the first time faced a nuclear threat to its homeland.

Deterrence   Whereas a strategy of compellence relies on an offensive threat aimed at persuading an adversary to relinquish something without resistance, *deterrence* seeks to dissuade an adversary from undertaking some future action. The chief assumption of deterrence theory is that the defender has the ability to punish an adversary with unacceptably high costs if it launches an attack. The key elements of deterrence are:

■ **Capabilities**. The possession of military resources that signal to the adversary that threats of military retaliation are possible.

■ **Credibility**. The belief that the actor is willing to act on its declared threats.

■ **Communication**. The ability to send a potential aggressor the clear message that the threat will be carried out.

A deterrence strategy depends on obtaining the unquestionable ability to inflict intolerable damage on an opponent. This means that a state seeking to deter an enemy must build its weapons to acquire a *second-strike capability*, which necessitates having sufficient destructive weapons to ensure that the country can withstand an adversary's

Corbis

WEAPONS FOR WAR AND PEACE Shown here is a U.S. test of a nuclear bomb in 1954, when only the United States and the Soviet Union had nuclear capabilities. Today, the capacity to wage war with weapons of mass destruction has spread to many countries, and the diffusion is transforming the global balance of power. What to do with such weapons for war and for peace is the central concern of realist theorizing, which looks on the acquisition of military power and its consequences as the most important dimension of world politics.

first strike and still retaliate with a devastating counterattack. To guarantee that an adversary is aware that a second-strike capability exists, deterrence rationalizes an unrestrained search for sophisticated retaliatory capabilities. As President Kennedy explained in 1961, "only when arms are sufficient beyond doubt can we be certain without doubt that they will never be employed."

The phrase *mutual assured destruction (MAD)* was coined to describe the strategic balance that emerged between the United States and the Soviet Union after the near nuclear exchange during the 1962 Cuban Missile Crisis. Regardless of who struck first, the other side could destroy the attacker. Under these circumstances, initiating a nuclear war was not a *rational choice*; the frightening costs outweighed any conceivable benefits. As Soviet leader Nikita Khrushchev put it, "If you reach for the push button, you reach for suicide." Safety, in former British Prime Minister Winston Churchill's words, was "the sturdy child of terror and survival the twin brother of annihilation."

Today, a strategy of deterrence is reflected in U.S.-led efforts to construct a defensive shield against ballistic missiles (see Map 8.4). Using an integrated system of ground, sea, and space-based radars and weapons, this defense technology detects, intercepts, and destroys weapons

second-strike capability

a state's capacity to retaliate after absorbing an adversary's first-strike attack with weapons of mass destruction.

mutual assured destruction (MAD)

A condition of mutual deterrence in which both sides possess the ability to survive a first strike with weapons of mass destruction and launch a devastating retaliatory attack.

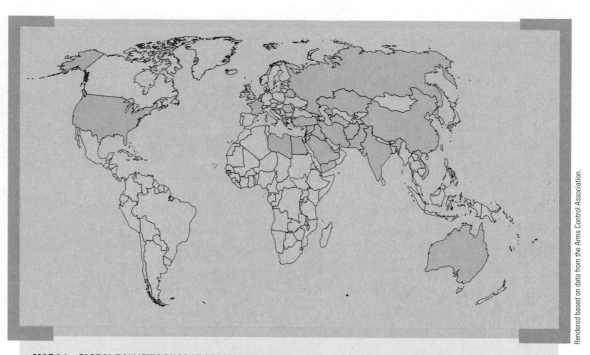

MAP 8.4 GLOBAL BALLISTIC MISSILE CAPABILITIES The map above shows countries with ballistic missiles. Although the direct threat is limited, such military capacity is widely feared. "The number of long-range missiles fielded by China and Russia has decreased 71 percent since 1987. The number of medium-range ballistic missiles pointed at U.S. allies in Europe and Asia has fallen 80 percent. Most countries that have any ballistic missiles at all have only short-range Scud missiles—which travel less than 300 miles and are growing older and less reliable every day" (Cirincione, 2008, p. 68). Nonetheless, by 2013 the United States will have spent in excess of $157 billion on missile defense, including an extra $1 billion to deter North Korea (Missile Defense Agency, 2013b; Shanker et al., 2013).

ballistic missile defense

A planned antiballistic missile system using space-based lasers that would destroy enemy nuclear missiles before they could enter Earth's atmosphere.

launched in fear, anger, or by accident. The goal of *ballistic missile defense* (BMD), in U.S. President Reagan's words, is to make nuclear weapons "impotent and obsolete" and to shift nuclear strategy away from mutual assured destruction. The United States' pursuit of antiballistic missile defense currently includes 26 Aegis BMD ships distributed between the Atlantic and Pacific theaters, with plans for extensive growth and improvements, including shore-based interceptor missiles in Europe and Japan as well as an improved SM-3 Block II missiles capable of taking out longer-range ballistic missiles (Missile Defense Agency, 2013a).

Critics question the allocation of resources to BMD. As former director of Operational Test and Evaluation for the Department of Defense Philip Coyle noted in 2006, it has shown "no demonstrated capability to defend the United States against enemy attack under realistic conditions." Others worry that BMD undermines the deterrence strategy, rather than complements it, and may lead to more nuclear missiles worldwide instead of fewer.

"Russia is concerned that these more potent Block II missile-defense interceptors might be capable of neutralizing some Russian nuclear forces and will, therefore, upset the delicate balance of arms agreed to in New START" (Butt, 2011)—an arms control treaty ratified in 2010 that would further scale back Cold War nuclear arsenals. In May 2011, then–Russian President Medvedev warned that "Russia will need to speed up the development of its nuclear strike capabilities if the United States does not convince Moscow its missile defense system isn't aimed at Russia" (Eshchenko and Tkachenko, 2011). However, Russian concerns were partly relieved when, in March 2013, the United States canceled part of its missile defense deployments under pressure from the Kremlin, which continues to cite missile defense in Europe as a major hurdle to nuclear arms reduction (Herszenhorn and Gordon, 2013).

Preemption   Strategic planning continues to find new ways of dealing with the constant danger of emergent military threats. The United States has led the way in forging new strategies to deal with global terrorism and belligerent enemies in the post-9/11 world. From that threat has emerged the *preemptive warfare* strategy, which calls for striking a potential enemy before it undertakes armed aggression.

As posited in the 2002 *U.S. National Security Strategy*, "traditional concepts of deterrence will not work against a terrorist enemy whose avowed tactics are wanton destruction and the targeting of innocents; whose so-called soldiers seek martyrdom in death; and whose most potent protection is statelessness." A preemptive strategy calls for attacking a potential enemy before it engages in armed aggression, either with or without the support of allies and international institutions. "We must take the battle to the enemy," President George W. Bush exhorted, "and confront the worst threats before they emerge."

Although international law affords states the legal right to defend themselves against aggression as well as imminent attacks, critics charge that beneath the language of military preemption lies a more radical policy of preventive war (see Chapter 9). A preemptive military attack entails the use of force to quell or mitigate an impending strike by an adversary. *Preventive warfare* entails the use of force to eliminate any possible future strike, even if there is no reason to believe that the capacity to launch an attack currently exists. Whereas the grounds for preemption lie in evidence of a credible, imminent threat, the basis for prevention rests on the suspicion of an incipient, contingent threat (Kegley and Raymond, 2004).

According to critics, the preventive use of military force sets a dangerous precedent. Predicting an adversary's future behavior is difficult because its leadership's intentions are hard to discern, information about long-term goals may be shrouded in secrecy, and signals of its policy direction may be missed in an oversupply of unimportant intelligence information. If suspicions about an adversary become a justifiable cause for military action, then every truculent leader would have a rough-and-ready pretext for ordering a first strike.

In 2009, President Barack Obama signaled a shift from the preemptive and unilateral policies of the prior administration. In its place, he called for an approach that maintained America's military strength but also sought to broaden engagement with the global community. Calling nuclear proliferation and nuclear terrorism "a threat that rises above all others in urgency," he sought to renew American diplomacy, with a willingness to engage in dialogue in order to advance U.S. interests (Allison, 2010; Ferguson 2010).

The ever-present threat of armed aggression raises timeless questions about the conditions under which, and the purposes for which, using military force is justified. What does prudent caution require when ruthless countries and nameless, faceless enemies pursue indiscriminate, suicidal attacks against innocent noncombatants? How can force be used to influence an adversary's decision-making calculus? What conditions affect the success of coercive diplomacy?

preemptive warfare

A quick first-strike attack that seeks to defeat an adversary before it can organize an initial attack or a retaliatory response.

Carnegie Council Video:
Preemptive Warfare

preventive warfare

Strictly outlawed by international law, a war undertaken by choice against an enemy to prevent it from suspected intentions to attack sometime in the distant future—if and when the enemy might acquire the necessary military capabilities.

Carnegie Council Video:
Preventive War

COERCIVE DIPLOMACY THROUGH MILITARY INTERVENTION

Coercive diplomacy in international bargaining is the threat or use of limited force to persuade an opponent to stop pursuing an activity it is already undertaking. Drawing on aspects of a strategy of compellence, threats to use arms are made to force an adversary to reach a compromise or, even better, to reverse its policies. The goal is to alter the target state's costs and benefits calculation, so that the enemy is convinced that acceding to demands will be better than defying them. This result may be accomplished by delivering an ultimatum that promises immediate and significant escalation, or by issuing a warning and gradually increasing pressure on the target (Craig and George, 1990).

Coercive diplomacy's reliance on the threat of force is designed to avoid the bloodshed and expense associated with traditional military campaigns. Orchestrating the mix of threats and armed aggression can be done in various ways. The methods range from traditional *gunboat diplomacy* to threaten an enemy by positioning navies and/or armies near its borders to "tomahawk diplomacy" by striking an adversary with precision-guided cruise missiles. These are among the instruments of coercive diplomacy in the arsenal of military options envisioned by realist policy makers to pursue power.

Intervention can be practiced in various ways—physically through direct entry of military forces into another country, indirectly by broadcasting propaganda to the target's population, or through *covert operations*. Global actors also can take a *unilateral* or *multilateral* approach to intervention. Overt military intervention is the most visible method of interference inside the borders of another country. For that reason, it is also the most controversial and costly.

Interventions have been frequently, if episodically, occurring since World War II (see Figure 8.5). This fluctuation suggests that military interventions rise and fall in response to both changing global circumstances as well as shifting perceptions about the advantages and disadvantages of intervention as an effective method of coercive diplomacy.

Each act of military intervention had a different rationale and produced different results. Past cases raise tough questions about the use of military intervention for coercive diplomacy. Does the record show that the actions met the goals of the intervening states, such as successfully punishing countries so that they no longer violated their citizens' human rights? Have they for the most part restored order to war-torn societies? Or, on the whole, have they made circumstances worse?

These questions are hotly debated now because of the prevalence of failed states. The great powers have not reached a consensus about the whether to intervene in sovereign states when tyrants victimize innocent civilians. Why? Primarily because these interventions undermine state sovereignty and the deeply entrenched *nonintervention norm*. The United Nation's call for a "new commitment to intervention" stirred up the percolating debate about military intervention, even in the name of morality, justice, and human rights.

Today, policy makers disagree about the appropriate use of military coercion. Research on coercive diplomacy suggests that its success depends upon each specific context.

gunboat diplomacy

A show of military force, historically naval force, to intimidate an adversary.

covert operations

Secret activities undertaken by a state outside its borders through clandestine means to achieve specific political or military goals with respect to another state.

nonintervention norm

A fundamental international legal principle, now being challenged, that traditionally has defined interference by one state in the domestic affairs of another as illegal.

Carnegie Council Video:
Nonintervention Norm

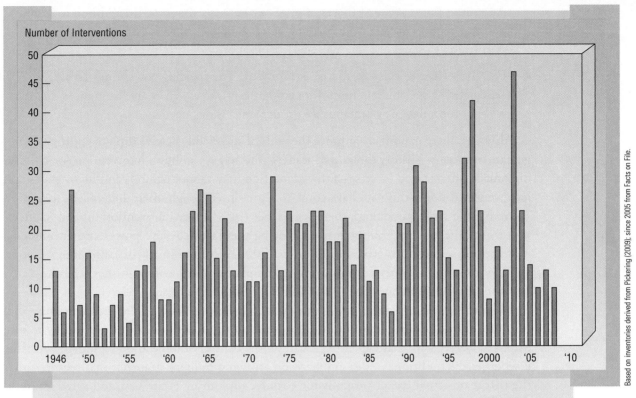

Number of Interventions

FIGURE 8.5   THE CHANGING INCIDENCE OF UNILATERAL MILITARY INTERVENTION FOR COERCIVE DIPLOMATIC PURPOSES SINCE 1945 As this evidence shows, states have frequently sent their troops into the sovereign territory of other states in order to influence the target, even though military intervention has been traditionally prohibited by international law. The frequency of this forceful coercive diplomacy fluctuates from year to year, and suggests that the fluctuations are dependent on the personal choices of the leaders authorizing their country's use of national armed forces for military engagement outside their borders.

The following conditions are thought to favor the effective use of coercive diplomacy (Art, 2005; George, 1992):

- **Clarity of user objectives**. The coercing power's demands must be clearly understood by the target state.

- **Asymmetry of motivation favoring the user**. The coercing power must be more highly motivated than the target by what is at stake. Military coercion tends to be effective when it occurs prior to the target making a firm commitment on the issue at hand, and when factions exist within the target state's government. It is far more difficult for a coercing power to reverse something that has already been accomplished by the target state.

- **Opponent's fear of escalation and belief in the urgency for compliance**. The coercing power must convince the adversary mind that compliance with its demand is an urgent matter. Two factors are important in affecting an adversary's perceptions: (1) the coercing power's reputation for successfully using armed force in the past and (2) its capability to increase pressure to a level that the target would find intolerable. Coercion generally fails when the target has the ability to absorb the punishment delivered by the coercing state.

- **Adequate domestic and international support for the user.** In addition to having political support at home, the coercing power is helped when it can also count on support from key states and international organizations.

- **Clarity on the precise terms of settlement.** The coercing power must be able to articulate the specific conditions for ending the crisis, as well as give assurances that it will not formulate new demands for greater concessions once the target capitulates.

Although these conditions improve the odds of successful coercive diplomacy, they do not guarantee success. History shows that leaders who rely on military intervention for coercive diplomacy often start a process that they later find they cannot control, and many states that have ventured down this path have come to regret it. Although often undertaken to address severe human rights conditions, there is evidence that military intervention instead "contributes to the rise of state repression by enhancing the state's coercive power and encouraging more repressive behavior" (Peksen, 2012, p. 558). In the aftermath of failed interventions, confidence in this military method of coercive diplomacy frequently vanishes, and the search for other means to exercise power in world politics has intensified.

Most realists, and many others, continue to put lasting faith in the realist premise that it is safer to rely on the force of arms than on the force of arguments to successfully resolve disputes. Yet security may depend as much on the control of force as on its pursuit. At issue is whether the traditional realist emphasis on arms and military strategies that require either the threat or actual use of weapons for coercive diplomacy is the best and safest route to national and international security. To be sure, the traditional realist reliance on military capabilities to increase national security continues to resonate in world capitals. However, other realists recommend an alternative path—one that sees national interests served most, not by the acquisition and use of arms, but rather by the acquisition of allies in order to maintain a balance of power among rivals that will prevent any transnational actor from using force against the others. This, these other realists believe, provides the safest path to security. Are they right?

> *Warfare is not a question of brute strength, but rather of winning and losing friends.*

> —Count Diego Sarmiento Gondomar, Spanish ambassador to London in 1618

REALIST INTERPRETATIONS OF ALLIANCES IN WORLD POLITICS

Alliances in world politics require agreements between parties in order for them to cooperate. For that reason, it may seem that *liberal theory*, with its emphasis on the possibility of self-sacrifice for mutual gain, might provide a key to understanding why and how states join together in alliances. According to liberal theory, states may form an alliance even if their immediate interest is not realized in order to maximize their long-term collective interest.

Realism, however, provides the dominant lens through which the dynamics of alliance formation and decay, and the impact of these dynamics on global security, are most often interpreted. As you have learned, realism portrays world politics as a struggle for power under conditions of anarchy by competitive rivals pursuing only their own self-interests (and *not* for moral principles and global ideals such as improving the security and welfare of *all* throughout the globe). Realists picture *alliances* as temporary, opportunistic agreements to cooperate that predictably come into being when two or more parties face a common security threat. "An alliance (or alignment) is a formal (or informal) commitment for security cooperation between two or more states, intended to augment each member's power, security, and/or influence" (Walt, 2009, p. 86; see also Fordham, 2010).

Realism provides the most compelling explanation of the coldly calculating motives underlying decisions about alliances, which realists see first and foremost as a method for states to protect themselves from threats posed by predatory common enemies and as a mechanism by which a "balance of power" can be maintained. "Regarding the origins and purposes of alliances, realists are doggedly parsimonious, taking states as rational, security-maximizing actors whose self-interested behavior is largely determined by the structure of the international system" (Byrne, 2013). Realism posits that military alliances are forged when the parties perceive that the advantages of an alliance outweigh the disadvantages. When facing a common threat, alliances provide their members with the means of reducing their probability of being attacked (deterrence), obtaining greater strength in case of attack (defense), and precluding their allies from aligning with the enemy (Snyder, 1991).

alliances

Coalitions of two or more states that combine their military capabilities and promise to coordinate their policies to increase mutual security.

Carnegie Council Video: Alliances

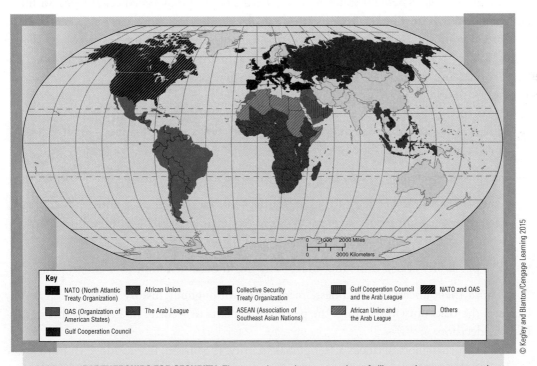

© Kegley and Blanton/Cengage Learning 2015

Key
- NATO (North Atlantic Treaty Organization)
- OAS (Organization of American States)
- Gulf Cooperation Council
- African Union
- The Arab League
- Collective Security Treaty Organization
- ASEAN (Association of Southeast Asian Nations)
- Gulf Cooperation Council and the Arab League
- African Union and the Arab League
- NATO and OAS
- Others

MAP 8.5   PARTNERSHIPS FOR SECURITY The map above shows a number of alliances that were created, in part, to integrate joint regional military or economic security interests and promote cooperation. Highlighting the importance of alliances in U.S. national security strategy, President Obama once said "We will be steadfast in strengthening those old alliances that have served us so well.... As influence extends to more countries and capitals, we must also build new partnerships, and shape stronger international standards and institutions."

These advantages notwithstanding, realists often see a downside and counsel against forming alliances, as Britain's Lord Palmerston did in 1848 when he advised that states "should have no eternal allies and no perpetual enemies." Under anarchy a state must rely on *self-help* for its own security, and cannot really count on allies to come to its defense if attacked. Moreover, alliances bind a state to a commitment that may later become disadvantageous.

As realist theoretician Thucydides counseled, "One has to behave as friend or foe according to the circumstances," and these choices are made on a complex geostrategic playing field in which today's enemy may be tomorrow's ally and where fears of entrapment, abandonment, or betrayal are ever present. This is why "wise and experienced statesmen usually shy away from commitments likely to constitute limitations on a government's behavior at unknown dates in the future in the face of unpredictable situations" (Kennan, 1984a, p.238). Because conditions are certain to change sooner or later and the usefulness of all alliances is certain to change once the common threat that brought the allies together declines, the realist tradition advises states not to take a fixed position on temporary convergences of national interests and, instead, to forge alliances only to deal with immediate threats.

When considering whether joining a new alliance is a rational choice in which the benefits outweigh the costs, heads of state usually recognize that allies can easily do more harm than good. Arguing that whereas a state "may safely trust to temporary alliances for extraordinary emergencies" it is an illusion "to expect or calculate real favors from nation to nation," the first president of the United States, George Washington, advised that the United States should "steer clear of permanent alliances." Many realists similarly advise states against forming alliances for defense, basing their fears on five fundamental flaws:

- Alliances enable aggressive states to combine military capabilities for war.

- Alliances threaten enemies and provoke the creation of counteralliances, which reduces the security of both coalitions.

- Alliance formation may draw otherwise neutral parties into opposed coalitions.

- Once states join forces, they must control the behavior of their own allies to discourage each member from reckless aggression against its enemies, which would undermine the security of the alliance's other members.

- The possibility always exists that today's ally might become tomorrow's enemy.

Despite their uncertain usefulness, many states throughout history have chosen to ally because, the risks notwithstanding, the perceived benefits to security in a time of threat justified the decision.

To best picture how alliances affect global security, it is instructive to move from the state level of analysis, which views alliance decisions from the perspective of an individual state's security, to the global level of analysis (recall Chapter 1) by looking at the impact of alliances on the frequency of interstate war. This view focuses attention on the possible contribution of alliance formation to maintaining the balance of power.

REALISM AND THE BALANCING OF POWER

The concept of a balance of power has a long and controversial history. Supporters envision it as an equilibrating process that maintains peace by counterbalancing any state that seeks military superiority, distributing global power evenly through *alignments* or shifts by nonaligned states to one or the other opposed coalitions. Critics deny the effectiveness of the balance of power, arguing that it breeds jealousy, intrigue, and antagonism.

At the core of "balance of power" is the idea that national security is enhanced when military capabilities are distributed so that no single state is strong enough to dominate all others. If one state gains inordinate power, balance-of-power theory predicts that it will take advantage of its strength and attack weaker neighbors, thereby giving compelling incentive for those threatened to unite in a defensive coalition. According to the theory, the threatened states' combined military strength would then deter (or, if need be, defeat) the state seeking to expand. Thus, for realists, laissez-faire competition among states striving to maximize their national power yields an international equilibrium, ensuring the survival of all by checking the hegemonic ambitions of any.

Balance-of-power theory is also founded on the realist premise that weakness invites attack and that countervailing power must be used to deter potential aggressors. Realists assume that the drive for power guides every state's actions. It follows that all countries are potential adversaries and that each must strengthen its military capability to protect itself. Invariably, this reasoning rationalizes the quest for military superiority, because others pursue it as well. This rationale springs from the realist belief that a system revolving around suspicion, competition, and anarchy will breed caution; uncertainty creates restraints on the propensity for war. As President George Washington once noted, "It is a maxim founded on the universal experience of mankind that no nation is to be trusted farther than it is bound by its interest."

The use of alliances to balance power is intrinsically tied to shifts in the global structure of the international system. Military power can be distributed around one or more power centers in different ways—an idea scholars call *polarity* (recall Chapter 4). Historically, these have ranged from *unipolarity*, where there is a high concentration of power in the hands of a single hegemon, to *multipolarity*, where the power distribution is highly dispersed among multiple actors. Examples of *unipolarity* include regional empires such as the Roman Empire, as well as the United States in the years immediately following World War II when it was without rival and no state could counterbalance it. An example of the latter is the approximate equality of power held by the European powers at the conclusion of the Napoleonic Wars in 1815.

In between these two ends of the continuum is *bipolarity*—the division of the balance of power into two coalitions headed by rival military powers, each seeking to contain the other's expansion. In 1949, when the Soviets broke the U.S. monopoly on atomic weapons, a redistribution of power began to emerge. Military capabilities became concentrated in the hands of two competitive "superpowers" whose capacities to destroy anyone else made comparisons with the other great powers meaningless.

alignments

The acceptance by a neutral state threatened by foreign enemies of a special relationship short of formal alliance with a stronger power able to protect it from attack.

Carnegie Council Video:
Alignments

Animated Learning Module:
The Balance of Power

Both superpowers attached great importance to balancing power by recruiting new allies. The formation of the *North Atlantic Treaty Organization (NATO)*, linking the United States to the defense of Western Europe, and the Warsaw Pact, linking the former Soviet Union in a formal alliance with its Eastern European client states, occurred due to this *polarization*. The opposing blocs formed in part because the superpowers competed for allies and in part because the less powerful states looked to one superpower or the other for protection.

To balance power, realists recognize that national actors need to see the value of rapidly shifting alliances. Although balancing is occasionally described as an automatic, self-adjusting process, most realists see it as the result of deliberate choices undertaken by national leaders to maintain equilibrium among contending states. This requires adhering to rules of decision making.

Rules for Rivals in the Balancing Process

It is necessary for all leaders to constantly monitor changes in states' relative capabilities so that policies about arms and allies can be adjusted to rectify power imbalances (see Map 8.6). Such choices must be made by rational, self-interested actors who recognize the costs and benefits of various strategic options. Many theorists have attempted to specify a set of rules that leaders must heed in order to effectively balance other states. These rules include:

- **Stay vigilant.** Constantly watch foreign developments in order to identify emerging threats and opportunities. Because international anarchy makes each state responsible for its own security and because states can never be sure of one another's intentions, self-interest encourages them to maximize their relative power. As Morton Kaplan (1957, p. 35) wrote: "Act to increase capabilities but negotiate rather than fight … [At the same time, states should] fight rather than pass up an opportunity to increase capabilities."

- **Seek allies whenever your country cannot match the armaments of an adversary.** States align with each other when they adopt a common stance toward some shared security problem. An alliance is produced when they formally agree to coordinate their behavior under certain specified circumstances. States sitting on the sidelines, *free riders*, cannot as rational actors risk *nonalignment*. If they refuse to ally, their own vulnerability will encourage an expansionist state to attack them sooner or later.

- **Remain flexible in making alliances.** Formed and dissolved according to the strategic needs of the moment, alliances must be made without regard to similarities of culture or ideological beliefs (Owen, 2005), and past experiences should not predispose states to accept or reject *any* potential partner. Nowhere is this philosophy better seen than in the role Great Britain once played as a *balancer* in European diplomacy. From the seventeenth through the early twentieth century, the British shifted their weight from one side of the continental balance to the other, arguing that they had no permanent friends and no permanent enemies, just a permanent interest in preventing the balance from tipping either way (Dehio, 1962). As described by Winston Churchill, Britain's goal was to "oppose the strongest, most aggressive, most dominating power on the continent. … [It] joined with the less strong powers, made a combination among them, and thus defeated and frustrated the continental military tyrant whoever he was, whatever nation he led."

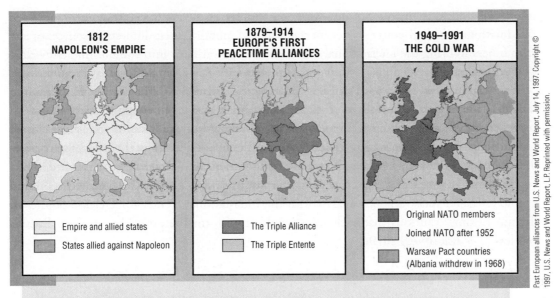

Past European alliances from U.S. News and World Report, July 14, 1997. Copyright © 1997, U.S. News and World Report, L.P. Reprinted with permission.

MAP 8.6   CHANGING EUROPEAN ALLIANCES When relationships and conditions change, new alliances form and established alliances dissolve as transnational actors—all obsessed with the power of their rivals—realign. Pictured here are three distributions of power in past European alliances.

■ **Oppose any state that seeks hegemony.** The purpose of engaging in balance-of-power politics is to survive in a world of potentially dangerous great powers. If any state achieves absolute mastery over everyone else, it will be able to act freely. Under such circumstances, the territorial integrity and political autonomy of other states will be in jeopardy. By joining forces with the weaker side to prevent the stronger side from reaching preponderance, states can preserve their independence. As Joseph Nye (2008) phrased it, "Balance of power is a policy of helping the underdog because if you help the top dog, it may eventually turn around and eat you." Over the last few years, China and Russia have sought to put their Cold War rivalries behind them, strengthen bilateral ties, and rise as a counterbalance to U.S. global dominance. In a meeting with then–Russian Prime Minister Vladimir Putin in March 2010, then–Chinese Vice President Xi Jinping expressed his view that "China and Russia should in the future facilitate the establishment of a multipolar world and democratization of international relations."

**Video Activity:
Shifting Alliances
in Iran**

■ **Be charitable in victory.** In the event of war, the winning side should not eliminate the defeated. Looking forward rather than backward, it should do as little damage as possible to those it has vanquished because yesterday's enemy may be needed as tomorrow's ally. Victors that couple firmness regarding their own interests with fairness toward the interests of others encourage defeated powers to work within the postwar balance of power. Similarly, states that win at the bargaining table can stabilize the balance of power by granting the other side compensation in return for its concessions.

These realist policy prescriptions urge states to check the ambitions of any great power that threatens to amass overwhelming power, because aspiring hegemons are a potential threat to everyone. Human beings and states, they argue, are selfish by nature, but balancing rival interests stabilizes their interactions. Weakness, realists insist, invites aggression. Thus, when faced with unbalanced power, leaders of states should mobilize their domestic resources or ally with others to bring the international distribution of power back into equilibrium (Schweller, 2004; Waltz, 1979).

The resistance of Germany, France, and many other countries to the 2003 U.S. decision to launch a preemptive war to prevent Iraq from acquiring and using weapons of mass destruction—especially as evidence of Iraq's possession of such weapons, ties to the 9/11 terrorist attacks, or intention to wage war were highly questionable—illustrates the balancing process. The alarm of countries in the Baltic, such as Estonia, Latvia, and Lithuania, to France's decision to sell Mistral-class assault ships to Russia that would enter service in 2015 provides another example. Kaarel Kaas, a policy analyst with the International Center for Defense Studies in Talinn, Estonia, cautions that such ships would "transform the power balance" on Russia's borders (*The Economist*, 2010i, p. 54).

Difficulties with the Maintenance of a Balance of Power

Can balancing power help to preserve world order, as most realists believe? Critics of balance-of-power theory raise several objections to the proposition that balancing promotes peace:

bandwagoning

The tendency for weak states to seek alliance with the strongest power, irrespective of that power's ideology or type of government, in order to increase their security.

- Scholars argue that the theory's rules for behavior are contradictory (Riker, 1962). On the one hand, states are urged to increase their power. On the other hand, they are told to oppose anyone seeking preponderance. Yet sometimes *bandwagoning* with (rather than balancing against) the dominant state can increase a weaker country's capabilities by allowing it to share in the spoils of a future victory. History suggests that states that are most content with the status quo tend to balance against rising powers more than do dissatisfied states.

- Balance-of-power theory assumes policy makers possess accurate, timely information about other states. Recall that the concept of "power" has multiple meanings. Tangible factors are hard to compare, such as the performance capabilities of the different types of weapons found in an adversary's arsenal. Intangible factors, such as leadership skills, troop morale, or public support for adventuresome or aggressive foreign policies, are even more difficult to gauge. The uncertainty of power balances due to difficulties in determining the strength of adversaries and the trustworthiness of allies frequently causes military planners to engage in worst-case analysis, which can spark an arms race. The intense, reciprocal anxiety that shrouds balance-of-power politics fuels exaggerated estimates of an adversary's strength. This, in turn, prompts each side to expand the quantity and enhance the quality of its weaponry. Critics of realism warn that if a serious dispute occurs between states locked in relentless arms competition under conditions of mutually assured suspicions, the probability of war increases.

- Balance-of-power theory assumes that decision makers are risk-averse—when confronted with countervailing power, they refrain from fighting because the dangers of taking on an equal are too great. Yet, as *prospect theory* (see Chapter 3) illuminates, national leaders evaluate risks differently. Some are risk-acceptant. Rather than being deterred by equivalent power, they prefer gambling on the chance of winning a victory, even if the odds are long. Marshaling comparable power against adversaries with a high tolerance for risk will not have the same effect as it would on those who avoid risks.

■ The past performance of balance-of-power theory is checkered. If the theory's assumptions are correct, historical periods during which its rules were followed should also have been periods in which war was less frequent. Yet a striking feature of those periods is their record of warfare. After the 1648 Peace of Westphalia created the global system of independent territorial states, the great powers participated in a series of increasingly destructive general wars that threatened to engulf and destroy the entire multistate global system. As Inis L. Claude (1989, p. 78) soberly concludes, it is difficult to consider these wars "as anything other than catastrophic failures, total collapses, of the balance-of-power system. They are hardly to be classified as stabilizing maneuvers or equilibrating processes, and one cannot take seriously any claim of maintaining international stability that does not entail the prevention of such disasters." Indeed, the historical record has led some theorists to construct the *hegemonic stability theory* as an alternative to the balance of power theory. This theory postulates that a single, dominant hegemon can guarantee peace better than a rough equality of military capabilities among competing great powers (Ferguson, 2004; Mandelbaum, 2006a).

FAST FRIENDS OR TEMPORARY PLAYMATES? On March 26 and 27, 2013, the BRICS (Brazil, Russia, India, China, and South Africa) held their fifth annual summit in Durban, South Africa. Seen as a balancing maneuver, this cooperative venture is a product of the growing desire to have greater influence in shaping the global economy and the political order. Yet while the group has economic heft, its political clout is uncertain. Says former Indian ambassador to the U.S. Lalit Mansingh, "They don't see eye to eye on many international issues. There is no common cementing principle among them." This picture shows, from left, Indian Prime Minister Manmohan Singh, Chinese President Xi Jinping, South African President Jacob Zuma, Brazilian President Dilma Rousseff, and Russian President Vladimir Putin.

A significant problem with the balance-of-power system is its haphazard character. The potential for great power harmony to be replaced by great power rivalry is what alarms many realist observers. A dangerous power vacuum could result if the world witnesses "the end of alliances," when formal military ties fade away and are replaced by informal shifting alignments among the competitors (Menon, 2007). These difficulties associated with balancing power lead most realists to conclude that international conflict and competition is a permanent feature of world politics.

WHAT LIES AHEAD?

Sooner or later, America's predominance will inevitably fade, and some new distribution of power will develop. The probable consequences of such a transformation in world politics are not clear. Some forecast the return of a bipolar pattern of direct opposition, with a new Sino-Russian bloc, European-Russian entente, or Sino-Japanese alliance countering the United States (Brzezinski, 2004).

Others see a more complex multipolar pattern of balance-of-power competition, where the United States, China, Japan, Russia, India, and the European Union would constitute six centers of global power. According to this image of the future, as power becomes more equally distributed, each player will become increasingly assertive, independent, and competitive. An enlarged global chessboard of multiple geo-strategic relationships will develop and lead to uncertainty about others' allegiances. The major players align together against others on particular issues, as their interests dictate. But behind the diplomatic smiles and handshakes, one-time friends and allies begin to grow apart, formally "specialized" relations begin to dissolve, and former enemies forge friendly ties and begin making a common cause against other common threats. "In this complex international reality, fixed alliances and formal organizations may count for less than shifting coalitions of interest" (Patrick, 2010, p. 51).

Much counterbalancing and shifting in flexible and fluid alliances is occurring. For example, friction grew between the United States and its closest allies over how to pursue the war on terrorism, particularly with regard to the war in Iraq. As a measure of how sensitive particular issues can be among great powers, both the European Union's foreign affairs commissioner, Christopher Pattern, and the German foreign minister, Joschka Fischer, at the time castigated President Bush for treating America's coalition partners as subordinate "satellites." In an effort to renew partnerships that had been strained because of the Iraq war, President Obama acknowledged that in "recent years, we've allowed our alliance to drift." At a NATO summit marking the 60th anniversary of the alliance, he called for all countries to play a part in fighting Al Qaeda, reminding the leaders of the 28 countries: "we have a mutual interest in ensuring that organizations like Al Qaeda cannot operate."

It is difficult to confidently predict what the twenty-first century will look like and whether it will be chaotic or stable. Realists insist that the tragic struggle for security among great powers will continue (Mearsheimer, 2001). Their expectations have been strengthened by China's rapid rise toward becoming the globe's biggest economy and the growing fears that this coming financial clout will translate into Chinese *hard power* and a military threat. If the future belongs

MAKE NEW FRIENDS BUT KEEP THE OLD Global summits provide foreign leaders an opportunity to meet and listen to each other and strengthen alliances. "It's an opportunity," explained Denis McDonough, U.S. White House chief of staff, "to re-energize our alliances to confront the looming threats of the twenty-first century." Pictured here are leaders from around the world at the Nuclear Security Summit held in Seoul, South Korea, in March 2012. Leaders gathered to discuss ways to foil the threat of nuclear terrorism and the trafficking of nuclear material.

to China, counterbalancing by the other great powers in an anti-Chinese coalition is likely (Kugler, 2006). Likewise, realists think that great power competition will continue because the American military giant is unlikely to quietly accept a diminished stature.

Whatever ensues, this crucial question is certain to command attention at the center of debate: whether international security is best served by states' military search for their own national security or whether, instead, the military pursuit of security through arms, alliances, and the balance of power will sow the seeds of the world's destruction. In the next chapter of *World Politics*, turn your attention away from the balance-of-power politics of realism to examine what liberal theorists say about institutional reforms that they contend lead to a more orderly world.

Simulation:
International Relations
Post 9/11

> *Those who scoff at "balance-of-power diplomacy" should recognize that the alternative to a balance of power is an imbalance of power—and history shows us that nothing so drastically escalates the danger of war as such an imbalance.*
>
> **—Richard M. Nixon, U.S. president**

STUDY. APPLY. ANALYZE.

Key Terms

alignments
alliances
balancer
ballistic missile defense
bandwagoning
blowback
brinkmanship
coercive diplomacy
compellence
covert operations
free riders

gunboat diplomacy
horizontal nuclear proliferation
human security
massive retaliation
military-industrial complex
multiple independently
    targetable reentry vehicles
    (MIRVs)
mutual assured destruction (MAD)
national security
nonalignment

nonintervention norm
nonlethal weapons (NLWs)
nonproliferation regime
North Atlantic Treaty
    Organization (NATO)
Nth country problem
Nuclear Nonproliferation
    Treaty (NPT)
nuclear winter
opportunity costs
power potential

preemptive warfare
preventive warfare
private military services
proliferation
relative burden of
    military spending
revolution in military
    technology (RMT)
second-strike capability
smart bombs
vertical nuclear proliferation

Suggested Readings

Allison, Graham. (2010) "Nuclear Disorder: Surveying Atomic Threats," *Foreign Affairs* 89:74–85.

Coker, Christopher. (2012) *Warrior Geeks: How 21st Century Technology Is Changing the Way We Fight and Think About War.* New York: Columbia University Press.

Dombrowski, Peter, and Eugene Gholz. (2007) *Buying Military Transformation: Technological Innovation and the Defense Industry.* New York: Columbia University Press.

Finnemore, Martha. (2009) "Legitimacy, Hypocrisy, and the Social Structure of Unipolarity: Why Being a Unipole Isn't All It's Cracked Up to Be," *World Politics* 61, no. 1:58–85.

Gartzke, Erik, and Matthew Kroenig. (2009) "A Strategic Approach to Nuclear Proliferation," *Journal of Conflict Resolution* 53:151–160.

Singer, P. W. (2009) *Wired for War: The Robotics Revolution and Conflict in the 21st Century.* New York: The Penguin Press.

Shearman, Peter. (2013) *Power Transition and International Order in Asia: Issues and Challenges.* New York, NY: Routledge.

Snyder, Glenn H. (2007) *Alliance Politics.* Ithaca: Cornell University Press.

Walt, Stephen M. (2009) "Alliances in a Unipolar World," *World Politics* 61, no. 1:86–120.

Suggested Videos

CourseMate

Carnegie Council Video

Bacevich, Andrew J. "Washington Rules: America's Path to Permanent War."

Cha, Victor D. "North Korea: What Next?"

Doyle, Michael W. and Koh, Harold H, "Striking First: Preemption and Prevention in International Conflict."

Jentleson, Bruce W. "The End of Arrogance: America in the Global Competition of Ideas."

Rose, Gideon, "How Wars End: Why We Always Fight the Last Battle."

CourseMate

Log in to CourseMate to access the following study tools for this chapter:

- Interactive Quiz
- eBook
- Flashcards & Key Term Crossword Puzzle
- Chapter Audio Summary
- Carnegie Council Videos

- Video Activities
- Simulation
- Animated Learning Module
- Case Study
- International Relations NewsWatch

"There are only two forces in the world, the sword and the spirit. In the long run the sword will always be conquered by the spirit."

—*Napoleon Bonaparte, former French emperor*

CHAPTER 9

The Quest for Peace through International Law and Collective Security

SEEKING ALTERNATIVES TO WAR Shown here, demonstrators gather in Seoul, South Korea, to call for the nations of the world to seek nonviolent solutions to conflict. Liberals, and many constructivists, are dissatisfied with the world and would like to change it. They have mobilized to exert pressure to contain arms races, warfare, and world poverty, among other causes.

Jason Lee/Reuters

QUESTIONS TO CONSIDER

▪ *What perspective does liberalism provide about the prospects for peace?*

▪ *What insights does constructivism offer about global peace?*

▪ *How can arms control and disarmament contribute to a more peaceful world?*

▪ *How are international organizations a force for peace?*

▪ *How do rules of law influence and address the use of force?*

▪ *What role do diplomatic responses play in resolving conflict?*

You overlook the incredibly low chances, purchase a lottery ticket, and hit an enormous jackpot. You are now very, very rich! What next? Remembering your pledge to try to make the world a better place before you die, you decide to put your ethical principles above power. To make a difference, you decide to invest your newfound wealth in projects that will "give peace a chance." Congratulations! You are joining Andrew Carnegie, Bill Gates, Warren Buffet, and other exceptionally wealthy philanthropists who generously chose to give large portions of their fortunes to causes that attempt to change the world for the better.

On what ventures should you invest your fortune? There are numerous choices. You could seek, for example, to provide humanitarian relief for refugees, fight worldwide poverty and disease, join others in seeking to stem the threat of global warming, or subsidize a global campaign to educate all youth throughout the world. The needs are endless. Sorting through your moral values, however, you conclude that the greatest threat to the world is the awesome danger of armed aggression. Acting on this conviction, you make it your mission to help others find better ways than violence to settle conflict. Reliance on weapons of war and balances of power has been tried since the beginning of time, but never with lasting success. So now you have found your cause—finding peaceful methods for settling potentially violent disputes.

In the quest to better understand nonviolent approaches to world security, you draw insights from policy makers and philosophers who have spent their lifetimes probing the same question you are now asking yourself—how to do good in a wicked world. This chapter presents some of the major ways in which liberal international thought directly challenges the assumptions underlying realist thinking about world politics. Also, from constructivist and identity perspectives, it looks at the importance of progressive ideas and norms in shaping international behavior and collective conceptions of world politics. What are the consequences if liberal and constructivist roads to world order—specifically disarmament, collective security through international organizations, and the management of conflict through negotiation and international law—are pursued? These questions will guide our discussion.

> *Although a more assertive world means more antagonists and demagogues, it also means more negotiators and regional leaders with a stake in keeping the peace. If that impulse can be organized and encouraged, the world will be a better place for it.*
>
> **—Fareed Zakaria, political journalist**

LIBERAL AND CONSTRUCTIVIST ROUTES TO INTERNATIONAL PEACE

Summarizing the principal approaches to the control of armed conflict, political scientist Kimberly Hudson (2009, p. 1) points out that:

> Changing attitudes toward sovereignty are evident in the emerging norms of "sovereignty as responsibility," the "responsibility to protect," and the "responsibility to prevent," as well as in the work of international relations theorists in the liberal and constructivist schools. Unlike the realists, … who tend to view international relations as the a-moral, rational pursuit of narrow self-interest by rational unitary sovereign states, liberals emphasize

interdependence and the possibility of cooperation, while constructivists stress the centrality of ideas as important for explaining and understanding international relations.

The various paths to peace that liberal thinkers depict differ greatly in their approach to world order, but they all share a fear of states' historic propensity to wage war. Resting on the liberal premises that principled moral behavior ultimately reaps higher rewards for all because fair treatment promotes peace and cooperation, liberal theory leads us to emphasize the role of collaboration and rule making in shaping behavior in world politics.

To understand how international norms and rules are created, *constructivism* informs us that popular ideas have meaningful consequences, and that when a favorable climate crystallizes around the preferred conduct for inter-state relations, those constructed images influence perceptions about the rules by which world politics should be governed. Whereas realists, and even liberals, emphasize the material underpinnings of war and peace, constructivists take into account both the material and communicative sources. As ideas "do not float freely (but) are embedded in an elaborate set of rules, norms, regimes and institutions" (Kolodziej, 2005, p. 297), the constructivist perspective often compliments the liberal emphasis on institutional and normative paths to peace, and the idea that constraints on the development and spread of weapons of war are critical to global security. For this reason, and consistent with constructivist theory, many experts see international law and collective security regimes mirroring changes in the most popular constructions of images about the ways in which states are habitually acting or should act toward one another in any particular period of history.

Keep these perspectives in mind as you contemplate the benefits and liabilities of alternative roads to peace. Here, rivet your focus on the hope that reduction in armaments will lead to less armed conflict and a safer and more secure world.

A FERVENT CALL FOR PEACE Liberal and constructivist views on war and peace are influenced by the importance of shared ethics and morality around the globe. Shown here, mourners gather to remember the 11 victims of a bomb blast at a café in Pune, India. Many Indians blame Pakistan, and a previously unheard of Pakistani militant group, Lashkar-e-Taiba Al Alami, claimed responsibility.

BEATING SWORDS INTO PLOWSHARES

The realist road to national security counsels, "If you want peace prepare for war." On the surface this makes intuitive sense. If a country is militarily stronger than its rivals, it is not very likely to be attacked. However, what would be the likely consequences if all countries adhered to this advice? It is possible that a country would become less secure, not more, as it builds its military might.

That is the deduction of liberal thought. In this construction, the *security dilemma* figures prominently—when a country builds armaments, alarmed neighbors mistrust its claims that the weapons are only for defensive purposes and out of fear begin to vigorously arm themselves. This results in an *arms race* that leaves no state more secure. All of the arming parties are now more vulnerable—wanting peace, war preparations increase the likelihood of war. Jesus Christ expressed this liberal conviction when he warned, "For all those who take up the sword perish by the sword" (Matthew 26:52). Centuries earlier, the Hebrew prophet Isaiah similarly voiced a recommendation that is now inscribed on the United Nations (UN) headquarters in New York City: "the nations shall beat their swords into plowshares" (Isaiah 2:4).

This liberal axiom and advice has been echoed many times. For example, Sir John Frederick Maurice wrote in his memoirs, "I went into the British Army believing that if you want peace you must prepare for war. I now believe that if you prepare thoroughly for war you will get it." The French political philosopher Charles de Montesquieu expressed the same liberal conviction when he observed that the quest for a preponderance of power in relation to rivals "inevitably becomes a contagious disease; for, as soon as one state increases what it calls its forces, the others immediately increase theirs, so that nothing is gained except mutual ruination."

The destructiveness of today's weapons has inspired many people to embrace the conclusion that reducing the weapons of war can increase the prospects for global peace. Although there is no single constructivist position on armaments or armed conflict, there is a widespread interest in moving beyond a limited traditional conception of security to one that takes into account the consequence of progressive ideas and human creativity. Constructivists "argue that violent political behavior and thereby its resolution and future prevention could be explained and even understood by focusing on the role of norms and ideas as determinants of such behavior" (Conteh-Morgan, 2005, p. 72).

Many feminist scholars are critical of the role of weapons of mass destruction in ensuring global security. In particular, the "antiwar feminist" tradition rejects and tries to change the social processes that associate norms of masculinity with militarized violence and war making (see Chapter 2). "It calls for ways of thinking that reveal the complicated effects on possessor societies of developing and deploying these weapons, that portray the terror and potential suffering of target societies, and that grapple with the moral implications of the willingness to risk such massive destruction" (Cohn and Ruddick, 2008, p. 459).

There is optimism that by reducing the supply of arms, armed conflict will be less likely and will result in a more secure world. These reforms are advanced even while liberal policy makers accept the notion that it is morally defensible to use constrained and proportional armed force to repel an imminent military attack by an adversary (Mapel, 2007). But in thinking about the control of the spread of weapons around the world, keep in mind that it is not strictly a

arms race

The buildup of weapons and armed forces by two or more states that threaten each other, with the competition driven by the conviction that gaining a lead is necessary for security.

tenet of liberal or constructivist theory. Although realists are reluctant to view arms control as a path to peace, most policy makers who have negotiated arms limitations have been realists who perceived such treaties as prudent tools to promote security by balancing military power to minimize the threat of war.

Disarmament versus Arms Control as Routes to Peace

Several distinctions must be made in this approach to international security. The first is between the terms "disarmament" and "arms control." Sometimes the terms are used interchangeably. They are not, however, synonymous. *Disarmament* is ambitious. It aims to reduce or eliminate armaments or classes of armaments completely, usually by negotiated reciprocal agreements between two or more rivals, in an effort to prevent their use in warfare.

Arms control is less ambitious. Arms control is designed to regulate arms levels either by limiting their growth or by restricting how they might be used. It results from agreements between potential enemies to cooperate in order to reduce the probability that conflicting interests will erupt in warfare, and to reduce the scope of violence in any armed conflict that may nonetheless occur.

Both liberalism and realism see limitations on weapons as useful. Where they part ways is in their respective postures toward the advantages of disarmament versus arms control. Liberals are more willing to take a leap of faith and consider disarmament as a workable possibility for peace. Because arms control is based on recognition that a true conflict of interest between rivals exists, it is favored by realists who see a positive contribution potentially made when enemies negotiate an agreement to balance their weapons and through that balancing build mutual confidence.

Controlling war by reducing weapons inventories is hardly a novel idea. Yet, until recently, few states have negotiated disarmament agreements. True, some countries in the past have reduced their armaments. For example, in 600 BCE the Chinese states formed a disarmament league that produced a peaceful century for the league's members. Canada and the United States disarmed the Great Lakes region through the 1817 Rush–Bagot Agreement. Nonetheless, these kinds of achievements have been relatively rare in history. Most disarmaments have been involuntary, the product of reductions imposed by the victors in the immediate aftermath of a war, as when the Allied powers attempted to disarm a defeated Germany after World War I.

In addition to differentiating between arms control and disarmament, you should also distinguish between *bilateral agreements* and *multilateral agreements*. Because the former involves only two countries, such agreements are often easier to negotiate and to enforce than are the latter, which are agreements between three or more countries. As a result, bilateral arms agreements tend to be more successful than multilateral agreements.

By far the most revealing examples are the superpower agreements to control nuclear weapons. This chapter will look briefly at the record of Soviet–American negotiations before examining the checkered history of multilateral arms control and disarmament.

Bilateral Arms Control and Disarmament

The Cold War between the Soviet Union and the United States never degenerated into a direct trial of military strength. One of the reasons was the series of more than 25 arms control

disarmament

Agreements to reduce or destroy weapons or other means of attack.

Carnegie Council Video:
Disarmament

arms control

Multilateral or bilateral agreements to contain arms races by setting limits on the number and types of weapons states are permitted.

CourseMate

Carnegie Council Video:
Arms Control

bilateral agreements

Exchanges between two states, such as arms control agreements negotiated cooperatively to set ceilings on military force levels.

multilateral agreements

Cooperative compacts among three or more states to ensure that a concerted policy is implemented toward alleviating a common problem, such as levels of future weapons capabilities.

Strategic Arms Limitation Talks (SALT)

Two sets of agreements reached during the 1970s between the United States and the Soviet Union that established limits on strategic nuclear delivery systems.

Intermediate-Range Nuclear Forces (INF) Treaty

The U.S.–Russian agreement to eliminate an entire class of nuclear weapons by removing all intermediate and short-range ground-based missiles and launchers with ranges between 300 and 3500 miles from Europe.

Strategic Arms Reduction Treaty (START)

The U.S.–Russian series of negotiations that began in 1993 and, with the 1997 START-III agreement ratified by Russia in 2000, pledged to cut the nuclear arsenals of both sides by 80 percent of the Cold War peaks, in order to lower the risk of nuclear war.

Strategic Offensive Reductions Treaty (SORT)

The U.S.–Russian agreement to reduce the number of strategic warheads to between 1700 and 2200 for each country by 2012.

agreements that Moscow and Washington negotiated in the wake of the Cuban Missile Crisis. Beginning with the 1963 Hot Line Agreement, which established a direct radio and telegraph communications system between the two governments, Soviet and American leaders reached a series of modest agreements aimed at stabilizing the military balance and reducing the risk of war. Each of these bilateral treaties lowered tensions and helped build a climate of trust that encouraged efforts to negotiate further agreements.

The most important agreements between the superpowers were the *Strategic Arms Limitation Talks (SALT)* of 1972 and 1979; the *Intermediate-Range Nuclear Forces (INF) Treaty* of 1987; the *Strategic Arms Reduction Treaty (START)* of 1991, 1993, 1997, and 2010; and the *Strategic Offensive Reductions Treaty (SORT)* of 2002. The first two agreements stabilized the nuclear arms race, and the remaining agreements reduced each side's stockpile of nuclear weapons. Even with these initial steps, at the end of the Cold War in 1991, the United States still had more than 9500 nuclear warheads and Russia had about 8000. It was then that disarmament began in earnest (see Figure 9.1). Since their 1986 peak, the sizes of the two superpowers' nuclear arsenals have declined by over 90 percent, and they will decline much further if the terms of the new Strategic Arms Reduction Treaty, which entered into force on February 5, 2011, are implemented. According to this agreement, both sides will reduce strategic warheads to 1550 in seven years—which is a 74 percent reduction from the limit established by the 1991 START treaty and a 30 percent reduction from the maximum 2200 allowed under the previous SORT accord.

This achievement has inspired other nuclear powers to discontinue building and expanding their nuclear arsenals. Most nuclear powers have not increased their stockpile of nuclear weapons, and 40 countries that have the technical ability to construct nuclear arsenals have

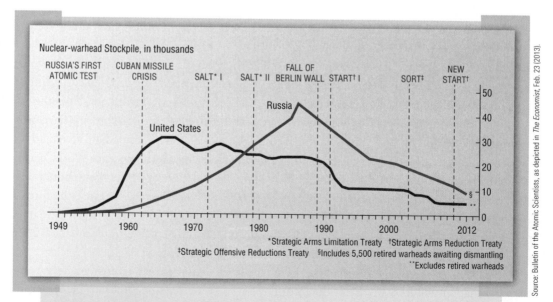

FIGURE 9.1 SHRINKING THE STOCKPILE The overall record of successful bilateral arms control and even disarmament between the United States and Russia attests to the possibilities for rival military powers to contain by agreement a dangerous arms race. As shown here, the nuclear warhead stockpiles of both countries have been reduced significantly in the post–Cold War period. However, the fragility of these agreements underscores the difficulties associated with maintaining and implementing such commitments.

renounced nuclear weapons. That said, there is always a temptation to rearm in response to new threats, and as a result many fear that continued disarmament is a tenuous prospect (Ferguson, 2010; Lodal, 2010). In fact, the progress achieved by both Russia and the United States in limiting their nuclear arsenals is threatened by their political dispute over the United States' missile defense system in Europe. In April 2013, Russian Deputy Prime Minister Dmitry Rogozin called the defense system an "excessive" and "provocative" weapon that creates a need for the Russians to develop an effective military counterweight (Groll, 2013). Nonetheless, the progress made by the United States and Russia in reducing their nuclear weapons stockpiles illustrates the possibility for rival military powers to take steps to de-escalate a risky arms race.

Multilateral Arms Control and Disarmament

History provides many examples of multilateral arms control and disarmament efforts. As early as the eleventh century, the Second Lateran Council prohibited the use of crossbows in fighting. The 1868 St. Petersburg Declaration prohibited the use of explosive bullets. In 1899 and 1907, International Peace Conferences at The Hague restricted the use of some weapons and prohibited others. The leaders of the United States, Britain, Japan, France, and Italy signed treaties at the Washington Naval Conferences (1921–1922) agreeing to adjust the relative-tonnage of their fleets.

Nearly 30 major multilateral agreements have been signed since World War II (see Table 9.1). Of these, the 1968 Nuclear Nonproliferation Treaty (NPT), which prohibited the transfer of nuclear weapons and production technologies to nonnuclear weapons states, stands out as particularly important. This 2400-word contract that some say saved the world is historically the most symbolic multilateral arms control agreement.

TABLE 9.1	Major Multilateral Arms Control Treaties Since 1945		
Date	Agreement	Number of Parties (signed, 2013)	Principal Objectives
1959	Antarctic Treaty	49	Prevents the military use of the Antarctic, including the testing of nuclear weapons
1963	Partial Test Ban Treaty	137	Prohibits nuclear weapons in the atmosphere, outer space, and underwater
1967	Outer Space Treaty	137	Outlaws the use of outer space for testing or stationing any weapons, as well as for military maneuvers
1967	Treaty of Tlatelolco	33	Creates the Latin American Nuclear Free Zone by prohibiting the testing and possession of nuclear facilities for military purposes
1968	Nuclear Nonproliferation Treaty	190	Prevents the spread of nuclear weapons and nuclear-weapons-production technologies to nonnuclear weapons states
1971	Seabed Treaty	117	Prohibits the development of weapons of mass destruction and nuclear weapons on the seabed beyond a 12-mile coastal limit
1972	Biological and Toxic Weapons Convention	179	Prohibits the production and storage of biological toxins; calls for the destruction of biological weapon stockpiles

(Continued)

TABLE 9.1	Major Multilateral Arms Control Treaties Since 1945 (Continued)		
1977	Environmental Modifications Convention (ENMOD Convention)	92	Bans the use of technologies that could alter Earth's weather patterns, ocean currents, ozone layer, or ecology
1980	Protection of Nuclear Material Convention	146	Obligates protection of peaceful nuclear material during transport on ships or aircraft
1981	Inhumane Weapons Convention	115	Prohibits the use of such weapons as fragmentation bombs, incendiary weapons, booby traps, and mines to which civilians could be exposed
1985	South Pacific Nuclear Free Zone (Roratonga) Treaty	13	Prohibits the testing, acquisition, or deployment of nuclear weapons in the South Pacific
1987	Missile Technology Control Regime (MTCR)	34	Restricts export of ballistic missiles and production facilities
1990	Conventional Forces in Europe (CFE)	30	Places limits on five categories of weapons in Europe and lowers force levels
1990	Confidence- and Security-Building Measures Agreement	53	Improves measures for exchanging detailed information on weapons, forces, and military exercises
1991	UN Register of Conventional Arms	101	Calls on all states to submit information on seven categories of major weapons exported or imported during the previous year
1992	Open Skies Treaty	35	Permits flights by unarmed surveillance aircraft over the territory of the signatory states
1993	Chemical Weapons Convention (CWC)	190	Requires all stockpiles of chemical weapons to be destroyed
1995	Treaty of Bangkok	10	Creates a nuclear-weapon-free zone in Southeast Asia
1995	Wassenaar Export-Control Treaty	40	Regulates transfers of sensitive dual-use technologies to nonparticipating countries
1996	Southeast Asian Nuclear Free Zone Treaty	10	Prevents signatories in Southeast Asia from making, possessing, storing, or testing nuclear weapons
1996	Comprehensive Test Ban Treaty (CTBT)	180	Bans all testing of nuclear weapons
1996	Treaty of Pelindaba	52	Creates an African nuclear-weapon-free zone
1997	Antipersonnel Landmines Treaty (APLT)	160	Bans the production and export of landmines and pledges plans to remove them
1998	Protocol IV of the Inhumane Weapons Convention	100	Bans some types of laser weapons that cause permanent loss of eyesight
1999	Inter-American Convention on Transparency in Conventional Weapons Acquisitions	21	Requires all 34 members of the Organization of American States (OAS) to annually report all weapons acquisitions, exports, and imports
2005	Nuclear Nonproliferation Treaty Review Conference	123 (delegates)	Final communiqué voices approval to continue support for the NPT treaty
2007	Treaty on Nuclear Free Zone in Central Asia (Treaty of Semipolinsk)	5	Obligates parties not to acquire nuclear weapons
2008	Convention on Cluster Munitions	110	Prohibits the use, production, stockpiling, and transfer of cluster munitions
2010	Nuclear Nonproliferation Treaty Review Conference	189 (delegates)	Reaffirmed support for the NPT accord

Based on data from SIPRI Yearbook (2013).

With 190 signatory countries, the NPT has had considerable success promoting nuclear nonproliferation, and efforts to bolster and extend this nonproliferation persist. In April 2010, the United States hosted a nuclear security summit where 47 countries established a four-year timetable for securing bomb-usable fissile material and agreed that "nuclear terrorism is one of the most challenging threats to international security" (*The Economist*, 2010j, p. 67). Two years later, at the second Nuclear Security Summit in Seoul, South Korea, progress seemed to be slowing. The new benchmarks commanded only weak commitments and the reduction in stocks of fissile materials had only seen minor declines since the 2010 meeting (*The Economist*, 2012d). The latest trends indicate that rather than aligning with the ideals set forth in the NPT, many countries are taking measures to enhance their nuclear arsenals (Nuclear Threat Initiative, 2013).

There have been several notable setbacks to the NPT. Though not signatories, in 1998 India and Pakistan broke the NPT's barriers to become nuclear powers and are presently locked in a spiraling arms race (see "A Closer Look: The Future of Nuclear Weapons"). Likewise, despite initially signing the treaty, North Korea violated the NPT with its secret development of nuclear weapons.

Fears of nuclear proliferation have been further inflamed by Iran's pursuit of nuclear capabilities. In September 2009, Iran test-fired missiles capable of striking Israel, Europe, and American bases in the Persian Gulf. The United Nations subsequently adopted new sanctions against Iran, including a prohibition on Iranian investment in uranium mining and activity involving ballistic missiles capable of delivering nuclear weapons.

Further speculation about Iranian military capabilities was raised by Iran's announced test-firing of a land-to-sea ballistic missile in April 2013. Many countries in the Middle East have a vested in interested in preventing Iran from becoming a nuclear power, but perhaps none more vocal than Israel. In addition to Israel's Prime Minister Benjamin Netanyahu stating that his country is prepared to attack Iran if international pressure to constrain the development of Iranian nuclear capacity is unsuccessful, Israel has begun to enhance its *second-strike capability* with submarines purchased from Germany (Federman, 2013). Despite such concern, however, there is still considerable doubt that Iran will be able to develop the nuclear materials necessary for a functioning nuclear weapon in the near future (Hymans, 2012).

The control and disarmament of nuclear arms face three intimidating obstacles—the insecurity of states, the idea that nuclear weapons are the great equalizer, and the proliferation risk that occurs when a nuclear power builds civilian reactors for a nonnuclear state (Ferguson, 2010). Furthermore, some states that signed the original agreement wonder whether the deal they were handed by the "nuclear club" in 1968 was fair. They observe the failure of the original nuclear powers to honor their pledge to disarm and perceive the NPT as "an instrument for the haves to deny the have-nots" (Allison, 2010, p. 80).

Over 4400 nuclear warheads remain (SIPRI, 2013), and countries in the Global South such as Saudi Arabia, the United Arab Emirates, and Egypt have indicated intent to explore nuclear options, albeit peaceful ones (Coll, 2009). Given this trend, it is all the more alarming that "new nuclear states, with a nascent arsenal and lack of experience in nuclearized disputes, play the 'nuclear card' significantly more often than their more experienced nuclear

THE FUTURE OF NUCLEAR WEAPONS

According to realism, the dynamics of arms competition are rooted in the security dilemma. Recall that in an anarchic international system, each country must ensure its own survival—and this demands that countries strive to become more powerful than their potential opponents. Yet, as described by the imagery of the *spiral model*, this enhancement of military capabilities for defensive purposes tends to result in escalating arms races that diminish the security of all. Sir Edward Grey, British foreign secretary before World War I, described this process well:

> The increase in armaments, that is intended in each nation to produce consciousness of strength and a sense of security, does not produce these efforts. On the contrary, it produces a consciousness of the strength of other nations and a sense of fear. Fear begets suspicion and distrust and evil imaginings of all sorts, 'til each government feels it would be criminal and a betrayal of its own country not to take every precaution, while every government regards every precaution of every other government as evidence of hostile intent (Wight, 2002, p. 254).

Consider the ongoing arms competition between Pakistan and India. With efforts under way to double its nuclear weapons arsenal by 2021, relations between Pakistan and India remain tense. Pakistani officials say that their efforts are not intentionally aggressive, but instead are a response to what they see as a threat from India, which is also increasing its nuclear stockpile and spending $50 billion on its military over the next five years (Bast, 2011). This rivalry was further exacerbated in 2012 when both states test-launched nuclear-capable missiles (Abbot, 2012). Yet while tensions remain, Pakistani Prime Minister Nawaz Sharif, although having previously overseen the emergence of Pakistan as a nuclear power, in 2013 called for warmer relations with India (Georgy, 2013).

Liberal theory posits that security may depend as much on the control of force as its pursuit. So how do countries avoid or pull out of an arms race? Expanding confidence-building measures that reduce fear and suspicion—including increased transparency and a global culture of disclosure—is critical to countering the uncertainties of the security dilemma and establishing a foundation of trust for future disarmament. In a world where nuclear proliferation and arms completion continue to pose a threat to global security, in the words of U.S. President Dwight D. Eisenhower, "disarmament, with mutual honor and confidence, is a continuing imperative."

WATCH THE VIDEO:

**Carnegie Council Video:
The Irony of Nuclear Weapons?**

YOU DECIDE:

1. Are nuclear weapons the scourge of international relations? Or, do they provide a valuable deterrent effect?

2. Are arms races doomed to end in violent conflict? What measures can be taken to ameliorate such competition?

3. Will disarmament bring about a more peaceful world?

---

spiral model

A metaphor used to describe the tendency of efforts to enhance defense to result in escalating arms races.

counterparts, making them more likely to reciprocate militarized disputes" (Horowitz, 2009, p. 235).

The ability and will to stem further nuclear proliferation remains in doubt, and in recognition of these serious trends, President Obama challenged the world to renew its commitment to confronting nuclear proliferation. He underscored the high stakes of this issue, warning that "Some argue that the spread of these weapons cannot be stopped…. Such fatalism is a deadly adversary. For if we believe that the spread of nuclear weapons is inevitable, then in some way we are admitting to ourselves that the use of nuclear weapons is inevitable."

The Problematic Future of Arms Control and Disarmament

The obstacles to arms control and disarmament are formidable. Critics complain that these agreements frequently regulate only obsolete armaments or ones that the parties to the agreement have little incentive to continue developing in the first place. Even when agreements are reached on modern, sophisticated weapons, the parties often set ceilings higher than the number of weapons currently deployed, so they do not have to slash their inventories.

A second pitfall is the propensity of limits on one type of weapon system to prompt developments in another system. Like a balloon that is squeezed at one end but simply expands at the other, constraints on certain parts of a country's arsenal can lead to enhancements elsewhere. An example can be seen in the 1972 SALT I agreement, which limited the number of intercontinental ballistic missiles possessed by the United States and Soviet Union. Although the number of missiles was restricted, no limits were placed on the number of nuclear warheads that could be placed on each missile. Consequently, both sides developed *multiple independently targeted reentry vehicles* (MIRVs). In short, the quantitative freeze on launchers led to qualitative improvements in their warhead delivery systems.

Furthermore, slow and ineffective ability of the global community to ban some of the most dangerous and counterproductive weapons reduces optimism in the future of meaningful arms control. Consider the case of *antipersonnel landmines (APLs)* that cannot discriminate between soldiers and civilians. It is thought that more than 100 to 300 million landmines are scattered in more than seventy countries (with another 100 million in stockpiles). It is estimated that about one mine exists for every 50 people in the world and that each year they kill or maim more than 26,000 people—almost all of them civilians. That is a rate of one victim occurring every 20 minutes.

antipersonnel landmines (APLs)

Weapons buried below the surface of the soil that explode on contact when any person—soldier or citizen—steps on them.

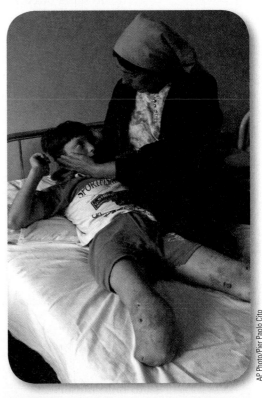

AP Photo/Pier Paolo Cito

A LEGACY OF WAR Antipersonnel mines are triggered by the contact or presence of a person. Indiscriminate weapons of war that do not recognize a ceasefire or termination of hostilities, they kill or cause injuries such as destroyed limbs, burns, and blindness. Pictured here is a 12-year old victim, Burin, in a hospital with his mother where he is being treated for the loss of his right leg and other serious wounds that he received while picking strawberries in a field in southern Kosovo.

In 1994, not a single state would endorse a prohibition on these deadly weapons. It took peace activist Jody Williams to organize the International Campaign to Ban Landmines, which led to the *Convention on the Prohibition of the Use, Stockpiling, Production and Transfer of Antipersonnel Mines*, which opened for signature in December 1997. For her efforts, Williams received the Nobel Peace Prize. But the United States, Russia, and other great powers stubbornly resisted the APL convention until a coalition of NGO peace groups mounted sufficient pressure for them to produce this important treaty (still without U.S. acceptance). Now signed by 161 states, the challenge of enforcing the ban and removing APLs remains staggering.

A final problem facing those advocating arms control and disarmament is continuous innovation in the defense industry. By the time that limits are negotiated on one type of weapon, a new generation of weapons has emerged. Modern technology is creating an ever-widening range of novel weapons—increasingly smaller, deadlier, and easier to conceal.

Why do states often make decisions to arm that apparently imprison them in the grip of perpetual insecurity? On the surface, the incentives for meaningful arms control seem numerous. Significant controls would save money, reduce tension, decrease environmental hazards, and diminish the potential destructiveness of war. However, most countries are reluctant to limit their armaments because the self-help international system requires each state to protect itself. Thus, states find themselves caught in a vicious cycle summarized by two basic principles: (1) "Don't negotiate when you are behind. Why accept a permanent position of number two?" and (2) "Don't negotiate when you are ahead. Why accept a freeze in an area of military competition when the other side has not kept up with you?" (Barnet, 1977).

Realists and liberal theorists both agree that the world could be a better place if countries would see their self-interests served by international cooperation. But they hold differing views about the prospects for cooperation. Realism insists that national security is best protected by developing military capabilities and not by reducing armaments or military spending as advocated by liberalism. Realists regard treaties as dangerous in an anarchical world in which the promises of self-interested rivals cannot be trusted. They counsel against putting faith in arms control treaties, because deception and broken promises are to be expected by ruthless leaders in the global jungle. Thus, instead of holding commitments to arms control agreements that cannot be enforced, realists advise reliance on unilateral self-help through military preparedness.

The logic underlying the well-known "Prisoner's Dilemma" illuminates the circumstantial barriers to international cooperation

Prisoner A

	cooperate	defect
cooperate	2, 2 win-win	4, 1 lose more-win more
defect	1, 4 win more-lose more	3, 3 lose-lose

(Prisoner B labels the rows)

FIGURE 9.2 THE PRISONER'S DILEMMA The matrix depicts the results that will occur depending on whether each prisoner chooses to cooperate with his accomplice by remaining silent or defect by confessing to the district attorney. Because both prisoners want to spend as little time incarcerated as possible, their preferences are rank ordered from the most preferred outcome to the least preferred as follows: (1) immunity from prosecution; (2) six months in prison; (3) five years in prison; and (4) ten years in prison. The first number shown in each cell is Actor A's outcome; the second number is B's outcome.

that exist among distrustful transnational actors (see Figure 9.2). To illustrate, imagine that two suspects following an armed robbery are taken into police custody and placed in separate cells by the district attorney, who is certain that they are guilty but only has sufficient evidence to convict them on an illegal weapons charge. The district attorney tells both prisoners that there are two choices: confess to the robbery or remain silent. If one prisoner confesses and the other doesn't, he will be given immunity from prosecution for providing evidence, whereas his accomplice will get a sentence of 10 years in prison. If both confess, they will be given a reduced sentence of five years. If neither confesses, they each will be convicted on the weapons charge but serve only six months in prison.

Faced with this situation, what should each prisoner do? They both want as little time behind bars as possible, and they are being interrogated separately so they cannot communicate. Furthermore, neither prisoner is sure that he can trust the other. This situation, which can be roughly applied to interactions between transnational actors, has some interesting consequences.

Although the optimal strategy for both prisoners would be to tacitly cooperate with each other and keep quiet so each receives only a six-month sentence (the win-win outcome of 2, 2 in the matrix), the suspects face incentives in this situation that incline each to turn on the other and provide incriminating evidence to the district attorney. First, there is an offensive incentive to defect by confessing and thereby securing an outcome for oneself (immunity) that is even better than the one available if the partners stick together (a six-month prison sentence for both). Second, there is a defensive incentive to defect grounded in the fear of being double-crossed by an accomplice who squeals and thereby winding up with the worst outcome (10 years in prison) while the partner goes free.

Not wanting to be a "sucker" who spends a decade incarcerated while his partner goes free, according to the logic of the Prisoner's Dilemma, both prisoners conclude that it is in their self-interest to defect and testify against one another in an effort to "win more." Consequently, they both receive a less optimal result (the lose-lose outcome 3, 3 in the matrix—five years in prison) than if they had tacitly cooperated and remained silent. The dilemma is that seemingly rational calculations by each individual actor can yield collectively worse results for both than had they chosen other strategies.

Many realist theorists liken arms races to the Prisoner's Dilemma. Instead of prisoners, consider two countries that have roughly equal military capabilities, are uncertain of whether they can trust one another, and are currently facing two choices: cooperate in lowering arms spending or defect by increasing arms spending. Suppose that each country prefers to have a military advantage over the other and fears being at a serious disadvantage, which would happen if one increased arms spending while the other reduced expenditures (the win more-lose more outcomes 4, 1 and 1, 4 depicted in Figure 9.2). By cooperating to lower arms spending they could devote more resources to other national needs such as education and health care (the outcome 2, 2), but given offensive and defensive incentives that are similar to those tempting the two prisoners in our earlier example, they both conclude that it is in their individual self-interest to play it safe and arm. As a result of their joint defection (outcome 3, 3), they end up worse off by locking themselves into an expensive arms race that may destabilize the prevailing balance of power.

CourseMate

**Simulation:
Prisoner's Dilemma**

Although this version of the Prisoner's Dilemma game is a simplification that does not take into account what might happen in repeated plays over time (see Axelrod, 1984), it highlights for you some of the difficulties in reaching mutually beneficial arms control agreements among self-interested actors who distrust their peers. This mindset was very evident in U.S. decisions at the turn of the century to reject an array of international treaties designed to control the threat of nuclear weapons. During 2001 alone, the United States decided to abrogate the 1972 Anti-Ballistic Missile (ABM) Treaty, withdraw from a UN conference to impose limits on illegal small arms trafficking, and reject proposed enforcement measures for the 1972 Biological Weapons Convention. This disregard for arms control set a standard for other states to follow.

Especially troubling was the U.S. repudiation of the 1972 ABM treaty, which was regarded by many as the cornerstone of nuclear arms control, as that announcement was the first time in modern history that the United States had renounced a major international accord. It ignited fears that a global chain reaction of massive repudiations of arms control agreements by other states would follow. For example, in 2007 Russia threatened to quit the INF missile treaty and to place a moratorium on the CFE treaty. However, while acknowledging a continued commitment to defensive military preparation, U.S. President Barack Obama indicated a renewed interest in controlling the spread of deadly weapons, stating, "We are spending billions of dollars on missile defense. And I actually believe that we need missile defense … but I also believe that, when we are only spending a few hundred million dollars on nuclear proliferation, then we're making a mistake."

The tendency of states to prioritize improving their weapons over controlling them is illustrated by the prevalence of nuclear tests (see Map 9.1 and Figure 9.3). At the start of 2013, the eight known nuclear states had conducted a total of 2055 nuclear explosions since 1945—an average of one test every 12 days, though there is suspicion that many tests are not reported (SIPRI, 2013). Both China and the United States regularly conduct zero-yield nuclear experiments and are suspected of conducting explosive tests so small that they cannot be detected. Moreover, the Partial Test Ban Treaty of 1963, which prohibited atmospheric and underwater testing but not underground explosions, did not slow the pace of testing. Over three-fourths of all nuclear tests took place after the ban went into effect. For instance, showing no sign of abandoning its nuclear ambitions, North Korea conducted an underground nuclear test on February 12, 2013.

The past record of arms control and disarmament has dispirited liberal and constructivist reformers who hope that negotiated compromises will curtail the global arms race. It appears that realism, and its abiding emphasis on peace through military preparations, is trumping liberalism's premise that weapons acquisitions are not a safe road toward world order. Someday, however, Woodrow Wilson's cause of world disarmament may yet triumph. As long as the threat of armed conflict haunts the world, leaders are unlikely to think it prudent to disarm. Many liberals and constructivists perceive other paths to peace as more promising. The construction of international organizations for collective security benefits from a more encouraging history, in part because so many military crises require multilateral cooperation to be peacefully managed.

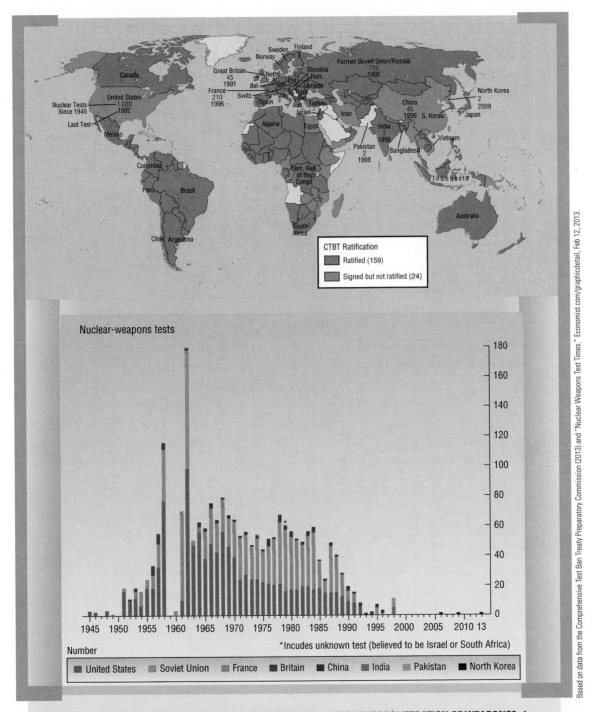

Based on data from the Comprehensive Test Ban Treaty Preparatory Commission (2013) and "Nuclear Weapons Test Times," Economist.com/graphicdetail, Feb 12, 2013.

MAP 9.1 and FIGURE 9.3   TRICK OR TREATY? CAN ARMS CONTROL STOP THE PROLIFERATION OF WEAPONS? As indicated in the timeline, nuclear testing has declined dramatically since the 1960s. This commitment to arms control is reflected in support for the Comprehensive Test Ban Treaty. Shown in the map, as of May 2013, 183 states had signed the Comprehensive Test Ban Treaty (CTBT); 159 had ratified it. However, Pakistan, India, and North Korea have still not signed, and many others—including the United States, China, Iran, and Israel—have not ratified the treaty. Fears of intensified nuclear arms rivalry and a potential wave of new testing remain.

MAINTAINING COLLECTIVE SECURITY THROUGH INTERNATIONAL ORGANIZATIONS

One of the prime rationales for the formation of *international organizations* is the preservation of peace. An institutional pathway to international peace is sculpted in liberal and constructivist thinking, with liberals focusing on interdependence and cooperation and constructivists emphasizing the centrality of ideas and norms. These approaches are voiced as alternatives to the balancing of power advocated by realist thinkers. The global community has usually trodden down paths to peace through international organizations when each previous balance of power has collapsed in large-scale warfare (as all past balances of power have done sooner or later).

Note that classical realism vigorously opposes relying on international organizations. Realism, it should be recalled, prizes the sovereign independence of states as a core value and berates any international organization as a barrier to states' foreign policy autonomy, freedom, and flexibility of unilateral action. Indeed, realism rejects prescriptions for the global community to "get organized" by creating institutions *above* states as a route to global stability. The only exception to this realist posture is when great powers have elected to create supranational multilateral institutions to manage military power in international relations, and this *only* when the great powers forming them were certain that the organizations would be managed authoritatively *by* them for their own self-interests (Claude, 1962).

For liberal and constructivist reformers, *collective security* is conceived as an alternative to the balance-of-power politics favored by realists. By definition, collective security requires collective decisions for collective goals, such as containing armed conflict, which is guided by the principle that an act of aggression by any state will be met with a unified response from the rest. As former U.S. Secretary of State Henry Kissinger explained, "collective security assumes that every nation perceives every challenge to the international order in the same way, and is prepared to run the same risk to preserve it." International organizations are seen as key to peaceful conflict management as "organizations with interventionist capabilities encourage disputing members to attempt peaceful conflict resolution" (Shannon, 2009, p. 145).

Collective security is based on a creed similar to that voiced by Alexandre Dumas's d'Artagnan and his fellow Musketeers: "One for all and all for one!" In order for collective security to function in the rough-and-tumble international arena, its advocates usually translate the Musketeer creed into the following rules of statecraft:

- **All threats to peace must be a common concern to everyone**. Peace, collective security theory assumes, is indivisible. If aggression anywhere is ignored, it eventually will spread to other countries and become more difficult to stop; hence, an attack on any one state must be regarded as an attack on all states.

- **Every member of the global system should join the collective security organization**. Instead of maneuvering against one another in rival alliances, states should link up in a single "uniting" alliance. Such a universal collectivity, it is assumed, would possess the international legitimacy and strength to keep the peace.

- **Members of the organization should pledge to settle their disputes through peaceful means**. Collective security is not wedded to the status quo. It assumes that peaceful change is possible when institutions are available to resolve conflicts of interest. In addition to providing a mechanism for the mediation of disagreements, the collective security organization would also contain a judicial organ authorized to issue binding verdicts on contentious disputes.

- **If a breach of the peace occurs, the organization should apply timely and robust sanctions to punish the aggressor**. A final assumption underpinning this theory holds that members of the collective security organization would be willing and able to give mutual assistance to any state suffering an attack. Sanctions could range from public condemnation to economic boycott to military retaliation.

Putting the pieces of these premises together, this approach to international peace through collective security organizations aims to control anarchical self-help warfare by guaranteeing every state's defenses through collective regulation. Perhaps ironically, therefore, liberal reformers accept the use of military might—not to expand state power, but rather to deter potential aggressors by confronting them with armed force organized by the united opposition of the entire global community. Might *can* be used to fight for right.

The League of Nations, United Nations, and Collective Security

Perhaps more than any other event, World War I discredited the realist argument that peace was a by-product of a stable balance of power. Citing arms races, secret treaties, and competing alliances as sources of divisive tension, many liberals viewed power balancing as a *cause* of war instead of as an instrument for its prevention. U.S. President Woodrow Wilson voiced the strongest opposition to balance-of-power politics; Point XIV of his Fourteen Points proposal for postwar peace called for "a general association of nations for the purpose of preserving the political independence and territorial integrity of great and small states alike." This plea led to the formation of the League of Nations, a precursor to the United Nations, to replace the balance of power with a global governance system for world order in which aggression by any state would be met by a united response.

Yet long before Wilson and other reformers called for the establishment of a League of Nations, the idea of collective security had been expressed in various peace plans. Between the eleventh and thirteenth centuries, for example, French ecclesiastic councils held in Poitiers (1000), Limoges (1031), and Toulouse (1210) discussed rudimentary versions of collective security. Similar proposals surfaced in the writings of Pierre Dubois (1306), King George Podebrad of Bohemia (1462), the Duc de Sully (1560–1641), and the Abbé de Saint-Pierre (1713). The belief that an organized "community" of power would be more effective in preserving peace than shifting alliances aimed at balancing power served as a foundation for these proposals.

To the disappointment of its advocates, the League of Nations never became an effective collective security system. It was not endorsed by the United States, the very power that had most championed it in the waning months of World War I. Moreover, its members disagreed

peacekeeping

The efforts by third parties such as the United Nations to intervene in civil wars and/or inter-state wars or to prevent hostilities between potential belligerents from escalating, so that by acting as a buf-fer, a negotiated settlement of the dispute can be reached.

Carnegie Council Video:
Peacekeeping

preventive diplomacy

Diplomatic actions taken in advance of a predictable crisis to prevent or limit violence.

Carnegie Council Video:
Preventive Diplomacy

peacemaking

The process of diplomacy, media-tion, negotiation, or other forms of peaceful settlement that arranges an end to a dispute and resolves the issues that led to conflict.

peace building

Post-conflict actions, predomi-nantly diplomatic and economic, that strengthen and rebuild governmental infrastructure and institutions in order to avoid renewed recourse to armed conflict.

over how to define "aggression," as well as how to share the costs and risks of mounting an organized response to potential aggressors. Although the League failed to realize its lofty goal, the principles of collective security embedded in the League of Nations guided the subsequent formation of the United Nations.

Like the League, the United Nations was established to promote international peace and security after a gruesome world war. The goal was to construct, in the words of U.S. President Harry Truman, "a permanent partnership … among the peoples of the world for their com-mon peace and common well-being." The architects of the United Nations were painfully aware of the League's disappointing experience with collective security. They hoped a new structure would make the United Nations more effective than the defunct League.

Recall from Chapter 6 that the UN Charter established a Security Council of 15 members, a General Assembly composed of representatives from all member states, and an administra-tive apparatus (or Secretariat) under the leadership of a secretary-general. Although the UN's founders voiced support for collective security, they were heavily influenced by the idea of a *con-cert* of great powers that together would manage global issues. The UN Charter permitted any of the Security Council's five permanent members (the United States, the Soviet Union [now Russia], Great Britain, France, and China) to veto and thereby block proposed military actions.

Because the Security Council could approve military actions only when the permanent members fully agreed, the United Nations was hamstrung by great power rivalries, especially between the United States and the Soviet Union. During the Cold War, "it became a formula for political paralysis" (Urquhart, 2010, p. 26), with more than 230 Security Council vetoes stopping action of any type on about one-third of the UN's resolutions. Because the UN's structure limited its ability to function as a true collective security organization, during the Cold War the United Nations fell short of many of its ambitious ideals.

Nevertheless, like any adaptive institution, the United Nations found other ways to over-come its compromising legal restrictions and lack of great power cooperation that inhibited its capacity to preserve world order. For example, in contrast to peace enforcement as in the Korean War, the United Nations undertook a new approach, termed *peacekeeping*, that aimed at separating enemies (Urquhart, 2010). The UN Emergency Force (UNEF), authorized in 1956 by the *Uniting for Peace Resolution* in the General Assembly in response to the Suez crisis, was the first of many other peacekeeping operations.

Furthermore, in 1960 Secretary-General Dag Hammarskjöld sought to manage security through what he termed *preventive diplomacy* by attempting to resolve conflicts before they became a cri-sis, in contrast to ending wars once they erupted. Frustrated with the superpowers' prevention of the United Nations from playing "as effective and decisive a role as the charter certainly envisaged for it," in 1989 Secretary-General Javier Pérez de Cuéllar pursued *peacemaking* initiatives. These programs were designed to end fighting so that the UN Security Council could then establish opera-tions to keep the peace. Later, UN Secretary-General Kofi Annan concentrated the UN's efforts on *peace building* by creating conditions that would make renewed war unlikely, while at the same time working on peacemaking (ending fighting already under way) and managing the UN's *peace operations* to police those conflicts in which the threat of renewed fighting between enemies is high. These endeavors have emphasized *peace enforcement* operations, relying on UN forces that are trained and equipped to use military force if necessary without the prior consent of the disputants.

For over four decades, the United Nations was a victim of superpower rivalry. However, the end of the Cold War removed many of the impediments to the UN's ability to act to preserve peace. For example, in 1999, the Security Council swung into action to authorize military coercion to force Iraq to withdraw from Kuwait, which it had invaded. This successful collective security initiative jump-started optimism for the usefulness of the UN's peacekeeping leadership. After 1990, the United Nations launched over three times as many peacekeeping missions as it had in its previous 40 years of its existence. On average, since 1990 it has managed almost six operations each year (see Map 9.2).

peace operations

A general category encompassing both peacekeeping and peace enforcement operations, undertaken to establish and maintain peace between disputants.

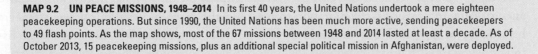

Author created map based on data from the United Nations

MAP 9.2   UN PEACE MISSIONS, 1948–2014 In its first 40 years, the United Nations undertook a mere eighteen peacekeeping operations. But since 1990, the United Nations has been much more active, sending peacekeepers to 49 flash points. As the map shows, most of the 67 missions between 1948 and 2014 lasted at least a decade. As of October 2013, 15 peacekeeping missions, plus an additional special political mission in Afghanistan, were deployed.

**peace
enforcement**

*The applica-
tion of military
force to warring
parties, or the
threat of its use,
normally pursuant
to international
authorization, to
compel compliance
with resolutions
or with sanctions
designed to
maintain or restore
peace and order.*

Carnegie Council Video:
Peace Enforcement

Although liberals have great hope for the United Nations as a means of promoting human rights and a global rule of law (Mertus, 2009b), the constraints that it faces as an organization may be due in part to its continued emphasis on sovereignty and dependence on power politics. From a realist perspective, the "UN was founded to perpetuate the global dominance of Britain and America while accommodating the unwelcome emergence of the Soviet Union … as an institution whereby power politics could be pursued by other means" (Gray, 2010, p. 79; Mazower, 2009). In order to fundamentally enhance the ability of the United Nations to function as a truly global authority, its members may need to relinquish their individual prerogatives and grant greater authority to the United Nations (Weiss et al., 2009). UN analyst Brian Urquhart (2010, p. 28) embraces this view, which he sees as critical to the continued relevance of the United Nations in the age of globalization:

> If governments really considered the effectiveness of the United Nations an urgent priority, this (state sovereignty) would be the first problem they would have to tackle. As it is, one can only wonder which of the great global problems will provide the cosmic disaster that will prove beyond doubt, and probably too late, that our present situation demands a post-Westphalian international order.

In 1945, there were few global problems that a single state could not successfully address alone. Today, the world faces intimidating challenges such as nuclear proliferation, international terrorism, global pandemics, environmental deterioration, and resource scarcities—global problems that require cooperative solutions. "As a universal organization, the United Nations should be uniquely suited to provide leadership and coordinate action on such matters, but the capacity of its members to use it as a place for cooperating on dangerous global problems has been limited and disappointing" (Urquhart, 2010, p. 26).

It is not only the interests of the Security Council's permanent members that constrain the United Nations, but also its limited infrastructure and financial resources. For the United Nations to succeed, the world community must match the means given to it with the demands made on it. In support of the UN's 67 peacekeeping operations since 1948, expenditures have totaled almost $84.33 billion. For the period from July 2012 through June 2013, the budget support to more than 113,000 UN peacekeeping personnel was $7.33 billion. To put this in perspective, compare this to U.S. military spending during the same period, which was $685.3 billion.

This represents a ninefold increase in UN peacekeepers since 1999, on what amounts to less than half of 1 percent (0.42 percent) of global military spending. UN peacekeeping forces are generally less expensive than the costs of troops deployed by countries in the Global North, NATO, or regional organizations. According to U.S. National Security Advisor Susan Rice "If the US was to act on its own—unilaterally—and deploy its own forces in many of these countries; for every dollar that the US would spend, the UN can accomplish the Mission for twelve cents."

Despite its imperfections, the United Nations remains the only global institution effective at organizing international collaboration to meet security crises in situations where states are unwilling or unprepared to act alone. However, the use of regional security organizations is rising as regional IGOs are stepping into the breach in those situations where UN Blue Helmets have not been given the necessary support to do the job.

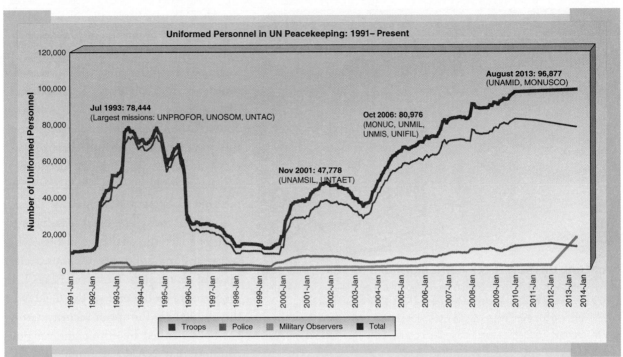

Based on data from United Nations Peacekeeping Operations, 2013.

FIGURE 9.4   THE INCREASING DEMAND FOR "PEACE" The preceding chart shows a clear trend in the demand for peacekeepers over time, as the total number of personnel involved in peacekeeping missions—often referred to as "Blue Helmets" because of their blue helmets or berets—has increased fivefold since 1999. The other trend lines show two of the other key functions increasingly performed by these personnel: military observers (who monitor conditions on the ground and have no mandate to engage militarily) and police. At the end of August 2013, uniformed personnel included 82,127 troops, 12,930 police, and 1802 military observers who were contributed by 116 countries.

Regional Security Organizations and Collective Defense

If the United Nations reflects the lack of shared values and common purpose characteristic of a divided global community, perhaps regional organizations, whose members already share some interests and cultural traditions, offer better prospects. The kinds of wars raging today do not lend themselves to being controlled by a worldwide body because these conflicts are now almost entirely civil wars. The United Nations was designed to manage international wars *between* states; it was not organized or legally authorized to intervene in internal battles *within* sovereign borders.

Regional IGOs are different. Regional IGOs see their security interests vitally affected by armed conflicts within countries in their area, and historically they have shown the determination and discipline to police these bitter intrastate conflicts. The "regionalization" of peace operations is a global trend. As 2013 began, no less than 53 peace missions served by 233,642 military and civilian personnel were carried out by regional organizations and UN-sanctioned coalitions of states (SIPRI, 2013). Hence, regional security organizations can be expected to play an increasingly larger role in the future security affairs of their regions.

The North Atlantic Treaty Organization (NATO) is the best-known regional security organization. Others include the Organization for Security and Cooperation in Europe (OSCE),

AP Photo/Aaron Favila

A LIBERAL MILITARY INTERVENTIONIST ROAD TO PEACE? Although many states and IGOs have been reluctant to intervene militarily in internal conflicts outside their spheres of influence, NATO's intervention in Libya in 2011 proved an exception. In this case, the UN Security Council argued that Muammar Gaddafi's response to the popular uprising—replete with the use of anti-aircraft guns against protestors and his promise to "cleanse Libya house by house" of the rebel "cockroaches"—rose to the level of crimes against humanity. While the decision to intervene generated controversy, it proved to be pivotal in helping to ultimately end the Gaddafi regime. Pictured here, protesters called for the withdrawal of U.S. and NATO troops from Libya.

CourseMate

Video:
A Long-Term Decision

the ANZUS pact (Australia, New Zealand, and the United States), and the Southeast Asia Treaty Organization (SEATO). Regional organizations with somewhat broader political mandates beyond defense include the Organization of American States (OAS), the League of Arab States, the Organization of African Unity (OAU), the Nordic Council, the Association of Southeast Asian Nations (ASEAN), and the Gulf Cooperation Council.

Many of today's regional security organizations face the challenge of preserving consensus and solidarity without a clear sense of its mission. Consider NATO. In the years since the end of the Cold War, the ambiguous European security setting has been marked by ethnic and religious conflicts that NATO was not originally designed to handle. Its original charter envisioned only one purpose—mutual self-protection from the Soviet Union. It never defined policing intrastate conflict as a goal.

Consequently, until 1995, when NATO took charge of all military operations in Bosnia-Herzegovina from the United Nations, it was uncertain whether the alliance could adapt to the new security environment. Since that intervention, NATO *has* redefined itself. In 1999, it intervened to police the civil violence in Kosovo. In 2001, for the first time invoking its Article 5, which requires collective defense of a member under attack, NATO joined the war in Afghanistan in a strong show of support for the United States following the terrorist attacks on 9/11. More recently, in March 2011, NATO took over responsibility for military operations in Libya that were initially conducted by the United States, France, and Britain.

Today, NATO has grown considerably, with its membership expanding from the 12 founding members in 1949 to the current 28 members through six rounds of enlargement in 1952, 1955, 1982, 1999, 2004, and 2009 (see Map 9.3). There are a number of countries in Eastern Europe that are candidates for future membership, and many feel that it is in NATO's and Europe's interest to integrate Russia into the membership as well.

Additionally, NATO has transformed itself to become both a *military* alliance for security both between states and within them and for containing the spread of global terrorism, as well as a *political* alliance that encourages the spread of democracy. Although NATO is widely seen as a proxy for the Global North, collective security operations under its authority convey a legitimacy that *unilateral* interventions tend to lack. "This is particularly the case for Britain and France, whose colonial histories bring enormous baggage in the Middle East and North

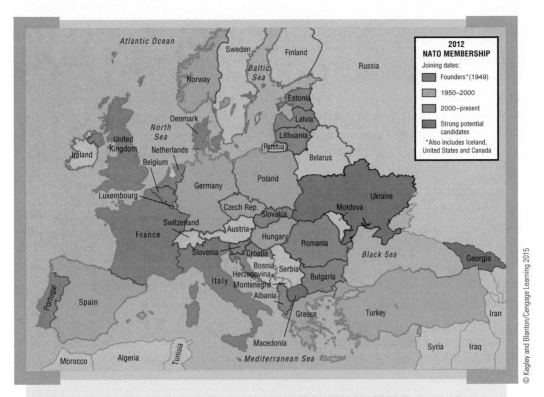

MAP 9.3   THE ENLARGED NATO IN THE NEW GEOSTRATEGIC BALANCE OF POWER The twenty-first-century geo-strategic landscape has been transformed by NATO's expansion to 28 full members, with Albania and Croatia formally joining as the newest members on April 1, 2009. As shown in this map, NATO now casts its security umbrella across and beyond Europe in its endeavor to create a collective security regime, including states that were once its enemies. Former NATO Secretary-General Jaap de hoop Scheffer emphasized the continued importance of security through multinational cooperation, proclaiming that "NATO is alive and kicking because it still has a unique job to do: to be the place where Europe and North America stand together, consult together and act together to ensure their common security."

Africa—not to mention the United States, with its own more recent complicated history in the region" (Joyner, 2011).

Nonetheless, as is the case with the United Nations and other regional organizations, NATO faces barriers to its success as a collective security organization. NATO is most capable of conducting successful peacekeeping operations only when it's most powerful members reach agreement about any proposed operation. In the case of Libya, the mandate as approved by the UN Security Council resolution was narrowly focused on civilian protection in order to secure tacit approval through abstentions, and avoid direct opposition, from Russia and China.

Second, the scope of NATO's mission is constrained as it is unlikely to target any country that is a great power or has a military alliance with one. Its traditional foe, Russia, agrees that in the twenty-first century, NATO and Russia should work together to confront terrorism, nuclear proliferation, piracy, and the illegal drug trade. However, "Russia is still far from reconciled to NATO's presence in countries that it regards as being within its 'sphere of privileged interests'" (*The Economist*, 2010a, p. 67).

The reluctance of its European members to sufficiently provide for their own militaries poses a major problem for NATO. Instead, they remain dependent upon the United States to take the lead in military operations and provide most of the weapons. The United States accounts for almost three-fourths of all military spending by NATO countries. Further, the limited investment by other NATO members is frequently matched by limited political will. In Afghanistan, many European states imposed restrictions and were reluctant participants in NATO's International Security Assistance Force (ISAF). American fighting forces ruefully quipped that the alliance mission's initials equated to "I Saw America Fight."

"In a post-Soviet world, there is growing resentment in Washington about NATO effectively paying for the defense of wealthy European nations" (Shanker and Erlanger, 2011). As former U.S. Secretary of Defense Robert Gates warned, "The blunt reality is that there will be dwindling appetite and patience in the U.S. Congress—and in the American body politic writ large—to expend increasingly precious funds on behalf of nations that are apparently unwilling to devote the necessary resources or make the necessary changes to be serious and capable partners in their own defense." NATO is an important institution that has shown an ability to adapt to changing global circumstances, but this will be tested if the United States shifts its interests away from Europe and toward Asia in the years to come (*The Economist*, 2012e).

Collective security organizations represent a major liberal path to international peace. Liberals have also long advocated that international law be strengthened in order to more capably provide for world order. Let us now consider the place of international law in world politics and the rules that have been fashioned to control by legal methods armed conflict within and between states.

LAW AT THE INTERNATIONAL LEVEL

War—one state's attack, by choice, against another state, without imminent threat and therefore not in self-defense—would seem to be an evil and dangerous practice that the global community would automatically prohibit, right? Likewise, does the international community have an obligation to protect innocent citizens from abuse and atrocities committed by their own state? Actually, no, or at least the idea that it should has only gained ground in recent history.

Core Principles of International Law

International law has been conceived and written mostly by realists, who have placed the privileges of the powerful as their primary concern and have historically advocated that the use of force should be an acceptable practice to protect a dominant state's position in the global hierarchy. As Henry Wheaton (1846) wrote, "every state has a right to force."

No principle of international law is more important than *state sovereignty*. Recall that sovereignty means that no authority is legally above the state, except that which the state voluntarily confers. Ever since the 1648 Treaty of Westphalia, states have tried to preserve the right to perform within their territories in any way the government chooses. That norm is the basis for all other legal rules; the key concepts in international law all speak to the rules by which sovereign states say they wish to abide. In fact, as conceived by theoreticians schooled in the realist tradition since the seventeenth century, the rules of international law express codes of conduct designed to protect a state's freedom to preserve its sovereign independence and act in terms of their perceived national interests.

Although the 1948 *Universal Declaration of Human Rights* addressed concerns about the state's treatment of individual people, states remain supreme. Accordingly, most rules address the rights and duties of states, not people. As Gidon Gottlieb has observed, "Laws are made to protect the state from the individual and not the individual from the state." For instance, the principle of *sovereign equality* entitles each state to full respect by other states as well as equal protection by the system's legal rules. The right of independence also guarantees states' autonomy in their domestic affairs and external relations, under the logic that the independence of each presumes the independence of all. Similarly, the doctrine of *neutrality* permits states to avoid involvement in others' conflicts and coalitions.

Furthermore, the noninterference principle forms the basis for the *nonintervention norm*, which requires states to refrain from uninvited activities within another country's territory. This sometimes-abused classic rule gives governments the right to exercise jurisdiction over practically all things on, under, or above their bounded territory. In fact, international law was so permissive toward the state's control of its own domestic affairs that, before 1952, "there was no precedent in international law for a nation-state to assume responsibility for the crimes it committed against a minority within its jurisdiction" (Wise, 1993). A citizen was not protected against the state's abuse of human rights or *crimes against humanity*.

Although international law has deficiencies, this does not mean that it is irrelevant or useless. States themselves find international law useful and expend a lot of effort to shape its evolution. This behavior demonstrates that countries interpret international law as real law and obey it most of the time (Joyner, 2005).

Consider this analogy: Children playing "tag" in the backyard create rules of the game. These rules might designate that the tree is out of bounds, the swing set is a safe base, once touched a player is "frozen" and cannot move, and so forth. There is no enforcement mechanism or real punishment for violating the rules, but the rules help organize the game, create certain expectations, and make it a pleasurable interaction.

Along these same lines, a primary reason why states value international law and affirm their commitment to it is that, as constructivist theory elucidates, they need a common understanding of the "rules of the game." Law helps shape expectations, and rules reduce uncertainty, which enhances predictability in international affairs. These communication functions serve every member of the global system by allowing for states to trust one another.

Even the most powerful states usually abide by international laws because they recognize that adherence pays benefits that often outweigh the costs of expedient rule violation. Those international actors that obey the rules receive rewards, whereas those that ignore international law or opportunistically break customary norms engender penalties for doing as they please. International reputations are important, and contribute to a state's *soft power*. States that routinely violate international legal rules are likely to find that other countries will be reluctant to cooperate with them. Violators also must fear the retaliation of those they victimize, as well as the loss of prestige. For this reason, only the most ambitious or reckless state is apt to flagrantly disregard accepted standards of conduct.

sovereign equality

The principle that states are legally equal in protection under international law.

neutrality

The legal doctrine that provides rights for states to remain nonaligned with adversaries waging war against each other.

crimes against humanity

A category of activities, made illegal at the Nuremberg war crime trials, condemning states that abuse human rights.

Carnegie Council Video: Crimes Against Humanity

Limitations of the International Legal System

Legal theoretician William Cobden observed that "International law is an institutional device for communicating to the policymakers of various states a consensus on the nature of the international system." Nonetheless, to liberal theoreticians, putting the state ahead of the global community was a serious flaw that undermined international law's potential effectiveness. Many theorists consider the international legal system institutionally defective due to its dependence on state participation. Because formal legal institutions are weak at the global level, critics point to several major limitations.

First, in world politics, no legislative body is capable of making truly binding laws. Rules apply only when states willingly observe or embrace them in the treaties to which they voluntarily subscribe. Generally accepted as the authoritative definition of the "sources of international law," Article 38 of the Statute of the International Court of Justice declares that international law derives from (1) custom, (2) international treaties and agreements, (3) national and international court decisions, (4) the writings of legal authorities and specialists, and (5) the "general principles" of law recognized since the Roman Empire as part of "natural law" and "right reason."

Second, in world politics, no judicial body exists to authoritatively identify and record the rules accepted by states, interpret when and how the rules apply, and then identify violations. Instead, states are responsible for performing these tasks themselves. The World Court does not have the power to perform these functions without the state's consent, and the United Nations cannot speak on judicial matters for the global community as a whole (even though it has recently defined a new scope for Chapter VII of the UN Charter that claims the right to make quasi-judicial authoritative interpretations of global laws).

Finally, in world politics there is no executive body capable of enforcing the rules. Enforcement usually occurs through the unilateral self-help actions of the victims of a transgression or with the assistance of their allies or other interested parties. No centralized enforcement procedures exist, and compliance is voluntary. The whole system rests, therefore, on states' willingness to abide by the rules to which they consent and on the ability of each to use retaliatory measures to punish violations of the norms and behaviors they value.

Beyond the barriers to legal institutions that sovereignty poses, further weaknesses reduce confidence in international law:

- **International law lacks universality**. An effective legal system must represent the norms shared by those it governs. According to the precept of Roman law, *ubi societas, ibi jus* (where there is society, there is law), shared community values are a minimal precondition for forming a legal system. Yet the contemporary international order is incredibly diverse culturally and ideologically and, as a consequence, lacks consensus on common values. The simultaneous functioning of often-incompatible legal traditions throughout the world undermines the creation of a universal, cosmopolitan culture and legal system.

- **Under international law, legality and legitimacy do not always go hand in hand**. As in any legal system, in world politics what is legal is not necessarily legitimate. Although legality is important in determining an action's legitimacy, other values play a role—such as popular normative acceptance of international law as having authority. Moreover, the legality of an action does not always imply wisdom or usefulness. "The UN Security Council's decision to deny weapons to victims of ethnic and religious abuse in Yugoslavia in the early 1990s, for example, was legal but arguably illegitimate, whereas NATO's unauthorized use of force to prevent abuses in Kosovo was illegal but arguably legitimate" (Sofaer, 2010, p. 117).

■ **International law is an instrument of the powerful to oppress the weak**. In a voluntary consent system, the rules to which the powerful willingly agree are those that serve their interests. These rules therefore preserve the existing global hierarchy (Goldsmith and Posner, 2005). As Marxist theory posits, "the form of international law consists of the struggle between states' view of legal right, and the view that prevails will depend on which state happens to be stronger" (Carty, 2008, p. 122).

■ **International law is little more than a justification of existing practices**. When a particular behavior pattern becomes widespread, it becomes legally obligatory; rules of behavior become rules *for* behavior (Leopard, 2010). Eminent legal scholar Hans Kelsen's (2009, p. 369) contention that "states ought to behave as they have customarily behaved" reflects *positivist legal theory* that when a type of behavior occurs frequently, it becomes legal. In fact, positive legal theory stresses that law is socially constructed. States' customary practices are the most important source from which laws derive in the absence of formal machinery for creating international rules.

positivist legal theory

A theory that stresses states' customs and habitual ways of behaving as the most important source of law.

■ **International law's ambiguity reduces law to a policy tool for propaganda purposes**. The vague, elastic wording of international law makes it easy for states to define and interpret almost any action as legitimate. "The problem here," observes Samuel S. Kim (1991, p. 111), "is the lack of clarity and coherence [that enables] international law [to be] easily stretched, … to be a flexible fig leaf or a propaganda instrument." This ambivalence makes it possible for states to exploit international law to get what they can and to justify what they have obtained.

Consequently, states themselves—not a higher authority—determine what the rules are, when they apply, and how they should be enforced. This raises the question that most concerns liberal advocates of world law: When all are above the law, are any truly ruled by it? It is precisely this problem that prompts reformers to restrict the sovereign freedom of states and expand their common pursuit of shared legal norms in order to advance collective global interests over the interests of individual states.

The Judicial Framework of International Law

To be sure, liberal and constructivist reformers have a long way to go in order to fulfill their dream of seeing international law strengthen so that it can more effectively police international conflict. However, reformers take heart from recent trends that have enabled international law to increase its capacity to manage the threat of war within states, between states, and through global terrorism—and they question those cynics who still contend that international law is and should remain irrelevant to states' use of armed force. They argue that:

AP Images

WAR CRIMES AND THE LOSS OF GLOBAL LEGITIMACY
In 2004, scandal erupted when more than 1000 graphic photos taken at the Abu Ghraib prison in Baghdad were televised worldwide, ostensibly showing U.S. personnel torturing Iraqi prisoners. Similar methods—including electric shocks, prolonged exposure to frigid temperatures, and simulated drowning—were purportedly used to interrogate terror suspects detained at the U.S. Guantanamo Naval Base. Both became a negative symbol of U.S. power in the Muslim world, and cast doubt upon American commitment to moral and ethical principles.

■ International law is not intended to prevent *all* warfare. Aggressive war is illegal, but defensive war is not. It is a mistake, therefore, to claim that international law is broken whenever war breaks out—though whether a war is seen as defensive or aggressive is often a matter of which side the participant is on in the conflict.

■ Instead of doing away with war, international law preserves it as a sanction against breaking rules. Thus, war is a method of last resort to punish aggressors and thereby maintain the global system's legal framework.

■ International law is an institutional substitute for war. Legal procedures exist to resolve conflicts before they erupt into open hostilities. Although law cannot prevent war, legal procedures often make recourse to violence unnecessary by resolving disputes that might otherwise escalate to war.

In order for the rule of law to gain strength in world politics, it is also necessary to strengthen the international adjudicative machinery to enhance its effectiveness and legitimacy. The *International Court of Justice (ICJ)*, known as the World Court, was created in 1945 as the highest judicial body on Earth—the only international court with universal scope and general jurisdiction. The court is highly regarded in principle: One hundred ninety-two states are party to the statute of the court, and more than three hundred bilateral or multilateral treaties have given the World Court jurisdiction in resolving disputes arising from the interpretation and application of international law.

A weakness in the World Court is that it can make rulings only on disputes freely submitted by the states themselves; the court cannot rule on cases that states do not bring forward. State sovereignty is protected, and many states have traditionally been hesitant to use the court because ICJ decisions are considered final—there is no opportunity to appeal. This is why between 1946 and 2013, states granted the court permission to hear only 153 cases, about one-fourth of which the disputants withdrew before the court could make a ruling.

The trends in the World Court's activity are not encouraging to advocates of world law. Whereas the number of sovereign states since 1950 has tripled, the court's caseload has not seen a similar increase. To illustrate, over half of today's states have never appeared before the ICJ, and that only the Global North's liberal democracies have actively agreed to litigate before the court (the United States, 22 cases; Britain, 13; France, 13; Germany, 7; and Belgium, 5),

International Court of Justice (ICJ)

The primary court established by the United Nations for resolving legal disputes between states and providing advisory opinions to international agencies and the UN General Assembly.

with Central America following closely behind (Nicaragua, 8; and Honduras, 6). Once the court has ruled on these cases, the disputants have complied with ICJ judgments only a little more than half of the time. This record suggests that although approval for using the court of law to resolve international conflicts is increasingly voiced, most states remain reluctant to voluntarily use judicial procedures to settle their most important international disputes.

However, attempts to bring armed conflict under more potent legal controls are now spread across the jurisdiction of several other international judicial bodies. It bodes well that the global community has radically revised international law to prevent the horror of civilian casualties and contain the mass slaughter that has increasingly taken place, and it now holds leaders of countries accountable for war crimes as war criminals. International law prohibits leaders from allowing their militaries to undertake actions in violation of certain principles accepted by the international community, such as the protection of innocent noncombatants.

Before these recent developments in international law, when violations occurred, little could be done except to verbally condemn those acts because international law exempted leaders from legal jurisdiction under the doctrine of "sovereign immunity." This was true even when their commands ignored the laws of the appropriate conduct of war. Although they might behave as criminals, leaders traditionally have been treated with respect (perhaps because they were the only people with whom negotiations could be held to settle disputes). This tradition has now been rejected on legal grounds, as reflected in the premise of the Nuremberg International Military Tribunal (which tried World War II German Nazi war criminals) that "crimes against international law are committed by men, not by abstract entities, and only by punishing individuals who commit such crimes can the provisions of international law be enforced."

The *international criminal tribunals* formed in 1993 signaled to would-be perpetrators that the global community would not tolerate these atrocities. The International Criminal Tribunal for the former Yugoslavia (ICTY) was established in 1993, followed by the International Criminal Tribunal for Rwanda (ICTR) in 1994. One of the most famous tribunal detainees was Slobodan Milosevic. Milosevic was the former Yugoslav president who perpetrated four wars in the 1990s that killed more than 250,000 and tore the Balkans apart—he died of a heart attack in March 2006 in his Hague prison cell while facing trial. Both the ICTY and the ICTR were set up by the United Nations on an ad hoc basis for a limited time period and a specific jurisdiction, and underscored the need for a permanent global criminal court.

With the ratification of the Rome Statute by 116 countries (there are now 139 signatories, with Tunisia becoming the newest member on June 24, 2011), the *International Criminal Court (ICC)* was launched in 2002 as an independent court of last resort that investigates and prosecutes terrible mass crimes such as genocide, crimes against humanity, and war crimes that have been committed since the court's inception (see Map 9.4). The ICC only pursues a case when a state's courts are unwilling or unable to do so, and brings charges only against individuals as opposed to states.

To date, the ICC has opened investigations into atrocities in Uganda, the Democratic Republic of Congo, the Central African Republic, and Darfur. Despite resistance from some members of the African Union, the ICC ruled in February 2010 that Sudanese President Omar al-Bashir could be charged with genocide for his part in the five-year campaign of violence in Sudan's Darfur region that, according to UN estimates, cost 300,000 people their lives and

international criminal tribunals

Special tribunals established by the United Nations to prosecute those responsible for wartime atrocities and genocide, bring justice to victims, and deter such crimes in the future.

International Criminal Court (ICC)

A court established by international treaty for indicting and administering justice to people committing war crimes.

Simulation: Rwanda

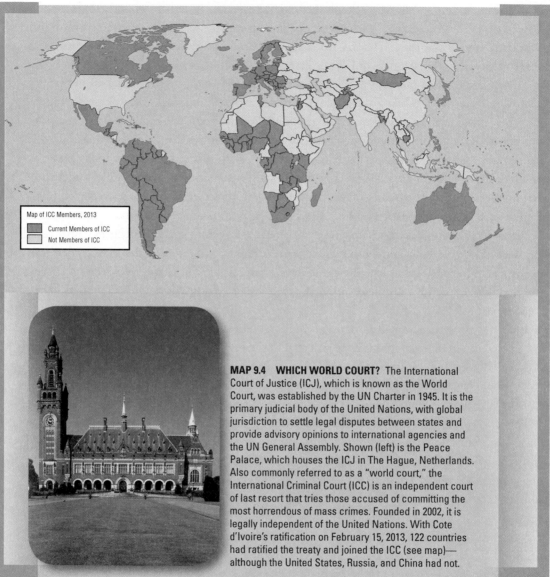

MAP 9.4 **WHICH WORLD COURT?** The International Court of Justice (ICJ), which is known as the World Court, was established by the UN Charter in 1945. It is the primary judicial body of the United Nations, with global jurisdiction to settle legal disputes between states and provide advisory opinions to international agencies and the UN General Assembly. Shown (left) is the Peace Palace, which houses the ICJ in The Hague, Netherlands. Also commonly referred to as a "world court," the International Criminal Court (ICC) is an independent court of last resort that tries those accused of committing the most horrendous of mass crimes. Founded in 2002, it is legally independent of the United Nations. With Cote d'Ivoire's ratification on February 15, 2013, 122 countries had ratified the treaty and joined the ICC (see map)—although the United States, Russia, and China had not.

Map of ICC Members, 2013
- Current Members of ICC
- Not Members of ICC

© Kegley and Blanton/Cengage Learning 2015

Dorling Kindersley/Getty Images

forced another 2.5 million from their homes. More recently, in May 2012, the U.N.'s Special Court for Sierra Leone convicted former Liberian President Charles Taylor and sentenced him to 50 years in prison for his role in arming rebels in Sierra Leone in exchange for "blood diamonds."

The ICC is gaining legitimacy as the appropriate court of last resort for cases involving crimes against humanity, genocide, and war crimes, but it is often criticized for the length of time it takes for cases to be brought to trial, and it lacks the independent ability to enforce its decisions or physically detain the accused. Given the politically complex nature of its mission, it is critical that the ICC avoid accusations of caving to political pressure or showing bias (Struett, 2012). Among the most prominent legal issues facing the court is the need to refine

CourseMate

Video Activity:
A Ticking Bomb

the vague definition of "crimes of aggression," a sensitive issue that runs counter to the interests of many states. Nonetheless, the criminalization of rulers' *state-sponsored terrorism* raises the legal restraints on the initiation and conduct of war to an all-time high, widening the scope of acts now classified as *war crimes*.

> *Governments that block the aspirations of their people, that steal or are corrupt, that oppress and torture or that deny freedom of expression and human rights should bear in mind that they will find it increasingly hard to escape their own people, or where warranted, the reach of international law.*
>
> —William Hague, British politician

LEGAL AND DIPLOMATIC RESPONSES TO ARMED CONFLICT

Many people are confused by international law because it both prohibits and justifies the use of force. The confusion derives, in part, from the just war tradition in "Christian realism," in which the rules of war are philosophically based on *morals* (principles of behavior) and *ethics* (explanations of why these principles are proper). Therefore, it is important to understand the origins of just war theory and the way it is evolving today, and to also consider how the rules of law shape military interventions and negotiated solutions to international disputes.

Just War Doctrine

In the fourth century, St. Augustine questioned the strict view that those who take another's life to defend the state necessarily violate the commandment "Thou shalt not kill." He counseled that "it is the wrong-doing of the opposing party which compels the wise man to wage just wars." The Christian was obligated, he felt, to fight against evil and wickedness. To St. Augustine, the City of Man was inherently sinful, in contrast to the perfect City of God. Thus, in the secular world, it was sometimes permissible to kill—to punish a sin by an aggressive enemy (while still loving the sinner) to achieve a "just peace." Pope Nicholas I extended this realist logic in 866 when he proclaimed that any defensive war was just.

The modern *just war doctrine* evolved from this perspective, as developed by such humanist reformers as Hugo Grotius. He challenged the warring Catholic and Protestant Christian powers in the Thirty Years' War (1618–1648) to abide by humane standards of conduct and sought to replace the two "cities," or ethical realms of St. Augustine, with a single global society under law. For Grotius, a just war was only one fought in self-defense to punish damages caused by an adversary's blatant act of violence: "No other just cause for undertaking war can there be excepting injury received."

For war to be moral it must also be fought by just means without harm to innocent noncombatants. The modern version of just war doctrine evolved from this distinction and consists of two categories, *jus ad bellum* (the justice of a war) and *jus in bello* (justice in a war). The former sets the legal criteria by which a leader may initiate a war. The latter specifies restraints on the range of permissible tactics to be used in fighting a just war.

war crimes

Acts performed during war that the international community defines as crimes against humanity, including atrocities committed against an enemy's prisoners of war, civilians, or the state's own minority population.

Carnegie Council Video:
War Crimes

morals

Principles clarifying the difference between good and evil and the situations in which they are opposed.

ethics

Criteria for evaluating right and wrong behavior and the motives of individuals and groups.

Carnegie Council Video:
Ethics

just war doctrine

The moral criteria identifying when a just war may be undertaken and how it should be fought once it begins.

jus ad bellum

A component of just war doctrine that establishes criteria under which a just war may be initiated.

Carnegie Council Video:
Jus Ad Bellum

jus in bello

A component of just war doctrine that sets limits on the acceptable use of force.

Carnegie Council Video:
Jus In Bello

At the core of the just war tradition is the conviction that the taking of human life may be a "lesser evil" when it is necessary to prevent further armed aggression (Ignatieff, 2004b). Christian theologian St. Thomas More (1478–1535) contended that the assassination of an evil leader responsible for starting a war was justified if it would prevent the loss of innocent lives. This premise shapes contemporary discussions of public international law (Wills, 2004) and provide the foundation for a number of other key principles:

- All other means to a morally just solution of conflict must be exhausted before a resort to arms can be justified.

- War can be just only if employed to defend a stable political order or a morally preferable cause against a real threat or to restore justice after a real injury has been sustained.

- A just war must have a reasonable chance of succeeding in these limited goals.

- Only a legitimate government authority can proclaim a just war.

- War must be waged for the purpose of correcting a wrong rather than for revenge.

- Negotiations to end a war must be continued as long as fighting continues.

- Particular people in the population, especially noncombatants, must be immune from intentional attack.

- Only legal and moral means may be employed to conduct a just war.

- The damage likely to be incurred from a war may not be disproportionate to the injury suffered.

- The final goal of the war must be to reestablish peace and justice.

These ethical criteria continue to color thinking about the rules of warfare and the circumstances under which the use of armed force is legally permissible. U.S. President Theodore Roosevelt counseled that "a just war is in the long run far better for a nation's soul than a most prosperous peace obtained by acquiescence in wrong and injustice." However, the advent of nuclear, chemical, and biological weapons of mass destruction that violate many of these principles has created a heated debate about the relevance of the just war doctrine (Hensel, 2007), which has been further exacerbated by the trend toward intrastate conflicts involving both state and nonstate actors (Hudson, 2009).

Advanced technological innovations have blurred many of the lines between acceptable and unacceptable conduct in war. For example, insurgent terrorists and now the armies fighting them are increasingly relying on Improvised Explosive Devices (IEDs) planted on animal carcasses, mobile

WAR AND THE BIRTH OF MODERN INTERNATIONAL LAW Enraged by inhumane international conditions that he witnessed during his lifetime, Dutch reformer Hugo Grotius (1583–1645) wrote *De Jure Belli et Pacis (On the Law of War and Peace)* in 1625 in the midst of the Thirty Years' War. His treatise called on the great powers to resolve their conflicts by judicial procedures rather than on the battlefield and specified the legal principles he felt could encourage cooperation, peace, and more humane treatment of people.

cell phones, or human cadavers in addition to IEDs left in the open in order to kill with minimal risk to the attacker. Today's IEDs, first invented by the United States and now available on the global black market, are cheap and easy-to-make gadgets such as garage-door openers used to detonate bombs. How can international law control such innovative new ways of perpetrating violence when the aggressors using them cannot be treated as criminals? Because the containment and prevention of violence has become the chief purpose of armies today, leaders and scholars are struggling to revise just war doctrine to deal with the new strategic realities of contemporary weapons and warfare (J. Johnson, 2005).

As Figure 9.5 shows, since World War I the international community has increasingly rejected the traditional right of states to use military force to achieve their foreign policy objectives. Just war theory reflects the continuing quest to place legal constraints on the use of

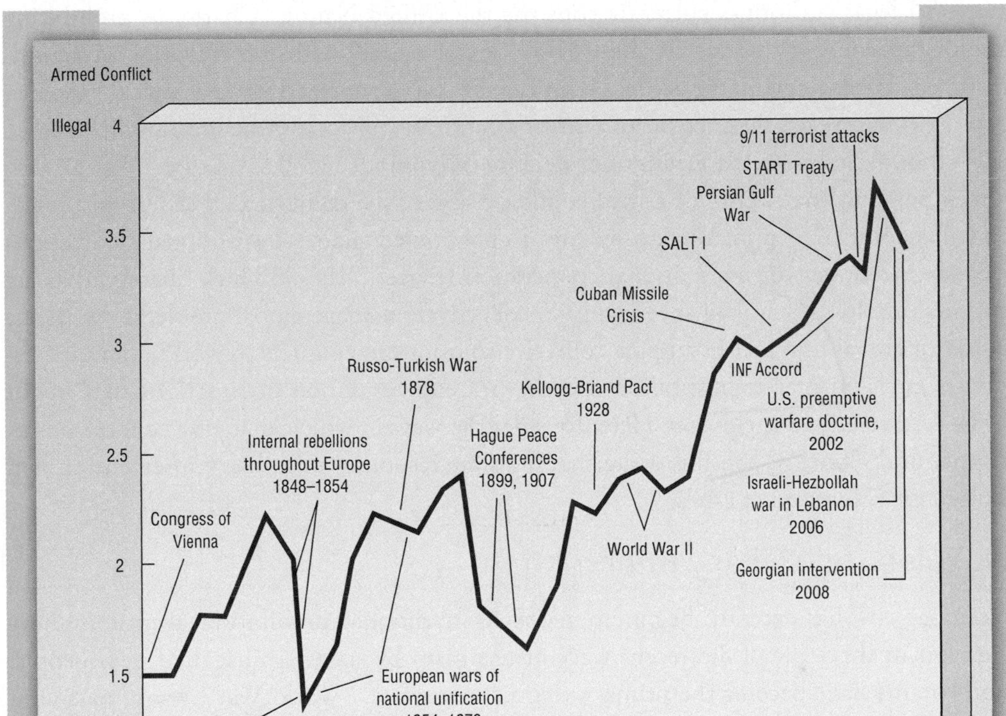

Adapted and updated from the Transnational Rules Indicators Project (TRIP), a time-series data set, as described in Charles W. Kegley, Jr., and Gregory A. Raymond, *When Trust Breaks Down* (Columbia: University of South Carolina Press, 1990).

FIGURE 9.5 THE LEGAL PROHIBITION AGAINST INITIATING WARS, 1815–2011 Legal restraints on the historic right of states to start a war have fluctuated over time, but have increased steadily since World War I when that carnage prompted the global community to make wars of conquest illegal. Since 9/11, these legal prohibitions have been questioned in the aftermath of the U.S. efforts to promote preemption as a legal right to repel the potential aggression of another state or nonstate terrorist network even before its threat of attack is imminent, which blurs the distinction between preemptive war and preventive war.

armed force in order to create a moral consensus about the conditions under which ends justify means, even though vehement disagreements continue today about what criteria should be accepted. These differences became especially evident in the heated debate after the U.S. preemptive invasion of Iraq in 2003. Many condemned the U.S. invasion as a breach of international law, calling the United States a "rogue nation" and an outlaw state (Hathaway, 2007; Paust, 2007). Others disagreed (Elsthain, 2003), however, with some suggesting that U.S. intent in waging war was justifiable as Saddam Hussein intentionally let the United States believe Iraq had weapons of mass destruction.

The U.S. invasion of Iraq made the legality of the use of force a hot topic, and concerns emerged regarding the preemptive and preventive use of force. The Bush administration's support for preventive action that included the use of force against states that either supported or failed to oppose terrorism was particularly controversial, since such use of force is generally viewed as a violation of international law. "The International Court of Justice (ICJ) and most international legal authorities currently construe the United Nations Charter as prohibiting any use of force not sanctioned by the UN Security Council, with the exception of actions taken in self-defense against an actual or imminent state-sponsored 'armed attack'" (Sofaer, 2010, p. 110). However, the doctrine of *military necessity* still accepts the use of military force as legal—though only as a last recourse for defense (Raymond, 1999).

Liberal paths to the control of armed conflict embrace the conviction that war and international instability are primarily caused by deeply rooted global institutional deficiencies that reduce incentives for international cooperation (Barrett, 2007). Thus, liberals advocate institutional methods that pool sovereignty to collectively manage global problems. With the expansion of global norms that support collective solutions to conflicts in world politics, constructivists envision greater possibilities for the peaceful resolution of situations that might otherwise lead to armed aggression. Here, consider the ways in which changing conceptions of sovereignty and global responsibility are shaping state responses to military intervention and the diplomatic resolution of crises.

New Rules for Military Intervention

International law has recently begun to revise its traditional prohibition against military intervention in the wake of the recent wave of terrorism by states against their own people. Noncombatants have become the primary victims in warfare. "World War I was a mass-conscription, democratic war with a vengeance, but it still was limited in its direct effect on civilians. The ratio of soldiers to civilians killed between 1914 and 1918 was about 90 to 10. In World War II, the ratio was 50-to-50. In recent years, it has been 90 civilian casualties to every 10 military losses—a reversal of the World War I ratio" (Pfaff, 1999, p. 8).

The belief that governments have a right, even an obligation, to intervene in the affairs of other states under certain conditions for humanitarian purposes has won advocates. This "responsibility to protect" norm has been advocated by former Australian foreign minister Gareth Evans, who counsels that our goal should be "to institutionalize the idea that all states have an obligation to shield their own citizens from mass atrocities, and that if a state fails to do so, it falls to other states to take on that obligation" (Malcomson, 2008, p. 9; see also Doyle, 2011). Contemporary international law has defined military intervention as a right

---

military necessity

The legal principle that violation of the rules of warfare may be excused for defensive purposes during periods of extreme emergency.

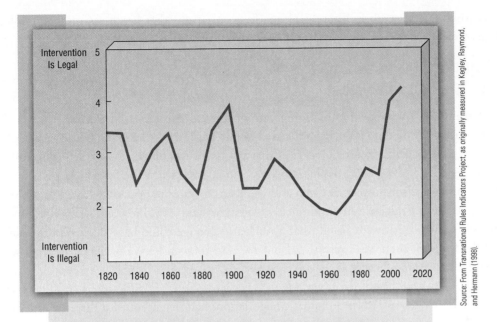

Source: From Transnational Rules Indicators Project, as originally measured in Kegley, Raymond, and Hermann (1998).

FIGURE 9.6   THE CHANGING STATUS OF THE NONINTERVENTION NORM IN INTERNATIONAL LAW SINCE 1820 Over time, the legality of intervening in sovereign states has changed, as measured by changes in international law about the prevailing consensus regarding rules for international conduct. Since 1960, international law has adopted an increasingly permissive posture toward this form of coercive diplomacy for a variety of purposes, including humanitarian aid, preventing genocide, protecting civil liberties, promoting democracy through "reform interventions," and combating global terrorism.

and a duty to alleviate human suffering, stop genocide and ethnic cleansing, and prevent the repression by states of basic human rights and civil liberties (Feinstein and Slaughter, 2004; Finnemore, 2003).

The result has been the collapse of the Westphalian principle that what a state does within its own borders is its own business. International law has relaxed its restrictive definition that delimits when the global community can legally use military intervention to intervene in other states (see Figure 9.6). The world has made a choice on genocide, declaring organized savagery illegal: Over the last 50 years, near-universal support for humanitarian intervention has emerged as a legal right to protect *human rights*—political rights and civil liberties are now recognized by the global community as inalienable and universally applicable. This shift permits states and international organizations to punish acts of genocide by reinterpreting the traditional rule against external interference in another state's domestic affairs to make outside intervention permissible. This includes even the right to military invasion and occupation.

This sea change suggests that international law develops and changes most rapidly when global problems arise that require collective solutions and legal remedies. The spread of genocide and atrocities in failed states and countries ruled by tyrants has spawned new sets of legal rules that attempt to arrest these dangers and to permit interventions within these countries. Likewise, the rising frequency of global crises has pushed efforts to rewrite

CourseMate

Animated Learning Module:
The Use of Force

crisis

A situation in which the threat of escalation to warfare is high and the time available for making decisions and reaching compromised solutions in negotiations is compressed.

Carnegie Council Video:
Crisis

negotiation

Diplomatic dialogue and discussion between two or more parties with the goal of resolving, through give-and-take bargaining, perceived differences of interests and the conflicts they cause.

Carnegie Council Video:
Negotiation

tit-for-tat strategy

a bargaining approach that consistently reciprocates in kind the offers or threats made by the other party in a negotiation, with equivalent rewards returned and equivalent punishing communications returned in retaliation.

international law so as to facilitate diplomatic negotiations that bring about a nonviolent settlement of disputes.

International Crises and the Negotiated Settlement of Disputes

Crises have been very frequent in modern history. When a crisis erupts, the capacity for reaching coolheaded rational decisions is reduced. The threat of force causes stress and reduces the amount of time available to reach decisions that might successfully end the *crisis* peacefully.

Consider the 1962 Cuban Missile Crisis, which occurred when the Soviet Union installed medium-range nuclear missiles in Cuba and the United States responded with a naval blockade. The danger of nuclear war rose quickly. After the fact, U.S. President John F. Kennedy estimated that the odds were 50–50 that a nuclear exchange could have destroyed the entire world. And, often, such crises resulting from *coercive diplomacy* have escalated to the use of force when bargaining failed and the adversaries took up arms.

The problem that liberal reformers identify is that these crises and armed conflicts could potentially have been settled by diplomatic negotiations had that avenue for dispute settlement been tried. To liberals, it is always better to talk about percolating divisive issues at a negotiating table than to let anger and anxieties sizzle and tempt the disputants to take up arms. Only through discussion and bargaining can positions be clarified and, possibly, concessions and compromises be reached that terminate the threat of warfare.

Embedded in international law, *negotiation* is a process of bargaining between two or more actors in an effort to deal with an issue or situation and reach an agreement. At a basic, elementary level, negotiation entails an exchange of communications, with discussion flowing back and forth between the bargaining parties. As an approach to conflict management, the goal is to facilitate communication between the parties regarding their intentions and goals, and produce options that address the interests of those involved. In the give-and-take required to negotiate a solution, there is a strong tendency for some level of reciprocity to emerge from the action-and-reaction sequence of communications—to return in kind or degree the kind of friendly or hostile communication received from the other party.

Note that, for this reason, reciprocated communications can produce greater cooperation or greater conflict. The Chinese translation of the word "crisis" means both "opportunity" and "danger," and efforts to negotiate compromises provide an opportunity to produce a positive agreement or to produce a dangerous negative outcome that heightens threats and tensions. That is why negotiation is not a sure-fire way to resolve global conflicts and crises.

Still, negotiations make the settlement of disputes possible by providing reciprocated concessions between disputants. Russia's President Vladimir Putin offered wise counsel, saying that "Today to be successful, one must be able to reach agreements. The ability to compromise is not a diplomatic politeness but rather taking into account and respecting your partner's legitimate interests." Reciprocated gestures of goodwill and empathy for the opponent's situation pave the way for a compromise. Indeed, a common bargaining approach to induce the other party to reach agreements is through a *tit-for-tat strategy* that responds to any cooperative offer by immediately reciprocating it with an equal offer; the reward through repetitive concessions can facilitate a mutually satisfactory agreement.

Winston Churchill, Franklin D. Roosevelt, and Joseph Stalin, 1945

Richard Nixon and Leonid Brezhnev, 1972

Ronald Reagan and Mikhail Gorbachev, 1988

Boris Yeltsin and Bill Clinton, 1994

Vladimir Putin and George W. Bush, 2002

Dmitri Medvedev and Barack Obama, 2009

DIPLOMACY DIALOGUES To liberal reformers, direct negotiations between adversaries are a crucial step on the path to make peace a possibility. Talks allow both sides to put their interests on the bargaining table and discuss issues openly—far better than resolving them on the battlefield. As shown here, despite times of open hostility and opposing interests, diplomatic summits between the United States and Russia help to keep conflicts between the two great military powers "cold." Although tensions persist, diplomacy is "worth a try. For this truth hasn't changed since the Cold War: when Russia and the United States don't get along, the rest of the world has every right to feel uneasy" (Ghosh, 2009, p. 14).

British diplomatic historian Sir Harold Nicolson defined diplomacy as "the management of the relations between independent states by the process of negotiation." Diplomacy aims to revolve international disputes peacefully, which is why liberals favor it. Conversely, realists, for whom the state's primary interest is the pursuit of power, believe that threats of war preserve peace better than diplomatic efforts. Marxism takes a similarly pessimistic view of diplomatic approaches to peace, declaring, "when equal rights collide, force decides" (Carty, 2008, p. 122). Chinese former foreign minister Zhou Enlai spoke to this view when he echoed Clausewitz, saying "all diplomacy is the continuation of war by other means."

Diplomacy requires great intelligence, information, imagination, flexibility, ingenuity, and honesty to successfully maintain peaceful negotiations. Compounding the challenge is the common liability that while diplomats are sent to negotiate for their countries, no matter what their skill or sincerity, they cannot succeed unless they have the full backing of their government's authority. Furthermore, public scrutiny can cripple negotiations. Sometimes secrecy is necessary to make concessions and reach compromises without losing face; "unless covenants are arrived at secretly," warned U.S. President Richard M. Nixon, "there will be none to agree to openly."

NEGOTIATING WITH A NEGOTIATOR ABOUT NEGOTIATION U.S. President George H. W. Bush meets with Charles Kegley, one of the authors of *World Politics*. The major topics they discussed: the uses and limits of methods of dispute settlement without the use of military force. These include diplomatic negotiations, international courts, collective security, and other methods of conflict resolution that are advocated by policy makers whose image of world politics is informed by liberal and constructivist theories.

As former-UN Secretary-General Dag Hammarskjöld similarly cautioned, "The best results of negotiation cannot be achieved in international life any more than in our private world in the full glare of publicity with current debate of all moves, unavoidable misunderstandings, inescapable freezing of positions due to considerations of prestige and the temptation to utilize public opinion as an element integrated into the negotiation itself." These problems, potholes, and pitfalls notwithstanding, liberals prefer negotiation when trying to facilitate international peace. The alternative—the coercive use of military power—is ethically unacceptable to people seeking to avoid war.

Fortunately, those playing the game of international politics have been inventive in creating supplementary methods that enable negotiations to reduce the threat of war. All are now nested in laws accepted by the global community:

- **Mediation**. When a third-party outside actor, either another state or a group of states in an intergovernmental organization (IGO), participate directly in negotiations between the disputants to aid them in recognizing their shared interests and proposing solutions based on these common interests.

- **Good offices**. When two conflicting parties have a history of relatively peaceful negotiations, often a "good office" will be provided by a third party as neutral ground for negotiation. In these circumstances, the good office provider does not participate in the actual negotiations.

- **Conciliation**. When two or more conflicting parties wish to negotiate a dispute resolution but wish to maintain control over the final compromise, often a third party will assist both sides during the negotiations and attempt to offer unbiased opinions and suggestions to help achieve a solution while remaining neutral and refraining from proposing a solution.

- **Arbitration**. When disputing parties are willing to allow a third party to make a binding decision to resolve their dispute, a temporary ruling board considers both sides' arguments and reaches a decision.

- **Adjudication**. Perhaps the most formal of the dispute resolution options, this approach is roughly the equivalent of arguing a case in court and accepting a binding decision or ruling by a judge.

Mediation has a particularly strong track record of terminating international crises (Bercovitch and Gartner, 2008), and history shows that it works best when democracies or international institutions perform the negotiating service, due in part to the influence of democratic social norms of conflict resolution (Mitchell et al., 2008; Shannon, 2009). Greater involvement of women in international negotiations may also enhance the prospects for dispute resolution (see "Controversy: Can Women Improve Global Negotiations and the Prospects for World Peace?"). More pessimistically, negotiated resolutions to global crises have proven less successful when ethnic groups have been a player in the crisis that led to armed aggression (Ben-Yehuda and Mishali-Ran, 2006).

> *The quest for international security involves the unconditional surrender by every nation, in a certain measure, of its liberty of action, its sovereignty that is to say, and it is clear beyond all doubt that no other road can lead to such security.*
>
> —Albert Einstein, Nobel Prize-winning physicist

CourseMate

Video Activity: Protecting Our Citizens

INSTITUTIONS, NORMS, AND WORLD ORDER

Liberal and constructivist perspectives on war and peace, armed conflict, and international security are fundamentally shaped by the importance attached to shared ethics and morality in world politics. Liberalism places the power of principle over the principle of power (Kegley, 1992) because it is based on the idea that peace depends on actions driven by moral convictions. Such emphasis is also embedded in the fabric of many world religions, including Christianity, as seen in Jesus Christ's proclamation "Blessed are the peacemakers, for they shall be called sons of God."

The liberal road to peace begins with a dedication to doing what is right and not doing what is wrong, and constructivism, although itself conventionally thought of as ethically neutral, serves as a means for explaining systems of ethical beliefs. This differs greatly from much realist theorizing that "holds international politics to be beyond the concern of morality" (Suganami, 1983).

Future generations will likely judge whether disarmament agreements, multilateral international organizations, and international law can lead to a collective response to the multitude of

CAN WOMEN IMPROVE GLOBAL NEGOTIATIONS AND THE PROSPECTS FOR WORLD PEACE?

Feminist theory stresses the importance of gender in studying world politics, and explores the extent to which a "masculine" conceptualization of key ideas—such as power, interest, and security—shapes the way transnational actors conduct foreign affairs. While recognizing the influence of a masculine tradition in world politics, some feminist scholarship posits that in practice there is on average no significant difference in the capabilities of men and women. Others, however, claim that differences exist and are contextual, with each gender being more capable than the other in certain endeavors. Does this apply to international negotiation? Do women bring strengths to the bargaining table and enhance the prospects for conflict resolution? Or are men better suited to conflict management?

Since the 1990s, feminist scholars have pointed to the different ways in which gender identity shapes international decision making (Ackerly and True, 2008; Bolzendahl, 2009; Peterson and Runyan, 2009). With its emphasis on the role of power in an amoral pursuit of narrow self-interest by rational actors, realism portrays a competitive world in which a masculine approach to decision making reigns. Power is typically viewed as the ability to influence another to do what you want them to do, and in this context the accumulation of power is achieved through greater strength and authority, and at the expense of others. Men tend to have independent self-schemas that lead them to define themselves as distinct from others, and in decision making "tend to focus on end gains, making the achievement of personal preferences and goals the primary negotiation objective" (Boyer et al., 2009, p. 27). Thus, men are often comfortable negotiating in situations in which controlled conflict is expected.

Some argue that, due to their traditional social roles, women have interdependent self-schemas and a nurturing orientation that gives them valuable perspectives that are an asset to conflict negotiation and mediation. How women frame and conduct negotiations is influenced by "a relational view of others, an embedded view of agency, an understanding of control through empowerment, and problem-solving through dialogue" (Kolb, 1996, p. 139). As women are likely to "define themselves more through their relationships than do men, their actions and rhetoric within the negotiation process may be more oriented toward maintaining and protecting these relationships" (Boyer et al., 2009, p. 27). Moreover, women understand events in a context that accounts for relationships as well as evolving situations. Eschewing the realist perspective of power achieved through competition, women tend to be more inclined to a liberal view of mutual empowerment achieved through cooperative interactions that construct connections and understandings. Not only are women more likely to cooperate with one another, "increasing the flow of information between the negotiators is essential to achieving a superior solution in an integrative bargain ... and women are more likely to use these methods" (Babcock and Laschever, 2003, pp. 169–170).

If gender differences produce different processes and outcomes in international negotiation, then many hypothesize that increasing the number of women involved in decision making may bring fresh perspectives to conflict management (Anderlini, 2007). Rooted in the premise that women bring certain values to negotiation and mediation that are derived from their gendered socialization experiences, and that these insights and policy prescriptions have been absent due to the exclusionary nature of international negotiations

(Continued)

CAN WOMEN IMPROVE GLOBAL NEGOTIATIONS AND THE PROSPECTS FOR WORLD PEACE? (Continued)

(Hudson, 2005), the intent of UN Resolution 1325 is to "increase the participation of women at decision-making levels in conflict resolution and peace processes" in the interest of generating new perspectives and options for lasting conflict resolutions.

For social constructivists, "men and women's roles are not inherent or predetermined, but rather a social fact that can change through practice, interaction, and the evolution of ideas and norms" (Boyer et al., 2009, p. 26). Perhaps as greater numbers of women are included in international negotiations where men have traditionally dominated, both will benefit from the perspectives of the other, and the role of diplomacy in preventing and resolving conflict will be enhanced.

WHAT DO YOU THINK?

- *As a lead mediator trying to resolve an intractable conflict between two countries, what value would you place on having women at the bargaining table?*

- *Might the role of women in negotiation vary across different regions of the world? How might culture influence the empowerment and legitimacy of women at the negotiating table?*

- *Consider two U.S. foreign policy figures: former Secretary of State Hillary Clinton and President Barack Obama. How would you categorize their negotiating tendencies? Do they fit the gender mold as described here? Why or why not? What lessons for conflict resolution do they have to offer?*

global needs. What is clear is that countries are making bold efforts to unite in a common civic culture behind common values to construct global institutions to jointly protect themselves against the many problems they face in common. They appear to increasingly accept the once radical liberal view that, as Kofi Annan argues, "a new, broader definition of national interest is needed" that would unify states to work on common goals that transcend national interests.

If the paths you have explored in this chapter are pursued, will the belief that peace is best preserved through ethical policies break the violent historical pattern? The world waits for an answer. But what is clear at this time is that the global agenda facing the world is huge. The biggest problems facing humanity are transnational, and none can be solved effectively with a unilateral national response. A multilateral approach is required to address the staggering number of global problems that require peaceful management through collective solutions.

In Part 4, you will have an opportunity to look at trends in the economic, human, and environmental conditions that prevail as the cascading globalization of world politics accelerates. This survey can aid in understanding the world as it presently exists and allow you to contemplate, as caring and responsible global citizens, the prospects for transformations that could create a better world.

Simulation:
Collective Security Problem

STUDY. APPLY. ANALYZE.

Key Terms

antipersonnel landmines (APLs)
arms control
arms race
bilateral agreements
conciliation
crimes against humanity
crisis
disarmament
ethics

Intermediate-Range Nuclear Forces (INF) Treaty
International Criminal Court (ICC)
International Court of Justice (ICJ)
international criminal tribunals
jus ad bellum
jus in bello
just war doctrine
military necessity
morals

multilateral agreements
negotiation
neutrality
peace building
peace enforcement
peacekeeping
peacemaking
peace operations
positivist legal theory
preventive diplomacy

sovereign equality
spiral model
Strategic Arms Limitation Talks (SALT)
Strategic Arms Reduction Treaty (START)
Strategic Offensive Reductions Treaty (SORT)
tit-for-tat strategy
war crimes

Suggested Readings

Armstrong, David, and Jutta Brunée. (2009) *Routledge Handbook of International Law.* New York: Taylor & Francis.

Chatterjee, Deen K., ed. (2013) *The Ethics of Preventive War.* Cambridge, UK: Cambridge University Press.

Cohn, Carol, and Sara Ruddick. (2008) "A Feminist Ethical Perspective on Weapons of Mass Destruction." In *Essential Readings in World Politics,* 3rd edition. Karen A. Mingst and Jack L. Snyder, editors, New York: W.W. Norton & Company, pp. 458–477.

Diehl, Paul F., and J. Michael Greig. (2012) *International Mediation.* Cambridge, UK: Polity Press.

Evans, Gareth. (2008) *The Responsibility to Protect: Ending Mass Atrocity Crimes Once and for All.* Washington, DC: Brookings Institution Press.

Hudson, Kimberly A. (2009) *Justice, Intervention and Force in International Relations: Reassessing Just War Theory in the 21st Century.* New York: Taylor & Francis.

Jolly, Richard, Louis Emmerij, and Thomas G. Weiss (2009) *UN Ideas That Changed the World.* Bloomington, IN: Indiana University Press.

Puchala, Donald, Katie Verlin Laatikainen, and Roger A. Coate. (2007) *United Nations Politics.* Upper Saddle River, NJ: Prentice Hall.

Simmons, Beth. (2009) *Mobilizing for Human Rights: International Law in Domestic Politics.* New York: Cambridge University Press.

Suggested Videos

Carnegie Council Video

Betts, Richard K. "The World Ahead: Conflict or Cooperation?"

Dhanapala, Jayantha, and David C. Speedie. "After START— What Next? David Speedie Interviews Jayantha Dhanapala."

Doyle, Michael W., and Harold H. Koh. "Striking First: Preemption and Prevention in International Conflict."

Kupchan, Charles A. "How Enemies Become Friends: The Sources of Stable Peace."

Romano, Cesare P. R., Stephen M. Schwebel, and Daniel Terris. "The International Judge: An Introduction to the Men and Women Who Decide the World's Cases."

Vocke, William. "Can Moral Injury Be a Wound of War?"

CourseMate

Log in to CourseMate to access the following study tools for this chapter:

- Interactive Quiz
- eBook
- Flashcards & Key Term Crossword Puzzle
- Chapter Audio Summary
- Carnegie Council Videos

- Video Activities
- Simulation
- Animated Learning Module
- Case Study
- International Relations NewsWatch

PART 4

HUMAN SECURITY, PROSPERITY, AND RESPONSIBILITY

"It has been said that arguing against globalization is like arguing against the laws of gravity."

—*Kofi Annan, former UN secretary-general*

CHAPTER 10
The Globalization of International Finance

SEEKING GLOBAL FINANCIAL STABILITY AND GROWTH In continued response to the 2008 global financial crisis, the leaders of the G-20—an informal group of the 20 largest economies that meets periodically to discuss the coordination of financial policy— met in St. Petersburg, Russia, in September 2013 to discuss initiatives to calm global financial markets and stimulate growth. World leaders focused on measures to spur balanced and sustainable economic growth through effective regulation, jobs creation and investment, and the bolstering of trust and transparency.

dpa picture alliance / Alamy

QUESTIONS TO CONSIDER

- *What is globalization, and how does it affect the global economy?*
- *What limitations and trade-offs do states face in navigating the global financial system?*
- *What was the Bretton woods system?*
- *What are the causes and consequences of the 2008 global financial crisis?*
- *What is the future of the international financial architecture?*

M oney makes the world go "round." "Money is a root of all evil." "All that glitters is not gold." "Money can't buy you happiness." "There's hell in not making money."

You have all heard these old sayings at one time or another. Even though such aphorisms and clichés are somewhat contradictory, they all contain elements of truth. Your challenge is to separate fact from fiction by determining the place of money in your life and in the world around you. This task will depend heavily on your personal values and preferences. However, the quality of your conclusions will depend on your analytic skills in evaluating how money affects the many dimensions of world politics—and your own personal financial fate.

Today more than ever, money truly *is* moving around the world, and with increasing speed. The rapidity of global finance directly affects your quality of life. When you make a purchase, the odds are now very high that the goods have been produced overseas. What is more, when you buy a sandwich, a sweater, a car, or the gasoline to make it run, the cost is very likely to be affected by the rate at which your own country's currency is valued and exchanged for the currency of the producer abroad. Should you have the opportunity to travel abroad, you will instantly discover how the global exchange of national currencies will determine whether you can afford to attend a rock concert or buy that extra bottle of wine.

This chapter introduces you to the global financial system. It looks at the processes governing currency exchanges, particularly on how the transfer of money across borders affects levels of national prosperity and human security. Note that this topic is part of the larger one of international economics in general, and it serves as an introduction to international trade, which will be discussed in Chapter 11. Neither dimension of international economics—money nor trade—can be considered without the other. They are inextricably linked, and only by looking at both together can you understand how money and markets drive the rise and fall of individual and national wealth. You will be looking at a phenomenon as old as recorded history and inspecting how it influences life in the twenty-first century.

Financial markets are like the mirror of mankind, revealing every hour of each working day the way we value ourselves and the resources of the world around us.

—Niall Ferguson, British historian

INTERPRETING CONTEMPORARY ECONOMIC CHANGE

When changes occur in the world, they force people to think about and interpret world politics in fresh ways. Of all the many recent changes, perhaps none has been more continually invasive and far reaching than those occurring in the economic world. In fact, to some analysts, *geo-economics* (the geographic distribution of wealth) will replace *geopolitics* (the distribution of strategic military and political power) as the most important axis around which international competition, and ultimately the globe's destiny, will revolve (see Chapter 4).

geo-economics

The relationship between geography and the economic conditions and behavior of states that define their levels of production, trade, and consumption of goods and services.

globalization

The integration of states through increasing contact, communication, and trade, as well as increased global aware-ness of such integration.

Carnegie Council Video: Globalization

The growth of interdependence between each state's economy can be viewed as part of a trend toward *globalization* that began more than a century ago, and as states' economies have become more closely linked, traditional ideas about states, currency exchange mechanisms, trade, and markets have had to be reexamined in a new light (see Map 10.1). Bond purchases by Chinese investors, or even statements about future purchases, influence the relative value of currencies worldwide. Financial crises in the United States can likewise create turbulence in markets around the world. Revolutionary activity in the Middle East causes rapid increases in world oil prices. These are only a few of the consequences of globalization, and the undercurrents of the global economy have assumed increasing importance as they are inextricably linked to world politics.

Although some regard globalization as little more than a euphemism for capitalism (Petras and Veltmeyer, 2004), it is a multifaceted phenomenon that encompasses the development of interconnected material relations, the increasing rapidity with which they take place, and the shift in public perception of these changes. These multiple facets are evident in sociologist Fran Tonkiss' (2012) definition of economic globalization as "the increasing integration of circuits of goods, production, image, information, and money across national borders … character-ized not only by high level of trade, but by increasing levels of foreign direct investment and outsourcing, as well as the complex linkage of financial transactions across space."

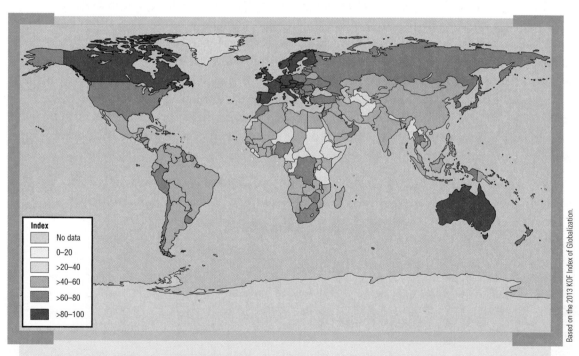

Based on the 2013 KOF Index of Globalization.

Index
- No data
- 0–20
- >20–40
- >40–60
- >60–80
- >80–100

MAP 10.1   GLOBALIZATION AROUND THE WORLD This map depicts the extent of globalization across the globe and is rendered from the 2013 Index of Globalization released by the KOF Swiss Economic Institute. The index is based on 24 different measures of economic, social, and political aspects of globalization, such as trade flows, personal contacts across borders, and participation in international organizations. As shown here, globalization varies across countries and regions. European countries are among the most global (18 of the 20 most globalized countries are from that region). The United States ranked 34th, with a globalization index score of 74.76 out of 100. There are also some trends among the least globalized, as they tend to be underdeveloped and largely autocratic regimes such as Bhutan, Liberia, and Comoros.

Globalization is thus shorthand for a cluster of interconnected phenomena, and you will find the term used to describe a process, a policy, a predicament, or the product of vast international forces producing massive worldwide changes. Moreover, most analysts would probably agree that globalization is a permanent trend leading to the probable *transformation* of world politics—the end of one historic pattern and the beginning of a new one. A political journalist Thomas L. Friedman (2007c, p. 48–9) argues, globalization will have a profound impact upon the global system as a whole:

> This new era of globalization will prove to be such a difference of degree that it will be seen, in time, as a difference in kind ... it will be remembered as one of those fundamental changes—like the rise of the nation-state or the Industrial Revolution—each of which, in its day, produced changes in the role of individuals, the role and form of governments, the way we innovated [and] the way we conducted business.

Given the broad and multifaceted scope of globalization, this chapter, as well as the remaining chapters in *World Politics*, will deal with different dimensions of globalization and their implications. Nowhere is this integration more apparent than in the world of international finance and capital. We will next focus our attention on the dynamics of the *international monetary system* through which currencies and credits are calculated as capital moves freely across national boundaries by way of investments, trade, foreign aid, and loans.

The importance of money flows from it being a link between the present and the future.

—**John Maynard Keynes, British economist**

MONEY MATTERS: THE TRANSNATIONAL EXCHANGE OF MONEY

Part of the equation on which global economic destiny depends is the character of *laissez-faire* capitalism, which posits that free-market mechanisms—with a minimum of state intervention—are foundational to the "dynamism that produces capitalism's vast economic and cultural benefits" (Muller, 2013:31). For its part, the state seeks to provide some operational rules for the system as well as measures to mitigate the more disruptive effects of the marketplace upon its citizenry. In the area of currency exchanges, a number of governments have taken some tentative steps in creating rules for adjusting their currencies with one another and stabilizing wide fluctuations in their exchange rates.

However, the process through which money is exchanged between countries does not have strong supranational regulatory institutions. Moreover, states often have very limited ability to control either those transactions or the relative value of their currencies on the world market. At the same time, these transactions, as noted above, are escalating at a furious rate. But what does this really mean, and what are its implications?

The Globalization of Finance

Global finance encompasses a broad variety of transactions, including international loans, foreign aid, remittances, and currency trading, as well as cross-border investments such as the

CourseMate

**Case Study:
International
Political Economy:
Globalization**

**international
monetary
system**

*The financial
procedures used
to calculate the
value of curren-
cies and credits
when capital is
transferred across
borders through
trade, investment,
foreign aid, and
loans.*

CourseMate

Carnegie Council Video:
International Monetary
System

purchase of stocks, bonds, or derivatives. It also includes financial services that are conducted across borders. Another major facet of global finance is *foreign direct investment* (FDI)—transactions "involving significant control of producing enterprises" (Cohen, 2005) ranging from the purchase of a substantial share of a foreign company's stock to setting up production facilities in another country (see Chapter 5).

globalization of finance

The increasing trans-nationalization of national markets through the worldwide integration of capital flows.

This *globalization of finance* refers to the increasing trans-nationalization and centralization of these markets through integrating worldwide capital flows. The most fundamental characteristic of this emerging system of financial arrangements is that it is not centered on any single state. Thus, globalization implies the growth of a single, unified *global* market. Whereas telecommunications specialists talk about the "death of distance," financial specialists talk about the "end of geography" because geographic location is no longer a barrier to finance.

Evidence of financial globalization abounds. Although trade has grown dramatically, since World War II the volume of cross-border capital flows has increased even more. In 2012 there were $1.4 trillion in global FDI flows. Although this is still below the levels reached before the 2008 global financial crisis, it is triple the level of FDI in 1997 and almost 10 times the amount of FDI in 1980 (OECD, 2013b).

arbitrage

The selling of one currency (or product) and purchase of another to make a profit on changing exchange rates.

Moreover, growth in the *arbitrage* market, in which currencies are bought and sold for profit based off differences and fluctuations in their relative values, has been truly staggering. Since 1973 this market has grown 60 times faster than the value of world trade (McGrew, 2008), and it routinely handles over $4 trillion worth of currency on a daily basis (Malmgren and Stys, 2011). By way of comparison, the total value of all goods and services produced in the United States during 2011—its *GDP (Gross Domestic Product)*—was $15.0 trillion. Viewed another way, the amount of currency that circulates in four days is greater than the total yearly production of the U.S. economy.

GDP (Gross Domestic Product)

Total value of all goods and services produced in a country within a year

Today, even more speculative financial instruments have exponentially increased the size and scope of these capital flows. For example, by 2011 the total value of all the stock markets in the world was $54.6 trillion, which was somewhat less than actual global GDP of $70 trillion. During that same time, the bond market (the means through which governments and corporations accumulate debt) was valued at $158 trillion, or just over twice the value of global GDP (Roxburgh, Lund, and Piotrowski, 2011; IMF, 2012a). Yet the value of the derivatives market—newer financial instruments that are essentially "side bets" placed on the prospective future value of assets such as stocks and bonds—was much greater. As many derivatives transactions are private contracts and thus not formally declared, it is somewhat difficult to get an accurate figure of the total value of these transactions (Sivy, 2013). Nonetheless, the more conservative estimates of the value of derivatives bought and sold during 2012 is between $600 and $700 trillion (*The Economist*, 2013). In other words, the market for these purely speculative financial instruments was almost ten times larger than the actual amount of goods and services produced in the world! In short, "Planet Finance is beginning to dwarf Planet Earth" (Ferguson, 2008, p. 4).

Global flows of capital are not entirely new. In an early form of globalization, a network of financial centers flourished along the Baltic and North Seas, and city-states such as Lübeck, Hamburg, and Bergen dominated finance and trading. At the turn of the nineteenth century, London replaced Amsterdam as the world's leading financial center, and by the early twentieth century New York began to rival London—antecedents of today's shifting of financial hubs to Tokyo, Singapore, and Dubai. Moreover, international financial crises are nothing new; economist Charles Kindlberger (2000) notes that the "manics, panics, and crashes" of global finance began in the early seventeenth century, with 27 major financial crises occurring before the beginning of the twentieth century.

The difference is the speed and breadth of finance capital flows throughout the entire globe. For example, many stock purchases are handled by high frequency trading firms (HFTs) that rely on computer programs to execute many trades in a short period of time—some firms measure their trading speed in picoseconds (trillionths of a second; Malmgren and Stys, 2011). The combination of rapid, computer-driven trading and the sheer volume of shares processed can produce rapid swings in global stock markets for very idiosyncratic reasons.

For example, a momentary crash occurred around 1:08 p.m. on April 23, 2013, when someone hacked the Associated Press' Twitter account and reported that two explosions had just occurred at the U.S. White House and that President Obama had been hurt. Over the course of two minutes the U.S. stock market plummeted $200 billion. By 1:13, as investors discovered the story was false, the stock market recovered and the Dow Jones Industrial Average (an index widely used to evaluate how the stock market is doing) closed the day at a net gain (Lauricella et al., 2013).

Politically, the global capital market reveals limitations in the power of the state. The volume of currencies traded far exceeds the actual amount of reserve currencies held by governments, which limits the ability of governments to influence exchange rates. In 2011, exchange rate tensions increased when the U.S. government, as well as the G-20, pressured the Chinese government to reexamine the value of its currency, the Yuan, and to modify the rate at which it would be exchanged in the future. Although acknowledging that China "needs a market-based exchanged rate regime," the governor of the People's Bank of China, Zhou Xiaochuan, countered that the process would have to occur "in a gradual way ... rather than shock therapy." In April 2012 China made significant progress toward reforming its exchange rate policies and liberalizing its financial markets (Qing, 2012). Although this is still an issue of contention between the United States and China, there is optimism about continued reforms and the many benefits that lie therein (He, 2013).

The globalization of finance also has implications for international trade (see Chapter 11), and there is considerable debate about the monetary factors underlying trade transactions. Indeed, the linkage between exchange rates and trade is at the heart of the debate over the valuation of the Yuan, as its relatively low exchange rate reduces the relative cost of Chinese goods shipped abroad and thus gives them a competitive advantage over goods produced in other countries. As will be discussed in the next section, the currency exchange rate directly influences price and thus affects the flow of international trade. Indeed, the international monetary system is the most critical factor facilitating international trade, as such transactions could not exist without a stable and predictable method for calculating the value of sales and investments.

Commercial liberals, the branch of liberalism that focuses on the positive spillovers that result from economic ties (see Chapter 2), argue that the open exchanges of currencies across borders benefits all countries. Yet the globalization of finance does not affect all countries equally. Though a vast majority of global capital goes to the Global North and East, all countries are mutually vulnerable to rapid transfers of capital in this globalized system.

As the financial crisis of 2008 has shown, the Global North is hardly without its problems (Laeven and Valencia, 2012). Yet the Global South is typically the most dependent and vulnerable to shifts in the financial marketplace. Of the 431 systemic banking, currency, or debt crises that occurred since 1970, 341 have been in the developing world (Laeven and Valencia, 2012). In accordance with neoliberal institutionalist approaches, this multitude of crises suggests why bankers and economists have called for more reliable multilateral mechanisms for policy coordination to better manage the massive movement of cross-border capital. This was the raison d'être for the G-20, a grouping of the 20 largest economies that was formed in the aftermath of the Asian financial crisis.

In assessing the implications of capital mobility for the global system, as well as the global economy as a whole, it is thus necessary to understand the international monetary system and the processes through which the relative value of each state's currencies are set. With that in mind, we will next examine the core concepts of the global monetary system, some of the key issues and dilemmas surrounding monetary policy, and its recent historical context.

Monetary Policy: Key Concepts and Issues

Monetary and financial policies are woven into a complex set of relationships between states and the global system, and involve fairly esoteric terminology. To help you to better understand these issues, Table 10.1 lays out some of the key concepts related to monetary policy and the role of currency. As you read through these explanations, keep in mind that these are not separate phenomena but a related set of factors through which the global financial system operates.

To begin to put together how these factors are related, and the importance of a state's *monetary policy* in determining its well-being, we will consider why a country's *exchange rate* fluctuates frequently and the challenges states face in dealing with these fluctuations. As you will see, states face a variety of "trade-offs" in navigating monetary policies, and must seek a difficult balance between competing values, goals, and priorities. Moreover, states are ultimately limited in their ability to control monetary outcomes.

Money works in several ways and serves different purposes. First, money must be widely accepted, so that people earning it can use it to buy goods and services from others. Second, money must store value, so that people will be willing to keep some of their wealth in the form of that particular currency. Third, money must act as a standard of deferred payment, so that people will be willing to lend money knowing that, when the money is repaid in the future, it will still have purchasing power.

Movements in a state's exchange rate occur, in part, when changes develop in the people's assessment of a national currency's underlying economic strength or the ability of its government to maintain the value of its money. A deficit in a country's balance of payments, for example, would likely cause a decline in the value of its currency relative to that of other countries. This happens when the supply of the currency is greater than the demand for it. Similarly, when those engaged in international economic transactions change their expectations about a currency's future value, they might reschedule their lending and borrowing. Fluctuations in the exchange rate could then follow.

monetary policy

The decisions made by states' central banks to change the country's money supply in an effort to manage the national economy and control inflation, such as changing the amount of money in circulation and raising or lowering interest rates.

exchange rate

The rate at which one state's currency is exchanged for another state's currency in the global marketplace.

TABLE 10.1	Understanding Currency: Basic Terms and Concepts
Term	**Concept**
Balance of Payments	A calculation summarizing a country's financial transactions with the external world, determined by the level of credits (export earnings, profits from foreign investment, receipts of foreign aid) minus the country's total international debits (imports, interest payments on international debts, foreign direct investments, and the like).
Budget Deficit	Yearly amount of debt necessary to fund a balance-of-payments deficit. Money is most commonly raised by selling bonds to foreign and domestic investors.
National Debt	Cumulative amount of debt that a country owes its various bondholders, both foreign and domestic.
Balance of Trade	The difference in the value of the goods a country sells (exports) minus the goods it purchases (imports). If a country imports more than it exports, it is said to have a balance-of-trade deficit. For example, in 2011 the United States exported just over $2.06 trillion in goods and services and imported just over $2.66 trillion, for a balance-of-trade deficit of about $600 billion (WDI, 2013).
Central Bank	The primary monetary authority within a state. It is responsible for issuing currency, setting monetary policy, acting as a bank for the government, and helping to administer the state's banking industry.
Monetary Policy	Central bank policy tools for managing economies. Policies fall into two basic categories—altering the money supply (the amount of money in circulation) and adjusting interest rates (the relative "price" for using money). An expansionary monetary policy would entail such things as selling additional bonds and lowering interest rates. Such policies would make money relatively more plentiful and less expensive to borrow.
Fiscal Policy	Governmental policy tools for managing economies. Basic policy options are taxation and spending. An expansionary fiscal policy would consist of lowering taxes and/or increasing spending, whereas a "tight" or contractionary policy would involve raising taxes and/or decreasing spending.
Devaluation	The lowering of the official exchange rate of one country's currency relative to other currencies. This is generally done to increase exports, as devaluation lowers the relative prices of a country's exports. However, it can also reduce the spending power of citizens within that country.
Exchange Rate	The rate at which one state's currency is exchanged for another state's currency in the global marketplace. For example, on October 17, 2012, for one U.S. dollar you would have received 0.76euro or 12.8 Mexican pesos. Exchange rates are subject to constant fluctuations. Daily changes are generally quite small, although they can vary greatly over the long run. For example, on June 28, 2001, the U.S. dollar was worth 1.17 euros and 9.08 Mexican pesos.
Fixed Exchange Rate	A system in which a government sets the value of its currency at a fixed rate for exchange in relation to another country's currency (usually the U.S. dollar) or another measure of value (such as a group of different currencies or a precious metal such as gold) so that the exchange value is not free to fluctuate in the global money market.
Floating Exchange Rate	System in which the relative value of a country's currency is set by market forces. In principle, the value of a country's currency is indicative of the underlying strengths and weaknesses of its economy.
Fixed-but-Adjustable Exchange Rate System	A system in which a government fixes its currency in relation to that of another country's currency but may still change the fixed price to reflect changes in the underlying strengths and weaknesses of its economy. The general expectation is that such changes are rare and only occur under specially defined circumstances.
Inflation	A decrease in the value of money, which increases the prices paid for goods and services. It is generally expressed in percentages and calculated on a yearly basis. Inflation reduces the buying power of citizens, as it decreases the value of their currency. Very high levels of inflation (hyperinflation) can cause severe disruptions within a society, as the currency becomes largely worthless. For example, in 2010 the inflation rate for Zimbabwe was over 12,000 percent. The following year, Zimbabwe abandoned its currency and adopted the dollar.
Capital Controls	Government attempts to limit or prevent global capital transactions. Examples range from placing taxes on foreign exchanges to outright bans on the movement of capital out of a country. These policies are generally intended as a means to "insulate" an economy from the global capital market.

Arbitrage speculators who buy and sell money also affect the international stability of a country's currency. Speculators make money by guessing the future value of currencies. If, for instance, they believe that the Japanese yen will be worth more in three months than it is now, they can buy yen today and sell them for a profit three months later. Conversely, if they believe that the yen will be worth less in three months, they can sell yen today for a certain number of dollars and then buy back the same yen in three months for less money. As is the case with global capital flows, the globalization of finance allows investors to rapidly move funds from one currency to another in order to realize gains from differences in states' interest rates and the declining value of other currencies. Short-term financial flows are now the norm: the International Monetary Fund estimates that more than 80 percent of futures (speculative markets based on the future values of assets) and arbitrage transactions are completed in one week or less, providing significant profit opportunities in a short time period.

In the same way that governments try to protect the value of their currencies at home, they often try to protect them internationally by intervening in currency markets. Their willingness to do so is important to importers and exporters, whose success may depend on predictability in the value of the currencies in which they deal to carry out transnational exchanges. Governments intervene when their central banks buy or sell currencies to change the relative value of their own. Unlike speculators, however, governments should not try to manipulate exchange rates so as to gain unfair advantages because that could tarnish their reputations as custodians of monetary stability. In any event, the extent to which governments can ultimately affect their currencies' value in the face of large transnational movements of capital is increasingly questionable (see Figures 10.1 and 10.2).

Within this system, governments are faced with the difficult task of balancing the demands of the global currency market with the need to manage their economies. There are many difficulties in navigating these channels, and states face three main sets of competing values, or "trade-offs"—inflation versus unemployment, strong versus weak currency valuation strategies, and the competing values of stability versus autonomy. These trade-offs, as well as the policy tools that are involved, are shown in Table 10.2.

Governments attempt to manage their currencies to prevent inflation. Inflation occurs when the government creates too much money in relation to the goods and services produced in its economy. As explained in Table 10.1, high degrees of inflation can undercut the ability of a currency to effectively serve as a store of value or medium of exchange. However, the creation of money—whether through increasing the *money supply* or lowering interest rates—does serve to stimulate the economy. Alternatively, restrictive monetary policy is very useful in curbing inflation or helping the government reduce debt. Yet such actions slow an economy down, which can result in increased unemployment and even recessions. This is one of the most commonly noted trade-offs associated with monetary policy—inflation versus unemployment.

A related dilemma regards currency values, specifically whether states should seek to maintain "strong" or relatively "weak" currencies. In a flexible exchange rate regime, the exchange rate for a given currency ideally reflects the health of its economy (or lack thereof). As mentioned, states are generally expected to refrain from manipulating the value of their currencies, or the currencies of other countries, in order to maintain predictability and stability. However, there are benefits to maintaining a weak currency, through such means as capital controls,

money supply

The total amount of currency in circulation, calculated to include demand deposits, such as checking accounts in commercial banks, and time deposits, such as savings accounts and bonds.

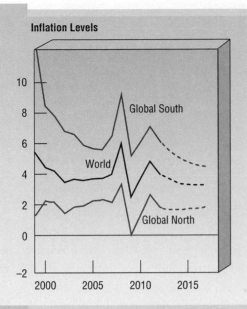

Inflation Levels

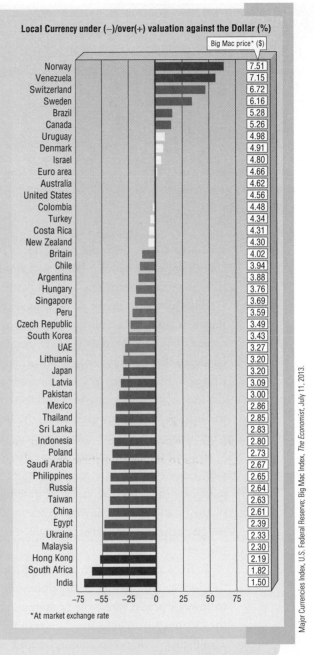

Local Currency under (−)/over(+) valuation against the Dollar (%)

Country	Big Mac price* ($)
Norway	7.51
Venezuela	7.15
Switzerland	6.72
Sweden	6.16
Brazil	5.28
Canada	5.26
Uruguay	4.98
Denmark	4.91
Israel	4.80
Euro area	4.66
Australia	4.62
United States	4.56
Colombia	4.48
Turkey	4.34
Costa Rica	4.31
New Zealand	4.30
Britain	4.02
Chile	3.94
Argentina	3.88
Hungary	3.76
Singapore	3.69
Peru	3.59
Czech Republic	3.49
South Korea	3.43
UAE	3.27
Lithuania	3.20
Japan	3.20
Latvia	3.09
Pakistan	3.00
Mexico	2.86
Thailand	2.85
Sri Lanka	2.83
Indonesia	2.80
Poland	2.73
Saudi Arabia	2.67
Philippines	2.65
Russia	2.64
Taiwan	2.63
China	2.61
Egypt	2.39
Ukraine	2.33
Malaysia	2.30
Hong Kong	2.19
South Africa	1.82
India	1.50

−75 −55 −25   0   25   50   75

*At market exchange rate

Major Currencies Index, U.S. Federal Reserve; Big Mac Index, *The Economist*, July 11, 2013.

FIGURE 10.1 AND FIGURE 10.2   CALCULATING THE CHANGING COSTS OF GOODS IN THE GLOBAL ECONOMY People from the United States who travel abroad must use currency exchange rates to convert the price of their purchases abroad to the value of U.S. dollars, and sometimes they are alarmed at the higher price. Economists usually calculate currency exchange rates in terms of purchasing power of parity (PPP) because that index of the value of exchange rates measures the cost of identical goods or services in any two countries. Shown on the right, this index uses a McDonald's Big Mac, which is available for sale in more than 130 countries. On July 11, 2013, the least expensive burger could be purchased in India for $1.50 versus an average price of $4.56 in the United States. In Venezuela, the same burger costs $7.15. Inflation also affects the cost of goods and services, as a general increase in the level of prices means that each unit of currency purchases less. As shown by the figure on the left, while inflation is higher in the Global South than the Global North, overall inflation levels have declined since the 2008 global financial crisis.

fixing exchange rates, or even currency devaluations. Although a weaker currency has a negative effect on the spending power of the domestic consumers, it makes exporting industries more competitive since their goods become relatively less expensive in the global marketplace as compared to those countries with a stronger currency. This has been a major source of controversy regarding the Chinese currency, as critics contend that the unduly low exchange rate creates unfair competition in the global marketplace. Alternatively, currencies that are

TABLE 10.2	Conflicting Goals in Financial Policy	
Trade-Off	**Policy Tools**	**Dilemma**
Inflation vs. unemployment	Monetary policy (interest rates and money supply)	Stimulative (expansionary) policies may create inflation. Restrictive (tight) monetary policies may cause unemployment.
Strong vs. weak currency	Capital controls Choice of exchange rate regime Currency devaluation Monetary policy	Any choice hurts some segments within the country, such as exporting industries or consumers.
Currency stability vs. policy autonomy	Choice of exchange rate regime	Cannot have both stability and autonomy in an open economy.

relatively strong face the opposite dilemma—though their consumers have relatively more spending power, both at home and abroad, their exporting industries suffer, and they are more likely to run a balance-of-trade deficit.

This speaks to the trade-off that is at the core of global monetary policy, namely, the choice between currency stability and policy autonomy. The basic problem is that in a system where capital flows freely (that is, there are no substantial capital controls), it is impossible to have both stability and autonomy. In principle, each has advantages. Stable exchange rates ensure that a country's currency can perform the primary functions of a currency cited earlier, and the lack of volatility provides both policy makers and potential investors with expectations for the future. Autonomy gives states the flexibility to pursue monetary policies that best suit their particular economic situation, such as the use of expansionary policies to stimulate growth.

A flexible exchange rate regime gives states autonomy to conduct their own monetary policies. For example, all else being equal, the market would respond to expansionary monetary policy by lowering the exchange rate of a currency (as the currency would be relatively more plentiful and/or offer lower interest rates). In this case, autonomy is gained, although there is no guarantee of stability, as the currency is subject to the vicissitudes of the global currency markets.

A fixed exchange rate regime provides currency stability, yet it gives states practically no freedom to conduct monetary policy. For example, if a country with a fixed exchange rate were to lower interest rates, the exchange rate could not move to take the decreased demand for the currency into account. As a result the country would have a balance-of-payments deficit. To fill this deficit, the country would need to intervene into the foreign exchange market to reduce the oversupply of currency—a "tight" monetary policy that would essentially undo the initial policy—or get rid of the fixed exchange rate altogether. The United States near the end of the Bretton Woods era, Argentina in the late 1990s, and Greece in 2010–2012 all faced such dilemmas.

States thus have to balance competing interests when creating monetary policy—the desire to help their economy grow with the necessity to maintain their currencies, the relative utility of strong versus weak currency valuation, and the incompatibility of stability and policy autonomy. Moreover, all states face these dilemmas within the context of a global monetary system over which they have very little actual control. It is helpful to keep these trade-offs and limitations on state power in mind as you consider the monetary policies of the Bretton Woods era, as well as some of the current issues in international finance.

BRETTON WOODS AND BEYOND

In July 1944, 44 of the states allied against the Axis powers met at Bretton Woods, a New Hampshire resort, to devise new rules and institutions that would govern international trade and monetary relations after World War II. As the world's preeminent economic and military power, the United States played the leading role.

The perceived causes of the economic catastrophes of the previous decade, as well as the states' beliefs about the need for active U.S. leadership, shaped the proposals. The United States sought free trade, open markets, and monetary stability—all central tenets of what would become the "Bretton Woods system"—based on the theoretical premises of *commercial liberalism*, which advocates free markets with few barriers to trade and capital flows.

Britain also played an important role at the conference. Led by John Maynard Keynes—whose theories about the state's role in managing inflation, unemployment, and growth still influence economic thinking around the world—the British delegation won support for the principle of strong government action when states face economic problems. This ideology conforms less closely with liberalism than the principles of *mercantilism*, which assigns states a greater role in managing economic interactions as a strategy for acquiring national wealth (see Chapter 5 and Chapter 11).

Despite these differences, the rules established at Bretton Woods reflected a remarkable level of agreement. They rested on three political bases. First, power was concentrated in the rich Western European and North American countries, which reduced the number of states needed to reach decisions. The onset of the Cold War helped cement Western unity along these lines. Second, a compromise was reached between the contrasting ideologies of the United States and Britain. In particular, the emergent order honored both commercial liberal preferences for an open international economy and the more mercantilist desires for active state involvement in their domestic economies. This mix of ideologies that underpinned the Bretton Woods order was eventually termed *embedded liberalism* (Ruggie, 1982). Third, Bretton Woods worked because the United States assumed the burdens of hegemonic leadership, which others willingly accepted.

Commercial liberalism's preference for open markets spread worldwide during this time and remains dominant today. Thus, it is still useful to characterize the contemporary international economic system as a *Liberal International Economic Order (LIEO)*—one based on such free-market principles as openness and free trade. Three institutions were formed to maintain the LIEO. The General Agreement on Tariffs and Trade (GATT), which later became the World Trade Organization (WTO), was formed to encourage trade liberalization. The International Bank for Reconstruction and Development, which later became the World Bank, and the International Monetary Fund (IMF) were created to bolster financial and monetary relations (see Chapter 5).

embedded liberalism

Dominant economic approach during the Bretton Woods system, which combined open international markets with domestic state intervention to attain such goals as full employment and social welfare.

Liberal International Economic Order (LIEO)

The set of regimes created after World War II, designed to promote monetary stability and reduce barriers to the free flow of trade and capital.

Lou-Foto/Alamy

GROWING FROM ECONOMIC INTEGRATION New skyscrapers—a symbol of economic growth—dot the skyline of Beijing, China, which is recognized as one of the globe's leading financial centers. Former World Trade Organization Director-General Pascal Lamy remarked that "the wealth of the great Merchant Cities extends far beyond money. As cities open to trade and traders, these communities have served as centers for the exchange of ideas and culture as well as goods and services."

Financial and Monetary Aspects of the Bretton Woods System

speculative attacks

Massive sales of a country's currency, caused by the anticipation of a future decline in its value.

fixed exchange rates

A system in which a government sets the value of its currency in relation to another country's currency at a fixed rate of exchange and does not allow it to fluctuate in the global money market.

The global economic collapse of the 1930s provided important lessons for monetary relations. In particular, as the major economies contracted in the late 1920s, they found themselves unable to maintain their fixed exchange rate regimes. The resulting flexible currency regime was highly unstable, replete with *speculative attacks* on currencies and currency devaluations. Eventually states began to close off their monetary and trade regimes from the global market, and the global economy collapsed into "closed imperial blocks" (Ravenhill, 2008, p. 12).

To avoid repeating history, the leaders sought to construct a common set of practices regarding monetary and currency policy to help simplify international trade and finance. The negotiating parties agreed that the postwar monetary regime should be based on *fixed exchange rates*, and governments were tasked with maintaining this new currency regime. To provide a stabilization fund to help countries offset short-term balance-of-payments problems, they set up what eventually became the International Monetary Fund (IMF). The IMF was to function somewhat like a global credit union—countries contributed to the fund and were able to draw capital from it to help them maintain a balance-of-payments equilibrium, and hence exchange rate stability. Along somewhat similar lines, they established the International Bank for Reconstruction and Development, later known as the World Bank, to provide capital for longer-term development and recovery projects.

Today the IMF and World Bank continue to be important, if controversial, players in the global monetary and financial systems. Eighty-five percent of their state members belong to both IGOs, which serve as "lenders of last resort" to members facing financial crises, if those seeking assistance agree to meet the often-painful loan conditions (see "Controversy: The IMF, World Bank, and Structural Adjustment Policies"). In the period immediately after World War II, these institutions commanded too little authority and too few resources to cope with the enormous devastation of the war.

The United States stepped into the breach. The U.S. dollar became the key to the hegemonic role that the United States eagerly assumed as manager of the international monetary system. Backed by a vigorous and healthy economy, a fixed relationship between gold and the dollar (pegged at $35 per ounce of gold), and the U.S. commitment to exchange gold for dollars at any time (known as "dollar convertibility"), the dollar became a universally accepted "parallel currency." It was accepted in exchange markets as the reserve used by monetary authorities in most countries and by private banks, corporations, and individuals for international trade and capital transactions.

To maintain the value of their currencies, central banks in other countries used the dollar to raise or depress their value. Thus, the Bretton Woods monetary regime was based on fixed-but-adjustable exchange rates (see Table 10.1) that were pegged to the dollar and gold, which ultimately required government intervention to maintain.

To get U.S. dollars into the hands of those who needed them most, the Marshall Plan provided Western European states billions of dollars in aid to buy the U.S. goods necessary to rebuild their war-torn economies. The United States also encouraged deficits in its own balance of payments as a way of providing *international liquidity*. Such liquidity was intended

international liquidity

Reserve assets used to settle international accounts.

MONEY MATTERS Currency now moves effortlessly across borders, and the globalization of international finance is wreaking havoc on the efforts of state governments to control rapid fluctuations in economic conditions. Shown here is an example of how financial policies sometimes unleash hostile feelings: As part of the Occupy Wall Street movement, May Day protestors expressed popular outrage and frustration over the corrupt and fraudulent practices of financial institutions, as well as the failure of governments to hold them accountable. Pictured left, around 32,000 people took to the streets in Tokyo on May 1, 2013 to protest economic conditions for the common man. Pictured right, a police lieutenant confronts protestors in New York City.

CONTROVERSY

THE IMF, WORLD BANK, AND STRUCTURAL ADJUSTMENT POLICIES: IS THE "CURE" WORSE THAN THE "DISEASE"?

The protests in Greece, which have taken place since 2010, are perhaps the most visible example of contentious action against the IMF and World Bank. In some instances, such as the 2003 Black Friday protests in Bolivia in which 33 people were killed, the violence can turn deadly. In the case of Indonesia in 1998, such protests and riots can sometimes even contribute to overturning a government.

Why is there so much controversy surrounding organizations whose primary purpose is to spur development within the Global South, and whose mission statements include such laudable goals as "global poverty reduction and the improvement of living standards" and fostering "economic growth and high levels of employment"?

The greatest sources of tension are structural adjustment policies (SAPs)—the strings attached to IMF and World Bank financial assistance. The basic goal of SAPs is to help countries repay their foreign debts through a combination of fiscal and monetary policy reforms, as well as increased participation in the global economy. SAPs were first introduced in the early 1980s as a way of helping countries in Latin America recover from the debt crisis. Since then, over 100 countries have undertaken some type of SAP (Abouharb and Cingranelli, 2007). SAPs utilize a common policy "playbook":

- Fiscal "austerity" (reductions in state spending)
- A decreased role of the state in the economy, including a reduction in the overall size of the public sector as well as the privatization of state-run industries (most commonly utilities)
- Monetary policy changes, including increased interest rates and currency devaluation
- Trade liberalization measures, such as the cessation of tariffs and nontariff barriers to foreign trade

The overall goal of SAPs is to help the target state resolve its balance-of-payments problems by reducing spending and increasing capital flow. Although this "playbook" is in line with basic macroeconomic principles for reducing deficits, the political and economic results of these measures have been subject to a great deal of criticism.

SAPs—which are often enacted very rapidly—are very recessionary, particularly in the short run. Decreases in government spending often translate into decreases in government jobs (and thus increased unemployment), as well as decreased levels of support for education, health care, and economic welfare. Interest rate increases make it more expensive for citizens to acquire loans, and currency devaluation lowers individual spending power. In many instances, reducing state subsidies may result in drastic increases in the prices that citizens pay for basic services, such as electricity and water, or goods that were formerly subsidized, including fuel and food. For example, in 2001 Ghana was forced to increase its water prices by 95 percent, while Nicaragua was forced to increase its by 30 percent (Grusky, 2001). These difficulties can be further exacerbated by trade liberalization, as inefficient domestic industries are likely unable to compete with their foreign competitors. As a result, these industries may be forced to cut jobs or close down entirely.

Politically, participation in SAPs is also problematic. The IMF and World Bank are largely controlled by the states of the Global North—indeed the policy mix represented by

(Continued)

THE IMF, WORLD BANK, AND STRUCTURAL ADJUSTMENT POLICIES: IS THE "CURE" WORSE THAN THE "DISEASE"? (Continued)

the IMF is often referred to as the "Washington Consensus." Countries in the Global South may view these institutions as another manifestation of "neocolonialism," which serves more to meet the interests of global investors and corporations rather than the needs of the citizens in the Global South. Indeed, in many instances privatization of industries results in many large state-run companies being sold to multinational corporations from the Global North. For example, when Bolivia was forced to privatize its water industry, the contract was awarded to a company controlled by Bechtel (Forero, 2005), while water privatization contracts in Argentina were picked up by Enron (Nichols, 2002).

Criticisms against the IMF have primarily focused on individual cases. However, studies have begun to systematically examine the impact of SAPs upon their recipient states. The empirical results paint an overwhelmingly negative picture—SAPs have been linked to reductions in social spending, greater income inequality, and lower levels of economic growth (Vreeland, 2003). Moreover, the social unrest that can occur due to SAPs is often met with state repression (Abouharb and Cingranelli, 2007).

Although acknowledging, and currently reforming, their imperfect record, the World Bank and the IMF defend their role in the international financial system. Pointing to successes, such as in Poland, officials note that the IMF has played a key role in helping countries recover. Moreover, countries only apply for help when they are in financial trouble, and thus it is hard to blame these organizations for problems that the country was facing anyway. Finally, political leaders may find it expedient to "scapegoat" the IMF and the World Bank, which can provide them with "cover" for enacting necessary, though unpopular, economic policies. Ultimately, as argued by IMF economist Kenneth Rogoff, countries would be much worse off if they isolated themselves from the global economy. "Perhaps poor nations won't need the IMF's specific macroeconomic expertise—but they will need something awfully similar" (Rogoff, 2003).

WHAT DO YOU THINK?

- *What do the controversies surrounding SAPs reveal about the "trade-off" between stability and policy autonomy? Inflation versus unemployment?*

- *What steps, if any, could be taken to improve the developing world's perception of the IMF?*

- *How would the various theories of development, particularly the modernization and dependency approaches, view the IMF?*

to enable these countries to pursue expansionary monetary and fiscal policies, as well as to facilitate their participation in the global economy.

In addition to providing liquidity, the United States assumed a disproportionate share of the burden in rejuvenating Western Europe and Japan. It supported European and Japanese trade competitiveness, permitted certain forms of protectionism (such as Japanese restrictions on importing U.S. products), and accepted dollar discrimination (as the European Payments Union did by promoting trade within Europe at the expense of trade with the United States). The United States willingly agreed to pay these costs of leadership because subsidizing economic growth in Europe and Japan increased the U.S. export markets and strengthened the West against communism's possible popular appeal.

The End of Bretton Woods

Although this system worked well initially, it grew overly burdensome. By the 1960s, it had become apparent that the system would ultimately be unsustainable. As use of the dollar—as well as the amount of dollars in circulation—continued to expand, the resulting U.S. balance-of-payments deficit became increasingly problematic. Unlike other countries, the United States was not able to adjust the value of its currency because it was pegged to gold. Although strict adherence to a fixed exchange regime supposedly limits the policy autonomy of a state—as noted in Table 10.2—the United States nonetheless began to pursue expansionary macroeconomic policies during the 1960s to finance policies such as the Vietnam War and increased social spending. Such spending further exacerbated the balance-of-payments deficit. By 1970, the total amount of foreign claims for dollars, $47 billion, was over four times the value of gold holdings in the United States (Oatley, 2012, p. 217). This gap between the amount of dollars in circulation and the amount of dollars actually supported by gold holdings was known as *dollar overhang*. Simply put, although the dollar was officially "as good as gold," the monetary reality was far different.

dollar overhang

The condition that precipitated the end of the Bretton Woods era, in which total holdings of dollars outside of the U.S. central bank exceeded the amount of dollars actually backed by gold.

This left the Bretton Woods system in a tenuous position, and the United States with few options. Tight monetary policies on behalf of the United States would have reduced the balance-of-payments deficit. However, given the scope of the deficit, such cuts would have dealt a major shock to the U.S. economy. Such policies would have international ramifications as well since reducing the supply of dollars would damage countries that relied on the dollar for liquidity purposes. Another potential option, currency devaluation, could conceivably have reduced the balance-of-payments problem. This option was also problematic, as its effect could be undone if other states likewise devalued their currencies (so as not to give the United States any advantage in selling goods on the world marketplace). Although some of the other major economies were willing to intervene to support the dollar, there were limits to what these countries would do, and it was widely known that the status quo was not sustainable.

The architecture of the international finance system must be reformed to reduce the susceptibility to crises. The ultimate key is not economics or finance, but politics—the art of developing support for strong policy.

—**Robert Rubin, former U.S. secretary of the treasury**

Floating Exchange Rates and Financial Crises

floating exchange rates

An unmanaged process in which governments neither establish an official rate for their currencies nor intervene to affect the value of their currencies and instead allow market forces and private investors to influence the relative rate of exchange for currencies between countries.

In 1971, U.S. President Richard Nixon cut this Gordian knot by abruptly announcing—without consulting allies—that the United States would no longer exchange dollars for gold. With the price of gold no longer fixed and dollar convertibility no longer guaranteed, the Bretton Woods system gave way to a system based on *floating exchange rates*. Market forces, rather than government intervention, now determined currency values. A country experiencing adverse economic conditions now sees the value of its currency fall in response to the choices of traders, bankers, and businesspeople. This was expected to make exports cheaper and imports more expensive, which in turn would pull the currency's value back toward equilibrium—all without the need for central bankers to support the value of its currency.

Although flexible exchange rates give governments the autonomy to conduct their own fiscal and monetary policies, these same market forces hold governments accountable for their policies and actions. Exposure to the market thus exerts a "disciplinary effect on the conduct of policies, because international capital flows adversely respond to imprudent macroeconomic policies" (IMF, 2005). As a result, states should be forced to closely monitor their fiscal and monetary policies to avoid balance-of-payments deficits and inflation.

Those expectations were not met. Beginning in the late 1970s, escalating through the 1980s, and persisting to the present, a wave of financial crises—both in currency and banking—occurred (see Map 10.2). In the Global South, the situation was particularly grim during the 1980s and 1990s. A massive debt crisis in Latin America, as well as unsustainable debt levels throughout the developing and transitioning economies, raised alarms throughout the global financial system.

Yet the debt picture within the developing world has improved markedly during the twenty-first century. Debt reduction programs such as the Heavily Indebted Poor Countries (HIPC) Initiative, which began in 1996 and targeted debt levels in 40 developing countries whose debt load was at least 280 percent of their GDP, as well as the Multilateral Debt Relief Initiative (MDRI), which provided debt forgiveness for developing countries, contributed to this improvement. Increased export performance, as well as higher prices for many of the commodities sold by these countries, similarly enhanced economic conditions. Overall, the external debt of the Global South decreased from 37.9 percent of GNI (Gross National Income) in 2000 to 22.1 percent in 2011 (World Bank, 2013j).

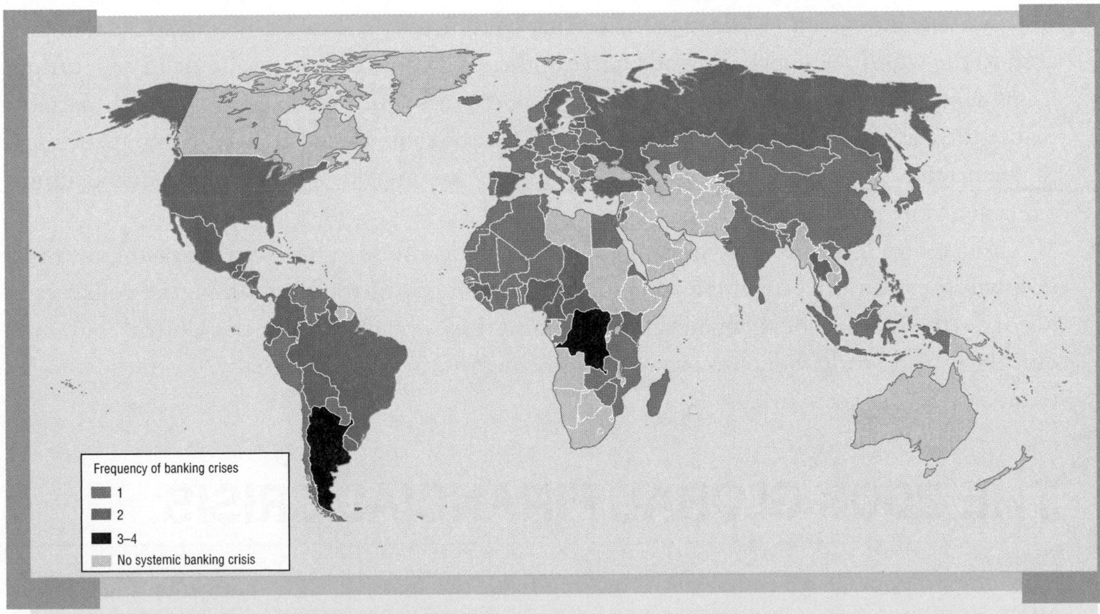

Adapted from International Monetary Fund Working Paper "Systemic Banking Crises Database: An Update" by Luc Laeven and FabiÁn Valencia

MAP 10.2 FINANCIAL CRISES SINCE BRETTON WOODS This map shows the global distribution and frequency of systemic banking crises, a type of financial crisis, marked by significant financial distress in the banking system such as bank runs and liquidations. In all, 147 banking crises occurred between 1970 and 2011. Most tend to have a regional focus and, until the 2008 global financial crisis, generally took place in the Global South.

Yet high debt levels have been endemic in many developed countries since the turn of the century, due in no small part to the 2008 global financial crisis. In the G-7 countries in the Global North, external debt is 126 percent of GNI, almost six times the level for countries in the Global South (World Bank, 2013j). Greece, for example, has perennially dealt with debt issues, and controversy still surrounds the tight fiscal policies that the country is forced to enact to reduce its debt. Indeed, since 2009, Greece has cut its total government spending by over 32 percent (Trading Economics, 2013). These cuts have translated into massive layoffs of government employees, decreased spending on social services—including a 40 percent reduction in public health expenditures (Stuckler and Basu, 2013)—increased taxes, and higher ages for retirement. So far, although it has cut its debt from 170 percent of its GDP to 157 percent, further drastic measures are still necessary to get this debt under control (Eurostat, 2013; see "A Closer Look: The Greek Financial Crisis"). In addition to generating controversy, such measures have shrunk the Greek economy and increased unemployment, which stood around 27 percent in 2013 (Trading Economics, 2013).

Even the most powerful countries are vulnerable. The United States may be the reigning hegemon with the globe's largest economy, but it borrows more than 46 cents of every dollar that it spends (Dinan, 2013). By March of 2013, the United States' total debt to foreign investors stood at around $16 trillion, which is 107 percent of the total U.S. GDP (U.S. Department of Treasury, 2013). By way of comparison, although the United States has the largest foreign debt in the world, its debt as a percentage of GDP is the 35th largest in the world, behind Japan and many Western European countries (CIA, 2013).

Given the large volumes of debt, as well as the rapidity with which currencies flow across borders, conditions have been ripe for financial crises, whether due to poor government practices (such as taking on too much debt) or the massive "boom and bust" patterns of global investment and currency markets. In all, since the demise of the Bretton Woods monetary system, there have been 147 financial crises that have directly affected as many as 120 countries around the world. Moreover, the total losses in these crises have been great. Since 1970, output losses of each crisis—that is, the deviation of post-crisis GDP growth from growth patterns before the crises—averaged 23 percent of GDP (Laeven and Valencia, 2012). To put such loss in perspective, in the absence of a financial crisis, these countries would have produced almost a quarter more goods and services.

To better understand the dynamics and far-reaching effects of financial crises, the next section will focus on the causes, effects, and aftermath of one of the largest financial collapses in history—the 2008 Global Financial Crisis. This crisis, which began in the United States and quickly spread worldwide, has produced subsequent crises in more than 20 other countries (Laeven and Valancia, 2012).

THE 2008 GLOBAL FINANCIAL CRISIS

The global financial system is still recovering from the massive crisis that came to a head in 2008. Myriad economic and political factors caused this crash, and the particulars of the crisis, especially the investment instruments themselves, are incredibly complex. Indeed, former chair of the U.S. Federal Reserve Alan Greenspan noted that a key cause of the crisis was the inability

A Closer Look

THE GREEK FINANCIAL CRISIS

Since 2010, Athens has been rocked with protests and riots. Demonstrators have thrown furniture, rocks, and even yogurt at police, who have responded with the widespread use of tear gas and clubs to disperse the crowds. Such protests are a response to the passage of austerity measures, including massive cutbacks in health and education spending, layoffs of public employees, the privatization of state-run industries, and tax increases on such items as heating oil (Donadio, 2011). The Greek economy is in a tailspin—the official unemployment rate is 26.8 percent overall and over 62.5 percent for workers under age 25. As one protester put it, "I'm here because I don't have hope .... I have two kids in university. What is their future?" (Donadio and Sayare, 2011).

The Greek government has passed painful measures in order to avoid defaulting on Greece's foreign debt, which had risen to about $583.3 billion (17 percent of annual GDP) by the beginning of 2013. The crisis was initially set off in December 2009 when President Papandreou "revised" his estimate of the Greek budget deficit from 6.7 percent of GDP to 12.7 percent, which severely undercut confidence in his government. Yet the accumulation of this debt was driven by several longer-term factors, including heavy government spending, an inefficient and corrupt tax collection system, a largely uncompetitive industrial base, ready access to cheap credit, and lax enforcement of EU financial rules (Nelson, Belkin, and Mix, 2010). To avoid default (failure to repay debts), it is estimated that Greece will have to change its budget deficit to a budget surplus of 7.5 percent. This represents a huge—and arguably unattainable—turnaround (Manasse, 2011). Yet many argue that the country is "too big to fail" and that debt default will hurt markets throughout the EU as well as the rest of the world.

The role of private investment banks, such as Goldman Sachs, in this crisis has generated controversy. Recent reports indicate that over the past decade they have helped Greece hide portions of its debt from public view through a complex array of derivatives and side deals, such as paying Greece to trade away future rights to long-term government revenues such as airport fees and lottery proceeds. Indeed, Greece's "original sin" regarding its entry into the euro zone was to hide debt through these methods in order to meet entrance requirements (Story, Thomas, and Schwartz, 2010). Yet such measures are legal, as there are no regulations that govern how a country handles is sovereign debt. As one IMF analyst noted, "if a government wants to cheat, it can cheat" (Story et al., 2010).

WATCH THE VIDEO:

Carnegie Council Video:
Greece, Goldman, and
Financial Transparency?

YOU DECIDE:

1. What policies should the Greek government enact?
2. What role do international institutions play in preventing, or facilitating recovery from, financial crises?
3. What does this situation reveal about the global financial system?

of the world's "most sophisticated investors" and regulators—the people who actually created and worked with these instruments—to understand them (Comisky and Madhogarhia, 2009).

Yet the broad dynamics of the crisis are hardly unprecedented, as they resemble the basic cycle described in Kindleberger's sweeping history of financial crises (Kindleberger, Aliber, and Solow, 2005). The first phase of a crisis cycle is "displacement," which refers to a change in the system that alters profit opportunities and creates new opportunities for financial gain. There were several developments that brought increased attention to the mortgage and securities markets during the beginning of the century, including massive cash holdings by states such as China and the OPEC members, the real estate boom in the United States, extremely low interest rates in the United States, and new investment instruments that banks and investment firms had created for themselves. These factors were inextricably linked—the initial dilemma that led to this crisis was how to put to use the "giant pool of money" (Glass and Davidson, 2008) held by China, the OPEC states, and other investors.

U.S. interest rates were extremely low, which meant that investing in dollars—traditionally considered the safest move for investors with large amounts of money—was not sufficiently profitable (U.S. Treasury bills at the time were only yielding 1 percent). At the same time, the low interest rates also meant that mortgages were less expensive for U.S. homeowners and that businesses had access to very inexpensive loans that could be leveraged for investment purchases. As housing prices were increasing, buying new or larger homes (financed by mortgages) was a good investment. Sensing opportunity, banks created instruments to link the "pool" of money to the housing market, by selling securities based off of the value of these mortgages to large investors. As a result, the investors made a higher rate of return from the mortgages, homeowners reaped the benefits of lower interest rates, and banks made billions of dollars as intermediaries.

The second phase of the crisis—the so-called "boom" period in which money pours into these new opportunities—thus began. As the investors and bankers continued to reap profits, the "pool of money" became ever larger, and trillions of dollars continued to flow into this market. To further service the "pool," banks began to invent more investment instruments (essentially different ways to "bundle" these mortgages and securities together), and huge derivative markets based on the performance of these instruments began to emerge.

This led to the "overtrading" stage, which involves "pure speculation for a price rise, an overestimate of prospective returns," and excessive leveraging or "gearing," where additional debt is taken on purely for the purposes of making investments (Kindleberger, 2000). At some point in this process, the market for traditional mortgages became saturated; basically everyone who was willing and able to purchase and/or refinance a home had already done so. Yet the "pool" continued to grow, and demand for these securities continued to increase.

To keep the market going, banks began to sell mortgages to "subprime" buyers who would have never qualified for mortgages under normal circumstances. Lending regulations were loosened so that prospective borrowers no longer had to provide proof of their ability to actually pay off their mortgages. Now, rather than having to show actual proof of income, such as paycheck stubs or bank statements, borrowers were only asked to provide estimates of their financial holdings and future earnings (these were disparagingly known as "liar's loans"). The rationalization for doing this was that even if some loans were not repaid, there would still be a sufficient flow of capital to keep the overall securities serviced. Even if the loans defaulted, the banks would get the real estate, which was considered at the time to be an ever-appreciating asset.

For their part, investment banks continued to use a mind-boggling array of speculative instruments based off the mortgage securities, including derivatives linked to the performance of mortgage-backed securities, as well as so-called "synthetic" securities, which were essentially repackaged derivatives based off the derivatives based on the securities themselves. The market for collateralized debt obligations (CDOs), which functioned as de facto insurance for the mortgage-backed securities and the various derivatives, boomed. Given the panoply of instruments, and their cross purposes, for many investment banks it was a "no lose" situation—they made fees for processing all of these investment flows, and even if the securities crashed, they could still recoup their losses via the CDOs. Investment banks further maximized their profits, as well as their exposure, through excessive use of leveraging to obtain additional investments. By 2007, the five largest investment banks (Bear Stearns, Goldman Sachs, Lehman Brothers, Merrill Lynch, and Morgan Stanley) were leveraged at an average of over 30 to 1, meaning that they owned assets, purchased through taking out loans, worth over 30 times the total equity of their firms (Government Accounting Office, 2009).

However, in 2007 and 2008, the "revulsion" or "panic" stage set in due to several directly related factors: increasing loan defaults by homeowners, plummeting real estate values, and severe liquidity problems of banks that were too entangled in this process. As homeowners failed to repay the mortgages, banks quickly found themselves without a stream of income from mortgage holders and holding properties of declining value that they were unable to sell. For their part, the highly-leveraged investment banks found themselves facing debt loads over 30 times greater than their own net worth. As the mortgage market began to fall, the speculative markets and instruments built around it—whose total cash value was many times more than the value of the mortgages themselves—also collapsed. As a result, banks and investors literally ran out of money, and the credit market in the United States, and much of the world, collapsed.

Though financial crises are not new to the global financial system, the 2008 global financial crisis has had a particularly profound and broad-reaching impact. First, the sheer amount of money involved is staggering—according to some estimates, the U.S. government alone devoted $13 trillion to help bailout its own financial sector, including direct financial assistance to the banks as well as selling bonds to help increase the supply of money (French, 2009). The crisis drove global FDI and trade to unprecedented declines in 2009—FDI outflows fell approximately 42 percent, and world trade slipped over 12 percent. In all, total global output, as measured by GDP, contracted by 2.3 percent in 2009—the worst worldwide decrease since World War II (IMF Survey, 2009; WTO, 2010b). Global markets are still recovering from this crisis, as none of these indices have returned to 2007 levels. For example, UNCTAD estimates that FDI levels will not return to 2007 levels until after 2015 (UNCTAD, 2013).

Second, this crisis originated in the United States, and "much of the world … blames U.S. financial excesses for the global recession" (Altman, 2009, p. 2). Given the leading role of the United States in maintaining the liberal financial order, the crisis has brought into question the ability of the United States to lead. Although some argue that the United States will eventually reemerge as "locomotives for global economic growth" (Altman 2013: 8), others predict a U.S. decline in the wake of the crisis (Keohane, 2012).

The 2008 global financial crisis also raised questions about the role of the dollar as the leading currency in the global financial system. According to the IMF, at the end of 2012, 62 percent of all foreign exchange reserves (money that states hold to help them maintain their balance of payments) were in dollars. Seventeen countries use the dollar as their currency, and another 49 anchor or "peg" the value of their currency to the dollar in some way (IMF, 2012b; 2013b). While the value of the dollar on the world market has rebounded since the beginning of the crisis, some of the leading economies in the world—most notably China—have suggested that the dollar be replaced as the major currency of the global marketplace.

Nonetheless, the dollar still holds the "exorbitant privilege" (Eichengreen, 2011a) of being the global currency of choice, and its status is largely unthreatened (Stokes 2013). Potential competitors are not without their own problems. Special drawing rights (SDRs), the composite "currency" used by the IMF for its reserve, would be impractical for individual countries to use (Bosco 2011). The euro is still struggling as several of its members, including Greece, Italy, Portugal, and Spain, deal with their own financial problems. For its part, the Chinese currency markets are largely closed to foreign investors, even as some reforms are taking place (*The Economist*, 2011i; Pei, 2013). Yet even talk of using these alternatives implies an underlying lack of confidence in the U.S. economy and its leadership.

On a broader scale, the crisis has raised doubts about the ideological underpinnings of the global financial system: the free-market–oriented "Washington Consensus." Although the free exchanges of currencies and the free movement of capital are viewed as foundational to liberal economics, the financial crisis has served to undercut basic belief regarding the efficacy of the marketplace. Among the larger economies of the world, the ones that fared the best in the crisis were India and China, arguably the two major countries most insulated from the global financial order. Interestingly enough, Moldova, a very small country with a "cash-only system" (Tayler, 2009) of finance—banks and credit cards are largely nonexistent and savings are generally stored under mattresses or in drawers—was ranked by a leading financial journal as the fifth most stable economy in the world in 2009. As Roger Altman, a former U.S. Treasury Department official and a leading adviser to President Clinton, remarked, "the long movement towards market liberalization has stopped," and "globalization itself is reversing. The long-standing wisdom that everyone wins in a single world market has been undermined" (2009, p. 2).

Some analysts go so far as to argue that a "Beijing Consensus," in which the state plays a much heavier role in the marketplace, may be seen as a possible alternative to the commercial liberalism of the Washington Consensus (Halper, 2010). Along those lines, state responses to the 2008 global financial crisis raised broader issues regarding the role of government in managing their economies. Some countries, such as the United Kingdom and Spain, instituted austerity measures—"tight" fiscal policies such as cutting public spending—in order to reduce excessive debt levels and thus prevent inflation. Others, such as the United States, focused more on stimulus spending to prompt economic recovery. Both policy pathways created political controversy, such as the widespread protests in the United Kingdom in response to the government cutting jobs and housing subsidies (Kilkenny 2013), the Tea Party groups in the United States that spoke out against government spending, and the Occupy Wall Street movement that protested the inadequate efforts of the U.S. government to make the economic system more equitable.

In addition to exemplifying the trade-off associated with the proper balance of fiscal and monetary tools, in this case the "inflation versus unemployment" trade-off, the use of austerity or spending policies raised broader issues about the proper role of the state in the global economy. To some, austerity policies represented an abdication of the embedded liberalism policies upon which the Bretton Woods order was founded (Bugaric, 2013). Moreover, these policies brought into focus the challenges that a state faces in trying to navigate its public interest in a largely free market that—left to its own devices—may increase economic inequality and, thus, damage the cohesion of societies (Muller, 2013). States, thus, find themselves in a double bind as they balance the somewhat contradictory needs to "unleash creative capitalism and … intervene directly to make certain markets work optimally" (Breznitz and Zysman, 2013, p. 1) to attain broader societal goals.

To many, the crisis has revealed strengths in the theoretical perspectives critical of commercial liberalism. Marxists have long noted the inherent instability of capitalism, its susceptibility to speculative panics, and the need for strong state intervention in the financial system. Along these lines, the 2008 global financial crisis revealed deep structural flaws in the capitalist order, particularly the tendency to overinvest, which creates an inherently unstable system (Kotz, 2013). Further questioning the effectiveness of liberal economics, Cuban President Raul Castro, forcefully argued that it has "failed as an economic policy" and that "any objective analysis raises serious questions about the myth of the goodness of the market and its deregulation … and the credibility of the financial institutions." As one analyst concludes, global capitalism is "in an ideological tailspin," and the crisis "has spawned a resurgence of interest in Karl Marx" (Panitch, 2009, p. 140).

For their part, feminist scholars note that males are both primarily responsible for the crisis and suffering the most from its effects. This sector of the economy was largely driven by males (Griffin 2013), and traditionally "male" traits—risk taking, aggression, and hypercompetitiveness—were driving factors behind the speculative surges that helped to create the financial crisis. Many have critically pointed to "a testosterone-filled trading culture" (Scherer, 2010) and wondered if "the presence of more women on Wall Street might have averted the downturn" (Kay and Shipman, 2009).

Just as the crisis was driven by male dominance, the current financial crisis will have a disproportionate impact upon males. In the United States, for example, over 80 percent

WOMEN AND GLOBAL FINANCE Only 4 percent of Fortune 500 companies have a woman as CEO, and all of the large banks—from Citigroup to Goldman Sachs—employ just a few women in senior positions. Within the U.S. finance and insurance industries, women comprise only 14 percent of executive officers and board directors (Goudreau, 2013). Pictured left is Margaret Whitman, chief executive officer of Hewlett-Packard, who was ranked in June 2013 as the most powerful woman CEO of a Fortune 500 company. Pictured right is Christine Lagarde, a former French minister of finance, who is the first woman to serve as managing director of the IMF.

of the job losses since November 2008 fell upon men, as traditionally male sectors (for example, construction and manufacturing) were the hardest hit. Indeed, some have termed the current crisis a "he-cession." As one scholar concludes, the financial crisis "will be not only a blow to the macho men's club called finance capitalism that got the world into the current economic catastrophe; it will be a collective crisis for millions and millions of working men around the globe" (Salam, 2009, p. 66).

There may also be geopolitical ramifications. To the extent that the crisis weakens the economic and ideological power of the United States and its Western allies, the United States is less able to assert itself in international negotiations. The crisis has also served to improve the relative global position of China, whose share of world markets increased during the global recession to almost 10 percent in 2010 and an anticipated 12 percent by 2014, making it the world's largest exporter. The economic crisis and U.S. recession drastically increased China's prominence as the largest holder of U.S. debt securities, as its share of the total U.S. debt increased almost 50 percent from 2008—as of March 2013 China held more than $1.2 trillion in U.S. debt (U.S. Department of Treasury, 2013b).

The crisis may contribute to a more multipolar financial order, as Europe continues to struggle while the Global South weathered the financial crisis better than expected. Despite the steep fiscal crises faced by the United Kingdom, Portugal, Ireland, Spain, and particularly Greece (see "A Closer Look: The Greek Financial Crisis"), the German economy has become increasingly competitive on the world stage. As for the Global South, its stock markets quickly rebounded from the crisis, private capital flows quickly resumed, and debt levels remained substantially lower than those of many countries in the Global North.

WHITHER THE INTERNATIONAL FINANCIAL ARCHITECTURE?

Financial crises have traditionally been followed by a multitude of suggestions for reform. For example, "after the East Asian crisis, such debates filled library shelves with myriad proposals for a new global financial architecture" (Pauly, 2005, p. 199). In dealing with the 2008 global financial crisis, efforts were made to improve the rather informal system of financial cooperation between states.

In particular, whereas such matters were traditionally discussed among the seven or eight largest economies (the so-called "G-7" or "G-8"), a much larger group consisting of the 20 largest economies (the "G-20") met to discuss ways to deal with the financial crisis. The rationale behind the larger group was that the larger emerging economies of the world, such as Argentina, Brazil, Indonesia, and Saudi Arabia, should have input into forging a common response to the crisis.

For the great difference between an ordinary casino where you can go into or stay away from, and the global casino of high finance, is that in the latter all of us are involuntarily engaged in the days' play.

—Susan Strange, economist and international relations scholar

What these and other proposals seek is a mechanism for creating the currency stability and flexibility on which prosperity depends. However, there is little agreement about how to bring about reforms. With the spread of democracy throughout the globe, most governments now face increasing domestic pressures to sacrifice such goals as exchange rate stability for unemployment reduction. So it seems likely that realizing a new financial system will remain elusive.

The mixed results of the G-20 summits in the aftermath of the crisis illustrate the difficulty in bringing about any fundamental change. Despite their common interest in recovering from the current crisis and averting future crises, the members have not been able to agree on a common set of policies to help their own economies recover and did not want to establish a supranational regulatory body to deal with global financial exchanges. Rather, the primary focus was on narrower policy issues. The 2009 meetings focused on how individual countries should approach debt reduction. Whereas some members, such as the United States, favored continued fiscal stimulus and expressed concern that pushing austerity measures too far might undermine economic recovery, others focused on the debt crises in Europe and pressed for reducing government spending and cutting national deficits in half by 2013. Thus far, the G-20 has continued along this "micro" route, focusing more on individual issues, such as tax evasion (Jolly, 2013), and providing a forum for discussing more contentious policy issues, such China's exchange rate regime (Clover et al., 2013).

Overall, while it has been useful as a common forum for the major economies, the G-20 has stopped short of providing any common institutions or financial architecture. Moreover, its recommendations sometimes run afoul of the policies of the IMF—for example, the G-20 has been supportive in its recommendations for the use of capital controls in the Global South, a policy tool that has traditionally been met with skepticism by the IMF (Gallagher, 2011).

For its part, the IMF is aware of the widespread criticism of its policies (see "Controversy: The IMF, World Bank, and Structural Adjustment Policies") and has undertaken some reform to help strengthen and legitimize its role in the global financial system. It has sought to give individual countries more flexibility by loosening up the conditionality requirements to better take into account the specific needs of each recipient (IMF, 2009). It has also been very forthright in admitting its failure to foresee the 2008 global financial crisis and is trying to develop a more effective "early warning system" for financial crises (Beattie, 2011; IMF, 2011). The IMF is also working on reforming its voting system, with the goal being to give China and India more influence within the organization as their financial contribution to the IMF continues to increase (Wroughton, 2013). These reforms would go a long way toward countering the criticism that the United States and Europe largely run the organization (Mallaby, 2011).

Although most analysts view these changes with optimism (Stiglitz, 2011), there is still much to do. The IMF is still unable to deal with many of the key issues underlying the global financial system, such as the presence of massive balance-of-payments imbalances among many of the world's economies—although it should be noted that some countries, most notably China, maintain huge surpluses. Many feel that such a situation encourages instability in investment flows (Eichengreen, 2011b). Additionally, there is only piecemeal regulation of investment banks, allowing ample room for abuse.

Thus, though some reforms are being enacted, much work remains. Using a baseball metaphor to describe the progress of the IMF and G-20, President Obama noted that "Instead of hitting home runs, we're hitting singles" (Kirk, 2010b). We are, thus, left with a troubling situation: global investment flows continue to proliferate, and there is every reason to expect that the currency dilemmas facing the world will continue to intensify. Yet a fundamental reform of the present international financial system remains unlikely in the near future.

Given the difficulties in putting together such a structure, and the lack of confidence that many countries still have in international financial institutions, some argue that regional solutions to financial issues may be a better alternative (Desai and Vreeland, 2011). Indeed, the EU "solved" the problems of erratic exchange rate fluctuations in 2002 by creating a *regional currency union* centered around its common currency, with the hope that a single currency would make the EU a single market for business, and that the euro would promote economic growth, cross-border investment, corporate innovation and efficiency, and political integration.

To some extent the euro has been successful. It has quickly become the second most popular *reserve currency* in existence, accounting for just under 24 percent of the world's total currency reserves (IMF, 2013b). However, it may not serve as a suitable model for other countries and regions. The EU's common currency represents much more than an economic policy; it is the end result of a decades-long process of economic integration. The euro remains

regional currency union

The pooling of sovereignty to create a common currency (such as the EU's euro) and single monetary system for members in a region, regulated by a regional central bank within the currency bloc.

reserve currency

Currency held in large amounts by governments for the purpose of setting international debts and supporting the value of their national currency.

Muchtar Zakaria/AP Photo

SURRENDERING TO THE IMF? A controversy surrounding multilateral institutions, such as the IMF, is that their policies are seen as another way in which powerful states of the Global North seek domination over those in the Global South. In this picture, taken on January 15, 1998, Indonesian President Suharto signs an agreement for a $43 billion assistance and reform package, while IMF Managing Director Michel Camdessus looks on. This picture proved damaging for both Suharto and the IMF. Indonesians, who place a great value on symbolism and body language, viewed the picture as a humiliating loss of face for the president, who was forced out of office four months later. It was also an economic and public relations disaster for the IMF, helping to solidify negative opinions of the IMF within the developing world (Camdessus later apologized for his arm-crossing and his stance).

controversial even in Europe, especially among important EU states (Britain, Denmark, and Sweden, among others, so far have rejected it). To critics it is also an overly ambitious *political* change designed to create a European superstate and thereby erase the economic and political sovereignty of European states. Moreover, some EU states have struggled with the euro in the wake of the global financial crisis. For example, along the lines of the "trade-offs" noted earlier, in adopting the euro, Greece sacrificed policy autonomy for currency stability. In dealing with their financial problems, Greek officials are unable to increase their money supply and are faced with drastic austerity measures to resolve their balance-of-payments problems. Yet if Greece chose "autonomy" by taking a "euro zone holiday" (Feldstein, 2010), its currency would be very unstable and would most likely collapse.

Though the euro may not be a solution for all, there has been some movement toward regionalized monetary funds, which could function as a "lender of last resort" that could be "better placed to coordinate economic actions" (Desai and Vreeland, 2011, p. 114) given their proximity to the country in need of relief. Along those lines, it may be the case that a regional body could be better suited to help troubled countries maintain their credit ratings, as they are better situated to use informal pressure, rather than strict conditionality measures, to encourage countries to service their debts. Within the developing world, such organizations could also help to foster a regional identity—unlike the IMF and World Bank, they would not be perceived as being driven by a few developed countries. Efforts have been made toward developing regional funds in East Asia, Latin America, Africa, and the Middle East. Ideally, these organizations could serve to supplement the IMF and World Bank to provide some stability to the global financial order.

Though such organizations may prove useful in helping countries to respond to financial crises, many of the factors underlying the instability of the global financial system—the lack of a common set of financial practices and regulations, the rapid and "manic" nature of the global capital and arbitrage markets, and the policy "trade-offs" involving fiscal and monetary policies—remain.

This means that the debate over currency and monetary policies will remain as intense as ever. Further adding to this turbulence is the related, and contentious, arena of international trade. It is that twin dimension of economic globalization that we will consider next in Chapter 11.

STUDY. APPLY. ANALYZE.

Key Terms

arbitrage
dollar overhang
embedded liberalism
exchange rate
fixed exchange rates

floating exchange rates
geo-economics
globalization
globalization of
finance

gross domestic product
(GDP)
international liquidity
international monetary
system

Liberal International
Economic Order
(LIEO)
monetary policy
money supply

regional currency
union
reserve currency
speculative attacks

Suggested Readings

Chinn, Menzie and Jeffry Freiden. (2011) *Lost Decades: The Making of America's Debt Crisis and the Long Recovery.* New York: W.W. Norton and Company, Inc.

Dowell Jones, Mary, and David Kinley. (2011) "Minding the Gap: Global Finance and Human Rights," *Ethics & International Affairs* 25, no. 2 (Summer):183–210.

Eichengreen, Barry. (2011) *Exorbitant Privilege: The Rise and Fall of the Dollar and the Future of the International*

Monetary System. New York: Oxford University Press.

Erturk, Korkut. (2009) "Decouple the World from the Dollar," Carnegie Council, http://www.carnegiecouncil.org/publications/articles_papers_reports/0070.html.

Lewis, Michael. (2011) *The Big Short: Inside the Doomsday Machine.* New York: W.W. Norton.

Oatley, Thomas. (2012) *International Political Economy*, 5th edition. New York: Pearson.

Raffer, Kunibert. (2004) "Internationa: Financial Institutions and Financial Accountability," *Ethics & Internationa: Affairs* 18, no. 2 (Summer):61–77.

Reinhart, Carmen M. and Kenneth S Rogoff. (2009) *This Time Is Different Eight Centuries of Financial Folly.* Princeton, NJ: Princeton University Press.

World Bank. (2013) *Capital for the Future: Saving and Investment in an Interdependent World.* Washington, DC: World Bank.

Suggested Videos

CourseMate

Carnegie Council Video

Cassidy, John. "How Markets Fail: The Logic of Economic Calamities."

Devin Stewart Interviews Ian Bremmer. "The End of the Free Market."

Donaldson, Thomas, Neal Flieger, Stephen Jordan, Seamus McMahon, and Christian Menegatti.

"Restoring Trust in the Global Financial System."

Farmer, Roger E. A. "How the Economy Works: Confidence, Crashes and Self-Fulfilling Prophecies."

Sormon, Guy. "Economics Does Not Lie: A Defense of the Free Market in a Time of Crisis."

Stiglitz, Joseph E., Bert Koenders, and Jose Antonio Ocampo. "Reform of the International Monetary and Financial System."

Vocke, William. "The Power of Economic Models."

CourseMate

Log in to CourseMate to access the following study tools for this chapter:

- Interactive Quiz
- eBook
- Flashcards & Key Term Crossword Puzzle
- Chapter Audio Summary
- Carnegie Council Videos

- Video Activities
- Simulation
- Animated Learning Module
- Case Study
- International Relations NewsWatch

"Globalization has changed us into a company that searches the world, not just to sell or to source, but to find intellectual capital—the world's best talents and greatest ideas."

—*Jack Welch, former CEO of General Electric*

CHAPTER 11
International Trade in the Global Marketplace

GLOBALIZATION AND CARBONATION
Multinational corporations are major players in the globalization of the world economy. Coca-Cola—one of the most recognizable brands in the world—illustrates this, as the global reach of its product is massive. According to company reports, over 1.7 billion servings of Coca-Cola are consumed daily. Shown here are some of its products in China, which is one of its most important growth markets and accounted for 7 percent of its global volume in 2011. Coca-Cola has been active there for over 80 years, has plans to invest more than $4 billion in China by 2014, and employs 50,000 local Chinese workers in 42 plants located in China (Xinhuanet, 2013).

QUESTIONS TO CONSIDER
- *What are the causes and consequences of the globalization of trade?*
- *What are the characteristics of the two major contending trade strategies?*
- *How can economic policy be used as a tool of foreign policy?*
- *How can states circumvent commercial liberalism? What are the consequences?*
- *Will confidence in free trade and the progression of the liberal trade order prevail?*

As you struggle to make payments on your college tuition, your father calls with some bad news: his employer has decided to move its production to India in order to save money by hiring lower-paid foreign workers where there are no trade unions. Now your father faces unemployment. The downside of globalized international trade has been brought home, and the quality of your life is declining. Or so it would appear as you contemplate your future clad in Levi jeans no longer produced in the United States and Calvin Klein shirts made in China. Trying to find meaning in the whirlwind of international trade going on around you, you race off to your international economics course, where you hope you can derive some insight. And you are in luck. Your professor's lesson today: "The Impact of International Trade on Global and National Circumstances." She introduces her topic by telling you that trade across national borders is the biggest part of the globalization of world politics. She begins by quoting former World Bank president Paul Wolfowitz: "I like globalization; I want to say it works, but it's hard to say that when 600,000,000 people are slipping backwards."

You learn that scholars also hold competing views about the consequences of the globalization of international trade. To construct an objective evaluation of these rival interpretations, consider leading ideas about various trade policies, which are rooted in past thinking. In this chapter, you will focus on the contest between liberalism and mercantilism, two dominant sets of values that underlie the different trade strategies states pursue in their quest for power and wealth. However, the best place to start is by identifying emerging trends in the globalization of international trade.

> *We must ensure that the global market is embedded in broadly shared values and practices that reflect global social needs, and that all the world's people share the benefits of globalization.*
>
> **—Kofi Annan, former secretary-general of the United Nations**

GLOBALIZATION AND TRADE

Evidence of global trade is as close to you as the clothes you wear and the coffee you drink. Yet how can we gauge the true extent to which commerce has become more global? Is the increase in international trade really significant, or is it just an artifact of the increased amount of total goods—both foreign and domestic—now available to us? Fortunately, there is a relatively straightforward index that provides insights into the degree of *trade integration* in the world economy. The commonly used measure of trade integration is simply the extent to which the growth rate in world trade increases faster than the growth rate of world gross domestic product (GDP). As trade integration grows, so does globalization, because states' interdependence increases as their exports account for an increasing percentage of their GDP (the value of the goods and services produced within a given country).

trade integration

The difference between growth rates in trade and gross domestic product (GDP).

The index of trade integration reveals that international trade has become increasingly global over the past decades. For example, since World War II, the world economy (as measured by GDP) has expanded by a factor of six while global trade has increased twenty times and, in 2011, world exports amounted to almost $18 trillion (Samuelson, 2006; 2012). As shown in

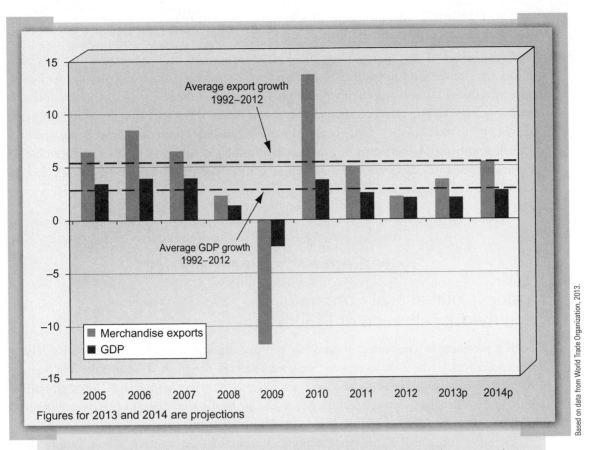

FIGURE 11.1   THE GROWTH OF GLOBAL TRADE INTEGRATION 2005–2014 When the annual percentage change in the volume of world trade grows faster than the annual growth rate of the combined world economy, "trade integration" increases. As shown in this figure, world trade generally grows faster than GDP. However, in 2009 world trade declined dramatically by 12.2 percent, a casualty of the 2008 global financial crisis. The 2010 rebound was just as dramatic, with a 13.8 percent surge in export volume. Yet growth slowed to 2 percent in 2012, with expectations of only 3.3 percent growth in 2013 (WTO, 2013a).

Figure 11.1, these trends persist, as the growth in world trade consistently exceeds the growth of global GDP. Although the general trend is toward greater integration, countries differ in the degree to which their economies participate in global commerce. Global trade integration has become most rapid as a result of the increasing participation of the Global South in world trade, which, in turn, fuels economic growth in the Global North. The Global South's share of global exports in manufactured products has grown from 10 percent in 1980 to 33.4 percent in 2011 (WDI, 2013), fueled predominantly by Asia's growth in the share of new export products.

Trade in services (intangible products such as tourism and banking financial assistance) and telecommunications is increasing as well. Such commercial ties have expanded more than threefold since 1980. However, the spread of information technology, the ease with which new business software can be used, and the comparatively lower wage costs in developing economies are among the many reasons why the World Bank predicts that developing countries will capture an increasing share of world trade in services. Countries with significant numbers of educated, English-speaking citizens, such as India, are already operating call centers and consumer assistance hotlines for Global North companies.

Trade is one of the most prevalent and visible aspects of the globalized world economy. However, globalization is a multifaceted phenomenon, encompassing a variety of often interrelated actions. There is a close relationship between trade and the global financial markets, as exchange rates set the values for traded goods, and capital flows are often necessary to finance these commercial activities. Trade is also inextricably linked to two other important aspects of globalization: the globalization of production and the globalization of labor. Understanding these components of globalization, as well as their relationship with trade, is important to understanding the complex world economy.

> *Global interdependence today means that economic disasters in developing countries could create a backlash on developed countries.*
>
> **—Atal Bihari Vajpayee, former prime minister of India**

Trade, Multinational Corporations, and the Globalization of Production

Selling products to consumers in another country often requires companies to establish a presence abroad, where they can produce goods and offer services. Traditionally, the overseas operations of *multinational corporations* (see Chapter 5) were "appendages" of a centralized hub. Today the pattern is more diffuse. Made feasible by the revolution in communication and transportation, production facilities are located around the world.

Consider the global nature of the production of Dell computers, whose supply chain involves eight countries outside of the United States (see Map 11.1). Every Dell computer that is sold is, in effect, generating trade between nine different countries. "As economist Richard Baldwin notes …, 'the formation of global production networks and supply chains has changed the center of gravity of the world economy'" (Baldwin et al., 2013, p. 3) Trade is no longer viewed as a bilateral interaction but as part of a broader, multi-country chain of production and commerce.

globalization of production

Transnationalization of the productive process, in which finished goods rely on inputs from multiple countries outside of their final market.

This *globalization of production* is transforming the *international political economy*. It once made sense to count trade in terms of flows between countries, and that practice continues because national account statistics are still gathered using states as the unit of analysis. But that picture increasingly fails to portray current realities. Countries do not really trade with each other; corporations do. Altogether MNCs are now responsible for about one-fourth of the world's production and two-thirds of global exports. Indeed, a substantial portion of current global trade is *intra-firm trade*, that is, commerce that takes place *between* an MNC's cross-border affiliates. For example, more than 40 percent of the total trade of the United States is of this nature (Lanz and Miroudot, 2011).

intra-firm trade

Cross-national trade of intermediate goods and services within the same firm.

MNCs are the primary agents in the globalization of production. By forming strategic corporate alliances with companies in the same industry and merging with one another, they often become massive NGOs that rival states in financial resources (see Table 6.1). As they facilitate large commercial flows across national borders, these global conglomerates are also integrating national economies into the worldwide market. In the process, the movement of investments

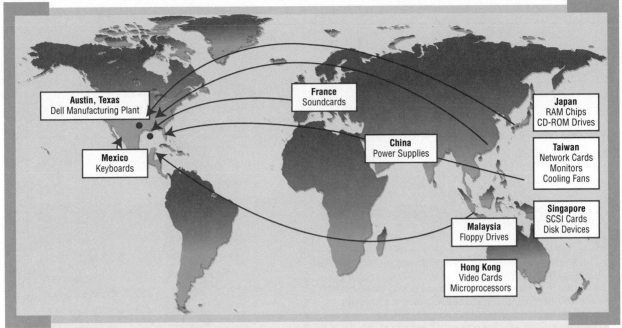

MAP 11.1   THE GLOBAL SUPPLY CHAIN The globalization of production means that it is often hard to discern exactly where a good is "from." This map shows the supply chain for the production of Dell computers. Supply chains such as this have a significant influence on the world economy, reflecting increasing levels of cross-border integration and the "networked" nature of interdependence. Thomas Friedman even goes so far as to offer a "Dell Theory" of conflict prevention, which posits that states that are part of common major supply chains are less likely to go to war.

across borders is facilitating a level of social homogeneity by causing "countries to adopt similar institutions and practices to organize economic life.... FDI is a conveyor of norms, technologies, and corporate practices" (Prakash and Potoski, 2007, p. 738). In short, FDI affects global identities as well as global trade.

Although the ultimate effects of FDI are controversial (see Chapter 5), many agree that the *globalization of production* will only increase. FDI flows throughout the world since 1970 increased one-hundred-fold by 2000 to $1.4 trillion, and peaked at over $1.9 trillion in 2007. FDI levels plummeted to $1.1 trillion in 2009 as a result of the global financial crisis of 2008, although they have since recovered to $1.65 trillion in 2011 (WDI, 2013). Due to the continuing turmoil in the global economy, FDI levels continued to fluctuate, dropping to $1.35 trillion by the end of 2012 (UNCTAD, 2013).

Within these broad trends, the rise of the Global South as a fully engaged participant in FDI stands out. Developing countries are increasingly the recipients of investments from abroad. Between 1995 and 2011, net inflows of FDI to developing countries increased almost fourfold, from $98 billion to over $648 billion. The Global South countries are also investing outside of their own borders. In 2011, net outflows of FDI from developing countries reached about 26.9 percent of total FDI outflows, after peaking in 2010 at 31.8 percent (Al-Sadig, 2013).

The recent financial crisis has heightened this pattern. Although the developed countries experienced a 25 percent drop in FDI inflows, investment into the Global South continued to

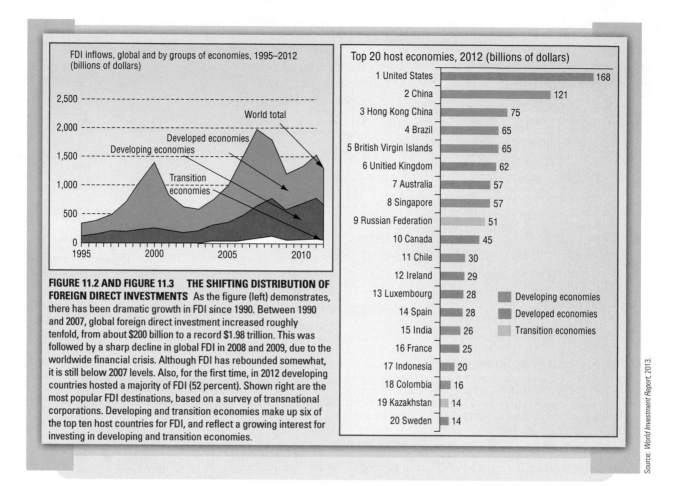

FDI inflows, global and by groups of economies, 1995–2012 (billions of dollars)

Top 20 host economies, 2012 (billions of dollars)

1 United States	168
2 China	121
3 Hong Kong China	75
4 Brazil	65
5 British Virgin Islands	65
6 Unitied Kingdom	62
7 Australia	57
8 Singapore	57
9 Russian Federation	51
10 Canada	45
11 Chile	30
12 Ireland	29
13 Luxembourg	28
14 Spain	28
15 India	26
16 France	25
17 Indonesia	20
18 Colombia	16
19 Kazakhstan	14
20 Sweden	14

Developing economies
Developed economies
Transition economies

FIGURE 11.2 AND FIGURE 11.3   THE SHIFTING DISTRIBUTION OF FOREIGN DIRECT INVESTMENTS As the figure (left) demonstrates, there has been dramatic growth in FDI since 1990. Between 1990 and 2007, global foreign direct investment increased roughly tenfold, from about $200 billion to a record $1.98 trillion. This was followed by a sharp decline in global FDI in 2008 and 2009, due to the worldwide financial crisis. Although FDI has rebounded somewhat, it is still below 2007 levels. Also, for the first time, in 2012 developing countries hosted a majority of FDI (52 percent). Shown right are the most popular FDI destinations, based on a survey of transnational corporations. Developing and transition economies make up six of the top ten host countries for FDI, and reflect a growing interest for investing in developing and transition economies.

Source: *World Investment Report, 2013.*

grow (WIPS, 2009). However, large differences exist among the companies investing overseas to expand their global financial presence and trade, as well as among the targets of FDI inflows (see Figures 11.2 and 11.3).

The Globalization of Labor

globalization of labor

Integration of labor markets, predicated by the global nature of production as well as the increased size and mobility of the global labor force.

Goods cannot be produced without labor. The globalization of production is thus inextricably linked to the *globalization of labor*. Labor is a particularly contentious aspect of globalization because it directly links individuals with the global economy, as illustrated by issues such as undocumented immigration (see Chapter 12), the use of child labor, and *outsourcing*.

The globalization of labor has emerged as a result of related changes in the world economy and global demographics. As evident from the growing volume of global FDI, an increasing amount of productive capital is mobile and can readily change locations according to the firm's desires as well as the perceived advantages of prospective host countries. Businesses are increasingly able to use labor from multiple countries and to switch locations when conditions change.

At the same time, there is mobility in the workforce as individuals move from one country to another. Although completely accurate estimates of migrant flows are virtually impossible to obtain, the UN estimates that around 215 million people work outside of their home

Carnegie Council Video: Globalization of Labor

countries. Moreover, the overall size of the global workforce has increased greatly over the past few decades. By 2011, the total size of the global labor force was 3.26 billion people, having increased more than fourfold since 1980. Much of this growth occurred in the BRICS countries as well as some Southeast Asian states (WDI, 2013). Comparing these two figures reveals that the mobility of labor, while substantial, is far less than the mobility of capital, as only a small portion of the overall labor pool actually relocates to another country.

Taken at face value, this does not bode well for global labor. In terms of supply and demand, the increased labor supply—in the absence of equal increases in demand—acts to depress the "price" of labor (wages). The ability of capital to seek out global sources of labor at a lower cost, termed "global sourcing" or more commonly outsourcing, has commonly occurred in many industrial sectors, particularly lower-skilled manufacturing ones where labor is more readily substitutable.

Yet outsourcing in higher-skill industry areas—from information technology to legal research— is also prominent. In Gurgaon, India, for example, lawyer Ritu Solanki earns $50 an hour working for a legal-outsourcing company to draft contracts and legal memos. By comparison, a London law firm would likely charge up to $400 an hour for the same type of work. Because of this, law firms and corporate legal departments are beginning to look to outsourcing as a way to cut costs. According to Indian estimates, legal-process outsourcing grew from $146 million in 2006 to $440 million in 2010, with expected growth to $1.1 billion in 2014 (*The Economist,* 2010n, p. 69).

In seeking a broader assessment of this issue, the basic question is the extent to which globalization undermines labor's bargaining power in seeking to obtain two main goals: living wages and worker rights. Though the simple logic of supply and demand—that increased labor supply serves to lower the "price" of labor—bodes poorly for wage levels, it oversimplifies the situation by treating labor as a relatively homogeneous and interchangeable good. Such a view ignores a key factor in business decisions—labor productivity. For example, it would not make sense for a corporation to move to a place where labor is 50 percent less expensive if the productivity of that labor was 75 percent less than the current labor force, as such a move would result in a net increase in operating expenses. Wages are thus not the only factor that determines where global capital will locate.

Bringing this to bear on outsourcing—which involves corporate use of gaps in wages across countries to maximize profitability—there is evidence that the practice is becoming less effective. In addition to differences in productivity across countries, some corporations are beginning to rediscover the advantages of producing goods close to where they are ultimately sold, as higher labor costs may be offset by several factors, such as lower inventory requirements, quicker customer service, and lower transport costs. As a result, the practice of *nearsourcing* is on the rise (Asbury, 2013).

Furthermore, there is evidence that the gap between labor costs across countries tends to lessen in the long run. As skill and education levels, and thus productivity, have increased in the Global South, countries that have traditionally been abundant sources of cheap labor have seen sharp increases in labor costs over the past few years. For example, since 2002 the wages of unskilled workers in China have increased 12 percent annually. In many of the industrial areas of China, the cost of labor will be equal to that of the United States by 2015 (LeBeau, 2013). To the extent that this connotes the expansion of a middle class in China (Ranasinghe, 2013), such trends offer support for the liberal economic perspective that global commerce—despite

nearsourcing

Locating production or services closer to where the goods or services are sold, in order to increase efficiency.

its disruptive effects in the short term—may lead to development and economic prosperity in the long run.

That said, empirical studies of this issue indicate that globalization is problematic for low-skilled labor, which is more readily interchangeable across countries. Yet even though some workers may face lower wages, globalization acts to increase the purchasing power of these workers. In concordance with liberal economic theory, global commerce enables consumers to purchase a greater selection of goods at lower prices than would be the case without globalization. Indeed, a recent IMF study found that though globalization had lowered the wage levels in some states, the losses were offset by increases in their purchasing power. In short, though globalization "reduced labor's share of the pie, it has made the whole pie bigger" (*The Economist*, 2007b, p. 84).

A similar dynamic occurs between the globalization of labor and labor rights. In this case the concern is that competition for capital and the increased supply of labor could have an adverse effect on labor rights, including the right to form unions (collective bargaining) and to legal protections from morally questionable labor practices such as the use of child labor and slave labor. Anecdotal evidence about "sweatshops" and the repression of union rights in the name of profit abound; companies as varied as Unocal, Walt Disney, Nike, and Apple have suffered embarrassment and financial costs for their associations with poor labor practices.

REUTERS/Kham

STRUGGLES WITH GLOBALIZATION After decades of communist rule, Vietnam has opened up to the global economy, enjoying rapid growth since 1990. This is due in part to the influx of foreign capital, as Vietnam is known as a "cheaper-than-china" location for foreign direct investment (Bloomberg, 2011). Yet difficulties remain, and repression of labor rights is endemic. This is particularly the case among the female labor force, which provides a majority of the labor in light-manufacturing industries. Shown above, employees work on an assembly line in a shoe factory in a village outside of Hanoi.

Yet comprehensive studies reveal a more complex reality. MNCs, for example, often bring in better technology and labor policies than domestic corporations (Graham, 2000). To the extent that they are drawn to skilled labor pools, they can also encourage countries to increase the skill and productivity of their labor force via education and healthcare reforms (Blanton and Blanton, 2012a; Mosley, 2011). Moreover, increased foreign investment has been found to be related to decreased incidents of child labor (Neumayer and de Soysa, 2005).

Though most studies have found the *globalization of production* and the *globalization of labor* to be—on balance—positive developments for societies, the gains have not been spread equally across or within societies. As noted by economist Dani Rodrik (2008), "Globalization has exposed a deep fault line between groups who have the skills and mobility to flourish in global markets and those who either do not have these advantages or perceive the expansion of unregulated markets as inimical to social stability."

Yet whatever the overall relationship between globalization and social well-being, fears about globalization persist. Though it creates winners and losers, the negative consequences of globalization—companies "outsourcing" their work or using child labor—are quite visible and strike people profoundly. A statement by an American whose software-testing job was outsourced to India is telling: "The fact that they not only outsourced my job, but my entire industry, makes me feel powerless and paralyzed.... Frankly, this situation has created problems that are way too big for one person like me to solve" (Cook and Nyhan, 2004). Alternatively, the gains from globalization, such as less expensive products and the gradual diffusion of technologies, are often unnoticed as their benefits are widely dispersed and shared by all. Thus, though globalization may be good for societies as a whole, the losers of globalization attract much more attention than the winners. As we will see, similar dynamics are apparent in many of the controversies surrounding trade policy.

CHILD LABOR IN A GLOBAL SYSTEM Globalization is sped not only by the rapid expansion of technology but by the availability of cheap labor in some countries that take advantage of their people's low wages to make products highly competitive in the globalized marketplace. Here, a child labors under hazardous conditions and at extremely low wages in Bangladesh, producing goods that cost less than those made where labor unions protect workers.

CONTENDING TRADE STRATEGIES

As you have learned, international trade is a far-reaching and hotly debated dimension of globalization, and the differing sides of the trade debates each offer their own set of policy prescriptions. To understand the trade strategies that states may pursue, it is important to understand the aspects of economic liberalism and mercantilism, and the historical context of the global trade order, that guide their international economic decisions.

The Shadow of the Great Depression

reciprocity

Mutual or reciprocal lowering of trade barriers.

nondiscrimination

Principle that goods produced by all member states should receive equal treatment, as embodied in the ideas of most-favored nation (MFN) and national treatment.

The institutional basis for the post–World War II economic order began at the 1944 meeting at Bretton Woods, New Hampshire (see Chapter 10). Over the course of the next three years, the leaders founded the liberal economic order based around convertible currencies and free trade. While the International Monetary Fund and the World Bank emerged as the leading financial institutions, the task of liberalizing world trade later fell to the General Agreement on Tariffs and Trade (GATT).

The basic mission of the GATT was to encourage free trade among countries by reducing trade barriers and serving as a common forum for resolving trade disputes. The GATT had three primary principles: reciprocity, nondiscrimination, and transparency. *Reciprocity* calls for the mutual lowering of trade barriers, so countries that lowered their tariffs could expect their trading partners to do the same. According to the *nondiscrimination* principle, all members have the same level of access to the markets of other member states. In practice, nondiscrimination had two specific forms, the *most-favored nation (MFN) principle* and national treatment. The MFN principle holds that the tariff preferences granted to one state must be granted to all others—in other words, there could be no "favored nation" among members. National treatment means that foreign goods are treated the same as domestic goods, and that countries are not able to enact policies, such as taxes or other regulations, to give their domestic products any advantage over foreign products. Finally, the GATT called for *transparency* in trade policy, meaning that trade regulations and barriers need to be clearly articulated.

Iain Masterton / Alamy

Overall, the GATT was successful in liberalizing trade. When the institution was formed, the primary barrier to trade was tariffs (taxes on imported goods). In a series of successive meetings or "rounds" held from 1947 to 1994, the average tariff levels were lowered from 40 percent to just below 5 percent. When the Uruguay Round was concluded in 1994 the GATT became the World Trade Organization (WTO), which further strengthened the organization by giving it the power to settle disputes between members. This dispute settlement mechanism gave the WTO the ability to enforce its rules, and the WTO has settled hundreds of disputes among its members since 1994. In addition to gaining additional power as an institution, the organization has

CASCADING GLOBALIZATION: COMMUNIST CHINA CHOOSES TO CONVERT TO CAPITALISM AND CONSUMERISM Shown here is one example of China's growing consumerism: a view of the huge South China Mall in Dongguan, the world's biggest shopping center. Opened in 2005, the mall has 7.1 million feet of leasable shopping area, and includes windmills and theme parks. In all, China has two of the world's ten largest malls (Emporis, 2012). China has now long embraced America's "shop-'til-you-drop" ethos and is overtaking the United States in many areas of consumer spending (Ranasinghe, 2013).

grown stronger in terms of members—since 1947 its membership has grown from 23 countries to 159.

Although liberalization has spread as a policy principle around the world (Simmons and Elkins, 2004), not all states consistently support the liberal tenet that governments should not actively manage trade flows. Indeed, *commercial liberalism* (see Chapter 10) is under attack in many states, including some of liberalism's supposed proponents, which are under domestic pressure to protect industries and employment at home.

Next, we will review the basic philosophical beliefs that undergird trade policy and the role of trade within the global political system so that we can assess some of the specific policy tools that states use in international trade.

The Clash between Liberal and Mercantilist Values

How should states cope in the globalized political economy to best manage economic change? The choices force governments to reconcile the overriding need for state cooperation in liberalizing trade if they are to maximize their wealth with each state's natural competitive desire to put its own welfare first. Many controversies in the international political economy are ultimately reducible to differences between liberalism and mercantilism. A comparison of their divergent theoretical positions on five central questions illuminates the issues of debate that divide these schools today (see Table 11.1).

Commercial Liberalism   Commercial liberalism proceeds from the idea that humans are naturally inclined to cooperate. Thus, progress through mutually beneficial exchanges is possible, both to increase prosperity and to enlarge individual liberty under the law. In commercial liberalism, economic activity can contribute to global welfare, and the major problems of capitalism (boom-and-bust cycles, trade wars, poverty, and income inequalities) can be managed. One of the globe's "great causes" (Bhagwati, 2004) is to promote free international trade to lift the poor from poverty and to expand political liberties.

Adam Smith laid the foundations for commercial liberalism in 1776 when he wrote the now-classic *The Wealth of Nations*. In it, he argued how the "invisible hand" of an unregulated market, guided by humanity's natural tendency to "truck, barter, and exchange" in pursuit of private interest, could serve the globe's collective, or public, interest by creating efficiency and gains. According to Smith, if individuals rationally pursue their own self-interest, they will maximize societal interests as well.

most-favored nation (MFN) principle

The central GATT principle of unconditional nondiscriminatory treatment in trade between contracting parties underscoring the WTO's rule requiring any advantage given by one WTO member to also extend it to all other WTO members.

transparency

With regard to free trade, the principle that barriers to trade must be visible and thus easy to target.

TABLE 11.1	Key Differences between Liberalism and Mercantilism	
	Liberalism	**Mercantilism**
Economic Relations	Harmonious	Conflictual
Major Actors	Households, firms	States
Goal of Economic Activity	Maximize global welfare	Serve the national interest
Priority of Economics vs. Politics	Economics determines politics	Politics determines economics
Explanation for Global Change	A dynamic, ever-adjusting equilibrium	The product of shifts in the distribution of states' relative power

absolute advantage

The liberal economic concept that a state should specialize only in the production of goods in which the costs of production are lowest compared with those of other countries.

Regarding trade between states, the key concept Smith fostered was the idea of *absolute advantage*, the belief that countries should produce goods in which their cost of production is lowest in comparison with other countries. As Smith reasoned, "If a foreign country can supply us with a commodity cheaper than we ourselves can make it, better buy it off them with some part of the produce of our own industry, employed in a way in which we have some advantage." Though the idea was revolutionary, it raises an obvious dilemma—what if a country does not have an absolute advantage in anything?

comparative advantage

The concept in liberal economics that, even if a state does not have an absolute advantage in the production of any good, a state will still benefit if it specializes in the production of those goods that it can produce at a lower opportunity cost.

David Ricardo, an eighteenth-century political economist, addressed this issue with his concept of *comparative advantage*. Ricardo argued that all parties, even those with no absolute advantage in anything, can benefit from trade. How? According to the principle of comparative advantage, countries should specialize in whichever good has a lower *opportunity cost* (the value of whatever the country forgoes producing). In other words, a country should focus on the production of goods that it produces comparatively cheaply, rather than other goods that it could conceivably produce but only at a higher cost.

This was a very profound concept with important implications for liberal theory as well as the discipline of economics. Comparative advantage shows that trade benefits all parties that partake in it. This principle is the basis for commercial liberalism's claim that free trade will enable all countries to achieve economic progress together.

To show how trade can produce benefits for both partners, consider a brief hypothetical situation involving China and the United States, each of which produce textiles and automobiles, but with different worker productivity (output per hour) for each country, as shown in the first column of Table 11.2.

Clearly, China has an absolute advantage in both products, as its workers are more productive at producing both textiles and automobiles than American workers. Does that mean that two countries cannot benefit from trading with each other? No; as long as the two countries have some difference in the relative costs they face in producing the goods they can still both gain from specialization and trade.

Following the logic of comparative advantage, each country should produce the item for which it has the lower opportunity cost relative to the other country. Viewing the first column in terms of opportunity cost, the "cost" of China producing each additional automobile is three units of textiles. Alternatively, by producing one less automobile, China can produce three more units of textiles. However, it only "costs" the United States two units of textiles for each additional automobile, and the United States only gains two units of textiles by producing one less automobile. The United States thus has a smaller disadvantage in automobile production, as its opportunity cost for automobile production (two units of textiles) is less than the

TABLE 11.2	Comparative Advantage and the Gains from Trade							
	Work Productivity per Hour		**Before Specialization**		**Specialization, No Trade**		**Specialization with Trade**	
Country	Textiles	Autos	Textiles	Autos	Textiles	Autos	Textiles	Autos
China	9	3	900	300	990	270	910	300
U.S.	4	2	400	200	320	240	400	210

opportunity cost faced by China for the same production (three units of textiles). Put another way, though the United States is at a disadvantage in the production of both goods, its disadvantage is comparatively less in automobiles.

The remaining scenarios show specifically how trade can benefit each country by enabling it to further specialize in producing the good in which it has a comparative advantage. Imagine a hundred workers in each industry without specialization or trade (the second column). Next, specialize production by shifting 10 Chinese workers from automobile to textile production and 20 Americans from textile production to automobiles (third column). The fourth column shows how both countries can then benefit from trade. If we permit trade between the two countries, then 80 units of textiles are sold or exported to the United States, and 30 U.S. automobiles are exported to China. By shifting Chinese resources into textiles, U.S. resources into automobiles, and allowing trade, the same total allocations will cause both textile and automobile output to increase by 10 units each. Resources are now being used more efficiently and both countries benefit—China ends up with more textiles than before specialization and trade, and with the same number of automobiles. The United States finds itself with more automobiles and the same number of textiles. Achieving greater output with the same number of workers means that both countries enjoy higher living standards.

The assumption implicit in liberalism is that markets succeed according to their own logic. This provides a fairly straightforward set of policy recommendations. For liberals, minimal state regulation of the national economy will maximize growth and prosperity. The best government is one that stays out of business, and politics should be separate from the economic market. A free market is the foundation for broad-based, steady economic growth that allows democratic institutions to flourish (Naím, 2007). As Benjamin Franklin once quipped, "No nation was ever ruined by trade."

There is at least one problem, however. Although liberal theory promises that the "invisible hand" will maximize efficiency so that everyone will gain, it does not promise that everyone will gain equally. Instead, "everyone will gain in accordance with his or her contribution to the whole, but … not everyone will gain equally because individual productivities differ. Under free exchange, society as a whole will be more wealthy, but individuals will be rewarded in terms of their marginal productivity and relative contribution to the overall social product" (Gilpin, 2001).

This holds true between states as much as within them. The gains from international trade are distributed quite unequally, even if the states are acting in accordance with comparative advantage. Globalization has not benefited middle-income countries as much as richer and poorer states (Garrett, 2004). Commercial liberal theory ignores these differences, as it is most concerned with *absolute gains* for all rather than *relative gains*. Mercantilist theory, in contrast, is more concerned with the political competition among states that determines how economic rewards are distributed.

Mercantilism

Mercantilism is essentially an economic extension of realist thinking. Unlike liberals, who focus on the rationality of the marketplace, mutual gains, and a minimal role for the state, mercantilists see the need for power politics as a determinant of economics and posit that the government has an important role to play in ensuring the state's economic well-being (see Chapter 5).

Classic mercantilism emerged in the late fifteenth century during the first wave of colonialism (Wallerstein, 2005). Classic mercantilists viewed gold and silver accumulation as the route to state power and wealth, and advocated imperialism as a means to that end. In the early nineteenth century, what we now call mercantilism (also called economic nationalism) emerged largely as a response to the rise of liberalism—indeed, one of the leading mercantilist works, Friedrich List's *National System of Political Economy*, can be seen as a direct critique of Smith's *The Wealth of Nations*. Although economic nationalists draw from some of the core ideas of liberalism, such as the importance of productivity, the benefits of specialization, and the efficiency of the marketplace, they draw a different set of political conclusions.

In particular, mercantilists diverge from liberal thought in three main ways:

- Whereas liberals view wealth and economic growth as ends in themselves, mercantilists view them as instruments of national power. This is very much in line with the realist emphasis on national interest, which posits that "economic activities are and should be subordinate to the goal of state building and the interests of the state" (Gilpin, 2001).

- While liberal thought expounds the gains of specialization, it implicitly treats all specializations as equal in value. Mercantilists question this assumption, positing that "the power of producing wealth is therefore infinitely more important than wealth itself" (List, 1841). For example, during the early years of the United States, Treasury Secretary Alexander Hamilton recommended that the United States specialize in manufacturing instead of agriculture, as it would better serve U.S. national interests. As opposed to agriculture, manufacturing required higher levels of technological advancement. Such industrialization would thus increase the "diversity of talents" in the country and, as a result, industrial capabilities would more readily convert to military might.

- Mercantilists view the state as playing an active and vital role in the economy. Since some specializations are superior to others, states can encourage the development of certain industries by subsidizing them and "protecting" them from foreign competition. As Hamilton (1791) noted, in key instances of national interest, the "public purse must supply the deficiency of private resources."

This perspective yields a different set of economic policies. Whereas commercial liberals emphasize the mutual benefits of cooperative economic agreements, mercantilists focus on *zero-sum* competition and are therefore more concerned that the gains realized by one party in a trade exchange will come at the expense of the other trade partner. For mercantilists, relative gains are more important than both parties' absolute gains. Although mercantilists recognize the superior efficiency of free trade, they have a more guarded view of its political benefits. They view free trade as an acceptable practice for a powerful country, in that it often serves to solidify that country's power. For growing countries, trade ties can sometimes be manipulated to the economic advantage of the more powerful, more developed state (Hirschman, 1945).

In many instances, practicing liberal trade can undermine national security and long-term economic development. Indeed, as mercantilists point out, powerful countries who profess liberal ideals, most notably the United States and the United Kingdom, were quite protectionist when their industries were developing. U.S. President Abraham Lincoln was an ardent protectionist who doubted the benefits of international trade and viewed tariffs as a way to protect the U.S. industrial base. He succinctly noted that his "politics are short and sweet, like the old woman's dance. I am in favor of a national bank … and a high protective tariff." In short, "(w)hile American industry was developing, the country had no time for laissez-faire. After it had grown strong, the United States began preaching laissez-faire to the rest of the world" (Fallows, 1993).

TRADE AND GLOBAL POLITICS

Trade plays a central role in the global system. In addition to being a key facet of economic globalization, it has many implications for the global political system. Indeed, a lot of scholarship on the international political economy deals with some aspect of the relationship between trade and world politics. With that in mind, let us briefly touch upon some of the key concepts and issues at the systemic and state levels of analysis (see Chapter 1).

At the systemic level, one of the most influential theories of global trade is *hegemonic stability theory*. Hegemonic stability theory, which is also used in theories of global conflict (see Chapter 7), is based on the proposition that free trade and international peace depend upon a single predominant great power, or *hegemon*, that is willing and able to use its economic and military might to enforce rules for international interaction. A hegemon is much more than a powerful state; rather, it refers to an instance where a single state has a preponderance of economic and military power, a dominant ideology shared by the world, and the willingness to exert its power and influence.

The underlying assumption of hegemonic stability theory is that a stable and prosperous global economy approximates a collective or *public good* in that it provides shared benefits from which no one can be excluded. If all share a public good, why does it require a hegemon to provide it? This is due to the problematic nature of providing public goods, or the *collective action dilemma*. In this dilemma, the provision of public goods is problematic due to two basic problems, accountability and rationality. First, although a public good generates benefits, there are certain costs associated with providing or maintaining it. If the benefit has a large group of potential recipients, it is not possible to hold any single party accountable for paying its portion of the cost to provide this good. The recipients are thus faced with a dilemma: why should they have to pay for the good when they can enjoy it without paying for it? If we assume that the actors are rational, then they would seek to enjoy the good as free riders that reap the benefits without paying any of the cost. However, if everyone is "rational," then no one will pay to maintain the good, and it will eventually disappear.

Thinking about the cost of a public park helps to clarify this principle. If there were no central government to provide for park maintenance, individuals themselves would have to cooperate to keep the park in order (the trees trimmed, the lawn mowed, litter removed, and so on). Some, however, may try to come and enjoy the benefits of the park without pitching in. If enough people realize that they can get away with this—that they can enjoy a beautiful park without helping to maintain it—it will not be long before the once beautiful park looks shabby. If even this basic form of cooperation is hard to sustain, imagine the difficulties in perpetuating cooperation in the international system.

public good

Collective goods, such as clean air or sunlight, whose use is nonexclusive and nonrival in nature; thus, if anyone can use the good, it is available to all.

collective action dilemma

Paradox regarding the provision of collective goods in which, if there is no accountability for paying the costs of maintaining or providing the good, it may cease to exist.

The same logic applies to the collective good of the liberal international economy. Since many states enjoy the collective good of an orderly, open, free-market economy, there are often free riders. A hegemon, however, may tolerate free riders, partly because the benefits that the hegemon provides, such as a stable global currency, encourage other states to accept the hegemon's dictates. Moreover, the hegemon may view maintaining the system as worthwhile, even if it bears a disproportionate share of the cost. Thus, both the hegemon and the smaller states gain from the situation. If the costs of leadership begin to multiply, however, a hegemon tends to become less tolerant of free riders. In such a situation, cooperation is increasingly seen as one-sided, or zero-sum, because most of the benefits come at the expense of the hegemon. The open global economy could then crumble amid a competitive race for individual gain at others' expense.

The theory is thus quite parsimonious in that it explains very broad political and economic trends on the basis of one condition—hegemonic leadership. Although theorists may disagree about how many instances of hegemony have existed throughout history, there is widespread agreement about the most recent case—the United States during the post–World War II period. Studies within this area have considered the issue of a U.S. decline from hegemony, and its implication for the world economic order (Keohane, 1984; Shifrinson and Beckley, 2013; Wallerstein, 2002; Zakaria, 2009).

At the state level of analysis, studies have assessed the relationship between trade and military conflict, with the preponderance supporting the *commercial liberalism* argument that trade ties tend to discourage military conflict (Hegre, Oneal, and Russett, 2010; Lupu and Traag, 2013; Mousseau, 2013). The basic argument is that trade interdependence increases the opportunity costs of violence—in addition to the more obvious costs that accompany military conflict, the presence of trade ties implies that a country would also forgo the benefits of trade if it takes military action against a trading partner (see "Controversy: China and Taiwan—Can Economic Ties Overcome Strategic Rivalry?"). On a broader scale, Russett and Oneal (2001) posit that trade, alongside democracy and international organizations, is a key part of the "Kantian triad" that encourages lasting peace between states.

Within states, trade liberalization is beneficial to societies, as it is positively related to economic growth, levels of democratization, life expectancy, education, human rights, and food security, and negatively related to child labor, poverty, and environmental degradation (Bhagwati, 2008b; Wolf, 2005). "Despite all the misgivings about international trade, the fact remains that countries in which the share of economic activity related to exports is rising grow one and a half times faster than those with more stagnant exports" (Naím, 2007, p. 95). This accounts for the continuing popularity of the liberal belief that the exponential growth of trade contributes enormously to economic prosperity, as the last 60 years suggest.

These payoffs notwithstanding, states still have many reasons to try to increase their own domestic standard of living through trade protectionism. Some states feel as though free trade is neither free nor fair because it does not benefit everyone equally. Although the overall trend is toward increased liberalization, many states remain unwilling to open their domestic markets to foreign competition because they are also unwilling to reform their home markets. According to the Heritage Foundation's Index of Economic Freedom, at the start of 2013 only five countries, or just under 3 percent, of the 185 states were "free." Thirty (16 percent)

CONTROVERSY

CHINA AND TAIWAN—CAN ECONOMIC TIES OVERCOME STRATEGIC RIVALRY?

In 1949 Chiang Kai-shek and his party, the Kuomintang (KMT), lost the Chinese Civil War and retreated from Mainland China to Taiwan with one to two million followers and troops. Since then, Taiwan has exercised *de facto*, if not *de jure*, sovereignty in international affairs. Ever since it lost its status as a recognized member of the United Nations (UN) in 1971, Taiwan has long sought broad international recognition as a sovereign state. For its part, China views Taiwan as a "breakaway province" that is rightfully a part of China. The Chinese emphatically adhere to the "One China" principle—that there is only one Chinese nation, of which Taiwan is a part. As such, any formal declaration of Taiwanese independence is viewed as an act of war. In 2005 China passed an Anti-Secession Law, which formalized this long-standing commitment to use "nonpeaceful means" if Taiwan declares formal independence.

Given these fundamental political differences, relations between China and Taiwan, or "Cross-Strait" relations, have been tarnished with suspicion and hostility. At its worst, the area has been on the brink of outright war. In 1958, China bombarded several offshore islands that are part of Taiwan, which nearly brought the United States, a close military ally of Taiwan, into war with China. Before Taiwan's first democratic elections in 1996, China test-fired missiles near two major Taiwanese ports, again risking military hostilities with both Taiwan and the United States. President Clinton responded by deploying aircraft carrier battle groups in the area.

The current strategic situation remains precarious in many respects. Reports indicate that China has a growing arsenal of more than 1200 missiles pointed at Taiwan (Capaccio, 2013). Despite its much smaller size, Taiwan has a powerful military—one report ranks it as the 18th most powerful in the world (globalfirepower.com, 2013). It is also a leading recipient of U.S. arms and Taiwan itself is currently producing 50 medium-range missiles that will be used to target Chinese military installations (Agence France-Presse, 2013).

Yet at the same time, the economies of China and Taiwan have become ever more closely integrated. Bilateral trade has increased dramatically since 2000, from $31.3 billion to over $121.6 billion in 2012 (Kan and Morrison, 2013). China is currently Taiwan's largest trading partner, responsible for 21.9 percent of Taiwan's total trade volume, while Taiwan ranks as China's fifth largest trading partner. Moreover, China is the leading location for Taiwanese FDI, having hosted over $150 billion in investment since 1988 (Roberge, 2009).

How can these contrasting patterns—traditionally labeled as "hot economics, cold politics"—be reconciled? From the theoretical viewpoint of liberalism, we would expect that economic interdependence may be reducing the probability of military conflict between the two countries. Given the close integration between both sides, any military conflict would be very costly to both countries, as it would damage large portions of both economies. Moreover, economic ties serve to empower business interests that have a vested concern in maintaining peaceful relations between the two countries. This could eventually cause the policy preferences of both countries to converge (Kastner, 2010). Finally, economic interdependence provides each country with a means to engage in "costly signaling," that is, a way to have conflicts through economic rather than political

(Continued)

CHINA AND TAIWAN—CAN ECONOMIC TIES OVERCOME STRATEGIC RIVALRY? (Continued)

means. Indeed, one study cites such ties as a reason that the 2000 elections in Taiwan did not attract the same military action as the 1996 elections (Gartzke and Li, 2003).

There is some evidence that relations have improved between the two countries. For example, in 2009 China allowed Taiwan to attend a meeting of the World Health Assembly, which marked the first time Taiwan was allowed to participate in any meeting of an UN-affiliated organization (Bush, 2011). Experts widely note that "mutual fear" between the two countries has abated, and some speculate that some type of peace agreement between the two countries may be possible within the next few years (Saunders and Kastner, 2009). However, deep-seated political differences persist. For example, survey results indicate that a vast majority of Taiwanese prefers the current status quo between the two countries, whereas mainlanders prefer that the two countries become one nation (Bush, 2011). Thus, key political issues remain unresolved, even in the face of economic integration. Furthermore, rising tensions about territorial claims in the South China Sea may embroil Taiwan and China in conflict. Time will tell whether optimists or pessimists are correct.

WHAT DO YOU THINK?

- *What does this case suggest about the ability of economic ties to prevent military conflict?*

- *What insights would a realist or constructivist perspective have on this case?*

- *As the United States is closely integrated with both countries, what policies do you think it should follow regarding cross-strait relations?*

Note: Prepared with the advice and assistance of William C. Vocke, Ph.D.

were "mostly free," and the remaining countries (81 percent) were "moderately free," "mostly unfree," or "repressed" (see Map 11.2).

Although governments may face political pressure to close off their economies, such policies frequently have negative consequences. Economically closed countries tend to be the poorest and the most corrupt. Indeed, many countries with low levels of economic freedom, such as Myanmar, Chad, and North Korea, are also some of the most corrupt countries in the world (Transparency International, 2013). These patterns underscore the influence of a state's internal conditions on its international economic policies, and suggest that the future preservation of a global free-trade regime may be compromised in the absence of increasing numbers of free governments and free economies.

Trade can also function as a foreign policy tool for states, and it is readily used as both a "carrot" and a "stick" in interstate relations. Trade ties, and granting of preferential access to markets, are commonly established with developing countries as a way to help them compete in the global market and thereby achieve economic growth. Leading examples include the WTO's Generalized System of Preferences, which exempts developing countries from some of

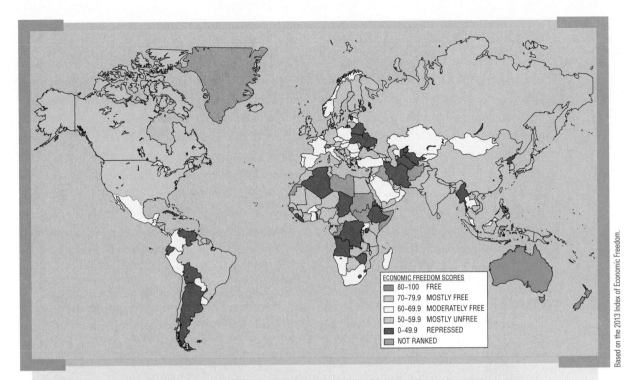

Based on the 2013 Index of Economic Freedom.

ECONOMIC FREEDOM SCORES
- 80–100   FREE
- 70–79.9   MOSTLY FREE
- 60–69.9   MODERATELY FREE
- 50–59.9   MOSTLY UNFREE
- 0–49.9   REPRESSED
- NOT RANKED

MAP 11.2   ECONOMIC FREEDOM IN THE WORLD Economic liberals and mercantilists portray two different visions of international economics, one in which the market has virtually free reign and the other in which the state actively intervenes to regulate and manipulate market forces. Yet the reality is more nuanced, as there are differences in the degree to which free markets operate within each state. This map depicts economic freedom as measured by the 2013 Index of Economic Freedom. By using measures across 10 economic areas, including government policies on trade, labor, investment, and property rights, the Economic Freedom Index assesses the extent to which countries promote competition, individual empowerment, and nondiscrimination. Although there are differences in the degree to which economic freedom is enjoyed across countries, there appears to be a strong relationship between economic freedom and prosperity.

the nondiscrimination and reciprocity principles of the organization; the Lomé Convention, which gives seventy-one developing countries preferential access to the EU markets; and the African Growth and Opportunities Act, which gives sub-Saharan African countries duty-free access to the U.S. market.

Economic sanctions—deliberate actions against a target country to deprive it of the benefits of economic relations—are the most common way that trade can be used as a "stick" for *coercive diplomacy*. Sanctions have a long history; as President Woodrow Wilson argued in 1919, "A nation that is boycotted is a nation that is in sight of surrender. Apply this economic, peaceful, silent, deadly remedy and there will be no need for force.... It does not cost a life outside the nation boycotted but it brings a pressure upon the nation which, in my judgment, no modern nation could resist" (Hufbauer et al., 2007; see also Rowe, 2010).

Sanctions are used frequently and have proliferated rapidly since the end of the Cold War. Indeed, the number of sanctions imposed since 1990 is roughly equal to the number imposed between 1900 and 1990 (Drezner, 2011). Politically, sanctions are an expedient tool because they are relatively easy to enact (as opposed to military conflict) and are viewed as largely "cost free" by the sender country.

economic sanctions

Punitive economic actions, such as the cessation of trade or financial ties, by one global actor against another to retaliate for objectionable behavior.

Carnegie Council Video: Economic Sanctions

A considerable amount of research has been devoted to sanctions, and most scholars are skeptical of their utility as a strategic tool. First, sanctions "are seldom effective in impairing the military potential" of their targets (Hufbauer, Schott, and Elliot, 1990, p. 94), and are rarely successful as a substitute for warfare. Moreover, only small numbers of sanctions achieve any of their stated policy goals; the percentage of successful sanctions ranges between 5 and 33 percent, depending on how "success" is measured (Elliott, 1998; Pape, 1997).

Although they have little effect on the regimes of targeted countries, sanctions can impose significant costs on their citizens. For example, U.S. sanctions against Iraq during the 1990s were argued to be "sanctions of mass destruction" (Mueller and Mueller, 1999), as resultant food and medicine shortages were linked to the deaths of an estimated 250,000 Iraqi children (Garfield, 1999). Although this may be an extreme case, studies show a consistently negative relationship between economic sanctions and the social welfare of citizens in the target states (Allen and Lektzian, 2013; Peksen, 2011).

To minimize such humanitarian concerns, policy makers have started to use more narrowly targeted sanctions, known as "smart sanctions," which they try to focus more closely on specific elements of the target country, such as the freezing assets or only stopping strategically significant commerce, such as arms shipments, rather than all economic relations. Although

Miguel Alvarez/AFP/Getty Images

STICKS AND STONES OF ECONOMIC STATECRAFT In 1962, the United States extended sanctions on Cuba to a near-total commercial, economic, and financial embargo. Although the Cold War has been over for decades, these sanctions persist, costing the U.S. economy somewhere between $1.2 and $3.6 billion annually (Hanson, et al., 2013). Pictured are protestors demanding the end of the blockade of Cuba. Their banner reads, "Cuba is America—End the Blockade!" In 2010, the United States loosened sanctions to permit U.S. companies to export services and software used for personal communications over the Internet. Restrictions for U.S. travel into Cuba have also been loosened, particularly for students and educators (Higgins, 2011).

smart sanctions may reduce the harm to civilians, there is little evidence that they are any more effective (Drezner, 2011; Gordon, 2011).

While the overall verdict on sanctions is quite negative, research does point out some complexities on the potential use of sanctions as a policy tool. First, some argue that much of the sanctions literature suffers from "selection effects." By focusing only on strategically motivated sanctions that are actually enacted, the number of cases examined is limited, which could lead to results that understate the actual effectiveness of sanctions. Studies that examine a broad sample of sanctions, including those over issues such as economic and environmental disputes and that focus on the threat (rather than the imposition) of sanctions, suggest that their actual usefulness may be greater than previously thought (Bapat, Heinrich, Kobayashi, and Morgan, 2013; Lopez, 2012).

The focus on success versus failure may also be too simplistic a way to view the effectiveness of sanctions, or any tool of economic statecraft (Rowe, 2010). Policy makers have a variety of tools at their disposal, all of which have costs and benefits. Stated policy goals, particularly strategic goals such as territorial concessions or regime change, may be too costly to carry out. In such cases, sanctions may be used as a symbol that a given country is "doing something," even if it is not likely to achieve its goal. Thus, "it is not enough to show the disadvantages of sanctions, one must show that some other policy option is better" for a given situation (Baldwin 1999/2000, p. 84).

THE FATE OF FREE TRADE

Global trade continues to proliferate and protectionism is at a historically low level. Yet arguments for protectionism still resonate, feeding in part off societal feelings of insecurity about the global economy. Such arguments are particularly tempting in times of economic downturn, as foreign trade makes a ready target for blame. Even in many economically open countries, protectionist pressures inevitably increase when jobs are lost. Such was reflected in U.S. Congresswoman Maxine Waters' (D-CA) call to "bring jobs back home," and the widespread skepticism that the conservative U.S. "Tea Party" movement has toward trade agreements (*The Economist*, 2010q). The age-old debate between free traders and mercantilists is thus likely to persist as a global issue.

As is the case with international finance (see Chapter 10), there is an esoteric vocabulary attached to trade policy issues. Thus, before assessing current issues facing the world trading order, it is helpful to develop an understanding of the "trade tricks" countries can use to influence trade flows.

Trade Tricks

Trade liberalization has played a key role in the growth of the global economy since World War II, and there is virtual unanimity among economists regarding the potential benefits of free trade. As Nobel Prize–winning economist Paul Krugman noted, "If there were an Economist's Creed, it would surely contain the affirmations 'I Understand the Principle of Comparative Advantage' and 'I Advocate Free Trade'" (1987, p. 131).

protectionism

Barriers to foreign trade, such as tariffs and quotas, that protect local industries from foreign competition.

Carnegie Council Video:
Protectionism

tariffs

Tax assessed on goods imported into a country.

import quotas

Numerical limit on the quantity of particular products that can be imported.

export quotas

Barriers to free trade agreed to by two trading states to protect their domestic producers.

orderly market arrangements (OMAs)

Voluntary export restrictions through govern-ment-to-govern-ment agreements to follow specific trading rules.

voluntary export restrictions (VERs)

Protectionist measure in which exporting countries agree to restrict shipments of a particular product to a country to deter it from imposing an even more burden-some import quota.

However, free trade is politically less attractive than mercantilism. This is to the result of the nature of the costs and benefits that accompany free trade. In the aggregate, the societal benefits of free trade greatly outweigh the costs. Yet these benefits, particularly the consumer gains from imports, are spread throughout an entire society and are often not noticed. For example, though foreign trade may enable you to save 10 dollars on a sweatshirt, you are probably unaware that imports are the reason behind your savings. There is thus little incentive to politically organize in the interests of imports—if you discovered that the price of sweatshirts had risen by 10 dollars, you would probably not take the time to organize "pro-import" protest marches.

However, the "costs" of free trade are quite concentrated and visible. It is quite common, for example, to hear about plants closing and people losing jobs due to competition with cheaper imports. There are thus greater political incentives to organize against free trade and for these forces to influence the political process. In short, "bad economics is often the cornerstone of good politics" (Drezner, 2000, p. 70).

Given this dilemma, trade squabbles are likely to continue, as states have political incentives to enact mercantilist policies. This section will explain some of these policy tools, all of which fall under the broad rubric of *protectionism*—policies designed to "protect" domestic industries from foreign competition.

- *Tariffs*—taxes placed on imported goods—are the most well-known protectionist policy tools. Although average tariff levels have greatly decreased due to WTO agreements and intervention, they are still occasionally employed. For example, in 2002 President Bush imposed tariffs ranging from 8 percent to 30 percent on steel imports.

- *Import quotas* limit the quantity of a particular product that can be imported from abroad. In the late 1950s, for example, the United States established import quotas on oil, arguing that they were necessary to protect U.S. national security. Hence the government, rather than the marketplace, determined the amount and source of imports.

- *Export quotas* usually result from negotiated agreements between producers and consumers and restrict the flow of products (e.g., shoes or sugar) from the former to the latter. Along those lines, *orderly market arrangements (OMAs)* are formal agreements through which a country accepts limiting the export of products that might impair workers in the importing country, often under specific rules designed to monitor and manage trade flows. Exporting countries are willing to accept such restrictions in exchange for concessions from the would-be importing countries. The Multi-Fiber Arrangement (MFA) was an example of an elaborate OMA that restricted exports of textiles and apparel. It originated in the early 1960s, when the United States formalized *voluntary export restrictions (VERs)* with Japan and Hong Kong to protect domestic producers from cheap cotton imports. The quota system was later extended to other importing and exporting countries and then, in the 1970s, to other fibers, when it became the MFA. The MFA expired in 1995.

- As quotas and tariffs have been reduced, a broader category of trade restrictions known as *nontariff barriers (NTBs)* has been created to impede imports without direct tax levies. These cover a wide range of creative government regulations designed to shelter particular domestic industries from foreign competition, including health and safety regulations, government purchasing procedures, and subsidies. Unlike tariffs and quotas, NTBs are more difficult to detect and dismantle.

■ Two particularly popular forms of NTBs, both meant to offset policies of exporting countries, are *countervailing duties* and *antidumping duties*. Countervailing duties impose tariffs to offset alleged subsidies, and their use is fairly common to offset agricultural subsidies. Antidumping duties counter competitors' sale of products below their cost of production. For example, in May 2013, WTO members created a review board to review accusations that China had imposed antidumping duties on high-performance stainless steel seamless tubes from Japan (WTO Dispute Settlement, 2013).

■ Among developing countries whose domestic industrialization goals may be hindered by the absence of protection from the Global North's more efficient firms, the *infant industry* argument is often used to justify mercantilist trade policies. According to this argument, tariffs or other forms of protection are necessary to nurture young industries until they eventually mature and lower production costs to successfully compete in the global marketplace. *Import-substitution industrialization* policies, which were once popular in Latin America and elsewhere, often depended on protection of infant industries (see Chapter 5).

■ In the Global North, creating comparative advantages now motivates what is known as *strategic trade policy* as a mercantilist method to ensure that a country's industries remain competitive. Strategic trade policies focus government subsidies toward particular industries so they gain comparative advantages over foreign producers. A notable example of this strategy is Airbus, a European company that builds wide-bodied airplanes. The company was founded in large part by France, Germany, and the United Kingdom, and has been heavily subsidized during much of its existence.

Although economic liberalism is based upon free trade, realist theory helps to account for the state's impulse to pursue mercantilist policies. Recall that realism argues that states often compete rather than cooperate because international anarchy without global governance feeds states' distrust of each other. Moreover, states seek self-advantage and economic primacy. In this sense, mercantilist strategic trade is a prime example of this realist explanation of states' concern for self-interest and relative gains, as it "focuses on economic development as a matter of strategic significance" (Holstein, 2005).

The Uneasy Coexistence of Liberalism and Mercantilism

Given the political advantages of mercantilism, states often have a hard time resisting the calls of domestic industries and interest groups for protection. They do so even if, according to liberalism, their relations with their trade partners will deteriorate and all will suffer in the long run, as trade partners retaliate with the many clever and innovative counterprotectionist actions.

The result is that states simultaneously pursue liberalism and mercantilism. Such a paradoxical approach to trade policy reflects the state's determination to reap the benefits of interdependence while minimizing costs. It also reveals the tension between states and markets,

---

nontariff barriers (NTBs)

Measures other than tariffs that discriminate against imports without direct tax levies and are beyond the scope of international regulation.

countervailing duties

Government tariffs to offset suspected subsidies provided by foreign governments to their producers.

antidumping duties

Taxes placed on another exporting state's alleged selling of a product at a price below the cost to produce it.

infant industry

Newly established industries ("infants") that are not yet strong enough to compete against mature foreign producers in the global.

strategic trade policy

Government support for particular domestic industries to help them gain competitive advantages over foreign producers.

between the promise that everyone will benefit and the fear that the benefits will not be equally distributed. The absence of a world government encourages each state to be more concerned with how it fares as compared to other states—its relative gains—than collectively with its absolute gains.

America's trade competitors have long noted that the United States, the principal advocate of free trade in the post–World War II era, has often failed to live up to its own rhetoric. There are various ways in which the United States uses its foreign economic tools to intervene in global trade markets and protect its own economy. For instance, a major portion of U.S. foreign aid is tied to the purchase of U.S. goods and services. A quote from a 2003 report by the U.S. Agency for International Development (USAID) is telling: "The principal beneficiary of America's foreign assistance programs has always been the United States. Close to 80 percent of USAID's contracts and grants go directly to American firms" (Easterly and Pfutze, 2008; Terlinden and Hilditch, 2003). This turns foreign aid into a de facto subsidy for domestic corporations.

Security goals also figure into U.S. trade liberalization efforts. The African Growth and Opportunities Act (AGOA) has been particularly contentious in this regard. The original mandate of the AGOA was to encourage democratic governance and respect for human rights (Blanton and Blanton, 2001), though strategic interests have reportedly supplanted this emphasis. For example, when the United States was seeking UN Security Council approval for military operations in Iraq, the AGOA was used to leverage the support of African members of the Security Council—"The message was clear: either you vote with us or you lose your trade privileges" (Deen, 2009).

Additionally, although overall tariff levels in the United States are lower than those in the developing world, the United States, like the rest of the developed countries, still protects several key sectors, most notably agriculture. Between 1995 and 2012, farmers in the United States received around $256 billion dollars in agriculture subsidies (EWG, 2013). Such mercantilist tactics are damaging to the liberal trade regime, given the United States' liberal rhetoric and its stature as the globe's leading economic superpower. This is particularly troubling for developing countries, as they often have very powerful agricultural sectors as well. The gap between the ideals and the actions of the Global North also brings back vestiges of colonialism and past hypocrisy on the part of the rich countries. "Perhaps the greatest hypocrisy," writes Ian Campbell (2004, p. 112), "is that the United States, which preaches the merits of free trade more strongly than almost any other country, spends tens of billions of dollars to prevent its own markets from being free."

To free-trade liberals, as well as Marxists, the trade game is rigged by the routine and lucrative corruption known as "rent-seeking" in which governments impose handicaps on competitors. *Rents* that create obstacles to participants in the global marketplace harm everyone, but especially the poor (Klein, 2007). A team of forecasting experts (National Intelligence Council, 2004) predicts that by 2020 "the benefits of globalization won't be global.... Gaps will widen between those countries benefiting from globalization economically ... and those underdeveloped nations or products within nations left behind [despite the likelihood that] the world economy is projected to be about 80 percent larger in 2020 than it was in 2000."

rents

Higher-than-normal financial returns on investments that are realized from market imperfections, such as governmental influence.

TRIUMPH OR TROUBLE FOR THE GLOBAL ECONOMY

The pressures on free trade notwithstanding, "rapid globalization has done nothing to undermine the confidence liberals have always placed in trade. No serious economist questions the case for international integration through flows of goods and services, though there is a lively argument over how integration through trade can be brought about" (Crook, 2003, p. 3). Will that confidence prevail? To better assess this key issue, let us next examine the progression of the liberal trade order, as well as the current issues it faces.

The Development of the WTO

Although it is difficult to maintain a liberal trade regime, and there are problems with the global trading system, it has a better developed architecture than the global financial system. As discussed in Chapter 10, the financial arrangement established by the Bretton Woods order broke down in 1971, and the current system is prone to "manics, panics, and crashes" (Kindleberger, 2000)—currencies fluctuate according to the dictates of the markets, there are only discussion forums to address issues of financial and monetary cooperation, and the IMF merely provides for the monitoring of financial systems and crisis management for countries that are in dire financial straits. It does not set broad-based, enforceable rules and practices for global financial flows.

By contrast, the WTO provides a well-developed institutional structure for the world trading system. The GATT/WTO has had a rather tumultuous and uneven history and has been criticized for its lack of progress throughout its existence. The 1950s were declared a "lost decade" and "postmortems" were written during the Uruguay Round negotiations as well as the ongoing, albeit stalled, Doha Round (Stiles, 2005; Pakpahan, 2013). In the aftermath of the financial crisis, legal scholar Richard Steinberg declared that "As a location for trade negotiation, the WTO is dead" (Steinberg, 2009).

Yet to paraphrase Mark Twain, rumors of the institution's death have been "greatly exaggerated," and the WTO soldiers on. During the Bretton Woods era, successive meetings or "rounds" of the GATT were very successful in cutting tariffs. The initial Geneva Round of negotiations in 1947 reduced tariffs by 35 percent, while successive rounds of negotiations in the 1950s, 1960s (the Kennedy Round), 1970s (Tokyo Round), and the 1980s and 1990s (Uruguay Round) virtually eliminated tariffs on manufactured goods. Currently, less than 0.25 percent of total world trade is subject to tariffs (Ali et al., 2011).

The Doha Round, which officially began in 2002, has a very ambitious agenda for trade liberalization that addresses many of the remaining nontariff barriers as well as other trade-related items on the global agenda, including intellectual property rights, environmental issues, trade in services, and trade-related investment measures. Another sign of success is its expanding membership. The WTO currently has 159 members, while another 25 states have "observer" status and have taken significant measures toward gaining WTO membership (see Map 11.3).

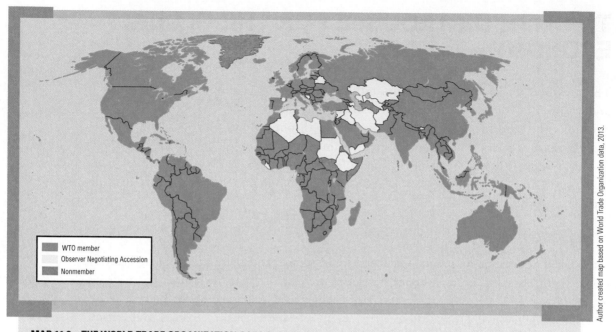

MAP 11.3   THE WORLD TRADE ORGANIZATION GOES GLOBAL When the GATT began in 1949, it had 23 members. As of July 2013, 159 countries were members of the World Trade Organization. In addition, 25 "observers" are in the process of negotiating to become formal members (such as Yemen). Despite the controversies surrounding the WTO, its near universal membership attests to the appeal of the institution among political leaders.

The Uruguay Round transformed the GATT into the WTO, a rules-based regime with a powerful dispute resolution mechanism that arbitrates trade-related conflicts among members and holds them accountable for mercantilist measures. The WTO has handled more than 459 disputes since 1995 (WTO, 2013c) and can hold even its most powerful members accountable for their trade practices. For example, the WTO played a pivotal role in forcing the United States to rescind its 2002 steel tariffs—according to a WTO ruling, had the United States not ended the protection of its steel markets, the EU would have been able to impose some $4 billion worth of trade sanctions against the United States (Becker, 2003).

In addition to having policy "sticks" to bring member states in line, the "carrot" of WTO membership, which brings with it access to the markets of the 159 member states, can serve to open up societies and improve the quality of state governance. Recent additions to the WTO—Russia, Laos, China, and Saudi Arabia—underwent reform of their trading regimes, including increased accountability and transparency of their trade policies, in order to make it through the accession process to join the WTO. According to Peter Sutherland, a founding director of the WTO, countries change "dramatically—and mostly for the better—in the context of acceding to the WTO" (2008, p. 127). Political effects continue after accession, as studies have found WTO membership to be positively related to some democratic processes, such as political participation as well as free and fair elections (Aaronson and Abouharb, 2011; Aaronson and Zimmerman, 2007).

Yet the WTO is to a large extent a victim of its success. When the GATT was formed it contained 23 members and was charged with one central goal—reducing tariffs. As tariffs have declined as a policy tool across most industrial sectors, the WTO has turned its attention to industries that previous rounds had left largely untouched and has begun to address a broad variety of nontariff barriers (NTBs) that impede foreign trade. Expansion into each of these areas has proven politically difficult, albeit for somewhat different reasons.

Despite the economic advantages of liberal trade, it is often politically advantageous to protect industries through mercantilist policies. Such is the case with agriculture, which has long been "the most distorted sector of the world economy" (Panagariya, 2005, p.1277), as many states subsidize their agricultural producers and enact various measures to protect them from foreign competition. Although worldwide liberalization of agriculture could actually double agricultural exports from both the Global North and Global South (Grant and Boys, 2011), states are unwilling to pay the political costs of removing subsidies and other barriers to agricultural trade. In some instances, steps taken to liberalize agriculture are met with waves of protest and even riots, as exemplified by the discord in South Korea over U.S. beef imports (Sang-Hun, 2008), as well as protests in Russia over potential imports of genetically modified products (Russia Times, 2012).

DOES THE WTO "KILL FARMERS"? The liberalization of agriculture has been one of the most intractable items on the WTO agenda and often triggers visceral responses to any potential "threat" to the status quo. South Korea is certainly no exception to this, particularly with regard to its rice market. This photo, taken at the 2003 WTO Ministerial Conference in Cancun, Mexico, shows South Korean rice farmer Lee Kyung Hae (at left, with sign) protesting rice liberalization. Shortly after this picture was taken, Lee, a longtime advocate for rice farmers, publicly stabbed himself in the heart as a dramatic display of his opposition to trade liberalization; he died shortly thereafter.

The so-called "cotton wars" between the United States and Brazil illustrate the competing pressures highlighted by liberalism and mercantilism. The United States has long subsidized cotton production, and Brazil, seeking access to the U.S. market, has filed—and won—many disputes with the WTO (Schnepf, 2011). However, the United States continually appealed these rulings, and refused to remove the subsidies. After eight years of disputes, the United States was presented with an ultimatum: either end cotton subsidies or face punitive tariffs on a wide variety of goods it exports to Brazil, ranging from beauty products to automobiles (Politi and Wheatley, 2010). Faced with two politically difficult options, removing cotton subsidies or starting a "trade war" with Brazil, the United States found a rather innovative solution. In exchange for Brazil dropping its trade dispute, it agreed to make payments to both the U.S. and Brazilian cotton farmers. Thus, in addition to keeping their multibillion dollar subsidies to U.S. farmers, U.S. trade officials agreed to provide Brazilian cotton producers with annual payments of over $150 million (Joffe-Walt, 2013).

As the WTO has begun to focus on nontariff barriers to trade, it has found itself addressing issues that go beyond the traditional dichotomy of free trade versus protectionism. For example, concerns related to labor and environmental standards link trade to broader controversies about core human rights and development (see A Closer Look: Trade and the Environment). As trade policy specialist I. M. Destler posits, a "new politics" of international trade has emerged. These new issues involve "not the balance to be struck among economic interests and goals, but rather the proper balance between economic concerns and other societal values." Often brought together under the umbrella of fair trade, these other goals and values do not neatly fall into arguments for or against free trade; survey research indicates even supporters of liberal trade still view fair trade measures, such as labor and environmental rights protections, as important (Ehrlich, 2011). These matters are far more difficult to reconcile, and pose "a challenge that longstanding trade policy institutions were ill-equipped to meet or even to understand" (Destler, 2005, p. 253).

Additionally, increased WTO membership has created further challenges. Traditionally GATT/WTO negotiations followed a "club model" (Esty, 2002) in which a small group of trade officials—typically the United States, European Union, and Japan—ironed out policy, with other countries largely following their lead. Rounds were largely private affairs, with the public paying little or no attention to them. For example, the conclusion of the Tokyo Round in 1979, which was widely heralded by experts as a sweeping victory for trade liberalization, was reported on page 18 of the Business Section (Section D) of the *Washington Post*—hardly prime placement for news items.

This is no longer the case. As evidenced by the massive protests that have become ubiquitous at every meeting, WTO rounds now attract a great deal of public attention. At the same time, the power structure in the organization has also become much more *multipolar*. The Global South has been very active in the international trade system; it currently conducts about a third of total world trade (WDI, 2013). Thus, developing states, particularly the "G-5" emerging economies—China, India, Brazil, Mexico, and South Africa—have become very assertive in trade negotiations (Meltzer, 2011).

The WTO thus faces an interesting dilemma—having largely succeeded in its goal of lowering tariffs, and having attracted almost every state into the organization, it is now tasked with getting an increasing number of states to agree on a large number of very difficult and contentious issues. Indeed, the most recent round of WTO negotiations, the Doha Round, was begun only after seven years of pre-negotiations, and has been ongoing since 2002. It faces a variety of major obstacles and an uncertain future (Bhatia, 2011; Pakpahan, 2013). The current global economic context has hardly served to make these matters easier.

World Trade and the Global Financial Crisis

In assessing global trade, it is important to keep the global context in mind, as recent issues and struggles have occurred in the aftermath of the largest financial crisis since the Great Depression. World trade fell 9 percent in 2008—the first time that annual world trade has decreased since 1982—and declined an additional 12.2 percent in 2009. This decrease in trade was steeper and more sudden than the drop that accompanied the Great Depression (Eichengreen and O'Rourke, 2009). In 2010, global trade came back very strongly, growing 13.8 percent, though trade since then is on track to only grow by 4.5 percent (WTO, 2012; 2013d). Examining the effects of the 2008 global financial crisis on world trade can provide an understanding of how facets of economic globalization, particularly trade and finance, interact. It also demonstrates the resilience of liberal trade norms even in times of economic crisis.

A Closer Look

TRADE AND THE ENVIRONMENT

A great deal of controversy surrounds the relationship between trade and the environment. Critics charge that globalization, of which free trade is a part, leads to a "race to the bottom" in environmental standards, as countries are encouraged to enhance their competiveness by lessening environmental regulations. Yet many studies find that trade can actually lead to improved environmental conditions, as it contributes to the diffusion of advanced technologies and environmentally friendly practices, a process termed the "California effect" (Prakash and Potoski, 2007; Vogel, 1995).

At the root of the trade/environment controversy is a substantial gap in global governance. The Marrakesh Agreement, which founded the WTO, calls for the organization to "protect and preserve the environment." Moreover, Article XX of the original GATT mandate allows for countries to enforce trade laws "necessary to protect human, animal or plant life or health" and that relate "to the conservation of exhaustible natural resources." Beyond this vague mandate, the WTO has no explicit set of environmental rules to guide its decisions. Rather, the principle of national treatment implies that goods are to be treated equally for trade purposes, no matter how they were made. Thus, to discriminate against a country's product because of the way it is manufactured constitutes protectionism. For example, the WTO ruled that U.S. labeling of "dolphin safe" tuna unfairly discriminated against Mexican tuna, which did not use dolphin-safe nets. The WTO also ruled against other U.S. environmental laws, such as provisions for "turtle-safe" shrimp harvesting methods and gasoline standards—although supporting the laws themselves, the panel nonetheless ruled that they were being enforced in a manner that unfairly targeted certain countries.

This highlights a key dilemma. States obviously have a right to maintain environmental standards and practices, yet there is wide variance in how states choose to do this. Given these differences, how can the line be drawn between legitimate environmental regulation and attempts to use such regulation as a "convenient additional excuse for raising trade barriers" (Anderson, 1996)?

WATCH THE VIDEO:

Carnegie Council Video:
Climate Protectionism
and Competitiveness

YOU DECIDE:

1. What does this reveal about the difficulties of reconciling free trade and the environment?
2. How can global trade be reconciled with the need to protect the environment?
3. Is the WTO the best forum to decide these issues?

The 2008 global financial crisis caused a historic drop in world trade levels due to three primary factors. First, the crisis led to a downturn in the overall world economy, which created a huge fall in consumer demand. There was less of a market for foreign goods, as well as products in general. The globalization of production, in particular the nature of supply chains, further magnified this effect. For example, for each unit decrease in the sales of Dell computers in the United States, trade between nine countries is reduced. Global supply chains thus mean that trade reduction has a "multiplier effect," and that the pain of trade contractions is shared among a large group of companies and states.

Additionally, with the collapse in credit markets, trade finance dried up; international trade often requires short-to-medium-term credit that was no longer readily available. Exporters, for example, may need short-term loans during the time period between when their goods are produced and when the revenue from their sales makes it back. In some instances, if neither seller nor buyer can obtain credit to facilitate the transactions, trade will not occur (Auboin, 2009; Chauffour and Malouche, 2011). The end result was a contraction in trade that was "sudden, severe, and synchronized" (Baldwin and Evenett, 2009) across the major trading states.

Economic downturns tend to encourage protectionism. The Great Depression pushed the United States to enact the Smoot-Hawley Act of 1932, which increased U.S. tariffs by 50 percent and contributed to a collapse in world trade. There were some short-term responses that raised concerns. Of particular note was the emergence of *murky protectionism* (Baldwin and Evenett, 2009; Drezner, 2009). This refers to more subtle NTBs that may not be direct violations of WTO laws, but are rather "abuses of legitimate discretion" on behalf of policy makers that serve to reduce trade.

**murky
protectionism**

*Nontariff barriers
to trade that
may be "hidden"
in government
policies not directly
related to trade,
such as environ-
mental initiatives
and government
spending.*

One of the more notable examples was the U.S. "bailout" of its domestic automobile industries with $30 billion in subsidies. Many foreign governments, whose economies were also suffering and whose industries were also requesting assistance, quickly pounced on the bailouts as a violation of free-trade principles. As former French President Sarkozy argued, "you cannot accuse any country of being protectionist when the Americans put up $30 billion to support their automotive industry." Along these lines, the governments of other automobile-producing states passed almost $13 billion in subsidies to their own industries (Gamberoni and Newfarmer, 2009).

Yet a rush toward broader protectionism never occurred, and world trade rebounded rapidly in 2010. There were several reasons global trade did not fall prey to protectionism and collapse. Although some protectionist policies were enacted, they were narrowly focused measures; at the peak of the crisis, the various protectionist measures only affected 2 percent of world imports. As former WTO director-general Pascal Lamy noted, "governments acted with great restraint." Although the WTO was but one of many factors that helped avert a collapse of trade, the organization's multilateral order was nonetheless important, as "its system of rules and disciplines, agreed to over 60 years of negotiations, held firm" (Lamy, 2011).

While the liberal trade order stayed intact, the Doha Round continues to stagnate, with no end in sight. Supporters of the Doha Round argue that the continued process is necessary to help the WTO "modernize" to better take into account the emerging economies and continue to reach out into different areas of the world economy (Lamy, 2011). Moreover, according to Indonesian Minister of Trade Mari Pangestu (2011), although there are some "unbridgeable gaps," countries already agree on a majority of the key issues, particularly in agriculture and food security. Moreover, many emerging countries are waiting for the "deliverables" that only completion of the Doha Round can provide.

Yet a growing number of analysts take a gloomier view of the Doha Round, arguing that "it is time for the international community to recognize that the Doha Round is doomed" (Schwab, 2011 p. 104; Rodrik, 2011). Overly broad and ambitious rounds may no longer be possible given the size of the organization and the growing power of many of its members. To some, the Round's lack of progress is actually hurting the WTO, and the organization would be better off ending the round and the "all or nothing" approach it represents (Schwab, 2011). It raises questions about whether the practices and priorities of the WTO accurately reflect the structure of world trade, and whether there are alternate governance structures—regional, plurilateral, or bilateral—that may more effectively encourage global trade.

Although threats to liberal trade remain, they have taken on different forms. While traditional measures of trade protectionism are increasingly rare, murky protectionism remains an area of concern—in addition to government subsidies of troubled industries, other government practices, such as export incentives as well as health, environmental, and safety regulations, may distort global trade in a manner that violates the spirit, if not the letter, of WTO principles. As economist Simon Evenett (2013, p. 71) concludes, while concerns over traditional forms of protectionism remain, "for the most part they are not where the action has been since the onset of the global economic crisis." Rather, "this time around it is the turn of murky protectionism."

Moreover, an increasing portion of world trade, particularly in growing economies such as those of the BRICS countries, is within supply chains. More than 60 percent of world merchandise trade is trade in components—that is, parts of finished products that represent portions of a larger production chain (Baldwin, Kawai, and Wignaraja, 2013, p. 16; see also Gereffi and Lee, 2012; World Bank, 2013). Since the production processes are increasingly split across different countries, participation in global trade becomes less a matter of shipping finished products and more one of participating in global supply chain networks. In short, a large portion of world trade is no longer about selling goods to other countries, but about making goods with other countries (Baldwin, 2011). Within this context, liberalization—through regional or even unilateral measures—is now the key to joining these chains as they develop.

The increased importance of supply chains has importance for state policies as well as the WTO. Multinational corporations control many of these chains, hence FDI as well as its relation to global trade becomes increasingly important to potential host countries. For the WTO, this underscores the need to change its emphasis from "20th century trade issues" (Baldwin, 2013, p. 25) such as tariffs and agriculture to areas more directly related to the formation of supply chains, including FDI policies as well as trade facilitation—the administrative "nuts and bolts of international trade" (Lamy, 2013), including customs and shipping regulations.

Given the ambitious goals and almost universal membership of the WTO, as well as the difficulty it has encountered in successfully completing the Doha round, a number of alternate institutional structures have evolved which are narrower in either membership or scope. We will now turn to these different organizations, paying particular focus to the most prevalent trade institutions, regional trade agreements (RTAs).

Regional and Plurilateral Trade Arrangements: Supplement or Substitute for the WTO?

In the absence of progress by the WTO, regional and bilateral trade agreements—efforts by pairs or small groups of states to deepen their trade ties with one another—have become a popular alternative for governing commerce (see Map 11.4). The EU was the earliest and most successful example of regional integration, and similar, albeit less successful, initiatives occurred in the Global South during the 1960s and 1970s. However, the rapid proliferation of *regional trade agreements (RTAs)* and bilateral trade agreements did not begin in earnest until the early 1990s—according to the WTO, the number of trade agreements in force increased over tenfold since 1990. As of January 10, 2013, the WTO had been notified of 546 RTAs, and 354 agreements were in force (WTO, 2013e).

Such agreements are ubiquitous; only Somalia, Mongolia, the Democratic Republic of the Congo, and Mauritania remain unaffiliated with any RTA. There is also some evidence that RTAs increase trade among members. For example, trade among the full members of Mercosur—Argentina, Brazil, Paraguay, and Uruguay (there are also six associate members)—increased to $44.2 billion in 2010 from only $8 billion in 1990. Another large trade block, the 10-member Association of Southeast Asian Nations (ASEAN) has seen expansion of trade among its member, with a total of $598 billion intra-ASEAN trade in 2012 (Ng, 2013). Politically, regional trade agreements are much easier to implement because they involve fewer actors and are often encouraged by politically powerful export-oriented industrial sectors (Dur, 2010).

regional trade agreements (RTAs)

Treaties that integrate the economies of members through the reduction of trade barriers.

World Trade Organization

Participation in Goods and Services RTAs

0
1
40

Based on World Trade Organization, 2013.

MAP 11.4   MEMBERSHIP IN REGIONAL TRADE AGREEMENTS RTAs have proliferated since the 1990s, and they have emerged worldwide as a means of expanding trade ties between groups of states. As shown here, many states, particularly in the Global South, join multiple RTAs. In the Global North, many of the EU countries belong to over 30 different RTAs. Membership often falls along geographic lines—for example, most of the RTAs to which the United States belongs are within the Western Hemisphere. They may also codify groups of countries that have traditionally had trade relations, as evidenced by the Lomé Convention, which joins EU members and the wide variety of states that were formerly colonial holdings.

Many RTAs are consistent with WTO principles, and are viewed as catalysts to trade because they encourage trade liberalization, albeit among smaller groups of states. Indeed, political leaders commonly assume that there is no natural conflict between bilateralism, regionalism, and multilateralism. For example, Robert Zoellick, a former president of the World Bank, argued that through a process of "competitive liberalization," the formation of bilateral and regional trade deals could pressure countries into strengthening multilateral institutions. Moreover, political struggles over these trade deals, such as NAFTA and the bilateral trade agreements between the United States and South Korea, are framed largely as a struggle between free trade and protectionism, with the trade agreements representing the former (Destler, 2005). Along the lines of liberal theory, the development of bilateral and regional trade agreements is also politically effective—whatever its economic effects, the economic integration serves to strengthen foreign policy ties among member states and reduce the probability of conflict (Aydin, 2010; Mousseau, 2013).

Yet others who support a multilateral trading order are less sanguine about these agreements. Politically, they argue that such agreements represent a "chimera" in which "attention and lobbying has been diverted to inconsequential deals" (Bhagwati, 2008a) at the cost of pushing for multilateralism. Legally, as countries often join multiple RTAs, the end result of these various deals is a confusing and sometimes contradictory "spaghetti bowl" of regulations, which creates a muddled legal foundation for trade (Suominen, 2013). Finally, although the WTO has specific legal provisions for RTAs, they violate the core principle of nondiscrimination and MFN, as they give some WTO members advantages over others. Economist Jagdish Bhagwati (2008a), who has long argued that such agreements are "termites in the trading system," humorously noted:

> I discovered that the European Union, which started the pandemic (of regionalism) … applied its MFN tariff to only six countries—Australia, New Zealand, Canada, Japan, Taiwan, and the United States—with all other nations enjoying more favorable tariffs. I asked Pascal Lamy, who was then the E.U. trade commissioner, 'Why not call it the LFN (least favored nation) tariff?'

Plurilateral agreements, issue-specific treaties created between a group of WTO members, represent a more "à la carte" approach to trade liberalization (Hoekman, 2013). WTO statutes have long allowed for these agreements, which were originally referred to as "codes." Currently there are only a handful of these agreements, including the Information Technology Agreement (ITA), which began in 1996 between 29 countries, and the Government Procurement Agreement (GPA), which was also enacted in 1996 and currently has 43 members.

plurilateral agreements

Treaties between a subset of WTO members that apply only to a specific issue.

Some see these agreements as a promising way forward for the WTO in that they provide a more flexible forum for addressing a single issue of contention (Bacchus, 2012). Plurilateral negotiations are open to all WTO members, though participation is voluntary and only those who specifically sign onto the agreement are subject to enforcement. It thus brings together countries that share at least some agreement over a given issue. Given the smaller membership, these agreements are also more flexible and quicker to implement or change (Hoekman and Mavriodis, 2012; Nakatomi, 2013).

Ideally, a plurilateral approach can be helpful to the WTO, as agreement in a given area could spread and provide the impetus to attain a "critical mass" of support within the organization as a whole (Saner, 2012). Moreover, unlike PTAs, plurilateral agreements are negotiated within the context of the WTO, thus reducing the chance of potential contradictions between these agreements and broader WTO statutes. Some economists note that plurilateralism could be applied to a broad variety of trade-related issues such as services, trade-related investment measures, and electronic commerce (Nakatomi, 2013).

Overall, although the liberal commercial order has proven robust, the WTO encounters continued difficulties in expanding its power and legitimacy within a more multipolar system. Such problems in the trading system provide some corroboration to the realist viewpoint that there are definite limits to the strength of international organizations, as countries will focus on their domestic interests when threats arise, be they economic or political. Yet at the same time, a liberal case can be made—for the WTO to maintain legitimacy during such tumultuous times does attest to its underlying strength and utility within the global economy. Whatever the current "balance" between the two, the perennial battle between mercantilism and liberalism will continue, and countries and organizations will continue to grapple with how to balance trade interests with noneconomic concerns such as human rights and the environment.

CourseMate

Case Study:
*The Promise
and Perils of
Interdependence*

This chapter, as well as the previous one, has shown that globalization is a "double-edged sword"—the same processes and ties that help our economies grow also ensure that crises have a diffuse effect. Moreover, you have seen the interdependent nature of the various facets of economic globalization, such as the linkages between global finance, production, labor, and trade. Yet globalization is more than just economics; it involves individuals and cultures. To understand that part of the broader puzzle of globalization, the next chapter will take you beyond the economics of globalization, by addressing the cultural and demographic dimensions of our global society.

STUDY. APPLY. ANALYZE.

Key Terms

absolute advantage
antidumping duties
collective action dilemma
comparative advantage
countervailing duties
economic sanctions
export quotas
globalization of labor

globalization of production
import quotas
infant industry
intra-firm trade
most-favored nation (MFN)
    principle
murky protectionism
nearsourcing

nondiscrimination
nontariff barriers (NTBs)
orderly market arrangements
    (OMAs)
plurilateral agreements
protectionism
public good
reciprocity

regional trade agreements (RTAs)
rents
strategic trade policy
tariffs
trade integration
transparency
voluntary export restrictions
    (VERs)

Suggested Readings

Bhagwati, Jadish. (2008) *In Defense of Globalization*. New York: Oxford University Press.

Breznitz, Dan, and John Zysman, eds. (2013) *The Third Globalization: Can Wealthy Nations Stay Rich in the Twenty-First Century?* New York, NY: Oxford University Press.

Hernandez-Truyol, Berta Esperanza, and Stephen J. Powell. (2012) *Just Trade:*

A New Covenant Linking Trade and Human Rights. New York: NYU Press.

Irwin, Douglas. (2009) *Free Trade under Fire*, 3rd edition. Princeton, NJ: Princeton University Press.

Rodrik, Dani. (2011) *The Globalization Paradox: Democracy and the Future of the World Economy*. New York: W.W. Norton.

Stiglitz, Joseph, and Andrew Charlton. (2006) *Fair Trade for All: How Trade Can*

Promote Development. New York: Oxford University Press.

Wenar, Leif. (2011) "Clean Trade in Natural Resources," *Ethics & International Affairs* 25, no. 1 (Spring): 27–39.

World Trade Organization. (2013f) *World Trade Report 2013: Factors Shaping the Future of World Trade*. Geneva: WTO.

Suggested Videos

Steward, Devin T., and Ian Bremmer. "The End of the Free Market."

Stiglitz, Joseph. "Fair Trade for All: How Trade Can Promote Development."

Vocke, William. "Global Ethics Corner: Populism, Protectionism, and China."

Vocke, William. "Global Ethics Corner: Trade Liberalization and the Financial Crisis."

Vocke, William. "Global Ethics Corner: Buy American? Is There a Choice?"

CourseMate

Log in to CourseMate to access the following study tools for this chapter:

- Interactive Quiz
- eBook
- Flashcards & Key Term Crossword Puzzle

- Chapter Audio Summary
- Carnegie Council Videos
- Video Activities
- Simulation

- Animated Learning Module
- Case Study
- International Relations NewsWatch

"In the globalized world that is ours, maybe we are moving towards a global village, but that global village brings in a lot of different people, a lot of different ideas, lots of different backgrounds, lots of different aspirations."

—*Lakhdar Brahimi, UN envoy and advisor*

CHAPTER 12

The Demographic and Cultural Dimensions of Globalization

MAGNUM/Jonas Bendiksen

THE DIFFERENCE BETWEEN HAVES AND HAVE-NOTS Of the seven billion people in the world, one out of every seven lives in slums. Pictured here, children dance in one of the squatter communities that surround Caracas, a city of 3.2 million people in Venezuela. The provision of better housing, social services, and education is a major challenge to improving human security and realizing benefits from urbanization.

QUESTIONS TO CONSIDER

- *What are the most salient characteristics of population change around the world?*
- *How is global migration shaping the world?*
- *How has globalization influenced the spread of disease?*
- *How has information technology affected world politics?*
- *What is the future of globalization? Is it helpful or harmful?*

Everyone in the world is becoming more alike each and every day. It really is a small world, after all. As you probably have at one time or another imagined, beneath the skin every human being is essentially similar. We all share the same planet. And we all tend to respond to the same experiences that almost everyone feels at one time or another—love, fear, alienation, or a sense of a common community and destiny. Everyone also certainly shares a similar aspiration for a better world, as expressed by world futurist Rafael M. Salas: "The final binding thought is to shape a more satisfying future for the coming generations, a global society in which individuals can develop their full potential, free of capricious inequalities and threats of environmental degradation."

There is increasing optimism that this hope will be fulfilled. Why? One explanation is that growing numbers of people throughout the world are pursuing these human goals because globalization is bringing all humanity together as never before in bonds of interdependence. Do you, like them, think that breaking down barriers and boundaries can bring people together in a human family that recognizes no East, West, North, or South, but every individual as part of the same human race? Should you, therefore, practice morals instead of cutthroat politics? And if that goal is your passion, should you, like many others joining together in *nongovernmental organizations* (NGOs) across the globe, promote progress toward more prudent policies rather than blind partisanship?

Is this rising global awareness and activism warranted? Is the vision by which people are increasingly defining themselves as global citizens reasonable? Will a truly global society come into being in your lifetime, propelled by the pressure of cascading globalization that is tearing down visions of separate states, nations, and races that throughout history have so divided humanity? This chapter opens a door to evaluating the prospect for such a jaw-dropping development. You will be asked to consider if global trends might transform the world, and the world politics that condition this.

Once you have glimpsed the world as it might be, as it ought to be, as it's going to be (however that vision appears to you), it is impossible to live compliant and complacent anymore in the world as it is.

—**Victoria Safford, Unitarian minister**

POPULATION CHANGE AS A GLOBAL CHALLENGE

demography

The study of population changes, their sources, and their impact.

To formulate your interpretation of this human dimension of globalization and world politics, it is instructive to first look at how changes in world population are a part of the globalization of world politics.

"Chances are," notes an expert in *demography*, Jeffrey Kluger (2006), "that you will never meet any of the estimated 247 human beings who were born in the past minute … In the minute before last, however, there were another 247. In the minutes to come, there will be another, then another, then another. By next year at this time, all those minutes will have produced millions of newcomers in the great human mosh pit. That kind of crowd is very hard to miss."

Carnegie Council Video:
Demography

As the population on this planet increases, globalization is bringing us closer together in a crowded *global village* where transnational challenges characterize our borderless world. Evidence strongly suggests that unrestrained population growth will result in strife and environmental degradation (see Chapters 7 and 14). Population change also forces reconsideration of standards for ethics (the criteria by which right and wrong behavior and motives should be distinguished). Some people regard the freedom to parent as a human right. Others claim that controls on family size are necessary because an unregulated population will "parent" a crowded and unlivable future world without the resources necessary to sustain life for all people. For this reason, politics—the exercise of influence in an attempt to resolve controversial issues in one's favor—surrounds debate about population policies. To understand why the globalization of population has become such a controversial issue, it is helpful to trace the global trends in population growth that have made this topic so problematic.

World Population Growth Rates

The rapid growth of world population is described by a simple mathematical principle that Reverend Thomas Malthus noticed in 1798: unchecked, population increases in a geometric or exponential ratio (e.g., 1 to 2, 2 to 4, 4 to 8), whereas subsistence increases in only an arithmetic ratio (1 to 2, 2 to 3, 3 to 4). When population increases at such a geometric rate, the acceleration can be staggering. Carl Sagan illustrated this principle that governs growth rates with a parable he termed "The Secret of the Persian Chessboard":

> The way I first heard the story, it happened in ancient Persia. But it may have been India, or even China. Anyway, it happened a long time ago. The Grand Vizier, the principal adviser to the King, had invented a new game. It was played with moving pieces on a board of 64 squares. The most important piece was the King. The next most important piece was the Grand Vizier—just what we might expect of a game invented by a Grand Vizier. The object of the game was to capture the enemy King, and so the game was called, in Persian, shahmat—shah for king, mat for dead. Death to the King. In Russia it is still called shakhmaty, which perhaps conveys a lingering revolutionary ardor. Even in English there is an echo of the name—the final move is called "checkmate." The game, of course, is chess.
>
> As time passed, the pieces, their moves and the rules evolved. There is, for example, no longer a piece called the Grand Vizier—it has become transmogrified into a Queen, with much more formidable powers.
>
> Why a king should delight in the creation of a game called "Death to the King" is a mystery. But, the story goes, he was so pleased that he asked the Grand Vizier to name his own reward for such a splendid invention. The Grand Vizier had his answer ready: He was a humble man, he told the King. He wished only for a humble reward. Gesturing to the eight columns and eight rows of squares on the board he devised, he asked that he be given a single grain of wheat on the first square, twice that on the second square, twice that on the third, and so on, until each square had its complement of wheat.
>
> No, the King remonstrated. This is too modest a prize for so important an invention. He offered jewels, dancing girls, palaces. But the Grand Vizier, his eyes becomingly lowered, refused them all. It was little piles of wheat he wanted. So, secretly marveling at the unselfishness of his counselor, the King graciously consented.
>
> When the Master of the Royal Granary began to count out the grains, however, the King was in for a rude surprise. The number of grains starts small enough: 1, 2, 4, 8, 16, 32, 64, 128, 256, 512, 1,024.... But by the time the 64th square is approached, the number becomes

colossal, staggering. In fact the number is nearly 18.5 quintillion grains of wheat. Maybe the Grand Vizier was on a high fiber diet.

How much does 18.5 quintillion grains of wheat weigh? If each grain were 2 millimeters in size, then all the grains together would weigh around 75 billion metric tons, which far exceeds what could have been stored in the King's granaries. In fact, this is the equivalent of about 150 years of the world's present wheat production (Sagan, 1989, p. 14).

The story of population growth is told in its statistics. The annual rate of population growth in the twentieth century increased from less than 1 percent in 1900 to a peak of 2.2 percent in 1964. It has since dropped to about 1.3 percent and is expected to drop slightly more to 1.1 percent between now and 2015, when 74 million new people (the equivalent to the population of Turkey) will be added each year. In terms of absolute numbers, the world population has grown dramatically in the twentieth century. Even in the past 20 years the population has grown from 6.1 billion in 2000 to 7.0 billion in 2011 and is expected to reach 7.6 billion by 2020 (WDI, 2013). Robert S. McNamara, as World Bank president, noted that "If one postulates that the human race began with a single pair of parents, the population has had to double only thirty-one times to reach its huge total." Plainly, the planet is certain to have many people by the mid-twenty-first century, well beyond the roughly 7 billion in 2014.

The size of the global population is shaped by worldwide fertility rates and cannot stabilize until it falls below *replacement-level fertility*. That will not happen until the total *fertility rate*, the worldwide average number of children born to a woman, falls to 2.1. Though a "global reduction in childbearing and birth rates is now under way" (Eberstadt, 2010, p. 55)—with the total fertility rate having dropped from 4.8 in 1965 to 2.4 today—world population is projected to continue to surge because of "population momentum" resulting from a large number of women now entering their childbearing years.

Like the inertia of a descending airliner when it first touches down on the runway, population growth simply cannot be halted even with an immediate, full application of the brakes. "Large families in an earlier generation mean that there will be more mothers in the current one and therefore more children, even if families are smaller and the underlying impetus towards growth has dropped" (Parker, 2010, p. 28). Not until the size of the generation giving birth to children is no larger than the generation among which deaths are occurring will the population "airplane" come to a halt. But through intentional and sustained efforts of birth control, "by about 2020, the global fertility rate will dip below the global replacement rate for the first time" (*The Economist*, 2010a, p. 29), though the population by then may have topped 8 billion (Wall, 2013).

Changes in life expectancy also account for global population growth. "Over the course of the twentieth century, global life expectancy at birth more than doubled, soaring from about 30 years in 1900 to about 65 years in 2000" (Eberstadt, 2010, p. 55). By 2015, life expectancy at birth is expected to reach 75 years. Improvements in general health conditions have led to declines in mortality, and the global population has grown as people have lived longer lives.

World population will reach 9.3 billion by 2050, at which point it is expected to stabilize. In the meantime, regional differences will become more prominent, with 90 percent of the population growth over the next 15 years occurring in the Global South (see Figure 12.1).

Case Study: The State of the World Population

replacement-level fertility

One couple replacing themselves on average with two children so that a country's population will remain stable if this rate prevails.

fertility rate

The average number of children born to a woman (or group of women) during her lifetime.

Carnegie Council Video: Fertility Rate

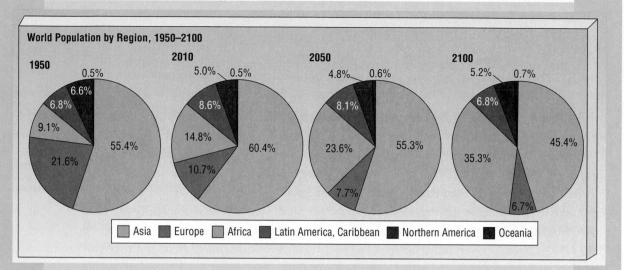

Source: Adapted from the United Nations Population Division

FIGURE 12.1   WORLD POPULATION GROWTH PROJECTIONS TO THE YEAR 2100 It took until the early 1800s for world population to reach 1 billion people, and today another billion people are added every 12 to 14 years. World population is expected to reach 9.3 billion in 2050 and continue to rise to 10.1 billion by 2100. The distribution of world population is also anticipated to change significantly. As the figure shows, Africa is expected to experience rapid population growth and account for over a third of global population by 2100; Europe is expected to continue to decline from almost 22 percent in 1950 to less than 7 percent in 2100.

Demographic Divisions: Youth Bulges and Aging Populations

The global population continues to expand, though the growth is much more rapid in the developing Global South countries (which are least able to support their existing populations) than in the wealthy Global North, where population is declining gradually despite increasingly longer life spans. Of the population growth the world has experienced since 1900, most—80 percent since 1950—has been in the Global South. This portends fulfillment of the "demographic divide," which is based on the probability that the population of the Global North will fall (from 23 percent of total world population in 1950 and 15.5 percent in 2020) to only 10 percent by 2050 (WDI, 2013; 2010).

Sub-Saharan Africa and Western Europe illustrate the force of two different pictures of population momentum. Africa's demographic profile is one of rapid population growth, as each new age group (cohort) contains more people than the one before it. Thus, even if individual African couples choose to have fewer children than their parents, Africa's population will continue to grow because there are now more men and women of childbearing age than ever before. In the past 50 years the population of sub-Saharan Africa more than tripled from 230 million to 820 million (World Bank, 2013e).

In contrast, Europe's population is growing slowly because recent generations have been smaller than preceding ones. In fact, Europe has moved below replacement-level fertility to become a stagnant population with low birthrates and a growing number of people who survive beyond middle age. A product of an extended period of low birthrates, low death rates, and increased longevity, Europe is best described as an aging society, where the low birthrates and aging populations have caused alarm that the number of European newborns will not be sufficient to renew populations or bear the financial burden of supporting an aged society.

Consider the demographic divide between the Global South and Global North as a whole. Fertility rates in the Global South are, on average, almost a full 1 percent higher than the Global North. Because each cohort is typically larger than the one before it, the number of young men and women entering their reproductive years continues to grow (see Figure 12.2). Although the average age is increasing faster in the Global South than in the Global North—in the less developed countries the population of people over the age of 65 will rise to 35 percent by 2050—people under 30 presently constitute more than 70 percent of the population in much of Africa (Lin, 2012), and children under the age of 15 constitute about 28 percent of the population throughout the Global South (WDI, 2013).

High birthrates pose challenges for economic growth and political stability, and some see a low birthrate as a prerequisite for successful development. It is difficult for public policy to meet citizens' needs and generate national wealth as "soaring unemployment, endemic poverty,

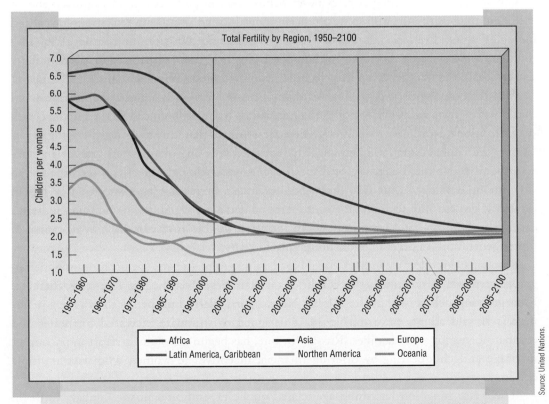

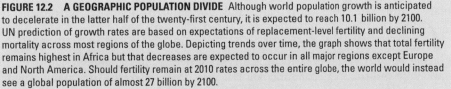

FIGURE 12.2   A GEOGRAPHIC POPULATION DIVIDE Although world population growth is anticipated to decelerate in the latter half of the twenty-first century, it is expected to reach 10.1 billion by 2100. UN prediction of growth rates are based on expectations of replacement-level fertility and declining mortality across most regions of the globe. Depicting trends over time, the graph shows that total fertility remains highest in Africa but that decreases are expected to occur in all major regions except Europe and North America. Should fertility remain at 2010 rates across the entire globe, the world would instead see a global population of almost 27 billion by 2100.

Source: United Nations.

and flailing schools are quite simply impossible to combat when every year adds more and more people" (Potts and Campbell, 2009, p. 30). Furthermore, as a *youth bulge* develops wherein a burgeoning youth population in the Global South faces poor economic conditions and a lack of resources to provide for a family, many are turning to religious fundamentalism to counter their frustration and despair and are propelling an Islamic revival. Particularly in conjunction with economic stagnation, youth bulges have been linked to a greater involvement in terrorism and crime (Schuman, 2012). As Michelle Gavin, an international affairs fellow with the Council on Foreign Relations, explains: "If you have no other options and not much else going on, the opportunity cost of joining an armed movement may be low."

At the same time, a revolution in longevity is unfolding, with life expectancy at birth worldwide at a record-high of 70 years and rising (WDI, 2013). Life expectancy at birth is expected to rise to 75 years by 2015. This is creating an increasingly aged world population, and changing the contours of the global community. By 2025, 9 percent of the population in the Global South will be 65 or older—a 45 percent increase since 2008. In the Global North, this demographic trend is even more pronounced, with about 20 percent of the population likely to be 65 years or older by 2025 (World Bank, 2011).

Global aging is occurring at rates never before seen, in part because of improvements in medicine and health care, with some physicians now distinguishing between chronological and biological aging. Even the number of people who reach age 80 is on the rise. In 1950, 14.5 million people had seen their 80th birthday. By 2009, the number had risen to 101.9 million, and by 2050, the number is expected to be almost 395 million (*Time*, 2010).

Although the "aging and graying" of the human population is a global population trend that poses its own set of public policy dilemmas, it is more pronounced in the Global North than the Global South (see Map 12.1). There are concerns that, due to its rapidly aging populations, the Global North will be especially burdened by rising old-age dependency and face an array of economic, budgetary, and social challenges. Although the effects are expected to vary among developed countries, these could include a decreasing labor supply; a decline in economic growth and per capita income; increased demand for public expenditures on health care, long-term care, and pensions; and an increased need to invest in the human capital of future generations in order to boost overall productivity.

Resolving this dilemma in the Global North will require, in part, the promotion of demographic renewal by creating better conditions for families. Over the past few years, there has been growing debate within the Global North, particularly Europe, as to whether policy makers should adopt "pro-natal" policies designed to stimulate increased birthrates and combat norms for small families. Russia, for one, has begun a sustained effort to encourage marriage and childbearing by offering financial incentives to women who have multiple children.

It will also hinge on reforming age-related public expenditures in the Global North, in particular health care, long-term care, and government-supported retirement pensions. As described by the European Commission's 2012 Aging Report:

> An aging population raises challenges for our societies and economies, culturally, organizationally and from an economic point of view. Policy makers worry about how living

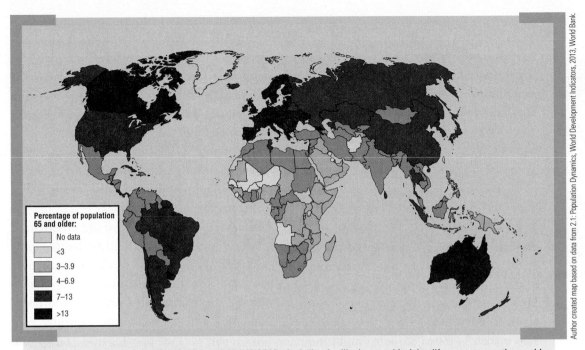

Percentage of population
65 and older:

	No data
	<3
	3–3.9
	4–6.9
	7–13
	>13

MAP 12.1   AGING AND GRAYING AROUND THE WORLD As falling fertility is met with rising life expectancy, the world moves toward a major demographic transformation—global aging—wherein elderly people constitute an increasing percentage of a state's population. "It will challenge the ability of many countries to provide a decent standard of living for the old without imposing too big a burden on the young" (Jackson, 2013). As the map shows, this transformation is already well under way in the Global North. In Germany, for example, 21 percent of the population is 65 or above as compared to only 2 percent in Angola.

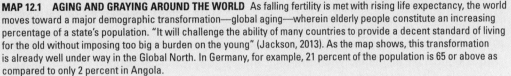

standards will be affected as each worker has to provide for the consumption needs of a growing number of elderly dependents. Markets worry about fiscal sustainability and the ability of policy makers to address timely and sufficiently these challenges in several Member States. The seriousness of the challenge depends on how our economies and societies respond and adapt to these changing demographic conditions. Looking ahead, policy makers need to ensure long-term fiscal sustainability in the face of large but predictable challenges, as well as significant uncertainty. This is all the more true as Europe has experienced the deepest recession in decades, which is putting an unprecedented stress on workers and enterprises and has had a major negative impact on public finances (European Commission, 2012, p. 21).

The resulting differences in demographic momentums are producing quite different population profiles in the developed and the developing worlds, and "twenty-first century international security will depend less on how many people inhabit the world than on how the global population is composed and distributed: where populations are declining and where they are growing, which countries are relatively older and which are more youthful, and how demographics will influence population movements across regions" (Goldstone, 2010, p. 31). The poor Global South is home to a surplus of youth, with rising birthrates and growing populations; the rich Global North is aging, with falling

Alexei Filippov/ITAR-TASS

FROM RUSSIA WITH LOVE In response to Russia's demographic crisis, policy makers are offering married couples incentives to procreate. With September 12th declared Family Contact Day throughout Russia in an effort to encourage marital intimacy, the governor of the Ulyanovsk region coined it the "Day of Conception" and offered prizes to couples that give birth nine months later on June 12, Russia's Independence Day. Shown here is a couple on the Bench of Reconciliation in a Moscow park, which is curved to promote physical contact and help couples to work out their differences.

birthrates and declining populations. In the Global South, the working-age population will shoulder the burden of dependent children for years to come, while in the Global North it is the growing proportion of elderly adults who will pose a dependency burden.

It is easy to see how this facet of globalization is *not* making people in the world more alike. Variation in the geographical distribution of population is increasing the differences in the quality of life experienced around the planet, and this demographic diversity is the result of different changes in the key determinants of population growth and structure—fertility, mortality, and migration. Let us now consider how the movement of people, both across and within countries, shapes global population structures.

GLOBAL MIGRATION TRENDS

The movement of populations across borders has reached unprecedented proportions, and has raised a host of moral issues, such as the ethnic balance inside host countries, the meaning of citizenship and sovereignty, the distribution of income, labor supply, *xenophobia*, the impact of multiculturalism, and protection of basic human rights and prevention of exploitation. Furthermore, the potential for large flows of migrants and refugees from *failed states*—countries whose governments no longer enjoy support from their rebelling citizens and from displaced peoples who either flee the country or organize revolts to divide the state into smaller independent units—to undermine democratic governance and state stability poses a potential threat (see Chapters 6 and 7). The governments of sovereign states are losing their grip on regulating the movement of foreigners inside their borders, and no multilateral IGOs for meaningful global governance exist to deal with the consequences of the escalating migration of people (and labor) around the globe. Porous borders create ambiguous ethics about mass migration movements, but one consequence is clear: there are both winners and losers through the globalization of migration.

CourseMate

Carnegie Council Video:
Xenophobia

A Quest for Sustenance and Freedom

People most commonly migrate in search of better jobs. For host countries, this can contribute to economic growth. For the home countries, many of which are poor Global South countries, the growing flow of *remittances*, or money that migrants earn while working abroad and then send to their families in their home countries, provides one of the biggest sources of foreign currency (Lopez et al., 2010; Singer, 2010). In 2011, migrants from the Global South sent home $358.4 billion (WDI, 2013).

Yet there are worries that migration may reduce the job opportunities for natives and place a strain on public services. These fears are exacerbated by the weak global economy, and many countries have adopted measures intended to stem the flow of peoples across borders (Koser, 2010; Traynor and Hooper, 2011). Construction continues in the United States to extend the line of barrier fences along the border with Mexico. In 2009, the European Parliament implemented controversial immigration rules that allow illegal immigrants to be detained up to 18 months and then expelled. Italy and France called for changes to tighten Europe's Schengen open-border treaty in 2011 in response to the more than 25,000 migrants who entered Italy from North Africa, many of whom also crossed into other European countries. Even countries in the Global South, such as Nigeria, have taken steps to counter what is seen as a security threat posed by large flows of illegal immigrants (Ekhoragbon, 2008).

Another trend in our "age of migration" is the flight of people not in search of economic opportunity but out of fear of persecution. *Refugees* are individuals whose race, religion, nationality, membership in a particular social group, or political opinions make them targets of persecution in their homelands and who, therefore, migrate from their country of origin, unable to return. According to the UN High Commissioner for Refugees (UNHCR), at the start of 2012, the world's refugee population was 15.2 million, of whom 10.4 million fell under UNHCR's mandate and 4.8 million Palestinian refugees fell under the responsibility of the

refugees

People who flee for safety to another country because of a well-founded fear of political persecution, environmental degradation, or famine.

CourseMate

Carnegie Council Video:
Refugees

DESPERATE REFUGEES ON THE RUN Over the last decade, about 15 million refugees each year have become homeless people in search of sanctuary. Shown left, these Somali women and their children are among more than 6000 refugees that sought safety and shelter in May 2012 as Somali and African Union forces fought against Al-Shababb insurgents in the Afgooye corridor in Somalia. Pictured right is actress Angelina Jolie meeting with women in refugee camps in the Democratic Republic of Congo in March 2013. As a Special Envoy for the United Nations High Commissioner for Refugees (UNHCR), an agency that currently assists over 20 million refugees in roughly 120 countries, Jolie attracts global attention to the fight against rape as a tool of warfare. As she explains: "The hope and the dream is that … it is known that if you abuse women, if you rape women, you will be accountable for your actions. This will be a crime of war and you won't just get away with it."

genocide

The attempt to eliminate, in whole or in part, an ethnic, racial, religious, or national minority group.

ethnic cleansing

The extermination of an ethnic minority group by a state.

Carnegie Council Video:
Ethnic Cleansing

Simulation:
Globalization

United Nations Relief and Works Agency for Palestinian Refugees in the Near East (UNRWA). Other "persons of concern" are internally displaced persons (IDPs), which the UNHCR estimated to total a staggering 29.5 million worldwide (see Figure 12.3). Additionally, though not considered displaced per se, there are about stateless people worldwide and 895,000 asylum seekers (UNHCR, 2012). This does not include the additional millions of children and women kidnapped by crime rings in the huge sex-trafficking trade and smuggled across borders as captives for prostitution.

Refugees and displaced persons alike are often the victims of war and political violence. For example, *genocide* in Rwanda in 1994 drove more than 1.7 million refugees from their homeland; the persecution, *ethnic cleansing*, and armed conflict that accompanied the breakup of the former Yugoslavia uprooted nearly 3 million victims, moving Europe to the list of continents with large numbers of refugees—over 6 million—for the first time since World War II. More recently, the UNHCR estimates that Afghan and Iraqi refugees comprise almost half of all refugees. At the start of 2012, around one out of every four refugees in the world was from Afghanistan, and 1.2 million Iraqis sought refuge in other countries (UNHCR, 2012).

A large proportion of the world's refugees and displaced people flee their own homelands when ethnic and religious conflicts erupt in failed states where governments fail to preserve

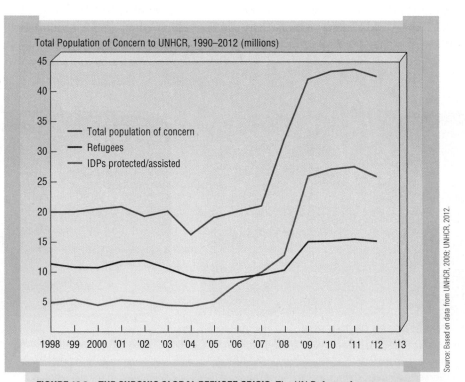

Source: Based on data from UNHCR, 2009; UNHCR, 2012.

FIGURE 12.3   THE CHRONIC GLOBAL REFUGEE CRISIS The UN Refugee Agency (UNHCR) defines "persons of concern" as refugees and internally displaced persons (IDPs). The problem is huge and has become steadily worse since 2004, climbing to over 42.5 million forcibly displaced people at the start of 2012 (UNHCR, 2012). Of all the refugees, around 50 percent reside in Asia and about a quarter reside in Africa.

law and order. In addition, millions of refugees flee their homelands because when disaster strikes they are denied basic human rights such as police protection, access to fair trials in courts, and public assistance. A combination of push-and-pull forces now propels migration trends. Human rights violations, environmental degradation, unemployment, overpopulation, famine, war, and ethnic conflict and *atrocities* within states—all push millions beyond their homelands (see Map 12.2).

Migrants also are pulled abroad by the promise of political freedom elsewhere, particularly in the democratically ruled Global North countries. "We are now faced with a complex mix of global challenges that could threaten even more forced displacement in the future," explains António Guterres, the UN High Commissioner for Refugees. "They range from multiple new conflict-related emergencies in world hot spots to bad governance, climate-induced environmental degradation that increases competition for scarce resources and extreme price hikes that have hit the poor the hardest and are generating instability in many places" (*International Herald Tribune*, 2008, p. 3).

Yet today's refugees are not finding safe havens; shutting the door is increasingly viewed as the preferred solution, and xenophobia is on the rise (see "A Closer Look: Global Migration and the Quest for Security"). Among both developed and developing countries, there is a growing unwillingness to provide refuge for those seeking a better life. With a weakening global economy, people are ever more resistant to foreigners competing for domestic jobs and resources. Moreover, as security concerns since 9/11 have escalated

atrocities

Brutal and savage acts against targeted citizen groups or prisoners of war, defined as illegal under international law.

**Video:
A Ticking Bomb**

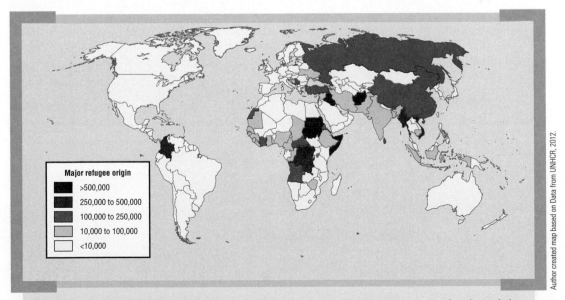

Author created map based on Data from UNHCR, 2012.

Major refugee origin
- >500,000
- 250,000 to 500,000
- 100,000 to 250,000
- 10,000 to 100,000
- <10,000

MAP 12.2   FROM WHENCE DO THEY FLEE? Oppressive and violent conditions cause many people to leave their homes in the interest of security and survival. At the start of 2012, 2.7 million refugees were from Afghanistan, the leading country of origin of the world's refugees. Iraq was the second largest country of origin, responsible for 1.4 million refugees. Somali and Sudanese refugees followed as third and fourth, respectively, with over 1 million and 500,000 refugees. Although it is commonly assumed that Western states admit the most refugees from conflict, evidence indicates instead that the majority flee to neighboring countries in the Global South. Indeed, the UNHCR estimates that between 75 and 93 percent of refugees remain within their region of origin.

A Closer Look

GLOBAL MIGRATION AND THE QUEST FOR SECURITY

As unrest flowed across northern Africa in Spring 2011, more than 25,000 migrants fled to Italy by way of the tiny island of Lampedusa. Most were Tunisians seeking refuge from the economic strife and political upheaval in their country.

The heavy influx of northern Africans posed problems for the conservative Italian government, which had taken a hard stand against illegal immigration. To Italy's frustration, the other members of the EU were unwilling to share the illegal immigration burden. Italy's request that the EU apply an emergency rule that would relocate the refugees across the various EU member states was blocked. In an effort to address its immigration crisis, Italy repatriated some of the migrants to their home country. For thousands of others, it issued national residence permits. This not only allowed the North Africans to remain in Italy, but it also enabled them to travel within Europe's border-free Schengen area to other countries.

This latter action angered France, as thousands of migrants traveled from Italy in the hopes of joining relatives in France. As tension between Italy and France accelerated, the leaders of the two countries at the time—French President Nicolas Sarkozy and Italian Prime Minister Silvio Berlusconi—collectively called for reform of the open-border Schengen treaty that allowed legal residents of most EU countries to travel across borders with only minimal border checks. Although both wish to see the treaty persist, they argued that it was necessary to allow temporary controls to be enacted when exceptional circumstances arise. In a joint letter to senior EU officials, they argued that the "situation concerning migration in the Mediterranean could rapidly transform into a crisis that would undermine the trust that our compatriots have in the [principle] of freedom of travel within Schengen." They further sought commitment to a "principle of solidarity" among the EU member states, with assurances that other EU countries would assist the southern states along the Mediterranean in dealing with problems posed by mass immigration.

WATCH THE VIDEO:

CourseMate

Carnegie Council Video:
Global Migration: Open the
Doors or Build the Walls?

YOU DECIDE:

1. Does global migration help or hurt the host country?

2. How can democracies reconcile conflicting principles—support for the fundamental right of people to emigrate versus a commitment to the absolute right of sovereign states to control their borders?

3. Is your stance on global migration compatible with the principle of a global "Responsibility to Protect?"

worldwide, the linkage drawn between refugees and the probability of terrorism has tightened immigration controls.

Not only have countries in the Global North restricted the flow of people across borders, but the Global South is also increasingly unwilling to bear the burden of hosting refugees. This places blame for insecurity on the victims—refugees seeking refuge—because "as a general rule, individuals and communities do not abandon their homes unless they are confronted with serious threats to their lives and liberty. Flight from one's country is the ultimate survival strategy.... Refugees serve both as an index of internal disorder and the violation of human rights and humanitarian standards" (Loescher, 2005, p. 47).

That said, efforts to stem the tide of migrants have not reversed the trend of people seeking *sanctuary*. During 2011, a total of 876,100 applications for *asylum* or refugee status were submitted to governments and UNHCR offices in 171 countries (UNHCR, 2012). This represented a 3 percent increase from the previous year in the number of people seeking sanctuary, after an 11 percent decrease the prior year. With more than 107,000 asylum applications, South Africa is the globe's largest recipient of individual applications, followed by the United States and France. Furthermore, approximately 17,700 asylum applications were submitted by unaccompanied children in 69 countries, mostly from Afghan and Somali children (UNHCR, 2012).

The ethical issue is whether in the future the wealthy countries will respond to the plight of the needy with indifference or with compassion. How will *human security* be reconciled with *national security*? The welfare and survival of everyday people are endangered, and the need for their protection is increasing.

sanctuary

A place of refuge and protection.

asylum

The provision of sanctuary to safeguard refugees escaping from the threat of persecution in the country where they hold citizenship.

Urbanization

When considering migration patterns and interpreting demographic projections, it is also important to examine the geographic concentration of people within countries. Known as *population density*, this measures how close together people are living. Some countries and regions are very crowded and others are not. For example, Monaco is the most congested country in the world, with 17,714 people for each square kilometer, and people in Greenland have the most space to spread out, with less than one person for each square kilometer (WDI, 2013).

Today, about half the world lives in cities, and the urbanization of the world is accelerating and spreading. At the start of 2011, 3.6 billion people, about 52 percent of the total world population, lived in urban areas, with a projected urban population growth rate of 2.1 percent (WDI, 2013). The United Nations predicts that by 2050, 6.3 billion people—two-thirds of the population—will live in an urban environment (UNDESA, 2012).

Referring to rapid urbanization, economist Edward Glaeser (2011) quips that "the world isn't flat, it's paved." Already 80 percent of the populations in the Global North live in big cities that are getting bigger (WDI, 2013), but cities are growing fastest in the developing Global South countries. "Every month 5 million people move from the countryside to a city somewhere in the developing world" (*The Economist*, 2011f, p. 91). This is particularly notable in Asia and the Pacific, where three of the world's ten most global cities are located.

population density

The number of people within each country, region, or city, measuring the geographical concentration of the population as a ratio of the average space available for each resident.

megacities

Metropolitan areas where the population is more than 10 million people.

This urbanizing trend is producing a related kind of demographic divide: the increasing concentration of people in giant *megacities* where populations exceed 10 million (see Figure 12.4). As the percentage of world population residing in dense urban agglomerations increases worldwide, the "*dualism*" between city dwellers and those living in the rural and poor periphery will make the urbanized core cities more similar to each other in outlooks,

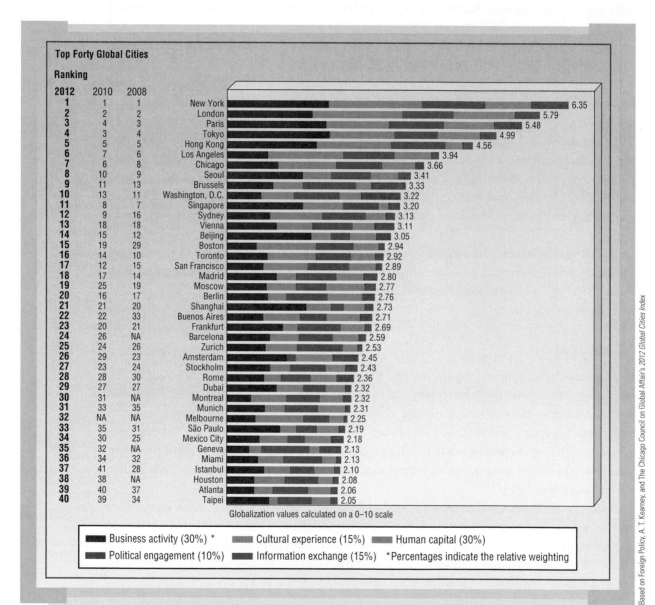

Based on Foreign Policy, A. T. Kearney, and The Chicago Council on Global Affair's 2012 Global Cities Index

FIGURE 12.4   THE TOP FORTY GLOBAL CITIES "The world today is more about cities than countries, and a place like Seoul has more in common with Singapore and Hong Kong than it does with smaller Korean cities" (Hales and Pena, 2012, p. 4). Based on the 2012 Global Cities Index, the figure depicts global engagement of major world metropolitan areas across five dimensions: business activity, human capital, information exchange, cultural experience, and political engagement. There is stability at the top of the rankings, with New York, London, Tokyo, and Paris placing in the top 10 ranked cities across all three time periods. At least three Asian cities have appeared in the top 10 each time, reflecting Asia's continued importance in world affairs.

values, and lifestyles. People in megacities are already communicating and computing with one another more frequently than they do with people living in the countryside within their own states. "The process of urbanization, through which populations are increasingly concentrated in towns and cities, is an apparently inexorable transition and associated with rising living standards. No highly developed society is primarily rural" (Skeldon, 2010, p. 25). Indeed, many positive externalities can result from urbanization: "proximity makes people more inventive, as bright minds feed off one another; more productive, as scale gives rise to finer degrees of specialization; and kinder to the planet, as city-dwellers are more likely to go by foot, bus or train" (*The Economist*, 2011f, p. 91; Glaeser, 2011).

However, urbanization and the growth of megacities can pose challenges for national governance. Balance-of-power politics falls short in helping us to understand the implications of how globalization enables major cities to challenge national sovereignty and pull away from their home states:

> Taken together, the advent of global hubs and megacities forces us to rethink whether state sovereignty or economic might is the new prerequisite for participating in global diplomacy. The answer is of course both, but while sovereignty is eroding and shifting, cities are now competing for global influence alongside states (Khanna, 2010, p.126).

The world is witnessing a surge in urbanization, where capital flows, supply chains, and telecommunications link global cities and denationalize international relations. Today, Hamburg and Dubai have cemented a partnership to expand shipping ties and life sciences research. Likewise, Abu Dhabi and Singapore have forged new commercial partnerships.

The power and influence of cities, however, are not unique to the contemporary period. Sociologist Saskia Sassen points out that, in ages past, nations and empires did not restrain cities but instead served as filters for their global ambitions. In Europe, it was in the largely autonomous Renaissance cities of Bruges and Antwerp that the innovative legal foundations for a transnational stock exchange were first developed, providing a basis for international credit and global trade networks and reflecting the ability of the cities to conduct their own "sovereign" diplomacy (Khanna, 2010; Sassen, 2008).

Though cities can serve as engines for growth and development, they can also pose risks to human security. Millions of urban squatters pour into megacities each year, and economic inequality and urban blight is rampant in major metropolitan areas. Migrants live in slums in destitution and squalor next to stunning high rises and private gated communities in cities such as Sao Paulo, Shanghai, and Istanbul. "Indian billionaire Mukesh Ambani, the world's fourth-richest person, is reportedly spending close to $2 billion on the construction of his 27-story home—complete with hanging gardens, a health center, and helipads—all with a bird's eye view of Mumbai's largest slum, Dharavi" (Khanna, 2010, p. 126).

The impact of global urbanization is also likely to aggravate health and environmental problems, straining supplies of clean water, shelter, and sanitation. If urbanization throughout the global community continues at its current pace, which is almost certain, this trend will lead to still another kind of *transformation* in the world. Threats, such as the outbreak of a widespread and deadly disease, could produce a *population implosion*. Next we will look at examples of life-threatening diseases that are sweeping a globe without borders.

population implosion

A rapid reduction of population that reverses a previous trend toward progressively larger populations; a severe reduction in the world's population.

R. Kiedrowski/Arco Images GmbH/Age Fotostock

FEELING THE PULSE OF HUMANITY At over 7 billion people at the start of 2014, the world's population continues to grow. Half live in cities, and urbanization continues to rise. In 1975, only three cities in the world exceeded 10 million people. The UN predicts that by 2025, there will be 37 megacities and all but 8 will be in the Global South (Mead, 2012). Pictured here, vendors, pedestrians, and vehicles vie for space on the streets of Kokata, India, a city of 16 million people.

NEW PLAGUES? THE GLOBAL IMPACT OF DISEASE

Although infant and child mortality rates remain discouragingly high in many developing countries, at least they are decreasing. On a global level, life expectancy at birth has increased each year since 1950, climbing by UN estimates to 70 years (WDI, 2013). However, this rising longevity could reverse if globally transmittable diseases cut into the life spans made possible by improvements in health care, nutrition, water quality, and public sanitation.

Throughout history, the spread of bacteria, parasites, viruses, plagues, and diseases to various ecospheres, regardless of state borders, has suspended the development of or brought down once-mighty states and empires (Kolbert, 2005). In our age of globalization, a disease such as drug-resistant strains of tuberculosis (TB), which affects 125 out of every 100,000 people around the world (WDI, 2013), knows no borders. It can spread with a sneeze or a cough on an international flight. Likewise, there are about 219 million cases of malaria each year, leading to more than 660,000 deaths in 2010 (*WHO Malaria Report*, 2012). Because communicable diseases cause 27 percent of deaths worldwide (WDI, 2013), global health is a concern and a threat to human security (see Figure 12.5).

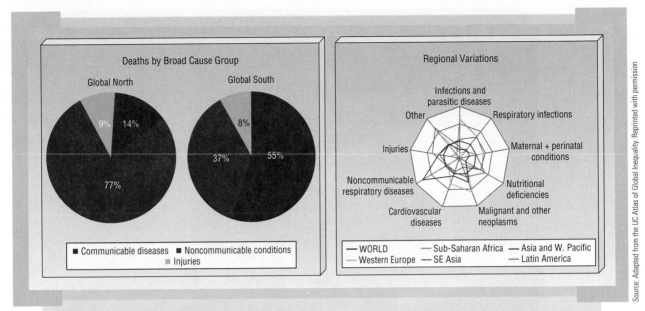

Source: Adapted from the UC Atlas of Global Inequality. Reprinted with permission

FIGURE 12.5   THE BURDEN OF DISEASE Globally, one out of three people dies from infectious disease. Yet a death divide is apparent between the Global North and the Global South. Shown on the left, over half of deaths in the Global South are caused by communicable disease, with HIV/AIDS as the most common culprit. In the Global North, people tend to live longer and die from noncommunicable conditions such as cardiovascular disease and cancer. On the right, the radar graph shows regional differences in the cause of death.

The grim possibility that virulent disease will decimate the world's population because we all share a common global environment is nowhere more evident than in the spread of the *human immunodeficiency virus (HIV)*, which causes *acquired immune deficiency syndrome (AIDS)*. Since the 1970s onset of the AIDS pandemic, the UN estimates that "every day more than 8,000 people die of AIDS. Every hour almost 600 people become infected. Every minute a child dies of the virus." Today, 55.8 million people worldwide between the ages of 15 and 49 have HIV (WDI, 2013), although some regions of the world suffer more from the disease than others. Sub-Saharan Africa, which is home to just over 10 percent of the global population, holds 67 percent of the people living with HIV/AIDS (Iqbal and Zorn, 2010).

The circumstances are tragic, and stopping the tragedy is "a moral duty." Fortunately, there are signs that this pandemic is losing momentum as fewer deaths are occurring due to HIV/AIDS every year (Purlain, 2013). During 2011, 1.7 million people died from AIDS-related illnesses—down from a peak of 2.3 million in 2005 (UNAIDS, 2013). This does not mean that the epidemic is vanishing: in many of the most seriously AIDS-affected countries, deaths are projected to overtake births and cause population decreases in the next few years. Thus, as world public health expert Laurie Garrett notes, "Tackling the world's diseases has become a key feature of many nations' foreign policies."

Sadly, there are many diseases that pose significant threats to human well-being and remind us of the permeability of our national borders. As the second leading cause of death from an infectious disease (ranking only behind HIV), the World Health Organization declared tuberculosis

human immuno-deficiency virus (HIV)

A virus that can lead to the lethal acquired immune deficiency syndrome (AIDS).

acquired immune deficiency syndrome (AIDS)

An often fatal condition that can result from infection with the human immunodeficiency virus (HIV).

Carnegie Council Video: Acquired Immune Deficiency Syndrome (AIDS)

AP Photo

DOES GLOBALIZATION MAKE THE WHOLE WORLD SICK? The dangerous threat of a global flu pandemic "ranks higher than a major terrorist attack, even one involving weapons of mass destruction" (*Newsweek*, 2005). Shown here is a cause for global alarm: at a market in Shanghai, workers sleep with their chickens, and close contact with infected birds is the primary source of deadly hybrids of human and animal viruses.

(TB) a major health emergency, and since 1993 has led efforts to improve TB care and control. Tuberculosis is an airborne infectious disease that, though preventable and curable, claims the lives of millions of people. An estimated 8.7 million new cases of TB, with 1.4 million deaths, were reported in 2011. The disease is most prevalent in Asia and Africa, with almost 40 percent of the cases worldwide occurring in India and China. However, considerable progress has been made toward halting and reversing the global tuberculosis epidemic. "The TB mortality rate has decreased 41 percent since 1990 and the world is on track to achieve the global target of a 50 percent reduction by 2015" (WHO, 2012b).

Malaria is also a major threat to global health, with the Centers for Disease Control and Prevention reporting 300 to 500 million cases of malaria annually, of which over 1 million result in death (Lyons, 2010). This is tragic because the disease, which is transmitted by mosquitoes to human beings, is largely preventable and treatable. Efforts to combat the spread of the disease include distributing millions of insecticide-treated bed nets.

Over the past decade, there have also been deadly outbreaks of influenza that have generated global concern. What makes influenza different from other global diseases is the frightening ease with which it spreads. Some strains, such as avian flu, spread from birds to human beings. Experts believe that this disease is spread through the direct handling of chickens and the processing of meat, and worry that a new strand may spread easily from human to human (Mo, 2013). Another recent deadly strain, known as H1N1 or swine flu, crossed the species barrier between pigs and people. First appearing in Mexico in March 2009 and then spreading quickly to the United States, by its peak in 2010 it had appeared in at least 214 countries and overseas territories. Although the pandemic is now over, it highlighted the challenges faced by public officials as they seek to identify and enact protective measures for the population. A number of countries, particularly China and Russia, took vigorous quarantine measures against people who had traveled to countries suffering from high numbers of infected people.

The spread and control of infectious diseases such as AIDS, tuberculosis, malaria, cholera, Lassa fever, ebola, lymphatic filariasis, avian flu, mad cow disease, and swine flu have established themselves on the radar screen of policy makers throughout the world. Additionally, noncommunicable diseases—such as cancer, stroke, and diabetes—are on the rise, and it is estimated that by 2030 they will be the "leading cause of death and disability in every region of the world" (Bollyky, 2012). These diseases will not vanish from sight anytime soon and are a stark reminder of the transnational threats that remain ever present in our borderless world and necessitate global cooperation and coordination.

A relationship exists between the health of individuals within a state and that state's national security. A population's health is of utmost importance to the state's ability to survive.

—Jeremy Youde, global health expert

THE GLOBAL INFORMATION AGE

Pessimists predict that one result of globalization is competition between states as they seek to preserve their sovereign independence, retain the allegiance of their citizens, resist the homogenizing forces now sweeping the world, and ensure their own national security. In a contrasting, more optimistic scenario, *liberal theory* anticipates a globalization of cultures that transcends contemporary geopolitical boundaries and erodes the meaning of national identity and sovereignty by creating "global citizens" who assign loyalty to the common interests of all peoples. Trends in the cultural dimension of globalization are generating changes in how people construct their identities and encourage a more *cosmopolitan* perspective. The major source of this global transformation is the growing speed and flow of communications, which is a hallmark of the *global village*—a metaphor used by many to portray a future in which borders will vanish and the world will become a single community.

In the age of global communication, the meaning of "home" and "abroad" and of "near" and "far" vanishes, promoting changes in people's images of community and their own identity. Will cellular phones, the Internet, blogs, and other means of transnational communication portend consensus and, perhaps, an integrated global village? Or is this vision, in which shared information breeds understanding and peace, unattainable? Or worse, will the unconstrained interconnectiveness of globalization do away with private life, erasing what remains of identity, individualism, and independence?

cosmopolitan

An outlook that values viewing the cosmos or entire world as the best polity or unit for political governance and personal identity, as opposed to other polities such as one's local metropolis or city of residence (e.g., Indianapolis or Minneapolis).

THE WORLD AT ONE'S FINGERTIPS As a primary information highway, the Internet fuels globalization and allows individuals to become part of a "digital public" that transcends national borders and identities (Tiessen, 2010). More than 73.4 percent of citizens in the Global North are Internet users, as are 21.5 percent of people in the Global South (WDI, 2012), and Internet usage continues to grow. This photo of a Huli tribal chief from Papua New Guinea presenting his new website illustrates how the spread of information technology facilitates the global flow of ideas and information.

The Evolution of Global Communications

The increased ease and volume of international communications is creating "the death of distance" and radically altering people's decisions about where to work and live, as well as their constructed images of "us" and "them." No area of the world and no arena of politics, economics, society, or culture are immune from the pervasive influence of *communication technology*. Personal computers and the "wireless world" of mobile phones have facilitated communication between people in areas as diverse as rural communities in the Global South and the technology-intensive countries in the Global North. "More than 50 percent of the world's population has access to some combination of cell phones (5 billion users) and the Internet (2 billion). These people communicate within and across borders, forming virtual communities that empower citizens" (Schmidt and Cohen, 2010, p. 75).

cyberspace

A metaphor used to describe the global electronic web of people, ideas, and interactions on the Internet, which is unencumbered by the borders of the geopolitical world.

The result of this expanding worldwide use of the Internet is the creation of *cyberspace*, a global information superhighway allowing people everywhere to communicate freely as they surf the Web, exchange emails, and join social networking sites. The increasing number of Internet users (by about a million *weekly*) is promoting a cultural revolution by giving most of the world access to unfiltered information for the first time. This creates a single globe, united in shared information. This face of globalization submerges borders and breaks barriers. It lays the foundation for a smaller, shrinking, and flatter world and propels "an exciting new era of global interconnectedness that will spread ideas and innovations around the world faster than ever before" (Giles, 2010, p. 4).

The growth of Internet *blogs* and active diarists, known as "bloggers," who share their opinions with a global audience adds to the influence of what has become known as "the information age." Drawing on the content of the international media and the Internet, bloggers weave together an elaborate network with agenda-setting power on issues ranging from human rights in China to the secretive U.S. surveillance of the Internet to the violent response to anti-government protest in Turkey. "What began as a hobby is evolving into a new medium that is changing the landscape for journalists and policymakers alike" (Drezner and Farrell, 2006).

This trend is accelerating by leaps and bounds with the rapid diffusion of iPods, text messaging, and Twitter, which "has managed to transcend basic instant messaging and social networking" (Kutcher, 2009, p. 60). In countries where the government restricts access to social media, such as China, copycat websites have sprung up to facilitate communication. Added to this is the enormous popularity of *podcasts*, which allow people to create their own website channels and share multimedia versions of new uploads with users throughout the world, and social networking sites such as Facebook, which enable people to share information with their friends and associates.

If one constant stands out, it is continuous change in technological innovation. The rapid pace of *information technology* development drives globalization. It will make today's methods of communicating look ancient in a few years and, in the process, transform how people communicate as well as which countries lead (and prosper) and which follow.

Enthusiasts believe that the advantages of the global communications revolution are a blessing for humanity. When people around the world are connected through the revolution in digital communications, the shared information propels human development and productivity. Proponents also see the globalized digital revolution as producing many side payoffs: reducing oppressive dictators' authority, allowing small businesses to compete globally, empowering transnational activists to exercise more influence, and providing opportunities for a diversity of voices and cultures. For example, in 2011, through the use of information technology such as Twitter, Facebook, and the online video-sharing site YouTube, Egyptians were able to organize protest demonstrations, document to the world images of repression, and bring to life a digital people's movement for freedom. These actions ultimately toppled Egyptian President Hosni Mubarak from power. As famous actor and Twitter enthusiast Ashton Kutcher optimistically noted, "Right now the word *revolution* is spelled with 140 characters." Expressing a similar sentiment, UN Secretary-General Ban Ki-moon observed that some dictators "are more afraid of tweets than they are of opposing armies."

On the other hand, there is a "dark side" to the global communications revolution. While social media can spur protest movements, the speed at which they develop has a negative consequence in that there is typically not sufficient time to build a strong enough core of leaders, robust structure, and devoted members to not just seize power but wield it effectively once there is victory. "Twitter-lutionaries are good at toppling regimes, but in the Mideast and North Africa, they're losing out to the Islamists, who've built protest movements the old-fashioned way" (Freeland, 2012, p. 64).

blogs

Online diaries, which spread information and ideas worldwide in the manner of journalists.

podcasts

Audio and visual programs that individuals make and distribute as digital downloads.

Additionally, as historian Niall Ferguson (2011, p. 9) notes, "social networks might promote democracy, but they also empower the enemies of freedom." Critics complain that the growing electronic network has created a new global condition known as *virtuality*. In such a world, one can conceal one's true identity, which threatens to make the activities of international organized crime and terrorist groups easier:

> The world's most repressive regimes and violent transnational groups—from al Qaeda and the Mexican drug cartels to the Mafia and the Taliban—are effectively using technology to bring on new recruits, terrify local populations, and threaten democratic institutions. The Mexican drug cartels, in order to illustrate the consequences of opposition, spread graphic videos showing decapitations of those who cooperate with law enforcement, and al Qaeda and its affiliates have created viral videos showing the killings of foreigners held hostage in Iraq (Schmidt and Cohen, 2010, p. 78).

Some also worry that "privateness will become passé [through] the spread of surveillance technology and the rise of Websites like YouTube, which receives more than 65,000 video uploads daily and is driving a trend toward cyber-exhibitionism" (*Futurist*, 2007, p. 6). New privacy issues are likely to arise as researchers and corporations figure out how to use all of the information about a user's location that can be determined through information technology services offered by Internet providers and cell phone companies. "You may use your phone to find friends and restaurants, but somebody else may be using your phone to find you and find out about you" (Markoff, 2009, p. 1). Similarly, online social networks, such as Facebook, which has a global membership that would place it as the world's third most populous country, encourage users to share information. Then, the networks mine the data on members' personal preferences (Fletcher, 2010).

In the name of national security, governments are also developing extensive surveillance systems that discreetly monitor activities, many in public spaces. One example is the high-tech surveillance program in China, known as "Golden Shield," which can identify dissent and allow the government to address it before it turns into a mass movement. Using people-tracking technology supplied by American corporations such as General Electric, IBM, and Honeywell, the goal is to create "a single, nationwide network, an all-seeing system that will be capable of tracking and identifying anyone who comes within its range" (Klein, 2008, p. 60).

The United States' extensive surveillance of Internet communications, which became the focus of considerable international criticism in 2013, is another example. The U.S. National Security Agency (NSA), Federal Bureau of Investigation (FBI), and Central Intelligence Agency (CIA) secretly collected millions of records from U.S. telecommunications and technology firms. While some defend the program as a necessary violation of privacy to fight terrorism and major crime, critics charge that it was an overreach of authority and a threat to democracy. U.S. Senator Mark Udall of the Senate Intelligence Committee summarized these concerns, saying "You have a law that's been interpreted secretly by a secret court that then issues secret orders to generate a secret program. I just don't think this is an American approach to a world in which we have great threats." Adding further to global furor, evidence emerged indicating that the emails and phone messages of national delegates at the G-20 economic meetings in 2009 were intercepted by the British signals intelligence agency (GCHQ) in order to give their country an advantage at the meetings (MacAskill et al., 2013).

The Politics and Business of Global Communication

The more-than-$1-trillion global telecommunications industry is without question the major vehicle for the rapid spread of ideas, information, and images worldwide. That impact accelerated after the World Trade Organization (WTO) created the World Telecom Pact in 1997. This *regime* ended government and private telecommunications monopolies in many states, and the resulting cuts in phone costs were widely seen as a catalyst of the world economy's expansion.

Advances in information technology and the expansive scope of global media have augmented this development. Yet, contrary to conventional wisdom that the media has the ability to drive a country's foreign policy, the type of power that media wields over international affairs is arguably limited. Scholarship shows that the media influence what people *think about* more than *what they think*. In this way, the media primarily function to set the agenda of public discussion about public affairs instead of determining public opinion.

It is through *agenda setting* that the media demonstrably shape international public policy (see Gilboa, 2002). For example, global broadcasts of the ruthless repression and illegitimate tactics associated with Mugabe's bid for reelection in Zimbabwe in 2008 ignited a worldwide chain reaction to aid that country's refugees and pressure the government to reform. Similarly, reports by professional journalists and individual activists helped to fan Iranian resistance and protest over the declared electoral victory of incumbent president Mahmoud Ahmadinejad in 2009. Likewise, in 2011, social media helped fan popular dissent and organize demonstrations by providing communication and inspiration during the "Arab Spring."

These examples of the power of information technology in international politics aside, some people caution that this kind of "virtual diplomacy" has real limitations. Not only can it constrain the policy options available to global decision makers, but it can provide biased or incomplete information that may contribute to an inaccurate or limited understanding of global problems.

Moreover, though ours is often described as the information age, a remarkably large portion of the available information is controlled by a *cartel* of huge multinational media corporations. Headquartered mostly in the rich Global North, these industry leaders are merging to combine their resources and, in the process, expanding their global reach. They keep "us fully entertained and perhaps half-informed, always growing here and shriveling there, with certain of its members bulking up, while others slowly fall apart or get digested whole. But while the players tend to come and go—always with a few exceptions—the overall leviathan itself keeps getting bigger, louder, mightier, forever taking up more time and space, in every street, in countless homes, in every other head" (Miller, 2006). The world's population is a captive audience, and the information presented by these corporate giants shapes our values and our images of what the world is like.

agenda setting

The thesis that by their ability to identify and publicize issues, the communications media determine the problems that receive attention from governments and international organizations.

Carnegie Council Video: Agenda Setting

cartel

A convergence of independent commercial enterprises or political groups that combine for collective action, such as limiting competition, setting prices for their services, or forming a coalition to advance their group's interests.

A counterpoint to the "McWorld" of transnational media consumerism is "*jihad*"—a world driven by "parochial hatreds," not "universalizing markets" (Barber, 1995). Because globalized communications and information may be used as tools for terrorism and revolution as well as for community and peace, the creation of a world without boundaries, where everybody will know everything about anybody's activities, will not necessarily be a better world. You should ask: Would the world be better or worse if it were to become an increasingly impersonal place, with rootless individuals who have declining connections to their own country's culture and history?

> *People from all over the world will draw knowledge and inspiration from the same technology platform, but different cultures will flourish on it. It is the same soil, but different trees will grow. The next phase of globalization is going to be more glocalization—more and more local content made global.*

—**Thomas L. Friedman, international journalist**

GLOBALIZATION AND THE GLOBAL FUTURE

Rapid globalization, propelled in large measure by revolutions in technology, is almost certain to continue. Expect the controversies about globalization's alleged virtues and vices to heighten as finance, trade, population, labor, communications, and cultures continue to converge globally.

Although globalization has narrowed the distance between the world's people, some have gained and others have lost ground. The global village is not proving to be an equally hospitable home for everyone. Indeed, levels of satisfaction with cascading globalization vary widely, as do the levels to which countries and people are linked by globalization's multiple forces (see Figure 12.6). Winners in the game downplay the cost of global integration, and critics deny globalization's benefits. The debate about globalization's problematic impact is intensifying, but without resolution, as contenders are hardening their positions without listening to the counterarguments.

You have now taken into account a number of the dimensions of globalization—in international economics, demography, global communication, and the potential spread of universal values for the entire world. If the trends you have surveyed actually do culminate for the first time in a global consensus uniting all of humanity, these values and understandings might unify all people on Earth into a common global culture. This could conceivably prepare the way for a global *civil society*, even with the eventual emergence of supranational institutions to govern all of humanity.

Yet this worldview and set of predictions strike fear into the hearts of many people who experience *cognitive dissonance* when they confront a frightening vision that challenges their customary way of thinking about world affairs. These people (and there are multitudes) strenuously reject the idea that the traditional system of independent sovereign states can or should

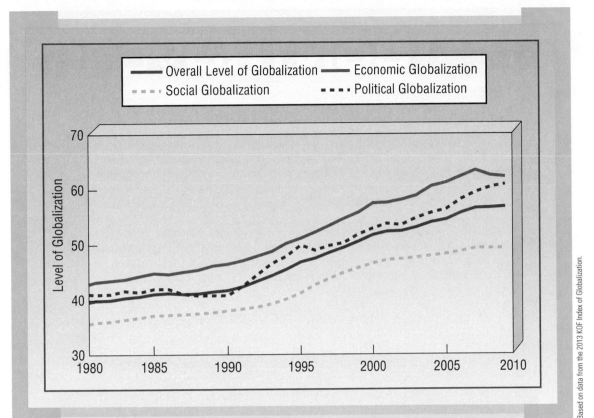

FIGURE 12.6   LEVELS OF GLOBALIZATION In an effort to take stock of globalization's progress, the *2013 KOF Index of Globalization* examines the political, social, and economic dimensions of globalization by looking at multiple indicators spanning trade, business, politics, and information technology to determine the ranking of 207 countries. Since the 1970s, there has been an upward trend in all three dimensions of globalization, with a strong increase after the end of the Cold War. The latest global economic and financial crisis has slowed the pace of the economic globalization process, although social and political globalization continues to rise.

be replaced by a global community with strong supranational regulatory institutions that enhance global governance.

So conclude your inspection of globalization's influence on world politics by evaluating the available evidence and sorting out the balance sheet of globalization's costs and benefits (see "Controversy: Is Globalization Helpful or Harmful?"). What do prevailing trends tell you? Is Thomas Friedman's "flat world" concept that globalization has emasculated the state just as an "electronic herd" tramples down traditional state borders valid? Or is Daniel Drezner (2007) more accurate in arguing that "states make the rules" and that powerful governments are still in control of shaping global destiny because "great powers cajole and coerce those who disagree with them into accepting the same rulebook"?

Globalization is real, for better or for worse. Many people recommend globalization for international public policy, because they believe that its consequences are basically good for

**Case Study:
Interdependence and
Future International
Politics**

IS GLOBALIZATION HELPFUL OR HARMFUL?

To many students of international relations, globalization has two faces, one positive and one negative. To those whose perceptions focus on globalization's benefits, globalization helps to break down traditional divisions of humanity—between races, nations, and cultures—that are barriers to peace, prosperity, and justice. To others, globalization is a harmful phenomenon, breeding such things as global disease and threats to local job security, and therefore a force to be resisted.

Imagine yourself writing a report such as the evaluation that the International Labour Organization undertook when it challenged itself to provide "new thinking to break the deadlock and bridge the divide about the globalization debate." To frame your analysis, see if your evaluation would support or question the World Commission's conclusion (Somavia, 2004, p. 6):

> Globalization can and must change. [We acknowledge] globalization's poten-
> tial for good—promoting open societies, open economies, and freer exchange
> of goods, knowledge, and ideas. But the Commission also found deep-seated
> and persistent imbalances in the current workings of the global economy that
> are ethically unacceptable and politically unsustainable. The gap between
> people's income in the richest and poorest countries has never been wider . . .
> More than one billion people are either unemployed, underemployed, or
> working poor. Clearly, globalization's benefits are out of reach for far too
> many people.

An alternative exercise would be to make an ethical assessment about the morality of globalization. This is what the philosopher Peter Singer (2004) did in applying as a crite-rion the utilitarian principle that it is a moral duty to maximize the happiness and welfare of all human beings and even animal welfare. Singer sees great benefit from the erosion of state sovereignty and the idea that the entire world should be the unit of ethical analysis. His conclusion springs from a UN report that observed, "In the global village, someone else's poverty very soon becomes one's own problem: illegal immigration, pollution, conta-gious disease, insecurity, fanaticism, terrorism." Under globalization, altruism and concern for others pay dividends, whereas narrow selfish behavior causes the selfish competitor counterproductive harm.

Or try one last thought experiment. Think like an economist. Would your economic analysis of globalization agree with the conclusions of famous social scientist Jagdish Bhagwati (2004)? Richard N. Cooper (2004, pp. 152–53) summarizes Bhagwati's liberal theoretical position and propositions:

> (Bhagwati) addresses a slate of charges against globalization ... before turning
> to fixes for globalization's downsides: improving governance, accelerating social
> agendas, and managing the speed of transitions. He concedes a few points to glo-
> balization's critics but, wielding logic and fact, demolishes most of the allegations
> made against it. His conclusion: that the world, particularly its poorest regions,
> needs more globalization, not less.... To the claim that globalization increases
> poverty, Bhagwati's response is, "rubbish."

humankind. However, critics argue that globalization's costs far outweigh its benefits. As the pace of globalization has become a recognized force in world politics, it also has become a topic of heated debate. Globalization has hit a political speed bump, provoking intense critical evaluation of globalization's causes, characteristics, and consequences, and inspiring fresh ethical examination of the elevated interdependence of countries and human beings. The uncertain wisdom and morality of globalization may be the most discussed issue on today's global agenda, receiving even more attention than poverty, disease, urbanization, or the preservation of identity.

The age of globalization has far-reaching implications for humanity. In the next chapter of *World Politics*, you will consider the circumstances of the 7 billion human beings striving throughout the world to sustain themselves, improve the human condition, and protect their right to life, liberty, and happiness.

AP Photo/Richard Vogel

THE MAKING OF A GLOBAL CULTURE?   Some people regard globalization as little more than the spread of values and beliefs of the globe's reigning hegemon, the United States. Shown here is one image that fuels that point of view—an enormous inflated Santa Claus in front of a hotel in downtown Hanoi, Vietnam—a predominantly Buddhist city still subscribing to the communist principles, emphasizing the greed of market capitalism and the class divisions it is believed to create. The sale of Christmas trees is rising there, too.

STUDY. APPLY. ANALYZE.

Key Terms

acquired immune deficiency syndrome (AIDS)

agenda setting

asylum

atrocities

blogs

cartel

cosmopolitan

cyberspace

demography

ethnic cleansing

fertility rate

genocide

global village

human immunodeficiency virus (HIV)

megacities

podcasts

population density

population implosion

refugees

replacement-level fertility

sanctuary

virtuality

xenophobia

Suggested Readings

Bromley, Daniel, and Glen Anderson. (2013) *Vulnerable People, Vulnerable States: Redefining the Development Challenge.* London: Routledge.

Carns, Katie. (November 25, 2009) "Globalization and Opportunity," Carnegie Council.

Friedman, Thomas L. (2007) *The World Is Flat: A Brief History of the 21st Century.* New York: Farrar, Straus, and Giroux.

Glaeser, Edward. (2011) *Triumph of the City: How Our Greatest Invention Makes Us Richer, Smarter, Greener, Healthier and Happier.* New York: Penguin.

Grewal, David Singh. (Spring 2009) "Network Power: The Social Dynamics of Globalization," Carnegie Council.

Risse, Mathias. (2008) "On the Morality of Immigration," *Ethics & International Affairs* 22, no. 1 (Spring):25–33.

Trask, Bahira Sherif. (2010) *Globalization and Families: Accelerated Systemic Social Change.* New York: Springer.

UNHCR. (2011) *UNHCR Global Trends.* Geneva: UN High Commissioner for Refugees.

World Bank. (2013f) *Atlas of Global Development,* 4th edition. Washington, DC: World Bank.

Suggested Videos

Carnegie Council Video

Grewal, David Singh. "Network Power: The Social Dynamics of Globalization."

Kotkin, Joel. "The Next Hundred Million: America in 2050."

Vocke, William. "Egypt: Democracy or Demography?"

Vocke, William. "How Real Is Virtual?"

CourseMate

Log in to CourseMate to access the following study tools for this chapter:

- Interactive Quiz
- eBook
- Flashcards & Key Term Crossword Puzzle
- Chapter Audio Summary
- Carnegie Council Videos
- Video Activities
- Simulation
- Animated Learning Module
- Case Study
- International Relations NewsWatch

"To deny people their human rights is to challenge their very humanity."

—*Nelson Mandela, former president of South Africa*

CHAPTER 13

The Promotion of Human Development and Human Rights

FOR THE PEOPLE Governments make choices about the priority placed on human development. In mid-June 2013, over a million protestors across 80 cities in Brazil took to the streets, and what began as grievance over a rise in bus fares expanded to include poor public services, especially health care and education, as well as high taxes, inflation, rising food prices, and government corruption. Given these profound deficiencies, as shown here, many Brazilians feel that it is wrong for the government to spend an anticipated $26 billion on projects related to the World Cup in 2014 and the Olympics in 2016.

REUTERS/Jeslei Marcelino

QUESTIONS TO CONSIDER

- *What role do individuals play as actors in world politics?*
- *How does human security vary around the world today?*
- *What groups are most vulnerable to human rights abuse? What threats do they face?*
- *What are the causes and consequences of gender inequality?*
- *What is the international community's role in promoting and enforcing human rights?*

Surfing the Web last night, you came across a number of news articles that depicted the daily horrors some people face. From living in conditions of squalor and poverty to suffering the raping and pillaging of paramilitary forces, you are stunned and sickened at the trials and tribulations that many less fortunate people must endure. Like most people, you hope for a better future for all humanity. So what can be done to promote moral values and reform world politics?

For many people the future is bleak, resembling what the English political philosopher Thomas Hobbes described when he talked of life as "solitary, poor, nasty, brutish, and short." The opportunities and choices that are most basic to freedom from fear and poverty are unavailable for most people in the Global South's poorest countries. They experience slower rates of development and less *human security* than in the Global North, and the prospects of the "have-nots" are not improving.

Given the serious deprivations facing so many people, there are many reasons for concern. The denial of the inalienable rights to which all humans are presumably entitled—the "life, liberty, and the pursuit of happiness" of which the U.S. Declaration of Independence speaks—attests to the extent that fundamental human security is not being met. This problem prompted Mary Robinson, the former United Nations (UN) high commissioner for human rights, to "call on global actors—corporations, governments and the international financial organizations—to join with globalized civil society and share responsibility for humanizing globalization."

> *Every human life is precious.... it is not just about our criminal justice system, which we also want to be proportionate and restorative; it is about the type of society that we want to build—a society that values every person, and one that doesn't give up on its people.*
>
> **—Laurence Lien, member of Parliament of Singapore**

PUTTING PEOPLE INTO THE PICTURE

Until relatively recently in the theoretical study of world politics, the needs of the faceless billions of everyday people were neglected. That past theoretical legacy pictured the mass of humanity as marginalized victims or left them invisible by painting their fates as controlled by forces over which hapless people have little influence. French world-systems historian Fernand Braudel (1973, p. 1244) wrote that "when I think of the individual, I am always inclined to see him imprisoned within a destiny in which he himself has little hand, fixed in a landscape in which the infinite perspectives of the long-term stretch into the distance both behind and before."

When thinking about world affairs, the average person has long been relegated to a mere "subject" whom rulers were traditionally permitted to manipulate to advance their states' interests. That vision has been rejected throughout the world. A consensus has emerged that now supports the view that people are important, that they have worth, and, therefore, that *ethics* and *morals* belong in the study of international relations. As ethicist Ronald Dworkin (2001,

p. 485) defined, "Ethics includes convictions about what kinds of lives are good or bad for a person to lead, and morality includes principles about how a person should treat other people." These principles apply to interstate relations, and they are at the heart of analyses of human security in world politics.

That consensus notwithstanding, many observers embrace the traditional realist assumption that vast global forces render people powerless. Realists recognize that people participate politically but claim they have no real power because an invisible set of powerful forces described before as the "system" gives most human beings only superficial involvement without granting real influence.

Denying the importance and influence of individual human *agency* seems increasingly strange, because classic thinking about the world has long been concentrated on people and the essential characteristics of human nature. As anthropologist Robert Redfield (1962) argued, "Human nature is itself a part of the method [of all analysis]. One must use one's own

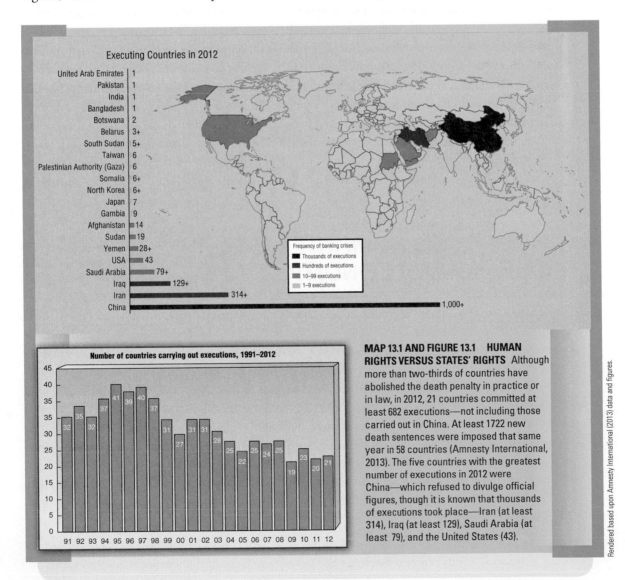

MAP 13.1 AND FIGURE 13.1   HUMAN RIGHTS VERSUS STATES' RIGHTS Although more than two-thirds of countries have abolished the death penalty in practice or in law, in 2012, 21 countries committed at least 682 executions—not including those carried out in China. At least 1722 new death sentences were imposed that same year in 58 countries (Amnesty International, 2013). The five countries with the greatest number of executions in 2012 were China—which refused to divulge official figures, though it is known that thousands of executions took place—Iran (at least 314), Iraq (at least 129), Saudi Arabia (at least 79), and the United States (43).

Rendered based upon Amnesty International (2013) data and figures.

human rights

The political rights and civil liberties recognized by the international community as inalienable and valid for individuals in all countries by virtue of their humanity.

📱 CourseMate

Carnegie Council Video:
Human Rights

humanity as a means to understanding. The physicist need not sympathize with his atoms, nor the biologist with his fruit flies, but the student of people and institutions must employ [one's] natural sympathies in order to discover what people think or feel." This requires a humanistic interpretation that gives people status and value. Moreover, in the global community a *civil society* is emerging. A normative consensus has emerged concerning the inherent moral worth and status of humans and the concomitant obligation of states to recognize and protect that status (Fields and Lord, 2004).

How can we create a world that is free of poverty and persecution? If you, as a student of international affairs, are to understand the forces behind the prevailing trends in world politics, it is important to consider the conditions that humanity faces. This chapter will introduce you to information about the human condition to enable you to evaluate the unfolding debate about the role of humans as actors on the global stage, the prospect for human development, and the ethics of *human rights*. Will humanity be valued? Will human welfare and rights be protected?

These are critical questions. Where does humanity fit into the prevailing and most popular *paradigms* or theoretical orientations that policy makers and scholars construct about world politics? For the most part, classical realism focuses solely upon the state and its ruler's sovereign freedom and, except for building its image of international reality from a pessimistic conception of human nature, it ignores the role of leaders and the *nongovernmental organizations* (NGOs) that people form. Liberals attach more importance to humans, following the ethical precept of German philosopher Immanuel Kant that people should be treated as ends and not means, and that human rights and human dignity should be safeguarded. *Constructivism* goes further; it makes humanity the primary level of analysis and emphasizes how human ideas define identities that in turn impart meaning to material capabilities and the behavior of actors (see Chapter 2).

HOW DOES HUMANITY FARE? THE HUMAN CONDITION TODAY

"Man is born free, and everywhere he is in chains," bemoaned political philosopher Jean Jacques Rousseau in his famous 1762 book, *Social Contract*. Times have since changed, but in many respects Rousseau's characterization of the human condition remains accurate. How should we evaluate the depth of human deprivation and despair against this fact? Can the poorest proportion of humanity sever their chains of disadvantage in order to realize their human potential and obtain the high ideals of human security, freedom, and dignity?

The inequalities and disparities evident in people's standards of living cannot help but to evoke sympathy for the difficult conditions many people face, especially in the less developed Global South countries. One American graduate student, when working on his Ph.D., confronted this reality during his field research in South America. Brian Wallace found a reality far different from his own experience of growing up in the southern United States. In 1978 he was moved to write:

> I spent the first 24 years of my life in South Carolina. When I left for Colombia [South America], I fully expected Bogotá to be like any large U.S. city, only with citizens who spoke

Spanish. When I arrived there I found my expectations were wrong. I was not in the U.S., I was on Mars! I was a victim of culture shock. As a personal experience this shock was occasionally funny and sometimes sad. But after all the laughing and the crying were over, it forced me to reevaluate both my life and the society in which I live.

Colombia is a poor country by American standards. It has a per capita GNP of $550 and a very unequal distribution of income. These were the facts that I knew before I left.

But to "know" these things intellectually is much different from experiencing firsthand how they affect people's lives. It is one thing to lecture in air conditioned classrooms about the problems of world poverty. It is quite another to see four-year-old children begging or sleeping in the streets.

It tore me apart emotionally to see the reality of what I had studied for so long: "low per capita GNP and maldistribution of income." What this means in human terms is children with dirty faces who beg for bread money or turn into pickpockets because the principle of private property gets blurred by empty stomachs.

It means other children whose minds and bodies will never develop fully because they were malnourished as infants. It means street vendors who sell candy and cigarettes 14 hours a day in order to feed their families.

It also means well-dressed businessmen and petty bureaucrats who indifferently pass this poverty every day as they seek asylum in their fortified houses to the north of the city.

It means rich people who prefer not to see the poor, except for maids and security guards.

It means foreigners like me who come to Colombia and spend more in one month than the average Colombian earns in a year.

It means politicians across the ideological spectrum who are so full of abstract solutions or personal greed that they forget that it is real people they are dealing with.

Somewhere within the polemics of the politicians and the "objectivity" of the social scientists, the human being has been lost.

Despite wide differences that enable a proportion of humanity to enjoy unprecedented standards of living, the daunting scale of poverty and misery is evident throughout the world, from which only a small fraction of people have any hope of escaping in the near term (see Map 13.2 and Figure 13.2). One indicator of this reality is money. According to the World Bank's definition of extreme poverty as income of $1.25 or less a day, about 1.2 billion people (about 20.6 percent of the world) live in extreme poverty and another 2.5 billion (about 36 percent of world population) seek to survive on two dollars or less a day (WDI, 2013).

Income inequality is a serious global problem from which many other difficulties and disputes result, and that problem is deeply entrenched: Consumption patterns show that the division between the rich and the poor is growing. About one-fifth of the globe's wealthiest people consume anywhere from two-thirds to nine-tenths of its resources. These proportions reflect the World Bank's estimates that only 24.3 percent of the households in low-income and middle-income countries have a computer, compared to 77.3 percent of the population in high-income countries. Country infrastructure similarly reflects this divide in affluence—only 38.4 percent of the roads are paved in the Global South as compared to 84.6 percent in the Global North (WDI, 2013).

A select few are prospering in comparison with the many who are barely surviving, and "there is some evidence that the forces of globalization in trade, investment and the labor forces are working to increase" the gap between rich and poor people, much as it appears to widen the gap between the wealthy Global North and poor Global South countries (Babones

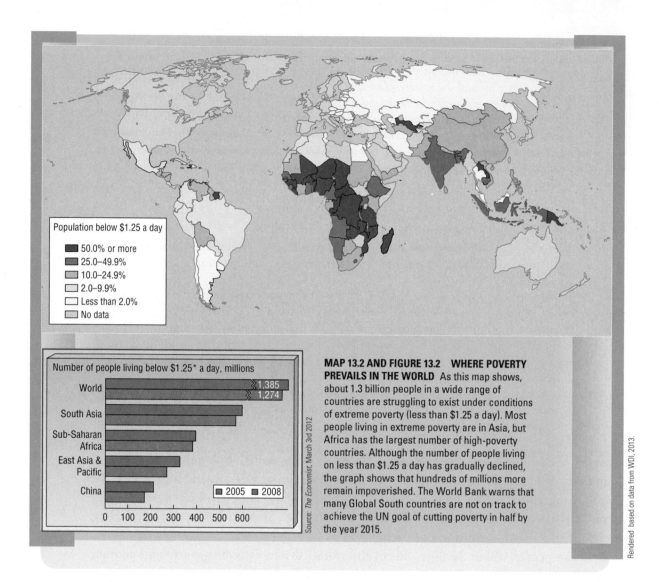

Population below $1.25 a day

- 50.0% or more
- 25.0–49.9%
- 10.0–24.9%
- 2.0–9.9%
- Less than 2.0%
- No data

Number of people living below $1.25* a day, millions

World	1.385 / 1.274
South Asia	
Sub-Saharan Africa	
East Asia & Pacific	
China	

0 100 200 300 400 500 600

■ 2005 ■ 2008

Source: *The Economist*, March 3rd 2012

MAP 13.2 AND FIGURE 13.2   WHERE POVERTY PREVAILS IN THE WORLD As this map shows, about 1.3 billion people in a wide range of countries are struggling to exist under conditions of extreme poverty (less than $1.25 a day). Most people living in extreme poverty are in Asia, but Africa has the largest number of high-poverty countries. Although the number of people living on less than $1.25 a day has gradually declined, the graph shows that hundreds of millions more remain impoverished. The World Bank warns that many Global South countries are not on track to achieve the UN goal of cutting poverty in half by the year 2015.

Rendered based on data from WDI, 2013.

and Turner, 2004, p. 117; also see Chapter 5). "One-fifth of humanity lives in countries where many people think nothing of spending $2 a day on a cappuccino. Another fifth of humanity survives on less than $1 a day and lives in countries where children die for want of a simple anti-mosquito bed net," according to the United Nations Development Programme (UNDP). This trend has produced a world in which the poorest fifth of the global population produces and consumes a mere 2 percent of the world's goods and services, creating vast inequalities: "A homeless person panhandling for two U.S. dollars a day on the streets of Boston would sit in the top half of the world in income distribution" (Dollar, 2005, p. 80).

The extreme suffering of people in many parts of the world, especially in the low-income countries of the Global South, manifests itself in many areas. For example, life expectancy in the Global South averages 68 years, whereas in the Global North it is 80 years. In the Global South, infant mortality rates are the highest in the world, agriculture remains the dominant form of productive activity, and 53 percent of people live in rural areas even as the world is undergoing rapid urbanization (WDI, 2013). Former World Bank President James Wolfensohn (2004) acknowledged the growing threat of global poverty, noting that "2 billion people have no access to clear water; 120 million children never get a chance to go to school; over 40 million people in the developing countries are HIV-positive with little hope of receiving treatment for this dreadful disease. So the world is at a tipping point: either we recommit to deliver on the goals, or the targets will be missed, the world's poor will be left even further behind—and our children will be left to face the consequences."

Against this grim picture are trends that inspire hope. For some segments of humanity things have improved: On average, people in developing countries are healthier, better educated, and less impoverished—and they are more likely to live in a multiparty democracy. Since 1990 life expectancy in developing countries has increased by five years, from 63 to 68. In the same period, primary school completion rates increased to 89 percent from 78 percent. In all, almost 600 million people have escaped the worst poverty since the early 1980s (WDI, 2013). These human development gains should not be underestimated. Nor should they be exaggerated.

To make the promotion of human development a global priority, a precise measure of human welfare is needed. How can human welfare—its level and the prospects for humanity's escape from poverty—best be gauged?

> *Poverty is the worst form of violence.*
>
> **—Mahatma Gandhi, Indian nationalist leader**

Measuring Human Development and Human Security

The human dimension of development first gained attention in the 1970s, partly in response to the growing popularity of *dependency theory* (see Chapter 5). This theory, popular among some leaders in the Global South, attributes persistent poverty to the exploitation caused by dependent relationships of the less developed countries with the wealthy Global North. It also reflects the realization that more is not necessarily better. Advocates of the basic *human needs* perspective sought new ways to measure development beyond those focusing exclusively on economic indicators such as the average income for each person in each country.

The *Human Development Index (HDI)* measures states' comparative ability to provide for their citizens' well-being. The HDI, as the UNDP most recently defines it, seeks to capture as many aspects of human development as possible in one simple composite index and to rank human development achievements. Although no multiple-indicator index (a detailed set of statistical measures) can perfectly monitor the progress of human development, the HDI comes close as an estimating procedure. It measures three dimensions of human welfare— living a long and healthy life, being educated, and having a decent standard of living.

The HDI is a more comprehensive measure than per capita income and has the advantage of directing attention from material possessions toward human needs. Income is only a means to human development, not an end. It is not the sum total of human life. Thus, by focusing on aspects of human welfare beyond average income for each person—by treating income as a proxy for a decent standard of living—the HDI provides a more complete picture of human life than does income alone. By this measure, the evidence provides a basic profile of the extent to which humanitarian aspirations are succeeding or failing.

human needs

Those basic physical, social, and political needs, such as food and freedom, that are required for survival and security.

Human Development Index (HDI)

An index that uses life expectancy, literacy, average number of years of schooling, and income to assess a country's performance in providing for its people's welfare and security.

Carnegie Council Video: Human Development Index (HDI)

The HDI ranges from 0 to 1. The HDI value for a country shows the distance that it has already traveled toward the maximum possible value of 1 and allows for comparison with other countries. The difference between the value achieved by a country and the maximum possible value shows how far it has to go, and the challenge for every country is to find ways to improve. When we look at the ability of countries to contribute to the human development of the people living within their borders, as measured by the HDI, we see a revealing picture of the way personal welfare is provided (see Figure 13.3). These indicators show that consumption

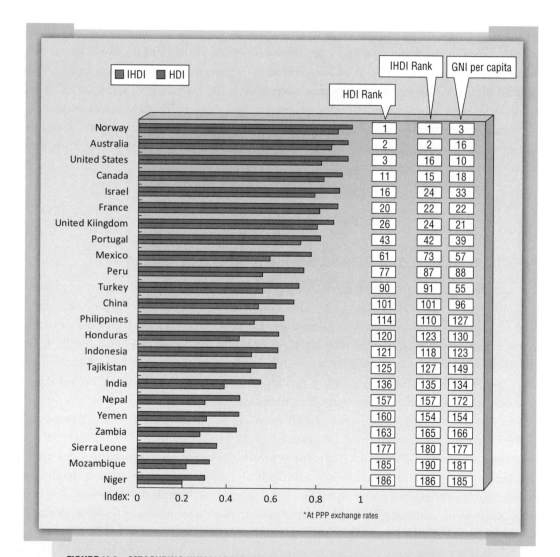

FIGURE 13.3   MEASURING HUMAN DEVELOPMENT: WHAT IS QUALITY OF LIFE? When using the human development index to measure the human welfare and development of people within various populations, notice how countries can rank somewhat differently than when using an aggregate measure such as the gross national income (GNI) per capita. The inequality-adjusted human development index further takes into account the effect of variation in the human condition within a country upon human development. Norway ranks very high and Niger ranks very low on all three measures, but other countries, such as Tajikistan and Nepal, have seen falling per capita incomes while also improving life expectancy and school enrollment (UNDP, 2013).

is not the same as human welfare and that economic growth does not automatically produce human development.

To further assess human welfare, in 2010 the *Inequality-adjusted Human Development Index (IHDI)* was added to take into account the effect of inequality in the distribution of health, education, and income upon human development within a society. In a country with perfect equality, the HDI score and the IHDI score are equivalent; in a country where there is significant inequality, the IHDI score is lower than the HDI score, which means that the haves and have-nots live in very different conditions.

In Latin America, there is up to a 38.5 percent regional drop in human development due to inequality in income. Differences in life expectancy across Sub-Saharan Africa are linked to a 39 percent decrease in human development for those with the lowest expected length of life. In South Asia, high levels of inequality in education have a profound negative effect—up to a 42 percent decrease—upon the human development of some of its people (UNDP, 2013). Generally, countries that have lower levels of human development suffer from higher levels of multidimensional inequality. Conversely, countries in the Global North experience the least inequality in human development.

The HDI focuses on people and their capabilities, rather than economic growth alone, as the central criteria for assessing the development of a country:

> The HDI can also be used to question national policy choices, asking how two countries with the same level of GNI per capita can end up with such different human development outcomes. For example, the Bahamas and New Zealand have similar levels of income per person, but life expectancy and expected years of schooling differ greatly between the two countries, resulting in New Zealand having a much higher HDI value than the Bahamas. These striking contrasts can directly stimulate debate about government policy priorities (UNDP, 2011).

However, a problem with the HDI is that "it does not include measures of the other aspects of human development such as leisure, security, justice, freedom, human rights, and self respect. It would be possible to register a high HDI in a zoo or even in a well-run prison. And, although at low incomes illness often leads to death, the HDI has no independent indicator of morbidity, the absence of which is surely one of the most basic needs. Life can be nasty, brutish, and long" (Streeten, 2001). Thus, despite its strengths as an indicator of human well-being around the world, there are many important aspects of human security and human rights that it does not assess.

So, what factors affect people's ability to live a good life? And why does human development vary greatly in the countries of the world? Let us consider several explanations.

Globalization, Democratization, and Economic Prosperity

The rapid transfer of global capital and investment across borders is integrating the world's economies and has led some to speculate that globalization will provide a cure for the chronic poverty faced by the majority of humanity. There exists "a widely shared image of globalization—a worldwide process of converging incomes and lifestyles driven by ever-larger international flows of goods, images, capital, and people as formidable equalizers [because] greater economic openness has made small parts of the changing world full-fledged members

Inequality-adjusted Human Development Index (IHDI)

An index that accounts for the impact of inequality on the human development of people in a country.

Simulation: Measuring Development

of the global village … so that globalized islands of prosperity are thriving in many developing nations" (Heredia, 1999).

However, critics of globalization complain that it is the culprit—that globalization actually causes relative deprivation rather than cures it. They see globalization as a part of the problem of human suffering, not the solution. Capital may flow more freely around the world, but it flows most slowly to the places and people where it is most scarce. In their constructed image of the consequences of globalization, a more global economy increases inequality in some countries, particularly in the Global South.

Critics decry the "human harms" wrought by globalization, arguing that "nothing is more certain than the inequality and exploitation generated by a totally free market. The inequalities that global capitalism generates are inequities because they violate the principles of egalitarian individualism …" and create "risks of injury and incapacitation that strike at the very being of human beings" (Boli, Elliott, and Bieri, 2004, p. 395). Economist John Maynard Keynes noted these tensions, stating that the "political problem of mankind is to combine three things: economic efficiency, social justice and individual liberty" It is argued that not only does globalization fail to benefit the people that most need help, but also, as economist Rombert Weakland lamented, "The poor are paying the price for everyone else's prosperity."

Yet, where human development has expanded, one factor stands out—the degree to which countries rule themselves democratically and protect citizens' civil liberties. Where democracy thrives, human development and human rights also tend to thrive. Recall the states where democracy and political liberties exist (see Chapter 7, Figure 7.1). At the start of 2013, 118 countries—well over half of the countries in the world (61 percent)—were democratic, providing their citizens with a broad range of political liberties (Freedom House, 2013).

Now compare the location where people benefit from such freedom with Map 13.3, which shows the various levels of human development in countries across the globe. The two go hand in hand: Where democracy flourishes, human development flourishes. But in autocratic governments not ruled by the will of the people, human development fails to occur and human rights are frequently denied.

Along with democratization, rising economic prosperity within a country clearly increases the pace of human development, as previously shown in Figure 13.3, which displays the wealth of each person for countries based on *purchasing power parity (PPP)* exchange-rate comparisons. This is why levels of human development are generally highest in the Global North, where economic prosperity on average is also highest (as opposed to the low-income Global South). Although it is still a source of debate, evidence also supports the conclusion that those countries that respect human rights encourage trade that reduces poverty (Blanton and Blanton, 2007; Ibrahim, 2013). But the exceptions demonstrate the general rule that a country's regime type, and its protection of the civil and political liberties of its population, make a crucial difference in achieving levels of human development.

Some question the "trickle-down" hypothesis (that if the rich first get richer, eventually the benefits will trickle down to help the poor) while accepting the evidence that meeting basic human needs ultimately promotes long-term economic growth. Others maintain that redistributive policies aimed at enhancing human welfare and growth-oriented policies focusing on "trickle-down" benefits function at cross-purposes because the latter can only be attained at the expense of the former.

purchasing power parity (PPP)

An index that calculates the true rate of exchange among currencies when parity— when what can be purchased is the same—is achieved; the index determines what can be bought with a unit of each currency.

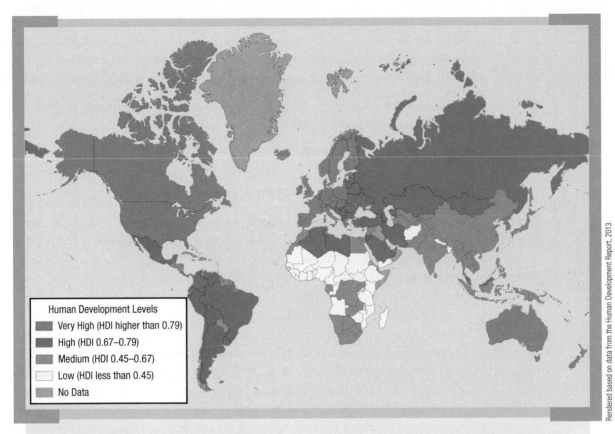

Rendered based on data from the Human Development Report, 2013.

Human Development Levels
- Very High (HDI higher than 0.79)
- High (HDI 0.67–0.79)
- Medium (HDI 0.45–0.67)
- Low (HDI less than 0.45)
- No Data

MAP 13.3   THE MAP OF HUMAN DEVELOPMENT This map measures the level of human development in the countries of the world, using the HDI scale. Note the wide variation. Although some Global South countries have made big gains in the past quarter-century (following political reforms leading to greater democracy and economic reforms leading to free markets), a gap in people's quality of life and in their levels of human development is apparent and parallels, to some degree, the gap between the Global North and the Global South.

Many now recommend fostering human development through a "*Third Way*" strategy that combines the efficiency of a free-enterprise capitalistic market with the compassion of governmental economic planning and regulation in an effort to cooperatively produce the greatest good for the greatest number. Proponents agree that this mixed approach would enable a free market to generate rapid growth while providing a safety net for those most in need of assistance, and that this formula is the best solution for engineering economic growth with a moral human purpose.

HUMAN RIGHTS AND THE PROTECTION OF PEOPLE

Most states have publicly embraced "the universalist claim that all human beings have the same moral status; to accept universal human rights [is to make on states] the moral demand to respect the life, integrity, well-being and flourishing of ... *all* human beings" (Vandersluis and Yeros, 2000a). This claim was expressed in the ringing words of the 1948 Universal Declaration of Human Rights: "Recognition of the inherent dignity and of the equal and inalienable rights of all members of the human family is the foundation of freedom, justice, and peace in the world." This treaty expressed the idea that people should be empowered and therefore no longer reduced to "simply hapless victims of fate, devoid of any historical agency" (Saurin, 2000).

> *Freedom means the supremacy of human rights everywhere. Our support goes to those who struggle to gain those rights or keep them.*
>
> **—Franklin Delano Roosevelt, U.S. president**

Internationally Recognized Human Rights

The body of legal rules and norms designed to protect individual human beings is anchored in the ethical requirement that every person should be treated with equal concern and respect. As the most authoritative statement of these norms, the 1948 *Universal Declaration of Human Rights* "establishes a broad range of civil and political rights, including freedom of assembly, freedom of thought and expression, and the right to participate in government. The declaration also proclaims that social and economic rights are indispensable, including the right to education, the right to work, and the right to participate in the cultural life of the community. In addition, the preamble boldly asserts that 'it is essential, if man is not to be compelled to have recourse, as a last resort, to rebellion against tyranny and oppression, that human rights should be protected by the rule of law'" (Clapham, 2001).

These rights have since been codified and extended in a series of treaties, most notably the *International Covenant on Civil and Political Rights* and the *International Covenant on Economic, Social, and Cultural Rights*. There are many ways to classify the rights listed in these treaties. International ethicist Charles Beitz (2001, p. 271) groups them into five categories:

- **Rights of the person**. "Life, liberty, and security of the person; privacy and freedom of movement; ownership of property; freedom of thought, conscience, and religion, including freedom of religious teaching and practice 'in public and private'; and prohibition of slavery, torture, and cruel or degrading punishment."

- **Rights associated with the rule of law**. "Equal recognition before the law and equal protection of the law, effective legal remedy for violation of legal rights, impartial hearing and trial, presumption of innocence, and prohibition of arbitrary arrest."

- **Political rights**. "Freedom of expression, assembly, and association; the right to take part in government; and periodic and genuine elections by universal and equal suffrage."

- **Economic and social rights**. "An adequate standard of living; free choice of employment; protection against unemployment; 'just and favorable remuneration'; the right to join trade unions; 'reasonable limitation of working hours'; free elementary education; social security; and the 'highest attainable standard of physical and mental health.'"

- **Rights of communities**. "Self-determination and protection of minority cultures."

Although the multilateral treaties enumerating these rights are legally binding on the states ratifying them, many have either not ratified them or have done so only with significant caveats.

AP Photo/Heri Juanda

CRUEL AND UNUSUAL, OR SIMPLY USUAL? The UN Human Rights Commission holds annual sessions that deal with accusations that some UN members are violating human rights treaties. This photo shows the kind of human rights abuse that some countries practice: a man being punished for gambling by Shariah law authorities in Jantho, Aceh Province, in Indonesia. Stipulated in Islam's holy book, the Quran, caning is practiced in some Muslim countries.

When states specify caveats, they are expressing agreement with the broad declarations of principle contained in these treaties while indicating that they object to certain specific provisions and elect not to be bound by them. The United States, for example, ratified the International Covenant on Civil and Political Rights with reservations in 1992, but it has not ratified the International Covenant on Economic, Social, and Cultural Rights. Countries that agree with the general principle that all human beings possess certain rights that cannot be withheld may still disagree on the scope of these rights. Thus, some emphasize rights associated with the rule of law and political rights, whereas others stress the importance of economic and social rights.

Unfortunately, not everyone enjoys the human rights recognized by international law. Three groups for whom respect for human rights remains particularly problematic are indigenous peoples, women, and children.

The Precarious Life of Indigenous Peoples

As you learned in the Chapter 6 introduction to *nonstate actors, indigenous peoples* are representative of one type of ethnic and cultural group that were once native to a geographic location. In most cases indigenous peoples were at one time politically sovereign and economically self-sufficient. Today, largely without a homeland or self-rule, an estimated 370 million indigenous peoples are living in more than 90 countries worldwide, each of which has a unique language and culture and strong, often spiritual, ties to an ancestral homeland (UNDESA, 2013).

Many indigenous peoples feel persecuted because their livelihoods, lands, and cultures are threatened. The Turkish mass killing of Armenians, Hitler's slaughter of Jews (and other

Case Study:
International Law and Organization: Indigenous Peoples

AP Photo/Karel Prinsloo

ETHNIC CLEANSING In 1994, ethnic conflict escalated to genocide in Rwanda as the Hutu militia attacked the Tutsi, and later as the Tutsi-dominated Rwandan Patriotic Front retaliated against the Hutus. This photo depicts the results of one such bloodbath, where as many as 800,000 Tutsis died.

groups), the Khmer Rouge slaughter of Cambodians, and the Hutu slaughter of the Tutsi of Rwanda all exemplify the atrocities committed during the twentieth century.

In describing the tragedy of the Nazi holocaust, Polish jurist Raphael Lemkin coined the word *genocide* from the Greek word *genos* (race, people) and the Latin *caedere* (to kill), and called for it to be singled out as the most grievous violation of human rights, a heinous crime that the international community would be morally responsible for punishing. "When any state or movement claims the right to decide what groups have the right to exist, it poses a threat to all groups" (Smith, 2010, p. 434). Genocide focuses on the destruction of groups, not individuals per se, and has several dimensions, including physical (the annihilation of members of a group), biological (measures taken to reduce the reproductive capacity of a group), and cultural (efforts to eliminate a group's language, literature, art, and other institutions).

Ethnocentrism often underlies genocidal policies. "Brute force realpolitik," concludes Manus Midlarski (2006), "often provides a rationale rooted in ethnocentrism for the physical extermination of victim minorities by leaders claiming genocide is a necessary 'altruistic punishment' for the good of the dominant nationality."

Various native peoples are now fighting back across the globe against the injustice they believe states have perpetrated against them. The members of these nonstate nations, however, are often outnumbered and divided about their objectives. Most indigenous movements only seek a greater voice in redirecting the policies and allocation of resources within existing states and are eliciting the support of NGOs and *intergovernmental organizations* (IGOs) to pressure states to recognize their claims and protect their rights.

Substantial numbers of indigenous movements in the last decade have successfully negotiated settlements resulting in *devolution*—the granting of regional political power that increases

ethnocentrism

A propensity to see one's nationality or state as the center of the world and therefore special, with the result that the values and perspectives of other groups are misunderstood and ridiculed.

devolution

States' granting of political power to minority ethnic groups and indigenous people in particular national regions under the expectation that greater autonomy will curtail the groups' quest for independence as a new state.

local self-governance. Examples include the Miskitos in Nicaragua, the Gagauz in Moldova, and most regional separatists in Ethiopia as well as in India's Assam region. Yet, as suggested by the hostilities between the Chechens and the Russian Federation, resolving clashes between aspiring peoples and established states can be extremely difficult.

The goal expressed in the UN Charter of promoting "universal respect for, and observance of, human rights and fundamental freedoms" is very challenging for many nationally diverse countries. The division of these states along ethnic and cultural lines makes them inherently fragile. Consider the degree to which minority groups compose many states: for example, the share of indigenous populations in Bolivia is 62 percent and 48 percent in Peru (The Hunger Project, 2009). Or consider the number of distinct languages spoken in some countries, with conspicuous examples in Papua New Guinea's 830 languages, Indonesia's 719, Nigeria's 514, India's 438, China's 292, and Mexico's 291 (*The Economist*, 2012g; see also Map 6.3).

Racism and intolerance are hothouses for fanaticism and violence. The belief that one's nationality is superior to all others undermines human rights. Although interethnic competition is a phenomenon that dates back to biblical times, it remains a contemporary plague. According to the Minorities at Risk Project (2011), since 1998, more than 283 politically motivated minority groups throughout the globe suffered in their home countries from organized discriminatory treatment and mobilized in collective action to defend and promote their self-defined interests. Some analysts predict that conflict within and between ethnically divided states will become a major axis on which twenty-first-century world politics will revolve.

Efforts to toughen domestic refugee legislation and criteria for granting asylum raise important ethical issues. Where will the homeless, the desperate, the weak, and the poor find *sanctuary*—a safe place to live where human rights are safeguarded? Will the rich countries act with compassion or respond with indifference? And more broadly, what is the best way to view human security and reconcile it with national security (see "Controversy: What Is Security?)? The policy proposals crafted to address these questions may involve controversial trade-offs, and point to the difficulties in appropriately responding to the global refugee crisis in particular (see Chapter 12), and human rights abuse in general.

Gender Inequality and Its Consequences

For more than three decades, global conferences have highlighted the critical role of women's human rights concerns (see Table 13.1). A global consensus has emerged that the status of women needs to improve if human rights and development are to progress. These conferences are signposts that increasingly depict gender equality and empowerment across political, social, and economic arenas as a fundamental right. They have introduced the world to the incontrovertible evidence that women's status in society, and especially their education, profoundly influences human development and that the treatment of women is a global rights issue that affects everyone.

As measured by the UNDP's *Gender Inequality Index (GII)*, women throughout the world continue to be disadvantaged relative to men across a broad spectrum (UNDP, 2013). The composite measure, which ranges from zero (no inequality) to one (extreme inequality), indicates that disparities between men and women persist across three dimensions: reproductive health, empowerment, and the labor market. *Gender inequality*—difference in living standards between men and women—erodes human development and human rights, and is

Simulation: Rwanda

Gender Inequality Index (GII)

An index that uses female reproductive health, political and educational empowerment, and participation in the labor market to assess the extent to which gender inequality erodes a country's human development achievements.

gender inequality

Differences between men and women in opportunity and reward that are determined by the values that guide states' foreign and domestic policies.

Carnegie Council Video: Gender Inequality

WHAT IS SECURITY?

How should security be defined? Policy makers disagree. Some see it primarily in military terms, others in human welfare terms. Underlying the disagreement is a different conception of what is most important on the global agenda. One tradition gives states first priority and assumes that protecting their territorial integrity must be foremost in the minds of national leaders. Others challenge this conception and place primacy on the security of individual people, arguing that social and environmental protection must be seen as a global priority.

In considering this question, remember the traditional realist view that national security is essentially the freedom from fear of attack by another country or nonstate terrorists. Realists maintain that armed aggression is the paramount security threat and that preparing for war to prevent war overrides all other security concerns. Safeguarding the state by military force matters most. Therefore, "security" is defined primarily in terms of each country's capacity to resist armed threats. This definition puts the protection of entire states' interests above those of individual people.

In contrast, "human security" has risen as a recent concept that focuses on protecting individuals from any threat. The Human Security Centre (2006, p. 35) elaborates this new conception that derives from liberal thought, explaining that "secure states do not automatically mean secure peoples. Protecting citizens from foreign attack may be a necessary condition for the security of individuals, but it is not a sufficient one. Indeed, during the last one hundred years far more people have been killed by their own governments than by foreign armies. All proponents of human security agree that its primary goal is a protection of individuals. But consensus breaks down over what threats individuals should be protected from ... The UN's Commission on Human Security argues that the threat agenda should be broadened to include hunger, disease, and natural disasters because these kill far more people than war, genocide and terrorism combined."

Extending this perspective, note that so-called "environmental security" is one of the many points of departure in the "human security" approach to national security, which stresses the threat of global environmental degradation to human well-being and welfare throughout the planet (see Chapter 14). That liberal position "rests primarily on evidence that there has been serious degradation of natural resources (fresh water, soils, forests, fishery resources, and biological diversity) and vital life-support systems (the ozone layer, climate system, oceans, and atmosphere) [and that] these global physical changes ... are comparable to those associated with most military threats that national security establishments prepare for" (Porter, 1995, p. 216).

WHAT DO YOU THINK?

- *To what extent are the "national security" approaches emphasized by realists and the "human security" approaches favored by liberals contradictory and in competition with one another? Might they instead be complementary and mutually reinforcing?*

- *What are some considerations that a feminist theorist would include in this debate? How might this affect your perception of security?*

- *As a policy maker, which aspects of security would you emphasize as the most likely guarantor of your country's well-being? Why?*

TABLE 13.1	Important Steps on the Path toward Human Rights and Women's Rights	

Year	Conference	Key Passage
1975	World Conference on International Women's Year (Mexico City)	Launched a global dialogue on gender equality and led to the establishment of the United Nations Development Fund for Women (UNIFEM)
1979	Convention on the Elimination of All Forms of Discrimination against Women (Women's Convention, New York)	Article 12 calls on countries to "take all appropriate measures to eliminate discrimination against women in the field of health care in order to ensure, on a basis of equality of men and women, access to health care services, including those related to family planning"
1980	Second World Conference on Women (Copenhagen)	Calls for governments to enact stronger measures that will ensure women's ownership and control of property, and will improve women's rights to inheritance, child custody, and recognition of nationality
1985	Third World Conference on Women (Nairobi)	Recognized the need for governments to bring gender concerns into the mainstream and develop institutional mechanisms to promote broad-based gender equality and empowerment of women
1993	United Nations World Conference on Human Rights (Vienna)	The Vienna Declaration includes nine paragraphs on "The Equal Status and Human Rights of Women," and for the first time recognizes that "violence against women is a human-rights abuse"
1995	United Nations Fourth World Conference on Women (Beijing)	Sets a wide-ranging, ambitious agenda for promoting human development by addressing gender inequality and women's rights
2004	NATO Conference on Trafficking in Humans (Brussels)	Seeks a convention to contain the growing problem of human trafficking and export of people across borders—particularly women and children
2004	United Nations Conference on Sexual and Reproductive Rights (New York)	Launches action plan to uphold women's "fundamental human rights including sexual and reproductive rights"
2005	United Nations World Conference on Women (Beijing)	110 Platform for Action charts strategies for empowerment of women and girls
2010	Commission on the Status of Women (New York)	Conducts a 15-year review of the implementation of the Beijing Declaration, and assesses the Platform for Action

reflected in differences found in female mortality and fertility rates, political power and educational attainment, and participation in the workforce. Women generally enjoy less access to advanced study and training in professional fields, are frequently relegated to less prestigious jobs, face formidable barriers to political involvement, and typically receive less pay than men.

Gender inequality varies enormously around the world, and is especially prevalent in three Global South regions: South Asia, the Middle East, and sub-Saharan Africa. At the start of 2013, gender inequality in the Netherlands was nominal, as indicated by a GII score of .045, whereas inequality was very high in Yemen and Niger, as shown by GII scores of .747 and .707, respectively (UNDP, 2013).

The need to extend women equal human rights is clear-cut. "When women are educated and can earn and control income, a number of good results follow: infant mortality declines, child health and nutrition improve, agricultural productivity rises, population growth slows, economies expand, and cycles of poverty are broken" (Coleman, 2010b, p. 13). When women and girls earn income, they reinvest 90 percent of it in the welfare of their families, buying books, bed nets, and medicines—as compared to men, who allocate only 30 to 40 percent of their income to fulfill similar functions (Gibbs, 2011). Yet despite the fact that "since the eighteenth century feminists, scholars, and activists have taken up the task of revealing just how much political life has been built on presumptions about femininity and masculinity … there is abundant evidence now that regimes and the states beneath them in fact have taken deliberate steps to sustain a sort of hierarchical gendered division of labor that provides them with cheapened, often completely unpaid, women's productive labor" (Enloe, 2001, p. 311).

Much the same holds true in politics: since 1900, only 15 percent of the world's countries have had one or more female heads of state (*Harper's*, 2008). Today, women continue to be vastly underrepresented in decision-making positions in government, even in democracies and developed countries. Gender differences in parliaments around the world are highly skewed in favor of men. At the start of 2013, women accounted for only 21 percent of all seats in parliament around the world, up from a mere 13 percent in 1990 (WDI, 2013; see also Map 13.4).

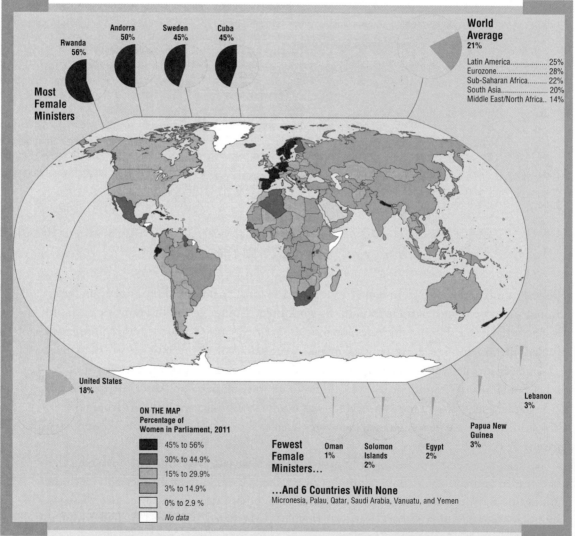

MAP 13.4   GENDER POLITICS There are now more women in government than ever before. The proportion of women in national parliaments grew by only 1 percent between 1975 and 1995, compared to 8 percent between 1998 and 2008. Nonetheless, gender parity remains scarce in democratic governance. There is only one woman for every four males in legislatures around the world, and in mid-2013 only 17 heads of state were female. According to the United Nations, "countries with 'first past the post' electoral systems without any type of quota arrangements will not reach the 40 percent threshold of women in public office until near to the end of this century" (UNIFEM, 2013).

Rendered based on data from World Development Indicators 2013.

In most societies, politics is seen "as a largely male sport—unarmed combat—and women are very often ignored or pushed aside in an effort to gain or consolidate power," explains former U.S. Secretary of State Hillary Clinton. Moreover, she continues, "where women are disempowered and dehumanized, you are more likely to see not just antidemocratic forces, but extremism that leads to security challenges," both within the home country and for the world at large. It is clear that "societies with greater equality are more likely to be prosperous and sustain stable democratic institutions" (Htun and Weldon, 2010, p. 207).

Further gender differences continue at the most basic levels of human development, and it is easy to conclude that women remain victims of human rights abuse and discrimination nearly everywhere. More girls than boys die at a young age, and females' access to adequate health care is more restricted (WDI, 2013). "In the Middle East and South Asia, women deemed insufficiently conservative in their dress are attacked with acid. Across Africa, the use of mass rape as an instrument of war has jumped from one conflict to another" (Coleman, 2010a, p. 128). Women continue to be the primary victims of sex trafficking and sexual violence, and not until 2001 did the International Criminal Court confirm "sexual enslavement" as a war crime—a fact that feminists point out as an example of the traditional disregard for women's human rights.

Protecting women's rights is difficult because the issues touch deeply entrenched, as well as widely divergent, religious and cultural beliefs. In many Islamic countries, for example, women must hide their faces with veils in public, and women and men are often completely separated in social and religious activities. As American sociologist Herbert Spencer says, "A people's condition may be judged by the treatment which women receive under it." For many in liberal Western countries that focus on social, political, and economic equality of the sexes, these traditions are difficult to understand.

HOW TO TRANSCEND THE GENDER GAP? Shown here are examples of how the empowerment of women is changing. Shown left is Dilma Rousseff, who was inaugurated as Brazil's first female president on January 1, 2011. Pictured right is U.S. major general Maggie Woodward, who, in 2011, became the first woman in U.S. history to command a military air campaign when the United States participated in attacks against Libya. When asked about her thoughts on being a role model, she responded "We're not going to get into the first-woman thing, are we? ... I hope I'm an inspiring figure to lots of little boys and girls" (Thompson, 2011, p. 38).

"Gender empowerment" is based on the conviction that only through realizing the full potential of *all* human beings can true human development occur, and that this includes women's human rights. Once this concept gained acceptance as a lens with which to construct a view of the core issues on the global agenda, gender issues became a central concern. Though grave threats to the rights and security of women and girls remain, there are signs that a transformation is under way. In many countries, significant efforts are being made to promote gender equality:

> Greater economic empowerment for women has been achieved through progressive legislation that has prohibited discriminatory practices, guaranteed equal pay, provided for maternity and paternity leave, and put in place protection against sexual harassment in the workplace. Governments have turned their back on the idea that violence against women is a private affair, with laws in every region now outlawing this scourge in its many manifestations. Legislation prohibiting discrimination based on sex with respect to inheritance and citizenship, laws that guarantee equality within the family and policies to ensure that women and girls can access services including health and education have also contributed to significant advances in women's standard of living (UNIFEM, 2011, p. 8).

Feminist theory, a departure from classical realist theory, seeks to rectify the ways conventional but distorted images of world politics are, as constructivism informs us, socially constructed (see Chapter 2). The objective is to show the world its neglect of gender and of women in global society and to offer an alternative theoretical vision that empowers women, secures their basic human rights, and challenges realist theories that honor the state and military power (Enloe, 2007; Tickner, 2010).

CourseMate

Video:
No Rights, No Dreams

Gendercide, Slavery, and Human Trafficking

Under normal circumstances, females live longer than males, and so there are more women than men in much of the world, even in poor regions such as much of Latin America and Africa. "Yet in places where girls have a deeply unequal status, they *vanish*" (Kristof and WuDunn, 2009, p. xv). In northern India and China, more than 117 boys continue to be born for every 100 girls due to a cultural partiality for sons, a modern preference for small families, and the availability of technology that enables couples to determine the gender of their unborn child. A growing number of countries, especially in Asia, are experiencing the effects of a generation of *gendercide*; Indian economist Amartya Sen estimates that well over 107 million females are "missing" due to abortion, murder, and death due to severe neglect. Over the last 50 years, more girls were killed precisely because of their gender than were men killed in all the wars of the twentieth century (Coleman, 2010a; Kristof and WuDunn, 2009).

gendercide

Systematic killing of members of a specific gender.

Another human rights horror to which women, as well as children, are particularly vulnerable is human trafficking (see Brysk and Choi-Fitzpatrick, 2013). Although many people assume that slavery is an obsolete practice, the reality is that trade in human beings is enormous. The growing modern-day slave trade crisscrosses the entire globe and, "despite more than a dozen international conventions banning slavery in the past 150 years, there are more slaves today than at any point in human history" (Skinner, 2010, p. 56).

Roughly 80,000 Africans were brought to the New World each year during the peak of the slave trade in the 1780s. By way of comparison, today, according to the U.S. State Department, between 600,000 and 800,000 people are trafficked across borders each year to suffer the fate of being bought and sold as sex slaves or bonded laborers (Coleman, 2010a). As Ethan Kapstein explains:

> Slavery and the global slave trade continue to thrive to this day; in fact, it is likely that more people are being trafficked across borders against their will now than at any point in the past. This human stain is not just a minor blot on the rich tapestry of international commerce. It is a product of the same political, technological, and economic forces that have fueled globalization. Just as the brutal facts of the Atlantic slave trade ultimately led to a reexamination of U.S. history—U.S. historiography until the 1960s had been largely celebratory—so must growing awareness of the modern slave trade spark a recognition of the flaws in our contemporary economic and governmental arrangements. The current system offers too many incentives to criminals and outlaw states to market humans and promises too little in the way of sanctions. Contemporary slavery typically involves women and children being forced into servitude through violence and deprivation (2006, p. 103).

The UN has found that the leading form of human trafficking, accounting for 79 percent of the slave trade, is sexual exploitation. Most of the victims are women and girls. The second leading form of human trafficking is forced labor (18 percent), and about one in five victims are children. Today, there are around 8.5 million child slaves. The vast majority of these children are held as forced labor, about a fourth work as child prostitutes, and around a half million are pressed into service as child soldiers (Aljazeera, 2011). "Children's nimble fingers are exploited to untangle fishing nets, sew luxury goods or pick cocoa," reports the UN. "Their innocence is abused for begging, or exploited for sex as prostitutes, pedophilia or child pornography. Others are sold as child brides or camel jockeys."

Although many victims of human trafficking are moved across continents, intraregional and domestic trafficking is far more common. Human trafficking is a lucrative criminal activity. According to Luis CdeBaca, who directs the U.S. State Department's Office to Monitor and Combat Trafficking in Persons, this shadow economy "turns a $32 billion annual profit for traffickers" (Ireland, 2010). It is the third largest illicit global business after trafficking in drugs and the arms trade (Obuah, 2006). "The lifetime profit on a brickmaking slave in Brazil is $8,700, and $2,000 in India. Sexual slavery brings the slave's owner $18,000 over the slave's working life in Thailand, and $49,000 in Los Angeles" (Hardy, 2013).

Children and Human Rights

Children are one of the most dependent and vulnerable groups in society, and their human rights are frequently violated. They face horrific neglect and abuse, as evident in their suffering from unmitigated hunger and illness, slavery for labor or sexual exploitation, and conscription as child soldiers. Amnesty International, a human rights NGO, describes conditions many children throughout the world face:

> Children are tortured and mistreated by state officials; they are arbitrarily or lawfully detained, often in appalling conditions; in some countries they are subjected to the death penalty. Countless thousands are killed or maimed in armed conflicts, many more have fled their homes to become refugees. Children forced by poverty or abuse to live on the streets are sometimes detained, attacked and even killed in the name of social cleansing. Many millions of children work at exploitative or hazardous jobs, or are the victims of child trafficking and forced prostitution. Because children are "easy targets", they are sometimes threatened, beaten or raped in order to punish family members who are not so accessible (Amnesty International, 2009b).

MODERN-DAY SLAVERY "More must be done to reduce the vulnerability of victims, increase the risks to traffickers, and lower demand for the goods and services of modern-day slaves" says Antonio Maria Costa, former executive director of the UN Office on Drugs and Crime. Shown on the left is a 17-year-old sex worker in Bangladesh after her service with a customer. She ran away from home to escape marriage at the age of fifteen, and sought work at a factory where she was deceived and sold to a brothel. Pictured on the right is actress Mira Sorvino who, in an effort to increase public awareness of human trafficking and generate greater commitment to combating the problem, was appointed by the United Nations as goodwill ambassador to combat human trafficking.

Human rights abuse of children takes place all across the globe. However, "weak states typically have worse human rights records than strong ones," as they lack the capacity to effectively protect human rights (Englehart, 2009, p. 163). They are often plagued by corruption, ineffectively police their territory, and are unable to provide basic services.

To bring about a transformation in the human condition, UNICEF contends that "improvements in public health services are essential, including safe water and better sanitation. Education, especially for girls and mothers, will also save children's lives. Raising income can help, but little will be achieved unless a greater effort is made to ensure that services reach those who need them most." Though child mortality has declined in every region of the world since 1960, almost 10 million children every year still do not live to see their fifth birthday. "Of these, the vast majority dies from causes that are preventable through a combination of good care, nutrition, and simple medical treatment" (World Bank, 2009, p. 44).

Most of the children who die every year live in the Global South, where death claims more than 5 in every 100 children under the age of five, as compared to the Global North, where less than 1 in 100 children die (WDI, 2013). Malnutrition lies at the root of more than half of the deaths of children worldwide; it weakens children's immune systems and leaves them vulnerable to illness and disease, such as malaria, pneumonia, diarrhea, measles, and AIDS (see Chapter 12). Yet "rapid declines in under-five mortality (more than 50 percent) have been seen in Latin America and the Caribbean, Central and Eastern Europe and the Commonwealth of Independent States (CEE/CIS), and East Asia and the Pacific. There remain, however, many countries with high levels of child mortality, particularly in sub-Saharan Africa and South Asia" (UNICEF, 2009).

Poor human rights conditions are exacerbated in countries where there is armed conflict. Not only are children often orphaned or separated from their families without food or care, but many are also direct participants in war. The United Nations (2013a) estimates that 300,000 boys and girls between the ages of seven and eighteen were recruited and used as child soldiers in over 50 countries in violation of international law. Because children are smaller than adults and more easily intimidated, they typically make obedient soldiers. Some are abducted from their homes, others fight under threat of death, and others join out of desperation or a desire to avenge the death of family members.

A United Nation's report on children and armed conflict released in May 2013 further highlights the harmful consequences for children, expressing concern that:

> the evolving character and tactics of armed conflict are creating unprecedented threats to children. The absence of clear front lines and identifiable opponents, the increasing use of terror tactics by some armed groups and certain methods used by security forces have made children more vulnerable. Children are being used as suicide bombers and human shields, while schools continue to be attacked, affecting girls' education in particular, and to be used for military purposes. In addition, children are being held in security detention for alleged association with armed groups. Furthermore, drone strikes have resulted in child casualties and have had a serious impact on the psychosocial health of children (UN, 2013b, p. 2).

In order to confront these consequences of armed conflict, it is essential that political leaders be committed to the welfare of children. On August 4, 2009, the UN Security Council unanimously adopted a resolution that expanded the secretary-general's annual report on grave violations of children by groups involved in armed conflict to include the names of groups that kill or maim children contrary to international law, or perpetrate grave sexual violence against children in wartime. "This is a major step forward in the fight against impunity for

Eros Haagland/The New York Times

Piers Benetar/Panos Pictures

HUMAN RIGHTS VIOLATIONS "Women between the ages of 15 and 44 are more likely to be maimed or killed by male violence than by war, cancer, malaria, and traffic incidents combined" (Coleman, 2010a, p. 127). Pictured (left) is Bibi Aisha, an Afghan woman whose husband cut off her nose and ears as punishment for running away from her abusive in-laws. Children are also victims of human rights violations. On the right, a starving farmer in Afghanistan, Akhtar Mohammed, watches his 10-year-old son, Sher, whom he traded to a wealthy farmer in exchange for a monthly supply of wheat. "What else could I do?" he asked. "I will miss my son, but there was nothing to eat."

crimes against children and a recognition of the reality of conflict today, where girls and boys are increasingly targeted and victimized, killed and raped, as well as recruited into armed groups" said former UN Special Representative for Children and Armed Conflict Radhika Coomaraswamy. In July 2011, the UN Security Council reaffirmed its commitment to the protection of children by unanimously adopting a resolution that denounced attacks or abuse against children and the recruitment of child soldiers.

The treatment of children has traditionally been seen as a "private" issue of family life that is firmly rooted in cultural values and traditions. Nonetheless, as innocents in our global society, many believe that security and sustenance are basic human rights to which children are entitled, and that the international community must help to protect these rights (see "A Closer Look: Insecurity in Childhood"). The Convention on the Rights of the Child (CRC) embraced these sentiments, which the United Nations adopted on November 20, 1989. The basic human rights that the CRC establishes for children everywhere, spelled out in 54 articles and two optional protocols, include:

- The right to survival
- The right to develop to the fullest
- The right to protection from harmful influences, abuse, and exploitation
- The right to participate fully in family, cultural, and social life

Emphasizing entitlement to human dignity and harmonious development, and ratified by all of the UN member states except the United States and Somalia, this treaty is widely seen as a major victory for human rights. As the human rights NGO Amnesty International enthusiastically proclaimed, "Here for the first time was a treaty that sought to address the particular human rights of children and to set minimum standards for the protection of their rights. It is the only international treaty to guarantee civil and political rights as well as economic, social, and cultural rights."

RESPONDING TO HUMAN RIGHTS

There are at least three arguments against making the promotion and enforcement of human rights a responsiebility of the global community. Realists reject promoting human rights because, as Executive Director of Amnesty International William Shulz explains, they "regard the pursuit of rights as an unnecessary, sometimes even a dangerous extravagance, often at odds with the national interest." Statists or legalists reject protecting human rights in other states because it represents an unwarranted intrusion into the domestic affairs of others and an infringement upon state sovereignty. Relativists or pluralists view human rights promotion as a form of moral imperialism (Blanton and Cingranelli, 2010; Donnelly, 2003).

Nonetheless, there is an "increasing willingness to regard concern for human rights violations as acceptable justification for various kinds of international intervention in the domestic affairs of states ranging from diplomatic and economic sanctions to military action" (Beitz, 2001, p. 269). As constructivists tell us, the evolution of global values can have a powerful impact on international behavior. "Virtually any explanation of the rise of human

A Closer Look

INSECURITY IN CHILDHOOD

In April 2012, UNICEF estimated that of the tens of thousands fleeing the violence in Syria, 50 percent of all refugees seeking shelter in Jordan, Lebanon, and Turkey were children and other young people. Beginning with public demonstrations in 2011 as part of the Arab Spring, the uprising in Syria escalated as the Syrian Army responded forcefully to the protestors' calls for the end of President Bashar al-Assad's regime. In what has become a major civil war, reports of the Syrian government intentionally targeting civilians—including the death and torture of innocent children and women—have emerged and been met with international condemnation.

Syria presents a grim example of the fate of many children who suffer physical and emotional trauma from violence and displacement. Tragically, this story is one that is repeated frequently in other countries throughout the world where children suffer from starvation, lack of education, life-threatening illness, physical abuse, forced labor, and sexual slavery. Yet to what extent does the global community have a *responsibility to protect* children around the world?

Advocates for intervention by the global community argue that "principled foreign policy defies the realist prediction of untrammeled pursuit of national interest" (Brysk, 2009, p. 4). Instead, it is necessary for state and nonstate actors to serve as a "global Good Samaritan" who, in the spirit of a fundamental Christian belief, "loves thy neighbor as thyself."

Calling for action from the global community, Executive Director Justin Forsyth of the NGO Save the Children urged "this indiscriminate killing must stop now. The world cannot sit back and allow this to happen. Children are suffering terribly in this conflict." Specific protection measures for children, provision of nutritional supplies, and support for education programs are needed. Underscoring the severity of the threats faced by many children such as those in Syria, UNICEF Executive Director Anthony Lake similarly urged a quick and decisive response to the crisis in Syria, asking, "How many more children need to die? Repeated calls for the protection of children by all parties in Syria have not yielded positive action. But we must voice again our outrage when seeing the murder of innocents … who are in no way responsible for the violence and must not be its victims."

WATCH THE VIDEO:

Carnegie Council Video:
Am I My Brothers' Keeper?

YOU DECIDE:

1. What are the consequences of serious violations of children's human rights and neglect of their human development for national development and global security?

2. What role should other states, IGOs, and NGOs play in addressing the condition of children throughout the world?

rights must take into account the political power of norms and ideas and the increasingly transnational way in which those ideas are carried and diffused" (Sikkink, 2008, p. 172).

The most common manifestations of this phenomenon are the expanding laws that regulate the practices that sovereign states may use. The human rights revolution has advanced moral progress by breaking states' monopoly on international affairs and over citizens. In this sense, liberalism triumphed and realism was repudiated, for the human rights movement has rejected the harsh realist vision expressed by Thomas Hobbes, who argued in the seventeenth century that because world politics is "a war of all against all, the notions of right and wrong, justice and injustice have there no place."

Moreover, international law has fundamentally revised the traditional realist conception of the state by redefining the relationship of states to humans. As former UN Secretary-General Kofi Annan notes, "States are now widely understood to be instruments at the service of their people, and not *vice versa*. When we read the Charter today, we are more than ever conscious that its aim is to protect individual human beings, not to protect those who abuse them."

If you are neutral in a situation of injustice, you have chosen the side of the oppressor.

—Archbishop Desmund Tutu, Nobel Prize winner

The Human Rights Legal Framework

The global community has expanded its legal protection of human rights significantly over the past sixty years. Multilateral treaties have proliferated as part of a global effort to construct a consensus on the rights of all humanity and put an end to human rights violations. Numerous conventions have been enacted that have increasingly recognized individual rights—asserting that people must be treated as worthy of the freedom and dignity traditionally granted by international law to states and rulers. Moreover, from the perspective of international law, a state is obligated to respect the human rights of its own citizens as well as those of another country, and the international community has the prerogative to challenge any state that does not respect these rights. Table 13.2 highlights eight international agreements, in addition to the Universal Declaration of Human Rights, which provide a foundation for the legal framework of international human rights.

TABLE 13.2	Core Conventions of the International Human Rights Legal Framework
1948	Universal Declaration of Human Rights
1965	International Convention on the Elimination of All Forms of Racial Discrimination (ICERD)
1966	International Covenant on Civil and Political Rights (ICCPR)
1966	International Covenant on Economic, Social, and Cultural Rights (ICESCR)
1979	Convention on the Elimination of All Forms of Discrimination against Women (CEDAW)
1984	Convention against Torture and Other Cruel, Inhumane or Degrading Treatment or Punishment (CAT)
1989	Convention on the Rights of the Child (CRC)
1990	International Convention on the Protection of the Rights of All Migrant Workers and Members of Their Families (ICRMW)
2006	Convention on the Rights of Persons with Disabilities (CRPD)

Among these treaties and instruments of international law, the Universal Declaration of Human Rights; the International Covenant on Economic, Social, and Cultural Rights; and the International Covenant on Civil and Political Rights together form the "International Bill of Human Rights." Additionally, there are hundreds of widely accepted legal instruments and political declarations across a broad array of human rights issues. They provide specific standards for the human rights protection of vulnerable groups such as women, children, migrant workers, and disabled persons and for the collective rights of minorities and indigenous groups. The United Nations and its members have been a driving force behind the development of a global human rights legal system. The International Labor Organization (ILO) and regional organizations, such as the African Union, the Inter-American Commission on Human Rights, and the European Court of Human Rights, also have established human rights protections.

The Challenge of Enforcement

Once the content of human rights obligations was enumerated in multilateral treaties, international attention shifted to monitoring their implementation and addressing violations. Unfortunately, "the deepening international human rights regime creates opportunities for rights-violating governments to display low-cost legitimating commitments to world norms, leading them to ratify human rights treaties without the capacity or willingness to comply with the provisions" (Hafner-Burton et al., 2008, p. 115; see also Powell and Staton, 2009). There are also some countries that endorse human rights treaties as merely a superficial symbolic commitment and continue to repress human rights.

Moreover, full agreement has yet to be reached on the extent to which the international community has a responsibility to intervene in order to enforce human rights. As the International Commission on Intervention and State Sovereignty noted in its report, *The Responsibility to Protect*, "If intervention for human protection purposes is to be accepted, including the possibility of military action, it remains imperative that the international community develop consistent, credible, and enforceable standards to guide state and intergovernmental practice." Although expanding global norms that elevate human security do much to advance human rights, critical policy questions remain about what steps can and should be taken to safeguard these rights and prevent violations (Ramcharan, 2010).

Humanitarian intervention encompasses the international community's actions to assist the population of a state that is experiencing severe human suffering caused by political collapse, deliberate government policy, or natural disaster (see Chapters 6 and 7). The principles that guide humanitarian intervention continue to be a matter of heated debate. The issue is not whether there exists a compelling need and moral obligation to express concerns about populations at risk of slaughter, starvation, or persecution; the issue is about how to craft a just response, when any response will comprise interference in the domestic affairs of a sovereign state. Humanitarian intervention is controversial because it pits the legal principle of territorial sovereignty against what some see as a moral responsibility to protect vulnerable populations from egregious violations of human rights.

Although the construction of global human rights norms has made great strides over the past sixty years, the enforcement of these laws has lagged. Within the United Nations, the Office of the High Commissioner for Human Rights (OHCHR) is responsible for implementing

humanitarian intervention

The use of peacekeeping troops by foreign states or international organizations to protect endangered people from gross violations of their human rights and from mass murder.

Carnegie Council Video:
Humanitarian
Intervention

international human rights agreements, overseeing major human rights programs, and providing global leadership in promoting and protecting human rights. It also supervises the Human Rights Council (HRC).

Created by the UN General Assembly on March 15, 2006, the HRC is a relatively new intergovernmental organization designed to evaluate allegations of human rights abuse and making recommendations about the best course of action. At that time, the United States, the Marshall Islands, and Palau voted against the resolution; Iran, Venezuela, and Belarus did not vote. There were concerns that the UNHCR did not have the ability to prevent states with poor human rights records from membership on the Council, and that the agency's mission undermined the principle of nonintervention.

In June 2008, the United States relinquished its observer status and disengaged from the HRC, much to the dismay of human rights advocates who felt that this greatly diminished the role of the IGO and sent a negative message about the importance of human rights around the world. In May 2009, however, the United States sought and was elected to a three-year term on the HRC. "While we recognize that the Human Rights Council has been a flawed body that has not lived up to its potential," explained former U.S. Ambassador to the United Nations Susan Rice, "we believe that working from within, we can make the council a more effective forum to promote and protect human rights."

Studies have shown that international organizations such as the United Nations "play an important role" in punishing human rights violators and "that seemingly symbolic resolutions of a politically motivated IO can carry tangible consequences" (Lebovic and Voeten, 2009, p. 79; see also Greenhill, 2010; Mertus, 2009). Nonetheless, despite the significant efforts to monitor human rights and enforce norms and agreements, the effectiveness of the United Nations and other intergovernmental organizations is constrained as they can exercise only the authority that member states delegate to them.

In response to these limitations, NGOs have assumed an important role in promoting human rights. They have developed an array of transnational advocacy networks and strategies designed to pressure governments to modify their behavior and conform to prevailing human rights norms and laws (Keck and Sikkink, 2008). As Ellen Lutz, executive director of *Cultural Survival* (an NGO that protects the human rights of indigenous peoples) explains:

> These organizations investigate human rights abuses wherever they occur, including in places enduring armed conflict. Because of their reputation for accuracy, their findings are relied on by the news media, many governments, and most intergovernmental institutions. While these NGOs hope their reports will bring about a change in the behavior of the government or other entity whose abuses they spotlight, their main targets are the policymakers who are in a more powerful position to put pressure on human rights violators. They lobby other governments to take human rights into account in their foreign aid and press the United Nations and other intergovernmental organizations to put pressure on rights abusers (Lutz, 2006, p. 25).

With greater openness to institutional activism in the post–Cold War era, human rights activists have pressed to strengthen enforcement mechanisms. Their efforts account, in part, for the establishment of UN tribunals that review gross human rights abuse, as in the cases of the former Yugoslavia and Rwanda, and the creation of the *International Criminal Court*. Activists are also credited with monitoring human rights situations and targeting a publicity

Omar Sobhani/Reuters/Landov

LIFE WITHOUT LIBERTY "The cost of liberty is less than the price of repression," African-American sociologist W. E. B. Dubois argued. Shown here are women protesting in Kabul, Afghanistan, to demand the repeal of a law authorizing a range of extreme human rights violations, including marital rape. Marching for rights and equality, Fatima Husseini said, "It means a woman is a kind of property, to be used by the man in any way that he wants."

"spotlight" on abusive practices to shame those who violate human rights into changing their behavior (Barry, Clay, and Flynn, 2012; Blanton and Blanton, 2012a; Murdie and Davis, 2012). "When citizens, even those who are relatively powerless by themselves, partner with non-governmental organizations (NGOs) and intergovernmental organizations (IGOs), they have promoted positive changes in human rights" (Smith-Cannoy, 2012, p. 3).

Although some individuals remain skeptical of claims that we all have transcendent moral obligations to humanity as a whole, others believe that every person, by virtue of being human, has certain inherent and inalienable rights that warrant international protection. Decrying the realist premise that human rights are at odds with national interest, Executive Director of Amnesty International William Schulz laments that "What they seem rarely to garner is that in far more cases than they will allow, defending human rights is a prerequisite to protecting that interest." Human rights buttress political and economic freedom, "which in turn tends to bring international trade and prosperity. And governments that treat their own people with tolerance and respect tend to treat their neighbors in the same way."

Promoting the rights and dignity of ordinary people around the world is a formidable challenge. Yet, as global security analyst David Rieff notes, "The old assumption that national sovereignty trumps all other principles in international relations is under attack as never before." As political scientist Alison Brysk (2009, p. 4) notes "Even in a world of security dilemmas, some societies will come to see the linkage between their long-term interest and the common good—at some times and places, states can overcome their bounded origins as sovereign security managers to act as 'global citizens.'" Because concerns for human rights have gained stature under international law and are being monitored more closely by IGOs and NGOs than ever before, we can expect human rights to receive continuing attention, as long as people are caught in emergency situations such as genocide or the threat of famine. Eleanor Roosevelt championed the *cosmopolitan* ideal, and her energetic leadership was largely responsible for global acceptance in 1948 of the Universal Declaration of Human Rights. When thinking about the human condition in the early twenty-first century, we can profit by the inspiration of her nightly prayer: "Save us from ourselves and show us a vision of a world made new."

John D. Rockefeller, Jr., once said, "I believe that every right implies a responsibility; every opportunity, an obligation; every possession, a duty." In the next chapter of *World Politics*, you will have an opportunity to look at another major issue that entails rights and responsibility to humanity. As the cascading globalization of our world accelerates, the human choices about our natural environment have consequences for the entire planet and affect the Earth's capability to sustain human life and security.

STUDY. APPLY. ANALYZE.

Key Terms

Suggested Readings

Blanton, Shannon Lindsey, and David L. Cingranelli. (2010) "Human Rights and Foreign Policy Analysis," in *The International Studies Compendium Project*, Robert Denemark et al. (eds.). Oxford: Wiley-Blackwell.

Brysk, Alison, and Austin Choi-Fitzpatrick, eds. *From Human Trafficking to Human Rights: Reframing Contemporary Slavery*. Philadelphia, PA: University of Pennsylvania Press.

Kristof, Nicholas D., and Sheryl WuDunn. (2009) *Half the Sky: Turning Oppression into Opportunity for Women Worldwide*. New York: Random House.

Føllesdal, Andreas, Johan Karlsson Schaffer, and Geir Ulfstein, eds. (2013) *The Legitimacy of International Human Rights Regimes: Legal, Political and Philosophical Perspectives*. Cambridge, UK: Cambridge University Press.

Mertus, Julie. (2009) *Human Rights Matters: Local Politics and National Human Rights Institutions*. Stanford, CA: Stanford University Press.

Pogge, Thomas. (2005) "World Poverty and Human Rights," *Ethics & International Affairs* 19, no. 1 (Spring):1–7.

Ramcharan, Bertrand. (2010) *Preventive Human Rights Strategies*. New York: Routledge.

Smith-Cannoy, Heather. (2012) *Insincere Commitments: Human Rights Treaties, Abusive States, and Citizen Activism*. Washington, DC: Georgetown University Press.

UNDP. (2013) *Human Development Report 2013*. New York: United Nations.

Suggested Videos

Goldhagen, Daniel Jonah. "Worse Than War: Genocide, Eliminationism, and the Ongoing Assault on Humanity."

Kennedy, Julia Taylor. "Handpicking Successors and the Brazilian Elections."

Moossy, Robert, Roger Plant, and Maria Suarez. "Forced to Labor: The Cost of Coercion."

Rodin, David. "How Rights Move: Losing and Acquiring Rights in the International Domain."

Vocke, William. "Your Income, Your Liberty, and Your Equality?"

CourseMate

Log in to CourseMate to access the following study tools for this chapter:

- Interactive Quiz
- eBook
- Flashcards & Key Term Crossword Puzzle
- Chapter Audio Summary
- Carnegie Council Videos
- Video Activities
- Simulation
- Animated Learning Module
- Case Study
- International Relations NewsWatch

"To waste, to destroy our natural resources, to skin and exhaust the land instead of using it so as to increase its usefulness, will result in undermining in the days of our children the very prosperity which we ought by right to hand down to them amplified and developed."

—*Theodore Roosevelt, U.S. president*

CHAPTER 14
Global Responsibility for the Preservation of the Environment

PRESERVING A LIFE-SUSTAINING RESOURCE Many of the world's waterways face serious pollution threats—from sources such as industrial wastewater, raw sewage, garbage, and oil spills—that pose great risk to human health and environmental sustainability. Shown here, two men scavenge from the floating garbage on the increasingly polluted Ciliwung River, which borders Jakarta, the capital of Indonesia.

Yue Yuewei/Xinhua Press/CORBIS

QUESTIONS TO CONSIDER

- *What are the major schools of thought surrounding the debate about environmental security?*
- *In what way are environmental issues transnational problems?*
- *What are some major ecopolitical issues surrounding climate change, biodiversity, and deforestation?*
- *What ecopolitical tensions arise over water, food, and energy resources?*
- *What are the prospects for sustainable development?*

"Where you stand depends on where you sit" is an aphorism used to describe the determinants of people's decisions (recall Chapter 3). Where do you stand on one of the more "hotly" debated issues created by a warming globe and deteriorating environment? You may already have strong feelings about this controversy. Many others do. On whichever side of the environmental debate you fall, there is at least one scholar and several politicians who share your opinion.

Some politicians, corporations, and scientists reject the idea that the planet is really in danger; they claim that there is not a real problem because technological innovation can reverse global warming (which they argue may not even be "real" because the long-term cyclical pattern of the Earth's evolution suggests that our present period of rising temperatures is temporary). These people claim that environmental deterioration and resource depletion have many people needlessly alarmed.

Most scientists are pessimistic and are now certain that the threat of global warming is real. They are themselves alarmed by optimists who fail to face the "clear and present danger" of environmental threats and undertake the reforms necessary to stem the tide of global change. The ecological threats that rivet the worried scientific community have led many to advocate immediate and sweeping changes by governments, before it is too late to save the human race from doom.

In this chapter, you have the opportunity to sharpen your own thinking by weighing the available evidence about prevailing global trends that affect the environment that we all share. So take a look at various dimensions of the planet's ecology now in transformation and base your stand on these global issues on information that can better ground your existing opinions. Consider also the extent to which humanity is responsible for preserving our global environment.

> *Earth provides enough to satisfy every man's needs, but not every man's greed.*
>
> **—Mohandas Gandhi, Indian peace activist**

FRAMING THE ECOLOGICAL DEBATE

The environment is linked to other priorities, such as security, economic prosperity, and social well-being. "Security" means freedom from fear, risk, and danger. Because fears of a nuclear holocaust and other forms of violence have long haunted the world, security has been conventionally equated with *national security*, the struggle for state power central to *realist theory* and its emphasis on armed conflict.

Environmental security broadens the idea of national security by focusing on the transnational nature of the perils that the global environment faces, such as global warming, ozone depletion, and the loss of tropical forests and marine habitats. These problems are just as much a threat to humanity as to the environment. Because environmental degradation undercuts economic well-being and quality of life, *liberalism* informs current thinking about how states can cooperate with international organizations (IGOs) and nongovernmental organizations (NGOs) to preserve the global environment. The liberal *epistemic community* has redefined

environmental security

A concept recognizing that environmental threats to global life systems are as dangerous as the threat of armed conflicts.

epistemic community

Scientific experts on a subject of inquiry such as global warming that are organized internationally as NGOs to communicate with one another and use their constructed understanding of "knowledge" to lobby for global transformations.

Carnegie Council Video:
Epistemic Community

politics of scarcity

The view that the unavailability of resources required to sustain life, such as food, energy, or water, can undermine security in degrees similar to military aggression.

Carnegie Council Video:
Politics of Scarcity

cornucopians

Optimists who question limits-to-growth perspectives and contend that markets effectively maintain a balance between population, resources, and the environment.

neo-Malthusians

Pessimists who warn of the global ecopolitical dangers of uncontrolled population growth.

the global commons

The physical and organic characteristics and resources of the entire planet—the air in the atmosphere and conditions on land and sea—on which human life depends and which is the common heritage of all humanity.

"security" in order to move beyond realism's conventional state-centric and militaristic portrayal of international politics.

Today, many experts urge people and governments to construct a broader definition of what really constitutes security, much like what the U.S. Department of Defense did in April 2007 when it warned that global warming should be regarded as a threat to American national security. This shift is compatible with liberal theory, which emphasizes that security should be defined as the capacity to protect quality of life. Out of conditions of global poverty and want emerge the so-called *politics of scarcity*, which anticipates that future international conflict will likely be caused by resource scarcities—restricted access to food, oil, and water, for example—rather than by overt military challenges. Moreover, insufficient or polluted resources will depress the living conditions of all of the people on the Earth, but particularly those in the Global South, where the ability and political will to address environmental challenges are limited.

These global environmental issues engage the competing perspectives of optimistic *cornucopians* and pessimistic *neo-Malthusians*. Cornucopians adhere to the belief that if free markets and free trade prevail, ecological imbalances that threaten humanity will eventually be corrected. For them, prices are the key adjustment mechanism that ultimately produces the greatest good for the greatest number of people.

Neo-Malthusians, on the other hand, have a lot in common with economic *mercantilism*, which argues that free markets fail to prevent excessive resource exploitation and that, accordingly, intervention by governing institutions is necessary. This latter perspective rejects the belief that the free market will always maximize social welfare.

The neo-Malthusian pessimists sounding the alarm about the signs of ecological deterioration, and the cornucopian optimists confidently extolling the virtues of free markets and technological innovation in saving the planet, portray very different visions of the global future. How we frame our understanding of environmental challenges will affect our policy prescriptions. It will also influence the extent to which the world community has the political will and capacity to cope with ecological problems and expand the possibilities for *human security*.

GLOBALIZATION AND THE TRAGEDY OF THE GLOBAL COMMONS

Ecologists—those who study the interrelationships of living organisms and the Earth's physical environment—use the term *the global commons* to highlight our growing interdependence, because they see the Earth as a common environment outside the political control of any single state or group. In a world where everything affects everything else, the fate of the global commons is the fate of all humanity. The planet's *carrying capacity*—the Earth's ability to support and sustain life—is at the center of this discussion. Lester R. Brown (2012, p. 9), the president of the Earth Policy Institute, has voiced serious concerns:

> Tonight there will be 219,000 people at the dinner table who were not there last night, many of them with empty plates. Tomorrow night there will be another 219,000 people. Relentless population growth is putting excessive pressure on local land and water resources in many countries, making it difficult if not impossible for farmers to keep pace.

Humanity faces enormous challenges of unprecedented scope and danger: arresting global climate change, preserving biodiversity, providing clean water, and restoring forests, fisheries, and other overly exploited renewable resources. No single cause is by itself responsible for the alarming trends in the global environment. Rather, many causes interact with each other to produce the dangers that are damaging the world's life systems upon which human existence depends. But among the ecologists who scientifically study the origins of planetary predicaments and problems, one explanation has become very popular—environmental degradation is seen, in part, as a product of the individual pursuit of private gain.

The *tragedy of the commons* is a popular term constructed to capture the human roots of the growing threats to the planet's resources and its delicately balanced ecological system. First articulated in 1833 by English political economist William Foster Lloyd, the concept was later popularized and extended to contemporary global environmental problems by human ecologist Garrett Hardin, in his famous 1968 article published in the journal *Science*. This approach emphasizes the impact of human behavior driven by the search for personal self-advantage. Although it stresses the importance of individual action and personal motivations, it also ascribes those motives to collectivities or groups such as corporations and entire countries.

carrying capacity

The maximum number of humans and living species that can be supported by a given territory.

tragedy of the commons

A metaphor, widely used to explain the impact of human behavior on ecological systems, that explains how rational self-interested behavior by individuals may have a destructive, undesirable collective impact.

AP Photo/Rafiq Maqbool

THE TOLL OF DISASTER Monsoon flooding and landslides in the mountainous northern region of India in mid-June 2013 led to the deaths of nearly 600 people and left 84,000 stranded as roads and bridges were destroyed or blocked by debris (Associated Press, 2013). While in some areas the devastation was attributed to the natural disaster, in others the floods and landslides were linked to inadequate government planning for the Himalayan region. "Deforestation, sand mining, stone quarrying and unregulated and excessive construction of buildings have caused havoc to the environment in Uttarakhand," said Indian social activist Medha Patkar. Shown here in that northern Indian state, a vehicle carefully moves along a road damaged by landslides.

The central question asked through the "commons" analogy is, what is the probable approach to resources held in common in an unregulated environment? If individuals (and corporations and countries) are interested primarily in advancing their own personal welfare, what consequences should be anticipated for the finite resources held in common for all?

Lloyd, and later Hardin, asked observers to consider what happened in medieval English villages, where the village green was typically considered common property on which all villagers could let their cattle graze. Freedom of access to the commons was a cherished village value. Sharing the common grazing area worked well as long as individuals (and their cattle) didn't reduce the land's usefulness to everyone else.

However, assuming that the villagers were driven by the profit motive and that no laws existed to restrain their greed, herders had incentive to increase their stock as much as possible. If pushed, individual herders might concede that the collective interest of all would be served if each contained the size of their herd rather than increasing it, so that the commons could be preserved. But self-restraint—voluntary reduction of the number of one's own cattle to relieve the pressure on the village commons—was not popular. This is especially true since there was no guarantee that others would do the same. By contrast, adding more animals to the village green would produce a personal gain whose costs would have to be borne by everyone.

Therefore, in accordance with economic *rational choice*, the individual pursuit of wealth encouraged all to increase indiscriminately the size of their herds, and it discouraged self-sacrifice for the common welfare. Ultimately, the collective impact of each effort to maximize individual gain was to place more cattle on the village green than it could sustain. In the long run, the overgrazed green was destroyed. The lesson? "Ruin is the destination toward which all men rush," Hardin (1968) concluded, "each pursuing his own best interest."

The tragedy of the commons has become a standard concept in ecological analysis because it aptly illuminates the sources of environmental degradation as well as many other global problems and predicaments. It is particularly applicable to the debate today about pressures on the global environment because the English common green is comparable to planetary "common property," such as the oceans and the atmosphere from which individual profit is maximized on the basis of a first-come, first-served principle. Overuse of common property is also highlighted, as when the oceans and atmosphere are used by some as a sink for environmental pollutants whose costs are borne by all.

Are the dynamics underlying the tragedy of the commons responsible for global ecological dangers? Many people think so. However, you have probably already noted that experts disagree about the moral and ethical implications of Hardin's interpretation. Note that the logical conclusion is that reforms are necessary if we are to save planet Earth. The needed changes will require both self-restraint on people's freedom of choice as well as a modicum of regulation in order to control the ruinous consequences of the tragedy of an unmanaged global commons.

Theorists adhering to realism and free-market mercantilism resolutely defend freedom of economic choice without regulation as the best path to realizing the greatest good for the greatest number. Theorists from these traditions believe that pursuing self-interest and personal profit will benefit all in the long run, producing more income and technological innovation than would otherwise occur under supervisory regulation of corporations, entrepreneurs, and investors. They also feel that minimal interference in the pursuit of personal gain is helpful to the preservation of the Earth's environment. According to their reasoning, the pursuit of private gain with little restraint is a virtue, not a vice.

Almost all religious moral traditions question this realist and mercantilist conclusion. Christianity, for example, follows ancient Hebrew ethics in defining greed as one of the seven deadly sins. As Timothy 6:10, the Bible warns, "For the love of money is the root of all evil." The predictable outcome of selfishness and blind dedication to personal financial gain over other values such as altruistic love and compassion for humankind is a path to certain ruin and sin. In this sense, religious traditions join some of the thinking underlying radical Marxist theorizing (see Chapter 2). These lines of thought argue that concern for the welfare of all provides happiness and benefits because only if community interests are protected can individuals realize their most precious personal interest in advancing such common values as the opportunity for maintaining a clean and sustainable environment.

Ecopolitics forces you to weigh rival perspectives and to evaluate competing values. Do you want income and prosperity? Of course—but at what cost? Countries and companies all seek wealth. Does this mean that their quest for profits justifies dumping toxic wastes into lakes, rivers, and oceans, and letting others bear the burden of these actions?

ON THE PRECIPICE OF EXTINCTION? In 2013 the International Union for Conservation of Nature (IUCN) reported that "Of the world's 5494 mammals, 78 are Extinct or Extinct in the Wild, with 191 Critically Endangered, 447 Endangered and 496 Vulnerable," and that the "current species extinction rate is between 1000 and 10,000 times higher than it would naturally be [without human activity]" (IUCN, 2013). Shown here is a "dead forest" in Madagascar, which has lost over 80 percent of its forest due mostly to slash-and-burn rice farming that also exhausts the soil and destroys the habitats of countless species.

These and other ethical questions bear directly on the debate about what is causing the degradation of the planetary commons and what, if anything, should be done to counter it, and at what cost. The next step is for you to characterize and estimate the nature and magnitude of environmental threats and challenges. Consider three interrelated clusters of problems on the global ecopolitical agenda: (1) climate change and ozone depletion, (2) biodiversity and deforestation, and (3) energy supply and demand. The clusters illustrate some of the obstacles to the preservation of common properties and renewable resources.

The Ecopolitics of the Atmosphere

The scores of government negotiators and nongovernmental representatives who converged in Rio de Janeiro in 1992 came in the wake of the hottest decade on record. For years, scientists had warned that global warming—the gradual rise in world temperature—would cause destructive changes in world climate patterns and that rising sea levels, melting glaciers, and freak storms would provoke widespread changes in global political and economic relationships. Perhaps because they had been burned by the chronic heat wave throughout the 1980s, negotiators agreed at Rio to a *Framework Convention on Climate Change*. Since then, fears have spread with the continuing rise in planetary temperatures and extreme weather events, and attention to the pollutants blamed for global warming has also risen.

Climate Change and Global Warming   Major gaps in knowledge about climate change remain, but most climate scientists are now convinced that the gradual rise in the Earth's temperature, especially evident since the late eighteenth century when the invention of power-driven machinery produced the Industrial Revolution, is caused by an increase in human-made gases that alter the atmosphere's insulating effects. The gas molecules, primarily carbon dioxide (CO_2) and chlorofluorocarbons (CFCs), form the equivalent of a greenhouse roof by trapping heat emitted from Earth that would otherwise escape into outer space. Since the eighteenth century, the emission of carbon dioxide has increased by almost 40 percent (EPA, 2013). Additionally, spreading deforestation contributes significantly to global warming as "the loss of trees accounts for 18 percent of annual carbon dioxide emission and is the second leading cause of the greenhouse effect" (Badwal, 2012).

As these gases are released into the atmosphere, they create a *greenhouse effect*, which has caused global temperatures to rise (see Figure 14.1). The average global temperature on the Earth's surface since the late 1800s has increased between 0.7 and 1.4 degrees Fahrenheit (0.4 to 0.8 degrees Celsius). The changing temperatures are expected to have a profound effect on animal and plant life across the world. Furthermore, "there is wide consensus that the 2 degrees Fahrenheit of global warming of the last century is behind the rise in seal levels, more intense hurricanes, more heat waves, and more droughts and deluges" (Begley, 2011, p. 43).

The globe's temperature is now projected to increase even more dramatically by 2100 if aggressive preventive action is not taken (see Map 14.1). The UN team of 600 hundred scientists from forty countries known as the Intergovernmental Panel on Climate Change (IPCC) predicts that, depending on greenhouse-gas emissions, global temperatures will probably rise about 2 to 12 degrees Fahrenheit by 2100, with longer and more intense heat waves along the way. The U.S. National Aeronautics and Space Administration (NASA) makes a similar forecast, anticipating that temperature may increase by 2.5 to 10.4 degrees Fahrenheit within that same time span.

greenhouse effect

The phenomenon producing planetary warming when gases released by burning fossil fuels act as a blanket in the atmosphere, thereby increasing temperatures.

Carnegie Council Video: Greenhouse Effect

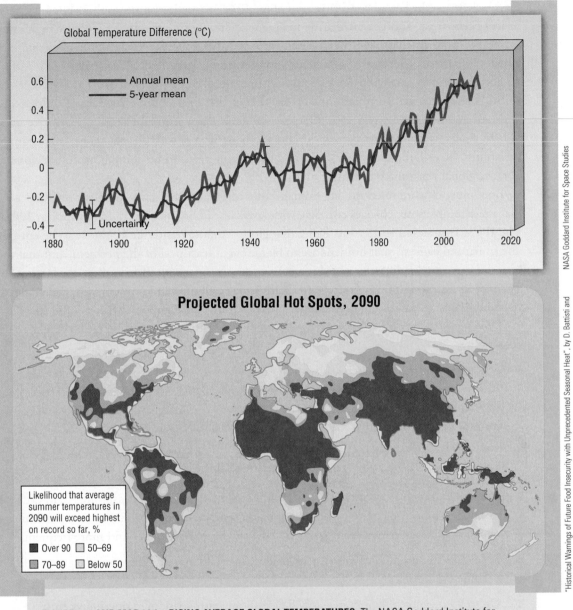

Global Temperature Difference (°C)

— Annual mean
— 5-year mean

Uncertainty

Projected Global Hot Spots, 2090

Likelihood that average summer temperatures in 2090 will exceed highest on record so far, %

■ Over 90   ☐ 50–69
▨ 70–89   ☐ Below 50

FIGURE 14.1 AND MAP 14.1   RISING AVERAGE GLOBAL TEMPERATURES The NASA Goddard Institute for Space Studies monitors average global surface temperatures around the world. Its records indicate that since 2000, as depicted in the graph above, nine of the ten warmest years since 1880 have occurred. With greenhouse gas emissions and atmospheric carbon dioxide levels on the rise, scientists predict that long-term temperatures will continue to increase. The map on the bottom projects the globe's most intense hot spots in 2090.

There is also scientific evidence that "we may see globally averaged temperature increases of 4 degrees Celsius—more than 7 degrees Fahrenheit—as early as the 2060s" (McKibben, 2011, p. 62). Although CO_2 is the principal greenhouse gas, concentrations of methane in the atmosphere are growing even more rapidly. Methane gas emissions arise from livestock populations, rice cultivation, and the production and transportation of natural gas. To the alarm of many scientists, the largest concentrations of methane are not in the atmosphere but are locked in ice, permafrost, and coastal marine sediments. This means that as the global temperature increases, more methane will be released into the atmosphere, which would then increase global temperatures because of methane's strong warming potential.

Some scientists insist the rise in global temperature is only part of a cyclical change the world has experienced for thousands of years. They are able to cite evidence of "sudden and dramatic temperature swings over the past 400,000 years, from warm climates to ice ages. [These] global warming skeptics say the climate changes we're seeing today reflect these natural variations" (Knickerbocker, 2007), and that cold water needs to be poured on all the "hot air" because global warming is a climate myth.

But "most climate scientists say human-induced greenhouse gases are at work—and note that these temperature changes correlate with levels of carbon dioxide" (Knickerbocker, 2007). The IPCC first stated in 1995 its belief that global climate trends are "unlikely to be entirely due to natural causes," that humans are to blame for at least part of the problem, and that the consequences are likely to be very harmful and costly. Speaking of his fellow climatologists, glaciologist Lonnie Thompson declared that "virtually all of us are now convinced that global warming poses a clear and present danger to civilization" (McKibben, 2011, p. 62).

The effects of continued rising temperatures around the globe will be both dramatic and devastating:

■ Sea levels will rise, mostly because of melting glaciers and the expansion of water as it warms up. This will produce massive flooding in vast areas of low-lying coastal lands, especially in Asia and the U.S. Atlantic coast. New York City could be submerged. Millions of people are likely to be displaced by major floods each year.

■ Winters will get warmer and heat waves will become increasingly frequent and severe, producing avalanches from melting glaciers in high altitudes.

■ Rainfall will increase worldwide, and deadly storms such as the devastating Asian cyclone in 2008 will become more common. As ocean temperatures continue to rise, hurricanes, which draw their energy from warm oceans, will become stronger and more frequent.

■ Because water evaporates more easily in a warmer climate, drought-prone regions will become even drier.

■ Up to 30 percent of living species will face an increasing risk of extinction as entire ecosystems vanish from the planet. A hotter Earth will drive some plant life to higher (or lower) latitudes and greater elevations, requiring farmers to change their crops and agricultural practices.

■ The combination of flooding and droughts will cause tropical diseases such as malaria and dengue fever to flourish in previously temperate regions that were formerly too cold for their insect carriers; "a warmer CO_2-rich world will be very, very good for plants, insects, and microbes that make us sick" (Begley, 2007).

■ The world will face increased hunger and water shortages, especially in the poorest countries. Africa will be the hardest hit, with up to 250 million people likely to suffer water shortages by 2020 (Bates et al., 2008).

MENAHEM KAHANA/AFP/Getty Images

AP Photo/Fang kuang

GLOBAL WARMING, CLIMATIC CATASTROPHES, AND MASS SUFFERING "Global warming is expected to make the climate warmer, wetter, and wilder. It is predicted that such climate change will increase the severity and frequency of climate-related disasters like flash floods, surges, cyclones, and severe storms" (Bergholt and Lujala, 2012, p. 147). Experiencing the worst snow storm in 20 years, Jerusalem was temporarily brought to a standstill in January 2013 (shown left). In July 2012, the heaviest rain storm to hit Beijing, China, in sixty-years caused widespread chaos (shown right). Many see the increase in extreme weather events such as these as evidence of global climate change.

Not all countries are contributing to global warming at the same rate. The high-income Global North states contribute more than half of global carbon emissions, in large measure because of their big buildings, millions of cars, and relatively inefficient industries. However, Asian dynamos China and India have rapidly increased their emissions as their economies have grown and generated increasing demands for fossil-fuel energy. In 2008, China surpassed the United States as the world's top emitter of greenhouse gases, with responsibility for 24 percent of all emissions (WDI, 2013). The International Energy Agency forecasts that the increase of greenhouse-gas emissions from 2000 to 2030 from China alone will nearly equal the increase from the entire industrialized world. India, though behind its Asian rival, already accounts for 75 percent of all greenhouse gas emissions in South Asia (World Bank, 2013g).

Compare the existing and new industrial giants' consumption of energy and production of greenhouse gases with those of the low-income Global South countries. They, too, are growing rapidly (see Chapter 5), and their appetite for fossil-fuel energy sources is on the rise. The Global South produces more than 62.6 percent of global energy and is responsible for 55.7 percent of the world's energy use (WDI, 2013). Thus, countries in all regions are contributing, at different rates, to the global trend in the growing level of carbon added to the atmosphere.

Rather than comparing rich and poor countries, the *Proceedings of the National Academy of Sciences* has suggested that "it is rich people, rather than rich countries, who need to change the most. The authors suggest setting a cap on total emissions, and then converting that cap into a global per-person limit.... So the high-living, carbon guzzling rich minority in India and China would not be able to hide behind their poor and carbon-thrifty compatriots" (*The Economist*, 2009l, p. 62). Although far too difficult to implement, the proposal highlights how the lower level of carbon emissions in the Global South masks the

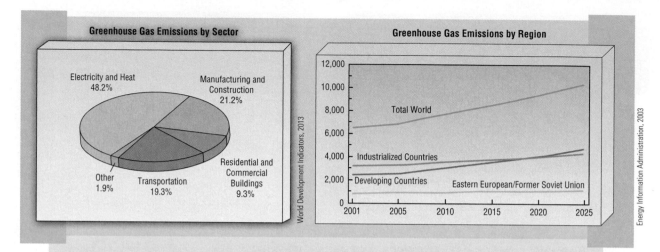

FIGURE 14.2 AND FIGURE 14.3   TRENDS IN GREENHOUSE GASES Concentrations of CO_2 in the atmosphere have risen by almost 40 percent since pre-industrial times, increasing from approximately 280 parts per million by volume (ppmv) in the eighteenth century to 399.89 ppmv in May 2013—the highest in at least 800,000 years (EPA, 2013; WDI, 2013). The figure on the left charts the sources of greenhouse-gas emissions by each major sector. The figure on the right identifies the distribution of carbon-equivalent greenhouse-gas emissions by region from 2001 and projected through the year 2025.

variation within states where the wealthy contribute at a far higher rate to environmental degradation than the poor.

These trends in greenhouse-gas emissions, as well as the changing percentage of world greenhouse-gas emissions by sector, suggest that the energy picture will change but that global warming and the environmental damage it causes are problems that are not likely to disappear any time soon (see Figures 14.2 and 14.3).

The politics of global warming are dramatically illustrated by the tensions between the countries trying to carve up the Arctic in order to reap economic payoffs from exploiting the resources that lie beneath the polar ice cap. Climate change affects the Arctic intensely, because the average temperature there has risen about twice as fast as that of the rest of the planet, with the melting of Arctic sea ice occurring more rapidly than projected by the IPCC, "largely because emissions of carbon dioxide have topped what the panel" expected (Begley, 2009a, p. 30). This trend is paving the way for a geopolitical struggle over ecopolitics among the five countries already laying claim to the resource-rich central zone (Russia, Norway, Canada, the United States, and Denmark).

The primary motive: possession of as much as one-fourth of the world's remaining oil and gas reserves buried beneath the seabed under Arctic ice. A "cold rush" is under way in the battle for the melting north (Funk, 2007). The disappearing ice also offers the possibility of new sea routes, at least for part of the year, which would significantly reduce the time it takes for ships to travel from Europe to Asia. "As global warming melts the Arctic ice, dreams of a short sea passage to Asia—and riches beneath the surface—have been revived. With Russia planting a flag on the ocean floor at the North Pole, Canada talking tough and Washington wanting to be a player, who will win the world's new Great Game?" (Graff, 2007). None of this international friction would have materialized had global warming not made competition for control of this geostrategic arena possible.

Ozone Depletion and Protection

The story of climate change is similar to states' efforts to cope with the depletion of the atmosphere's protective *ozone layer*. In this case, however, an international regime has emerged, progressively strengthened by mounting scientific evidence that environmental damage is directly caused by human activity.

Ozone is a pollutant in the lower atmosphere, but in the upper atmosphere it provides the Earth with a critical layer of protection against the sun's harmful ultraviolet radiation. Scientists have discovered a marked depletion of the ozone layer—most notably, an "ozone hole" over Antarctica that has grown to a size larger than the continental United States. They have conclusively linked the thinning of the layer to CFCs—a related family of compounds known as halons, hydrochlorofluorocarbons (HCFCs), methyl bromide, and other chemicals. Depletion of the ozone layer exposes humans to health hazards of various sorts, particularly skin cancer, and threatens other forms of marine and terrestrial life.

Scientists began to link halons and CFCs

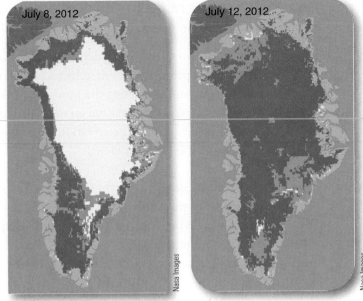

■ Melted ice

FEELING THE HEAT The IPCC has concluded that evidence of the Earth's rising temperatures is "unequivocal" and that global warming is more than 90 percent likely to be the product of human activity. Shown here is one possible consequence: dramatic melting of Greenland's surface ice sheet. Satellite maps show that on July 8, 2012 (shown left), about 40 percent of the ice sheet's surface had melted, and that by July 12 (shown right) a shocking 97 percent of the ice sheet had turned to slush. While this event may be due to a rare heat wave—there is evidence of similar events every 150 years—many worry that if such widespread thawing is due to climate change, it would result in rising seas. "Scientists estimate that if all of Greenland's ice sheet were to melt, the global sea level would rise by 23 feet" (Than, 2012).

to ozone depletion in the early 1970s. The 1987 landmark *Montreal Protocol on Substances That Deplete the Ozone Layer* treaty, which as of July 2013 had been ratified by 197 parties, has led to an amazing 90 percent reduction since the late 1980s in global atmospheric concentrations of chlorofluorocarbons (UNEP, 2011; WDI, 2007). The expansion of the ozone regime was made possible by growing scientific evidence and by having an active NGO epistemic community to actively promote the treaty. However, in spite of reductions in CFCs over the past 20 years, the ozone hole over Antarctica continues to expand, and depletion of the protective ozone shield is expected to continue before it begins to regenerate itself.

Production of CFCs in the Global North declined sharply in the 1990s as the largest producers (and consumers) of these ozone-damaging products began to phase them out. However, production in the Global South surged, and increased demand for refrigerators, air conditioners, and other products using CFCs offset the gains realized by stopping production in the Global North. Developed countries agreed to provide aid to help the developing countries adopt CFC alternatives, but they have failed to provide all of the promised resources. Without this support, many in the Global South may not be able to keep their end of the global bargain.

ozone layer

The protective layer of the upper atmosphere over the Earth's surface that shields the planet from the sun's harmful impact on living organisms.

The Ecopolitics of Biodiversity, Deforestation, and Water Shortages

Success at containing ozone depletion has raised hopes that other environmental threats can also be given priority over vested financial interests. Forests are critical in preserving the Earth's *biodiversity* and protecting the atmosphere and land resources. For these reasons, they have become a rising ecological issue on the global agenda. Some rules have emerged to guide international behavior in the preservation of biodiversity, but issues concerning forests have proven much more difficult to address.

biodiversity

The variety of plant and animal species living in the Earth's diverse ecosystems.

Threats to Global Biodiversity   Biodiversity, or biological diversity, is an umbrella term that refers to the Earth's variety of life. Technically, it encompasses three basic levels of organization in living systems: genetic diversity, species diversity, and ecosystem diversity. Until recently, public attention has focused almost exclusively on preserving species diversity by protecting ecosystems, including old forests, tall-grass prairies, wetlands, coastal habitats, and coral reefs.

Forests, especially tropical forests, are important to preserving biodiversity because they are home to countless species of animals and plants, many of them still unknown. Scientists believe that the global habitat contains between eight and ten million species. Of these, only about 1.5 million have been named, and most of them are in the temperate regions of North America, Europe, Russia, and Australia. Destruction of tropical forests, where two-thirds to three-fourths of all species are believed to live, threatens to destroy much of the world's undiscovered biological diversity and genetic heritage.

Many experts worry that the globe is relentlessly heading toward major species extinction. Of the nearly 300,000 plant species surveyed by the World Conservation Union, more than 8000 are threatened with extinction, mainly as a result of clearing land for housing, roads, and industries. The IPCC predicts that global warming increases the risk of extinction for almost 70 percent of species, with Arctic animals such as the polar bear at the most risk. Others doubt the imminence of a massive die-out, estimating that only a small fraction of the Earth's species have actually disappeared over the past several centuries. Indeed, optimistic cornucopians argue that species extinction may not be bad news, as new species may evolve that will prove even more beneficial to humanity (McKibben, 2006).

Because much of the Earth's biological heritage is concentrated in the tropics, the Global South also has a growing concern about protecting its interests in the face of efforts by MNCs to reap profits from the sale of biological products. MNCs in the Global North are major players in the so-called *enclosure movement* geared to privatize and commercialize the products derived from plant and animal genes that are the genetic bases for sustained life. Pharmaceutical companies in particular have laid claim to Global South resources. They actively explore plants, microbes, and other living organisms in tropical forests for possible use in prescription drugs. Concern in the Global South is centered on the idea that the genetic character of the many species of plants and animals should be considered a part of the global commons and therefore available for commercial use by all, for their medical benefit.

enclosure movement

The claiming of common properties by states or private interests.

Biogenetic engineering threatens to escalate the erosion of global diversity. Biological resources—animal and plant species—are distributed unevenly in the world. Map 14.2 shows

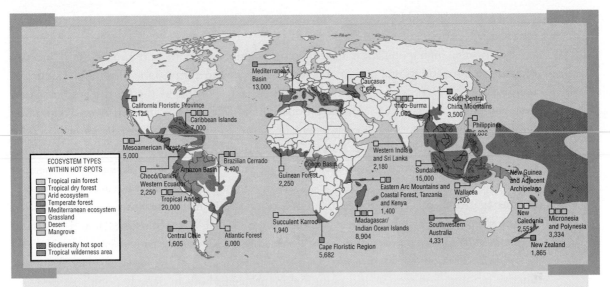

MAP 14.2   LOCATING BIODIVERSITY BASTIONS AND ENDANGERED HOT SPOTS This map provides a picture of global "danger zones" in identifying the estimated number of plant and animal species that are endangered in these biodiversity "hot spots." Former German Environment Minister Sigmar Gabriel estimated that "up to 150 species become extinct every day."

the major "biodiversity bastions," where more than half the Earth's species are found. They are located in primarily tropical wilderness territories laden with plant and animal species yet covering only 2 percent of the land. It also shows the location of "biodiversity hot spots," where human activity threatens to disturb and potentially destroy many species that international law defines as collective goods, a resource for all humanity from which everyone benefits. According to the UN, about 50,000 plant and animal species become extinct each year as the global community wrestles with the ethics of biodiversity preservation and management policies.

Shrinking Forests, Dust Bowls, and Water Shortages   Trends since the 1980s show considerable *deforestation* throughout much of the world. Over the past 8000 years, the World Resources Institute estimates almost half the forests once covering the Earth have been converted for ranching, farmland, pastures, and other uses, and that "one-fifth of the Earth's original forest remains in large, relatively natural ecosystems—what are known as 'frontier forests.'" Of the world's forests, 76.1 percent are located in the Global South (WDI, 2013). "Deforestation is occurring most rapidly in the remaining tropical moist forests of the Amazon, West Africa, and parts of Southeast Asia" (WDR, 2008, p. 191). Destruction of tropical rain forests in such places as Brazil, Indonesia, and Malaysia is a matter of special concern because much of the world's genetic heritage is found there.

Nonetheless, the Global South objects vigorously to the socially constructed view that the world's forests are a common property resource, the "common heritage of mankind." The developing countries feared that legally accepting this view would enable the Global North to interfere with the local management of their tropical forest resources. As Ogar Assam Effa, a tree plantation director in Nigeria, observes, "The developed countries want us to keep the forests, since the air we breathe is for all of us, rich countries and poor countries. But we breathe the air, and our bellies are empty." He asks "Can air give you protein? Can air give you

deforestation

The process of clearing and destroying forests.

carbohydrates? It would be easy to convince people to stop clearing the forest if there was an alternative" (Harris, 2008, p. A2).

Meanwhile, high population growth rates, industrialization, and urbanization increase pressure to farm forests and marginal land poorly suited to cultivation. This has led to deforestation and *desertification*, which turn an increasing portion of the Earth's landmass into deserts that are useless for agricultural productivity or wildlife habitats. "The world is running out of freshwater. There's water everywhere, of course, but less than three percent of it is fresh, and most of that is locked up in polar ice caps and glaciers, unrecoverable for practical purposes. Lakes, rivers, marshes, aquifers, and atmospheric vapor make up less than one percent of the Earth's total water, and people are already using more than half of the accessible runoff" (Finnegan, 2002, p. 43). Water demand and water use in many areas is far greater than the rate of natural replenishment, (see "A Closer Look: Global Water Shortages"), and this trend is expected to continue as demand seems destined to exceed supply by 56 percent by 2025.

Additionally, soil degradation has stripped billions of acres of the Earth's surface from productive farming. Soil erosion and pollution are problems both in densely populated developing countries and in the more highly developed regions of mechanized industrial agriculture. "Global demand for food is projected to double in the next fifty years as urbanization proceeds and income rises. But arable land per capita is shrinking" (WDI, 2007, p. 124). The threat will surely increase because land degradation is increasing and deforestation continues at about 44,000 square kilometers a year (WDI, 2013). Map 14.3 shows the trends across regions where desertification is occurring most rapidly.

desertification

The creation of deserts due to soil erosion, overfarming, and deforestation, which converts cropland to nonproductive, arid sand.

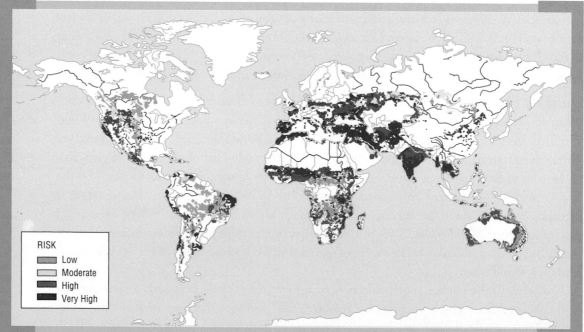

RISK
Low
Moderate
High
Very High

Adapted from U.S. Department of Agriculture

MAP 14.3   HUMAN-INDUCED DESERTS Desertification affects roughly 25 percent of the world's landmass, and in an effort to raise awareness and promote action, the United Nations launched the Decade for Deserts and the Fight against Desertification (2010–2020). This map displays the extent to which human activity, as opposed to natural environmental factors alone, is likely to lead to further desertification or degraded dry lands in regions across the globe.

A Closer Look

GLOBAL WATER SHORTAGES

March 22 marks World Water Day. Adopted by the United Nations in 1993, this annual observation draws global attention to the critical role of water in sustaining human life and well-being. Yet the "proportion of people living in countries chronically short of water, which stood at 8 percent (500 million) at the turn of the 21st century, is set to rise to 45 percent (four billion) by 2050" (Grimond, 2010, p. 3). Moreover, nearly one out of every five people in the world lacks access to safe drinking water. The World Health Organization estimates that millions of people die every year from diseases caused by poor water quality, inadequate sanitation, or poor hygiene. As a recent report by the UN World Water Assessment Programme concluded, "It is clear that urgent action is needed if we are to avoid a global water crisis."

Part of the problem is demographic. As the world's population has risen, the demand for water has also increased. With the simultaneous growth in urbanization, demand has exceeded the capacity of the already insufficient water supply and sanitation infrastructure in many cities throughout the Global South. By some estimates, "global water consumption is doubling every twenty years, and the United Nations expects demand to outstrip supply by more than 30 percent come 2040" (Interlandi, 2010, p. 42). Furthermore, as countries across the world become wealthier, their populations tend to shift from vegetarian to meaty diets, which include foods that use more water to produce. Additionally, "there is growing evidence that global warming is speeding up the hydrologic cycle—that is, the rate at which water evaporates and falls again as rain or snow.... It brings longer droughts between more intense periods of rain" (*The Economist*, 2009h, p. 60). With rising population and consumption, in the absence of serious water-conservation measures and cooperation among mutual water users for watershed preservation, water availability will become an ever-growing resource issue.

WATCH THE VIDEO:

Carnegie Council Video:
Has Water Become a
Right?

YOU DECIDE:

1. Is access to consumable water a basic human right?

2. What obligation, if any, do countries have to ensure the sustainability of freshwater resources for the world's 7 billion people?

3. What insights does the "tragedy of the commons" provide regarding this challenge?

In the Global North, reforestation has begun to alleviate some of the danger. This is not the case, however, in many cash-starved Global South countries where the reasons for rapid destruction vary. In Southeast Asia, forests are burned or cut for large-scale planting of palm to obtain the oil that is used in a wide array of products, including cosmetics and food processing. In Africa, individuals hack out small plots for farming (Harris, 2008). South American forests, most notably the Amazon, are generally burned for industrial-scale soybean farming or cattle grazing.

The Amazon continues to be cleared at an alarming pace amid heated national debate over whether to ease Brazil's Forest Code, which has required 80 percent of a landholding in the Amazon to remain forest. Supporters of the current law fear that change will lead to greater destruction of the Amazon rainforest, whereas those who seek to reduce the restrictions argue that the law presently inhibits economic development. As John Carter, founder of a nonprofit that promotes sustainable ranching in the Amazonian region, lamented "You can't protect it. There's too much money to be made tearing it down." However, a recent decline in deforestation, as well as sustained economic growth, provides hope that the link between deforestation and economic growth may be weakening (Butler, 2012).

And most recently, deforestation is being spurred by the global demand for biofuels. Although biofuels such as ethanol are often touted as being eco-friendly, critics point out that ethanol destroys forests, contributes to global warming, and inflates food prices. Moreover, the clearing and burning of tropical rain forests to make room for farms and ranches are doubly destructive because agriculture uses 70 percent of freshwater globally (WDI, 2013). From the viewpoint of climate change, green plants remove CO_2 from the atmosphere during photosynthesis. So the natural processes that remove greenhouse gases are also being destroyed when forests are cut down and, as the forests decay or are burned, the amount of CO_2 released into the atmosphere further increases. The Amazon rain forest is "an incomparable storehouse of carbon, the very carbon that heats up the planet when it's released into the atmosphere" (Grunwald, 2008, p. 40).

The Ecopolitics of Energy Supply and Demand

According to naturalist Loren Eiseley, human history can be thought of as our ascent up "the heat ladder," where "coal bested firewood as an amplifier of productivity, and oil and natural gas bested coal" (Owen, 2009, p. 21). Throughout the twentieth century, the demand for and consumption of oil—the primary fossil fuel supplying energy—spiraled upward. An abundant supply of cheap oil facilitated the recovery of Western Europe and Japan after World War II and encouraged consumers to use energy-intensive technologies, such as the private automobile.

FROM FARMLAND TO DUST BOWL Desertification has hit many areas hard, and "man-made climate change is also causing more droughts on top of those that occur naturally" (Begley, 2008, p. 53). In 2012, the UN Food and Agriculture Organization warned that drought in Central Africa had reduced cereal production by as much as 50 percent, placing more than 16 million people at risk of starvation.

An enormous growth in the worldwide demand for and consumption of energy followed. The International Energy Agency predicts that, even taking into account gains in efficiency (the United States has doubled its energy efficiency since the 1970s), the world will be using 50 percent more oil in 2030 than it does now. Although the Global North remains a major consumer of oil, this century has witnessed a globalization of demand, with 85 percent of the surge in oil demand occurring in emerging markets such as China, India, and the Middle East (Yergin, 2009).

The suppliers of oil have also changed over the past decade. Oil companies such as Chevron and ExxonMobil continue to be the "supermajors" within the oil industry, although others such as Amoco have disappeared. But traditional MNCs no longer maintain overriding control of the oil industry. Rather, "much larger state-owned companies, which, along with governments, today control more than 80 percent of the world's oil reserves. Fifteen of the world's 20 largest oil companies are state-owned" (Yergin, 2009, p. 92). Moreover, oil has moved from being just a physical commodity to now also being a financial asset, where there has been a massive growth in the number of oil investors and traders.

Old players such as the Organization of Petroleum Exporting Countries (OPEC) remain important, of course. To maximize profits, OPEC emerged as an important intergovernmental organization. Because the resources OPEC controls cannot be easily replaced, it has monopoly power. In March 1999, OPEC began to flex its economic muscles by reducing production and hence restricting the oil supply. Oil prices tripled within a year, showing that OPEC could still make oil a critical global political issue—as it has again since 2004 in an effort to use oil prices as an instrument of *coercive diplomacy* to influence, by the use of threats, the course of the unfolding war on terrorism.

Oil supplies assume great importance in world politics because oil is not being discovered at the same rate at which it is being used. For every two barrels pumped out of the ground, the giant oil companies discover only one new barrel. Production in the United States peaked thirty years ago, and in Russia peaked in 1987. About 70 percent of the oil consumed today was found 25 years ago or longer (Klare, 2008). Meanwhile, demand for oil keeps escalating, and the era of cheap and abundant oil has ended.

Or at least, that is what analysts thought when, on July 11, 2008, the price of a barrel of oil hit a high of $147.27. It was believed that the days of affordable oil were over. This may still be the case, but what we have now witnessed is that the price of oil as a commodity is extremely volatile. In December 2008, the price of oil had fallen to $32.40 per barrel; on July 11, 2009, exactly a year after the peak oil price, the price of oil was as low as $59.87 per barrel. By the middle of June 2013, the cost of a barrel of crude oil had risen again to just under $99. These dramatic price swings may be even more threatening than an end to cheap prices, as it introduces a great deal of instability into our global economic and political systems, affects an array of industries and the individual consumer, and makes it very difficult to plan future energy investments (see Figure 14.4). Despite our quest for stability, "the changing balance of supply and demand—shaped by economics, politics, technologies, consumer tastes, and accidents of all sorts—will continue to move prices" (Yergin, 2009, p. 95).

What strikes fear in the minds of those who study oil supply against rising demand is the widespread "illusion" of bountiful petroleum. Dwindling global oil reserves will likely limit sustained increases in production (Samuelson, 2008). This alarming predicament suggests that

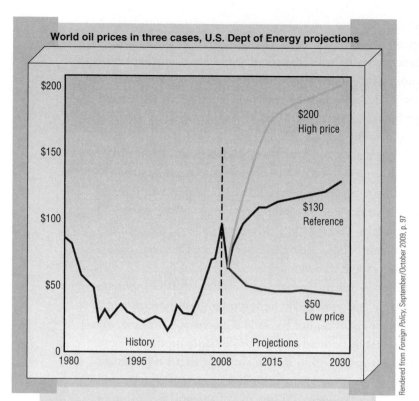

World oil prices in three cases, U.S. Dept of Energy projections

$200 High price

$130 Reference

$50 Low price

History   Projections

1980   1995   2008   2015   2030

Rendered from *Foreign Policy,* September/October 2009, p. 97

FIGURE 14.4   THE UPS AND DOWNS OF THE PRICE FOR OIL As seen here, there are three very different projections regarding world oil prices between now and 2030. Most analysts expect that oil demand will grow quickly as the world economy recovers. Price hikes could result from a number of factors: the restriction of oil supply by OPEC, the anticipation of future oil scarcity by traders, and the eagerness of the Global South for energy—which will likely account for 90 percent of the surge in demand over the next decade. There is also a possibility that prices may decline, however, due to rising oil output in Iraq and the United States (Macalister, 2012).

a "new geopolitics of oil" has arisen over how the oil producers will use their supplies in international bargaining with those oil-importing countries that are vulnerable to supply disruptions. The world today does not face the immediate threat of running out of oil; it faces instead the problem that over half of the proven oil reserves are now concentrated in a small number of OPEC countries that are drawing down their reserves at half the average global rate. It seems almost inevitable that OPEC's share of the world oil market will grow.

This means that OPEC is critical to global oil supply, the Middle East is critical to OPEC, and countries that depend on oil imports from this volatile and unstable source are highly vulnerable to disruptions. "As the center of gravity of world oil production shifts decisively to OPEC suppliers and state-centric energy producers like Russia, geopolitical rather than market factors will come to dominate the marketplace" (Klare, 2008, p. 19). Indeed, the war between Russia and Georgia in 2008 was seen by many "as an intense geopolitical contest over the flow of Caspian Sea energy to markets in the West."

Another challenge facing the world, starkly illustrated by the massive oil spill in the Gulf of Mexico in 2010, is how to balance the demand for oil against the environmental, economic, and health risks posed by drilling. A U.S. presidential commission "concluded that a cascade of technical and managerial failures—including a faulty cement job—caused the disaster" (Burdeau and Weber, 2011). Yet the public also used the ballot box to demonstrate their preference for cheap oil underwritten by risky drilling instead of a government committed to industry regulation. As political historian Sarah Elkind said, "This failure of government is government acting the way American people have said they want it to act."

Do we have the capacity and will to make changes in our energy production and consumption? In response to the threat of future shortages and the risk of heavy dependence on oil, the Global North may be on the verge of a potentially historic juncture that would overturn the pivotal place of oil in the global political economy. In 2008, China and Japan ended a longtime dispute by agreeing to jointly develop two natural gas fields in the East China Sea; in August 2009, Russia reached an agreement with Turkey to build a gas pipeline from the Black Sea to the Mediterranean via the Anatolian Peninsula. There is also an array of efforts under way to develop alternative clean-energy fuel sources, such as wind and solar power, to break our dependence on fossil fuels.

TOWARD SUSTAINABILITY AND HUMAN SECURITY

Across the globe, people desire to live in a clean and green environment and seek to avoid ones that are polluted, unhealthy, and prone to floods, hurricanes, tornadoes, and typhoons. Why, then, have human threats to the global ecology increased despite their conflictual relationship with human interests and values? Environmental activists argue that the Earth is at a critical point and even more attention to environmental preservation is needed.

> *Future prosperity and stability means rethinking how we exploit the planet's natural assets.*
>
> **—Ban Ki-moon, UN secretary-general**

The Quest for Sustainable Development

Environmental decay seems to recognize few borders; it is a worldwide problem, for both poor and rich countries. "Overall, there are considerable signs that the capacity of ecosystems to continue to produce many of the goods we depend on is declining," cautions the World Resources Institute (2009). That transformation makes protection of the planetary environment a necessity, but the solutions are hard to find when many people put their personal advantage ahead of those of all humanity. Recommended changes to protect and preserve planet Earth's ecology may be expensive, but it is important to try.

Sustainable development is now popularly perceived as an alternative to the quest for unrestrained growth. The movement began in earnest in 1972, when the UN General Assembly convened the first UN Conference of the Human Environment in Stockholm. Since then, conferences on a wide range of environmental topics have produced scores of treaties and created new international agencies to promote cooperation and monitor environmental developments.

The concept of sustainable development is directly traceable to *Our Common Future*, the 1987 report of the World Commission on Environment and Development, popularly known as the "Brundtland Commission" after the Norwegian prime minister who chaired it. The commission concluded that the world cannot sustain the growth required to meet the needs and aspirations of the world's growing population unless it adopts radically different approaches to basic issues of economic expansion, equity, resource management, and energy efficiency, among other areas of concern. Rejecting the "limits to growth" maxim popular among neo-Malthusians, it emphasized instead "the growth of limits." The commission defined a "sustainable society" as one that "meets the needs of the present without compromising the ability of future generations to meet their own needs."

sustainable development

Economic growth that does not deplete the resources needed to maintain life and prosperity.

Carnegie Council Video: Sustainable Development

Another milestone in the challenge to the then-dominant cornucopian social paradigm occurred at the 1992 Earth Summit in Rio de Janeiro, Brazil, on the twentieth anniversary of the Stockholm conference. The meeting brought together more than 150 states, 1400 non-governmental organizations, and 8000 journalists. Before the Earth Summit, the environment and economic development had been treated separately—and often regarded as being at odds with each other because economic growth frequently imperils and degrades the environment. In Rio, the concept of sustainability galvanized a simultaneous treatment of environmental and development issues.

Other international conferences have since punctuated the strong consensus behind the proposition that all politics—even global politics—are local, as what happens any place ultimately affects conditions every place, and accordingly that the protection of Earth's environment is a primary international security issue. In anticipation of the climate conference in Copenhagen in December 2009, UN Secretary-General Ban Ki-moon urgently called on members to concretely address climate change and greenhouse gas emissions, stating, "We must harness the political will to seal the deal on an ambitious new climate agreement.... If we get it wrong we face catastrophic damage to people, to the planet." Others recognized that the challenges to reaching a global agreement were great and anticipated that a comprehensive treaty would not be reached at the Copenhagen meeting (Bueno de Mesquita, 2009; Levi, 2009).

Many scholars and policy makers are convinced that threats to the preservation of the global commons likewise threaten our basic welfare and security. Sustainable development is crucial to striking a responsible balance for preserving the global environment and providing the resources needed to sustain human life and prosperity. Yet sustainability cannot be realized without substantial changes. Is that possible? Are individuals willing to sacrifice personal consumption for the common good? Will they sacrifice now to enrich their heirs? What approaches are under way?

Although the goal of sustainable development remains distant and frustrations about lost opportunities are mounting, governmental and nonstate actors' acceptance of the concept continues to inspire creative, environmentally sensitive responses. In a political world in which growing population means growing demand for energy, food, and other resources, the politics of scarcity becomes central. This is the vulnerability created by interdependent globalization. Left unchecked, threats to environmental security will compromise human security. "Though governments have an enormous role to play … nongovernmental organizations, philanthropists, the private sector, social entrepreneurs, and technologists can help" to overcome the adverse effects of environmental degradation (Brainard et al., 2009, p. 1). Consider next some key global initiatives to counter environmental degradation.

Feeding the Masses

According to the UN's Food and Agricultural Organization, in order to meet the growing demands of a global population that is expected to surpass 9 billion by 2050, food production must increase by at least 70 percent. But there are concerns that food insecurity is growing, and these fears are leading to political unrest. In 2008, the world witnessed widespread rioting in almost 40 countries as food prices soared and fears of food scarcity became pervasive. "Oddly enough, almost none of the food riots had emerged from a lack of food.... The riots had been generated by the lack of money to buy food" (Kaufman, 2009, p. 51). In 2011, world food prices again escalated (see Figure 14.5), surpassing the peak that they had reached three years prior and causing hardship for many already impoverished people across the world (see Map 14.4). Rising food prices were a major factor leading to the political unrest and protests in many Arab countries that year.

Three ominous trends fuel fears about future food scarcity: the rate of increase in crop yields appears to be slowing, agricultural research expenditures have diminished (especially in Africa), and global food supplies have begun to decline relative to demand as food prices have begun to increase (Runge and Runge, 2010). Some of the reasons for the rise in food prices are environmental. Erosion and deforestation make farming difficult (Daniel, 2011). Extreme weather events—such as droughts in China, Russia, and Argentina and flooding in Canada, Pakistan, and the United States—destroy agricultural crops and lead to disruptions in the market. Other causes of global food insecurity are the result of structural changes that are quite averse to change in the short term (see "Controversy: Why Is There Global Food Insecurity?").

Growth in population, and the explosion of megacities in the Global South, has created changes in diet that occur due to increased wealth and urbanization. Surging fuel prices—linked

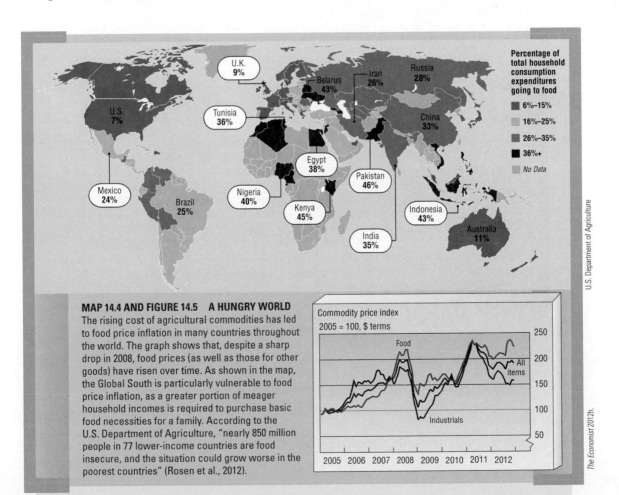

MAP 14.4 AND FIGURE 14.5   A HUNGRY WORLD
The rising cost of agricultural commodities has led to food price inflation in many countries throughout the world. The graph shows that, despite a sharp drop in 2008, food prices (as well as those for other goods) have risen over time. As shown in the map, the Global South is particularly vulnerable to food price inflation, as a greater portion of meager household incomes is required to purchase basic food necessities for a family. According to the U.S. Department of Agriculture, "nearly 850 million people in 77 lower-income countries are food insecure, and the situation could grow worse in the poorest countries" (Rosen et al., 2012).

U.S. Department of Agriculture

The Economist 2012h.

WHY IS THERE A GLOBAL FOOD CRISIS?

A quick trip to the grocery store is revealing—since 2003, bread prices have gone up almost 75 percent, pork prices have more than doubled, and the price of bananas has gone up over 40 percent (Dykman, 2008, p. 35). Globally, increased food prices have created civil unrest and a wave of humanitarian crises in the developing world. Between 2007 and the start of 2009, nearly forty countries had food riots—such as the "tortilla riots" in Mexico and the "pasta riots" in Italy (Landau, 2010). In 2011, rising food prices fed the unrest and anti-government protests that swept through many Arab countries (Zurayk, 2011). As fears of food scarcity spread, panic buying ensued and governments responded by enacting export bans and emergency price controls.

Such dilemmas, particularly for the poor, have led one observer to warn that food riots are likely to become commonplace (Ahmed, 2013). Furthermore, not only do persistently high and volatile food prices influence conditions of hunger and under-nutrition, they also contribute to health problems such as "obesity which may increase in the context of high prices as people opt for cheaper, less nutritious food to feed their families" (World Bank, 2013h).

What factors have pushed us into this impoverished "danger zone"? Looking at some of the primary root causes of food insecurity provides insight into the interconnected nature of global threats, the trade-offs inherent in trying to provide for human needs, as well as the ways in which the policies of individual governments and international organizations can influence the international system as a whole:

- **Environmental stress**. Changing demographics and climates contribute to the crisis. For example, increases in urbanization have resulted in increased stress on the agricultural sectors—not only is key agricultural land often incorporated into rapidly growing urban areas, but government support formerly targeted at agricultural sectors (such as assistance with irrigation and farm equipment) may be diverted to urban development (Teslik, 2008). One of the primary effects of climate change is an increase in "extreme weather" events, and such events have had a key role in damaging agricultural production. "The scientists tell us that if the world warms by 2°C—warming that may be reached in 20 to 30 years—that will cause widespread food shortages, unprecedented heat waves, and more intense cyclones" warned World Bank President Jim Yong Kim in June 2013. For example, droughts in China cut its wheat production by almost a third, and flooding in Ecuador played a key role in the recent rise of banana prices. There is also concern that "over the next 40 years farmers will find it harder to produce enough for everyone because of constraints on land, water and fertilizers" (*The Economist*, 2011e, p. 16). Additionally, as UN Secretary-General Ban Ki-moon notes, "Continued land degradation—whether from climate change, unsustainable agriculture or poor management of water resources—is a threat to food security, leading to starvation among the most acutely affected communities and robbing the world of productive land."
- **Government policies**. As noted in Chapter 11, governments have traditionally protected their agricultural markets through subsidies and tariffs, which have served to increase the price of many agricultural goods. Moreover, recent food shortages have resulted in a proliferation of another form of government intervention—limits on the export of agricultural products such as wheat and rice. Indeed, the UN World Food Programme found that 40 countries

(Continued)

WHY IS THERE A GLOBAL FOOD CRISIS? (Continued)

were currently engaging in such export bans (Teslik, 2008). These bans serve to decrease the world supply of these goods, which raises prices. Along these lines, government encouragement of biofuel production has had an impact upon food prices. "About 30 percent of the projected increases in global food prices over the next several decades can be attributed to increased biofuel production worldwide" (Runge and Runge, 2010, p. 14).

- **Prices.** The cost of agricultural inputs has risen greatly. Agriculture relies heavily on petroleum for many aspects of production as well as transport, and the sector has thus been hit hard by increases in energy prices. Moreover, fertilizer prices have also risen dramatically. For example, the price of nitrogen fertilizer has increased over 350 percent since 1999 (*Financial Times*, 2007).

- **Food consumption patterns.** In emerging markets, such as China, India, Russia, and Brazil, people have changed their eating habits as their countries have developed. In particular, these countries have greatly increased their consumption of meat and dairy products. For example, meat consumption in China, traditionally a vegetarian society, has more than doubled since 1980—and is now twice that of the United States—and dairy consumption has tripled (Larsen, 2012; Dymkan, 2008). Dairy consumption in Brazil doubled from 2005 to 2007 (*Financial Times*, 2007). This has contributed to increased demand for these products, as well as the inputs necessary for their production (such as cattle feed).

The dominant cornucopian social paradigm stressing the right to conspicuous consumption is under global attack, but many challenges remain to achieving sustainable development worldwide.

WHAT DO YOU THINK?

- *Of the causes of the food crisis mentioned here—environmental stress, government policies, prices of agricultural inputs, and food consumption patterns—which do you think is the most important to address in overcoming the crisis? Why?*

- *As a policy maker, how would you balance the need for addressing domestic poverty with the need to contribute to assisting with the international humanitarian food crisis?*

- *The food crisis raises a question fundamental to our existence: Is our world capable of supporting itself? What insights do realist, liberal, and constructivist theories provide as to our future prospects?*

to increased global demand for fuel and unrest in the Middle East and North Africa in 2011—have also contributed to rising food prices. However, it is unlikely that big increases in food production can be achieved "because there is little unfarmed land to bring into production, no more water and, in some places, little to be gained by heaping on more fertilizer" (*The Economist*, 2011d, p. 12).

This raises a vital issue—how should we respond to this crisis? As prices surge, issues of food security are garnering greater attention and rising on the political agenda. Calling for greater action by the global community, former French President Nicolas Sarkozy warned of dire consequences of inaction: "If we don't do anything, we run the risk of food riots in the poorest countries and a very unfavorable effect on global economic growth." Josette Sheeran, former executive director of the United Nations World Food Programme, similarly underscored these concerns, lamenting that "if we do not act quickly, the bottom billion will become the bottom two billion virtually overnight as their purchasing power is cut in half due to a doubling in food and fuel prices."

Many international organizations have begun to articulate some type of response. In 2011, the World Bank provided $1.5 billion in support to help 40 million people secure vegetables, meats, fruits, and cooking oil, and pledged to boost spending on agriculture to $7 billion a year (Sambidge, 2011). It exceeded this commitment in 2012, with $9.3 billion allocated to agriculture and related sectors, and projected increases in assistance of up to $10 billion by 2015 (World Bank, 2013i).

However, maintaining the political will to enact fundamental changes is always difficult. Developed countries, for example, are very resistant to reducing agricultural subsidies. Moreover, some of the suggested solutions, such as *genetic engineering* and *transgenic crops* and livestock, are quite controversial and not supported by a variety of countries and NGOs.

Though many of the solutions to food insecurity center on increasing the amount and quality of food produced, it is important to note that the "most recent famines have been caused not because food wasn't available but because of bad governance—institutional failures that led to poor distribution of the available food, or even hoarding and storage in the face of starvation elsewhere" (Banerjee and Duflo, 2011, p. 71). As Amartya Sen observed, "no substantial famine has ever occurred in any independent and democratic country with a relatively free press." Reform of national practices and policies is an intrinsic aspect of efforts to prevent and respond to food insecurity and promote sustainable development.

Converting to Renewable Sources of Energy

How countries meet their growing demand for energy directly influences the evolution and preservation of the global commons. A new and less destructive source of energy could soon emerge because of the advent of revolutionary new technologies that derive energy from the sun, wind, and other abundant and renewable sources of energy such as hydrogen. The impact of such a global transformation would be huge, overturning the past 125-year pattern in world energy development and consumption. Could the era of "big oil" really be ending? Together, widely fluctuating but rising oil prices and public alarm about global warming are pushing the world, however haltingly, toward cleaner and cheaper energy systems.

The supply of fossil fuels will not run out anytime soon, but the *externalities* or consequences of environmental and health threats make burning fossil fuels excessively dangerous. The combustion of oil and coal is traced to lung cancer and many other health hazards. And, what is more, it leads to air pollution, urban smog, and *acid rain* that damage forests, water quality, and soil. There are powerful incentives to harness technology to shift to renewable sources of energy. Solar, tidal, and wind power, as well as geothermal energy and bioconversion, are among the alternatives to oil most likely to be technologically and economically viable, as Figure 14.6 shows.

genetic engineering

Research geared to discover seeds for new types of plant and human life for sale and use as substitutes for those produced naturally.

transgenic crops

New crops with improved characteristics created artificially through genetic engineering that combine genes from species that would not naturally interbreed.

acid rain

Precipitation that has been made acidic through contact with sulfur dioxide and nitrogen oxides.

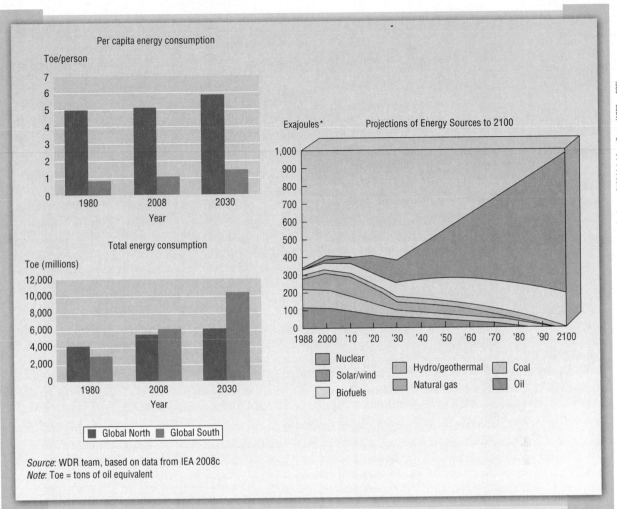

FIGURE 14.6   SUPPLYING THE WORLD'S GROWING ENERGY NEEDS BY THE YEAR 2100   The demand for energy continues to rise, requiring more energy than is ultimately available from nonrenewable resources. The Global North consumes, on average, four and a half times more energy per capita than the Global South (top left). However, the energy consumption of developing countries is on the rise—and is expected to account for 90 percent of the projected increase in global energy consumption over the next 20 years (bottom left). As a fossil-free energy supply becomes increasingly probable (right), it might become possible to tap renewable sources to meet the world's entire energy needs by the end of the twenty-first century.

Among known technologies, nuclear energy, wherein sustained nuclear processes generate electricity and heat, has often been championed as the leading alternative to fossil-fuel dependence (see Figure 14.7). Currently, existing nuclear plants provide about 19 percent of America's electricity (Nuclear Energy Institute, 2013). However, the United States is now spending billions of dollars to enhance nuclear plants to ease its dependence on the foreign suppliers that provided approximately 40 percent of the oil consumed in the United States in 2012 (U.S. Energy Information Administration, 2013).

However, safety and financial costs may limit the surge toward nuclear power; these problems have led some countries to reduce (or, like Germany, Sweden, and Spain, phase out)

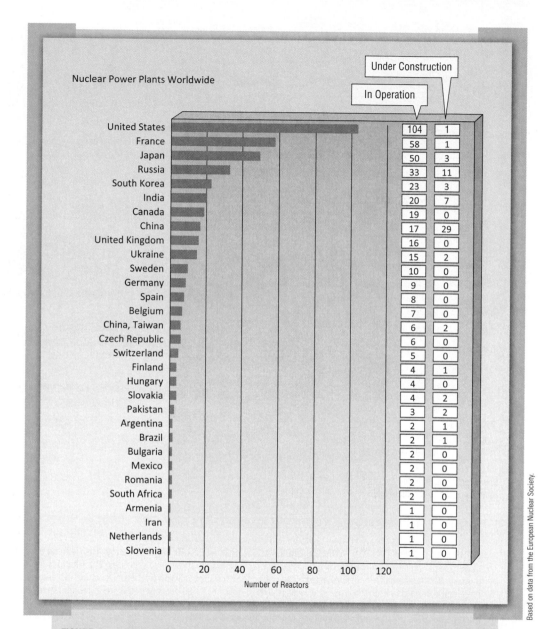

Based on data from the European Nuclear Society.

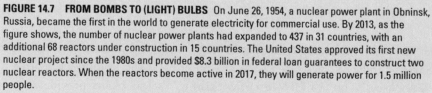

FIGURE 14.7 FROM BOMBS TO (LIGHT) BULBS On June 26, 1954, a nuclear power plant in Obninsk, Russia, became the first in the world to generate electricity for commercial use. By 2013, as the figure shows, the number of nuclear power plants had expanded to 437 in 31 countries, with an additional 68 reactors under construction in 15 countries. The United States approved its first new nuclear project since the 1980s and provided $8.3 billion in federal loan guarantees to construct two nuclear reactors. When the reactors become active in 2017, they will generate power for 1.5 million people.

their nuclear programs. Well-publicized nuclear accidents in the United States at the Three Mile Island nuclear power plant in Pennsylvania in 1979 and at Chernobyl in the Ukraine in 1986 and no less than five major accidents between 1995 and 1999 at Japan's 52 nuclear power plants (which supply about a third of Japan's electricity) dramatized the potential dangers of nuclear power.

Then, on March 11, 2011, a 9.0 earthquake and tsunami devastated Japan and caused extensive damage at its nuclear power stations. Some 70,000 people were forced to evacuate from a 12-mile radius of the Fukushima Daiichi nuclear power plant due to leaking radioactive materials. Since then, safety fears concerning nuclear power have spread around the world. In May 2011, Germany announced that it will close all of its nuclear power plants by 2022. Though 40 percent of Switzerland's electricity comes from nuclear power, it has also said that it will shut down its nuclear reactors as they reach their expected life span, with the last plant to be closed in 2034 (Mufson, 2011).

Concerns about the risks of nuclear power extend beyond safety. How and where to dispose of highly radioactive nuclear waste that comes from the 437 nuclear power plants is an unresolved issue virtually everywhere (European Nuclear Society, 2013). There are no safe procedures for handling the 52,000 tons of toxic radioactive nuclear waste, some of which will remain dangerous for hundreds of thousands of years. "Not in my back yard" (NIMBY) is a divisive cry on the global ecopolitical agenda; the Global North prefers to dump waste outside its own territory, and the Global South would prefer not to be the dump—but often is.

A related fear is that countries that do not currently possess nuclear know-how might develop nuclear weapons (see Chapter 8). Most nuclear-energy-generating facilities continue to produce weapons-grade material. Specifically, highly enriched uranium and plutonium present national security concerns because "with the underlying technical infrastructure able

Yanin Arthus Bertrand/Terra/CORBIS

THE UNFORGIVING COST OF NUCLEAR POWER FAILURE Shown here is the town of Pripyat, Ukraine, which was abandoned after the Chernobyl nuclear accident. Rather than learning from this lesson, and despite strong opposition from the public, Russia opened its borders to become the largest international repository for radioactive nuclear wastes, in the hope of earning billions of dollars over the next two decades.

to support both weapons and electrons, there is no clear way to ensure nuclear energy can be developed without also building capabilities for weapons" (*Vital Signs 2006–2007*, p. 34). This dilemma was highlighted as a significant concern with regard to North Korea's nuclear development program.

Other efforts to develop potential alternate fuel sources have also begun in hopes of breaking our dependence on fossil fuels. Recognizing the importance of such efforts, U.S. President Obama declared that "to truly transform our economy, protect our security and save our planet from the ravages of climate change, we need to ultimately make clean, renewable energy the profitable kind of energy." Thomas L. Friedman (2008) echoed this sentiment, arguing that countries clinging to fossil fuels will see their security and prosperity decline as compared to those that pioneer renewable-energy technologies. This emphasis reflects a shift over the past decade or two from a focus on conventional pollution issues to one on clean-energy opportunities.

Reflective white roofs that reduce air-conditioning costs by 20 percent, and hence produce far fewer carbon dioxide emissions, are becoming more popular as a way to save energy and fight global warming (Barringer, 2009). Seaweed and algae fields are touted as a potential wave of the future, as "algal oil can be processed into biodiesel or nonpetroleum gasoline, the carbohydrates into ethanol, and the protein into animal feed or human nutritional supplements. The whole biomass can generate methane, which can be combusted to produce electricity" (Gies, 2008, p. 3). Indonesia and the Philippines, located within the "Pacific Ring of Fire," are looking to harness volcanic power as a source of geothermal power. Indonesia has at least 130 active volcanoes, and according to Lester Brown, president of the Earth Policy Institute, "Indonesia could run its economy entirely on geothermal energy and has not come close to tapping the full potential" (Davies and Lema, 2008, p. 13).

And although presently too expensive for most people, Honda Motor has begun producing the world's first hydrogen-powered fuel-cell car. Says Takeo Fukui, president of Honda, "This is a must-have technology for the future of the earth" (Fackler, 2008, p. 16). Technological, economic, cultural, and environmental changes suggest that the early stage of a major energy transformation is under way, forced by supply scarcities and demand increases.

Conversion to renewable sources of energy represents a possible avenue away from global environmental degradation. Many believe this will not happen soon enough. They propose another path to reduce the dangers: forging international treaties among countries that provide for the protection of the environment and establish compliance mechanisms.

International Treaties for Environmental Protection   The 1992 Earth Summit in Stockholm was precedent-setting. From it, a separate treaty set forth a comprehensive agreement for preserving biodiversity throughout the world. It committed state governments to devise national strategies for conserving habitats, protecting endangered species, expanding protected areas, and repairing damaged ones. Since then, the world has attempted to cooperate through increasingly concerted efforts to reach agreements and to back them with ratified treaties to protect the sustained global commons.

Success breeds success. The *Biodiversity Treaty* was followed by other international efforts to deal with environmental problems through global agreements. A big example was the Kyoto Protocol of 2005, in which 156 countries accounting for at least 55 percent of global greenhouse emissions pledged to cut emissions of gases linked to global warming below 1990 levels by the year 2012. Only the United States refused to cooperate. In anticipation of the impending 2012 deadline for negotiating a successor to the Kyoto Protocol, the Global North committed to providing the Global South a total of $100 billion by 2020 to combat problems caused by climate change. However, the countries failed to reach a long-term binding agreement on global climate change, and the prospect for a post-2012 framework that enlarges prior targets is dim. Following the Durban climate talks in 2011, only 34 industrialized countries (responsible for only 15 percent of global greenhouse emissions) had agreed to a second commitment period beginning in 2013.

The number of international environmental treaties has grown exponentially in the last 130 years. However, many skeptics fear that these efforts are too little, too late, and that not enough is being done to save the global commons for future generations. Many question the ability of today's existing treaties to manage the environmental dangers they are meant to address. Some of them are weak and do not command the policy changes needed to remedy the various problems they identify. Of particular concern is the reluctant backing of the United States. Of the UN's 31 major global environmental agreements, the United States has only ratified one-third of them. Environmental protection activists worry that if the American hegemon refuses to lead, the prospects for strengthening the rules of the environmental preservation regime are dim.

CourseMate

**Simulation:
The Kyoto Treaty**

Trade, the Environment, and Sustainable Development

Multinational corporations are key players in the ecopolitics game that has the potential to determine the Earth's fate. Corporations rule globally, and they are strong advocates with powerful lobbyists of free trade. Is their power and quest supportive, or detrimental, to sustainable development? The question is especially pertinent in a rapidly globalizing world in which trade increasingly links politics, economics, ecology, and societies and cultures in webs of ever-tightening interdependencies.

Beyond the issue of the gains from and the costs of trade, environmentalists and liberal economists differ in their assessments concerning the wisdom of using trade to promote environmental standards. Liberal economists see such efforts as market distortions, whereas environmentalists view them as useful instruments for correcting market failures, such as the market's inability to compensate for environmental exploitation (for example, atmospheric pollution by chemical companies). Some countries, however, particularly in the Global South, view the use of trade mechanisms to protect the environment as yet another way the rich states block entry into lucrative Global North markets and keep the Global South permanently disadvantaged.

Trade-offs must sometimes be made between goals that, in principle, all seem designed to increase human well-being and security. However, another interpretation holds that trade encourages states to live beyond their means. According to some ecologists, trade magnifies the damaging ecological effects of production and consumption by expanding the market for commodities beyond state borders. Countries that have depleted their resource bases or passed strict laws to protect them can easily look overseas for desired products, in ways that shift the environmental stress of high consumption to other states' backyards.

PLAYING IN THE "POISON POND" Children play in the shadow of the former Union Carbide factory in Bhopal, India, the site of one of the worst industrial accidents in history. The "pond" in which they are playing was a sludge pit containing chemical by-products from the former pesticide plant. Although the chemical leakage at Bhopal, which resulted in more than 3000 deaths, occurred in 1984, the area—which still contains more than 400 tons of toxic waste—has yet to be cleaned up. The picture is a stark reminder of how environmental crises can long outlive the political will necessary to resolve them.

The tragedy of the commons suggests a bleak future. Is ruin the destination toward which humanity must rush? Or is a more optimistic scenario possible?

A trend is under way in the corporate global finance culture that bodes well for the potential for global corporations to recognize that their profits will improve with investment in and development of "green" products, for which there is rising consumer demand worldwide. Moreover, a new "code of corporate responsibility" is gaining acceptance in the context of green industries seeking to sell environmentally-friendly products, spawning a new era in the development of products designed to protect the environment (see Table 14.1). The possibility that the international political economy will provide economic incentives for producing products that can contribute to global environment sustainability has inspired hope that the environmental dangers may be contained. That hope is rising because some governments, corporations, and individuals are seeking local solutions to environmental sustainability.

A huge concern is that some very powerful states, advantageously positioned in the global hierarchy, are selfishly resisting painful and costly adjustments now. They are resisting reforms of their own existing environmental protection policies. Yet there are exceptions to this response to environmental degradation. Numerous countries have managed to balance the risk of short-term economic loss against the expectation of long-term economic growth by investing in costly renewable energy programs that can enable them to experience their economic growth. Consider Figure 14.8. It charts the rankings of countries according to the Environmental Performance Index. The score measures their investments in efforts to protect their future

TABLE 14.1	Green Performance Ranking of Global Corporations					
Rank	Company/ Sector/ Country	Environmental Impact Score	Environmental Management Score	Environmental Disclosure Score	GREEN SCORE	Principal Actions
1	Santander Brasil/ Financial/ Brazil	88.5	88.4	61.5	85.7	Santander has adopted the practice of investigating potential clients' environmental practices and correcting potential problems before approving any loans or lines of credit for that client.
2	Wipro/ Information Technologies and Services/ India	70.2	100.0	88.3	85.4	Wipro has a venerable history of environmental conservationism and plans to continue this tradition by making five of its locations "biodiversity zones" over the next several years. Additionally, Wipro's North Carolina data center was awarded LEED Gold—an indication of Wipro's commitment to sustainability.
3	Bradesco Financial/ Brazil	87.9	75.9	99.9	83.7	In addition to offering funding to companies that wish to begin environmental reforms and reducing its own environmental impact, Bradesco has started a nonprofit that has so far conserved 10 million hectares—almost 40,000 square miles—of the Amazon Rainforest.
4	IBM/ Information Technologies and Services/ United States	78.9	87.0	82.9	82.9	Successful history of improving operational efficiency, cutting its own power-use by 5.1 billion kilowatt hours in the 1990s and producing computer systems to help other businesses do the same.
5	National Australia Bank Financial/ Australia	82.0	79.5	99.8	82.7	Achieved carbon-neutrality by the end of 2010 and continues to address environmental considerations through recycling, other paper-saving initiatives, and incorporating environmental standards in the construction of new buildings.

(continued)

TABLE 14.1	Green Performance Ranking of Global Corporations (Continued)					
6	BT Group/ Telecommunications/ United Kingdom	77.3	84.2	99.8	82.7	Having reached a 59 percent reduction in carbon emissions, BT Group plans to further reduce emissions by 80 percent by 2020. Initiatives include creating wind farms to produce 25 percent of its energy consumption by 2016.
7	Munich Re/ Financial/ Germany	87.6	78.2	79.0	82.5	Munich Re has had a long history of environmental responsibility. This company has studied climate change since 1974 and has recently begun using its findings to help the insurance industry find ways of reducing its impact on the climate.
8	SAP/ Information Technologies and Services/ Germany	80.7	78.9	99.8	81.8	SAP produces energy-saving products that have been estimated to have saved 8 billion kilowatt hours of electricity from use—about $550 million worth of energy, not to mention costly environmental impacts.
9	KPN/ Telecommunications/ Netherlands	76.1	81.3	98.3	80.6	KPN currently meets nearly all of its energy needs through "green energy" and is on track to become completely carbon-neutral by 2020.
10	Marks & Spencer Group/ Retailers United Kingdom	65.7	92.0	95.8	80.5	Through a five-year sustainability program, this British retailer is carbon-neutral and does not contribute at all to landfill waste. Additionally, all of the fish sold by these stores come from "the "most sustainable sources available."

Source: Based on *Newsweek* Green Rankings 2012 of Global Companies, October 2012. The Green Score is a weighted average of the Environmental Impact Score (45 percent), which is based on over seven hundred metrics; the Environmental Management Score (45 percent), which assesses corporate initiatives and policies; and the Environmental Disclosure Score (10 percent), which is based on a survey of CEOs, academics, and environmental officers.

environments. Clearly, some countries see environmental sustainability as a priority that protects their interest more so than others.

The entire world stands at a critical juncture. The path humanity takes will affect human security far into the future. Evidence of serious ecological problems is getting harder and harder

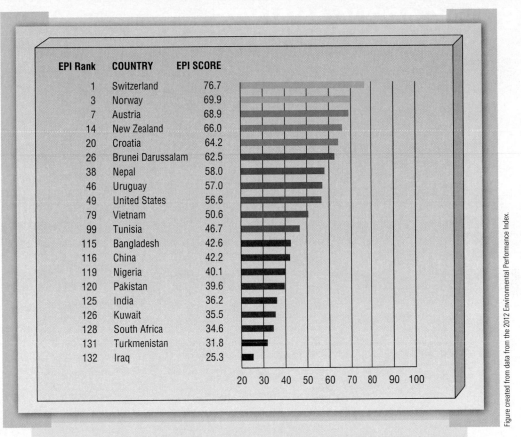

FIGURE 14.8   MEASURING NATIONAL COMMITMENTS TO ENVIRONMENTAL SUSTAINABILITY
Measures of environmental protection performance suggest some countries are doing much
more than many others to protect their environments. The Environmental Performance Index (EPI)
gauges the relative performance of countries across the categories of environmental health, air
pollution, water resources, biodiversity and habitat, productive natural resources, and climate
change. Pictured are the EPI ratings of selected countries that illustrate these differences.

Figure created from data from the 2012 Environmental Performance Index.

to ignore. Because the stakes are so high, all the pieces in the puzzle—population growth, natural
resources, technology, and changing preferences in lifestyles—must be addressed simultaneously.

If necessity really is the mother of invention, there is hope. The planet *must* be saved, or all
other opportunities will be closed, the global environment will face certain doom, and human
history will end. Therefore, the stakes are so high that perhaps solutions will be found. As the
world struggles, the debate about solutions is likely to continue on two tracks: between those
who think humankind's concentration should be geared toward trying to reverse environmental deterioration, and those who prefer to concentrate on creating new technologies to contain
environmental damage. Both strategies are urgently needed.

*Our entire planet, its land and water areas, the Earth's surface and its subsoil provide
today the arena for a worldwide economy, the dependence of whose various parts upon
each other has become indissoluble.*

—**Leon Trotsky, Russian communist theoretician**

STUDY. APPLY. ANALYZE.

Key Terms

acid rain
biodiversity
carrying capacity
cornucopians
deforestation

desertification
enclosure movement
environmental security
epistemic community
genetic engineering

greenhouse effect
neo-Malthusians
ozone layer
politics of scarcity
sustainable development

the global commons
tragedy of the commons
transgenic crops

Suggested Readings

Brainard, Lael, Abigail Jones, and Nigel Purvis, eds. (2009) *Climate Change and Global Poverty.* Washington, DC: Brookings Institution Press.

Brown, Lester B. (2012) *Full Planet, Empty Plates: The New Geopolitics of Food Scarcity.* New York: W. W. Norton & Co.

Friedman, Thomas L. (2008) Hot, Flat, and Crowded: Why We Need a Green *Revolution, and How It Can Renew America.* New York: Farrar, Straus and Giroux.

Hannigan, John. (2012) *Disasters Without Borders: The International*

Politics of Natural Disasters. Cambridge: Polity.

Hittner, Jeffrey. (2010, September 23) "Sustainability: An Engine for Growth," http://www.carnegiecouncil.org/resources/ethics_online/0049.html.

Levi, Michael A. (2009) "Copenhagen's Inconvenient Truth: How to Salvage the Climate Conference." *Foreign Affairs* 88, no. 5: 92–104.

Coyle, Eugene D. and Melissa J. Dark, eds. (2014) *Understanding the Global Energy Crisis.* West

Lafayette, IN: Purdue University Press.

Vanderheiden, Steve. (2011) "Globalizing Responsibility for Climate Change," *Ethics & International Affairs* 25, no. 1 (Spring):65–84.

World Bank. (2010) *World Development Report 2010: Development and Climate Change.* Washington, DC: The International Bank for Reconstruction and Development/The World Bank.

Suggested Videos

Carnegie Council Video

Ahmed, Saraz, et al. "Sustainable Societies."

Dorset, Steve. "Climate Change and the Precautionary Principle."

Powers, Jonathan. "Security Threat of Climate Change."

Stern, Nicholas. "Impact of Climate Change."

CourseMate

Log in to CourseMate to access the following study tools for this chapter:

- Interactive Quiz
- eBook
- Flashcards & Key Term Crossword Puzzle

- Chapter Audio Summary
- Carnegie Council Videos
- Video Activities
- Simulation

- Animated Learning Module
- Case Study
- International Relations NewsWatch

PART 5

THINKING ABOUT THE FUTURE OF WORLD POLITICS

Jay Directo/AFP/Getty Images

MOST CONJECTURES ABOUT THE GLOBAL FUTURE ARE BASED ON EXTRAPOLATION FROM EARLIER EVENTS AND EXPERIENCES. People usually speculate about future prospects based on their understanding of prevailing trends. What makes prediction so difficult is the sheer complexity and uncertainty surrounding world politics—some trends seem to move forward in the same direction, whereas others change direction; some trends intersect, whereas others diverge over time; and some trends are catalysts of others,

GLOBAL DESTINY: DELIGHT OR DESPAIR?

This photo captures the dramatic inequalities

that exist in many, if not all, cities across the

globe—some enjoying rising prosperity, some

living in desperate squalor. Both conditions

are products of prevailing trends in world

"There are many ways in which we are living in the most wonderful age ever. We can imagine we are heading toward a sort of science-fiction utopia, where we are incredibly rich and incredibly prosperous, and the planet is healthy. But there are other reasons to fear that we're headed toward a dystopia of sorts."

—*Ramez Naam, computer scientist*

CHAPTER 15
Looking Ahead at Global Trends and Transformations

NASA

ENVISIONING OUR GLOBAL DESTINY
This satellite image of the world at night portrays an integrated world community in a globe without borders, but with variation in the degree of prosperity and development. Against a landscape of trend and transformation, humanity faces many dilemmas in a globalized world. As former U.S. Secretary of State Hillary Clinton observed, "The challenges of change are always hard. It is important that we begin to unpack those challenges … and realize that we each have a role that requires us to change and become more responsible for shaping our own future."

QUESTIONS TO CONSIDER

- *Can observers accurately predict the most salient trends in world politics?*
- *What influences how people think about the future of world politics?*
- *What are the most important questions concerning the future of politics that need to be addressed?*
- *Are we headed toward a new world order or new world disorder?*

Many, sometimes conflicting, global trends are unfolding. Some point toward integration, and others to fragmentation; the world looks like it is coming together and at the same time it is coming apart. A new global system is on the horizon, but it is one whose characteristics have yet to develop definition. Uncertainty and unpredictability are today's prevailing mood. But one thing is certain: Seismic shifts that challenge the wisdom of old beliefs and traditions are under way. Because both turmoil and turbulence describe contemporary international affairs, they require asking unconventional questions about conventional ideas. They push us to think about the political, military, economic, demographic, and environmental pressures being brought to bear on the countries of the world, the people who reside in them, and their interactions.

Facing the future, you confront an awesome investigative challenge: anticipating and interpreting the probable future contours of world affairs and constructing compelling theoretical explanations of their causes and consequences. To do so, you must consider a number of unusual and controversial questions rising to the top of the global agenda throughout the world. Experts whose profession it is to help you may be somewhat informative. However, the rival conclusions boldly advanced by would-be prophets are not likely to be very definitive, and often diverge wildly.

Those caught up in revolutionary change rarely understand its ultimate significance.

—Boutros Boutros-Ghali, former UN secretary-general

GLOBAL TRENDS AND FORECASTS

Many problems and challenges are expected to confront humanity in the twenty-first century. As recognized by former UN Secretary-General Kofi Annan (2006, p. 205), "We face a world of extraordinary challenges—and of extraordinary interconnectedness. We are all vulnerable to new security threats, and to old threats that are evolving in complex and unpredictable ways." The UN's report, *A More Secure World* (2004, p. 2), further outlines the following six clusters of threats with which the world must be concerned now and in the decades ahead:

- Economic and social threats—including poverty, national debt, infectious disease, and environmental degradation

- Interstate conflict

- Internal conflict—including civil war, genocide, and other large-scale atrocities

- Nuclear, radiological, chemical, and biological weapons

- Terrorism

- Transnational organized crime

This inventory hints at what the world will be like in the years to come. To construct your own images of the future of world affairs, begin by thinking about the key questions that are likely to dominate international relations in the coming decades. The questions you identify will determine which scenarios and theories better inform your understanding of your global future. To assist you, *World Politics* concludes this final chapter with some additional questions to consider, and those questions will require you to weigh contending interpretations to intellectually prepare you to interpret the future of world politics.

HOW TO THINK ABOUT HOW PEOPLE THINK ABOUT THE WORLD

As you construct scenarios about different possible global futures, begin by keeping in mind that your images, like those of everyone, are heavily shaped by your prior perceptions of reality and the inherited values and expectations that underlie them (see Chapter 1). So proceed cautiously, but with an open mind to views that may be different from those you now hold. Take insight and wisdom from the following observations:

- "Any frontal attack on ignorance is bound to fail because the masses are always ready to defend their most precious possession—their ignorance."
   —Hendrik Willem van Loon, Dutch-American journalist

- "The most fatal illusion is the settled point of view. Since life is growth and motion, a fixed point of view kills anybody who has one."
   —Brooks Atkinson, American drama critic

- "Fanaticism consists in redoubling your effort when you have forgotten your aim."
   —George Santayana, Spanish philosopher

- "Men are more apt to be mistaken in their generalizations than in their particular observations."
   —Niccoló Machiavelli, seventeenth-century Italian realist theoretician

- "One of the sources of pride in being a human being is the ability to bear present frustrations in the interests of longer purposes."
   —Helen Merrel Lynd, American sociologist

- "The philosophies of one age have become the absurdities of the next, and the foolishness of yesterday has become the wisdom of tomorrow."
   —Sir William Osler, Canadian physician and educator

- "It is better to know some of the questions than all of the answers."
   —James Thurber, American writer

Armed with an understanding of how ideas about international relations are formed and retained, rejected, or replaced, imagine yourself at the end of a semester preparing to take the final exam in your course about international relations. Your entire grade, your instructor tells you, will be determined by only one question. Sitting nervously, you open your blue book and are astonished at the instructions: "(1) define the question that you wish had been asked in this exam for this course, and (2) then answer it; you will be graded on both the understanding you display in the kind of question you ask and the answers you provide." How would you respond?

Believe it or not, this kind of question is not fictional. It has been used to sort out candidates on exams for entry into the foreign service of several countries. There are really no right or wrong questions about international relations. Indeed, there is little agreement about the trends and issues that are the most important in international affairs, and no scholarly consensus exists about the questions that deserve the greatest attention today.

To stimulate your thinking, make a preliminary list, based on what you now know after reading *World Politics*, of what you believe will be the crucial questions about the future of the world. How would you go about interpreting your own questions? What rival theories (see Chapter 2) would you rely on to frame your analyses? This mental exercise will sharpen your critical thinking skills and tell you as much about yourself and your reasoned perspective as it does about your capacity to describe the present global condition, predict its future course, and explain *why* world politics is changing (or staying the same).

Rather than leave you in the lurch, *World Politics* puts itself to the same test. It concludes now by identifying a series of questions about the future that are high on the global agenda. As a further catalyst for framing your own thinking, look critically at these questions. How they are answered is widely expected to give shape to world politics throughout the remainder of the twenty-first century.

THE GLOBAL PREDICAMENT: KEY QUESTIONS ABOUT A TURBULENT WORLD

World Politics has argued that international relations are subject to recurring patterns. Despite changes and chaos, behavior by transnational actors is not random. It is governed by regular propensities, and this makes it possible to uncover "laws" or generalized action-and-reaction patterns. As realist theorist Hans J. Morganthau argued in his classic text *Politics Among Nations*, the past historical record speaks with sufficient continuity to make the scientific study of international politics a meaningful intellectual endeavor. There are some lessons about how countries interact that are constant across time and place. "These regularities and associated causal mechanisms attract considerable attention when they appear capable of accounting for and, better yet, of predicting, outcomes of importance to us" (Lebow, 2010, p. 4). It is the purpose of scholarship to uncover these patterns and influence sound policy decisions based on the lessons history provides.

Under certain conditions, it can be assumed that certain types of transnational actors respond in similar ways to the same types of stimuli. Yet, there are exceptions. Sometimes similar actors in similar situations make different decisions. Thus despite regularities in world politics, social scientists cannot draw on a body of uniform, deterministic laws to precisely predict the global future. "Generalization and specification are different undertakings, but they are neither necessarily dichotomous nor separate on the path toward discovery" (Yetiv, 2011, p. 94).

Another factor that makes it difficult to predict the future is the role of happenstance in world politics. The search for patterns in world politics "needs to be complemented by the investigation of ruptures … that undermine existing regularities and the understandings of the actors on which they are based" (Lebow, 2010, p. 5). History is replete with what Greek philosopher Aristotle called accidental conjunctions—situations in which things come together by chance. Consider, for example, the outbreak of World War I. Recall from Chapter 4 that one of the proximate causes of the war was Austrian Archduke Franz Ferdinand's assassination in Sarajevo on June 28, 1914. Earlier that day, several would-be assassins had failed to find an opportunity to kill the archduke and had apparently given up in frustration. When Ferdinand's motorcade made a wrong turn en route to visit patients in a city hospital, it stopped briefly in front of a café where Gavrilo Princip, one of the frustrated assassins, coincidentally had gone to get something to eat. Astonished to find the archduke's open-air car just 5 feet away, Princip fired two shots, killing the archduke and his wife. Given the political climate in Europe at the time, if Franz Ferdinand had not been assassinated, something else might have precipitated the war. But as political scientist Stuart Bremer (2000, p. 35) asks, "Who can say whether a different triggering event, a day, a month, or a year later, would have led to the same chain of events that produced World War I?"

Myriad possible futures lie ahead. Some are desirable; others, frightening. Although we cannot predict with certainty which one will materialize, we can narrow the range of possibilities by forecasting how current trends will likely develop and what steps may be taken to channel the course of events toward a global future we prefer.

The following six questions are designed to help you think about the future of world politics. Each question is based on information presented in previous chapters. When pondering the long-term implications of these questions, you are encouraged to:

- imagine what conceivable global futures are possible,

- determine which are the most probable, and

- consider what policies would be of the most help to bring about the global future you prefer.

The glorious thing about the human race is that it does change the world—constantly. It is the human being's capacity for struggling against being overwhelmed which is remarkable and exhilarating.

—Lorraine Hansberry, American author

Is Globalization a Cure or a Curse?

Why does it now appear that the world and the states within it are spinning out of control? One answer has to do with "globalization," a widely accepted socially constructed word understood as a transforming force that is creating sweeping governance crises in a new age of increasing interdependent complexity. *Globalization* captures the idea that everything on the planet is now more closely connected than ever before, but only within an unsteady institutional foundation that is largely unprepared for the future.

The integration of the globe in this transformed, interconnected, borderless world and common *cosmopolitan culture* has reduced old feelings of independence, identity, and autonomy, and driven many states to surrender some of their sovereignty in order to benefit from collaborative participation in a competitive global marketplace. "Globalization enables each of us, wherever we live, to reach around the world farther, faster, deeper, and cheaper than ever before and at the same time allows the world to reach into each of us farther, faster, deeper, and cheaper than ever before" (Friedman and Kaplan, 2002, p. 64). The message has been heard everywhere: borders and barriers cannot be revived in a nationalistic effort to isolate a country. "Join the world or become irrelevant" is the way that Edouard Balladur, former French prime minister, described "the end of nationalism."

Optimists, who are aware of the common destiny of all and the declining ability of many sovereign states to cope with global problems through unilateral *self-help* approaches, will energize efforts to put aside interstate competition. According to this reasoning, conflict will recede as humanity begins to better recognize that national borders and oceans provide little protection against the multitude of challenges that arise from the global revolution in travel, communications, and trade. These shared problems can only be managed through collective, multilateral cooperation. Globalization is creating a strong web of constraints on the foreign policy behavior of those who are plugged into the network of global transactions (Rodrik, 2011). Consequently, because globalization makes cooperation crucial to the well-being of everyone, the continued tightening of interstate linkages should be welcomed.

What is especially important about globalization is that when everyone depends on everyone else, all *must* work together. Global interdependence makes it imperative for states to renounce aggressive competition because they increasingly have a shared interest in cooperation and fewer and fewer incentives to fight. Globalization, optimists argue, is an irreversible motor of unity and progress, and ought to be promoted because it will ultimately increase the wealth of everyone everywhere (Norberg, 2006).

Pessimists, however, point out that globalization may be slowing down (Abdelal and Segal, 2007). Even if the present period of globalization continues, pessimists fret about how to cope with our "flat, hot, and crowded" planet Earth (Friedman, 2008). Moreover, despite the successes of globalization, it is often difficult to maintain the necessary political will to support global initiatives—particularly regarding economic globalization—and international organizations only imperfectly fill this gap. As economist Dani Rodrik (2011, p. 88) argues, "(T)he reality is that we lack the domestic and global strategies needed to manage globalizations' disruptions." Regardless of how compelling the need or how rewarding the benefits, increased contact and the integration of a single society of states may breed enmity, not amity.

Another issue with globalization concerns the distribution of its benefits. Critics of globalization posit that it favors advantaged states but constrains the prospects of weak states, producing new inequalities as the gap between the wealthy and the poor widens. "The problem," writes James Surowiecki (2007, pp. 137–138), "is that the number of countries that have dramatically improved their standard of living in the era of globalization is surprisingly small … It is not surprising that people are made unhappy by the sight of others getting richer while they stay the same or actually get poorer."

GOING GLOBAL Former UN Secretary-General Kofi Annan once noted "it has been said that arguing against globalization is like arguing against the laws of gravity." In your reading of *World Politics*, you have considered many facets of globalization and the positive and negative implications of the increasing interconnectedness of the globe's states and peoples. Shown here in Egypt are horse-drawn carriages parked in front of a McDonald's, reflecting a blending of cultures and economies, traditionalism and modernity. Although globalization certainly presents many challenges, it also provides opportunities to learn, prosper, and enjoy a world of great diversity and possibility.

CourseMate

Case Study: Interdependence and Future International Politics

Because its benefits may not be distributed equally, globalization may generate conflict between winners and losers. As neorealist theorist Kenneth Waltz observed, "interdependence promotes war as well as peace." Intertwined economies will sour relations more than sweeten them. Under conditions of fierce competition, scarcity, and resurgent nationalism, the temptation to seek isolation from globalization's assault on national autonomy by creating barriers to trade and other transactions may be irresistible. The temptation to achieve political benefits by military force will also persist. Thus, the tightening web of globalization has the potential to lead to either danger or to opportunity.

Will Technological Innovation Solve Pressing Global Problems?

The surge in globalization that followed on the heels of late-twentieth-century discoveries in microelectronics and information processing has unleashed revolutionary changes. "Biotechnology will dominate our lives during the next fifty years," predicts physicist philosopher Freeman Dyson (2007), "at least as much as computers have dominated our lives during the previous fifty years." The consequences of the technological revolution, however, are not certain. Technological innovations solve some problems but cause others. "Like any irrepressible force," observes Nobel laureate economist Wassily Leontief, "technology can bestow on us undreamed benefits but also inflict irreparable damage." It can increase productivity and economic output, but it can also displace workers and trigger social unrest and environmental damage.

Although acknowledging that there is often a significant time lag between the diffusion of new technology and the changes it causes in society, some people assert that technological innovation promises humanity a more secure and bountiful future (Fidler and Gostin, 2008). Indeed, the most optimistic members of this group believe that because of promising developments in such fields as biotechnology and digital software, humanity is entering the most innovative period in history. From their perspective, with patience, technological solutions will eventually be found that will ease the most serious problems facing the world today.

Malnutrition and disease, they note as an example, may still exist; but as a result of technological advances in agriculture and medicine, many people are alive today who might have perished otherwise. Agro-ecological innovation can enhance food production while also restoring rural economies and sustaining the natural resource base (Worldwatch Institute, 2013a). Others are hopeful about the potential role of technology in futuristic geo-engineering initiatives to curb global warming, such as "directly scrubbing the air with devices that resemble big cooling towers" (Victor et al., 2009, p. 68).

Technology is also profoundly important for the future of energy (see Chapter 14), both to identify alternative sources and more efficiently use existing resources. For example, researchers at MIT and Harvard have created an artificial leaf that is capable of producing energy from sunlight and water, and has self-healing capabilities (Quick, 2013). And as advanced technology becomes cheaper and more accessible, it is likely to have broad impact. Google, a multinational corporation that specializes in Internet-related products and services, is intentionally taking steps to expand its use of green energy because, even as traditional sources of power are becoming more expensive, green power is becoming more cost-effective (Kanellos, 2013). Perhaps such developments will reduce the need for states to compete over scarce energy resources, and thus lessen a potential source of global conflict.

In contrast to those who envision technological innovation as a way to increase economic growth and alleviate social welfare problems, some remain concerned that proposed technological solutions will only serve to compound current problems. Whereas genetically modified crops are seen by optimists as a way to reduce famine, pessimists worry about the public health consequences. Even the so-called green revolution had its drawbacks, they argue. Although fertilizers, pesticides, and herbicides initially increased crop yields in various Global South countries, they eventually spawned new problems such as contaminated water supplies. Without wise management, technological advances can have detrimental side effects.

Consider the world's fisheries. At first, larger ships and improved maritime technology resulted in increases in the amount of fish harvested from the world's oceans. Over time, however, many fisheries were depleted. Applying more technology could not increase catches once the ecosystem had collapsed. As one member of this school of thought has put it, "many of our new technologies confer upon us new power without automatically giving us new wisdom" (Gore, 2006, p. 247).

Likewise, critics decry the manner in which technological advancements have enabled governments to engage in widespread surveillance and targeted killings from afar. From the proliferation of drones to clandestine electronic surveillance programs, an urgent need arises for greater transparency and global discussion about what constitutes the legitimate use of such technology, and what is an unacceptable infringement upon state sovereignty, individual rights and due process. Reflecting upon the controversy surrounding the heavy use of drones by the United States, public policy expert Audrey Kurth Cronin (2013, p. 54) notes that while "there is nothing inherently wrong with replacing human pilots with remote-control operators … the problem is that the guidelines for how Washington uses drones has fallen well behind the ease with which the United States relies on them, allowing short-term advantages to overshadow long-term risks."

What do you think? Is the customary way of seeing technological discoveries as the engines of progress really valid? Or is the tendency to overrate the positive impact of new technology based on wishful thinking? "Learning how to make new technology is one thing; learning how to use it is another" (Shapin, 2007, p. 146). So, when you look at new technologies (stem cells, nanotechnology, human genomes, etc.), think counterfactually and imagine how things might turn out if new technologies had not been invented or how new ones might influence life on planet Earth for better or for worse.

What Types of Armed Conflict Will Become the Major Fault Line in the Geostrategic Landscape?

Prevalent practices tend to wither away when they cease to serve their intended purpose, as the examples of slavery, dueling, and colonialism illustrate. Trends point toward the possibility that this may also happen for interstate wars, which have almost disappeared in modern history. Even more impressively, the period since 1945 has been the longest span of great power peace since the sixteenth century. This achievement is raising expectations that large-scale warfare between countries will disappear and armed conflict between countries will become obsolete. Part of this confidence is based on the assumption that no sane national leader would dare to wage war against another state because any conceivable rewards would be greatly exceeded by the cost of mass destruction.

To be sure, most leaders are still preparing for traditional kinds of warfare against other states and are adhering to the abiding wisdom of ancient Greek philosopher Aristotle: "A people without walls is a people without choice." That said, the usefulness of traditional weapons of warfare against the emergent threats that now haunt the globe is questionable. How can countries effectively combat the dangers presented by faceless and invisible nonstate terrorists willing to die in suicide bombings for their cause? Can these attacks be deterred when the adversary lacks any obvious vulnerability? How does a state destroy an enemy with preemptive strikes when those adversaries have neither a location nor things of value to attack?

The old forms of military power still used by states today may be becoming impotent, and no level of military might can guarantee a state's safety. When countries' primary security problem is no longer an attack by another country but instead the threat of internal armed conflict or an attack by a transnational terrorist network such as Al Qaeda, states face the challenging question of how to fight wars against the unconventional military threats in today's world.

The conduct of war has undergone several "generational" changes since the Thirty Years' War drew to a close and gave birth to the modern state system. Whereas "third-generation" military thinking has influenced most countries since World War II, the threat of being attacked today by the military forces of another country has diminished, particularly in the Global North. Instead, a "fourth generation" of warfare has emerged in which states are pitted against nonstate actors in hostilities that lack front lines and clear distinctions between soldiers and civilians (Hammes, 2004). Unable to defeat conventional armies on the field of battle, irregular forces using unconventional tactics focus on their adversary's will, using patience, ingenuity, and gruesome acts of violence to compel their opponent to face the mounting costs of continuing a long, drawn-out struggle.

Both state and nonstate actors are also turning to information technology and the Internet as unconventional weapons of war. Across the globe, "military and intelligence organizations are preparing the cyber battlefield with things called 'logic bombs' and 'trapdoors,' placing virtual explosives in other countries in peacetime" (Clark and Knake, 2010, p. xi). The ability of high-tech weapons to rapidly attack and disable thousands of targets introduces the possibility of highly volatile crises. "We could face a cyber-attack that could be the equivalent of Pearl Harbor," warned former U.S. Secretary of Defense Leon Panetta, that could "take down our power grid system, take down our financial systems in this country, take down our government systems, take down our banking systems. They could virtually paralyze this country. We have to be prepared to deal with that."

Some political and military leaders, however, continue to think of warfare in third-generational terms, dismissing this new face of war as an annoyance that detracts from preparations for decisive, large-scale engagements (Woodward, 2006). Do the wars in Afghanistan and Iraq provide a glimpse into the future? Will most military clashes in the early twenty-first century follow their pattern?

Should the Global Community Intervene to Protect Human Rights?

Conflicts within countries are raging throughout the world. Many civilians are subject to widespread oppression and violence by governments presumably created to preserve law and order. Of great concern is whether the moral outrage of the global community will be sufficient to spur concerted peacekeeping and peacemaking interventions to end human rights abuses in those countries where acceptable standards of conduct in international law have been blatantly disregarded. Atrocities in many failed states each year expel tens of millions of refugees and displaced people from their homes. The global community is being put to a test of its true ideals and its capacity to defend them, at potentially high costs. Will a humanitarian concern for the victims targeted for extermination crystallize into a response? Or will the victims perish in a sea of indifference?

In principle, human rights law now provides unprecedented protection for people everywhere to live in freedom without fear. The traditional legal rule of state sovereignty and its corollary, the *nonintervention norm* against external interference in the internal affairs of states, have been revised. There is growing support within the international community for a global *responsibility to protect* those who suffer from mass abuse at the hands of their state governments. Former UN Secretary-General Kofi Annan described well the redefinition when he noted, "states are now widely understood to be instruments at the service of their people, and not vice versa."

STRINGER/AFP/Getty Images

WHEN DOES HUMAN RIGHTS ABUSE MATTER?
Great Britain and other European states increased foreign aid to Ethiopia in 2011, amid accusations of ignoring reports of "continuing ethnic cleansing, mass detentions, the widespread use of torture and extra-judicial killings by Ethiopian government forces" in order to further their own strategic interests with the key African ally (Waterfield, 2011). These actions raise deep concerns that the world's great powers will intervene to protect the human rights of ordinary people only when vital security interests or needed resources such as oil are threatened. Shown here, a civilian woman receives care after having been injured during a clash between Ethiopian troops and anti-government insurgents.

Principle is one thing; the reality of preventing human suffering is another. Will the major powers and nonstate actors in the globalized community back their expressed convictions with action to free humanity from the oppression of mass murder? Can they agree on rules for humanitarian intervention that define when it is legitimate to militarily respond to gross violations of human rights? As then Secretary-General Kofi Annan challenged the UN General Assembly in the wake of a decade marred by ethnic cleansing, genocide, massacres, and atrocious human rights abuse in countries such as Bosnia and Herzegovina, Haiti, Rwanda, Somalia, and Serbia (Slaughter, 2005), can the world "reach consensus—not only on the principle that massive and systematic violations of human rights must be checked, wherever they take place, but also on ways of deciding what action is necessary, and when, and by whom"? Contention over whether the international community should intervene to stop human suffering in Syria, which intensified following the alleged use of chemical weapons in 2013, shows that these questions remain unresolved.

The challenge is to transcend traditional notions of sovereignty and to construct a global consensus for intervention that, in the words of civil rights activist Dr. Martin Luther King, Jr., is based on the belief that "Injustice anywhere is a threat to justice everywhere." If the global community truly recognizes that all people have rights that transcend state borders and defines those human rights as the core of the community's "common global interests," then it will have to answer and act on essential unresolved questions: What is the common interest? Who shall define it? Who shall defend it? Under whose authority? And by what means of intervention?

Is the World Preparing for the Wrong War?

To preserve peace, one must prepare for war. That remains the classical realist formula for national security. But would states not be wiser to prepare to fight the conditions that undermine prosperity, freedom, and welfare rather than each other?

Leaders have long been loath to fall prey to the single-mindedness of preparing to compete with other states. As former French President Francois Mitterand once urged, "together we must urgently find the solutions to the real problems at hand—especially unemployment and underdevelopment. This is the battlefield where the outlines of the [future] will be drawn." India's former Prime Minister Indira Gandhi warned that "either nuclear war will annihilate the human race and destroy the Earth, thus disposing of any future, or men and women all over must raise their voices for peace and for an urgent attempt to combine the insights of different civilizations with contemporary knowledge. We can survive in peace and goodwill only by viewing the human race as one, and by looking at global problems in their totality." These prescriptions adhere to a fundamental premise, as expressed by Martti Ahtisaari, then president of Finland: "To deal with the great security challenges of our time, including population growth, the spread of weapons of mass destruction, crime, environmental degradation, and ethnic conflicts, we must resolutely adopt new methods of managing change and building global security."

These rhetorical positions reflect the problems and self-interests leaders face at home and abroad. Nonetheless, they reveal only the view of a limited number of people. The war of people against people goes on. Human security remains precarious.

A large percentage of humanity faces famine, poverty, and a denial of basic human rights. Millions are threatened by genocide and terrorism sponsored by their own governments. "As human activities disrupt a growing number of ecological systems, it will become increasingly clear that the biggest threat to national security," argues Erik Assadourian (2010, p. 117) of the WorldWatch Institute, is "the weakened state of the planet." Humankind may consequently self-destruct, not because it lacks opportunities, but because of its collective inability to see and to seize them. "Perhaps we will destroy ourselves. Perhaps the common enemy within us will be too strong for us to recognize and overcome," lamented eminent astronomer Carl Sagan (1988). "But," he continued, "I have hope.... Is it possible that we humans are at last coming to our senses and beginning to work together on behalf of the species and the planet?"

Is This the "End of History" or the End of Happy Endings?

To many observers, the history of world affairs is the struggle between tyranny and liberty. The contest has taken various forms since antiquity: between kings and mass publics, despotism and democracy, ideological principle and pragmatic politics. Labels are misleading and sometimes dangerous. However, they provide the vocabulary of diplomacy and inform theoretical discussion of governance and statecraft. History, in this image, is a battle for hearts and minds. It is an ideological contest for the allegiance of humanity to a particular form of political, social, and economic organization.

With the defeat of fascism in World War II and the collapse of the international communist movement a generation later, it has become fashionable to argue that the world had witnessed the end of a historic contest of epic proportions—and thus the triumph of liberalism and what Francis Fukuyama (1989, p. 3) called the end of history:

The twentieth century saw the developed world descend into a paroxysm of ideological violence, as liberalism contended first with the remnants of absolutism, then bolshevism and fascism, and finally an updated Marxism that threatened to lead to the ultimate apocalypse of nuclear war. But the [twentieth] century that began full of self-confidence in the ultimate triumph of Western liberal democracy [seemed] at its close to be returning full circle to where it started: ... to the unabashed victory of economic and political liberalism. The abrupt repudiation of communism raised expectations that history had indeed "ended," in the sense that liberal democratic capitalism had triumphed throughout most of the world. Liberals, inspired by the belief that "liberal democracy and a market-oriented economic order are the only viable options for modern societies" (Fukuyama, 1999b; see also Fukuyama, 2004), are heartened by the doubling of the number of countries that have multiparty elections, as well as by capitalism at home and in foreign trade since the mid-1980s. Free governments practicing free trade, they believe, can best create a sound world order. As Woodrow Wilson argued, making the world "safe for democracy" would make the world itself safe. From this liberal perspective, the diffusion of democratic capitalism bodes well for the future of world politics.

A less reassuring possibility is that history has not "ended" and that the battle between totalitarian and democratic governance is not truly over. "The continued spread of democracy in the twenty-first century is no more inevitable than it is impossible" (Mandelbaum, 2007). There are signals that the march of democracy's spread is stalling, and many countries are democracies in name only as they remain ruled by one-party despots who, although elected, disregard constitutional limits on their power and deny their citizens basic political, religious, and economic freedoms. What is more, new democracies often lack the rule of law, political parties, or a free news media, and as a consequence are unstable and warlike (Mansfield and Snyder, 2005b). This persistence of leaders unaccountable to the electorate suggests that we may *not* be witnessing history's end.

The global economic crisis has also led to renewed speculation about the merits and shortcomings of global capitalism. "If he were observing the current downturn, Marx would certainly relish pointing out how flaws inherent in capitalism led to the current crisis. He would see how modern developments in finance, such as securitization and derivatives, have allowed markets to spread the risks of global economic integration" (Panitch, 2009, p. 141). Although many countries are starting to regain their financial footing, the consensus on the virtues of commercial liberalism has been shattered. The free market economies most exposed to the global economy bore the brunt of the financial damage, whereas countries that were relatively less open—ranging from India and China to Moldova—were less affected by the downturn.

> *Change is the law of life. And those who look only to the past or present are certain to miss the future.*
>
> **—John F. Kennedy, U.S. president**

A NEW WORLD ORDER OR NEW WORLD DISORDER?

The paradox of contemporary world politics is that a world no longer haunted by the paralyzing fear of a looming all-out war between great powers now faces a series of challenges every bit as threatening and potentially unmanageable. Globalization has simultaneously enlarged the responsibilities and expanded the issues to be confronted. In a prosperous and stable period of history, when confidence in peace and economic growth was high, then–U.S. President Bill Clinton found it necessary to warn, "profound and powerful forces are shaking and remaking our world. And the urgent question of our time is whether we can make change our friend and not our enemy."

The changes in recent years have spawned transnational threats to world order, in addition to resurgent nationalism, ethnic conflict, failed states, and separatist revolts. These include contagious diseases, human and drug trafficking, climate change, gender inequality, energy

THE NEXT FRONTIER? India and China are joining the United States, Russia, Europe, and Japan as major players in space exploration. Will the quest for knowledge, territory, and power in space be characterized by similar opportunities, tensions, and interests that shape politics across the world? Pictured here is the first female Chinese astronaut, Liu Yang, during a departure ceremony on June 16, 2012. A famous Maoist maxim has it that women hold up half the sky. Her accomplishments show that they have now soared past it (Branigan, 2012).

and food scarcities, desertification and deforestation, youth bulges and aging populations, and financial crises and collapsing economies.

The potential impact of these additional threats is formidable, as emerging trends suggest that nonmilitary dangers will multiply alongside the continuing threat of arms and armed aggression in civil wars, as well as interstate wars in particular regions and terrorism in almost any place and at any time in the world. The distinction between geostrategic issues of security that pertain to matters of war and peace and global issues related to economic, social, demographic, and environmental aspects of relations between governments and people may disappear. How will humanity set priorities for action with so many interrelated issues and problems, all of which require attention if peace and prosperity with justice is to prevail?

This book has focused on global change. It has identified the most important changes under way that are leading to potential transformations in world politics. Change, as we have seen, can be abrupt or slow. It moves constantly, but at its own pace, and history reminds us that the evolutionary direction of global change is uncertain. Many trends are unfolding at the same time, and their combined impact can move the world along an unexpected trajectory. In addition, trends can reverse themselves, and each trend advances at its own rate. Some trends move very slowly in an evolutionary process that can only result in dramatic transformations over many centuries, whereas others exhibit short bursts of rapid change, interrupted by long periods without much change.

To appreciate the diverse ways trends may combine to affect each other, it is helpful for you to construct your images by both using memories of the past and by being inspired by visions of the future. In 1775, American revolutionary Patrick Henry underscored the importance of history, stating that there was "but one lamp by which my feet are guided, and that is the lamp of experience. I know of no way of judging the future but by the past." Decades later, in 1848, another patriot, Italian political leader Giuseppe Mazzini, stressed the importance of forward thinking when he observed, "great things are achieved by guessing the direction of one's century." All of us need both perspectives, and a keen awareness that our images of history and the future must avoid the temptation to see ourselves and our own country as we wish to see them, without taking into account how differently others might view us and our state.

It now appears that the collective impact of the divergent trends under way is signaling a major transformation in world politics. Yet, juxtaposed against the revolutionary is the stable—the enduring rituals, existing rules, established institutions, and entrenched customs that resist the pull of the momentous recent changes in world politics. Persistence and change coexist uneasily, and it is this mixture that makes the future so uncertain.

The outcomes of two races will determine the difference between the world that is and the world that will be. The first is the race between knowledge and oblivion. Ignorance stands in the way of global progress and justice. Advances in science and technology far outpace the ability to resolve the social and political problems they generate. Building the knowledge to confront these problems may therefore present the ultimate challenge. "The splitting of the atom," Albert Einstein warned, has "changed everything save our modes of thinking, and thus we drift toward unparalleled catastrophe. Unless there is a fundamental change in [our] attitudes toward one another as well as [our] concept of the future, the world will face unprecedented disaster."

"Knowledge is our destiny," philosopher Jacob Bronowski declared. If the world is to forge a promising future, it must develop more sophisticated knowledge. Sophistication demands that we see the world as a whole, as well as its individual parts; it does not permit picturing others according to our self-images or projecting onto others our own values. We must discard belief in a simple formula for a better tomorrow and resist single-issue approaches to reform. A willingness to tolerate ambiguity is essential.

The future of world politics also rests on the outcome of a race between states' ability to cooperate and their historic tendency to compete and fight. Only concerted international cooperation stands in the way of slipping back into military conflicts and ruthless competition. To meet the global challenges of the future, and to make wise decisions to implement needed changes for bringing about a world that is more secure and just, vision is required.

If our image of the future were different, the decisions of today would be different.
[An inspiring vision] will impel us to action. But if there is no commonly held
image of what is worth striving for, society will lack both motivation and direction.

—Willis Harman, policy analyst

The future is not fixed, and headlines are not trend lines. So we can overcome threatening present dangers by making wise and ethical choices. How, then, should we proceed?

"In times like these," futurologist David Pearce Snyder (2006, p. 17) counsels, "the best advice comes from ancient ideas that have withstood the test of time." As Greek philosopher Heraclitus observed 2500 years ago, "Nothing about the future is inevitable except change." Two hundred years later, ancient Chinese general Sun Tzu advised that "the wise leader exploits the inevitable." Their combined message is clear: "The wise leader exploits change."

Therefore, rather than fear the future, we should welcome its opportunities as we strive to build a more peaceful and just world. The moving words of former U.S. President John F. Kennedy thus describe a posture we might well assume: "However close we sometimes seem to that dark and final abyss, let no man of peace and freedom despair. For he does not stand alone.... Together we shall save our planet or together we shall perish in its flames. Save it we can, and save it we must, and then shall we earn the eternal thanks of mankind."

STUDY. APPLY. ANALYZE.

Suggested Readings

Bueno de Mesquita, Bruce. (2009) *The Predictioneer's Game: Using the Logic of Brazen Self-Interest to See & Shape the Future.* New York: Random House.

Carland, Maria Pinto, and Candace Faber, eds. (2008) *Careers in International Affairs.* Washington, DC: Georgetown University Press.

Denemark, Robert A., ed. (2010) *The International Studies Encyclopedia.* Boston, MA: Blackwell Publishing.

Detraz, Nicole. (2012) *International Security and Gender.* Malden, MA: Polity Press.

Haigh, Stephen Paul. (2013) *Future States: From International to Global Order.* Burlington, VT: Ashgate Publishing Company.

Glenn, Jerome C., Theodore J Gordon, and Elizabeth Florescu. (2011) *2011 State of the Future.* Washington, DC: The Millennium Project.

Lebow, Richard Ned. (2010) *Forbidden Fruit: Counterfactuals and International Relations.* Princeton, NJ: Princeton University Press.

The World Bank. (2013) *World Development Report 2013: Jobs.*

Washington, DC: The World Bank.

Worldwatch Institute. (2013b) *State of the World 2013: Is Sustainability Still Possible?* New York: Norton.

Yetiv, Steve. (2011) "History, International Relations, and Integrated Approaches: Thinking about Greater Interdisciplinarity," *International Studies Perspectives* 12, no. 2 (May):94–118.

Suggested Videos

Carnegie Council Video

Ancram, Michael. "Emerging Challenges in a Network World."

Bueno de Mesquita, Bruce. "The Predictioneer's Game: Using the

Logic of Brazen Self-Interest to See and Shape the Future."

Friedman, George. "The Next 100 Years: A Forecast for the 21st Century."

Khanna, Parag. "How to Run the World: Charting a Course to the Next Renaissance."

Nye, Joseph. "The Future of Power."

CourseMate

Log in to CourseMate to access the following study tools for this chapter:

- Interactive Quiz
- eBook
- Flashcards & Key Term Crossword Puzzle
- Chapter Audio Summary
- Carnegie Council Videos

- Video Activities
- Simulation
- Animated Learning Module
- Case Study
- International Relations NewsWatch

GLOSSARY

A

absolute advantage The liberal economic concept that a state should specialize only in the production of goods in which the costs of production are lowest compared with those of other countries (**Chapter 11**).

acid rain Precipitation that has been made acidic through contact with sulfur dioxide and nitrogen oxides (**Chapter 14**).

acquired immune deficiency syndrome (AIDS) An often fatal condition that can result from infection with the human immunodeficiency virus (HIV) (**Chapter 12**).

actor An individual, group, state, or organization that plays a major role in world politics (**Chapter 1**).

adjudication A conflict-resolution procedure in which a third party makes a binding decision about a dispute in an institutional tribunal (**Chapter 7**).

agency The capacity of an actor to make choices and achieve objectives (**Chapter 2**).

agenda setting The thesis that by their ability to identify and publicize issues, the communications media determine the problems that receive attention from governments and international organizations (**Chapter 12**).

agent-oriented constructivism A variant of constructivism that sees ideas and identities as influenced in part by independent actors (**Chapter 2**).

alignments The acceptance by a neutral state threatened by foreign enemies of a special relationship short of formal alliance with a stronger power able to protect it from attack (**Chapter 8**).

alliances Coalitions of two or more states that combine their military capabilities and promise to coordinate their policies to increase mutual security (**Chapter 8**).

anarchy A condition in which the units in the global system are subjected to few, if any, overarching institutions to regulate their conduct (**Chapter 1**).

antidumping duties Taxes placed on another exporting state's alleged selling of a product at a price below the cost to produce it (**Chapter 11**).

antipersonnel landmines (APLs) Weapons buried below the surface of the soil that explode on contact with any person—soldier or citizen—stepping on them (**Chapter 9**).

appeasement A strategy of making concessions to another state in the hope that, satisfied, it will not make additional claims (**Chapter 4**).

arbitrage The selling of one currency (or product) and purchase of another to make a profit on changing exchange rates (**Chapter 10**).

arbitration A conflict-resolution procedure in which a third party makes a binding decision between disputants through a temporary ruling board created for that ruling (**Chapter 7**).

armed conflict Combat between the military forces of two or more states or groups (**Chapter 7**).

arms control Multilateral or bilateral agreements to contain arms races by setting limits on the number and types of weapons states are permitted (**Chapter 9**).

arms race The buildup of weapons and armed forces by two or more states that threaten each other, with the competition driven by the conviction that gaining a lead is necessary for security (**Chapter 9**).

asylum The provision of sanctuary to safeguard refugees escaping from the threat of persecution in the country where they hold citizenship (**Chapter 12**).

asymmetric warfare Armed conflict between belligerents of vastly unequal military strength, in which the weaker side is often a nonstate actor that relies on unconventional tactics (**Chapter 7**).

atrocities Brutal and savage acts against targeted citizen groups or prisoners of war, defined as illegal under international law (**Chapter 12**).

autocratic rule A system of authoritarian or totalitarian government in which unlimited power is concentrated in a single leader (**Chapter 3**).

B

balance of power The theory that peace and stability are most likely to be maintained when military power is distributed to prevent a single superpower hegemon or bloc from controlling the world (**Chapter 2**).

balancer Under a balance-of-power system, an influential global or regional great power that throws its support in decisive fashion to a defensive coalition (**Chapter 8**).

ballistic missile defense A planned antiballistic missile system using space-based lasers that would destroy enemy nuclear missiles before they could enter Earth's atmosphere (**Chapter 8**).

bandwagoning The tendency for weak states to seek alliance with the strongest power, irrespective of that power's ideology or type of government, in order to increase their security (**Chapter 8**).

bargaining model of war An interpretation of war's onset as a choice by the initiator to bargain through aggression with an enemy in order to win on an issue or to obtain things of value, such as territory or oil (**Chapter 7**).

bilateral Interactions between two transnational actors, such as treaties they have accepted to govern their future relationship (**Chapter 5**).

bilateral agreements Exchanges between two states, such as arms control agreements, negotiated cooperatively to set ceilings on military force levels (**Chapter 9**).

biodiversity The variety of plant and animal species living in the Earth's diverse ecosystems (**Chapter 14**).

bipolarity A condition in which power is concentrated in two competing centers so that the rest of the states define their allegiances in terms of their relationships with both rival great power superstates, or "poles" (**Chapter 4**).

blogs Online diaries, which spread information and ideas worldwide in the manner of journalists (**Chapter 12**).

blowback The propensity for actions undertaken for national security to have the unintended consequence of provoking retaliatory attacks by the target when relations later sour (**Chapter 8**).

bounded rationality The concept that a decision maker's capacity to choose the best option is often constrained by many human and organizational obstacles (**Chapter 3**).

brinkmanship The intentional, reckless taking of huge risks in bargaining with an enemy, such as threatening a nuclear attack, to compel its submission (**Chapter 8**).

bureaucracy The agencies and departments that conduct the functions of a central government or of a nonstate transnational actor (**Chapter 3**).

bureaucratic politics model A description of decision making that sees foreign policy choices as based on bargaining and compromises among competing government agencies (**Chapter 3**).

Bush Doctrine The unilateral policies of the George W. Bush administration proclaiming that the United States will make decisions only to meet America's perceived national interests, not to concede to other countries' complaints or to gain their acceptance (**Chapter 3**).

C

carrying capacity The maximum number of humans and living species that can be supported by a given territory (**Chapter 14**).

cartel A convergence of independent commercial enterprises or political groups that combine for collective action, such as limiting competition, setting prices for their services, or forming a coalition to advance their group's interests (**Chapter 12**).

caucuses Informal groups that individuals in governments and other groups join to promote their common interests (**Chapter 3**).

civil society A community that embraces shared norms and ethical standards to collectively manage problems without coercion and through peaceful and democratic procedures for decision making aimed at improving human welfare (**Chapter 6**).

civil war Wars between opposing groups within the same country or by rebels against the government (**Chapter 7**).

clash of civilizations Political scientist Samuel Huntington's controversial thesis that in the twenty-first century the globe's major civilizations will conflict with one another, leading to anarchy and warfare similar to that resulting from conflicts between states over the past 500 years (**Chapter 6**).

classical liberal economic theory A body of thought based on Adam Smith's ideas about the forces of supply and demand in the marketplace, emphasizing the social and economic benefits when individuals pursue their own self-interest (**Chapter 5**).

coercive diplomacy The use of threats or limited armed force to persuade an adversary to alter its foreign and/or domestic policies (**Chapter 8**).

cognitive dissonance The general psychological tendency to

deny discrepancies between one's preexisting beliefs (cognitions) and new information (**Chapter 1**).

Cold War The 44-year (1947–1991) rivalry between the United States and the Soviet Union, as well as their competing coalitions, which sought to contain each other's expansion and win worldwide predominance (**Chapter 4**).

collective action dilemma Paradox regarding the provision of collective goods in which there is no accountability for paying the costs of maintaining or providing the goods (**Chapter 11**).

collective security A security regime agreed to by the great powers that set rules for keeping peace, guided by the principle that an act of aggression by any state will be met by a collective response from the rest (**Chapter 2**).

colonialism The rule of a region by an external sovereign power (**Chapter 4**).

commercial liberalism An economic theory advocating free markets and the removal of barriers to the flow of trade and capital as a locomotive for prosperity (**Chapter 7**).

communications technology The technological means through which information and communications are transferred (**Chapter 5**).

communism The Marxist ideology maintaining that, if society is organized so that every person produces according to his or her ability and consumes according to his or her needs, a community without class distinctions will emerge, sovereign states will no longer be needed, and imperial wars of colonial conquest will vanish from history (**Chapter 5**).

communist theory of imperialism The Marxist-Leninist economic interpretation of imperialist wars of conquest as driven by capitalism's need for foreign markets to generate capital (**Chapter 7**).

comparative advantage The concept in liberal economics that a state will benefit if it specializes in the production of those goods that it can produce at a lower opportunity cost (**Chapter 11**).

compellence A method of coercive diplomacy usually involving an act of war or threat to force an adversary to make concessions against its will **(Chapter 8)**.

complex interdependence A model of world politics based on the assumptions that states are not the only important actors, security is not the dominant national goal, and military force is not the only significant instrument of foreign policy. This theory stresses cross-cutting ways in which the growing ties among transnational actors make them vulnerable to each other's actions and sensitive to each other's needs **(Chapter 2)**.

concert A cooperative agreement among great powers to jointly manage the global system **(Chapter 4)**.

conciliation A conflict-resolution procedure in which a third party assists both parties to a dispute but does not propose a solution **(Chapter 9)**.

conflict Discord, often arising in international relations over perceived incompatibilities of interest **(Chapter 7)**.

consequentialism An approach to evaluating moral choices on the basis of the results of the action taken **(Chapter 2)**.

constitutional democracy Government processes that allow people, through their elected representatives, to exercise power and influence the state's policies **(Chapter 3)**.

constructivism A paradigm based on the premise that world politics is a function of the ways that states construct and then accept images of reality and later respond to the meanings given to power politics; as consensual definitions change, it is possible for either conflictual or cooperative practices to evolve **(Chapter 2)**.

containment A strategy of confronting attempts of a power rival to expand its sphere of influence, with either force or the threat of force, thereby preventing it from altering the balance of power **(Chapter 4)**.

cornucopians Optimists who question limits-to-growth analyses and contend that markets effectively maintain a balance between population, resources, and the environment **(Chapter 14)**.

cosmopolitan An outlook that values viewing the cosmos or entire world as the best polity or unit for political governance and personal identity, as opposed to other polities such as one's local metropolis or city of residence (e.g., Indianapolis or Minneapolis) **(Chapter 12)**.

countervailing duties Government tariffs to offset suspected subsidies provided by foreign governments to their producers **(Chapter 11)**.

coup d'etat A sudden, forcible takeover of government by a small group within that country, typically carried out by violent or illegal means with the goal of installing their own leadership in power **(Chapter 7)**.

covert operations Secret activities undertaken by a state outside its borders through clandestine means to achieve specific political or military goals with respect to another state **(Chapter 8)**.

crimes against humanity A category of activities, made illegal at the Nuremberg war crime trials, condemning states that abuse human rights **(Chapter 9)**.

crisis A situation in which the threat of escalation to warfare is high and the time available for making decisions and reaching compromised solutions in negotiations is compressed **(Chapter 9)**.

cultural conditioning The impact of national traditions and societal values on the behavior of states, under the assumption that culture affects national decision making about issues such as the acceptability of aggression **(Chapter 7)**.

cyberspace A metaphor used to describe the global electronic web of people, ideas, and interactions on the Internet, which is unencumbered by the borders of the geopolitical world **(Chapter 12)**.

cycles The periodic reemergence of conditions similar to those that existed previously **(Chapter 1)**.

D

decolonization the process by which sovereign independence was achieved by countries that were once colonies of the great powers **(Chapter 5)**.

defensive realism A variant of realist theory that emphasizes the preservation of power, as opposed to the expansion

of power, as an actor's primary security objective **(Chapter 2)**.

deforestation The process of clearing and destroying forests **(Chapter 14)**.

democratic peace The theory that although democratic states sometimes wage wars against nondemocratic states, they do not fight one another **(Chapter 7)**.

demography The study of population changes, their sources, and their impact **(Chapter 12)**.

dependency theory A theory hypothesizing that less developed countries are exploited because global capitalism makes them dependent on the rich countries that create exploitative rules for trade and production **(Chapter 2)**.

desertification The creation of deserts due to soil erosion, overfarming, and deforestation, which converts cropland to nonproductive, arid sand **(Chapter 14)**.

détente In general, a strategy of seeking to relax tensions between adversaries to reduce the possibility of war **(Chapter 4)**.

deterrence Preventive strategies designed to dissuade an adversary from doing what it would otherwise do **(Chapter 7)**.

developed countries A category used by the World Bank to identify Global North countries with an annual GNI per capita of $12,276 or more **(Chapter 5)**.

developing countries A category used by the World Bank to identify low-income Global South countries with an annual GNI per capita below $1005 and middle-income countries with an annual GNI per capita of more than $1005 but less than $12,276 **(Chapter 5)**.

development The processes, economic and political, through which a country develops to increase its capacity to meet its citizens' basic human needs and raise their standard of living **(Chapter 5)**.

devolution States' granting of political power to minority ethnic groups and indigenous people in particular national regions under the expectation that greater autonomy will curtail the groups' quest for independence as a new state (**Chapter 13**).

diasporas The migration of religious or ethnic groups to foreign lands despite their continuation of affiliation with the land and customs of their origin (**Chapter 6**).

digital divide The division between the Internet technology–rich Global North and the Global South in the proportion of Internet users and hosts (**Chapter 5**).

diplomacy Communication and negotiation between global actors that is not dependent upon the use of force and seeks a cooperative solution (**Chapter 2**).

disarmament Agreements to reduce or destroy weapons or other means of attack (**Chapter 9**).

diversionary theory of war The hypothesis that leaders sometimes initiate conflict abroad as a way of increasing national cohesion at home by diverting national public attention away from controversial domestic issues and internal problems (**Chapter 3**, **Chapter 7**).

dollar overhang Condition that precipitated the end of the Bretton Woods era, in which total holdings of dollars outside of the U.S. central bank exceeded the amount of dollars actually backed by gold (**Chapter 10**).

domino theory A metaphor popular during the Cold War that predicted that if one state fell to communism, its neighbors would also fall in a chain reaction, like a row of falling dominoes (**Chapter 4**).

dualism The separation of a country into two sectors, the first modern and prosperous and centered in major cities, and the second at the margin, neglected and poor (**Chapter 5**).

E

ecological fallacy The error of assuming that the attributes of an entire population—a culture, a country, or a civilization—are the same attributes and attitudes of each person within it (**Chapter 7**).

economic peace The premise that economic institutions associated with a contract-intensive economy are the

source of peace between countries (**Chapter 7**).

economic sanctions Punitive economic actions, such as the cessation of trade or financial ties, by one global actor against another to retaliate for objectionable behavior (**Chapter 11**).

embedded liberalism Dominant economic approach during the Bretton Woods system, which combined open international markets with domestic state intervention to attain such goals as full employment and social welfare (**Chapter 10**).

emerging powers Countries with rising political and economic capabilities and influence that seek a more assertive role in international affairs (**Chapter 5**).

enclosure movement The claiming of common properties by states or private interests (**Chapter 14**).

enduring internal rivalry (EIR) Protracted violent conflicts between governments and insurgent groups within a state (**Chapter 7**).

enduring rivalries Prolonged competition fueled by deep-seated mutual hatred that leads opposed actors to feud and fight over a long period of time without resolution of their conflict (**Chapter 1**).

environmental security A concept recognizing that environmental threats to global life systems are as dangerous as the threat of armed conflicts (**Chapter 14**).

epistemic community Scientific experts on a subject of inquiry such as global warming who are organized internationally as NGOs to communicate with one another and use their constructed understanding of "knowledge" to lobby for global transformations (**Chapter 14**).

ethics Criteria for evaluating right and wrong behavior and the motives of individuals and groups (**Chapter 9**).

ethnic cleansing The extermination of an ethnic minority group by a state (**Chapter 12**).

ethnic groups People whose identity is primarily defined by their sense of sharing a common ancestral nationality, language, cultural heritage, and kinship (**Chapter 1**, **Chapter 6**).

ethnic nationalism Devotion to a cultural, ethnic, or linguistic community (**Chapter 6**).

ethnicity Perceptions of likeness among members of a particular racial grouping leading them to prejudicially view other nationality groups as outsiders (**Chapter 6**).

ethnocentrism A propensity to see one's nationality or state as the center of the world and therefore special, with the result that the values and perspectives of other groups are misunderstood and ridiculed (**Chapter 13**).

European Commission The executive organ administratively responsible for the European Union (**Chapter 6**).

European Union (EU) A regional organization created by the merger of the European Coal and Steel Community, the European Atomic Energy Community, and the European Economic Community (called the European Community until 1993) that has since expanded geographically and in its authority (**Chapter 6**).

exchange rate The rate at which one state's currency is exchanged for another state's currency in the global marketplace (**Chapter 10**).

export quotas Barriers to free trade agreed to by two trading states to protect their domestic producers (**Chapter 11**).

export-led industrialization A growth strategy that concentrates on developing domestic export industries capable of competing in overseas markets (**Chapter 5**).

externalities The unintended side effects resulting from choices, such as inflation from runaway government spending, that are not taken into account at the time of the decision (**Chapter 3**).

F

failed states Countries whose governments have so mismanaged policy that their citizens, in rebellion, threaten revolution to divide the country into separate independent states (**Chapter 7**).

fascism A far-right ideology that promotes extreme nationalism and the establishment of an authoritarian society built around a single party with dictatorial leadership (**Chapter 4**).

feminist theory   Body of scholarship that emphasizes gender in the study of world politics (**Chapter 2**).

fertility rate   The average number of children born to a woman (or group of women) during her lifetime (**Chapter 12**).

First World   The relatively wealthy industrialized countries that share a commitment to varying forms of democratic political institutions and developed market economies, including the United States, Japan, the European Union, Canada, Australia, and New Zealand (**Chapter 5**).

fixed exchange rates   A system in which a government sets the value of its currency at a fixed rate for exchange in relation to another country's currency so that the exchange value is not free to fluctuate in the global money market (**Chapter 10**).

floating exchange rates   An unmanaged process in which governments neither establish an official rate for their currencies nor intervene to affect the value of their currencies, and instead allow market forces and private investors to influence the relative rate of exchange for currencies between countries (**Chapter 10**).

foreign aid   Economic assistance in the form of loans and grants provided by a donor country to a recipient country for a variety of purposes (**Chapter 5**).

foreign direct investment (FDI)   A cross-border investment through which a person or corporation based in one country purchases or constructs an asset such as a factory or bank in another country so that a long-term relationship and control of an enterprise by nonresidents results (**Chapter 5**).

free riders   Those who obtain benefits at others' expense without the usual costs and effort (**Chapter 8**).

G

game theory   Mathematical model of strategic interaction in which outcomes are determined not only by a single actor's preferences, but also by the choices of all actors involved (**Chapter 3**).

gender inequality   Differences between men and women in opportunity and reward that are determined by the values that guide states' foreign and domestic policies (**Chapter 13**).

Gender Inequality Index (GII)   An index that uses female reproductive health, political and educational empowerment, and participation in the labor market to assess the extent to which gender inequality erodes a country's human development achievements (**Chapter 13**).

gendercide   Systematic killing of members of a specific gender (**Chapter 13**).

genetic engineering   Research geared to discover seeds for new types of plant and human life for sale and use as substitutes for those produced naturally (**Chapter 14**).

genocide   The attempt to eliminate, in whole or in part, an ethnic, racial, religious, or national minority group (**Chapter 12**).

geo-economics   The relationship between geography and the economic conditions and behavior of states that defines their levels of production, trade, and consumption of goods and services (**Chapter 10**).

geopolitics   The relationship between geography and politics and its consequences for states' national interests and relative power (**Chapter 3**).

the global commons   The physical and organic characteristics and resources of the entire planet—the air in the atmosphere and conditions on land and sea—on which human life depends and that is the common heritage of all humanity (**Chapter 14**).

global level of analysis   An analytical approach that emphasizes the impact of worldwide conditions on foreign policy behavior and human welfare (**Chapter 1**).

Global North   A term used to refer to the world's wealthy, industrialized countries located primarily in the Northern Hemisphere (**Chapter 5**).

Global South   A term now often used instead of "Third World" to designate the less developed countries located primarily in the Southern Hemisphere (**Chapter 5**).

global system   The predominant patterns of behaviors and beliefs that prevail internationally and define the major worldwide conditions that heavily influence human and state activities (**Chapter 1**).

global village   A popular cosmopolitan perspective describing the growth of awareness that all people share a common fate because the world is becoming an integrated and interdependent whole (**Chapter 12**).

globalization   The integration of states through increasing contact, communication, and trade, as well as increased global awareness of such integration (**Chapter 10**).

globalization of finance   The increasing transnationalization of national markets through the worldwide integration of capital flows (**Chapter 10**).

globalization of labor   Integration of labor markets, predicated by the global nature of production as well as the increased size and mobility of the global labor force (**Chapter 11**).

globalization of production   Transnationalization of the productive process, in which finished goods rely on inputs from multiple countries outside of their final market (**Chapter 11**).

globally integrated enterprises   MNCs organized horizontally with management and production located in plants in numerous states for the same products they market (**Chapter 6**).

good offices   Provision by a third party to offer a place for negotiation among disputants but the party does not serve as a mediator in the actual negotiations (**Chapter 7**).

great powers   The most powerful countries, militarily and economically, in the global system (**Chapter 1**).

greenhouse effect   The phenomenon producing planetary warming when gases released by burning fossil fuels act as a blanket in the atmosphere, thereby increasing temperatures (**Chapter 14**).

gross national income (GNI) A measure of the production of goods and services within a given time period, which is used to delimit the geographic scope of production. GNI measures production by a state's citizens or companies, regardless of where the production occurs (**Chapter 5**).

Group of 77 (G-77) The coalition of Third World countries that sponsored the 1963 Joint Declaration of Developing Countries calling for reform to allow greater equality in North–South trade (**Chapter 5**).

groupthink The propensity for members of a group to accept and agree with the group's prevailing attitudes, rather than speaking out for what they believe (**Chapter 3**).

gunboat diplomacy A show of military force, historically naval force, to intimidate an adversary (**Chapter 8**).

H

hegemon A preponderant state capable of dominating the conduct of international political and economic relations (**Chapter 4**).

hegemonic stability theory A body of theory that maintains that the establishment of hegemony for global dominance by a single great power is a necessary condition for global order in commercial transactions and international military security (**Chapter 7**).

history-making individuals model An interpretation of world politics that sees foreign policy decisions that affect the course of history as products of strong-willed leaders acting on their personal convictions (**Chapter 3**).

horizontal nuclear proliferation An increase in the number of states that possess nuclear weapons (**Chapter 8**).

Human Development Index (HDI) An index that uses life expectancy, literacy, average number of years of schooling, and income to assess a country's performance in providing for its people's welfare and security (**Chapter 13**).

human immunodeficiency virus (HIV) A virus that can lead to the lethal acquired immune deficiency syndrome (AIDS) (**Chapter 12**).

human needs Those basic physical, social, and political needs, such as food and freedom, that are required for survival and security (**Chapter 13**).

human rights The political rights and civil liberties recognized by the international community as inalienable and valid for individuals in all countries by virtue of their humanity (**Chapter 13**).

human security A measure popular in liberal theory of the degree to which the welfare of individuals is protected and promoted, in contrast to realist theory's emphasis on putting the state's interests in military and national security ahead of all other goals (**Chapter 8**).

humanitarian intervention The use of peacekeeping troops by foreign states or international organizations to protect endangered people from gross violations of their human rights and from mass murder (**Chapter 13**).

I

ideology A set of core philosophical principles that leaders and citizens collectively construct about politics, the interests of political actors, and the ways people ought to behave (**Chapter 4**).

imperial overstretch The historic tendency for past hegemons to sap their own strength through costly imperial pursuits and military spending that weaken their economies in relation to the economies of their rivals (**Chapter 4**).

imperialism The policy of expanding state power through the conquest and/or military domination of foreign territory (**Chapter 2**).

import quotas Numerical limits on the quantity of particular products that can be imported (**Chapter 11**).

import-substitution industrialization A strategy for economic development that centers on providing investors at home incentives to produce goods so that demand for previously imported products from abroad will decline (**Chapter 5**).

indigenous peoples the native ethnic and cultural inhabitant populations within countries, referred to as the "Fourth World." (**Chapter 5**, **Chapter 6**).

individual level of analysis An analytical approach that emphasizes the psychological and perceptual variables motivating people, such as those who make foreign policy decisions on behalf of states and other global actors (**Chapter 1**).

individualistic fallacy The logical error of assuming that an individual leader, who has legal authority to govern, represents the people and opinions of the population governed, so that all citizens are necessarily accountable for the vices and virtues (to be given blame or credit) of the leaders authorized to speak for them (**Chapter 7**).

Inequality-adjusted Human Development Index (IHDI) To further assess human welfare, this index accounts for the effect of the inequality in the distribution of health, education, and income upon human development within a society (**Chapter 13**).

infant industry Newly established industries ("infants") that are not yet strong enough to compete against mature foreign producers in the global marketplace until in time they develop and can then compete (**Chapter 11**).

information age The era in which the rapid creation and global transfer of information through mass communication contributes to the globalization of knowledge (**Chapter 6**).

information technology (IT) The techniques for storing, retrieving, and disseminating recorded data and research knowledge through computerization and the Internet (**Chapter 5**).

information warfare Attacks on an adversary's telecommunications and computer networks to degrade the technological systems vital to its defense and economic well-being (**Chapter 7**).

intergovernmental organizations (IGOs) Institutions created and joined by states' governments, which give them authority to make collective decisions to manage particular problems on the global agenda (**Chapter 1**).

Intermediate-Range Nuclear Forces (INF) Treaty The U.S.–Russian agreement to eliminate an entire class of nuclear weapons by removing all intermediate and short-range ground-based missiles and launchers with ranges between 300 and 3500 miles from Europe (**Chapter 9**).

International Court of Justice (ICJ) The primary court established by the United Nations for resolving legal disputes between states and providing advisory opinions to international agencies and the UN General Assembly (**Chapter 9**).

International Criminal Court (ICC) A court established by the United Nations for indicting and administering justice to people committing war crimes (**Chapter 9**).

international criminal tribunals Special tribunals established by the UN prosecute those responsible for war time atrocities and genocide, bring justice to victims, and deter such crimes in the future (**Chapter 9**).

international liquidity Reserve assets used to settle international accounts (**Chapter 10**).

international monetary system The financial procedures used to calculate the value of currencies and credits when capital is transferred across borders through trade, investment, foreign aid, and loans (**Chapter 10**).

international regime Embodies the norms, principles, rules, and institutions around which global expectations unite regarding a specific international problem (**Chapter 2**).

interspecific aggression Killing others who are not members of one's own species (**Chapter 7**).

intra-firm trade Cross-national trade of intermediate goods and services within the same firm (**Chapter 11**).

intraspecific aggression Killing members of one's own species (**Chapter 7**).

irredentism A movement by an ethnic national group to recover control of lost territory by force so that the new state boundaries will no longer divide the group (**Chapter 4**).

isolationism A policy of withdrawing from active participation with other actors in world affairs and instead concentrating state efforts on managing internal affairs (**Chapter 4**).

J

jus ad bellum A component of just war doctrine that establishes criteria under which a just war may be initiated (**Chapter 9**).

jus in bello A component of just war doctrine that sets limits on the acceptable use of force (**Chapter 9**).

just war doctrine The moral criteria identifying when a just war may be undertaken and how it should be fought once it begins (**Chapter 9**).

K

Kellogg-Briand Pact A multilateral treaty negotiated in 1928 that outlawed war as a method for settling interstate conflicts (**Chapter 2**).

L

laissez-faire economics The philosophical principle of free markets and free trade to give people free choices with little governmental regulation (**Chapter 5**).

least developed of the less developed countries (LLDCs) The most impoverished countries in the Global South (**Chapter 5**).

levels of analysis The different aspects of and agents in international affairs that may be stressed in interpreting and explaining global phenomena, depending on whether the analyst chooses to focus on "wholes" (the complete global system and large collectivities) or on "parts" (individual states or people) (**Chapter 1**).

liberal feminism A category of feminist theory that sees men and women as equal in skills and capabilities, and focuses on the subordination of women under existing political, legal, and social institutions and practices (**Chapter 2**).

Liberal International Economic Order (LIEO) The set of regimes created after World War II, designed to promote monetary stability and reduce barriers to the free flow of trade and capital (**Chapter 10**).

liberalism A paradigm predicated on the hope that the application of reason and universal ethics to international relations can lead to a more orderly, just, and cooperative world; liberalism assumes that anarchy and war can be policed by institutional reforms that empower international organization and law (**Chapter 2**).

linkage strategy A set of assertions claiming that leaders should take into account another country's overall behavior when deciding whether to reach agreement on any one specific issue so as to link cooperation to rewards (**Chapter 4**).

long-cycle theory A theory that focuses on the rise and fall of the leading global power as the central political process of the modern world system (**Chapter 4**).

long peace Long-lasting periods of peace between any of the militarily strongest great powers (**Chapter 7**).

M

massive retaliation The Eisenhower administration's policy doctrine for containing Soviet communism by pledging to respond to any act of aggression with the most destructive capabilities available, including nuclear weapons (**Chapter 8**).

mediation A conflict-resolution procedure in which a third party proposes a nonbinding solution to the disputants (**Chapter 7**).

megacities Metropolitan areas where the population is more than 10 million people (**Chapter 12**).

mercantilism Political economic perspective that views international trade in zero-sum terms and calls for active state intervention into domestic economies (**Chapter 5**).

militant religious movements Politically active organizations based on strong religious convictions, whose members are fanatically devoted to the global promotion of their religious beliefs (**Chapter 6**).

military-industrial complex A combination of defense establishments, contractors who supply arms for them, and government agencies that benefit from high military spending, which act as a lobbying coalition to pressure governments to appropriate large expenditures for military preparedness (**Chapter 8**).

military necessity The legal principle that violation of the rules of warfare may be excused for defensive purposes during periods of extreme emergency (**Chapter 9**).

mirror images The tendency of states and people in competitive interaction to perceive each other similarly—to see others the same hostile way others see them (**Chapter 1**).

modernization A view of development popular in the Global North's liberal democracies that wealth is created through efficient production, free enterprise, and free trade, and that countries' relative wealth depends on technological innovation and education more than on natural endowments such as climate and resources (**Chapter 5**).

monetary policy The decisions made by states' central banks to change the country's money supply in an effort to manage the national economy and control inflation, such as changing the amount of money in circulation and raising or lowering interest rates (**Chapter 10**).

money supply The total amount of currency in circulation, calculated to include demand deposits, such as checking accounts in commercial banks, and time deposits, such as savings accounts and bonds (**Chapter 10**).

morals Principles clarifying the difference between good and evil and the situations in which they are opposed (**Chapter 9**).

most-favored-nation (MFN) principle The central GATT principle of unconditional nondiscriminatory treatment in trade between contracting parties underscoring the WTO's rule requiring any advantage given by one WTO member to also extend it to all other WTO members (**Chapter 11**).

multilateral agreements Cooperative compacts among many states to ensure that a concerted policy is implemented toward alleviating a common problem, such as levels of future weapons capabilities (**Chapter 9**).

multilateralism Cooperative approaches to managing shared problems through collective and coordinated action (**Chapter 4**).

multinational corporations (MNCs) Business enterprises headquartered in one state that invest and operate extensively in many other states (**Chapter 5**).

multiple advocacy The concept that better and more rational choices are made when decisions are reached in a group context, which allows advocates of differing alternatives to be heard so that the feasibility of rival options receives critical evaluation (**Chapter 3**).

multiple independently targetable reentry vehicles (MIRVs) A technological innovation permitting many weapons to be delivered from a single missile (**Chapter 8**).

multipolarity The distribution of global power into three or more great power centers, with most other states allied with one of the rivals (**Chapter 4**).

murky protectionism Nontariff barriers to trade that may be "hidden" in government policies not directly related to trade, such as environmental initiatives and government spending (**Chapter 11**).

mutual assured destruction (MAD) A condition of mutual deterrence in which both sides possess the ability to survive a first strike with weapons of mass destruction and launch a devastating retaliatory attack (**Chapter 8**).

N

nation A collectivity whose people see themselves as members of the same group because they share the same ethnicity, culture, or language (**Chapter 1**).

national character The collective characteristics ascribed to the people within a state (**Chapter 7**).

national interest The goals that states pursue to maximize what they perceive to be selfishly best for their country (**Chapter 2**).

national security A country's psychological freedom from fears that the state will be unable to resist threats to its survival and national values emanating from abroad or at home (**Chapter 8**).

nationalism A mind-set glorifying a particular state and the nationality group living in it, which sees the state's interest as a supreme value (**Chapter 4**).

nature versus nurture The controversy over whether human behavior is determined more by the biological basis of "human nature" than it is nurtured by the environmental conditions that humans experience (**Chapter 7**).

negotiation Diplomatic dialogue and discussion between two or more parties with the goal of resolving through give-and-take bargaining perceived differences of interests and the conflicts they cause (**Chapter 9**).

neoconservative A political movement in the United States calling for the use of military and economic power in foreign policy to bring freedom and democracy to other countries (**Chapter 2**).

neoliberalism The "new" liberal theoretical perspective that accounts for the way international institutions promote global change, cooperation, peace, and prosperity through collective programs for reforms (**Chapter 2**).

neo-Malthusians Pessimists who warn of the global ecopolitical dangers of uncontrolled population growth (**Chapter 14**).

neorealism A theoretical account of states' behavior that explains it as determined by differences in their relative power within the global hierarchy, defined primarily by the distribution of military power, instead of by other factors such as their values, types of government, or domestic circumstances (**Chapter 2**).

neutrality The legal doctrine that provides rights for states to remain nonaligned with adversaries waging war against each other (**Chapter 9**).

New International Economic Order (NIEO) The 1974 policy resolution in the United Nations that called for a North–South dialogue to open the way for the less developed countries of the Global South to participate more fully in the making of international economic policy **(Chapter 5)**.

newly industrialized countries (NICs) The most prosperous members of the Global South, which have become important exporters of manufactured goods as well as important markets for the major industrialized countries that export capital goods **(Chapter 5)**.

nonalignment A foreign policy posture that rejects participating in military alliances with an alliance bloc for fear it will lead to involvement in an unnecessary war **(Chapter 8)**.

nondiscrimination Principle that goods produced by all member states should receive equal treatment, as embodied in the ideas of most-favored nation (MFN) and national treatment **(Chapter 11)**.

nongovernmental organizations (NGOs) Transnational organizations of private citizens maintaining consultative status with the United Nations; they include professional associations, foundations, multinational corporations, or simply internationally active groups in different states joined together to work toward common interests **(Chapter 1)**.

nonintervention norm A fundamental international legal principle, now being challenged, that traditionally has defined interference by one state in the domestic affairs of another as illegal **(Chapter 8)**.

nonlethal weapons (NLWs) The wide array of "soft kill," low-intensity methods of incapacitating an enemy's people, vehicles, communications systems, or entire cities without killing either combatants or noncombatants **(Chapter 8)**.

nonproliferation regime Rules to contain arms races so that weapons or technology do not spread to states that do not have them **(Chapter 8)**.

nonstate nations National or ethnic groups struggling to obtain power and/or statehood **(Chapter 6)**.

nontariff barriers (NTBs) Measures other than tariffs that discriminate against imports without direct tax levies and are beyond the scope of international regulation **(Chapter 11)**.

norms Generalized standards of behavior that, once accepted, shape collective expectations about appropriate conduct **(Chapter 2)**.

North Atlantic Treaty Organization (NATO) A military alliance created in 1949 to deter a Soviet attack on Western Europe that since has expanded and redefined its mission to emphasize not only the maintenance of peace but also the promotion of democracy **(Chapter 8)**.

Nth country problem The expansion of additional new nuclear weapon states **(Chapter 8)**.

Nuclear Nonproliferation Treaty (NPT) An international agreement that seeks to prevent horizontal proliferation by prohibiting further nuclear weapons sales, acquisitions, or production **(Chapter 8)**.

nuclear winter The expected freeze that would occur in the Earth's climate from the fallout of smoke and dust in the event nuclear weapons were used, blocking out sunlight and destroying the plant and animal life that survived the original blast **(Chapter 8)**.

O

offensive realism A variant of realist theory that stresses that, in an anarchical international system, states should always look for opportunities to gain more power **(Chapter 2)**.

official development assistance (ODA) Grants or loans to countries from donor countries, now usually channeled through multilateral aid institutions such as the World Bank, for the primary purpose of promoting economic development and welfare **(Chapter 5)**.

opportunity costs The sacrifices that sometimes result when the decision to select one option means that the opportunity to realize gains from other options is lost **(Chapter 8)**.

orderly market arrangements (OMAs) Voluntary export restrictions through government-to-government agreements to follow specific trading rules **(Chapter 11)**.

outsourcing The transfer of jobs by a corporation usually headquartered in a Global North country to a Global South country able to supply trained workers at lower wages **(Chapter 6)**.

ozone layer The protective layer of the upper atmosphere over the Earth's surface that shields the planet from the sun's harmful impact on living organisms **(Chapter 14)**.

P

pacifism The liberal idealist school of ethical thought that recognizes no conditions that justify the taking of another human's life, even when authorized by a head of state **(Chapter 7)**.

paradigm Derived from the Greek *paradeigma*, meaning an example, a model, or an essential pattern; a paradigm structures thought about an area of inquiry **(Chapter 2)**.

peace building Postconflict actions, predominantly diplomatic and economic, that strengthen and rebuild governmental infrastructure and institutions in order to avoid renewed recourse to armed conflict **(Chapter 9)**.

peace enforcement The application of military force to warring parties, or the threat of its use, normally pursuant to international authorization, to compel compliance with resolutions or with sanctions designed to maintain or restore peace and order **(Chapter 9)**.

peace operations A general category encompassing both peacekeeping and peace enforcement operations undertaken to establish and maintain peace between disputants **(Chapter 9)**.

peaceful coexistence Soviet leader Nikita Khrushchev's 1956 doctrine that war between capitalist and communist states is not inevitable and that inter-bloc competition could be peaceful **(Chapter 4)**.

peacekeeping The efforts by third parties such as the United Nations to intervene in civil wars and/or interstate wars or to prevent hostilities between potential belligerents from escalating, so that by acting as a buffer a negotiated settlement of the dispute can be reached **(Chapter 9)**.

peacemaking   The process of diplomacy, mediation, negotiation, or other forms of peaceful settlement that arranges an end to a dispute and resolves the issues that led to conflict **(Chapter 9)**.

plurilateral agreement   Treaties between a subset of WTO members that apply only to a specific issue **(Chapter 11)**.

podcasts   Audio and visual programs that individuals make and distribute as digital downloads **(Chapter 12)**.

polarity   The degree to which military and economic capabilities are concentrated in the global system that determines the number of centers of power, or "poles." **(Chapter 3)**.

polarization   The formation of competing coalitions or blocs composed of allies that align with one of the major competing poles, or centers, of power **(Chapter 3)**.

policy agenda   The changing list of problems or issues to which governments pay special attention at any given moment **(Chapter 3)**.

policy networks   Leaders and organized interests (such as lobbies) that form temporary alliances to influence a particular foreign policy decision **(Chapter 3)**.

political economy   A field of study that focuses on the intersection of politics and economics in international relations **(Chapter 4)**.

political efficacy   The extent to which policy makers' self-confidence instills in them the belief that they can effectively make rational choices **(Chapter 3)**.

political integration   The processes and activities by which the populations of many or all states transfer their loyalties to a merged political and economic unit **(Chapter 6)**.

politics of scarcity   The view that the unavailability of resources required to sustain life, such as food, energy, or water, can undermine security in degrees similar to military aggression **(Chapter 14)**.

pooled sovereignty   Legal authority granted to an IGO by its members to make collective decisions regarding specified aspects of public policy heretofore made exclusively by each sovereign government **(Chapter 6)**.

population density   The number of people within each country, region, or city, measuring the geographical concentration of the population as a ratio of the average space available for each resident **(Chapter 12)**.

population implosion   A rapid reduction of population that reverses a previous trend toward progressively larger populations; a severe reduction in the world's population **(Chapter 12)**.

positivist legal theory   A theory that stresses states' customs and habitual ways of behaving as the most important source of law **(Chapter 9)**.

postcolonial feminism   a category of feminist theory that looks at differences in the experiences of women, and argues there is no universal feminine perspective or approach **(Chapter 2)**.

postmodern terrorism   To Walter Laqueur, the terrorism practiced by an expanding set of diverse actors with new weapons "to sow panic in a society to weaken or even overthrow the incumbents and to bring about political change" **(Chapter 6)**.

post-structural feminism   This category of feminism focuses on the ways in which gendered language and action pervade world politics **(Chapter 2)**.

power   The factors that enable one actor to change another actor's behavior against its preferences **(Chapter 1)**.

power potential   The capabilities or resources held by a state that are considered necessary to its asserting influence over others **(Chapter 8)**.

power transition theory   The theory that war is likely when a dominant great power is threatened by the rapid growth of a rival's capabilities, which reduces the difference in their relative power **(Chapter 7)**.

preemptive warfare   A quick first-strike attack that seeks to defeat an adversary before it can organize an initial attack or a retaliatory response **(Chapter 8)**.

preventive diplomacy   Diplomatic actions taken in advance of a predictable crisis to prevent or limit violence **(Chapter 9)**.

preventive warfare   Strictly outlawed by international law, a war undertaken by choice against an enemy to prevent it from suspected intentions to attack sometime in the distant future—if and when the enemy might acquire the necessary military capabilities **(Chapter 8)**.

private military services   The outsourcing of activities of a military-specific nature to private companies, such as armed security, equipment maintenance, IT services, logistics, and intelligence services **(Chapter 8)**.

proliferation   The spread of weapon capabilities from a few to many states in a chain reaction, so that an increasing number of states gain the ability to launch an attack on other states with devastating (e.g., nuclear) weapons **(Chapter 8)**.

prospect theory   A social psychological theory explaining decision making under conditions of uncertainty and risk that looks at the relationship between individual risk propensity and the perceived prospects for avoiding losses and realizing big gains **(Chapter 3)**.

protectionism   Barriers of foreign trade, such as tariffs and quotas, that protect local industries from competition for the purchase of products local manufacturers produce **(Chapter 11)**.

public good   Collective goods, such as clean air or sunlight, whose use is nonexclusive and nonrival in nature; thus if anyone can use the good it is available to all **(Chapter 11)**.

purchasing power parity (PPP)   An index that calculates the true rate of exchange among currencies when parity—when what can be purchased is the same—is achieved; the index determines what can be bought with a unit of each currency **(Chapter 13)**.

R

rapprochement   In diplomacy, a policy seeking to reestablish normal cordial relations between enemies **(Chapter 4)**.

rational choice Decision-making procedures guided by careful definition of situations, weighing of goals, consideration of all alternatives, and selection of the options most likely to achieve the highest goals (**Chapter 3**).

realism A paradigm based on the premise that world politics is essentially and unchangeably a struggle among self-interested states for power and position under anarchy, with each competing state pursuing its own national interests (**Chapter 2**).

realpolitik The theoretical outlook prescribing that countries should increase their power and wealth in order to compete with and dominate other countries (**Chapter 5**).

reciprocity mutual or reciprocal lowering of trade barriers (**Chapter 11**).

refugees People who flee for safety to another country because of a well-founded fear of political persecution, environmental degradation, or famine (**Chapter 12**).

regimes Norms, rules, and procedures for interaction agreed to by a set of states (**Chapter 6**).

regional currency union The pooling of sovereignty to create a common currency (such as the EU's euro) and single monetary system for members in a region, regulated by a regional central bank within the currency bloc (**Chapter 10**).

regional trade agreements (RTAs) Treaties that integrate the economies of members through the reduction of trade barriers (**Chapter 11**).

relative burden of military spending Measure of the economic burden of military activities calculated by the share of each state's gross domestic product allocated to military expenditures (**Chapter 8**).

relative deprivation Inequality between the wealth and status of individuals and groups, and the outrage of those at the bottom about their perceived exploitation by those at the top (**Chapter 7**).

relative gains Conditions in which some participants in cooperative interactions benefit more than others (**Chapter 2**).

remittances The money earned by immigrants working in rich countries (which almost always exceeds the income they could earn working in their home country) that they send to their families in their country (**Chapter 5**).

rents Higher-than-normal financial returns on investments that are realized from restrictive governmental interference or monopolistic markets (**Chapter 11**).

replacement-level fertility One couple replacing themselves on average with two children so that a country's population will remain stable if this rate prevails (**Chapter 12**).

reserve currency Currency held in large amounts by governments for the purpose of setting international debts and supporting the value of their national currency (**Chapter 10**).

responsibility to protect Unanimously adopted in a resolution by the UN General Assembly in 2005, this principle holds that the international community must help protect populations from war crimes, ethnic cleansing, genocide, and crimes against humanity (**Chapter 2**).

responsible sovereignty A principle that requires states to protect not only their own people but to cooperate across borders to protect global resources and address transnational threats (**Chapter 6**).

revolution in military technology (RMT) The sophisticated new weapons technologies that make fighting war without mass armies possible (**Chapter 8**).

roles The constraints written into law or custom that predispose decision makers in a particular governmental position to act in a manner and style that is consistent with expectations about how the role is normally performed (**Chapter 3**).

S

sanctuary A place of refuge and protection (**Chapter 12**).

schematic reasoning The process of reasoning by which new information is interpreted according to a memory structure, a schema, which contains a network of generic scripts, metaphors, and simplified characterizations of observed objects and phenomena (**Chapter 1**).

secession, or separatist revolts A religious or ethnic minority's efforts, often by violent means, to gain independent statehood by separating territory from an established sovereign state (**Chapter 6**).

second-strike capability A state's capacity to retaliate after absorbing an adversary's first-strike attack with weapons of mass destruction (**Chapter 8**).

Second World During the Cold War, the group of countries, including the Soviet Union, its (then) Eastern European allies, and China, that embraced communism and central planning to propel economic growth (**Chapter 5**).

security community A group of states whose high level of institutionalized or customary collaboration results in the settlement of disputes by compromise rather than by military force (**Chapter 6**).

security dilemma The tendency of states to view the defensive arming of adversaries as threatening, causing them to arm in response, so that all states' security declines (**Chapter 2**).

selective engagement A great power grand strategy using economic and military power to influence only important particular situations, countries, or global issues by striking a balance between a highly interventionist "global policeman" and an uninvolved isolationist (**Chapter 4**).

self-determination The liberal doctrine that people should be able to determine the government that will rule them (**Chapter 5**).

self-help The principle that because in international anarchy all global actors are independent, they must rely on themselves to provide for their security and well-being (**Chapter 2**).

small powers Countries with limited political, military, or economic capabilities and influence (**Chapter 5**).

smart bombs Precision-guided military technology that enables a bomb to search for its target and detonate at the precise time it can do the most damage (**Chapter 8**).

social constructivism A variant of constructivism that emphasizes the role of social discourse in the development of ideas and identities (**Chapter 2**).

socialization The processes by which people learn to accept the beliefs, values, and behaviors that prevail in a given society's culture (**Chapter 7**).

soft power The capacity to co-opt through such intangible factors as the popularity of a state's values and institutions, as opposed to the "hard power" to coerce through military might (**Chapter 4**).

sovereign equality The principle that states are legally equal in protection under international law (**Chapter 9**).

speculative attacks Massive sales of a country's currency, caused by the anticipation of a future decline in its value (**Chapter 10**).

sphere of influence A region of the globe dominated by a great power (**Chapter 4**).

spiral model A metaphor used to describe the tendency of efforts to enhance defense to result in escalating arms races (**Chapter 9**).

standard operating procedures (SOPs) Rules for reaching decisions about particular types of situations (**Chapter 3**).

standpoint feminism A category of feminism that sees women as experiencing a very different reality from that of men, and consequently holding a different perspective (**Chapter 2**).

state An independent legal entity with a government exercising exclusive control over the territory and population it governs (**Chapter 1**).

state level of analysis An analytical approach that emphasizes how the internal attributes of states influence their foreign policy behaviors (**Chapter 1**).

state sovereignty A state's supreme authority to manage internal affairs and foreign relations (**Chapter 1**).

state-sponsored terrorism Formal assistance, training, and arming of foreign terrorists by a state in order to achieve foreign policy and/or domestic goals (**Chapter 7**).

Strategic Arms Limitation Talks (SALT) Two sets of agreements reached during the 1970s between the United States and the Soviet Union that established limits on strategic nuclear delivery systems (**Chapter 9**).

Strategic Arms Reduction Treaty (START) The U.S.–Russian series of negotiations that began in 1993 and, with the 1997 START-III agreement ratified by Russia in 2000, pledged to cut the nuclear arsenals of both sides by 80 percent of the Cold War peaks, in order to lower the risk of nuclear war (**Chapter 9**).

Strategic Offensive Reductions Treaty (SORT) The U.S.–Russian agreement to reduce the number of strategic warheads to between 1,700 and 2,200 for each country by 2012 (**Chapter 9**).

strategic trade policy Government subsidies for particular domestic industries to help them gain competitive advantages over foreign producers (**Chapter 11**).

structural realism See *neorealism*, (**Chapter 2**).

structuralism The neorealist proposition that states' behavior is shaped primarily by changes in the properties of the global system, such as shifts in the balance of power, instead by individual heads of states or by changes in states' internal characteristics (**Chapter 4**).

survival of the fittest A realist concept derived from Charles Darwin's theory of evolution advising that ruthless competition is ethically acceptable to survive, even if the actions violate moral commands not to kill (**Chapter 7**).

sustainable development Economic growth that does not deplete the resources needed to maintain life and prosperity (**Chapter 14**).

T

tariffs Tax assessed on goods as they are imported into a country (**Chapter 11**).

terrorism Premeditated violence perpetrated against noncombatant targets by subnational or transnational groups or clandestine agents, usually intended to influence an audience (**Chapter 6**).

theocracy A country whose government is organized around a religious dogma (**Chapter 6**).

theory A set of hypotheses postulating the relationship between variables or conditions advanced to describe, explain, or predict phenomena and make prescriptions about how to pursue particular goals and follow ethical principles (**Chapter 2**).

Third Way An approach to governance advocated primarily by many European leaders who, although recognizing few alternatives to liberal capitalism, seek to soften the cruel social impact of free-market individualism by allowing government intervention in order to preserve social justice and prevent the deprivations caused by disruptions in the global economy (**Chapter 6**).

Third World A Cold War term to describe the less-developed countries of Africa, Asia, the Caribbean, and Latin America (**Chapter 5**).

tit-for-tat strategy A bargaining approach that consistently reciprocates in kind the offers or threats made by the other party in a negotiation, with equivalent rewards returned and equivalent punishing communications returned in retaliation (**Chapter 9**).

trade integration The difference between growth rates in trade and gross domestic product (**Chapter 11**).

tragedy of the commons A metaphor, widely used to explain the impact of human behavior on ecological systems, that explains how rational self-interested behavior by individuals may have a destructive and undesirable collective impact (**Chapter 14**).

transformation A change in the characteristic pattern of interaction among the most active participants in world politics of such magnitude that it appears that one "global system" has replaced another (**Chapter 1**).

transgenic crops New crops with improved characteristics created artificially through genetic engineering that combine genes from species that would not naturally interbreed (**Chapter 14**).

transnational relations   Interactions across state boundaries that involves at least one actor that is not the agent of a government or intergovernmental organization **(Chapter 2)**.

transnational religious movements   A set of beliefs, practices, and ideas administered politically by religious organizations to promote the worship of their conception of a transcendent deity and its principles for conduct **(Chapter 6)**.

transparency   With regard to free trade, the principle that barriers to trade must be visible and thus easy to target **(Chapter 11)**.

Truman Doctrine   The declaration by President Harry S. Truman that U.S. foreign policy would use intervention to support peoples who allied with the United States against communist external subjugation **(Chapter 4)**.

two-level games   A concept referring to the growing need for national policy makers to make decisions that will meet both domestic and foreign goals **(Chapter 3)**.

U

unilateralism   An approach to foreign policy that relies on independent, self-help strategies in foreign policy **(Chapter 4)**.

uni-multipolar   A global system where there is a single dominant power, but the settlement of key international issues always requires action by the dominant power in combination with that of other great powers **(Chapter 4)**.

unipolarity   A condition in which the global system has a single dominant power or hegemon **(Chapter 4)**.

unitary actor   A transnational actor (usually a sovereign state) assumed to

be internally united, so that changes in its domestic opinion do not influence its foreign policy as much as do the decisions that actor's leaders make to cope with changes in its global environment **(Chapter 3)**.

V

vertical nuclear proliferation   The expansion of the capabilities of existing nuclear powers to inflict increasing destruction with their nuclear weapons **(Chapter 8)**.

virtuality   Imagery created by computer technology of objects and phenomena that produces an imaginary picture of actual things, people, and experiences **(Chapter 12)**.

voluntary export restrictions (VERs)   A protectionist measure popular in the 1980s and early 1990s, in which exporting countries agree to restrict shipments of a particular product to a country to deter it from imposing an even more burdensome import quota **(Chapter 11)**.

W

war   A condition arising within states (civil war) or between states (interstate war) when actors use violent means to destroy their opponents or coerce them into submission **(Chapter 7)**.

war crimes   Acts performed during war that the international community defines as crimes against humanity, including atrocities committed against an enemy's prisoners of war, civilians, or the state's own minority population **(Chapter 9)**.

war weariness hypothesis   The proposition that fighting a major war is costly in terms of lost lives and income, and these costs greatly reduce a country's tolerance for undertaking

another war until enough time passes to lose memory of those costs **(Chapter 7)**.

world politics   The study of how global actors' activities entail the exercise of influence to achieve and defend their goals and ideals, and how it affects the world at large **(Chapter 1)**.

world-system theory   A body of theory that treats the capitalistic world economy originating in the sixteenth century as an interconnected unit of analysis encompassing the entire globe, with an international division of labor and multiple political centers and cultures whose rules constrain and share the behavior of all transnational actors **(Chapter 2)**.

X

xenophobia   The suspicious dislike, disrespect, and disregard for members of a foreign nationality, ethnic, or linguistic group **(Chapter 12)**.

Y

Yalta Conference   The 1945 summit meeting of the Allied victors to resolve postwar territorial issues and to establish voting procedures in the United Nations to collectively manage world order **(Chapter 4)**.

youth bulge   A burgeoning youth population, thought to make countries more prone to civil conflicts **(Chapter 7)**.

Z

zeitgeist   The "spirit of the times," or the dominant cultural norms assumed to influence the behavior of people living in particular periods **(Chapter 3)**.

zero-sum   An exchange in a purely conflictual relationship in which what is gained by one competitor is lost by the other **(Chapter 2)**.

Aaronson, Susan, and Rodwan Abouharb. (2011) "Unexpected Bedfellows: The GATT, the WTO and *Some* Democratic Rights," *International Studies Quarterly* 55(2): 379–408.

Aaronson, Susan, and Jamie Zimmerman. (2007) *Trade Imbalance: The Struggle to Weigh Human Rights Concerns in Trade Policymaking*. Cambridge: Cambridge University Press.

Abbot, Sebastian. (2012) "Pakistan Tests Missile Days after India's Launch," Associated Press (April 25). Available at: http://news.yahoo.com/pakistan-tests-missile-days-indias-launch-074942245.html.

Abdelal, Rawi, and Adam Segal. (2007) "Has Globalization Passed Its Peak?" *Foreign Affairs* 86 (January/February): 103–114.

Abedine, Saad, Joe Sterling, and Laura Smith-Spark. (2013) "U.N.: More Than 1.5 million Fled Syria, 4 million More Displaced Within Nation," *CNN* (May 18). Accessed June 3, 2013. Available at: http://edition.cnn.com/2013/05/17/world/meast/syria-civil-war/?hpt=hp_t1.

Abouharb, Rodwan, and David Cingranelli. (2007) *Human Rights and Structural Adjustment*. New York: Cambridge University Press.

Abramowitz, Morton. (2002) "The Bush Team Isn't Coping," *International Herald Tribune* (August 20): 6.

Acemoglu, Daron and James A. Robinson. (2012) *Why Nations Fail: The Origins of Power, Prosperity, and Poverty*. New York: Random House.

Ackerly, Brooke and Jacqui True. (2008) "Reflexivity in Practice: Power and Ethics in Feminist Research on International Relations," *International Studies Review* 10: 693–707.

Adams, Gordon, and Matthew Leatherman. (2011) "A Leaner and Meaner Defense: How to Cute the Pentagon's Budget While Improving Its Performance," *Foreign Affairs* 90(1): 139–52.

AFP. (2012) "China Shuts Coke Plant after Chlorine Reports," *AFP* (April 29). Accessed June 25, 2012. Available at: http://www.google.com/hostednews/afp/article/ALeqM5jyi25j7iM5ZD_1EGBEBBflzJyeVg?docId=CNG.dbf0c47a5473a69f8ee5b06a64081dce.21.

Agence France-Presse. (2013) "Report: Taiwan to Aim 50 Medium-Range Missiles at China," *DefenseNews* (March 18). Accessed July 27, 2013. Available at: http://www.defensenews.com/article/20130318/DEFREG03/303180012/Report-Taiwan-Aim-50-Medium-Range-Missiles-China.

Ahmed, Nafeez Mosaddeq. (2013) "Why Food Riots Are Likely to Become the New Normal," *The Guardian* (March 6). Accessed June 25, 2013. Available at: http://www.guardian.co.uk/environment/blog/2013/mar/06/food-riots-new-normal.

Ajami, Fouad. (2010) Review of *The Frugal Superpower* by Michael Mandelbaum. *Foreign Affairs* (1 November).

Alessi, Christopher and Stephanie Hanson. (2012) "Expanding China-Africa Oil Ties," Council of Foreign Relations (February 8). Last accessed November 22, 2013. Available at: http://www.cfr.org/china/expanding-china-africa-oil-ties/p9557.

Ali, Shimelse, Uri Dadush, and Rachel Esplin Odell. (2011) "Is Protectionism Dying?" *International Economics* (May).

Aljazeera. (2011) "Child Slaves," Aljazeera. Accessed June 24, 2013. Available at: http://www.aljazeera.com/programmes/slaverya21stcenturyevil/2011/10/20111010152040468529.html.

Allen, Susan Hannah and David J Lektzian. (2013) "Economic Sanctions: A Blunt Instrument?" *Journal of Peace Research*, 50(1): 121–135.

Allison, Graham T. (2010) "Nuclear Disorder: Surveying Atomic Threats." *Foreign Affairs* 89, no. 1 (January/February): 74–85.

——— (1971) *Essence of Decision: Explaining the Cuban Missile Crisis*. Boston: Little, Brown.

Allison, Graham T., and Philip Zelikow. (1999) *Essence of Decision: Explaining the Cuban Missile Crisis*, 2nd ed. New York: Longman.

Al-Sadig, Ali. (2013) "Outward Foreign Direct Investment and Domestic Investment: The Case of Developing Countries," *IMF Working Paper*. Accessed July 27, 2013. Available at: http://www.imf.org/external/pubs/ft/wp/2013/wp1352.pdf.

Altman, Daniel. (2005) "China: Both a Powerhouse and a Pauper," *International Herald Tribune* (October 8–9): 16.

Altman, Lawrence K. (2002) "AIDS Is Called a Security Threat," *International Herald Tribune* (October 2): 1, 10.

Altman, Roger. (2013) "The Fall and Rise of the West," *Foreign Affairs* (January/February). Accessed June 27, 2013.

Available at: http://www.foreignaffairs.com/articles/138463/roger-c-altman/the-fall-and-rise-of-the-west.

———— (2009) "Globalization in Retreat: Further Geopolitical Consequences of the Financial Crisis." *Foreign Affairs* 88(4): 2–16.

Altman, Roger C., and C. Bowman Cutter. (1999) "Global Economy Needs Better Shock Absorbers," *International Herald Tribune* (June 16): 7.

Amnesty International. (2012) *Death Penalty in 2011.* London: Amnesty International Publications. Available at: http://www.amnesty.org/en/death-penalty/death-sentences-and-executions-in-2011.

———— (2009a) *Death Sentences and Executions in 2008.* London: Amnesty International Publications.

———— (2009b) "Children's Rights: The Future Starts Here" Available at: http://www.amnesty.org/en/library/info/ACT76/014/1999/en.

Amoore, Louise (ed.). (2005) *The Global Resistance Reader: Concepts and Issues.* New York: Routledge.

Anderlini, Sanam N. (2007) *Women Building Peace: What They Do, Why It Matters.* Boulder, CO: Lynne Rienner.

Andersen, Camila. (2009) "New Rules of Engagement for IMF Loans," *IMF Survey Online.* Available at: http://www.voxeu.org/content/collapse-global-trade-murky-protectionism-and-crisis-recommendations-g20.

Anderson, Kym. (1996) "Social Policy Dimensions of Economic Integration: Environmental and Labour Standards," *NBER Working Paper No. 5702.* Cambridge, Mass: National-Bureau for Economic Research.

Andreas, Peter. (2005) "The Criminalizing Consequences of Sanctions," *International Studies Quarterly* 49 (June): 335–60.

Angell, Norman. (1910) *The Grand Illusion: A Study of the Relationship of Military Power in Nations to Their Economic and Social Advantage.* London: Weidenfeld & Nicholson.

Annan, Kofi. (2006) "Courage to Fulfill Our Responsibilities," pp. 205–09 in Helen E. Purkitt (ed.), *World Politics 05/06.* Dubuque, Iowa: McGraw-Hill/Dushkin.

———— (1999) "Two Concepts of Sovereignty," *Economist* (September 18): 49–50.

Appiah, Kwame Anthony. (2006) *Cosmopolitanism: Ethics in a World of Strangers.* New York: Norton.

Ariely, Dan. (2013) *The (Honest) Truth About Dishonesty: How We Lie to Everyone—Especially Ourselves.* New York: Harper.

———— (2010) *The Upside of Irrationality: The Unexpected Benefits of Defying Logic at Work and at Home.* New York: Harper Collins.

———— (2008) *Predictably Irrational: The Hidden Forces That Shape Our Decisions.* New York: Harper.

Arms Control Association. (2013) "Worldwide Ballistic Missile Inventories," *Arms Control Association.* Accessed June 13, 2013. Available at: http://www.armscontrol.org/factsheets/missiles.

Armstrong, David, and Jutta Brunée. (2009) *Routledge Handbook of International Law.* Taylor & Francis.

Arquilla, John. (2010) "The War Issue." *Foreign Policy* (March/April): 61–62.

Arreguín-Toft, Ivan. (2006) *How the Weak Wins Wars: A Theory of Asymmetric Conflict.* New York: Cambridge University Press.

Art, Robert J. (2005) "Coercive Diplomacy," pp. 163–77 in Robert J. Art and Robert Jervis (eds.), *International Politics,* 7th ed. New York: Pearson Longman.

Asbury, Neal. (2013) "The End of Outsourcing?" *The Manzella Report* (May 1). Accessed July 27, 2013. Available at: http://www.manzellareport.com/index.php/manufacturing/658-the-end-of-outsourcing.

Ash, Timothy Garton. (2004) *Free World: America, Europe, and the Surprising Future of the West.* New York: Random House.

Assadourian, Erik. (2010) "Government's Role in Design." *State of the World: Transforming Cultures, From Consumerism to Sustainability.* New York: W. W. Norton & Company.

Associated Press. (2013) "India Flood and Landslide Death Toll Nears 600 as Army Steps up Evacuations," *The Guardian* (June 21). Accessed June 25, 2013. Available at: http://www.guardian.co.uk/world/2013/jun/21/india-floods-uttarakhand-600-deaths.

ATKearney. (2012) "2012 Global Cities Index and Emerging Cities Outlook." Accessed August 8, 2012. Available at: http://www.atkearney.com/index.php/Publications/2012-global-cities-index-and-emerging-cities-outlook.html.

Auboin, Marc. (2009) "Restoring Trade Finance: What the G-20 Can Do." In *The Collapse of Global Trade, Murky Protectionism, and the Crisis: Recommendations for the G20,* Baldwin, Richard and Simon Evenett (eds.), London: VoxEU.org. Available at: http://www.voxeu.org/content/collapse-global-trade-murky-protectionism-and-crisis-recommendations-g20.

Auguste, Byron G. (1999) "What's So New about Globalization?" pp. 45–47 in Helen E. Purkitt (ed.), *World Politics 99/00,* 20th ed. Guilford, Conn.: Dushkin/ McGraw-Hill.

Australian Government Department of Foreign Affairs and Trade. (2012) "Taiwan Brief," Australian Government. Accessed June 25, 2012. Available at: http://www.dfat.gov.au/geo/taiwan/taiwan_brief.html.

Avlon, John. (2011) "The 21st-Century Statesman." *Newsweek.* Available at: http://www.thedailybeast.com/newsweek/2011/02/20/a-21st-century-statesman.html.

Axelrod, Robert M. (1984) *The Evolution of Cooperation.* New York: Basic Books.

Aydin, Aysegul. (2010) "The Deterrent Effects of Economic Integration," *Journal of Peace Research* 47(5): 523–33.

———— and Patrick M. Regan. (2012) "Networks of Third-Party Interveners and Civil War Duration," *European Journal of International Relations* 18 (3): 573–597.

Ayoob, Mohammed. (2004) "Third World Perspectives on Humanitarian Intervention," *Global Governance* 10 (January/March): 99–18.

———— (1995) *The Third World Security Predicament.* Boulder, Colo.: Lynne Rienner.

Babai, Don. (2001) "International Monetary Fund," pp. 412–18 in Joel Krieger (ed.), *The Oxford Companion to Politics of the World*, 2nd ed. Oxford: Oxford University Press.

Babcock, Linda and Sara Laschever. (2003) *Women Don't Ask: Negotiation and the Gender Divide.* Princeton: Princeton University Press.

Babones, Jonathan, and Jonathan H. Turner. (2004) "Global Inequality," pp. 101–20 in George Ritzer (ed.), *Handbook of Social Problems.* London: Sage.

Bacchus, James. (2012) "A Way Forward for the WTO," pp. 6–9 in Ricardo Meléndez-Ortiz, Chistophe Bellmann, and Miguel Rodriguez Mendoza (eds.), *The Future and the WTO: Confronting the Challenges*, edited by [G1]. Geneva, Switzerland: International Centre for Trade and Sustainable Development.

Bacevich, Andrew J. (2005). *The New American Militarism: How Americans Are Seduced by War.* New York: Oxford University Press.

———— (ed.). (2003) *The Imperial Tense.* Chicago: Ivan R. Dee/ Rowman & Littlefield.

———— (2002) *American Empire.* Cambridge, Mass.: Harvard University Press.

Badey, Thomas J. (ed.). (2005) *Violence and Terrorism 05/06*, 8th ed. Guilford, Conn.: Dushkin/McGraw-Hill.

Badwal, Karun. (2012) "Deforestation: A Major Threat to the Des-truction of Our Planet," *Earth Reform* (April 21). Accessed June 25, 2013. Available at: http://earthreform.org/deforestation-a-major-threat-to-the-destruction-of-our-planet/.

Baines, Erin K. (2004) *Vulnerable Bodies: Gender, the UN, and the Global Refugee Crisis.* Burlington, Ver.: Ashgate.

Bajoria, Jayshree. (2011) "Escalation and Uncertainty in Libya." *Council on Foreign Relations.* Available at: http://www.cfr.org/libya/escalation-uncertainty-libya/p24730.

Bakke, Kristen M. (2005) "Clash of Civilizations or Clash of Religions?" *International Studies Review* 7 (March): 87–89.

Baker, Aryn and Kajaki Olya. (2008) "A War That's Still Not Won," *Time* (July 7): 37–43.

Baker, Aryn and Loi Kolay. (2009) "The Longest War," *Time* (April 20): 25–29.

Baker, Peter and Dan Bilefsky. (2010) "Russia and U.S. Sign-Nuclear Arms Reduction Act." *The New York Times* (April 8): A8.

Baldwin, David A. (1999/2000) "The Sanctions Debate and the Logic of Choice," *International Security* 24 (Winter): 80–107.

———— (ed.). (1993) *Neorealism and Neoliberalism: The Contemporary Debate.* New York: Columbia University Press.

———— (1989) *Paradoxes of Power.* New York: Basil Blackwell.

Baldwin, Richard. (2011) 21st Century Regionalism: Filling the Gap between 21st Century Trade and 20th Century Trade Rules. Gevena, Switzerland: World Trade Organization.

———— and Simon Evenett. (2009) "Introduction and Recommendations for the G-20." In Baldwin, Richard and Simon Evenett (eds.) *The Collapse of Global Trade, Murky Protectionism, and the Crisis: Recommendations for the G20,.* London: VoxEU.org. Available at: http://www.voxeu.org/content/collapse-global-trade-murky-protectionism-and-crisis-recommendations-g20.

———— Masahiro Kawai, and Ganeshan Wignaraja, (eds.) (2013) *The Future of the World Trading System: Asian Perspectives.* London, UK: Centre for Economic Policy Research.

Bamford, James. (2005) *A Pretext for War: 9/11, Iraq, and the Abuse of America's Intelligence Agencies.* New York: Anchor Vintage.

Bandy, Joe, and Jackie Smith. (2004). *Coalitions Across Borders: Transnational Protest and the Neoliberal Order.* Lanham, Md: Rowman & Littlefield.

Banerjee, Abhijit, and Esther Duflo. (2011) "More Than 1 Billion People Are Hungry in the Word: But What If the Experts Are Wrong?" *Foreign Policy* (May/June): 66–72.

Bank for International Settlements (BIS). (2012) *Semiannual OTC Derivatives Statistics.* Available at: http://www.bis.org/statistic/derstats.htm.

Bapat, Navin A. (2011) "Transnational Terrorism, US Military Aid, and the Incentive to Misrepresent." *Journal of Peace Research* 48 (3): 202–18.

———— and T. Clifton Morgan. (2009) "Multilateral versus Unilateral Sanctions Reconsidered: A Test Using New Data," *International Studies Quarterly* 53 (4): 1468–2478.

———— Tobias Heinrich, Yoshiharu Kobayashi, and T. Clifton Morgan. (2013) "Determinants of Sanctions Effectiveness: Sensitivity Analysis Using New Data," *International Interactions: Empirical and Theoretical Research in International Relations*, 39(1): 79–98.

Baratta, Joseph Preston. (2005) *The Politics of World Federation.* New York: Praeger.

Barber, Benjamin R. (2003) *Fear's Empire.* New York: Norton.

———— (1995) *Jihad vs. McWorld.* New York: Random House.

Barbieri, Katherine. (2003) *The Liberal Illusion: Does Trade Promote Peace?* Ann Arbor: University of Michigan Press.

Barbieri, Katherine, and Gerald Schneider. (1999) "Globalization and Peace," *Journal of Peace Research* 36 (July): 387–404.

Barboza, David. (2005) "For China, New Malls Jaw-Dropping in Size," *International Herald Tribune* (May 25): 1, 4.

Bardhan, Pranab. (2005) "Giants Unchained? Not So Fast," *International Herald Tribune* (November 3): 6.

Barkin, Samuel. (2003) "Realist Constructivism," *International Studies Review* 5 (September): 328–42.

——— (2001) "Resilience of the State," *Harvard International Review* 22 (Winter): 40–46.

Barnes, Joe, Amy Jaffe, and Edward L. Morse. (2004) "The New Geopolitics of Oil," *National Interest* (Winter/Energy Supplement): 3–6.

Barnet, Michael. (2005) "Social Constructivism," pp. 251–270 in John Baylis and Steve Smith (eds.), *The Globalization of World Politics*, 3rd ed. New York: Oxford University Press.

Barnet, Richard J. (1980) *The Lean Years.* New York: Simon & Schuster.

——— (1977) *The Giants: Russia and America.* New York: Simon & Schuster.

Barnet, Richard J. and John Cavanagh. (1994) *Global Dreams: Imperial Corporations and the New World Order.* New York: Simon & Schuster.

Barnet, Richard J. and Ronald E. Müller. (1974) *Global Reach: The Power of the Multinational Corporations.* New York: Simon & Schuster.

Barnett, Michael. (2005) "Social Constructivism," pp. 251–70 in John Baylis and Steve Smith (eds.), *The Globalization of World Politics*, 3rd ed. New York: Oxford University Press.

Barnett, Thomas P. M. (2004) *The Pentagon's New Map.* New York: G. P. Putnam's Sons.

Bar-On, Tamir and Howard Goldstein. (2005) "Fighting Violence: A Critique of the War on Terrorism," *International Politics* 42 (June): 225–45.

Baron, Samuel H., and Carl Pletsch (eds.). (1985) *Introspection in Biography.* Hillsdale, N.J.: Analytic Press.

Barratt, Bethany. (2007) *Human Rights and Foreign Aid: For Love or Money?* New York: Routledge.

Barringer, Felicity. (2009) "Cool Roofs Offer a Tool in Fight against Global Heat," *International Herald Tribune* (July 29): 1.

Barrett, Scott. (2007) *Why Cooperate? The Incentive to Supply Global Public Goods.* New York: Oxford University Press.

Barry, Colin M., K. Chad Clay, and Michael E. Flynn. (2012) "Avoiding the Spotlight: Human Rights Shaming and Foreign Direct Investment," *International Studies Quarterly.* DOI: 10.1111/isqu.12039.

Bast, Andrew. (2011) "Pakistans' Nuclear Surge," *Newsweek* (May 23): 45–46.

Bates, B.C., Z.W. Kundzewicz, S. Wu, and J.P. Palutikof, (eds.) (2008) *Climate Change and Water*, Technical Paper of the Intergovernmental Panel on Climate Change, IPCC Secretariat, Geneva, 210 pp.

Battelle and R&D Magazine. (2012) "2013 Global R & D Funding Forecast," Battelle and *R & D Magazine.* Accessed May 29, 2013. Available at: http://www.battelle.org/docs/r-d-funding-forecast/2013_r_d_funding_forecast.pdf?sfvrsn=0.

——— (2008) "2009 Global R&D Funding Forecast," Battelle and *R&D Magazine.* Available at: http://www.battelle.org/news/pdfs/2009RDFundingfinalreport.pdf.

Baylis, John, and Steve Smith (eds.). (2005) *The Globalization of World Politics*, 3rd ed. New York: Oxford University Press.

Bayne, Nicholas, and Stephen Woolcock (eds.). (2004) *The New Economic Diplomacy.* Burlington, Ver.: Ashgate.

BBC. (2010) "Historic Taiwan-China Trade Deal Takes Effect."Available at: http://www.bbc.co.uk/news/world-asia--pacific-11275274 (September 12).

Beattie, Alan. (2011) "Watchdog Says IMF Missed Crisis Risks," *Financial Times* (February 9). Available at: http://www.ft.com/intl/cms/s/0/59421568-344e-11e0-993f-00144feabdc0.html#axzz1V7p2MKKP.

——— and Jean Eaglesham. (2009) "Still No Deadline for Doha Accord," *Financial Times* (April 2).

Becker, Elizabeth. (2003) "WTO. Rules against U.S. on Steel Tariff," *The New York Times* (March 27).

Beckman, Peter R., and Francine D'Amico (eds.). (1994) *Women, Gender, and World Politics.* Westport, Conn.: Bergin & Garvey.

——— (2005) "The Great Thrift Shift," *Economist* (September 24): 3.

Begley, Sharon. (2011) "I Can't Think!: The Twitterization of Our Culture Has Revolutionized Our Lives, but with an Unintended Consequence—Our Overloaded Brains Freeze When We Have to Make Decisions," *Newsweek* (March 7): 28–33.

——— (2010) "What the Spill Will Kill." *Newsweek* (June 14): 25–30.

——— (2009) "Climate-Change Calculus: Why It's Even Sores Than We Feared," *Newsweek* (August 3): 30.

——— (2009b) "Good Cop/Bad Cop Goes Green," *Newsweek* (May 4): 49.

——— (2008) "Global Warming Is a Cause of This Year's Extreme Weather," *Newsweek* (July 7/14): 53.

——— (2007) "Get Out Your Handkerchiefs," *Newsweek* (June 4): 62.

Behe, Michael J. (2005) "Rationalism and Reform," *First Things* (August/September): 75–79.

Beitz, Charles R. (2001) "Human Rights as a Common Concern," *American Political Science Review* 95 (June): 269–82.

Bell, James John. (2006) "Exploring the 'Singularity'," pp. 207–10 in Robert M. Jackson (ed.), *Global Issues 05/06.* Dubuque, Iowa: McGraw-Hill/Dushkin.

Bellamy, Alex J. and Paul D. Williams. (2005) "Who's Keeping the Peace?" *International Security* 29 (Spring): 157–97.

Benhabib, Seyla. (2005) "On the Alleged Conflict Between Democracy and International Law," *Ethics and International Affairs* 19(1): 85–100.

Benner, Thorsten, Stephan Mergenthaler, and Philipp Rotman. (2008) "Rescuing the Blue Helmets," *International Herald Tribune* (July 23): 6.

Bennett, Scott and Allan C. Stam. (2004) *The Behavioral Origins of War.* Ann Arbor: University of Michigan Press.

Benson, Michelle. (2007) "Extending the Bounds of Power Transition Theory," *International Interactions* 33 (July/September): 211–15.

Ben-Yehuda, Hemda and Meirav Mishali-Ran. (2006) "Ethnic Actors and International Crises," *International Interactions* 32 (January/March): 49–78.

Bercovitch, Jacob and Scott Sigmund Gartner. (2008) *International Conflict Mediation*. New York: Routledge.

Berdal, Mats and Mónica Serrano (eds.). (2002) *Transnational Organized Crime and International Security*. Boulder, Colo.: Lynne Rienner.

Bergen, Peter L. (2006) *The Osama bin Laden I Know*. New York: Free Press.

———— and Samuel P. Huntington (eds.). (2002) *Many Globalizations: Cultural Diversity in the Contemporary World*. Oxford: Oxford University Press.

Bergesen, Albert and Ronald Schoenberg. (1980) "Long Waves of Colonial Expansion and Contraction, 1415–1969," pp. 231–77 in Albert Bergesen (ed.), *Studies of the Modern World-System*. New York: Academic Press.

Bergholt, Drago and Paivi Lujala. (2012) "Climate-Related Natural Disasters, Economic Growth, and Armed Civil Conflict," *Journal of Peace Research* (49): 147–62.

Bergsten, C. Fred. (2009) "The Global Crisis and the International Economic Position of the United States," pp. 1–10 of *The Long-Term International Economic Position of the United States*, edited by Fred Bergsten. Washington, DC: Petersen Institute for International Economics.

———— (2005) *The United States and the World Economy*. Washington, DC.: Institute of International Economics.

———— (2004) "The Risks Ahead for the World Economy," *Economist* (September 11): 63–65.

Bernstein, Jeremy. (2010) "Nukes for Sale." *The New York Review* (May 13): 44–46.

Bernstein, Richard. (2003) "Aging Europe Finds Its Pension Is Running Out," *New York Times International* (June 29): 3.

Berthelot, Yves. (2001) "The International Financial Architecture—Plans for Reform," *International Social Science Journal* 170 (December): 586–96.

Bhagwati, Jagdish. (2008a) *Termites in the Trading System: How Preferential Agreements Undermine Free Trade*. New York: Oxford University Press.

———— (2008b) *In Defense of Globalization*. New York: Oxford University Press.

———— (2005) "A Chance to Lift the 'Aid Curse,'" *Wall Street Journal* (March 22): A14.

———— (2004) *In Defense of Globalization*. New York: Oxford University Press.

Bhatia, Ujal Singh. (2011) "Salvaging Doha," VoxEU.org (May 10). Available at: http://voxeu.org/index.php?q5node/6497.

Bijian, Zheng. (2005) "China's 'Peaceful Rise' to Great-Power Status," *Foreign Affairs* 84 (October): 18–24.

Bishop, William. (1962) *International Law*. Boston Little, Brown.

Bjerga, Alan. (2010) "Broadband Trumps Farmer Payments in Rural Aid." *Bloomberg*. Available at: http://www.bloomberg.com/news/2010-08-26/broadband-trumps-farmer-payments-as-obama-remakes-assistance-to-rural-u-s-.html.

Blackmon, Pamela. (2008) "Rethinking Poverty Through the Eyes of the International Monetary Fund and the World Bank." *International Studies Review* 10 (2): 179–202.

Blanton, Robert G. (2012) "Zombies and International Relations: A Simple Guide for Bringing the Undead into Your Classroom," *International Studies Perspectives* (14): 1–13.

Blanton, Robert G. and Shannon Lindsey Blanton. (2012a) "Rights, Institutions, and Foreign Direct Investment: An Empirical Assessment," *Foreign Policy Analysis* 8(4): 431–452.

———— (2012b) "Labor Rights and Foreign Direct Investment: Is There a Race to the Bottom?" *International Interactions* 38(3): 267–294.

———— (2009) "A Sectoral Analysis of Human Rights and FDI: Does Industry Type Matter?" *International Studies Quarterly* 53(2): 473–498.

———— (2008) "Virtuous or Vicious Cycle? Human Rights, Trade, and Development," pp. 91–103 in Rafael Reuveny and William R. Thompson (eds.), *North and South in the World Political Economy*. Malden, MA: Blackwell.

———— (2007) "Human Rights and Trade," *International Interactions* 33 (April/June): 97–117.

———— (2001) "Democracy, Human Rights, and U.S.-Africa Trade," *International Interactions* 27(2): 275–95.

Blanton, Shannon Lindsey. (2005) "Foreign Policy in Transition? Human Rights, Democracy, and U.S. Arms Exports," *International Studies Quarterly* 49 (December): 647–67.

———— (1999) "Instruments of Security or Tools of Repression? Arms Imports and Human Rights Conditions in Developing Countries," *Journal of Peace Research* 36 (March): 233–44.

Blanton, Shannon Lindsey and David L. Cingranelli. (2010) "Human Rights and Foreign Policy Analysis," in Robert Denmark et al. (eds.), *The International Studies Compendium Project*. Oxford: Wiley-Blackwell.

Blanton, Shannon Lindsey and Katharine Andersen Nelson. (2012). "Arms Transfers," in George Ritzer (ed.), *Encyclopedia of Globalization*. Oxford: Wiley-Blackwell.

Blanton, Shannon Lindsey and Robert G. Blanton. (2007) "What Attracts Foreign Investors? An Examination of Human Rights and Foreign Direct Investment," *Journal of Politics* 69 (1): 143–55.

Blanton, Shannon Lindsey and Charles W. Kegley, Jr. (1997) "Reconciling U.S. Arms Sales with America's Interests and Ideals," *Futures Research Quarterly* 13 (Spring): 85–101.

Blas, Lorena. (2013) "Angelina Jolie Visits Africa on a Mission to Fight Rape," *USA Today* (March 26). Accessed June 3, 2013. Available at: http://www.usatoday.com/story/life/people/2013/03/25/jolie-congo-rwanda-ape-war-weapon/2018539/.

Bloom, Mia. (2005) *Dying to Kill: The Allure of Suicide Terror.* New York: Columbia University Press.

Bloomberg News. (2011) "Vietnam Cheaper-than-China Appeal Diminishes as Labor Strikes." Available at: http://www.bloomberg.com/news/2011-06-15/vietnam-cheaper-than-china-appeal-diminshes-as-labor-strikes.html (June 15).

Blum, Andrew, Victor Asal, and Jonathan Wilkenfeld (eds.). (2005) "Nonstate Actors, Terrorism, and Weapons of Mass Destruction," *International Studies Review* 7 (March): 133–70.

Blustein, Paul. (2010) "R.I.P., WTO." *Foreign Policy* (January/February): 66.

Boehmer, Charles and Timothy Nordstrom. (2008) "Intergovernmental Organization Memberships: Examining Political Community and the Attributes of International Organizations," *International Interactions* 34: 282–309.

Boehmer, Charles, Erik Gartzke, and Timothy Norstrom. (2005) "Do International Organizations Promote Peace?" *World Politics* 57 (October): 1–38.

Boin, Arjen, Paul't Hart, Eric Stern, and Bengt Sunderlius. (2007) *The Politics of Crisis Management.* Cambridge, U.K.: Cambridge University Press.

Boli, John, and Frank L. Lechner. (2004) *World Culture.* London: Blackwell.

Boli, John, Michael A. Elliott and Franziska Bieri. (2004) "Globalization," pp. 389–415 in George Ritzer (ed.), *Handbook of Social Problems.* London: Sage.

Bollyky, Thomas. (2012) "Reinventing the World Health Organization," *Council on Foreign Relations* (March 23). Accessed August 8, 2012. Available at: http://www.cfr.org/global-health/reinventing-world-health-organization/p28346.

Bolton, M. Kent. (2005) *U.S. Foreign Policy and International Politics: George W. Bush, 9/11, and the Global-Terrorist Hydra.* Upper Saddle River, N.J.: Prentice Hall.

Bolzendahl, Catherine. (2009) "Making the Implicit Explicit: Gender Influences on Social Spending in Twelve Industrialized Democracies, 1980–1999," *Social Politics* 16: 40–81.

Boot, Max. (2013) "The Evolution of Irregular War: Insurgents and Guerrillas from Akkadia to Afghanistan," *Foreign Affairs* (March/April). Accessed June 3, 2013. Available at: http://www.foreignaffairs.com/articles/138824/max-boot/the-evolution-of-irregular-war#.

——— (2006) *War Made New.* New York: Gothan.

Borenstein, Seth. (2006) "Pentagon Accused of Wasteful Spending," *The Idaho Statesman* (January 24): Main 3.

——— (2005) "Mankind Is Using Up the Earth, Scientists Say," Columbia, S.C., *The State* (March 30): A8.

——— (2003) "U.S. to Revive Dormant Nuclear-Power Industry," Columbia, S.C., *The State* (June 16): A5.

Borer, Douglas A., and James D. Bowen. (2007) "Rethinking the Cuban Embargo," *Foreign Policy Analysis* 3 (April): 127–43.

Borgerson, Scott G. (2008) "Arctic Meltdown: The Economic and Security Implications of Global Warming," *Foreign Affairs* 87 (2): 63–77.

Borrows, Mathew and Jennifer Harris. (2009) "Revisiting the Future: Geopolitical Effects of the Financial Crisis," *Washington Quarterly* 32 (2): 37–48.

Bosco, David. (2011) "Dreaming of SDRs," *Foreign Policy.* Available at: http://www.foreignpolicy.com/articles/2011/09/07/dreaming_of_sdrs?page=0,0 (September 7). Last accessed November 22, 2013.

Boswell, Terry. (1989) "Colonial Empires and the Capitalist World-Economy," *American Sociological Review* 54 (April): 180–96.

Boyer, Mark A., Brian Urlacher, Natalie Florea Hudson, Anat Niv-Solomon, Laura L. Janik, Michael Butler, and Andri Ioannou. (2009) "Gender and Negotiation: Some Experimental Findings from an International Negotiation Simulation." *International Studies Quarterly* 53 (1): 23–47.

Boyle, Francis A. (2004) *Destroying World Order.* London: Clarity/Zed.

Bradsher, Keith. (2009) "China Gearing Up in Crisis to Emerge Even Stronger," *International Herald Tribune* (March 17): 1, 12.

Brainard, Lael, Abigail Jones, and Nigel Purvis, (eds.) (2009) *Climate Change and Global Poverty.* Washington, D.C.: Brookings Institution Press.

Branigan, Tania. (2012) "China's First Female Astronaut Shows How 'Women Hold Up Half the Sky,'" *The Guardian* (16 June). Accessed September 5, 2012. Available at: www.guardian.co.uk/world/2012/jun/17/china-woman-space-liu-yang.

Brams, Steven J. (1985) *Rational Politics: Decisions, Games, and Strategy.* Washington, D.C.: CQ Press.

Braudel, Fernand. (1973) *The Mediterranean and the Mediterranean World at the Age of Philip II.* New York: Harper.

Braveboy-Wagner, Jacqueline Anne (ed.). (2003) *The Foreign Policies of the Global South.* Boulder, Colo.: Lynne Rienner.

Breitmeier, Helmut. (2005) *The Legitimacy of International Regimes.* Burlington, Ver.: Ashgate.

Bremer, Ian. (2007) *The J Curve: A New Way to Understand Why Nations Rise and Fall.* New York: Simon and Schuster.

Bremer, Stuart A. (2000) "Who Fights Whom, When, Where, and Why?" pp. 23–36 in John A. Vasquez (ed.), *What Do We Know About War?* Lanham, Md.: Rowman & Littlefield.

Bremmer, Ian, and Nouriel Roubini. "A G-Zero World." Available at: http://www.americanfuture.net/journal-articles/foreign-affairs/2011-03-ian-bremmer-and-nouriel-roubini-a-g-zero-world/.

Breuning, Marike. (2007) *Foreign Policy Analysis: A Comparative Introduction.* New York: Palgrave Macmillan.

Bresnitz, Dan and John Zysman. (2013) *The Third Globalization: Can Wealthy Nations Stay Rich in the Twenty-First Century?* Oxford: Oxford University Press.

Brinkley, Joel. (2005) "As Nations Lobby to Join Security Council, U.S. Resists Giving Them Veto Power," *New York Times International* (May 15): 12.

Broad, Robin (ed.). (2002) *Global Backlash: Citizen Initiatives for a Just World Economy*. Lanham, Md.: Rowman & Littlefield.

Broad, William J. (2005) "U.S. Has Plans to Again Make Own Plutonium," *New York Times* (June 27): A1, A13.

Brody, William R. (2007) "College Goes Global," *Foreign Affairs* 56 (March/April): 122–133.

Bromley, Daniel, and Glen Anderson. (2013) *Vulnerable People, Vulnerable States: Redefining the Development Challenge*. London, UK: Routledge.

Bronfenbrenner, Urie. (1961) "The Mirror Image in Soviet-American Relations," *Journal of Social Issues* 17 (3): 45–56.

Brooks, David. (2007) "The Entitlements People," Columbia, S.C., *The State* (October 2): A7.

——— (2005a) "Hunch Power," *New York Times Book Review* (January 16): 1, 12–13.

——— (2005b) "Our Better Understanding of Who the Terrorists Are," Columbia, S.C., *The State* (August 6): A11.

Brooks, Doug, and Gaurav Laroia. (2005) "Privatized Peacekeeping," *The National Interest* 80 (Summer): 121–25.

Brown, John. (2006) "Beyond Kyoto," pp. 209–13 in Helen E. Purkitt (ed.), *World Politics 05/06*. Dubuque, Iowa: McGraw-Hill/Dushkin.

Brown, Justin. (1999) "Arms Sales: Exporting U.S. Military Edge?" *Christian Science Monitor* (December 2): 2.

Brown, Lester R. (2012) *Full Planet, Empty Plates: The New Geopolitics of Food Scarcity*. New York, NY: W. W. Norton & Company.

——— and Brian Halweil. (1999) "How Can the World Create Enough Jobs for Everyone?" *International Herald Journal* (September 9): 9.

Brunk, Darren C. (2008) "Curing the Somalia Syndrome: Analogy, Foreign Policy Decision Making, and the Rwandan Genocide," *Foreign Policy Analysis* 4 (July): 301–20.

Brysk, Alison and Austin Choi-Fitzpatrick, (eds.) (2012) *From Human Trafficking to Human Rights: Reframing Contemporary Slavery*. Philadelphia, PA: University of Pennsylvania Press.

Brysk, Alison. (2009) *Global Good Samaritans: Human Rights as Foreign Policy*. Oxford: Oxford University Press.

Brzezinski, Zbigniew. (2010) "From Hope to Audacity: Appraising Obama's Foreign Policy." *Foreign Affairs* 89, no. 1 (January/February): 16–30.

——— (2005) "George W. Bush's Suicidal Statecraft," *International Herald Tribune* (October 14): 6.

——— (2004) *The Choice: Global Domination or Global Leadership*. New York: Basic Books/Perseus.

Bueno de Mesquita, Bruce. (2009) *The Predictioneer's Game: Using the Logic of Brazen Self-Interest to See & Shape the Future*. New York: Random House.

Bugaric, Bojan. (2013) "Europe against the Left? On Legal Limits to Progressive Politics," *LSA 'Europe in Question' Discussion Paper Series* (May). Accessed June 27, 2013. Available at: http://www.lse.ac.uk/europeanInstitute/LEQS/LEQSPaper61.pdf.

Burdeau, Cain, and Harry R. Weber. (2011) "BP Sues Partners as Gulf Marks Year Since Spill," *Associated Press* (April 21). Available at http://www.washingtontimes.com/news/2011/apr/21/bp-sues-partners-gulf-marks-year-spill/.

Buruma, Ian. (2005) "The Indiscreet Charm of Tyranny," *New York Review of Books* 52 (May 12): 35–37.

Bush, Richard. (2011) "Taiwan and East Asian Security," *Orbis* 55(2): 274–89.

Bussmann, Margit, and Gerald Schneider. (2007) "When Globalization Discontent Turns Violent: Foreign Economic Liberalization and Internal War," *International Studies Quarterly* 51 (March): 79–97.

Butt, Yousaf. (2011) "Billions for Missile Defense, Not a Dime for Common Sense: At a Time of Tight Budgets, Doubling Down on a Risky, Easily Foiled Technology Is More Foolish Than Ever," *Foreign Policy* (June 10). Available at: http://www.foreignpolicy.com/articles/2011/06/10/billions_for_missile_defense_not_a_dime_for_common_sense?page50,1

Buzan, Barry. (2005) "The Dangerous Complacency of Democratic Peace," *International Studies Review* 7 (June): 292–93.

——— (2004) *From International to World Society? English School Theory and the Social Structure of Globalization*. Cambridge, UK: Cambride University Press.

——— and Gerald Segal. (1998) *Anticipating the Future*. London: Simon & Schuster.

——— and Ole Weaver. (2003) *Regimes of Power*. Cambridge: Cambridge University Press.

Byers, Michael and George Nolte (eds.). (2003) *United States Hegemony and the Foundations of International Law*. New York: Columbia University Press.

Byman, Daniel. (2005) *Deadly Connections: States That Sponsor Terrorism*. Cambridge: Cambridge University Press.

Byrne, Andrew. (2013) " Conflicting Visions: Liberal and Realist Conceptualisations of Transatlantic Alignment," *Transworld* (March). Accessed June 13, 2013. Available at: http://www.iai.it/pdf/Transworld/TW_WP_12.pdf.

Caldwell, Christopher. (2004) "Select All: Can You Have Too Many Choices?" *New Yorker* (March): 91–93.

Caldwell, Dan and Robert E. Williams, Jr. (2006) *Seeking Security in an Insecure World*. Lanham, Md.: Rowman & Littlefield.

Calvocoressi, Peter, Guy Wint, and John Pritchard. (1989) *Total War: The Causes and Courses of the Second World War*, 2nd ed. New York: Pantheon.

Campbell, Ian. (2004) "Retreat from Globalization," *National Interest* 75 (Spring): 111–17.

Canetti-Nisim, Daphna, Eran Halperin, Keren Sharvit, and Stevan E. Hobfoll. (2009) "A New Stress-Based Model of

Political Extremism: Personal Exposure to Terrorism, Psychological Distress, and Exclusionist Political Attitudes." *Journal of Conflict Resolution* 53 (3): 363–89.

Canton, James. (2007) *The Extreme Future*. New York Penguin.

Capaccio, Tony. (2013) "China's Anti-Carrier Missile Now Opposite Taiwan, Flynn Says," Bloomberg (April 18). Accessed July 27, 2013. Available at: http://www.bloomberg.com/news/2013-04-18/china-s-anti-carrier-missile-now-opposite-taiwan-flynn-says.html.

Caporaso, James A. (1993) "Global Political Economy," pp. 451–481 in Ada W. Finifter (ed.), *Political Science: The State of the Discipline II*. Washington, D.C.: American Political Science Association.

Caprioli, Mary. (2005) "Primed for Violence: The Role of Gender Inequality in Predicting International Conflict," *International Studies Quarterly* 49 (June): 161–78.

——— (2004) "Feminist IR Theory and Quantitative Methodology," *International Studies Review* 6 (June): 253–69.

Carr, E. H. (1939) *The Twenty-Years' Crisis, 1919–1939*. London: Macmillan.

Carter, Jimmy. (2005) *Our Endangered Values: America's Moral Crisis*. New York: Simon and Schuster.

Carty, Anthony. (2008) "Marxist International Law Theory as Hegelianism," *International Studies Review* 10 (March): 122–125.

Caryl, Christian. (2009) "1979: The Great Backlash." *Foreign Policy* (July/August): 50–64.

——— (2005) "Why They Do It," *New York Review of Books* 52 (September 22): 28–32.

Casetti, Emilio. (2003) "Power Shifts and Economic Development: When Will China Overtake the USA?" *Journal of Peace Research* 40 (November): 661–75.

Cashman, Greg and Leonard C. Robinson. (2007) *An Introduction to the Causes of War*. Lanham, Md.: Rowman & Littlefield.

Caspary, William R. (1993) "New Psychoanalytic Perspectives on the Causes of War," *Political Psychology* 14 (September): 417–46.

Cassese, Antonio and Andrew Clapham. (2001) "International Law," pp. 408–11 in Joel Krieger (ed.), *The Oxford Companion to Politics of the World,* 2nd ed. Oxford: Oxford University Press.

Cassidy, John. (2005) "Always with US?" *New Yorker* (April 11): 72–77.

Cassis, Youssef. (2007) *Capitals of Capital*. New York: Cambridge University Press.

Castles, Stephen, Mark J. Miller; Guiseppe Ammendola. (2003) *The Age of Migration: International Population Movements in the Modern World*. New York: The Guilford Press.

Castles, Stephen and Mark Miller. (2004) *The Age of Migration*, 3rd ed. London: Palgrave Macmillan.

Cavallo, Alfred. (2004) "Oil: The Illusion of Plenty," *Bulletin of the Atomic Scientists* (January/February): 20–22, 70.

CCEIA (Carnegie Council for Ethics in International Affairs). (2005) *Human Rights Dialogue*. Carnegie Council for Ethics in International Affairs, Series 2 (Spring) 1–34.

Cederman, Lars-Erik and Kristian Skrede Gleditsch. (2004) "Conquest and Regime Change," *International Studies Quarterly* 48 (September): 603–29.

Center for World Indigenous Studies. (2005) *The State of Indigenous People*. Olympia, Wash.: Center for World Indigenous Studies.

Central Intelligence Agency. (2012) *The World Factbook*. Available at: http://www.cia.gov/library/publications/the-world-factbook/.

——— (2010) *The World Factbook*. Available at https://www.cia.gov/library/publications/the-world-factbook/geos/us.html.

——— (2002) *Global Trends 2015*. Washington, D.C.: Central Intelligence Agency.

——— (2001) *Handbook of International Economic Statistics 2000*. Langley, Va.: Central Intelligence Agency.

CGD/FP (Center for Global Development/Foreign Policy). (2005) "Ranking the Rich," *Foreign Policy* (September/ October): 76–83.

Chaliand, Gérald, and Jean-Pierre Rageau. (1993) *Strategic Atlas*, 3rd ed. New York: Harper Perennial.

Chant, Sylvia and Cathy McIlwaine. (2009) *Geographies of Development in the 21st Century: An Introduction to the Global South*. Edward Elgar Publishing.

Chapman, Dennis. (2005) "US Hegemony in Latin America and Beyond," *International Studies Review* 7 (June): 317–19.

Chapman, Terrence and Scott Wolford. (2010) "International Organizations, Strategy, and Crisis Bargaining." *The Journal of Politics* 72, no. 1 (January): 227–42.

Charette, Robert N. (2008) "What's Wrong with Weapons Acquisitions?" IEEE Spectrum Special Report. Available at: http://www.spectrum.ieee.org/aerospace/military/whats-wrong-with-weapons-acquisitions/0

Chase-Dunn, Christopher and E. N. Anderson (eds.). (2005) *The Historical Evolution of World-Systems*. London: Palgrave.

Chauffour, Jean-Pierre and Mariem Malouch. (2011) *Trade Finance During the Great Trade Collapse*. Washington, DC: World Bank.

Chen, Lincoln, Jennifer Leaning, and Vasant Narasimhan (eds.). (2003). *Global Health Challenges for Human Security*. Cambridge, Mass.: Harvard University Press.

Chernoff, Fred. (2008) *Theory and Metatheory in International Relations*. London: Palgrave Macmillan.

——— (2004) "The Study of Democratic Peace and Progress in International Relations," *International Studies Review* 6: 49–77.

Chesterman, Simon (ed.). (2007) *Secretary or General?: The UN Secretary-General in World Politics*. New York: Cambridge University Press.

———, Michael Ignatieff, and Ramesh Thakur (eds.). (2005) *Making States Work: State Failure and the Crisis of Governance*. Tokyo: United Nations University Press.

China Post. (2010) "China may up missiles aimed at Taiwan to 1,900." Available at: http://www.chinapost.com.tw/taiwan/china-taiwan-relations/2010/07/22/265570/China-may.htm (July 22).

Chinn, Menzie, and Jeffry Freiden. (2011) *Lost Decades: The Making of America's Debt Crisis and the Long Recovery.* New York: W.W. Norton & Company.

Choi, Ajin. (2004) "Democratic Synergy and Victory in Wars, 1816–1992," *International Studies Quarterly* 48 (September): 663–82.

Choi, Seung-Whan, and Patrick James. (2005) *Civil–Military Dynamics, Democracy, and International Conflict.* New York: Palgrave Macmillan.

Chomsky, Noam. (2004) *Hegemony or Survival: America's Quest for Global Dominance.* New York: Metropolitan Books/Henry Holt.

Chua, Amy. (2008) *Day of Empire: How Hyperpowers Rise to Global Dominance—and Why They Fail.* New York: Doubleday.

Chuluv, Martin. (2010) "Iraq Violence Set to Delay US Troop Withdrawl." *Guardian* (May 12). Available at http://www.guardian.co.uk/world/2010/may/12/iraq-us-troop-withdrawal-delay.

CIA. (2013) *The World Factbook.* Central Intelligence Agency. Accessed June 27, 2013. Available at: https://www.cia.gov/library/publications/the-world-factbook/.

Cincotta, Richard P. and Robert Engelman. (2004) "Conflict Thrives Where Young Men Are Many," *International Herald Tribune* (March): 18.

Cirincione, Joseph. (2008) "The Incredible Shrinking Missile Threat," *Foreign Policy* (May/June): 68–70.

Clapham, Andrew. (2001) "Human Rights," pp. 368–70 in Joel Krieger (ed.), *The Oxford Companion to Politics of the World*, 2nd ed. New York: Oxford University Press.

Clark, Gregory. (2008) *A Farewell to Alms: A Brief Economic History of the World.* Princeton, N.J.: Princeton University Press.

Clark, Ian and Christian Reus-Smit. (2007) "Preface," *International Politics* 44 (March/May): 153–56.

Clarke, Michael. (2013) "Pakistan and Nuclear Terrorism: How Real Is the Threat?" *Comparative Strategy* 32 (2): 98–114.

Clarke, Richard A. (2004) *Against All Enemies.* New York: Simon & Schuster.

———— and Robert Knake. (2010) *Cyber War: The Next Threat to National Security and What to Do About It.* New York: HarperCollins.

Claude, Inis L., Jr. (1989) "The Balance of Power Revisited," *Review of International Studies* 15 (January): 77–85.

———— (1967) *The Changing United Nations.* New York: Random House.

———— (1962) *Power and International Relations.* New York: Random House.

Clemens, Michael A. (2007) "Smart Samaritans," *Foreign Affairs* (September/October): 132–40.

Cline, William. (2004) *Trade Policy and Global Poverty.* Washington D.C.: Institute for International Economics.

Clover, Charles, Robin Harding, and Alice Ross. (2013) "G20 Agrees to Avoid Currency Wars," *Financial Times* (February 17). Accessed June 27, 2013. Available at: http://www.ft.com/intl/cms/s/0/789439ae-784f-11e2-8a97-00144feabdc0.html#axzz2XRhfLrrQ.

Cobb, Roger, and Charles Elder. (1970) *International Community.* New York: Harcourt, Brace & World.

Cohen, Benjamin J. (ed.). (2005) *International Political Economy.* Burlington, Ver.: Ashgate.

———— (1973) *The Question of Imperialism.* New York: Basic Books.

Cohen, Daniel. (2006) *Globalization and its Enemies.* Cambridge, Mass.: MIT Press.

Cohen, Eliot A. (1998) "A Revolution in Warfare," pp. 34–46 in Charles W. Kegley, Jr., and Eugene R. Wittkopf (eds.), *The Global Agenda*, 4th ed. New York: McGraw-Hill.

Cohen, Joel E. (1998) "How Many People Can the Earth Support?" *New York Review of Books* 45 (October 8): 29–31.

Cohen, Roger. (2005) "Next Step: Putting Europe Back Together," *New York Times International* (June 5): Section 4, 3.

———— (2000) "A European Identity," *New York Times* (January 14): A3.

Cohen, Saul Bernard. (2003) *Geopolitics of the World System.* Lanham, Md.: Rowman & Littlefield.

Cohn, Carol and Sara Ruddick. (2008) "A Feminist Ethical Perspective on Weapons of Mass Destruction," pp. 458–477 in Karen A. Mingst and Jack L. Snyder (eds.), *Essential Readings in World Politics*, 3rd ed., New York: W.W. Norton & Company.

Colapinto, John. (2012) "Looking Good: The New Boom in Celebrity Philanthropy," *The New Yorker* (March 26): 56.

Cole, Juan. (2006) "9/11," *Foreign Policy* 156 (September/October): 26–32.

Coleman, Isobel. (2010) "The Better Half: Helping Woman Help the World." *Foreign Affairs* 89(1) (January/February): 126–130.

———— (2010) "The Global Glass Ceiling: Why Empowering Women Is Good for Business." *Foreign Affairs* 89, no. 3 (May/June): 13–20.

Coll, Steve. (2011) "Democratic Movements," *The New Yorker* (January 31): 21–22.

———— (2009) "Comment: No Nukes," *The New Yorker* (April 20): 31–32.

Collier, Paul. (2009). "The Dictator's Handbook," *Foreign Policy* (May/June): 146–49.

———— (2007) *The Bottom Billion.* New York: Oxford University Press.

———— (2005) "The Market for Civil War," pp. 28–32 in Helen E. Punkitt (ed.), *World Politics 04/05*. Dubuque, Iowa: McGraw-Hill/Dushkin.

———— (2003) "The Market for Civil War," *Foreign Policy* 136 (May/June): 38–45.

Comisky, Mike and Pawan Madhogarhia. (2009) "Unraveling the Financial Crisis of 2008." *PS: Political Science & Politics* 42: 270–75.

Commercial Appeal. (2012) "Pope Benedict Arrives in Cuba," *The Commercial Appeal* (March 27): A3.

Commission of the European Communities. (2009) *2009 Aging Report*. Luxembourg.

Conteh-Morgan, Earl. (2005) "Peacebuilding and Human Security: A Constructivist Perspective," *International Journal of Peace Studies* 10 (Spring/Summer): 69–86.

CRS (Congressional Research Service). (2012) *FY2013 Defense Budget Request: Overview and Context*. Washington, D.C.: Congressional Research Service (April 20; prepared by Stephen Daggett and Pat Towell).

———— (2011) *The Cost of Iraq, Afghanistan, and Other: Global War on Terror Operations Since 9/11*. Washington, D.C.: Congressional Research Service (March 29, prepared by Amy Belasco).

———— (2008) *Conventional Arms Transfers to Developing Nations, 2000–2007*. Washington, D.C.: Congressional Research Service (October 23; prepared by Richard F. Grimmett).

———— (2007) *Conventional Arms Transfers to Developing -Nations, 1999–2006*. Washington, D.C.: Congressional Research Service (September 26; prepared by Richard F. Grimmett).

Cook, John and Paul Nyhan. (2004) "Outsourcing's Long-Term Effects on U.S. Jobs an Issue," *Seattle Post-Intelligencer*. March 10.

Cooper, Richard N. (2004) "A False Alarm: Overcoming -Globalization's Discontents," *Foreign Affairs* 83 (January/February): 152–55.

Coplin, William D. (1971) *Introduction to International Politics*. Chicago: Markham.

———— (1965) "International Law and Assumptions about the State System," *World Politics* 17 (July): 615–34.

Copeland, Dale C. (2006) "The Constructivist Challenge to Structural Realism: A Review Essay," pp. 1–20 in Stefano Guzzini and Anna Leander (eds.), *Constructivism and International Relations*. New York: Rutledge.

Cornish, Edward. (2004) *Futuring: Re-Exploration of the Future*. Bethesda, Md.: World Future Society.

Correlates of War (COW). (2010) "News and Notes." Available at: http://www.correlatesofwar.org/.

Cortright, David and George A. Lopez (eds.). (2008) *Uniting against Terror*. Cambridge, Mass.: MIT Press.

Cox, Robert J. with Timothy J. Sinclair. (1996) *Approaches to World Order*. Cambridge: Cambridge University Press.

Coyne, Christopher J. (2007) *After War: The Political Economy of Exporting Democracy*. Palo Alto, Calif.: Stanford University Press.

Craig, Gordon A. and Alexander L. George. (1990) *Force and Statecraft*, 2nd ed. New York: Oxford University Press.

Crawford, Neta C. (2003) "Just War Theory and the U.S. Counterterror War," *Perspectives on Politics* 1 (March): 5–25.

Crenshaw, Martha. (2003) "The Causes of Terrorism," pp. 92–105 in Charles W. Kegley, Jr. (ed.), *The New Global Terrorism*. Upper Saddle River, N.J.: Prentice Hall.

Cronin, Audrey Kurth. (2013) "Why Drones Fail," *Foreign Affairs* (July/August). Accessed July 4, 2013. Available at: http://www.foreignaffairs.com/articles/139454/audrey-kurth-cronin/why-drones-fail.

Crook, Clive. (2003) "A Cruel Sea of Capital," *Economist* (May 3): 3–5.

———— (1997) "The Future of the State," *Economist* (September 20): 5–20.

Crump, Andy. (1998) *The A to Z of World Development*. Oxford: New Internationalist.

Cumming-Bruce, Nick. (2008) "World Refugee Population Jumps to 11.4 Million," *The New York Times* (June 17). Last accessed November 4, 2013. Available at: http://www.nytimes.com/2008/06/17/news/17iht-refuge.3.13776120.html?_r=0.

Daadler, Ivo H., and James M. Lindsay. (2005) "Bush's Revolution," pp. 83–90 in Helen E. Purkitt (ed.), *World Politics 04/05*. Dubuque, Iowa: McGraw-Hill/Dushkin.

———— (2004) "An Alliance of Democracies," *Washington Post* (May 24): B.07.

———— (2003) *America Unbound: The Bush Revolution in Foreign Policy*. Washington, D.C.: Brookings Institution Press.

Dadush, Uri, Shimelse Ali, and Rachel Esplin Odell. (2011) "Is Protectionism Dying?" Washington, D.C.: Carnegie Endowment for International Peace. Available at: http://carnegieendowment.org/files/is_protectionism_dying.pdf.

Dadush, Uri, and William Shaw. (2011) "The Poor Will Inherit the Earth," *Foreign Policy* (June 20). Available at: http://www.foreignpolicy.com/articles/2011/06/20/the_poor_will_inherit_the_ earth?hidecomments5yes.

———— (2011) *Juggernaut: How Emerging Powers Are Reshaping Globalization*. New York: Carnegie Endowment for International Peace.

Dafoe, Allan, John R. Oneal, and Bruce Russett. (2013) "The Democratic Peace: Weighing the Evidence and Cautious Inference," *International Studies Quarterly* 57 (1): 201–214.

Dahl, Robert Alan, Ian Shapiro, and Jose Antonio Cheibub. (2003) *The Democracy Sourcebook*. Cambridge: MIT Press.

D'Amico, Francine, and Peter R. Beckman (eds.). (1995) *Women in World Politics*. Westport, Conn.: Bergin and Garvey.

Daniel, Trenton. (2011) "Haiti Again Feels Pinch of Rising Food Prices," *Associated Press* (May 2). Available at: http://www.usatoday.com/news/world/2011-05-01-haiti-food-prices_n.htm.

Danner, Mark. (2005) "What Are You Going to Do with That?" *New York Review of Books* 52 (June 23): 52–57.

Davenport, Andrew. (2013) "Marxism in IR: Condemned to a Realist Fate?" *European Journal of International Relations* 19(1): 27–48.

Davies, Ed, and Karen Lema. (2008) "Pricey Oil Making Geothermal Projects More Attractive," *International Herald Tribune* (June 30): 13.

Davis, Julie Hirschfield, Laura Lilvan, and Greg Stohr. (2013) "Obama Faces Bipartisan Pressure on Drone Big Brother Fear," *Bloomberg* (March 7). Accessed June 17, 2013. Available at: http://www.bloomberg.com/news/2013-03-08/obama-faces-bipartisan-pressure-on-drone-big-brother-fear.html.

de las Casas, Gustavo. (2008) "Is Nationalism Good for You?" *Foreign Policy* (March/April): 51–57.

de Rugy, Veronique. (2012) "Depression-era Farm Subsidies Should End," *The Examiner* (June 7). Accessed June 25, 2012. Available at: http://washingtonexaminer.com/article/702816.

DeBardeleben, Joan. (2012) "Applying Constructivism to Understanding EU-Russian Relations," *International Politics*, 49(4): 418–433.

Debusman, Bernd. (2012) "America's Decline - Myth or Reality?" (April 20, 2012). Available at: http://www.reuters.com/article/2012/04/20/column-debusmann-idUSL2E8FK5IH20120420. Last accessed November 22, 2013.

Deen, Thalif. (2009) "Tied Aid Strangling Nations, Says U.N." Inter Press Service, July 6. Available at: http://ipsnews.net/interna.asp?idnews524509.

Deets, Stephen. (2009) "Constituting Interests and Identities in a Two-Level Game: Understanding the Gabcikovo-Nagymaros Dam Conflict" *Foreign Policy Analysis* 5 (January): 37–56.

Deffeyes, Kenneth. (2005) "It's the End of Oil," *Time* (October 31): 66.

Dehio, Ludwig. (1962) *The Precarious Balance*. New York: Knopf.

Dempsey, Judy. (2008) "War Scrambles Strategic Map of Europe," *International Herald Tribune* (August): 1, 3.

Denmark, Robert A., Jonathan Friedman, Barry K. Gills, and George Modelski (eds.). (2002) *World System History: The Social Science of Long-Term Change*. London: Routledge.

Deng, Yong, and Thomas G. Moore. (2006) "China Views Globalization: Toward a New Great-Power Politics," pp. 147–56 in Helen E. Purkitt (ed.), *World Politics 05/06*. Dubuque, Iowa: McGraw-Hill/Dushkin.

DeParle, Jason. (2007) "Migrant Money Flow," *New York Times* (November 18): Week in Review, 3.

DeRouen, Karl R. Jr., and Jacob Bercovitch. (2008) "Enduring Internal Rivalries: A New Framework for the Study of Civil War." *Journal of Peace Research* 45 (January): 55–74.

—— and Christopher Sprecher. (2006) "Arab Behaviour towards Israel: Strategic Avoidance or Exploiting Opportunities?" *British Journal of Political Science* 36 (3): 549–60.

Desai, Raj M. and James Raymond Vreeland. (2011) "Global Governance in a Multipolar World: The Case for Regional Monetary Funds," *International Studies Review* 13, no. 1 (March): 109–121.

De Soysa, Indra, Thomas Jackson, and Christin Ormhaug. (2009) "Does Globalization Profit the Small Arms Bazaar?" *International Interactions* 35: 86–105.

Destler, I. M. (2005) *American Trade Politics*, 4th ed. Washington, DC: Institute of International Economics.

Detraz, Nicole. (2012) *International Security and Gender*. Malden, Mass.: Polity Press.

Deutsch, Karl W. (1957) *Political Community and the North Atlantic Area*. Princeton, NJ: Princeton University Press.

Diamond, Jared. (2003) "Environmental Collapse and the End of Civilization," *Harper's* (June): 43–51.

Diamond, Larry. (2005) *Squandered Victory: The American -Occupation and the Bungled Effort to Bring Democracy to Iraq*. New York: Henry Holt.

Diehl, Paul F. (ed.). (2005) *The Politics of Global Governance*, 3rd ed. Boulder, Colo.: Lynne Rienner.

—— and J. Michael Greig. (2012) *International Mediation*. Cambridge: Polity Press.

Dietz, Mary G. (2003) "Current Controversies in Feminist Theory." *Annual Review of Political Science*. Vol. 6: 399–431.

Dillon, Dana. (2005) "Maritime Piracy: Defining the Problem," *SAIS Review* 25 (Winter/Spring): 155–65.

Dimerel-Pegg, Tijen and James Moskowitz. (2009) "US Aid Allocation: The Nexus of Human Rights, Democracy, and Development" *Journal of Peace Research* 46 (2): 181–98.

Dinan, Stephen. (2012) "U.S. Borrows 46 Cents of Every Dollar It Spends," *The Washington Times* (December 7). Accessed June 27, 2013. Available at: http://www.washingtontimes.com/news/2012/dec/7/government-borrows-46-cents-every-dollar-it-spends/.

DiRenzo, Gordon J. (ed.). (1974) *Personality and Politics*. Garden City, NY: Doubleday-Anchor.

Dittmer, Lowell. (2013) "Asia in 2012: The Best of a Bad Year?" *Asian Survey* 53(1): 1–11.

Dobson, William J. (2006) "The Day Nothing Much Changed," *Foreign Policy* 156 (September/October): 22–25.

DOD (Department of Defense). (2013) "United States Department of Defense Fiscal Year 2014 Budget Request." Accessed June 12, 2013. Available at: http://comptroller.defense.gov/budget.html.

Dolan, Chris. (2005) *In War We Trust: The Ethical Dimensions and Moral Consequences of the Bush Doctrine*. Burlington, VT.: Ashgate.

Dollar, David. (2005) "Eyes Wide Open: On the Targeted Use of Foreign Aid," pp. 80–83 in Robert J. Griffiths (ed.), *Developing World 05/06*. Dubuque, IA: McGraw-Hill/Dushkin.

—— and Aart Kraay. (2004) "Spreading the Wealth," pp. 43–49 in Robert Griffiths (ed.), *Developing World 04/05*. Guilford, CT: Dushkin/McGraw Hill.

Dombrowski, Peter and Eugene Gholz. (2007) *Buying Military Transformation*. New York: Columbia University Press.

Donadio, Rachel. (2011) "Greece Approves Tough Measures on the Economy," *New York Times* (June 29).

——— and Elisabetta Povoledo. (2009) "Earthquake Kills Scores in Italy," *International Herald Tribune* (April 7): 1.

——— and Scott Sayare. (2011) "Violent Clashes in the Streets of Athens," *The New York Times* (June 29): A8.

Donnelly, Sally B. (2005) "Foreign Policy," *Time Inside Business* (June): A17–A18.

Doran, Charles F. (2012) "Power Cycle Theory and the Ascendance of China: Peaceful or Stormy?" *SAIS Review* 32 (1): 73–87.

Dos Santos, Theotonio. (1971) "The Structure of Dependence," in K. T. Fann and Donald C. Hodges (eds.), *Readings in U.S. Imperialism*. Boston: Porter Sargent.

——— (1970) "The Structure of Dependence," *American Economic Review* 60 (May): 231–36.

Dougherty, James E. and Robert L. Pfaltzgraff, Jr. (2001) *Contending Theories of International Relations*, 5th ed. New York: Longman.

Dowd, Maureen. (2004) *Bushworld: Enter at Your Own Risk*. New York: G. P. Putnam's Sons.

Doyle, Michael W. (2011) "International Ethics and the Responsibility to Protect," *International Studies Review* 13: 72–84.

Draper, Robert. (2008) *Dead Certain: The Presidency of George W. Bush*. New York: Free Press.

Dreher, Axel, Noel Gaston, and Pim Martens. (2008) *Measuring Globalisation—Gauging its Consequences*. New York: Springer.

Drehle, David Von. (2011) "Don't Bet against the United States," *Time* (March 14): 34–35.

Drew, Jill. (2008) "Dalai Lama's Envoys in Beijing for Tibet Talks," *Washington Post* (July 1): A07.

Drezner, Daniel. (2011) "Sanctions Sometimes Smart: Targeted Sanctions in Theory and Practice," *International Studies Review* 13 (1): 96–108.

——— (2010a) *Theories of International Politics and Zombies*. Princeton, NJ: Princeton University Press.

——— (2010b) "Night of the Living Wonks," *Foreign Policy* (July/August): 34–38.

——— (2010c) "Why Is the WTO Protest-Free?" *Foreign Policy* (September 15). Available at: http://drezner.foreignpolicy.com/posts/2010/09/15/why_is_the_wto_protest_free.

——— (2009) "Backdoor Protectionism," *The National Interest Online*. Available at: http://www.nationalinterest.org/Article.aspx?id521192.

——— (2007) *All Politics Is Global*. Princeton, NJ: Princeton University Press.

——— (2000) "Bottom Feeders," *Foreign Policy* (November/December): 64–70.

——— and Henry Farrell. (2006) "Web of Influence," pp. 12–19 in Helen E. Purkitt (ed.), *World Politics 05/06*. Dubuque, IA: McGraw-Hill/Dushkin.

Drezner, Daniel, Gideon Rachman, and Robert Kagan. (2012) "The Rise or Fall of the American Empire," Foreign Policy (February 14). Last accessed November 23, 2013. Available at: http://www.foreignpolicy.com/articles/2012/02/14/the_rise_or_fall_of_the_american_empire?page=full.

Drost, Nadja. (2009) "Postcard: Medellin," *Time* (May 4): 8.

Druba, Volker. (2002) "The Problem of Child Soldiers," *International Review of Education* 48(3/4): 271–77.

Drucker, Peter F. (2005) "Trading Places," *The National Interest* 79 (Spring): 101–07.

Dunne, Tim. (2005) "Liberalism," pp. 185–203 in John Baylis and Steve Smith (eds.), *The Globalization of World Politics*, 3rd ed. New York: Oxford University Press.

Dupont, Alan. (2002) "Sept. 11 Aftermath: The World Does Seem to Have Changed," *International Herald Tribune* (August 6): 6.

Dur, Andreas. (2010) *Protectionism for Exporters: Power and Discrimination in Transatlantic Trade Relations 1930–2010*. Ithaca, NY: Cornell University Press.

Durch, William J. (2005) "Securing the Future of the United-Nations," *SAIS Review* 25 (Winter/Spring): 187–91.

Dworkin, Ronald. (2001) *Sovereign Virtue*. Cambridge, Mass.: Harvard University Press.

Dykman, Jackson. (2008) "Why the World Can't Afford Food," *Time* (May 19): 34–35.

Dyson, Freeman. (2007) "Our Biotech Future," *The New York Review of Books* 54 (July 19): 4–8.

Easterbrook, Gregg. (2002) "Safe Deposit: The Case for Foreign Aid," *New Republic* (July 29): 16–20.

Easterly, William. (2007) "The Ideology of Development," *Foreign Policy* (July/August): 31–35.

——— (2006) *The White Man's Burden: Why the West's Efforts to Aid the Rest Have Done So Much Ill and So Little Good*. New York: Penguin.

——— and Laura Freschi. (2009) "Unsung Hero Resurrects US Tied Aid Reporting." Accessed August 13, 2009. Available at http://blogs.nyu.edu/fas/dri/aidwatch/2009/02/unsung_hero_resurrects_us_tied.html.

——— and Tobias Pfutze. (2008) "Where Does the Money Go? Best and Worst Practices in Foreign Aid," *Journal of Economic Perspectives* 22(2): 29–52.

Easton, Stewart C. (1964) *The Rise and Fall of Western Colonialism*. New York: Praeger.

Eberstadt, Nicholas. (2011) "The Demographic Future: What Population Growth—and Decline—Means for the Global Economy," *Foreign Affairs* (November/December): 54–64.

——— (2004) "The Population Implosion," pp. 168–77 in Robert J. Griffiths (ed.), *Developing World 04/05*, Guilford, Conn: McGraw-Hill/Dushkin.

Economist. (2013) "Back to the Futures?" *The Economist* February 4): Accessed June 27, 2013. Available at: http://www.economist.com/blogs/freeexchange/2013/02/derivatives-markets-regulation.

——— (2012a) "New Rivers of Gold," *The Economist* (April 28): 77–78.

——— (2012b) "Rustling with Kalashnikovs," *The Economist* (March 24): 50.

——— (2012c) "Threat Multiplier: Dangerous Complacency about Nuclear Terrorism," *The Economist* (March 31). Accessed August 8, 2012. Available at: http://www.economist.com/node/21551465.

——— (2012d) "Bad Timing: An Atlantic Alliance with Less Ambition Looks Inevitable; But It Should Not Be Allowed to Fade Away," *The Economist* (March 31). Accessed September 4, 2012. Available at: http://www.economist.com/node/21551491.

——— (2012e) "Big Mac Index," *The Economist* (January 12). Available at: http://www.economist.com/blogs/graphicdetail/ 2012/01/daily-chart-3.

——— (2012f). "Global Poverty: A Fall to Cheer," *The Economist* (March 3): 81–2.

——— (2012g) "Speaking in Tongues," *The Economist*. Accessed June 24, 2013. Available at: http://www.economist.com/blogs/graphicdetail/2012/02/daily-chart-9.

——— (2011a) "Another Project in Trouble: First the Euro, Now Schengen. Europe's Grandest Integration Projects Seem to be Suffering," *The Economist* (April 30): 57.

——— (2011b) "Trade: Buy American Tea," *The Economist* (November 10). Available at: http://rss.economist.com/blogs/freeexchange/2010/11/trade.

——— (2011c) "Hope Over Experience," *The Economist* (January 15):83.

——— (2011d) "Crisis Prevention: What Is Causing Food Prices to Soar and What Can be Done about It?" *The Economist* (February 26): 12.

——— (2011e) "A Prospect of Plenty: For the First Time in History, the Whole of Mankind may Get Enough to Eat," *The Economist* (February 26): 16.

——— (2011f) "A Tale of Many Cities," *The Economist* (February 12): 91–92.

——— (2011g) "Threatening a Sacred Cow: America's Fiscal Crisis Has Put Defence Spending in the Crosshairs," *The Economist* (February 12): 33–34.

——— (2011h) "Ali Baba Gone, but What about the 40 Thieves?" *The Economist* (January 22): 31–33.

——— (2011i) "Redback and Forth," *The Economist* (August 20).

——— (2010a) "Harmony—for Now: There were Smiles and Handshakes in Lisbon, but the Road Ahead Is Bumpy," *The Economist* (November 27): 67–68.

——— (2010b) "Climbing Mount Publishable," *The Economist* (November 14): 95–96.

——— (2010c) "Fewer Dragons, More Snakes," *The Economist* (November 13): 27–29.

——— (2010d) "The Power of Nightmares," *The Economist* (June 26): 61–62.

——— (2010e) "It Takes Two," *The Economist* (April 3): 61–62.

——— (2010f) "Marching through Red Square," *The Economist* (May 22): 53–54.

——— (2010g) "An Awkward Guest-list," *The Economist* (May 1): 60–61.

——— (2010h) "Loaned Goals," *The Economist* (June 5): 67–68.

——— (2010i) "The Cruel Sea," *The Economist* (February 11): 54.

——— (2010j) "Old Worry, New Ideas," *The Economist* (April 17): 67.

——— (2010k) "Fear of the Dragon," *The Economist* (January 9): 73–75.

——— (2010l) "Counting Their Blessings," *The Economist* (January 2): 25–28.

——— (2010m) "By Fits and Starts," *The Economist* (February 6): 25–27.

——— (2010n) "Passage to India," *The Economist* (June 26): 69.

——— (2010o) "Economic and Financial Indicators," *The Economist* (May 1): 97–98.

——— (2010p) "Consensus Costs," *The Economist* (June 3). Available at: http://www.economist.com/node/16274169.

——— (2009a) "Go Forth and Multiply a Lot Less," *The Economist* (October 31): 29–32.

——— (2009b) "Agricultural Subsidies," *The Economist* (July 23): 93.

——— (2009c) "Cheesed Off," *The Economist* (July 18): 74.

——— (2009d) "Not Just Straw Men," *The Economist* (June 20): 63:65.

——— (2009e) "Cuba and the United States: It Takes Two to Rumba," *The Economist* (April 18): 39–40.

——— (2009f) "Taking the Summit by Strategy," *The Economist* (April 11): 42.

——— (2009g) "Mission: Possible," *The Economist* (April 11): 69.

——— (2009h) "Sin aqua non," *The Economist* (April 11): 59–61.

——— (2009i) "Coca-Cola and China: Hard to Swallow," *The Economist* (March 21): 68–69.

——— (2009j) "Not so Nano; Emerging-Market Multinationals," *The Economist* (March 28): 20.

——— (2009k) "Trickle-Down Economics," *The Economist* (February 21): 76.

——— (2009l) "Wanted: Fresh Air," *The Economist* (July 11): 60–62.

——— (2008a) "Winning or Losing? A Special Report on al-Qaeda," *The Economist* (July 19): 1–12.

——— (2008b) "Ireland's Voters Speak; The European Union," *The Economist* (June 21): 61.

——— (2007a) "Magnets for Money," *The Economist* (September 15): 3–4.

——— (2007b) "Finance and Economics: Smaller Shares, Bigger Slices," *The Economist* (April 7): 84.

——— (2007c) *Pocket World in Figures*, 2007 Edition. London: *The Economist*.

Economy, Elizabeth C. (2007) "The Great Leap Backward?" *Foreign Affairs* 86 (September/October): 38–59.

Edgerton, David. (2007) *The Shock of the Old: Technology and Global History Since 1900*. New York: Oxford University Press.

Eggen, Dan, and Scott Wilson. (2005) "Suicide Bombs Potent Tools of Terrorists," *Washington Post* (July 17): A1, A20.

Ehrlich, Sean. (2011) "The Fair Trade Challenge to Embedded Liberalism," *International Studies Quarterly* 54 (1): 1013–33.

Eichengreen, Barry. (2011a) *Exorbitant Privilege: The Rise and Fall of the Dollar and the Future of the International Monetary System*. Oxford, UK: Oxford University Press.

——— (2011b) "The G20 and Global Imbalances," VoxEU.org (June 26).

——— (2000) "Hegemonic Stability Theories of the International Monetary System," pp. 220–44 in Jeffrey A. Frieden and David A. Lake (eds.), *International Political Economy*. Boston: Bedford/St. Martin's.

Eichengreen, Barry and Kevin O'Rourke. (2009) "A Tale of Two Depressions," VoxEU.org, June 4. Available at: http://www.voxeu.org/index.php?q5node/3421.

Eisler, Riane. (2007) "Dark Underbelly of the World's 'Most Peaceful' Countries," *Christian Science Monitor* (July 26): 9.

Ekhoragbon, Vincent. (2008) "Nigeria: Influx of Illegal Immigrants Worries Immigration Service," Available at: http://allafrica.com/stories/200808080481.html.

Eland, Ivan. (2004) *The Empire Has No Clothes: U.S. Foreign Policy Exposed*. New York: Independent Institute.

Elliott, Kimberly Ann. (1998) "The Sanctions Glass: Half Full or Completely Empty?" *International Security* 23 (Summer): 50–65.

——— (1993) "Sanctions: A Look at the Record," *Bulletin of the Atomic Scientists* 49 (November): 32–35.

Elliott, Michael. (1998) "A Second Federal Democratic-Superpower Soon," *International Herald Tribune* (November 24): 8.

Ellis, David C. (2009) "On the Possibility of "International Community," VoxEU.org, *The International Studies Review* 11 (March): 1–26.

Elms, Deborah Kay. (2008) "New Directions for IPE: Drawing from Behavioral Economics," *International Studies Review* 10 (June): 239–265.

Elshtain, Jean Bethke. (2003) *Just War against Terror: The Burden of American Power in a Violent World*. New York: Basic Books.

Emporis. (2012) "Press Release: World's 10 Biggest Shopping Malls," Emporis. Accessed June 20, 2012. Available at: http://www.emporis.com/pdf/Pressrelease_20120207_ENG.pdf.

Engardio, Pete, Michael Arndt, and Dean Foust. (2006) "The Future of Outsourcing: How Its Transforming Whole Industries and Changing the Way We Work," in *Businessweek* (January 30).

Engelhardt, Henriette, and Alexia Prskawetz. (2004) "On the Changing Correlation between Fertility and Female Employment over Space and Time," *European Journal of Population* 20 (1): 1–21.

Englehart, Neil A. (2009). "State Capacity, State Failure, and Human Rights," *Journal of Peace Research* 46 (2): 163–80.

Enloe, Cynthia H. (2007) "The Personal Is International" pp. 202–206, in Karen A. Mingst and Jack L. Synder (eds.) *Essential Readings in World Politics*, 3rd ed. New York: W.W. Norton & Company.

——— (2004) *The Curious Feminist*. Berkeley: University of California Press.

——— (2001) "Gender and Politics," pp. 311–15 in Joel Krieger (ed.), *The Oxford Companion to Politics of the World*, 2nd ed. New York: Oxford University Press.

——— (2000) *Maneuvers: The International Politics of Militarizing Women's Lives*. Berkeley: University of California Press.

Enriquez, Juan. (1999) "Too Many Flags?" *Foreign Policy* 116 (Fall): 30–50.

EPA (2013). "Causes of Climate Change," *Environmental Protection Agency*. Accessed June 25, 2013. Available at: http://www.epa.gov/climatechange/science/causes.html.

Epatko, Larisa. (2012). "In Syria, Aid Groups Look for Break in Fighting to Deliver Supplies," PBS NewsHour. Last accessed November 22, 2013. Available at: http://www.pbs.org/newshour/rundown/2.012/03/syria-aid.html

Eshchenko, Alla, and Maxim Tkachenko. (2011) "Russia Threatens Nuclear Build-up over U.S. Missile Shield," *CNN* (May 18). Available at: http://articles.cnn.com /2011-05-18/world/russia.nuclear.missiles_1_missile-defense-missile-shield-europe-based-system?_s5PM:WORLD.

Esty, Daniel C., M. A. Levy, C. H. Kim, A. de Sherbinin, T. Srebotniak, and V. Mara. (2008) *2008 Environmental Performance Index*. New Haven, CT: Yale Center for Environmental Law and Policy.

Esty, Daniel. (2002) "The World Trade Organization's Legitimacy Crisis," *World Trade Review* 1 (1): 7–22.

Etzioni, Amitai. (2005) *From Empire to Community: A New Approach to International Relations*. London: Palgrave Macmillan.

Eurostat. (2013) "Eurostat," *European Commission*. Accessed June 27, 2013. Available at: http://epp.eurostat.ec.europa.eu/portal/page/portal/eurostat/home/.

European Commission. (2012) *The 2012 Ageing Report: Economic and Budgetary Projections for the 27 EU Member States (2010–2060)*. Brussels, Belgium: European Commission.

European Nuclear Society. (2013) "Nuclear Power Plants, Worldwide." Available at: http://www.euronuclear.org/info/encyclopedia/n/nuclear-power-plant-world-wide.htm.

European Union: Commission of the European Communities, *Communication from the Commission to the European Parliament, the Council, The European Economic and Social Committee and the Committee of the Regions. Dealing with the Impact of an Ageing Population in the EU*, April 14, 2009, COM (2009) 180 Final. Available at: http://eur-lex.europa.eu/LexUriServ/LexUriServ.do?uri5COM:2009:0180:FIN:EN:PDF.

Evans, Gareth. (2011) "Viewpoint: 'Overwhelming' Moral Case for Military Path," *BBC* (March 8). Available at: http://www.bbc.co.uk/news/world-africa-12676248.

——— (2008) *The Responsibility to Protect: Ending Mass Atrocity Crimes Once and for All.* Washington, DC: Brookings Institution Press.

Evans, Peter B. (2001) "Dependency," pp. 212–14 in Joel Krieger (ed.), *The Oxford Companion to Politics of the World*, 2nd ed. New York: Oxford University Press.

Evenett, Simon J. (2013) "Is Murky Protectionism a Real Threat to Asian Trade?" pp. 65–73 in Richard Baldwin, Masahiro Kawai, and Ganeshan Wignaraga (eds.), *The Future of the World Trading System: Asian Perspectives*. London, UK: Centre for Economic Policy Research.

Evenett, Simon J., and John Whalley. (2009) "Resist Green Protectionism—or Pay the Price at Copenhagen," in Baldwin, Richard, and Simon Evenett (eds.) *The Collapse of Global Trade, Murky Protectionism, and the Crisis: Recommendations for the G20*. London: VoxEU.org. Available at: http://voxeu.org/reports/Murky_Protectionism.pdf.

EWG. (2013) "EWG Farm Subsidies," *Environmental Working Group*. Accessed July 27, 2013. Available at: http://farm.ewg.org/.

Ewing, Jack, and Louise Story. (2011) "Finland Could Upend Fragile Consensus on Greece," *The New York Times*. Available at: http://www.nytimes.com/2011/08/29/business/global/finland-casts-doubt-on-aid-for-greece.html?ref5europeanfinancialstabilityfacility.

Fabbrini, Sergio. (2010) "Anti-Americanism and U.S. Foreign Policy: Which Correlation?" *International Politics* 47, no 6: 557–73.

Fackler, Martin. (2009) North Korea Vows to Produce Nuclear Weapons, *The New York Times* (June 14): A12.

——— (2008) "Honda Rolls Out Hydrogen-Powered Car," *International Herald Tribune* (June 18): 16.

Fahrenthold, David A., and Paul Kane. (2011) "Lawmakers Urging Speedy Pullout in Afghanistan Unlikely to Make Headway," *The Washington Post* (May 5). Available at: http://www.washingtonpost.com/politics/lawmakers_urging_speedy_pullout_in_afghanistan_unlikely_to_make_headway/2011/05/05/AFgvJf1F_story.html?nav5emailpage.

Fahrenthold, David A. and Paul Kane. (2011) "On Hill, Renewed Calls for Rapid Afghan Pullout," *Washington Post* (May 11).

Falk, Richard A. (2001a) "The New Interventionism and the Third World," pp. 189–98 in Charles W. Kegley, Jr., and Eugene R. Wittkopf (eds.), *The Global Agenda*, 6th ed. Boston: McGraw-Hill.

——— (2001b) "Sovereignty," pp. 789–91 in Joel Krieger (ed.), *The Oxford Companion to Politics of the World*, 2nd ed. Oxford: Oxford University Press.

——— (1970) *The Status of Law in International Society.* Princeton, N.J.: Princeton University Press.

Falk, Richard, and Andrew Strauss. (2001) "Toward Global Parliament," *Foreign Affairs* 80 (January/February): 212–18.

Fallows, James. (2005) "Countdown to a Meltdown," *The Atlantic Monthly* 51 (July/August): 51–63.

——— (2002) "The Military Industrial Complex," *Foreign Policy* 22 (November/December): 46–48.

——— (1993) "How the World Works," *The Atlantic* (December).

Farber, David (ed.). (2007) *What They Think of Us: International Perceptions of the United States Since 9/11.* Princeton, NJ: Princeton University Press.

Farrell, Theo. (2002) "Constructivist Security Studies: Portrait of a Research Program," *International Studies Review* 4 (Spring): 49–72.

Fathi, Nazila. (2009) "In Tehran, A Mood of Melancholy Descends," *The New York Times* (June 28): A6.

Federman, Josef. (2013) "Benjamin Netanyahu, Israel's Prime Minister, Says Iran Has Not Yet Reached 'Red Line,'" *Huffington Post* (April 29). Accessed June 17, 2013. Available at: http://www.huffingtonpost.com/2013/04/29/benjamin-netanyahu-israel-iran_n_3178864.html.

Feingold, David A. (2005) "Human Trafficking," *Foreign Policy* (September/October): 26–31.

Feinstein, Lee, and Anne-Marie Slaughter (2004) "A Duty to Prevent," *Foreign Affairs* 83 (January/February): 136–50.

Feldman, Noah. (2013). *Cool War: The Future of Global Competition.* New York: Random House.

Feldsten, Martin. (2010) "Let Greece Take a EuroZone 'Holiday,'" *Financial Times* (February 16).

Ferguson, Charles. (2010) "The Long Road to Zero: Overcoming the Obstacle to a Nuclear-Free World." *Foreign Affairs* 89(1) (January/February): 86–94.

Ferguson, Niall. (2011) "The Mash of Civilizations: Social Networks Might Promote Democracy, but They Also Empower the Enemies of Freedom," *Newsweek* (April 18): 9.

——— (2010) "Complexity and Collapse: Empires on the Edge of Chaos." *Foreign Affairs* 89, no. 2 (March/April): 18–32.

——— (2009) "The Axis of Upheaval," *Foreign Policy* (March/April): 56–58.

——— (2008) *The Ascent of Money.* New York: Penguin Press.

——— (2004) *Colossus: The Price of America's Empire.* New York: Penguin.

——— (2001) *The Cash Nexus.* New York: Basic Books.

Ferrell, Theo. (2002) "Constructivist Security Studies: Portrait of a Research Program." *International Studies Review* 4 (1):49–72.

Fetini, Alyssa. (2009) "Changing U.S.-Cuba Policy," *Time* (February 24).

Fidler, David P., and Lawrence O. Gostin. (2008) *Biosecurity in the Global Age*. Palo Alto, CA: Stanford University Press.

Fieldhouse, D. K. (1973) *Economics and Empire, 1830–1914*. Ithaca, NY: Cornell University Press.

Fields, A. Belden, and Kriston M. Lord (eds.). (2004) *Rethinking Human Rights for the New Millennium*. London: Palgrave.

Filkins, Dexter. (2009) "Afghan Women Protest Restrictive Law," *International Herald Tribune* (April 6): 1.

Financial Times. (2007) "Why Are Food Prices Rising," Available at: http://media.ft.com/cms/s/2/f5bd920c-975b-11dc-9e08–0000779fd2ac.html?from5textlinkindepth.

Finnegan, William. (2007) "The Countdown," *New Yorker* (October 15): 70–79.

——— (2002) "Leasing the Rain," *New Yorker* (April 18): 43–53.

Finnemore, Martha. (2013) "Constructing Norms of Humanitarian Intervention," in *Conflict After the Cold War: Arguments on Causes of War and Peace*, 4th edition. Rickard K Betts, ed. Boston, MA: Pearson. pp 262–279.

——— (2009) "Legitimacy, Hypocrisy, and the Social Structure of Unipolarity: Why Being a Unipole Isn't All It's Cracked Up to Be," *World Politics* 61: 58–85.

——— (2003) *The Purpose of Intervention: Changing Beliefs about the Use of Force*. Ithaca, N.Y: Cornell University Press.

Fishman, Ted C. (2005) *China, Inc.* New York: Scribner.

Flanagan, Stephen J., Ellen L. Frost, and Richard Kugler. (2001) *Challenges of the Global Century*. Washington, D.C.: Institute for National Strategic Studies, National Defense University.

Fletcher, Dan. (2010) "Friends Without Borders." *Time* (May 31): 32–38.

Flint, Colin (ed.). (2004) *The Geography of War and Peace*. New York: Oxford University Press.

Florida, Richard. (2007) "America's Looming Creativity Crisis," pp. 183–190 in Robert M. Jackson, ed., *Global Issues 06/07*. Dubuque, IA: McGraw-Hill Contemporary Learning Series.

——— (2005a) *The Flight of the Creative Class: The New Global Competition for Talent*. New York: HarperBusiness.

——— (2005b) "The World Is Spiky," *Atlantic Monthly* 296 (October): 48–52.

Flynn, Stephen. (2004) *America the Vulnerable*. New York: HarperCollins.

Fogel, Robert. (2010) "$123,000,000,000,000." *Foreign Policy* (January/February): 70–75.

Foley, Conor. (2008) *The Thin Blue Line: How Humanitarianism Went to War*. New York: Verso Books.

Føllesdal, Andreas, Johan Karlsson Schaffer, and Geir Ulfstein (eds.), (2013) *The Legitimacy of International Human Rights Regimes: Legal, Political and Philosophical Perspectives*. Cambridge, UK: Cambridge University Press.

Foster, Dennis M. and Jonathan W. Keller. (2013) "Leaders' Cognitive Complexity, Distrust, and the Diversionary Use of Force," *Foreign Policy Analysis* (May 2). DOI: 10.1111/fpa.12019

Forbes. (2013; various years) "The World's Biggest Public Companies," *Forbes*. Last accessed November 4, 2013. Available at: http://www.forbes.com/global2000/.

Fordham, Benjamin. (2010) "Trade and Asymmetric Alliances," *Journal of Peace Research* 47 (6): 685–696.

Foreign Policy /A.T. Kerney Inc. (2013) "The Failed States Index." Available at: http://ffp.statesindex.org/rankings-2013-sortable

——— (2008) "The Terrorism Index," *Foreign Policy* 168 (September/October): 79–85.

——— (2007) "Sanctioning Force," *Foreign Policy* (July/August): 19.

——— (2005) "Measuring Globalization," *Foreign Policy* (May/June): 52–60.

Forero, Juan. (2005) "Bolivia Regrets IMF Experiment," *International Herald Tribune*, (December 14).

Foust, Joshua and Ashley S. Boyle. (2012) "The Strategic Context of Lethal Drones: A Framework for Discussion," *American Security Project*. Accessed June 17, 2013. Available at: http://www.scribd.com/doc/102744195/The-Strategic-Context-of-Lethal-Drones.

Frank, Andre Gunder. (1969) *Latin America: Underdevelopment or Revolution*. New York: Monthly Review Press.

Frankel, Jeffrey. (2008) "The Euro Could Surpass the Dollar within Ten Years," VoxEU.org (March 18).

Frankel, Max. (2004) *High Noon in the Cold War: Kennedy, Khrushchev, and the Cuban Missile Crisis*. New York: Random House.

Frankel, Rebecca. (2011) "War Dog: There's a Reason They Brought One to Get Osama bin Laden," *Foreign Policy* (May 4). Available at: http://www.foreignpolicy.com/articles/2011/05/04/war_dog.

Frantz, Ashley. (2013) "Syria Death Toll Probably at 70,000, U.N. Human Rights Official Says," *CNN* (February 12). Accessed June 3, 2013. Available at: http://www.cnn.com/2013/02/12/world/meast/syria-death-toll/index.html.

Frasquieri, Manuel Hevia. (2011) The Seven-League Giant. Havana, Cuba: Editorial Capitan San Luis.

Frazier, Derrick V., and William J. Dixon. (2006) "Third-Party Intermediaries and Negotiated Settlements, 1946–2000," *International Interactions* 32 (December): 385–408.

Frederking, Brian, Michael Artine, and Max Sanchez Pagano. (2005) "Interpreting September 11," *International Politics* 42 (March): 135–51.

Freeland, Chrystia. (2012) "The Cost of Modern Revolution," *The Atlantic Magazine* (July/August). Accessed August 8,

2012. Available at: http://www.theatlantic.com/magazine/archive/2012/07/the-cost-of-modern-revolution/9035/.

Freedman, Lawrence. (2010) "Frostbitten: Decoding the Cold War, 20 Years Later." In *Foreign Affairs* (March/April).

——— (2005) "War," pp. 8–11 in Helen E. Purkitt (ed.), *World Politics 04/05.* Dubuque, Iowa: McGrawHill/Dushkin.

——— (2004) *Deterrence.* Cambridge, Mass: Polity Press.

Freedom House. (2013) *Freedom in the World 2013.* Available at: http://www.freedomhouse.org/report/freedom-world/freedom-world-2013

Freeman, Charles. (2010) "President Obama to Meet the Dalai Lama," *Center for Strategic and International Studies* (February 17). Accessed June 3, 2013. Available at: http://csis.org/publication/president-obama-meet-dalai-lama.

French, George. (2009) "A Year in Bank Supervision: 2008 and a Few of Its Lessons." *Supervisory Insights* 6 (1): 3–18.

Freud, Sigmund. (1968) "Why War," pp. 71–80 in Leon Bramson and George W. Goethals (eds.), *War.* New York: Basic Books.

Fried, John H. E. (1971) "International Law—Neither Orphan nor Harlot, Neither Jailer nor Never-Never Land," pp. 124–76 in Karl W. Deutsch and Stanley Hoffmann (eds.), *The Relevance of International Law.* Garden City, N.Y: Doubleday-Anchor.

Friedheim, Robert L. (1965) "The 'Satisfied' and 'Dissatisfied' States Negotiate International Law," *World Politics* 18 (October): 20–41.

Friedman, Benjamin M. (2005a) *The Moral Consequences of Economic Growth.* New York: Knopf.

——— (2005b) "Homeland Security," *Foreign Policy* (July/August): 22–28.

Friedman, George. (2011) *The Next Decade: Where We've Been... and Where We're Going.* New York: Doubleday, Random House.

Friedman, Jeffrey. (2007) *Global Capitalism: Its Rise and Fall in the Twentieth Century.* New York: Norton.

Friedman, Thomas L. (2008) *Hot, Flat, and Crowded: Why We Need a Green Revolution, and How It Can Renew America.* New York: Farrar, Straus and Giroux.

——— (2007a) "It's a Flat World, After All," pp. 7–12 in Robert M. Jackson, (ed.), *Global Issues 06/07.* Dubuque, Iowa: McGraw-Hill Contemporary Learning Series.

——— (2007b) *The World Is Flat 3.0: A Brief History of the 21st Century.* New York: Farrar, Straus, and Giroux.

Friedman, Thomas and Robert Kaplan. (2002) "States of Discord," *Foreign Policy* 129 (March/April): 64–70.

Friedmann, S. Julio, and Thomas Homer-Dixon. (2004) "Out of the Energy Box," *Foreign Affairs* 83 (November/December): 72–83.

Frum, David, and Richard Perle. (2004) *An End to Evil: How to Win the War on Terror.* New York: Random House.

Fukuyama, Francis. (2011) *The Origins of Political Order: From Prehuman Times to the French Revolution.* New York: Farar, Straus and Giroux.

——— (ed.). (2008) *Blindside: How to Anticipate Future Events and Wild Cards in Global Politics.* Washington, DC: Brookings Institution.

——— (2004) *State-Building: Governance and World Order in the 21st Century.* Ithaca, NY: Cornell University Press.

——— (1999a) *The Great Disruption: Human Nature and the Reconstitution of Social Order.* New York: Free Press.

——— (1999b) "Second Thoughts: The Last Man in a Bottle," *National Interest* 56 (Summer): 16–33.

——— (1992) "The Beginning of Foreign Policy," *New Republic* (August 17 and 24): 24–32.

Funk, McKenzie. (2007) "Cold Rush: The Coming Fight for the Melting North," *Harper's* (September): 45–55.

Futurist. (2007) "Forecasts From the Futurist Magazine." Available at: http://www.wfs.org/book/export/html/68.

Gall, Carlotta. (2008) "Afghan Highway Drenched in Blood," *The Commercial Appeal* (August 17): A18.

Gallagher, Kevin. (2011) "The IMF Must Heed G20 Decisions," *The Guardian* (November 29). Accessed June 27, 2013. Available at: http://www.guardian.co.uk/commentisfree/cifamerica/2011/nov/29/imf-must-heed-g20-decisions.

Gallagher, Maryann E. and Susan H. Allen. (2013) "Presidential Personality: Not Just a Nuisance," Foreign Policy Analysis (February): 1–21.

Galtung, Johan. (1969) "Violence, Peace, and Peace Research," *Journal of Peace Research* 6 (3): 167–91.

Gamberoni, Elisa and Richard Newfarmer. (2009) "Trade Protection: Incipient but Worrisome Trends," *World Bank Trade Note* 37. Available at: http://siteresources.worldbank.org/NEWS/Resources/Trade_Note_37.pdf.

Gambetta, Diego (ed.). (2005) *Making Sense of Suicide Missions.* New York: Oxford University Press.

Gamel, Kim. (2009) "FBI Notes: Saddam Hussein Sought Familiar Refuge," Associated Press (July 3). Available at: http://hosted.ap.org/dynamic/stories/u/us_saddam_fbi_interviews?site5ap&section5home&template5default&ctime52009–07–03–01–59–01.

Gardner, Richard N. (2003) "The Future Implications of the Iraq Conflict," *American Journal of International Law* 1997 (July): 585–90.

Garfield, Richard. (1999) "Morbidity and Mortality among Iraqi Children from 1990 through 1998." Available at: http://www.cam.ac.uk/societies/casi/info/garfield/dr-garfield.html.

Garrett, Geoffrey. (2004) "Globalization's Missing Middle," *Foreign Affairs* 83 (November/December): 84–96.

Garrett, Laurie. (2007) "The Challenge of Global Health," *Foreign Affairs* 86 (January/February): 14–38.

——— (2005) "The Scourge of AIDS," *International Herald Tribune* (July 29): 6.

——— (2000) *The Coming Plague: Newly Emerging Diseases in a World Out of Balance,* rev. ed. London: Virago.

Garrison, Jean. (2006) "From Stop to Go in Foreign Policy," *International Studies Review* 8 (June): 291–93.

Gartzke, Erik. (2007) "The Capitalist Peace," *American Journal of Political Science* 51 (1): 166–91.

Gartzke, Erik and Matthew Kroenig. (2009) "A Strategic Approach to Nuclear Proliferation," *Journal of Conflict Resolution* 53: 151–60.

Gartzke, Erik and Quan Li. (2003) "How Globalization Can Reduce International Conflict," in Nils Petter Gleditsch, Gerals Schneider, and Katherine Barbieri (eds.), *Globalization and Armed Conflict*. New York: Rowman & Littlefield Publishers, 123–40.

Gartzke, Erik and Alex Weisiger. (2013) "Permanent Friends? Dynamic Difference and the Democratic Peace," *International Studies Quarterly* 57 (1): 171–185.

Gayle, Damien. (2013) "The Incredible U.S. Military Spy Drone That's So Powerful It Can See What Type of Phone You're Carrying from 17,500 ft," *Daily Mail* (January 28). Accessed June 17, 2013. Available at: http://www.dailymail.co.uk/sciencetech/article-2269563/The-U-S-militarys-real-time-Google-Street-View-Airborne-spy-camera-track-entire-city-1-800MP.html.

Gazzaniga, Michael S. (2005) *The Ethical Brain*. New York: Dana Press.

Gebrekidan, Fikru. (2010) "Ethiopia and Congo: A Tale of Two Medieval Kingdoms," *Callaloo* 33 (1) (Winter): 223–38.

Gelb, Leslie H. (2009) *Power Rules: How Common Sense Can Rescue American Foreign Policy*. New York: HarperCollins.

——— and Morton H. Halperin. (1973) "The Ten Commandments of the Foreign Affairs Bureaucracy," pp. 250–59 in Steven L. Spiegel (ed.), *At Issue*. New York: St. Martin's.

Georgy, Michael. (2013) "Pakistan's Sharif Calls for Warmer Ties with India," *Reuters* (May 8). Accessed June 17, 2013. Available at: http://www.reuters.com/article/2013/05/08/us-pakistan-election-idUSBRE94704U20130508.

Gereffi, G. and J Lee. (2012) "Why the World Suddenly Cares about Global Supply Chains," *Journal of Supply Chain Management* 48(3): 24–32.

German, F. Clifford. (1960) "A Tentative Evaluation of World Power," *Journal of Conflict Resolution* 4 (March): 138–44.

Gershman, Carl. (2005) "Democracy as Policy Goal and Universal Value," *The Whitehead Journal of Diplomacy and International Affairs* (Winter/Spring): 19–38.

Gerson, Michael. (2006) "The View from the Top," *Newsweek* (August 21): 58–60.

Gertz, Bill. (2013) "U.S. Says Deal Violates International Accord," *The Washington Times* (March 21). Accessed June 12, 2013. Available at: http://www.washingtontimes.com/news/2013/mar/21/china-pakistan-reach-secret-reactor-deal-pakistan/?page=all.

Ghosh, Bobby. (2011) "Yemen: The Most Dangers Domino," *Time* (March 14): 44–49.

——— (2009) "Obama in Moscow," *Time* (July 13): 14.

Gibbs, Nancy. (2011) "The Best Investments: If You Really Want to Fight Poverty, Fuel Growth and Combat Extremism, Try Girl Power," *Time* (February 14): 64.

Gibler, Douglas M. (2007) "Bordering on Peace," *International Studies Quarterly* 51 (September): 509–532.

Giddens, Anthony. (1984) *The Constitution of Society: Outline of the Theory of Structuration*. Cambridge: Polity.

Gies, Erica. (2008) "New Wave in Energy: Turning Algae to Oil," *International Herald Tribune* (June 30): 3.

Gilbert, Alan. (2000) *Must Global Politics Constrain Democracy?* Princeton, NJ: Princeton University Press.

Gilboa, Eytan. (2005) "Global Television News and Foreign Policy," *International Studies Perspectives* 6 (August): 325–41.

——— (2003) "Foreign Policymaking in the Age of Global Television," *Georgetown Journal of International Affairs* 4 (Winter): 119–26.

——— (2002) "Global Communication and Foreign Policy," *Journal of Communication* 52 (December): 731–48.

Giles, Martin. (2010) "A World of Connections." *The Economist* (January 30): 3–4.

Gill, Stephen. (2001a) "Group of 7," pp. 340–41 in Joel Krieger (ed.), *The Oxford Companion to Politics of the World*, 2nd ed. Oxford: Oxford University Press.

——— (2001b) "Hegemony," pp. 354–86 in Joel Krieger (ed.), *The Oxford Companion to Politics of the World*, 2nd ed. Oxford: Oxford University Press.

Gilligan, Michael, and Stephen John Stedman. (2003) "Where Do the Peacekeepers Go?" *International Studies Review* 5 (4): 37–54.

Gilpin, Robert. (2004) "The Nature of Political Economy," pp. 403–10 in Karen A. Mingst and Jack L. Snyder (eds.), *Essential Readings in World Politics*, 2nd ed. New York: Norton.

——— (2002) *Global Political Economy: Understanding the International Economic Order*. Princeton, NJ: Princeton University Press.

——— (2001) "Three Ideologies of Political Economy," pp. 269–86 in Charles W. Kegley, Jr., and Eugene R. Wittkopf (eds.), *The Global Agenda*, 6th ed. Boston: McGraw-Hill.

——— (1981) *War and Change in World Politics*. Cambridge: Cambridge University Press.

Glaberson, William. (2001) "U.S. Courts Become Arbiters of Global Rights and Wrongs," *New York Times* (June 21): A1, A20.

Gladwell, Malcolm. (2001) *Blink*. New York: Little, Brown.

Glaeser, Edward. (2011) *Triumph of the City: How Our Greatest Invention Makes Us Richer, Smarter, Greener, Healthier and Happier*. New York: Penguin.

Glaser, Charles L. (2011) "Security Dilemma in Structural International Relations Theory," *The Encyclopedia of Peace Psychology* (November). DOI: 10.1002/9780470672532.wbepp245

Glasius, Marlies. (2009) "What Is Global Justice and Who Decides?: Civil Society and Victim Responses to the

International Criminal Court's First Investigations," *Human Rights Quarterly* 31: 496–520.

Glass, Ira and Adam Davidson. (2008) *This American Life: The Giant Pool of Money.* Radio Episode Aired on National Public Radio, May 9, 2008. Available at: http://www.thisamerican-life.org/extras/radio/355_transcript.pdf.

Gleditsch, Kristian Skrede. (2004) "A Revised List of Wars-Between and within Independent States, 1816–2002," *International Interactions* 30 (July/September): 231–62.

Glenn, Jerome C., Theodore J. Gordon, and Elizabeth Florescu. (2011) *2011 State of the Future.* Washington, DC: The Millennium Project.

Globalfirepower.com. (2013) *World Military Strength Ranking 2013.* Available at: globalfirepower.com.

——— (2009) *UN Finance,* Available at http://www.globalpolicy.org/un-finance.html.

——— (2006) *UN Finance,* Available at http://www.globalpolicy.org/finance/index.htm.

Goertz, Gary. (2003) *International Norms and Decision Making: A Punctuated Equilibrium Analysis.* Lanham, MD.: Rowman & Littlefield.

Goldberg, Jeffrey. (2005) "Breaking Ranks: What Turned Brent Scowcroft against the Bush Administration?" *New Yorker* (October 31): 52–65.

Goldsmith, Jack. (2008) *The Terror Presidency: Law and Judgment Inside the Bush Administration.* New York: Norton.

Goldsmith, Jack I., and Eric A. Posner. (2005) *The Limits of International Law.* New York: Oxford University Press.

Goldstein, Joshua S. (2005). *The Real Price of War.* New York: New York University Press.

——— (2002) *War and Gender.* Cambridge: Cambridge University Press.

Goldstone, Jack. (2010) "The New Population Bomb: The Four Megatrends That Will Change the World." *Foreign Affairs* 89, no. 1 (January/February): 31–43.

Gordon, John Steele. (2004) *An Empire of Wealth.* New York: HarperCollins.

Gordon, Joy. (2011) "Smart Sanctions Revisited," *Ethics & International Affairs* 25(3): 315–35.

Gore, Al. (2006) *An Inconvenient Truth: The Planetary Emergency and What We Can Do About It.* Emmaus, PA: Rodale.

Gottlieb, Gidon. (1982) "Global Bargaining," pp. 109–30 in Nicholas Greenwood Onuf (ed.), *Law-Making in the Global Community.* Durham, NC: Carolina Academic Press.

Goudreau, Jenna. (2013) "Eight Leadership Lessons from the World's Most Powerful Women," *Forbes* (March 21). Accessed June 27, 2013. Available at: http://www.forbes.com/sites/jennagoudreau/2013/03/21/eight-leadership-lessons-from-the-worlds-most-powerful-women/.

——— (2012) "With JPMorgan Chase's Ina Drew Out, Few Top Wall Street Women Left Standing," *Forbes* (May 14). Available at: http://www.forbes.com/sites/jenna goudreau/2012/05/14/with-jpmorgan-chases-ina-drew-out-few-top-wall-street-women-left-standing/.

Graff, James. (2007) "Fight for the Top of The World," *Time* (October 1): 28–36.

Graham, Edward. (2000) *Fighting the Wrong Enemy: Antiglobal Activists and Multinational Enterprises.* Washington, DC: Institute for International Economics.

Grant, Jason H. and Kathryn A. Boys. (2011) "On the Road to Doha," *Foreign Policy* (April 18). Accessed July 28, 2013. Available at: http://www.foreignpolicy.com/articles/2011/04/18/on_the_road_to_doha?page=0,1.

Grant, Ruth W., and Robert O. Keohane. (2005) "Accountability and Abuses of Power in World Politics," *American Political Science Review* 99 (February): 29–43.

Gray, John. (2010) "World Wide Web: The Myth and Reality of the United Nations." *Harper's Magazine* (June): 78–82.

Greenhill, Brian. (2010) "The Company You Keep: International Socialization and the Diffusion of Human Rights Norms." *International Studies Quarterly* 54: 127–45.

Greenstein, Fred I. (1987) *Personality and Politics.* Princeton, N.J.: Princeton University Press.

Gregory, Rob, Christian Henn, Brad McDonald, and Mika Saito. (2010) *Trade and the Crisis: Protect or Recover.* International Monetary Fund. Available at: http://www.imf.org/external/pubs/ft/spn/2010/spn1007.pdf.

Grey, Edward. (1925) *Twenty-Five Years, 1892–1916.* New York: Frederick Stokes.

Grieco, Joseph M. (1995) "Anarchy and the Limits of Cooperation: A Realist Critique of the Newest Liberal Institutionalism," pp. 151–71 in Charles W. Kegley, Jr. (ed.), *Controversies in International Relations Theory.* New York: St. Martin's.

Griffin, Penny. (2013) "Gendering Global Finance: Crisis, Masculinity, and Responsibility" *Men and Masculinities* 16 (1): 9–34.

Grimond, John. "For Want of a Drink," *The Economist* (May, 20, 2010): 3.

Groll, Elias. (2013) "Russia Is No Longer Worried about U.S. Missile Defense Systems," *Foreign Policy* (April 16). Accessed June 17, 2013. Available at: http://blog.foreignpolicy.com/posts/2013/04/16/russia_is_no_longer_worried_about_us_missile_defense_systems.

Grosby, Steven. (2006) *Nationalism.* New York: Oxford University Press.

Grunwald, Michael. (2009) "How Obama Is Using the Science of Change," *Time* (April 13): 28–32.

——— (2008) "The Clean Energy Scam," *Time* (April 7): 40–45.

Grusky, Sara. (2001) "Privatization Tidal Wave: IMF/World Bank Water Policies and the Price Paid by the Poor," *The Multinational Monitor* 22 (September). Available at: http://www.multinationalmonitor.org/mm2001/01september/sep-01corp2.htm.

Grussendorf, Jeannie. (2006) "When the Stick Works: Power in International Mediation," *International Studies Review* 8 (June): 318–20.

Gugliotta, Guy. (2004) "Scientists Say Warming to Increase -Extinctions," Columbia, S.C., *The State* (January 8): A6.

Gvosdev, Nikolas K. (2005) "The Value(s) of Realism," *The SAIS Review of International Affairs* 25 (Winter/Spring) 17–25.

Habermas, Jürgen. (1984) *The Theory of Communicative-Action*, 2 vols. Boston: Beacon Press.

Hafner-Burton, Emilie M., Kiyoteru Tsutsui, and John W. Meyer. (2008) "International Human Rights Law and the Politics of Legitimation: Repressive States and Human Rights Treaties," *International Sociology* 23 (January): 115–41.

Haggard, Stephan, and Beth A. Simmons. (1987) "Theories of International Regimes," *International Organization* 41 (Summer): 491–517.

Hales, Mike and Andres Pena. "2012 Global Cities Index and Emerging Cities Outlook." ATKearny. Accessed November 22, 2013. Available at http://www.atkearney.com/documents/10192/dfedfc4c-8a62-4162-90e5-2a3f14f0da3a

Hall, Anthony J. (2004) *The America Empire and the Fourth World.* Montreal: McGill-Queen's University Press.

Hall, John A. (2001) "Liberalism," pp. 499–502 in Joel Krieger (ed.), *The Oxford Companion to Politics of the World*, 2nd ed. Oxford: Oxford University Press.

Halper, Stephan. (2010) *The Beijing Consensus: How China's Authoritarian Model Will Dominate the Twenty-First Century.* New York: Basic Books.

Hamilton, Alexander. (1913 [1791]) *Report on Manufactures.* Washington, DC: U.S. Government. Accessed August 1, 2009. Available at books.google.com.

Hammes, Thomas X. (2004) *The Sling and the Stone: On War in the 21st Century.* St. Paul, Minn.: Zenith Press.

Hannah, Mark. (2009) "Issue Advocacy on the Internet, Part 1," *Mediashift.* (May 7). Available at: http://www.pbs.org/mediashift/2009/05/issue-advocacy-on-the-internet-part-1127.html.

Hannigan, John. (2012) *Disasters without Borders: The International Politics of Natural Disasters.* Cambridge: Polity.

Hanson, Daniel, Dayne Batten, and Harrison Ealey. (2013) "It's Time for the U.S. to End Its Senseless Embargo of Cuba," *Forbes* (January 16). Accessed July 27, 2013. Available at: http://www.forbes.com/sites/realspin/2013/01/16/its-time-for-the-u-s-to-end-its-senseless-embargo-of-cuba/.

Hanson, Victor Davis. (2003) *Ripples of Battle.* New York: Doubleday.

Hardin, Garrett. (1993) *Living within Limits.* Oxford: Oxford University Press.

—— (1968) "The Tragedy of the Commons," *Science* 162 (December): 1243–48.

Hardy, Quentin. (2013) "Global Slavery, by the Numbers," *The New York Times.* Accessed June 24, 2013.

Available at: http://bits.blogs.nytimes.com/2013/03/06/global-slavery-by-the-numbers/?_r=0.

Harknett, Richard J. and Hasan B. Yalcin. (2012). "The Structure for Autonomy: A Realist Structural Theory of International Relations." *International Studies Review* 14 (4): 499–521.

Harries, Owen. (1995) "Realism in a New Era," *Quadrant* 39 (April): 11–18.

Harris, Edward. (2008) "World Chopping Down Trees at Pace That Affects Climate," *The Cincinnati Enquirer* (February 3): A2.

Hartung, William. (2007) "Exporting Instability." *The Nation* (September 10–17): 8.

—— and Michelle Ciarrocca. (2005) "The Military Indus-trial-Think Tank Complex," pp. 103–7, in Glenn P. Hastedt (ed.), *American Foreign Policy 04/05*, 10th ed., Guiford, Conn: Dushkin/McGraw-Hill.

Hartzell, Caroline, and Matthew Hoddie. (2007) *Crafting Peace: Power-Sharing Institutions and the Negotiated Settlement of Civil Wars.* University Park, PA: The Pennsylvania State University Press.

Harvey, David. (2004) *The New Imperialism.* Oxford: Oxford University Press.

Haskin, Jeanne. (2005) *The Tragic Congo: From Decolonization to Dictatorship.* New York: Algora Publishing.

Hathaway, Oona A. (2007) "Why We Need International Law," *The Nation* (November 19): 35–39.

Hayden, Patrick. (2005) *Cosmopolitan Global Politics.* Burlington, Ver.: Ashgate.

Haynes, Jeffrey. (2005) *Comparative Politics in a Globalizing World.* Cambridge, UK: Polity.

—— (2004) "Religion and International Relations," *International Politics* 41 (September): 451–62.

He, Fan. (2013) "China Must Push Ahead with Exchange Rate Reforms," *East Asia Forum* (April 29). Accessed June 27, 2013. Available at: http://www.eastasiaforum.org/2013/04/29/china-must-push-ahead-with-exchange-rate-reforms/.

Hecht, Jeff. (2007). "Military Wings Ig-Nobel Peace Prize for 'Gay Bomb.'" *New Scientist.* Available at: http:// www.newscientist.com/article/dn12721.

Hedges, Chris. (2003) "What Every Person Should Know about War," *New York Times* (July 6). Available at: http://www.nytimes.com/2003/ 07/06/books/ chapters/0713-1st-hedges.html?pagewanted5all

Hegre, Håvard. (2004) "The Duration and Termination of Civil War," *Journal of Peace Research* 41 (May): 243–52.

—— John R. Oneal, and Bruce M. Russett. (2010) "Trade Does Promote Peace: New Simultaneous Estimates of the Reciprocal Efforts of Trade and Conflict," *Journal of Peace Research* 47(6): 763–774.

Hehir, J. Bryan. (2002) "The Limits of Loyalty," *Foreign Policy* (September/October): 38–39.

Hellion, Christophe. (2010) "The Creeping Nationalism of the EU Enlargement Policy." *Swedish Institute for European Policy Studies (SIEPS).* (November), No. 6.

Hellman, Christopher. (2009) "Analysis of the Fiscal Year 2010 Pentagon Spending Request," Center for Arms Control and Non-Proliferation. (May 8). Available at: http://www.armscontrolcenter.org/policy/missiledefense/articles/050809_analysis_fy2010_pentagon_request/.

Hensel, Howard M. (ed.). (2007) *The Law of Armed Conflict.* Burlington, Ver.: Ashgate.

Heredia, Blanca. (1999) "Prosper or Perish? Development in the Age of Global Capital," pp. 93–97 in Robert M. Jackson (ed.), *Global Issues 1999/00,* 15th ed. Guilford, Conn.: Dushkin/McGraw-Hill.

Heritage Foundation. (2013) "2013 Index of Economic Freedom." *The Heritage Foundation.* Available at: http://www.heritage.org/index/.

Hermann, Charles F. (1988) "New Foreign Policy Problems and Old Bureaucratic Organizations," pp. 248–65 in Charles W. Kegley, Jr., and Eugene R. Wittkopf (eds.), *The Domestic Sources of American Foreign Policy.* New York: St. Martin's.

Hermann, Margaret G. (2007) *Comparative Foreign Policy Analysis: Theories and Methods.* Upper Saddle River, N.J.: Prentice Hall.

——— (1976) "When Leader Personality Will Affect Foreign Policy," pp. 326–33 in James N. Rosenau (ed.), *In Search of Global Patterns.* New York: Free Press.

——— and Joe D. Hagan. (2004) "International Decision Making: Leadership Matters," pp. 182–88 in Karen A. Mingst and Jack L. Snyder (eds.), *Essential Readings in World Politics,* 2nd ed. New York: Norton.

——— and Charles W. Kegley, Jr. (2001) "Democracies and Intervention," *Journal of Peace Research* 38 (March): 237–45.

Hernandez-Truyol, Berta Esperanza, and Stephen J. Powell. (2012) *Just Trade: A New Covenant Linking Trade and Human Rights.* New York: NYU Press.

Herrmann, Richard K., and Richard Ned Lebow (eds.). (2004) *Ending the Cold War: Interpretations, Causation, and the Study of International Relations.* London: Palgrave Macmillan.

Hersh, Seymour M. (2005) "The Coming Wars: What the Pentagon Can Now Do in Secret," *New Yorker* (January 24 and 31): 40–47.

Herszenhorn, David M. and Michael R. Gordon. (2013) "U.S. Cancels Part of Missile Defense That Russia Opposed," *The New York Times* (March 16). Accessed June 13, 2013. Available at: http://www.nytimes.com/2013/03/17/world/europe/with-eye-on-north-korea-us-cancels-missile-defense-russia-opposed.html?_r=1&.

Hertsgaard, Mark. (2003) *The Eagle's Shadow: Why America Fascinates and Infuriates the World.* New York: Picador/Farrar, Straus & Giroux.

Herz, John H. (1951) *Political Realism and Political Idealism.* Chicago: University of Chicago Press.

Higgins, Michelle. (2011) "New Ways to Visit Cuba—Legally," *New York Times* (June 30): TR3.

Hillion, Christophe. (2010) *The Creeping Nationalisation of the EU Enlargement Policy.* Stockholm, Sweden: Swedish Institute for European Policy Studies. Available at: http://wider-europe.org/sites/default/files/attachments/events/SIEPS%20report.pdf

Hindle, Tim. (2004) "The Third Age of Globalization," pp. 97–98 in *The Economist, The World in 2004.* London: Economist.

Hironaka, Ann. (2005) *Neverending Wars.* Cambridge, MA: Harvard University Press.

Hirsh, Michael. (2003) *At War with Ourselves: Why America Is Squandering Its Chance to Build a Better World.* Oxford: Oxford University Press.

Hirschman, Albert. (1945) *National Power and the Structure of Foreign Trade.* Berkeley: University of California Press.

Hobson, John A. (1965 [1902]) *Imperialism.* Ann Arbor: University of Michigan Press.

Hodge, Carl Cavanagh. (2005) *Atlanticism for a New Century.* Upper Saddle River, NJ: Prentice Hall.

Hoekman, Bernard M. and Petros C. Mavroidis. (2012) "WTO 'à la carte' or WTO 'menu du jour'? Assessing the Case for Plurilateral Agreements." Accessed July 27, 2013. Available at: http://globalgovernanceprogramme.eui.eu/wp-content/uploads/2012/11/Hoekman_Mavroidis_Plurilaterals.pdf.

Hoffman, David E. (2011) "The New Virology: The Future of War by Other Means," *Foreign Policy* (March/April): 77–80.

Hoffman, Eva. (2000) "Wanderers by Choice," *Utne Reader* (July/August): 46–48.

Hoffmann, Matthew. (2009) "Is Constructivist Ethics and Oxymoron." *International Studies Review* 11 (2): 231–52.

Hoffmann, Stanley. (1998) *World Disorders.* Lanham, MD.: Rowman & Littlefield.

——— (1992) "To the Editors," *New York Review of Books* (June 24): 59.

——— (1971) "International Law and the Control of Force," pp. 34–66 in Karl W. Deutsch and Stanley Hoffmann (eds.), *The Relevance of International Law.* Garden City, N.Y: Doubleday-Anchor.

——— (1961) "International Systems and International Law," pp. 205–37 in Klaus Knorr and Sidney Verba (eds.), *The International System.* Princeton, N.J.: Princeton University Press.

——— with Frédéric Bozo. (2004) *Gulliver Unbound: America's Imperial Temptation and the War in Iraq.* Lanham, MD.: Rowman & Littlefield.

Hoge, James F., Jr. (2006) "A Global Power Shift in the Making," pp. 3–6 in Helen E. Purkitt (ed.), *World Politics 05/06.* Dubuque, IA: McGraw-Hill/Dushkin.

Hollander, Jack M. (2003) *The Real Crisis: Why Poverty, Not Affluence, Is the Environment's Number One Enemy.* Berkeley: University of California Press.

Holstein, William J. (2005) "One Global Game, Two Sets of Rules," *The New York Times* (August 14): BU9.

Holsti, Kalevi J. (2004) *Taming the Sovereigns: Institutional Changes in International Politics.* Cambridge: Cambridge University Press.

——— (1991) *Peace and War.* Cambridge: Cambridge University Press.

Holsti, Ole R. (2001) "Models of International Relations: Realist and Neoliberal Perspectives on Conflict and Cooperation," pp. 121–35 in Charles W. Kegley, Jr., and Eugene R. Wittkopf (eds.), *The Global Agenda*, 6th ed. Boston: McGraw-Hill.

Holt, Jim. (2005) "Time-Bandits," *New Yorker* (February 28): 80–85.

Homer-Dixon, Thomas. (2006) "The Rise of Complex Terrorism," pp. 214–20 in Thomas J. Badey (ed.), *Violence and Terrorism 06/07.* Dubuque, IA: McGraw-Hill.

Hooper, Charlotte. (2001) *Manly States.* New York: Columbia University Press.

Hopkins, Terence K., and Immanuel Wallerstein (eds.). (1996) *The Age of Transitions: Trajectory of World Systems 1945–2025.* London: Zed.

Horkheimer, Max. (1947) *Eclipse of Reason.* New York: Oxford University Press.

Horowitz, Michael. (2009) "The Spread of Nuclear Weapons and International Conflict: Does Experience Matter?" *Journal of Conflict Resolution* 53 (2): 234–257.

Hosenball, Mark. (2009) "The Danger of Escalation," *Newsweek* (April 27): 43.

Hough, Peter. (2004) *Understanding Global Security.* New York: Routledge.

House, Karen Elliot. (1989) "As Power Is Dispersed among Nations, Need for Leadership Grows," *Wall Street Journal* (February 21): A1, A10.

Howard, Michael E. (1978) *War and the Liberal Conscience.* New York: Oxford University Press.

Howell, Llewellyn D. (2003) "Is the New Global Terrorism a Clash of Civilizations?" pp. 173–84 in Charles W. Kegley, Jr. (ed.), *The New Global Terrorism.* Upper Saddle River, NJ: Prentice Hall.

——— (1998) "The Age of Sovereignty Has Come to an End," *USA Today* 127 (September): 23.

Htun, Mala, and S. Laurel Weldon. (2010) "When Do Governments Promote Women's Rights? A Framework for the Comparative Analysis of Sex Equality Policy." *Perspectives on Politics* 8(1) (March): 207–216.

Hudson, Kimberly A. (2009) *Justice, Intervention, and Force in International Relations: Reassessing Just War Theory in the 21st Century.* New York: Routledge.

Hudson, Natalie F. (2005) "En-Gendering UN Peacekeeping Operations," *International Journal* 60 (3): 785–807.

Hudson, Valerie M. (2012) *Sex and World Peace.* New York, NY: Columbia University Press.

——— (2007) *Foreign Policy Analysis: Classic and Contemporary Theory.* New York: Rowman & Littlefield Publishers.

Hufbauer, Gary Clyde, Jeffrey J. Schott, and Kimberly Ann Elliott. (1990) *Economic Sanctions Reconsidered*, 2nd ed. Washington, DC: Institute for International Economics.

——— and B. Oegg. (2007) *Economic Sanctions Reconsidered*, 3rd ed. Washington, DC: Institute for International Economics.

Hughes, Emmet John. (1972) *The Living Presidency.* New York: Coward, McCann and Geoghegan.

Hulsman, John C, and Anatol Lievan. (2005) "The Ethics of Realism," *The National Interest* 80 (Summer): 37–43.

Hulsman, John C., and A. Wess Mitchell. *The Godfather Doctrine: A Foreign Policy Parable.* Princeton, NJ: Princeton University Press.

Human Rights Dialogue (2005). Series 2 (Spring): 1–34. New York: Carnegie Council for Ethics in International Affairs.

Human Security Centre. (2006) *Human Security Brief 2006.* Vancouver: The University of British Columbia, Canada.

Hume, David. (1817) *Philosophical Essays on Morals, Literature, and Politics*, Vol. 1. Washington, D.C.: Duffy.

Hunt, Swanee, and Cristina Posa. (2005) "Women Making Peace," pp. 212–17 in Robert J. Griffiths (ed.), *Developing World 05/06.* Dubuque, IA: McGraw-Hill/Dushkin.

Huntington, Samuel P. (2005) "The Lonely Superpower" pp. 540–550 in G. John Ikenberry (ed.), *American Foreign Policy: Theoretical Essays.* New York: Pearson/Longman.

——— (2004) "The Hispanic Challenge," *Foreign Policy* (March/April): 30–45.

——— (2001a) "The Coming Clash of Civilizations, or the West against the Rest," pp. 199–202 in Charles W. Kegley, Jr., and Eugene R. Wittkopf (eds.), *The Global Agenda*, 6th ed. Boston: McGraw-Hill.

——— (2001b) "Migration Flows Are the Central Issue of Our Time," *International Herald Tribune* (February 2): 6.

——— (1996) *The Clash of Civilizations and the Remaking of World Order.* New York: Simon & Schuster.

——— (1991a) *The Third Wave: Democratization in the Late Twentieth Century.* Norman: University of Oklahoma Press.

——— (1991b) "America's Changing Strategic Interests," *Survival* (January/February): 5–6.

Hurwitz, Jon and Mark Peffley. (1987) "How Are Foreign Policy Attitudes Structured?" *American Political Science Review* 81 (December): 1099–1120.

Hutchings, Kimberly. (2008) "1988 to 1998: Contrast and Continuity in Feminist International Relations." *Millennium—Journal of International Studies* (37): 97–105.

Huth, Paul K. and Todd L. Allee. (2003) *The Democratic Peace and Territorial Conflict in the Twentieth Century.* Cambridge: Cambridge University Press.

Hymans, Jacques E. C. (2012) "Botching the Bomb: Why Nuclear Weapons Programs Often Fail on Their Own—and

Why Iran's Might, Too," *Foreign Affairs* (May/June). Accessed August 8, Available at: http://www.foreignaffairs.com/articles/137403/jacques-e-c-hymans/botching-the-bomb.

Ibrahim, Abadir M. (2013) "International Trade and Human Rights: An Unfinished Debate." German Law Journal 14: 321.

Ikenberry, G. John. (2011) *Liberal Leviathan: The Origins, Crisis, and Transformation of the American World Order*. Princeton, NJ: Princeton University Press.

Ignatieff, Michael. (2005a) "Human Rights, Power, and the State," pp. 59–75 in Simon Chesterman, Michael Ignatieff, and Ramesh Thakur (eds.), *Making States Work: State Failure and the Crisis of Governance*. Tokyo: United Nations University Press.

——— (2005b) "Who Are the Americans to Think That Freedom Is Theirs to Spread?" *New York Times Magazine* (June 28): 40–47.

——— (2004a) "Hard Choices on Human Rights," pp. 54–55 in *The Economist, The World in 2004*. London: Economist.

——— (2001a) "The Danger of a World without Enemies," *New Republic* 234 (February 26): 25–28.

——— (2001b) *Human Rights as Politics and Ideology*. Princeton, N.J.: Princeton University Press.

Ikenberry, G. John. (2011) "The Future of the Liberal World Order: Internationalism after America," *Foreign Affairs* (May/June): 56–68.

——— (2008) "The Rise of China and the Future of the West," *Foreign Affairs* 87 (January/February): 23–37.

——— (2004) "Is American Multilateralism in Decline?" pp. 262–82 in Karen A. Mingst and Jack L. Snyder (eds.), *Essential Readings in World Politics,* 2nd ed. New York: Norton.

Iklé, Fred Charles. (2007) *Annihilation from Within*. New York: Columbia University Press.

Independent Evaluation Office, International Monetary Fund. (2011) *IMF Performance in the Run-Up to the Financial and Economic Crisis*. Washington, DC: International Monetary Fund.

Interlandi, Janeen. (2010) "The Race to Buy Up the World's Water," *Newsweek* (18 October): 39–46.

International Labour Office. (2004) *Working Out of Poverty*. Geneva: International Labour Office.

International Monetary Fund (IMF). (2013a) *World Economic Outlook: Hopes, Realities, Risks*. Washington, DC: International Monetary Fund Publication Services.

——— (2013b) "Currency Composition of Official Foreign Exchange Reserves (COFER)" Accessed June 27, 2013. Available at: http://www.imf.org/external/np/sta/cofer/eng/cofer.pdf.

——— (2012a) "World Economic Outlook Database." Accessed June 21, 2012. Available at: http://www.imf.org/external/pubs/ft/weo/2012/01/weodata/index.aspx.

——— (2012b) "Currency Composition of Official Foreign Exchange Reserves (COFER)." Available at: http://www.imf.org/external/np/sta/cofer/eng/cofer.pdf.

——— (2011) "Global Financial Stability Report." *International Monetary Fund* (September 18). Available at: http://www.imf.org/external/pubs/ft/gfsr.

——— (2010) "Currency Composition of Official Foreign Exchange Reserves." Available at http://www.imf.org/external/np/sta/cofer/eng/cofer/pdf.

——— (2009) "Global Economy Contracts." *IMF Survey Online.* Available at: http://www.imf.org/external/pubs/ft/survey/so/2009/RES042209A.htm.

——— (2009) "De Facto Classification of Exchange Rate Regimes and Monetary Policy Frameworks". Available at: http://www.imf.org/external/np/mfd/er/2008/eng/0408.htm.

——— (2007) *World Economic Outlook: Spillovers and Cycles in the Global Economy.* New York: International Monetary Fund.

——— (2005) *World Economic Outlook, April 2005.* New York: International Monetary Fund.

Inglehart, Ronald and Christian Welzel. (2009) "How Development Leads to Democracy," *Foreign Affairs* 88 (March/April): 33–48.

International Herald Tribune. (2009) "Pakistan Hits Taliban Sites in Key Area Near Capital," *International Herald Tribune* (April 29): 1.

International Work Group for Indigenous Affairs. "The Indigenous World." Accessed June 3, 2013. Available at: http://www.iwgia.org/regions.

——— (2012) "The Indigenous World." Available at: http://www.iwgia.org/regions.

——— (2011) *The Indigenous World 2011.* (June 2). Available at: http://shop.iwgia.org/pi/The_Indigenous_World_2011_2125_80.aspx.

Iqbal, Zaryab and Christopher Zorn. (2010) "Violent Conflict and the Spread of HIV/AIDS in Africa." *The Journal of Politics* 72(1) (January): 149–162.

Irwin, Douglas. (2009) *Free Trade Under Fire*, 3rd ed. Princeton, NJ: Princeton University Press.

IUCN (International Union for the Conservation of Nature). (2012) "Biodiversity." Accessed August 8, 2012. Available at: http://www.iucn.org/what/tpas/biodiversity/.

Jackson, Derrick Z. (2007) "Spreading Fear, Selling Weapons," Columbia, S.C., *The State* (August 6): A9.

Jackson, Patrick. (2004) "Bridging the Gap: Towards a Realist-Constructivist Dialogue," *International Studies Review* 6: 337–352.

Jackson, Richard. (2013) "Balancing Adequacy and Sustainability: Lessons from the Global Aging Preparedness Index," *Over 65* blog (May 3). Accessed June 22, 2013. Available at: http://www.over65.thehastingscenter.org/balancing-adequacy-and-sustainability-lessons-from-the-global-aging-preparedness-index/.

Jacobson, Harold K. (1984) *Networks of Interdependence.* New York: Knopf.

Jaeger, Hans-Martin. (2007) "Global Civil Society and the Political Depoliticization of Global Governance," *International Political Sociology* 1 (September): 257–277.

Jaffe, Greg, and Jonathan Karp. (2005) "Pentagon Girds for Big Spending Cuts," *Wall Street Journal* (November 5): A7.

James, Barry. (2002a) "Summit Aims, Again, for a Better World," *International Herald Tribune* (August 8): 1, 8.

——— (2002b) "Talks to Tackle Threat to Biodiversity," *International Herald Tribune* (August 23): 1, 9.

Janis, Irving. (1982) *Groupthink: Psychological Studies of Policy Decisions and Fiascoes*, 2nd ed. Boston: Houghton Mifflin.

Janowski, Louis. (2006) "Neo-Imperialism and U.S. Foreign Policy," pp. 54–61 in John T. Rourke (ed.), *Taking Sides*. Dubuque, IA: McGraw-Hill/Dushkin.

Jenkins, Michael. (2009) "Linking Communities, Forests, and Carbon," in Lael Brainard et al. (eds.), *Climate Change and Global Poverty: A Billion Lives in the Balance?* Washington, DC: The Brookings Institution.

Jennings, Ralph. (2010) "China on Track to Aim 2,000 Missiles at Taiwan: Report." *Reuters* (19 July). Available at: http://www.reuters.com/article/2010/07/19/us-taiwan-china-idUSTRE66I13F20100719?feedType5RSS.

Jensen, Lloyd. (1982) *Explaining Foreign Policy*. Englewood Cliffs, N.J.: Prentice Hall.

Jentleson, Bruce and Ely Ratner. (2011) "Bridging the Beltway-Ivory Tower Gap" *International Studies* 13 (1): 6–11.

Jervis, Robert. (2008) "Unipolarity: A Structural Perspective," *World Politics* 61:188–213.

——— (2005) *American Foreign Policy in a New Era*. New York: Routledge.

——— (1992) "A Usable Past for the Future," pp. 257–68 in Michael J. Hogan (ed.), *The End of the Cold War*. New York: Cambridge University Press.

——— (1985c) *World Politics* 38 (October): 58–79.

——— (1976) *Perception and Misperception in World Politics*. Princeton, NJ: Princeton University Press.

Joffe-Walt, Chana. (2013) "The Cotton Wars," NPR (May 3). Accessed July 27, 2013. Available at: http://www.npr.org/blogs/money/2013/05/03/180912847/episode-224-the-cotton-wars.

Johnson, Chalmers. (2004a) *Blowback: The Costs and Consequences of American Empire*. New York: Henry Holt.

——— (2004b) *The Sorrows of Empire*. New York: Metropolitan Books/Henry Holt.

Johnson, James Turner. (2005) "Just War, as It Was and Is," *First Things* 149 (January): 14–24.

——— (2003) "Just War Theory: Responding Morally to Global Terrorism," pp. 223–38 in Charles W. Kegley, Jr. (ed.), *The New Global Terrorism*. Upper Saddle River, NJ: Prentice Hall.

Johnson, Robert. (2012) "For the First Time Ever Taiwan Has Cruise Missiles Aimed at Mainland China," *Business Insider* (May 29). Accessed June 25, 2012. Available at: http://www.businessinsider.com/for-the-first-time-ever-taiwan-has-cruise-missiles-aimed-at-mainland-china-2012–5.

Johnston, Michael. (2006) *Syndromes of Corruption*. Cambridge: Cambridge University Press.

Jolly, David. (2013) "G-20 Pushes for Measures to End Tax Evasion," *New York Times* (April 19). Accessed June 27, 2013. Available at: http://www.nytimes.com/2013/04/20/business/global/g-20-pushes-for-measures-to-end-tax-evasion.html?_r=0.

Jones, Bruce, Carlos Pascual, and Stephen John Stedman. (2009) *Power & Responsibility: Building International Order in an Era of Transnational Threats*. Washington DC: Brookings.

Jones, Dorothy V. (2002) *Toward a Just World*. Chicago: University of Chicago Press.

——— (1991) *Code of Peace: Ethics and Security in the World of the Warlord States*. Chicago: University of Chicago Press.

Jones, Terril Yue. (2013) "China Has 'Mountains of Data' about U.S. Cyber Attacks: Official," *Reuters* (June 5). Accessed June 7, 2013. Available at: http://news.yahoo.com/china-mountains-data-u-cyber-attacks-official-042422920.html.

Joyce, Mark. (2005) "From Kosovo to Katrina," *International Herald Tribune* (August 8): 6.

Joyner, Christopher C. (2005) *International Law in the 21st Century*. Lanham, Md.: Rowman & Littlefield.

Joyner, James. (2011) "Back in the Saddle: How Libya Helped NATO Get Its Groove Back," *Foreign Policy* (April 15). Available at: http://www.foreignpolicy.com/ articles/2011/04/15/back_in_the_saddle

Judis, John B. (2005) *The Folly of Empire*. New York: Scribner.

——— (2004) "Imperial Amnesia," *Foreign Policy* (July/August): 50–59.

Judt, Tony. (2007) "From Military Disaster to Moral High Ground," *New York Times* (October 7): 15.

——— (2005) "The New World Order," *New York Review of Books* 52 (July 14): 14–18.

——— and Denis Lacorne (eds.). (2005) *With US or against US: Studies in Global Anti-Americanism*. London: Palgrave Macmillan.

Juergensmeyer, Mark. (2003) "The Religious Roots of Contemporary Terrorism," pp. 185–93 in Charles W. Kegley, Jr. (ed.), *The New Global Terrorism*. Upper Saddle River, N.J.: Prentice Hall.

Justino, Patricia. (2009) "Poverty and Violent Conflict: A Micro-Level Perspective on the Causes and Duration of Warfare," *Journal of Peace Research* 46 (3): 315–33.

Kagan, Robert. (2007) *Dangerous Nation*. New York: Knopf.

Kahneman, Daniel. (2011) *Thinking, Fast and Slow*. New York: Farrar, Straus, and Giroux.

——— (2003) "Maps of Bounded Nationality," *American Economic Review* 93 (December):1449–1475.

Kaiser, David. (1990) *Politics and War*. Cambridge, MA: Harvard University Press.

Kam, Cindy D. and Elizabeth N. Simas. (2010) "Risk Orientations and Policy Frames," *Journal of Politics* 72(2): 381–396.

Kaminski, Matthew. (2002) "Anti-Terrorism Requires Nation Building," *Wall Street Journal* (March 15): A10.

Kan, Shirley A. and Wayne M. Morrison. (2013) "U.S.-Taiwan Relationship: Overview of Policy Issues," *Congressional Research Service* (July 23). Accessed July 27, 2013. Available at: http://www.fas.org/sgp/crs/row/R41952.pdf.

Kanellos, Michael. (2013) "Google Explains Why the Future of Energy Is Green," *Forbes* (March 20). Accessed July 4, 2013. Available at: http://www.forbes.com/sites/michaelkanellos/2013/03/20/google-explains-why-the-future-of-energy-is-green/.

Kaneko, Kaori. (2013) "Japan Wins Approval from Member Countries to Join Tran-Pacific Tade Talks," *Reuters* (April 20). Accessed May 29, 2013. Available at: http://www.reuters.com/article/2013/04/20/us-trade-asiapacific-japan-idUSBRE93J09Y20130420.

Kanet, Roger. (2010) "Foreign Policy Making in a Democratic Society." *International Studies Review* 12: 123–127.

Kant, Immanuel. (1964; 1798). *Anthropologie in Pragmatischer Hinsicht*. Darmstadt, Germany: Werke.

Kaplan, Morton A. (1957) *System and Process in International Politics*. New York: Wiley.

Kaplan, Robert D. (2012) "John J. Mearsheimer is Right (About Some Things)" Financial Review (February 10). Last accessed November 22, 2013. Available at: http://www.afr.com/p/lifestyle/review/john_mearsheimer_is_right_about_0gGV0Ha2WZnzbvW2Sp1XVN.

——— (2009a) "The Revenge of Geography" *Foreign Policy* (May/June): 96–105.

——— (2009b) "Center Stage for the Twenty-first Century," *Foreign Affairs* 88 (2): 16–32.

——— (2005a) "How We Would Fight China," *Atlantic Monthly* 295 (May): 49–64.

——— (2005b) "Supremacy by Stealth," pp. 91–100 in Helen E. Purkitt (ed.), *World Politics 04/05*. Dubuque, IA: McGraw-Hill/Dushkin.

Kapstein, Ethan B. (2006) "The New Global Slave Trade," *Foreign Affairs* 85 (November/December): 103–115.

——— (2004) "Models of International Economic Justice," *Ethics & International Affairs* 18 (2): 79–92.

Kapur, Devesh, and John McHale. (2003) "Migration's New Payoff," *Foreign Policy* (November/December): 49–57.

Karns, Margaret P., and Karen A. Mingst. (2004) *International Organizations*. Boulder, Colo: Lynne Rienner.

Kasher, Asa, and Amos Yadlin. (2005) "Assassination and Preventive Killing," *SAIS Review* 25 (Winter/Spring): 41–57.

Kassimeris, Christos. (2009) "The Foreign Policy of Small Powers" *International Politics* 46 (1):84–101.

Kastner, Scott L. (2010) "The Security Consequences of China-Taiwan Economic Integration," *Testimony before the U.S.-China Economic and Security Review Commission* (March 18).

——— and Phillip C. Saunders. (2012) "Is China a Status Quo or Revisionist State? Leadership Travel as an Empirical Indicator of Foreign Policy Priorities," *International Studies Quarterly* 56 (1): 163–177.

Kathman, Jacob D. (2010) "Civil War Contagion and Neighboring Interventions," *International Studies Quarterly* 54: 989–1012.

Katznelson, Ira and Helen V. Milner (eds.) (2002) *Political Science: State of the Discipline*. Centennial edition. New York: W.W. Norton & Company.

Kaufman, Frederick. (2009) "Let Them Eat Cash," *Harper's* (June): 51–59.

Kaufman, Joyce P. and Kristen P. Williams. (2007) *Women, the State, and War: A Comparative Perspective on Citizenship and Nationalism*. Lanham, MD: Lexington Books.

Kavanagh, Jennifer. (2011) "Selection, Availability, and Opportunity: The Conditional Effect of Poverty on Terrorist Group Participation," *Journal of Conflict Resolution* 55 (1): 106–132.

Kay, Katty and Claire Shipman. (2009) "Fixing the Economy Is Women's Work." *The Washington Post* (July 12). Available at: //http://www.washingtonpost.com/wp-dyn/content/article/2009/07/10/AR2009071002358.html.

Kearney, A. T. (2004) "Measuring Globalization" *Foreign Policy* (March/April): 54–69.

——— (2002) "Globalization's Last Hurrah?" *Foreign Policy* (January/February): 38–71.

Keating, Joshua. (2011) "How Do You Hire Mercenaries?: It Helps to Have Connections in Post-Conflict Countries," *Foreign Policy* (February 23). Available at: http://www.foreignpolicy.com/articles/2011/02/23/how_do_you_hire_mercenaries.

——— (2009) "The Longest Shadow" *Foreign Policy* (May/June): 28.

——— (2009b) "The New Coups" *Foreign Policy* (May/June): 28.

Keck, Margaret E., and Kathryn Sikkink. (2008) "Transnational Advocacy Networks in International Politics," pp. 279–90 in Karen A. Mingst and Jack L. Snyder (eds.), *Essential Readings in World Politics*, 3rd ed. New York: Norton.

——— (1998) *Activists Beyond Borders: Advocacy Networks in International Politics*. Ithaca, NY: Cornell University Press.

Keegan, John. (1999) *The First World War*. New York: Knopf.

——— (1993). *A History of Warfare*. New York: Knopf.

Kegley, Charles W., Jr. (ed.). (1995) *Controversies in International Relations Theory: Realism and the Neoliberal Challenge*. New York: St. Martin's.

——— (1994) "How Did the Cold War Die? Principles for an Autopsy," *Mershon International Studies Review* 38 (March): 11–41.

——— (1993) "The Neoidealist Moment in International Studies? Realist Myths and the New International Realities," *International Studies Quarterly* 37 (June): 131–46.

——— (1992) "The New Global Order: The Power of Principle in a Pluralistic World," *Ethics & International Affairs* 6: 21–42.

——— and Margaret G. Hermann. (2002) "In Pursuit of a Peaceful International System," pp. 15–29 in Peter J. Schraeder (ed.), *Exporting Democracy.* Boulder, Colo.: Lynne Rienner.

——— (1997) "Putting Military Intervention into the Democratic Peace," *Comparative Political Studies* 30 (February): 78–107.

Kegley, Charles W., Jr., and Gregory A. Raymond. (2007a) *After Iraq: The Imperiled American Imperium.* New York: Oxford University Press.

——— (2007b) *The Global Future,* 2nd ed. Belmont, Calif.: Wadsworth/Thomson Learning.

——— (2004) "Global Terrorism and Military Preemption: Policy Problems and Normative Perils," *International Politics* 41 (January): 37–49.

——— (2002a) *Exorcising the Ghost of Westphalia: Building World Order in the New Millennium.* Upper Saddle River, N.J.: Prentice Hall.

——— (2002b) *From War to Peace: Fateful Decisions in World Politics.* Belmont, Calif.: Wadsworth.

——— (1999) *How Nations Make Peace.* Boston: Bedford/ St. Martin's.

——— (1994) *A Multipolar Peace? Great-Power Politics in the Twenty-First Century.* New York: St. Martin's.

——— (1990) *When Trust Breaks Down: Alliance Norms and World Politics.* Columbia: University of South Carolina Press.

Kegley, Charles W., Jr., Gregory A. Raymond, and Margaret G. Hermann. (1998) "The Rise and Fall of the Nonintervention Norm: Some Correlates and Potential Consequences," *Fletcher Forum of World Affairs* 22 (Winter/Spring): 81–101.

Kegley, Charles W., Jr., with Eugene R. Wittkopf. (2006) *World Politics,* 10th ed. Belmont, Calif.: Wadsworth/Thomson Learning.

——— (1982) *American Foreign Policy,* 2nd ed. New York: St. Martin's.

Kekic, Laza. (2010) "The State of the State," *The Economist: The World in 2011* (November 22): 90.

Keller, Jonathan W. (2005) "Leadership Style, Regime Type, and Foreign Policy Crisis Behavior," *International Studies Quarterly* 49 (June): 205–31.

Kellman, Barry. (2007) *Bioviolence.* Cambridge: Cambridge University Press.

Kelsen, Hans. (2009) *General Theory of Law and State.* Cambridge, MA: Harvard University Press.

Kennan, George F. (1985) "Morality and Foreign Policy," *Foreign Affairs* 64 (Winter): 205–218.

——— (1984) *The Fateful Alliance.* New York: Pantheon.

——— ["X"]. (1947) "The Sources of Soviet Conduct," *Foreign Affairs* 25 (July): 566–82.

Kennedy, Paul. (2006) "The Perils of Empire," pp. 69–71 in Helen E. Purkitt (ed.), *World Politics 05/06.* Dubuque, IA: McGraw-Hill/Dushkin.

——— (1987) *The Rise and Fall of the Great Powers.* New York: Random House.

Keohane, Robert O. (2012) "Hegemony and after," *Foreign Affairs* (July/August). Accessed June 27, 2013. Available at: http://www.foreignaffairs.com/articles/137690/robert-o-keohane/hegemony-and-after.

——— (1998) "Beyond Dichotomy: Conversations between International Relations and Feminist Theory." *International Studies Quarterly* 42 (1): 193–197

——— (1984) *After Hegemony: Cooperation and Discord in the World Political Economy.* Princeton: Princeton University Press.

Keohane, Robert O., and Joseph S. Nye. (2013) "Power and Interdependence," in *Conflict after the Cold War: Arguments on Causes of War and Peace,* 4th edition. Richard K. Betts, ed. Boston, MA: Pearson. pp164–171.

——— (2001) *Power and Interdependence,* 3rd ed. New York: Addison WesleyLongman.

Keynes, John. (1936) *The General Theory of Employment, Interest, and Money,* Macmillan Cambridge University Press.

Khanna, Parag. (2010) "Beyond City Limits: The Age of Nations Is Over. The New Urban Era Has Begun," *Foreign Policy* (September/October): 120–123.

——— (2006) "United They Fall," *Harper's* (January): 31–40.

Kher, Unmesh. (2006) "Oceans of Nothing," *Time* (November 13): 56–57.

Kibbe, Jennifer D. (2004) "The Rise of Shadow Warriors." *Foreign Affairs* 83 (March/April): 102–15.

Kifner, John. (2005) "A Tide of Islamic Fury, and How It Rose," *New York Times* (January 30): Section 4, 4–5.

Kilkenny, Allison. (2013) "Thousands Protest the UK Government's Brutal Austerity," *The Nation* (April 1). Accessed June 27, 2013. Available at: http://www.thenation.com/blog/173602/thousands-protest-uk-governments-brutal-austerity#axzz2X9O8OVGt.

Kim, Dae Jung, and James D. Wolfensohn. (1999) "Economic Growth Requires Good Governance," *International Herald Tribune* (February 26): 6.

Kim, Samuel S. (1991) "The United Nations, Lawmaking and World Order," pp. 109–24 in Richard A. Falk, Samuel S. Kim, and Saul H. Mendlovitz (eds.), *The United Nations and a Just World Order.* Boulder, CO: Westview.

Kindleberger, Charles. (2001) *Manics, Panics, and Crashes: A History of Financial Crises,* 5th ed. Hoboken, NJ: John Wiley and Sons.

——— (2000) *Manics, Panics, and Crashes: A History of Financial Crises,* 4th ed. New York: John Wiley and Sons.

——— (1973) *The World in Depression, 1929–1939.* Berkeley: University of California Press.

————, Robert Ailber, and Robert Solow. (2005) *Manics, Panics, and Crashes: A History of Financial Crises*, 5th ed. Hoboken, NJ: Wiley.

King, Gary, and Langche Zeng. (2007) "When Can History be Our Guide?" *International Studies Quarterly* 51 (March): 183–210.

———— (2005) "Battle Splits Conservative Magazine," *New York Times* (13 March): 12.

Kingsbury, Kathleen. (2007) "The Changing Face of Breast Cancer," *Time* (October 15): 36–43.

Kinnas, J. N. (1997) "Global Challenges and Multilateral Diplomacy," pp. 23–48 in Ludwik Dembinski (ed.), *International Geneva Yearbook*. Berne, Switzerland: Peter Lang.

Kirk, Donald. (2010) "Obama's Asian Odyssey: Speaking in Home Runs but Never Reaching First Base," *WorldTribune.com* (November 15). Available at: www.worldtribune.com/worldtribune/WTARC/2010/ea_korea1124_11_15.asp.

Kissinger, Henry A. (2012a) *On China*, 2nd ed. New York, NY: Penguin Press.

———— (2012b) "The Future of U.S.-Chinese Relations: Conflict Is a Choice Not a Necessity," *Foreign Affairs* (March/April). Accessed August 8, 2013. Available at: http://www.foreignaffairs.com/articles/137245/henry-a-kissinger/the-future-of-us-chinese-relations.

———— (1979) *White House Years*. Boston: Little, Brown.

Rosenau (ed.) *International Politics and Foreign Policy*. New York: Free Press.

Klare, Michael. (2008) *Rising Powers, Shrinking Planet*. New York: Metropolitan Books.

———— (1994) *World Security: Challenges for A New Century*, 2nd ed. New York, NY: St. Martin's Press.

———— (1990) "An Arms Control Agenda for the Third World." *Arms Control Today* 20 (3) : 8–12.

Klein, Naomi. (2008) "China's All-Seeing Eye," *Rolling Stone* (May 29): 59–66.

———— (2007) *The Shock Doctrine: The Rise of Disaster Capitalism*. New York: Metropolitan Books/Henry Holt.

Klimová-Alexander, Ilona. (2005) *The Romani Voice in World Politics: The United Nations and Non-State Actors*. Burlington, VT.: Ashgate.

Kluger, Jeffrey. (2007) "What Makes Us Moral," *Time* (December 3): 54–60.

———— (2006) "The Big Crunch," pp. 24–25 in Robert M. Jackson (ed.), *Global Issues 05/06*. Dubuque, Iowa: McGraw-Hill/Dushkin.

———— (2001) "A Climate of Despair," *Time* (April 9): 30–35.

Knickerbocker, Brad. (2007) "Might Warming be 'Normal'," *Christian Science Monitor* (September 20): 14, 16.

Knight, W. Andy. (2000) *A Changing United Nations*. London: Palgrave.

Knorr, Klaus, and James N. Rosenau (eds.). (1969) *Contending Approaches to International Politics*. Princeton, N.J.: Princeton University Press.

Knorr, Klaus, and Sidney Verba (eds.). (1961) *The International System*. Princeton, NJ: Princeton University Press.

Knox, MacGregor, and Williamson Murray. (2001) *The Dynamics of Military Revolution: 1300–2050*. Cambridge: Cambridge University Press.

KOF Index of Globalization. (2013) "KOF Index of Globalization." Available at: http://globalization.kof.ethz.ch/static/pdf/rankings_2012.pdf.

Kohli, Atul. (2004) *State-Directed Development*. Cambridge: Cambridge University Press.

Kolb, Deborah M. (1996) "Her Place at the Table: Gender and Negotiation," pp. 138–144 in Mary Roth Walsh (ed.), *Women, Men, and Gender: Ongoing Debates*. New York: Hamilton.

Kolbert, Elizabeth. (2008) "What Was I Thinking? The Latest Reasoning about Our Irrational Ways," *The New Yorker* (February 25): 77–79.

———— (2005) "The Climate of Man-II," *New Yorker* (May 2): 64–73.

Kolodziej Edward. (2005). *Security and International Relations*. Cambridge: Cambridge University Press.

Koser, Khalid. (2010) "The Impact of the Global Financial Crisis on International Migration." *The Whitehead Journal of Diplomacy and International Relations* 11(1) (Winter/Spring): 13–20.

Kotz, David M. (2013) "The Current Economic Crisis in the United States: A Crisis of Over-Investment," *Review of Radical Political Economics* (June 6). Accessed June 27, 2013. Available at: DOI: 10.1177/0486613413487160.

Krauthammer, Charles. (2003) "The Unipolar Moment Revisited," *National Interest* 70 (Winter): 5–17.

Kristof, Nicholas D and Sheryl WuDunn. (2009) *Half the Sky: Turning Oppression into Opportunity For Women Worldwide*. New York: Vintage Books.

Kroenig, Matthew. (2009) "Exporting the Bomb: Why States Provide Sensitive Nuclear Assistance," *American Political Science Review* 103: 113–133.

Krueger, Alan B. (2007) *What Makes a Terrorist*. Princeton, N.J.: Princeton University Press.

Krueger, Anne O. (2006) "Expanding Trade and Unleashing Growth," pp. 4–19 in John T. Rourke (ed.), *Taking Sides*. Dubuque, IA: McGraw-Hill/Dushkin.

Krugman, Paul. (1987) "Is Free Trade Passé?" *Journal of Economic Perspectives* 1 (Autumn): 131–44.

Kugler, Jacek. (2006) "China: Satisfied or Dissatisfied, the Strategic Equation," paper presented at the Annual Meeting of the International Studies Association, March 22–25, San Diego.

———— (2001) "War," pp. 894–96 in Joel Krieger (ed.), *The Oxford Companion to Politics of the World*. 2nd ed. New York: Oxford University Press.

————, Ronald L. Tammen, and Brian Efird. (2004) "Integrating Theory and Policy," *International Studies Review* 6 (December): 163–79.

Kuhn, Patrick M., and Nils B. Weidman. (2013) "Unequal We Fight: The Impact of Economic Inequality within Ethnic Groups on Conflict Initiation," Draft at Princeton University. Accessed June 6, 2013. Available at: https://www.princeton.edu/politics/about/file-repository/public/KuhnWeidmann_PrincetonIRTalk.pdf.

Kuhnhenn, Jim. (2009) "Trillions Devoted to Bank Bailout," *The Commercial Appeal* (July 21): A1.

Kunzig, Robert. (2003) "Against the Current," *U.S. News & World Report* (June 2): 34–35.

Kupchan, Charles A. (2003) *The End of the American Era: U.S. Foreign Policy and the Geopolitics of the Twenty-First Century.* New York: Knopf.

——— and Clifford A. Kupchan. (2000) "Concerts, Collective Security, and the Future of Europe," pp. 218–265 in Michael Brown, et. al. (eds.), *America's Strategic Choices.* Cambridge, MA: The MIT Press.

——— (1992) "A New Concert for Europe," pp. 249–66 in Graham Allison and Gregory F. Treverton (eds.), *Rethinking America's Security.* New York: Norton.

Kurlantzick, Joshua. (2010) "Dazzled by Asia." *The Boston Globe* (February 7).

Kurzweil, Ray. (2005) *The Singularity Is Near: When Humans Transcend Biology.* New York: Penguin Group (USA).

Kutcher, Ashton. (2009) "Builders and Titans," *Time* (May 11): 60.

Kuwait Times. (2013) "Kuwait's Construction Projects Valued at $250.6bn," *Kuwait Times.* Accessed May 27, 2013. Available at: http://news.kuwaittimes.net/2013/05/15/kuwaits-construction-projects-valued-at-250-6bn/.

Lacayo, Richard. (2009) "A Brief History of: Photographing Fallen Troops," *Time* (March 16): 19.

Laeven, Luc and Fabian Valencia. (2010) "Resolution of Banking Crises: The Good, the Bad, and the Ugly." IMF Working Paper 10/146. Washington, D.C.: The International Monetary Fund.

——— (2008) "Systemic Banking Crises: A New Database." IMF Working Paper. Available at: http://www.imf.org/external/pubs/ft/wp/2008/wp08224.pdf.

Lamy, Pascal. (2013) "A Trade Facilitation Deal Could Give a $1 Trillion Boost to World Economy—Lamy," WTO (February 1). Accessed July 27, 2013. Available at: http://www.wto.org/english/news_e/sppl_e/sppl265_e.htm.

——— (2011) "Time for a System Upgrade." Available at: http://www.foreignpolicy.com/articles/2011/04/18/system_upgrade.

Landau, Julia. (2010) "Food Riots or Food Rebellions?: Eric Holt-Giménez Looks at the World Food Crisis." CommonDreams.org (March 25). Available at http://www.commondreams.org/view/2010/03/25–11.

Landes, David S. (1998) *The Wealth and Poverty of Nations: Why Are Some So Rich and Some So Poor?* New York: Norton.

Landler, Mark and David E. Sanger. (2009) "Leaders Reach $1 Trillion Deal," *International Herald Tribune* (April 3): 1,4.

Lanz, R. and S. Miroudot (2011) "Intra-Firm Trade: Patterns, Determinants and Policy Implications," *OECD Trade Policy Working Papers*, No. 114, OECD Publishing. Available at: http://dx.doi.org/10.1787/5kg9p39Irwnn-en.

Laqueur, Walter. (2006) "The Terrorism to Come," pp. 229–36 in Thomas J. Badey (ed.), *Violence and Terrorism 06/07.* Dubuque, IA: McGraw Hill/Dushkin.

——— (2003) "Postmodern Terrorism," pp. 151–59 in Charles W. Kegley, Jr. (ed.), *The New Global Terrorism.* Upper Saddle River, N.J.: Prentice Hall.

——— (2001) "Terror's New Face," pp. 82–89 in Charles W. Kegley, Jr., and Eugene R. Wittkopf (eds.), *The Global Agenda*, 6th ed. Boston: McGraw-Hill.

Larkin, John. (2005) "India Bets on Nuclear Future," *Wall Street Journal International* (November 4): A12.

Larsen, Janet. (2012) "Plan B Updates," *Earth Policy Institute* (April 24). Accessed June 25, 2013. Available at: http://www.earth-policy.org/plan_b_updates/2012/update102.

Lauricella, Tom, Christopher S. Stewart, and Shira Ovide. (2013) "Twitter Hoax Sparks Swift Stock Swoon," *The Wall Street Journal* (April 23). Accessed June 27, 2013. Available at: http://online.wsj.com/article/SB10001424127887323735604578441201605193488.html.

Leander, Anna. (2005) "The market for Force and Public Security: The Destabilizing Consequences of Private Military Companies" *Journal of Peace Research* 42 (5): 605–22.

LeBeau, Philip. (2013) "U.S. Manufacturing No More Expensive Than Outsourcing To China by 2015: Study," *Huffington Post* (April 19). Accessed July 27, 2013. Available at: http://www.huffingtonpost.com/2013/04/19/china-manufacturing-costs_n_3116638.html.

Lebovic, James H. (2004) "Uniting for Peace?" *Journal of Conflict Resolution* 48 (December): 910–36.

——— and Erik Voeten. (2009) "The Cost of Shame: International Organizations and Foreign Aid in the Punishing of Human Rights Violators" *Journal of Peace Research* 46 (1): 79–97.

Lebow, Richard Ned. (2010) *Forbidden Fruit: Counterfactuals and International Relations.* Princeton, N.J.: Princeton University Press.

——— (2003) *The Tragic Vision of Politics: Ethics, Interests, and Orders.* Cambridge: Cambridge University Press.

——— (1981) *Between Peace and War.* Baltimore: Johns Hopkins University Press.

Lechner, Frank and John Boli. (2007) *The Globalization Reader*, 3rd ed. Hoboken, NJ: Wiley-Blackwell.

Leffler, Melvyn. (2007) *For the Soul of Mankind: The United States, the Soviet Union, and the Cold War.* New York: Hill and Wang.

——— and Westad (ed.). (2009) *The Cambridge History of the Cold War.* Cambridge, UK: Cambridge University Press.

Legrain, Philippe. (2003) "Cultural Globalization Is Not Americanization," *Chronicle of Higher Education* (May 9): B7–B70.

Legro, Jeffrey W. (2007) *Rethinking the World: Great Power Strategies and International Order.* Ithaca, NY Cornell University Press.

―――― and Andrew Moravcsik. (1999) "Is Anybody Still a Realist?" *International Security* 24 (Fall): 5–55.

Lehrer, Jonah. (2012) "Groupthink: The Brainstorming Myth." The New Yorker (January 30).

Lektzian, David and Mark Souva. (2009) "A Comparative Theory Test of Democratic Peace Arguments, 1946–2000." *Journal of Peace Research* 46 (1): 17–37.

Lemke, Douglas. (2003) "Development and War," *International Studies Review* 5 (December): 55–63.

Lentner, Howard H. (2004) *Power and Politics in Globalization: The Indispensable State.* New York: Routledge.

Leopard, Brian D. (2010) *Customary International Law: A New Theory with Practical Applications.* New York: Cambridge University Press.

Leow, Rachel. (2002) "How Can Globalization Become 'O.K.' for All?" *International Herald Tribune* (February 15): 9.

Levi, Michael. (2009) "Copenhagen's Inconvenient Truth: How to Salvage the Climate Conference" *Foreign Affairs* 88 (September/October): 92–104.

―――― (2008) "Stopping Nuclear Terrorism," *Foreign Affairs* 87 (January/February): 131–40.

Levitt, Peggy. (2007) *God Needs No Passport.* New York: New Press.

Levy, Jack S. (2001) "War and Its Causes," pp. 47–56 in Charles W. Kegley, Jr., and Eugene Wittkopf (eds.), *The Global Agenda*, 6th ed. Boston: McGraw-Hill.

―――― (1989) "The Causes of War: A Review of Theories and Evidence," pp. 209–333 in Philip E. Tetlock, Jo L. Husbands, Robert Jervis, Paul C. Stern, and Charles Tilly (eds.), *Behavior, Society, and Nuclear War.* New York: Oxford University Press.

Lieber, Robert J. (2005) *The American Era.* New York: Cambridge University Press.

Lin, Justin Yifu. (2013) "Youth Bulge: A Demographic Dividend or a Demographic Bomb in Developing Countries?" World Bank blog (January 5). Accessed June 19, 2013. Available at: http://blogs.worldbank.org/developmenttalk/youth-bulge-a-demographic-dividend-or-a-demographic-bomb-in-developing-countries.

Lindberg, Todd (ed.). (2005) *Beyond Paradise and Power: Europe, America, and the Future of a Troubled Relationship.* New York: Routledge.

Lipson, Charles. (1984) "International Cooperation in Economic and Security Affairs," *World Politics* 37 (October): 1–23.

List, Friedrich. (1841) *National System of Political Economy.* Available at: http://socserv2.socsci.mcmaster.ca/~econ/ugcm/3ll3/list/list.

Lobe, Jim. (2013) "Drone Provoke Controversy in U.S.," *Inter Press Service New Agency.* Accessed June 12, 2013. Available at: http://www.ipsnews.net/2013/01/drones-provoke-growing-controversy-in-u-s/.

Lodal, Jan, et al. (2010) "Second Strike: Is the U.S. Nuclear Arsenal Outmoded?" *Foreign Affairs* 89(2) (March/April): 145–52.

Loescher, Gil. (2005) "Blaming the Victim: Refugees and Global Security," pp. 126–29 in Robert J. Griffiths (ed.), *Developing World 05/06.* Dubuque, IA: McGraw-Hill/Dushkin.

Lomborg, Bjørn. (2007) *Solutions for the World's Biggest Problems.* New York: Cambridge University Press.

―――― (ed.). (2004) *Global Crisis, Global Solutions.* Cambridge: Cambridge University Press.

Longman, Phillip. (2005) "The Global Baby Bust," pp. 173–79 in Robert J. Griffiths (ed.), *Developing World 05/06.* Dubuque, IA: McGraw-Hill/Dushkin.

Lopez, George A. (2012) "In Defense of Smart Sanctions: A Response to Joy Gordon," *Ethics & International Affairs* 26(1): 135–45.

Lopez, J. Humberto, et al. (2010) "Big Senders." *Foreign Policy* (January/February): 35.

Lorenz, Konrad. (1963) *On Aggression.* New York: Harcourt, Brace & World.

Lowrey, Annie. (2012) "U.S. Candidate Is Chosen to Lead the World Bank," *The New York Times* (April 16): B3.

Löwenheim, Oded. (2007) *Predators and Parasites.* Ann Arbor: Pluto Books, University of Michigan Press.

Lupovici, Amir. (2009) "Constructivist Methods: A Plea and Manifesto for Pluralism," *Review of International Studies* 35: 195–218.

Lupu, Yonatan and Vincent A Traag. (2013) "Trading Communities, the Networked Sructure of International Relations and the Kantian Peace," *Journal of Conflict Resolution* 57 (4): DOI:10.1177/0022002712453708.

Lutz, Ellen L. (2006) "Understanding Human Rights Violations in Armed Conflict," pp. 23–38 in Julie Mertus and Jeffrey W. Helsing (eds.), *Human Rights and Conflict: Exploring the Links Between Rights, Law, and Peacebuilding.* Washington, D.C.: United States Institute of Peace Press.

Lynch, Colum. (2008) "U.N. Chief to Prod Nations on Food Crisis," *Washington Post* (June 2): A07.

Lynn, Jonathan. (2008) "Diplomats See Reason for Hope in WTO Talks," *International Herald Tribune* (May 29).

Lyons, Daniel. (2010) "Short-Circuiting Malaria." *Newsweek* (April 19): 36–41.

Macalister, Terry. (2012) "Oil Demand in 2013 to Rise as World Economy Recovers, IEA says," *The Guardian* (December 12). Accessed June 25, 2013. Available at: http://www.guardian.co.uk/business/2012/dec/12/oil-demand-rise-2013-iea.

MacAskill, Ewen. (2011) "Barack Obama to Back Middle East Democracy with Billion in Aid: President Pledges Cash to Support Egypt and Tunisia after Criticism US Has been too Slow to Support Uprisings," *Guardian* (May 19). Available at: http:// www.guardian.co.uk/world/2011/may/19/barack-obama-middle-east-aid

―――― , Nick Davies, Nick Hopkins, Julian Borger, and James Ball. (2013) "GCHQ Intercepted Foreign

Politicians' Communications at G20 Summits," *The Guardian* (June 16). Accessed June 22, 2013. Available at: http://www.guardian.co.uk/uk/2013/jun/16/gchq-intercepted-communications-g20-summits.

Mackinder, Sir Halford. (1919) *Democratic Ideals and Reality.* New York: Holt.

Magee, Christopher and Tansa George Massoud. (2011) "Openness and Internal Conflict," *Journal of Peace Research* 48 (1): 59–72.

Mahan, Alfred Thayer. (1890) *The Influence of Sea Power in History.* Boston: Little, Brown.

Mahbulbani, Kishore. (2009) *The New Asian Hemisphere: The Irresistible Shift of Global Power to the East.* Basic Civitas Books.

——— (2005) "Understanding China," *Foreign Affairs* 84 (October): 49–60.

Malaquias, Assis V. (2001) "Humanitarian Intervention," pp. 370–74 in Joel Krieger (ed.), *The Oxford Companion to Politics of the World*, 2nd ed. New York: Oxford University Press.

——— (2008) "The Benefits of Goliath," pp. 55–64 in Eugene R. Wittkopf and James M. McCormick (eds.), *The Domestic Sources of American Foreign Policy.* Lanham, MD.: Rowman and Littlefield.

Malcomson, Scott. (2008) "Humanitarianism and Its Politicization," *International Herald* Tribune (December 13–14): 9.

Mallaby, Sebastian (2011) "The Wrong Choice to Head the IMF," *Council on Foreign Relations* (June 1). Available at: http://www.cfr.org/economics/wrong-choice-head-imf/p25166.

——— (2011) "The Wrong Choice to Head the IMF," *Washington Post* (June 1).

Malmgren, Harald and Mark Stys. (2011) "Computerized Global Trading 24/6: A Roller Coaster Ride Ahead?" *The International Economy* (Spring): 30–32.

Manasse, Paolo. (2011) "Greece, the Unbearable Heaviness of Debt," *Vox* (24 May). Available at: http://www.voxeu.org/index.php?q5node/6553.

Mandelbaum, Michael. (2010) *The Frugal Superpower: America's Global Leadership in a Cash-Strapped Era.* New York: PublicAffairs.

——— (2007) "Democracy without America," *Foreign Affairs* 86 (September/October): 119–30.

——— (2006a) "David's Friend Goliath," *Foreign Policy* (January/February): 49–56.

——— (2006b) *The Case for Goliath: How America Acts as the World's Government in the 21st Century.* New York: Public Affairs.

——— (2002) *The Ideas That Conquered the World: Peace, Democracy, and Free Markets in the Twenty-First Century.* New York: Public Affairs/Perseus.

Mankoff, Jeffrey. (2009) *Russian Foreign Policy: The Return of Great Power Politics.* New York: Rowman and Littlefield.

Mann, Charles C. (2005) "The Coming Death Shortage," *Atlantic Monthly* 295 (May): 92–102.

Mann, James. (2004) *Rise of the Vulcans: The History of Bush's War Cabinet.* New York: Viking.

Mansfield, Edward D., Helen V. Milner, and B. Peter Rosendorff. (2002) "Replication, Realism, and Robustness: Analyzing Political Regimes and International Trade," *American Political Science Review* 96 (March): 167–69.

———, and Brian M. Pollins (eds.). (2003) *Economic Interdependence and International Conflict.* Ann Arbor: University of Michigan Press.

———, and Jack Snyder. (2005a) *Electing to Fight.* Cambridge, MA.: MIT Press.

——— (2005b) "When Ballots Bring On Bullets," *International Herald Tribune* (November 29–30): 6.

Maoz, Zeev and Errol A. Henderson. (2013) "The World Religion Dataset, 1945–2010: Logic, Estimates, and Trends." *International Interactions*, 39(3): 265–91.

Mapel, David R. (2007) "The Right of National Defense," *International Studies Perspectives* 8 (February): 1–15.

Maplecroft. (2013) *Digital Inclusion Index.* Available at: http://maplecroft.com.

——— (2011) *Maplecroft Ranking Highlighting the 'Digital Divide' Reveals India Lagging Behind Brazil, Russia and China.* Available at: http://maplecroft.com/about/news/digital_inclusion_index.html.

Margolis, Max, and Alex Marin. (2010) "Venezuela and the Tyranny of Twitter." *Newsweek* (June 14): 6.

Markoe, Lauren and Seth Borenstein. (2005) "We Overpay by 20% for Military Goods," Columbia, S.C., *The State* (October 23): A1, A8.

Markoff, John. (2009) "A Map of the World, in 4 Billion Pockets," *International Herald Tribune* (February 188): 1, 11.

Markusen, Ann R. (2003) "The Case Against Privatizing National Security" *Governance* 16 (4): 471–501.

Marshall, Monty G., and Ted Robert Gurr. (2003) *Peace and Conflict 2003.* College Park, MD.: Center for International Development and Conflict Management.

Martel, William C. (2008) *Victory in War.* New York: Cambridge University Press.

Martell, Luke. (2007) "The Third Wave in Globalization Theory," *International Studies Review* 9 (Summer): 173–96.

Marx, Anthony W (2003) *Faith in Nation: Exclusionary Origins of Nationalism.* New York: Oxford University Press.

Masters, Jonathan. (2011) "Backgrounder: The International Monetary Fund," *Council of Foreign Relations.* Available at: http://www.cfr.org/economics/international-monetary-fund/p25303.

Mathews, Jessica T. (2000) "National Security for the Twenty-First Century," pp. 9–11 in Gary Bertsch and Scott James (eds.), *Russell Symposium Proceedings.* Athens: University of Georgia.

Matlock, Jack F. (2004) *Reagan and Gorbachev: How the Cold War Ended*. New York: Random House.

Mattes, Michaela, and Burcu Savun. (2010) "Information, Agreement Design, and the Durability of Civil War Settlements," *American Journal of Political Science* 54 (2) (April): 511–24.

May, Ernest R. (2000) *Strange Victory*. New York: Hill and Wang.

Mayall, James. (2001) "Mercantilism," pp. 535 and 540 in Joel Krieger (ed.), *The Oxford Companion to Politics of the World*, 2nd ed. New York: Oxford University Press.

Mazarr, Michael J. (1999) *Global Trends 2005*. London: Palgrave.

Mazower, Mark. (2009) *No Enchanted Palace: The End of Empire and the Ideological Origins of the United Nations*. Princeton, NJ: Princeton University Press.

Mazur, Amy G. (2002) *Theorizing Feminist Policy*. New York: Oxford University Press.

McCrae, R. R., and Paul T. Costa. (2003). *Personality in Adulthood: A Five-Factor Theory Perspective* (2nd ed.). New York: Guilford Press.

McDermott, Rose. (2013) "The Biological Bases for Aggressiveness and Nonaggressiveness in Presidents," *Foreign Policy Analysis* : 1–15.

———, James H. Fowler and Oleg Smirnov. (2008) "On the Evolutionary Origin of Prospect Theory Preferences." *The Journal of Politics* 70 (April): 335–50.

McGinnis, John O. (2005) "Individualism and World Order," *The National Interest* 28 (Winter): 41–51.

McGirk, Tim. (2010) "Armed Farces." *Time* (June 14): 52–55.

McGrew, Anthony. (2005) "The Logics of Globalization," pp. 207–34 in John Ravenhill (ed.), *Global Political Economy*. New York: Oxford University Press.

McGurn, William. (2002) "Pulpit Economics," *First Things* 122 (April): 21–25.

McNamara, Robert S. (2005) "Apocalypse Soon," *Foreign Policy* (May/June): 29–35.

Mead, Nick. (2012) "Rise of the Megacities," *The Guardian* (October 4). Accessed June 22, 2013. Available at: http://www.guardian.co.uk/global-development/interactive/2012/oct/04/rise-of-megacities-interactive.

Mead, Walter Russell. (2010) "The Carter Syndrome." *Foreign Policy* (January/February).

——— (2008) *God and Gold: Britain, America, and the Making of the Modern World*. New York: Knopf.

Mearsheimer, John J. (2004) "Anarchy and the Struggle for Power," pp. 54–72 in Karen A. Mingst and Jack L. Snyder (eds.), *Essential Readings in World Politics*, 2nd ed. New York: Norton.

——— (2001) *The Tragedy of Great Power Politics*. New York: Norton.

——— (1990) "Back to the Future: Instability in Europe after the Cold War," *International Security* 15 (Summer): 5–56.

——— and Stephen W. Walt. (2003) "An Unnecessary War," *Foreign Policy* (January/February): 50–58.

Meernik, James David. (2004) *The Political Use of Military Force in US Foreign Policy*. Burlington, VT.: Ashgate.

Melander, Erik. (2005) "Gender Equality and Intrastate Armed Conflict," *International Studies Quarterly* 49 (December): 695–714.

Melloan, George. (2002) "Bush's Toughest Struggle Is with His Own Bureaucracy," *Wall Street Journal* (June 25): A19.

Meltzer, Joshua. (2011) "The Future of World Trade." Available at: http://www.foreignpolicy.com/articles/2011/04/18/the_future_of_trade.

Mendelsohn, Jack. (2005) "America and Russia: Make-Believe Arms Control," pp. 205–9 in Glenn P. Hastedt (ed.), *America Foreign Policy 04/05*, 10th ed. Guilford, Conn.: Dushkin/McGraw-Hill.

Menkhaus, Ken. (2002) "Somalia: In the Crosshairs of the War on Terrorism," *Current History* (May): 210–18.

Menon, Rajan. (2007) *The End of Alliances*. New York: Oxford University Press.

Mentan, Tatah. (2004) *Dilemmas of Weak States: Africa and Transnational Terrorism in the Twenty-First Century*. Burlington, VT: Ashgate.

Merkelson, Suzanne, and Joshua E. Keating. (2011) "What Not to Wear: Five Countries Where the Term 'Fashion Police' Is Meant Literally," *Foreign Policy* (April 11). Available at: http://www.foreignpolicy.com/articles/2011/04/11/what_not_ to_wear.

Mertus, Julie. (2009a) *Human Rights Matters: Local Politics and National Human Rights Institutions*. Stanford, CA: Stanford University Press.

——— (2009b) *The United Nations and Human Rights: A Guide for a New Era*, 2nd ed. New York: Routledge.

de Mesquita, Bruce Bueno. (2009) "Recipe for Failure." *Foreign Policy* (November): 76–81.

Michael, Marie. (2001) "Food or Debt," pp. 78–79 in Robert J. Griffiths (ed.), *Developing World 01/02*. Guilford, CT.: Dushkin/McGraw-Hill.

Micklethwait, John, and Adrian Wooldridge. (2001) "The Globalization Backlash," *Foreign Policy* (September/October): 16–26.

Miller, Mark Crispin. (2006) "What's Wrong with This Picture?" pp. 115–17 in Robert M. Jackson (ed.), *Global Issues 05/06*. Dubuque, IA: McGraw-Hill/Dushkin.

Milner, Helen V., and Andrew Moravcsik. (2009) *Power, Interdependence, and Nonstate Actors in World Politics*. Princeton University Press.

Minorities at Risk Project. (2010) "Minorities at Risk Dataset." College Park, MD: Center for International Development and Conflict Management. Accessed June 3, 2013. Available at: http://www.cidcm.umd.edu/mar/.

Mintz, Alex. (2007) "Why Behavioral IR?" *International Studies Review* 9 (June): 157–72.

Missile Defense Agency (MDA). (2013a) "Elements," *Missile Defense Agency*. Accessed June 13, 2013. Available at: http://www.mda.mil/system/aegis_bmd.html.

——— (2013b) "Historical Funding for MDA FY85-13," *Missile Defense Agency*. Accessed June 13, 2013. Available at: http://www.mda.mil/global/documents/pdf/histfunds.pdf.

Mitchell, Sara McLaughlin, Kelly M. Kadera, and Mark J.C. Crescenzi (2008) "Practicing Democratic Community Norms: Third Party Conflict Management and Successful Settlements," pp. 243–64 in Jacob Bercovitch and Scott Sigmund Gartner (eds.), *International Conflict Mediation*. New York: Routledge.

Mo, Lavinia. (2012) "New Bird Flu May Be Capable of Human to Human Spread–Study," *Reuters* (May 24). Accessed June 22, 2013. Available at: http://www.reuters.com/article/2013/05/24/us-hongkong-birdflu-idUSBRE94N0AR20130524.

Modelski, George. (1964) "The International Relations of Internal War." In James N. Rosenau, ed., *International Aspects of Civil Strife*. Princeton, NJ: Princeton University Press : 14–44.

Modelski, George, and William R. Thompson. (1999) "The Long and the Short of Global Politics in the Twenty-First Century," *International Studies Review*, Special Issue, ed. by Davis B. Bobrow: 109–40.

Moens, Alexander. (2005) *The Foreign Policy of George W Bush*. Burlington, VT: Ashgate.

Moghadam, Reza. (2009) "Transcript of a Conference Call on the New Lending Framework for Low-Income Countries," International Monetary Fund. Available at: http://www.imf.org/external/np/tr/2009/tr072909a.htm.

Mohanty, Chandra Talpade. (1988) "Under Western Eyes: Feminist Scholarship and Colonial Discourse" *Feminist Review* 30 (Autumn): 61–88.

Møller, Bjørn. (1992) *Common Security and Nonoffensive Defense: A Neorealist Perspective*. Boulder, CO.: Lynne Rienner.

Mondak, Jeffery J. and Karen D. Halperin. (2013) "A Framework for the Study of Personality and Political Behaviour," *British Journal of Political Science* 38: 335–362.

Moon, Bruce E. (2008) "Reproducing the North-South Divide: The Role of Trade Deficits and Capital Flows," pp. 39–64 in Rafael Reuveny and William R. Thompson (eds.), *North and South in the World Political Economy*. Malden, MA: Blackwell.

Moorehead, Caroline. (2007) "Women and Children for Sale," *New York Review of Books* (October 11): 15–18.

Moran, Theodore H., Edward M. Graham, and Magnus Blomström (eds.). (2005) *Does Foreign Direct Investment Promote Development?* Washington, DC: Institute for International Economics.

Morgan, Patrick. (2005) *International Security: Problems and Solutions*. Washington, DC: CQ Press.

Morgan, T. Clifton, Navin A. Bapat, and Valentin Krustev. (2009) "The Threat and Imposition of Sanctions 1971–2000," *Conflict Management and Peace Science* 26 (1): 92–110.

Morgenthau, Hans J. (1985) *Politics Among Nations*, 6th ed. Revised by Kenneth W. Thompson. New York: Knopf.

——— (1948) *Politics among Nations*. New York: Knopf.

Morphet, Sally. (2004) "Multilateralism and the Non-Aligned Movement," *Global Governance* 10 (October/December): 517–37.

Morris, Ian. (2010) *Why the West Rules—For Now: The Patterson of History, and What They Reveal about the Future*. New York: Farrar, Straus and Giroux.

Morse, Edward L., and James Richard. (2002) "The Battle for Energy Dominance," *Foreign Affairs* 81 (March/April): 16–31.

Morton, David. (2006) "Gunning for the World," *Foreign Policy* (January/February): 58–67.

Mosley, Layna. (2011) *Labor Rights and Multinational Production*. Cambridge, UK: Cambridge University Press.

——— (2008) "Workers' Rights in Open Economies: Global Production and Domestic Institutions in the Developing World," *Comparative Political Studies* 41 (4/5): 674–714.

Mousseau, Michael. (2013) "The Democratic Peace Unraveled: It's the Economy," *International Studies Quarterly* (57): 180–197.

Mueller, John. (2004) *The Remnants of War*. Ithaca: Cornell University Press.

——— and Karl Mueller. (1999) "Sanctions of Mass Destruction," *Foreign Affairs* 78 (3): 43–52.

Mufson, Steven. (2011) "Germany to Close All of Its Nuclear Plants by 2022," *The Washington Post* (May 30). Available at: http://www.ashingtonpost.com/ business/economy/germany-to-close-all-of-its-nuclear-plants-by-2022/2011/05/30/AG0op1EH_story.html.

Mullenbach, Mark J. (2005) "Deciding to Keep Peace," *International Studies Quarterly* 49 (September): 529–55.

Muller, Jerry Z. (2013) "Capitalism and Inequality: What the Right and the Left Get Wrong," *Foreign Affairs* (March/April). Accessed June 27, 2013. Available at: http://www.foreignaffairs.com/articles/138844/jerry-z-muller/capitalism-and-inequality.

——— (2008) "Us and Them: The Enduring Power of Ethnic Nationalism," *Foreign Affairs* 87 (March/April): 18–35.

Münster, Johannes and Klaas Staal. (2011) "War with Outsiders Makes Peace Inside," *Conflict Management and Peace Science* 28 (2): 91–110.

Munz, Philip, Ioan Hudea, Joe Imad, and Robert J. Smith. (2009) "When Zombies Attack!: Mathematical Modeling of an Outbreak of Zombie Infection," *Infectious Disease Modeling Research Progress*. pp. 133–50.

Murdie, Amanda M. and David Davis. (2012) "Shaming and Blaming: Using Events Data to Assess the Impact of Human Rights INGOs," *International Studies Quarterly* 56(1): 1–16.

Murdoch, James C. and Todd Sandler. (2004) "Civil Wars and Economic Growth," *American Journal of Political Science* 48 (January): 138–51.

Murithi, Timothy. (2004) "The Myth of Violent Human Nature," *Peace & Policy* 8: 28–32.

Murray, Williamson, and Allan R. Millett. (2000) *A War to be Won.* Cambridge, Mass.: Harvard University Press.

Myers, Steven Lee and David M. Herszenhorn. (2013) "U.S.-Russian Diplomacy, with a Personal Touch," *New York Times* (May 17). Accessed May 18, 2013. Available at: http://www.nytimes.com.

Naím, Moisés. (2007) "The Free-Trade Paradox," *Foreign Policy* (September/October): 96–97.

———— (2006a) "The Five Wars of Globalization," pp. 61–66 in Robert M. Jackson (ed.), *Global Issues 05/06.* Dubuque, IA: McGraw-Hill/Dushkin.

———— (2006b) "The Most Dangerous Deficit," *Foreign Policy* (January/February): 94–95.

Nakatomi, Michitaka. (2013) "Plurilateral Agreements: A Viable Alternative to the WTO?" pp. 131–140 in Richard Baldwin, Masahiro Kawai, and Ganeshan Wignaraja (eds.), *The Future of the World Trading System: Asian Perspectives.* London, UK: Centre for Economic Policy Research.

Nardin, Terry. (2005) "Humanitarian Imperialism," *Ethics and International Affairs* 19 (No. 2, Special Issue): 21–26.

National Institute of Justice. (2012) "Transnational Organized Crime." Available at: http://www.nij.gov/topics/crime/transnational-organized-crime/welcome.htm.

———— (2007) "Transnational Organized Crime." Available at: http://www.nij.gov/topics/crime/transnational-organized-crime/welcome.htm.

National Intelligence Council (NIC). (2004) *Mapping the Global Future.* Washington, D.C.: National Intelligence Council.

NCTC. (National Counter-Terrorism Center). (2009) *2008 NCTC Report on Terrorism.* Washington, DC: National Counter-Terrorism Center.

———— (2007) *NCTC Report on Terrorist Incidents.* Washington, DC: National Counter-Terrorism Center.

Neack, Laura. (2004) "Peacekeeping, Bloody Peacekeeping," *Bulletin of the Atomic Scientists* 57 (July/August): 40–47.

Nelson, Rebecca, Paul Belkin and Derek Mix. (2010) *Greece's Debt Crisis: Overview, Policy Responses and Implications.* Washington, DC: Congressional Research Service.

Neumann, Iver B. (2007) "'A Speech That the Entire Ministry May Stand For,' or: Why Diplomats Never Produce Anything New," *International Political Sociology* 1 (June): 183–200.

Neumayer, Eric and Indra de Soysa. (2005) "Trade Openness, Foreign Direct Investment, and Child Labor," *World Development* 33(1): 43–63.

Newhouse, John. (2003) *Imperial America: The Bush Assault on World Order.* New York: Knopf.

Newell, Richard G. (2005) "The Hydrogen Economy," *Resources for the Future* 156 (Winter): 20–23.

Newsweek. (2008) "The United States Doesn't Have Any Oil," *Newsweek* (July 7/14): 44–45.

Nexon, Daniel H. (2009) "The Balance of Power in the Balance," *World Politics* 61: 330–59.

Ng, Rebecca. (2013) "Growing Inter-ASEAN Trade Creates New Opening for Marine Insurance," tradingcharts.com. Accessed June 1, 2013. Available at: http://futures.tradingcharts.com/news/futures/Growing_Inter_ASEAN_Trade_Creates_New_Opening_for_Marine_Insurance_198381908.html.

Nichols, Michelle. (2013) "Syria Death Toll at Least 80,000, Says U.N. General Assembly President," *Reuters* (May 15). Accessed June 3, 2013. Available at: http://in.reuters.com/article/2013/05/15/syria-crisis-un-deaths-idINDEE94E0CJ20130515.

Nicholls, Natsuko H., Paul K. Huth and Benjamin J. Appel. (2010) "When Is Domestic Political Unrest Related to International Conflict? Diversionary Theory and Japanese Foreign Policy, 1890–1941," *International Studies Quarterly* 54: 915–37.

Nichols, John. (2002) "Enron's Global Crusade," *The Nation* (March 4). Available at: http://www.thenation.com/doc/20020304/nichols.

Niebuhr, Reinhold. (1947) *Moral Man and Immoral Society.* New York: Scribner's.

9/11 Commission. (2004) *Final Report of the National Commission on Terrorist Attacks upon the United States: The 9/11 Commission Report.* New York: Norton.

Norberg, Johan. (2006) "Three Cheers for Global Capitalism," pp. 52–60 in Robert M. Jackson (ed.), *Global Issues 05/06.* Dubuque, IA: McGraw-Hill/Dushkin.

Norris, Robert S., and Hans M. Kristensen. (2009) "Nuclear Notebook: U.S. Nuclear Forces, 2009." *The Bulletin of the Atomic Scientists.* Available at: http://www.thebulletin.org/files/065002008.pdf.

Nossel, Suzanne. (2004) "Smart Power," *Foreign Affairs* 83 (March/April): 31–142.

Nuclear Energy Institute (NEI). (2013) "U.S. Nuclear Power Plants." Accessed August 10, 2012. Available at: http://www.nei.org/resourcesandstats/nuclear_statistics/U-S-Nuclear-Power-Plants.

Nuclear Threat Initiative (NTI). (2013) "Nuclear Nonproliferation Treaty Meeting Ends with Concerns on Disarmament," *Global Security Newswire* (May 3). Accessed June 17, 2013. Available at: http://www.nti.org/gsn/article/nuclear-treaty-meeting-ends-concerns-disarmament/.

Nye, Joseph S., Jr. (2008) "Soft Power and American Foreign Policy," pp. 29–43 in Eugene R. Wittkopf and James M. McCormick (eds.), *The Domestic Sources of American Foreign Policy.* Lanham, MD.: Rowman and Littlefield.

———— (2007) *Understanding International Conflicts*, 6th ed. New York: Pearson Longman.

———— (2005) *Power in the Global Information Age.* New York: Routledge.

———— (2004a) "America's Soft Learning Curve," pp. 31–34 in *The World in 2004*, London: Economist Newspapers.

———— (2004b) *Soft Power.* New York: Public Affairs.

———— (1990) *Bound to Lead: The Changing Nature of American Power.* New York: Basic Books.

Nygren, Bertil. (2012) "Using the Neo-classical Realism Paradigm to Predict Russian Foreign Policy Behaviour as a Complement to Using Resources," International Politics 49 (July): 517–529.

Oatley, Thomas. (2012) *International Political Economy*, 5th ed. New York: Norton.

O'Brien, Conor Cruise. (1977) "Liberty and Terrorism," *International Security 2* (Fall): 56–67.

Obuah, Emmanuel. (2006) "Combating Global Trafficking in Persons," *International Politics* 43 (April): 241–65.

OECD. (2013a) *OECDiLibrary.* Accessed May 29, 2013. Available at: http://www.oecd-ilibrary.org/development/development-aid-net-official-development-assistance-oda-2012_aid-oda-table-2012-1-en.

———— (2013b) "FDI in Figures," OECD (April). Accessed June 27, 2013. Available at: http://www.oecd.org/daf/inv/FDI%20in%20figures.pdf.

———— (2011) *Development: Aid Increases, but with Worrying Trends.* Paris: Organisation for Economic Co-operation and Development.

———— (2010) "Government Support to Farmers Rises Slightly in OECD Countries." OECD. Available at: http://www.oecd.org/document/34/0,3746,de_34968570_45565602_1_1_1_1,00.html.

———— (2007a) *Trends and Recent Developments in Foreign Direct Investment.* Paris: Organisation for Economic Co-operation and Development.

———— (2005) *Distribution of Aid by Development Assistance Committee (DAC) Members.* Paris: Organization for Economic Cooperation and Development.

Office of the High Commissioner for Human Rights. (2011) "Work Group on Indigenous Populations." Available at: http://www2.ohchr.org/english/issues/indigenous/groups/groups-01.htm.

Office of the Under Secretary of Defense. (2011) "Program Acquisition Costs by Weapon System." Accessed 18, June 2012. Available at: http://comptroller.defense.gov/defbudget/fy2012/FY2012_Weapons.pdf.

Olson, Laicie. (2011) *Analysis of Fiscal Year 2012 Defense Appropriations Bill as Approved by House Appropriations Committee.* The Center for Arms Control and Non-Proliferation (June 15). Available at: http://armscontrolcenter.org/policy/securityspending/articles/FY_2012_House_Defense_Approps_Committee/

Oneal, John R., and Jaroslav Tir. (2006). *International Studies Quarterly* 50 (December): 755–79.

Greenwood Onuf (ed.) *Law-Making in the Global Community.* Durham, NC: Carolina Academic Press.

Opello, Walter C, Jr. and Stephen J. Rosow. (2004) *The Nation-State and Global Order*, 2nd ed. Boulder, CO: Lynne Rienner.

O'Reilly, Kelly. (2013) "A Rogue Doctrine? The Role of Strategic Culture on US Foreign Policy Behavior," *Foreign Policy Analysis* 9: 57–77.

———— (2005) "U.S. Arms Sales and Purchaser's Governments," Occasional Paper, Walker Institute of International Studies. Columbia: University of South Carolina.

O'Reilly, Marc J. and Wesley B. Renfro. (2007) "Evolving Empire," *International Studies Perspectives* 8 (May): 137–51.

O'Rourke, Lindsey. (2009) "V-22 Osprey Tilt-Rotor Aircraft: Background and Issues for Congress," Washington, DC: Congressional Research Service. (July 14).

———— (2008) "The Woman behind the Bomb," *International Herald Tribune* (August 5): Op-Ed.

Ostler, Nicholas. (2003) "A Loss for Words," *Foreign Policy* (November/December): 30–31.

O'Sullivan, John. (2005) "In Defense of Nationalism," *The National Interest* 78 (Winter): 33–40.

Owen, David. (2009) "Comment: Economy vs. Environment," *The New Yorker* (March 30): 21–22.

Owen, John M., IV. (2005) "When Do Ideologies Produce Alliances?" *International Studies Quarterly* 49 (March): 73–99.

Oxfam International. (2011) "Oxfam to IMF: Your Loans Should Not Punish the World's Poorest Citizens." (June 16). Available at: http://www.oxfam.org/en/news/2008/pr080327_IMF_reform.

Pacala, Stephen, and Robert Socolow. (2004) "Stabilization Wedges: Solving the Climate Problem for the Next 50 Years with Current Technologies," *Science* 305 (August): 968–72.

Pakpahan, Beginda. (2013) "Can the WTO Deliver on Its Promise to Find a Breakthrough for Doha Round Talks in Bali?" *Global Policy Journal* (March 21). Accessed July 27, 2013. Available at: http://www.globalpolicyjournal.com/blog/21/03/2013/can-wto-deliver-its-promise-find-breakthrough-doha-round-talks-bali.

Palan, Ronen. "A World of Their Making: An Evaluation of the Constructivist Critique in International Relations," in *Review of International Studies* 26(4): 575–98.

Palmer, Glenn, and T. Clifton Morgan. (2007) "Power Transition, the Two-Good Theory, and Neorealism: A Comparison with Comments on Recent U.S. Foreign Policy," *International Interactions* 33 (July/September): 329–46.

Panagariya, Arvind. (2005) "Agricultural Liberalisation and the Least Developed Countries: Six Fallacies," *The World Economy* 28(9): 1277–1299.

———— (2003) "Think Again: International Trade," *Foreign Policy* (November/December): 20–28.

Pangestu, Mari. (2011) "No Plan B for Completing Doha." *East Asia Forum.* Available at: http://www.eastasiaforum.org/2011/06/01/no-plan-b-for-completing-doha.

Panitch, Leo. (2009) "Thoroughly Modern Marx," *Foreign Policy* (May/June): 140–43.

Papachristou, Harry. (2012) "Factbox: Greek Austerity and Reform Measures," *Reuters* (February 19). Available at: http://www.reuters.com/article/2012/02/19/us-greece-austerity-idUSTRE81I05T20120219.

Pape, Robert A. (2003) "The Strategic Logic of Suicide Terrorism," *The American Political Science Review*, 97.3 (August): 343–361.

Parker, Alice. (2010) "How to Live 100 Years," *Time* (February 22).

Parker, Georg, Guy Dinmore and Alan Beattie. (2009) "Leaders Seek Trade Deal by 2010," *Financial Times* (July 9, 2009). Available at: http://www.ft.com/cms/s/0/f42cf9e2-6c7e-11de-a6e6-00144feabdc0.html?nclick_check51.

Parker, John. (2010) "Another Year, Another Billion," *The Economist: The World in 2011* (December): 28.

Parker, Owen and James Brassett. (2005) "Contingent Borders, Ambiguous Ethics: Migrants in (International) Political Theory," *International Studies Quarterly* 49 (June): 233–53.

Patrick, Stewart. (2011) "The Brutal Truth," in *Foreign Policy* (July/August). Available at: http://www.foreignpolicy.com/articles/2011/06/20/the_brutal_truth.

——— (2010) "Irresponsilbe Stakeholders?: The Difficult of Integrating Rising Powers," *Foreign Affairs* (November/December): 44–53.

Patterson, Eric. (2005) "Just War in the 21st Century: Reconceptualizing Just War Theory after September 11," *International Politics* 42 (March): 116–34.

Paul, T. V., G. John Ikenberry, and John A. Hall (eds.). (2003) *The Nation-State in Question*. Princeton, NJ: Princeton University Press.

Pauly, Louis W. (2005) "The Political Economy of International Financial Crises," pp. 176–203 in John Ravenhill (ed.), *Global Political Economy*. New York: Oxford University Press.

Paust, Jordan J. (2008) *Beyond the Law*. New York: Cambridge University Press.

——— (2007) *Beyond the Law: The Bush Administration's Unlawful Responses in the War on Terror*. New York: Cambridge University Press.

Payne, Richard J. (2007) *Global Issues*. New York: Pearson Longman.

Peirce, Neal R. (2000) "Keep an Eye on 'Citistates' Where Economic Action Is," *International Herald Tribune* (January 11): 8.

——— (1997) "Does the Nation-State Have a Future?" *International Herald Tribune* (April 4): 9.

Peksen, Dursun. (2012) "Does Foreign Military Intervention Help Human Rights?" *Political Research Quarterly* 65 (3): 558–571.

——— (2011) "Economic Sanctions and Human Security: The Public Effect of Economic Sanctions," *Foreign Policy Analysis*, 7(3): 237–251.

Pells, Richard. (2002) "Mass Culture Is Now Exported from All Over to All Over," *International Herald Tribune* (July 12): 9.

Peterson, V. Spike. (2003) *A Critical Rewriting of Global Political Economy: Retrospective, Productive and Virtual Economies*. London: Routledge.

——— and Anne Sisson Runyan. (2010) *Global Gender Issues in the New Millennium*. 3rd ed. Boulder, CO: Westview Press.

——— (2009) *Global Gender Issues in the New Millennium*. 3rd ed. Boulder, CO: Westview Press.

——— (1993) *Global Gender Issues*. Boulder, CO.: Westview Press.

Petras, James. (2004) *The New Development Politics*. Williston, Vt.: Ashgate.

Petras, James and Henry Veltmeyer. (2004) *A System in Crisis: The Dynamics of Free Market Capitalism*. London: Palgrave.

Pfaff, William. (2001a) "Anti-Davos Forum Is Another Sign of a Sea Change," *International Herald Tribune* (July 25): 6.

——— (2001b) "The Question of Hegemony," *Foreign Affairs* 80 (January/February): 50–64.

——— (1999) "A Chronicle of Man's Descent into the Abyss of War." (September 7). Available at: http://articles.chicagotribune.com/1999-09-07/news/9909070157_1_war-crimes-civil-war-civilians.

Pfanner, Eric. (2008) "U.S. Will Trail Emerging Markets in Media Growth, Study Says." *New York Times* (June 18).

Pfetsch, Frank L. (1999) "Globalization: A Threat and a Challenge for the State," paper presented at the European Standing Conference on International Studies, Vienna, September 11–13.

Pham, J. Peter. (2005) "Killing to Make a Killing," *The National Interest* 81 (Fall): 132–37.

Phillips, Nicola (ed.). (2005) *Globalizing Political Economy*. London: Palgrave.

Piasecki, Bruce. (2007) "A Social Responsibility Revolution in the Global Marketplace," *Christian Science Monitor* (August 9): 9.

Piazza, James. (2008) "Incubators of Terror: Do Failed and Failing States Promote Transnational Terrorism?" *International Studies Quarterly* 52 (3).

Pickering, Jeffrey. (2009). "The International Military Intervention Dataset: An Updated Resource for Conflict Scholars" *Journal of Peace Research* 46(4): 589–99.

Pickering, Jeffrey and Mark Peceny. (2006) "Forging Democracy at Gunpoint," *International Studies Quarterly* 50 (September): 539–59.

Pei, Minxin. (2013) "China's Economic Reform: Don't Hold Your Breath," *CNNMoney* (May 28). Accessed June 27, 2013. Available at: http://management.fortune.cnn.com/2013/05/28/china-economy/.

Pogge, Thomas. (2005) "World Poverty and Human Rights," *Ethics & International Affairs* 19 (1): 1–7.

Politi, James and Jonathan Wheatley. (2010) "Tariff Move by Brazil Risks US Trade War," *Financial Times* (March 9). Accessed July 27, 2013. Available at: http://www.ft.com/intl/cms/s/0/c5da3202-2b1a-11df-93d8-00144feabdc0.html#axzz2aN0Zfze8.

Polsky, Andrew. (2010) "Staying the Course: Presidential Leadership, Military Stalemate, and Strategic Inertia." *Perspectives on Politics* 8(1): 127–39.

Porter, Gareth. (1995). "Environmental Security as a National Security Issue," pp. 215–22 in Gearoid O Tauthail, Simon Dalby and Paul Routledge (eds.), *The Geopolitics Reader*. New York, NY: Routledge.

Posen, Barry R. (2004) "The Security Dilemma and Ethnic Conflict," pp. 357–66 in Karen A. Mingst and Jack L. Snyder (eds.), *Essential Readings in World Politics*, 2nd ed. New York: Norton.

Potts, Malcom and Martha Campbell. (2009) "Sex Matters," *Foreign Policy* (July/August): 30–31.

Pouliot, Vincent. (2007) "'Sobjectivism': Toward a Constructivist Methodology," *International Studies Quarterly* 51: 359–84.

Pound, Edward T. and Danielle Knight. (2006) "Cleaning Up the World Bank," *US News & World Report* 140(12): 40–51.

Powell, Colin L. (1995) *My American Journey*. New York: Random House.

Powell, Emilia Justyna and Staton, Jeffrey K. (2009). " Domestic Judicial Institutions and Human Rights Treaty Violation," *International Studies Quarterly*. 53: 149–74.

Powell, Jonathan. (2011) "Global Instances of Coups from 1950 to 2010: A New Dataset." *Journal of Peace Research* 48(2): 249–59.

——— (2004) "United Nations—Much Maligned, but Much Needed," *International Herald Tribune* (February 26): 6.

Powers, Thomas. (1994) "Downwinders: Some Casualties of the Nuclear Age," *Atlantic Monthly* (March): 119–24.

Prakash, Aseem and Matthew Potoski. (2007) "Investing Up," *International Studies Quarterly* 51 (September): 723–44.

——— (2006) "Racing to the Bottom? Globalization, Environmental Governance, and ISO 14001," *American Journal of Political Science* 50 (2): 350–64.

Prempeh, E. Osei Kwadwo, Joseph Mensah, and Senyo B. S. K. Adjibolosoo (eds.). (2005) *Globalization and the Human Factor*. Burlington, Ver.: Ashgate.

Prestowitz, Clyde. (2005) *Three Billion New Capitalists*. New York: Basic Books.

——— (2003) *Rogue Nation: American Unilateralism and the Failure of Good Intentions*. New York: Basic Books/Perseus.

Price, Richard. (2003) "Transnational Civil Society and Advocacy in World Politics," *World Politics* 55 (July): 519–606.

Puchala, Donald J. (2003) *Theory and History in International Relations*. New York: Routledge.

Puchala, Donald, Katie Verlin Laatikainen, and Roger A. Coate. (2007) *United Nations Politics*. Upper Saddle River, NJ: Prentice Hall.

Puddington, Arch. (2010) "Freedom in the World 2010: Erosion of Freedom Intensifies." Washington, DC. Freedom House. Available at: http://www.freedomhouse.org/template.cfm?page5130&year52010.

Purlain, Ted. (2013) "HIV/AIDS Deaths Decrease in Sub-Saharan Africa," Vaccine News Daily (January 7). Last accessed November 23, 2013. Available at: http://vaccinenewsdaily.com/medical_countermeasures/325750-african-countries-reduce-new-hiv-infections-among-children-by-50-percent/.

Putnam, Robert D. (1988) "Diplomacy and Domestic Politics: The Logic of Two-Level Games," *International Organization* 42 (Summer): 427–60.

Qing, Koh Gui. (2012) "China Gives Currency More Freedom with New Reform," *Reuters* (April 14). Accessed June 27, 2013. Available at: http://www.reuters.com/article/2012/04/14/us-china-cbank-yuan-band-idUSBRE83D02020120414.

Quester, George H. (1992) "Conventional Deterrence," pp. 31–51 in Gary L. Guertner, Robert Haffa, Jr., and George Quester (eds.), *Conventional Forces and the Future of Deterrence*. Carlisle Barracks, PA: U.S. Army War College.

Quick, Darren. (2013) "Self-Healing 'Artificial Leaf' Produces Energy from Dirty Water," *Gizmag*. (April 10). Accessed July 4, 2013. Available at: http://www.gizmag.com/artificial-leaf-self-healing/27004/.

Quinn, David, Jonathan Wilkenfeld, Kathleen Smarick, and Victor Asal. (2006) "Power Play: Mediation in Symmetric and Asymmetric International Crises," *International Interactions* 32 (December): 441–70.

Quinn, Jane Bryant. (2002) "Iraq: It's the Oil, Stupid," *Newsweek* (September 30): 43.

Quinn, Michael J., T. David Mason, and Mehmet Gurses. (2007) "Sustaining the Peace: Determinants of Civil War Recurrence." *International Interactions* 33 (2): 167–93.

Quirk, Matthew. (2007) "The Mexican Connection," *The Atlantic* (April) 26–27.

Raasch, Chuck. (2009) "Obama Is America's First Global President, Historian Says," *USA Today News: Opinions* (April 7). Available at: http://www.usatoday.com/news/opinion/columnist/ raasch/2009–04–07–newpolitics_N.htm.

Rabkin, Jeremy A. (2005) *Law without Nations? Why Constitutional Government Requires Sovereign States*. Princeton, NJ: Princeton University Press.

Raloff, Janet. (2006) "The Ultimate Crop Insurance," pp. 166–68 in Robert J. Griffiths (ed.), *Global Issues 05/06*. Dubuque, IA: McGraw-Hill/Dushkin.

Ramcharan, Bertrand. (2010) *Preventive Human Rights Strategies*. New York: Routledge.

Ranasinghe, Dhara. (2013) "Consumer Spending Playing a Greater Role in China's Economy," *NBC News* (March 12). Accessed July 27, 2013. Available at: http://www.nbcnews.com/business/consumer-spending-playing-greater-role-chinas-economy-1C8827106.

Rapkin, David, and William R. Thompson, with Jon A. Christopherson. (1989) "Bipolarity and Bipolarization in the Cold War Era," *Journal of Conflict Resolution* 23 (June): 261–95.

Rasler, Karen A. and William R. Thompson. (2006) "Contested Territory, Strategic Rivalries, and Conflict Escalation," *International Studies Quarterly* 50 (March): 145–167.

——— (2005) *Puzzles of the Democratic Peace: Theory, Geopolitics, and the Transformation of World Politics.* London: Palgrave Macmillan.

Rathbun, Brian. (2012) "Politics and Paradigm Preferences: The Implicit Ideology of International Relations Scholars," *International Studies Quarterly* 56: 607–622.

Ravallion, Martin. (2004) "Pessimistic on Poverty?" *Economist* (April 10): 65.

Ravenhill, John. (2008) *Global Political Economy.* New York: Oxford University Press.

——— (2004) *Global Political Economy.* New York: Oxford University Press.

Raymond, Gregory A. (1999) "Necessity in Foreign Policy," *Political Science Quarterly* 113 (Winter): 673–88.

Redfield, Robert. (1962) *Human Nature and the Study of Society,* Vol. 1. Chicago: University of Illinois Press.

Regan, Patrick M., and Aida Paskevicute. (2003) "Women's Access to Politics and Peaceful States," *Journal of Peace Research* 40 (March): 287–302.

Reich, Robert B. (2010) "The Job Picture Still Looks Bleak," *Wall Street Journal* (April 12). Available at: http://online.wsj.com/article/SB10001424052702304222504575173780671015468.html.

——— (2007a) "How Capitalism Is Killing Democracy," *Foreign Policy* (September/October) 39–42.

——— (2007b) *Supercapitalism.* New York: Knopf.

Reid, T. R. (2004) *The United States of Europe: The New Superpower and the End of American Supremacy.* New York: Penguin.

Reimann, Kim D. (2006) "A View from the Top: International Politics, Norms and the Worldwide Growth of NGOs," *International Studies Quarterly* 50: 45–67.

Reinares, Fernando. (2002) "The Empire Rarely Strikes Back," *Foreign Policy* (January/February): 92–94.

Reinhart, Carmen M. and Kenneth S. Rogoff. (2009) *This Time Is Different: Eight Centuries of Financial Folly.* Princeton: NJ: Princeton University Press.

Reiter, Dan. (2009) *How Wars End.* Princeton, NJ: Princeton University Press.

——— (2003) "Exploring the Bargaining Model of War," *Perspectives on Politics* 1 (March): 27–43.

Renshon, Jonathan and Stanley A. Renshon. (2008) "The Theory and Practice of Foreign Policy Decision Making," *Political Psychology* 29: 509–36.

Reuveny, Rafael, and William R. Thompson. (2008) " Observations on the North-South Divide," pp. 1–16 in Rafael Reuveny and William R. Thompson (eds.), *North and South in the World Political Economy.* Malden, MA: Blackwell.

——— (2004) "World Economic Growth, Systemic Leadership and Southern Debt Crises," *Journal of Peace Research* 41 (January): 5–24.

——— (eds.) (2008) *North and South in the World Political Economy.* Malden, Mass.: Blackwell.

Revel, Jean-Francois. (2004) *Anti-Americanism.* San Francisco: Encounter.

Rich, Frank. (2004) "The Corporate-Military Whiz Kids," *International Herald Tribune* (January 24–25): 8.

Ridley, Matt. (2003) *Nature vs. Nurture: Genes, Experiences and What Makes Us Human.* New York: HarperCollins.

Riedel, Bruce. (2007) "Al Qaeda Strikes Back," *Foreign Affairs* 86 (May/June) 24–40.

Rieff, David. (2005) *At the Point of a Gun: Democratic Dreams and Armed Intervention.* New York: Simon & Schuster.

Rifkin, Jeromy. (2004) *The European Dream: How Europe's Vision of the Future Is Quietly Eclipsing the American Dream.* New York: Tarcher.

Riggs, Robert E., and Jack C. Plano. (1994) *The United Nations,* 2nd ed. Belmont, CA: Wadsworth.

Riker, William H. (1962) *The Theory of Political Coalitions.* New Haven, CT.: Yale University Press.

Riley-Smith, Jonathan. (1995) "Religious Warriors," *Economist* (December 23/January 1): 63–67.

Ripsman, Norrin M. (2005) "Two Stages of Transition from a Region of War to a Region of Peace," *International Studies Quarterly* 49 (December): 669–93.

——— and T. V. Paul. (2005) "Globalization and the National Security State," *International Studies Review* (June): 199–227.

Risse-Kappen, Thomas. (1996) "Identity in a Democratic Security Community: The Case of NATO," pp. 357–400 in Peter Katzenstein (ed.), *The Culture of National Security: Norms and Identity in World Politics.* New York, Columbia Press.

Roche, Douglas. (2007) "Our Greatest Threat," pp. 137–140 in Robert M. Jackson, ed., *Global Issues 06/07.* Dubuque, Iowa: McGraw-Hill Contemporary Learning Series.

Rochester, J. Martin. (2006) *Between Peril and Promise: The Politics of International Law.* Washington, DC: CQ Press.

Rodenbeck, Max. (2011) "Volcano of Rage," *The New York Review* (March 24): 4–7.

Rodrik, Dani. (2011) *The Globalization Paradox: Democracy and the Future of the World Economy.* New York: W. W. Norton.

——— (2008) *One Economics, Many Recipes: Globalization, Institutions, and Economic Growth.* Princeton, NJ: Princeton University Press.

Rogers, Simon. (2012) "Drones by Country: Who Has all the UAVs?" *The Guardian* (August 3). Accessed June 17, 2013. Available at: http://www.guardian.co.uk/news/datablog/2012/aug/03/drone-stocks-by-country.

Rogoff, Kenneth. (2003) "The IMF Strikes Back," *Foreign Policy* 134 (January/February): 38–46.

Rosato, Sebastian. (2003) "The Flawed Logic of Democratic Peace Theory." *The American Political Science Review* 97(4): 585–602.

Rose, Gideon. (2005) "The Bush Administration Gets Real," *International Herald Tribune* (August 19): 7.

Rosecrance, Richard. (2005) "Merger and Acquisition," *The National Interest* 80 (Summer): 65–73.

Rosen, Stacey, Shahla Shapouri, and Birgit Meade. (2012) "Global Food Security," *United States Department of Agriculture.* Accessed August 10. Available at: http://www.ers.usda.gov/topics/international-markets-trade/global-food-security.aspx.

Rosenau, James N. (1980) *The Scientific Study of Foreign Policy.* New York: Nichols.

Rosenberg, Justin. (2005) "Globalization Theory: A Post-Mortem," *International Politics* 42 (March): 2–74.

Rosenthal, Elisabeth. (2005) "Global Warming: Adapting to a New Reality," *International Herald Tribune* (September 12): 1, 5.

Rosenthal, Joel H. (2009, July 20) "Leadership as Practical Ethics," *The Essence of Ethics,* retrieved from http://www.carnegiecouncil.org/education/001/ethics/0003.html.

Ross, Dennis. (2007) *Statecraft and How to Restore America's Standing in the World.* New York: Farrar, Straus, and Giroux.

Ross, Michael L. (2004) "What Do We Know about Natural Resources and Civil War?" *Journal of Peace Research* 41 (May): 337–56.

Ross, Philip E. (1997) "The End of Infantry?" *Forbes* (July 7): 182–85.

Rostow, W. W. (1960) *The Stages of Economic Growth.* Cambridge: Cambridge University Press.

Rothkopf, David. (2012). *Power, Inc: The Epic Rivalry between Big Business and Government—and the Reckoning That Lies Ahead.* New York: Farrar, Straus, and Giroux.

——— (2005) *Running the World.* New York: Public Affairs.

Rousseau, Jean Jaques. (1976). *Social Contract.* London: Penguin Books.

Rowe, David M. (2010) "Economic Sanctions and International Security," *The International Studies Encyclopedia.* Denmark: Robert A. Blackwell Publishing, 2010. Blackwell Reference Online. Available at: http://www.isacompendium.com/subscriber/tocnode?id1g9781444336597_chunk_g97814443365977_ss1-4.

Roxburgh, Charles, Susan Lund, and John Piotrowski. (2011). *Mapping Global Capital Markets 2011.* McKinsey Global Institute. Available at: http://www.mckinsey.com/insights/mgi/research/financial_markets/mapping_global_capital_markets_2011.

Rubenstein, Richard E. (2003) "The Psycho-Political Sources of Terrorism," pp. 139–50 in Charles W. Kegley, Jr. (ed.), *The New Global Terrorism.* Upper Saddle River, NJ: Prentice Hall.

Rudolph, Christopher. (2005) "Sovereignty and Territorial Borders in a Global Age," *International Studies Review* 7 (March): 1–20.

Ruggie, John Gerald. (1982) "International Regimes, Transaction, and Change: Embedded Liberalism in the Postwar Economic Order." *International Organization* 36 (2).

Runge, Carlisle Ford and Carlisle Piehl Runge. (2010) "Against the Grain: Why Failing to Complete the Green Revolution Could Bring the Next Famine." *Foreign Affairs* 89(1) (January/February): 8–14.

Russett, Bruce. (2005) "Bushwhacking the Democratic Peace," *International Studies Perspectives* 6 (November): 395–408.

——— (2001a) "How Democracy, Interdependence, and International Organizations Create a System for Peace," pp. 232–42 in Charles W. Kegley, Jr. and Eugene Wittkopf (eds.), *The Global Agenda,* 6th ed. Boston: McGraw-Hill.

Russia Times. (2012) "'It's a trap!'—Russian Leftists Hold Protests against WTO Entry," *Russia Times.* Accessed July 27, 2013. Available at: http://rt.com/politics/leftists-hold-protests-entry-296/.

Rynning, Sten and Jens Ringsmose. (2008) "Why Are Revisionist States Revisionist? Reviving Classical Realism as an Approach to Understanding International Change," *International Politics* 45 (January): 19–39.

Sabastenski, Anna (ed.). (2005) *Patterns of Global Terrorism 1985–2004.* Great Barrington, Mass.: Berkshire.

Sachs, Jeffrey. (2005) *The End of Poverty.* New York: Penguin Press.

Sagan, Carl. (1989) "Understanding Growth Rates: The Secret of the Persian Chessboard," *Parade* (February 14): 14.

——— (1988) "The Common Enemy," *Parade* (February 7): 4–7.

Sageman, Marc. (2008) *Leaderless Jihad: Terror Networks in the Twenty-First Century.* Philadelphia: University of Pennsylvania Press.

——— (2004) *Understanding Terror Networks.* Philadelphia: University of Pennsylvania Press.

Salam, Reihan. (2009) "The Death of Macho," *Foreign Policy* (July/August): 65–71.

Sambanis, Nicholas. (2004) "What Is Civil War?" *Journal of Conflict Resolution* 48 (December): 814–58.

Sambidge, Andy. (2011) "Global Food Prices Rise 36% in Year, World Bank Says: Soaring Costs Partly Driven by Higher Fuel Costs Connected to Middle East Political Unrest," Arabian Business.com. Available at: http://www.arabianbusiness.com/global-food-prices-rise-36-in-year-world-bank-says-393963.html?sms_ss5 twitter&at_xt54da9251570d7fafa,0.

Samin, Amir. (1976) *Unequal Development.* New York: Monthly Review Press.

Samuelson, Robert J. (2012) "Can Globalization Survive 2013?" *The Washington Post* (December 30). Accessed July 27, 2013. Available at: http://articles.washingtonpost.com/2012-12-30/opinions/36071260_1_production-workers-capital-flows-cost-advantage.

——— (2008) "Learning from the Oil Shock." *Newsweek* (June 23): 39.

gust 8): A7.

——— (2006) "This Year Could Mark the End of Pax Americana," Columbia, SC: *The State* (December 19): A9.

Sandler, Todd. (2010) "New Frontiers of Terrorism Research: An Introduction." *Journal of Peace Research* 48: 279–86.

——— (2010) "Terrorism and Policy: Introduction." *Journal of Conflict Resolution*. 54(2): 203–13.

Sandler, Todd and Walter Enders. (2007) "Applying Analytical Methods to Study Terrorism," *International Studies Perspectives* 8 (August): 287–302.

Sands, Phillippe. (2005) *Lawless World: America and the Making and Breaking of Global Rules*. New York: Viking Penguin.

Saner, Raymond. (2012) "Plurilateral Agreements: Key to Solving Impasse of WTO/Doha Round and Basis for Future Trade Agreements within the WTO Context," *CSEND Policy Brief Nr. 7*. Accessed July 27, 2013. Available at: http://www.csend.org/site-1.5/images/files/CSEND_Policy_Brief_Nr_7_Plurilaterals_April_2012_1.pdf.

Sang-Hun, Choe. (2008) "Hundreds Injured in South Korean Beef Protest," *International Herald Tribune* (June 29).

Sanger, David E. (2009b) "Obama's Worst Pakistan Nightmare," *New York Times Magazine* (January 11).

——— (2005) "The New Global Dance Card," *New York Times* (September 18): Section 4, 3.

Sassen,, Saskia. (2008) *Territory, Authority, Rights: From Medieval to Global Assemblages*. Princeton, NJ: Princeton University Press.

Saul, John Ralstom. (2004) "The Collapse of Globalism and the Rebirth of Nationalism," *Harper's* 308 (March): 33–43.

Saunders, Phillip and Scott Kastner. (2009) "Bridge over Troubled Water? Envisioning China-Taiwan Peace Agreement," *International Security* 33 (4): 87–114.

Saurin, Julian. (2000) "Globalization, Poverty, and the Promises of Modernity," pp. 204–29 in Sarah Owen Vandersluis and Paris Yeros (eds.), *Poverty in World Politics*. New York: St. Martin's.

Savage, Charlie. (2011) "Attack Renews Debate over Congressional Consent" *The New York Times* (March 21): A14.

Saxton, Gregory D. (2005) "Repression, Grievances, Mobilization, and Rebellion," *International Interactions* 31 (1): 87–116.

Schelling, Thomas C. (2006) *Strategies of Commitment and Other Essays*. Cambridge, Mass.: Harvard University Press.

——— (1978) *Micromotives and Macrobehavior*. New York: Norton.

Scherer, Michael. (2010) "The New Sheriffs of Wall Street." *Time* (May 13). Available at: http://www.time.com/time/magazine/article/0,9171,1989144,00.html.

——— (1986) *The Cycles of American History*. Boston: Houghton Mifflin.

Schmidt, Blake and Elisabeth Malkin. (2009) "Leftist Wins Salvadoran Election for President" *International Herald Tribune* (March 19): 5.

Schmidt, Eric and Jared Cohen. (2010) "The Digital Disruption: Connectivity and the Diffusion of Power," *Foreign Affairs* (November/December): 75–85.

Schneider, Gerald, Katherine Barbieri, and Nils Petter Gleditsch (eds.). (2003) *Globalization and Armed Conflict*. Lanham, Md.: Rowman & Littlefield.

Schnepf, Randy. (2011) "Brazil's WTO Case against the U.S. Cotton Program," Congressional Research Service (June 21). Accessed July 27, 2013. Available at: http://www.fas.org/sgp/crs/row/RL32571.pdf.

Schraeder, Peter J. (ed.). (2002) *Exporting Democracy*. Boulder, Colo.: Lynne Rienner.

Schroeder, Paul W. (1989) "The Nineteenth-Century System," *Review of International Studies* 15 (April): 135–53.

Schulz, William F. (2001) *In Our Own Best Interest: How Defending Human Rights Benefits Us All*. Boston: Beacon Press.

Schwab, Susan. (2011) "After Doha: Why the Negotiations Are Doomed and What We Should Do About It," *Foreign Affairs* (May/June).

Schwarz, Benjamin. (2005) "Managing China's Rise," *Atlantic Monthly* 295 (June): 27–28.

Schweller, Randall L. (2004) "Unanswered Threats: A Neoclassical Realist Theory of Underbalancing," *International Security* 29 (Fall): 159–201.

——— (1999) "Review of *From Wealth to Power* by Fareed Zakaria," *American Political Science Review* 93 (June 1999): 497–99.

Scowcroft, Brent and Samuel R. Berger. (2005) "In the Wake of War: Getting Serious about Nation-Building," *The National Interest* 81 (Fall): 49–60.

Secor, Laura. (2005) *Sands of Empire*. New York: Simon and Schuster.

Selck, Torsten J. (2004) "On the Dimensionality of European Union Legislative Decision-Making," *Journal of Theoretical Politics* 16 (April): 203–22.

Sen, Amartya. (2006) *Identity and Violence: The Illusion of Destiny*. New York: Norton.

Sending, Ole Jacob and Iver B. Neumann. (2006) "Governance to Governmentality: Analyzing NGOs, States, and Power," *International Studies Quarterly* 50: 651–672.

Sengupta, Somini. (2005) "Hunger for Energy Transforms How India Operates," *New York Times International* (June 5): Section 4, 3.

Senese, Paul D. and John A. Vasquez. (2008) *The Steps to War*. Princeton, N.J.: Princeton University Press.

Serfaty, Simon. (2003) "Europe Enlarged, America Detached?" *Current History* (March): 99–102.

Sezgin, Yüksel. (2005) "Taking a New Look at State-Directed Industrialization," *International Studies Review* 7 (June): 323–325.

Shaffer, Gregory. (2009) "The Future of the WTO," University of Chicago Law School Faculty Blog, February 23, 2009. Available at: http://uchicagolaw.typepad.com/faculty/2009/02/future-of-the-wtorelevance.html.

Shah, Timothy Samuel. (2004) "The Bible and the Ballot Box: Evangelicals and Democracy in the 'Global South,'" *SAIS Review of International Affairs* 24 (Fall): 117–32.

Shambaugh, David. (2013) *China Goes Global: The Partial Power*. Oxford, UK: Oxford University Press.

Shane, Scott. (2005) "The Beast That Feeds on Boxes: Bureaucracy," *New York Times* (April 10): Section 4, 3.

Shaker, Thom, David E. Sanger, and Martin Fackler. (2013) " U.S. Is Bolstering Missile Defense to Deter North Korea," *The New York Times* (March 15). Accessed June 13, 2013. Available at: http://www.nytimes.com/2013/03/16/world/asia/us-to-bolster-missile-defense-against-north-korea.html?pagewanted=all.

Shanker, Thom and Steven Erlanger. (2010) "Blunt U.S. Warning Reveals Deep Strains in NATO," *The New York Times* (June 11): A1.

——— (2009) "Afghanistan Presents NATO a Choice of Fusion or Fracture," *International Herald Tribune* (April 3): 1.

Shannon, Megan. (2009) "Preventing War and Providing the Peace? International Organizations and the Management of Territorial Disputes," *Conflict Management and Peace-Science* 26 (2): 144–63.

Shannon, Thomas Richard. (1989) *An Introduction to the World-System Perspective*. Boulder, CO: Westview.

Shapin, Steven. (2007) "What Else Is New," *The New Yorker* (May 14): 144–48.

Shapiro, Ian. (2008) *Futurecast: How Superpowers, Populations, and Globalization Will Change the Way You Live and Work*. St. Martin's Press, New York.

Sharp, Travis. (2009) "Fiscal Year 2010 Pentagon Defense Spending Request: February 'Topline,'" Center for Arms Control and Non-Proliferation. (February 26). Available at: http://www.armscontrolcenter.org/policy/securityspending/articles/022609_fy10_topline_growth_decade/.

Shearman, Peter. (2013) *Power Transition and International Order in Asia: Issues and Challenges*. New York: Routledge.

Sheffer, Gabriel. (2003) *Diaspora Politics: At Home Abroad*. Cambridge: Cambridge University Press.

Shifrinson, Joshua R Itzkowitz, and Michael Beckley. (2012/2013) "Debating China's Rise and U.S. Decline," *International Security*, 37(3): 172–181.

Shiffman, Gary M. (2006) *Economic Instruments of Security Policy*. Basingstoke, U.K.: Palgrave MacMillan.

Shlapentorkh, Vladmir, Eric Shirae, and Josh Woods (eds.). (2005) *America: Sovereign Defender or Cowboy Nation?* Burlington, VT: Ashgate.

Shreeve, Jamie. (2005) "The Stem-Cell Debate," *New York Times Magazine* (April 10): 42–47.

Shuman, Michael. (2012) "The Jobless Generation," *Time* (April 16). Last accessed November 23, 2013. Available at: http://content.time.com/time/magazine/article/0,9171,2111232,00.html.

Shwayder, Maya and Lisa Mahapatra. (2013) "Drone: Which Countries Have Them for Surveillance and Military Operations?" *International Business Times* (May 18). Accessed June 17, 2013. Available at: http://www.ibtimes.com/drones-which-countries-have-them-surveillance-military-operations-map-1264271.

Siegle, Joseph T, Michael M. Weinstein, and Morton H. Halperin. (2004) "Why Democracies Excel," *Foreign Affairs* 83 (September/October): 57–71.

Sikkink, Kathryn. (2008). "Transnational Politics, International relations Theory and Human Rights," pp. 172–79 in Karen A. Mingst and Jack L. Snyder (eds.), *Essential Readings in World Politics*, 3rd ed. New York: Norton.

Simão, Licínia. (2012). "Do Leaders Still Decide? The Role of Leadership in Russian Foreign Policy," International Politics 49: 482–97.

Simmons, Beth A. and Allison Danner. (2010) "Credible Commitments and the International Criminal Court," *International Organization* 64 (2): 225–256.

Simmons, Beth A. and Zachary Elkins. (2004) "The Globalization of Liberalization: Policy Diffusion in the International Political Economy," *American Political Science Review* 98 (February): 171–89.

Simmons, Beth A. and Richard H. Steinberg. (2007) *International Law and International Relations*. New York: Cambridge University Press.

Simon, Herbert A. (1997) *Models of Bounded Rationality*. Cambridge, MA: MIT Press.

Singer, David. (2010) "Migrant Remittances and Exchange Rate Regimes in the Developing World." *American Political Science Review* 104(2) (May): 307–323.

Singer, Hans W. and Javed A. Ansari. (1988) *Rich and Poor Countries*, 4th ed. London: Unwin Hyman.

Singer, J. David. (2000) "The Etiology of Interstate War," pp. 3–21 in John A. Vasquez (ed.), *What Do We Know About War?* Lanham, Md.: Rowman & Littlefield.

——— (1991) "Peace in the Global System," pp. 56–84 in Charles W. Kegley, Jr. (ed.), *The Long Postwar Peace*. New York: HarperCollins.

——— (ed.). (1968) *Quantitative International Politics*. New York: Free Press.

Singer, P. W. (2013) "The Global Swarm," *Foreign Policy* (March 11). Accessed June 13, 2013. Available at: http://www.foreignpolicy.com/articles/2013/03/11/the_global_swarm.

——— (2010) "We, Robot: Is It Dangerous to Let Drones Fight Our Wars for Us?" *Slate* (May). Available at: http://www.slate.com/id/2253692.

——— (2009a) "Robots at War: The New Battlefield," *The Wilson Quarterly* (Winter).

——— (2009b) "Wired for War: The Robotics Revolution and Conflict in the 21ˢᵗ Century". The Penguin Press.

Singer, Peter. (2004) *One World: The Ethics of Globalization*, 2nd ed. New Haven, Conn.: Yale University Press.

SIPRI (Stockholm International Peace Research Institute). (2013) *SIPRI Yearbook*. New York: Oxford University Press.

——— (2012) *SIPRI Yearbook*. New York: Oxford University Press.

——— (2012b) "Trends in International Arms Transfers in 2011" (March, prepared by Paul Holtom, Mark Bromley, Pieter D. Wezeman, and Siemon T. Wezeman).

——— (2012c) "The SIPRI Top 100 Arms-Producing and Military Services Companies, 2010."

——— (2011) *SIPRI Yearbook*. New York: Oxford University Press.

——— (2009) *SIPRI Yearbook*. New York: Oxford University Press.

Sivard, Ruth Leger. (1991) *World Military and Social Expenditures* 1991. Washington, DC: World Priorities.

Siverson, Randolph M. and Julian Emmons. (1991) "Democratic Political Systems and Alliance Choices," *Journal of Conflict Resolution* 35 (June): 285–306.

Sivy, Michael. (2013) "Why Derivatives May be the Biggest Risk for the Global Economy," *Time* (March 27). Accessed June 27, 2013. Available at: http://business.time.com/2013/03/27/why-derivatives-may-be-the-biggest-risk-for-the-global-economy/.

Skeldon, Ronald. (2010) "Managing Migration for Development Is Circular Migration the Answer?" *The Whitehead Journal of Diplomacy and International Relations* 11(1) (Winter/Spring): 21–33.

Skinner, E. Benjamin. (2010) "The New Slave Trade." *Time* (January 18): 54–57.

——— (2008) "A World Enslaved," *Foreign Policy* (March/April): 62–67.

Sklair, Leslie. (1991) *Sociology of the Global System*. Baltimore: Johns Hopkins University Press.

Slackman, Michael. (2008) "Dreams Stifled, Egypt's Young Turn to Islamic Fervor," *The New York Times* (February 17): 1.

Slater, David. (2005) *Geopolitics and the Post-Colonial: Rethinking North-South Relations*. Malden, Mass: Blackwell.

Slaughter, Anne-Marie. (2005) "Help Develop Institutions and Instruments for Military Intervention on Humanitarian Grounds," *Restoring American Leadership:13 Cooperative Steps to Advance Global Progress*. Accessed July 4, 2013. Available at: http://www.princeton.edu/~slaughtr/Articles/Chapter5RALHumanitarian-Intervention_rev2.pdf.

Small, Melvin and J. David Singer. (1982) *Resort to Arms: International and Civil Wars, 1816–1980*. Beverly Hills, CA: Sage.

Smith, Adam. (1904) "An Inquiry into the Nature and Causes of the Wealth of Nations." Edwin Cannan, ed. *Library of Economics and Liberty*. Available at: http://www.econlib.org/library/Smith/smWN.html.

Smith, Jackie and Timothy Patrick Moran. (2001) "WTO 101: Myths about the World Trade Organization," pp. 68–71 in Robert J. Griffiths (ed.), *Developing World 01/02*. Guilford, CT: Dushkin/McGraw-Hill.

Smith, Michael J. (2000) "Humanitarian Intervention Revisited," *Harvard International Review* 22 (April): 72–75.

Smith, Roger W. (2010) "Review of *Genocide: A Normative Account* - by Larry May," *Ethics & International Affairs* 24(4) (Winter): 433–435.

Smith, Steve and Patricia Owens. (2005) "Alternative Approaches to International Theory," pp. 271–93 in John Baylis and Steve Smith (eds.), *The Globalization of World Politics*, 3rd ed. New York: Oxford University Press.

Smith, Tony. (2007) *Pact with the Devil: Washington's Bid for World Supremacy and the Betrayal of the American Promise*. New York: Routledge.

Smith-Cannoy, Heather. (2012) *Insincere Commitments: Human Rights Treaties, Abusive States, and Citizen Activism*. Washington, DC: Georgetown University Press.

Snyder, David Pearce. (2006) "Five Meta-Trends Changing the World," pp. 13–17 in Robert M. Jackson (ed.), *Global Issues 05/06*. Dubuque, IA: McGraw-Hill/Dushkin.

Snyder, Glenn H. (1991) "Alliance Threats: A Neorealist First Cut," pp. 83–103 in Robert L. Rothstein (ed.), *The Evolution of Theory in International Relations*. Columbia: University of South Carolina Press.

Snyder, Jack. (2005) "A Perfect Peace," *The Washington Post National Review Weekly Edition* (January 10): 33.

——— (2004) "One World, Rival Theories," *Foreign Policy* (November/December): 53–62.

Sobek, David. (2005) "Machiavelli's Legacy: Domestic Politics and International Conflict," *International Studies Quarterly* 49 (June): 179–204.

Sofaer, Abraham. (2010) "The Best Defense?: Preventive Force and International Security." *Foreign Affairs* 89(1) (January/February): 109–118.

Somavia, Juan. (2004) "For Too Many, Globalization Isn't Working," *International Herald Tribune* (February 27): 6.

Sorensen, Theodore C. (1963) *Decision Making in the White House*. New York: Columbia University Press.

Soros, George. (2003) *The Bubble of American Supremacy: Correcting the Misuse of American Power*. New York: Public Affairs.

Spar, Debora. (1999) "Foreign Investment and Human Rights." *Challenge* 42(1): 55–80.

Sperandei, Maria. (2006) "Bridging Deterrents and Compellence," *International Studies Review* 8 (June): 253–280.

Spiegel, Peter. (2013) "Hostility to the EU deepens," *Financial Times* (January 16). Accessed June 3, 2013. Available at: http://www.ft.com/intl/cms/s/0/d585cdaa-5fca-11e2-8d8d-00144feab49a.html#axzz2VB01jBjR.

Sprout, Harold and Margaret Sprout. (1965) *The Ecological Perspective on Human Affairs*. Princeton, NJ: Princeton University Press.

Spykman, Nicholas. (1944) *The Geography of Peace*. New York: Harcourt Brace.

Stark, Sam. (2007) "Flaming Bitumen: Romancing the Algerian War," *Harper's* (February): 92–98.

Starr, Harvey. (2006) "International Borders," *SAIS Review* 26 (Winter/Spring): 3–10.

——— and Benjamin Most. (1978) "A Return Journey: Richardson, 'Frontiers' and Wars in the 1945–1965 Era," *Journal of Conflict Resolution* 22 (September): 441–67.

Steans, Jill. (2006) *Gender and International Relations*. Cambridge, UK: Polity.

Steele, Brent J. (2007) "Liberal-Idealism: A Constructivist Critique," *International Studies Review* 9 (Spring): 23–52.

Stefan Halper (2010) *The Beijing Consensus: How China's Authoritarian Model Will Dominate the Twenty-First Century*. New York: Basic Books.

Steil, Benn and Manuel Hinds. (2009) *Money, Markets, and Sovereignty*. New Haven: Yale University Press.

Steinberg, Richard. (2009) "The Future of the WTO," University of Chicago Law School Faculty Blog, February 23. Available at: http://uchicagolaw.typepad.com/ faculty/2009/02/future-of-the-wtorelevance.html.

Stephenson, Carolyn M. (2000) "NGOs and the Principal Organs of the United Nations," pp. 270–94 in Paul Taylor and R. J. Groom (eds.), *The United Nations at the Millennium*. London: Continuum.

Stephenson, Max and Laura Zanotti. (2012) *Peacebuilding Through Community-Based NGOs: Paradoxes and Possibilities*. Boulder, CO: Kumarian Press.

Stewart, Devin T., Nikolas K. Gvosdev, and David A. Andelman. (2008) "Roundtable: The Nation-State" Carnegie Council, August 29. Available at: http://www.carnegiecouncil.org/resources/ethics_online/0024.html/:pf_printable.

Stiglitz, Joseph (2011) "The IMF Cannot Afford to Make a Mistake with Strauss-Kahn's Successor," *The Telegraph (UK)* (May 21).

——— (2006) *Making Globalization Work*. New York: Norton.

——— (2003) *Globalization and Its Discontents*. New York: Norton.

Stiglitz, Joseph and Andrew Charlton. (2006) *Fair Trade for All: How Trade Can Promote Development*. New York: Oxford University Press.

Stiles, Kendall. (2005) "The Ambivalent Hegemon: Explaining the 'Lost Decade' in Multilateral Trade Talks, 1948–1958," *Review of International Political Economy* 2 (1): 1–26.

Stohl, Rachel. (2005) "Fighting the Illicit Trafficking of Small Arms," *SAIS Review* 25 (Winter/Spring): 59–68.

Stokes, Doug. (2013) "Achilles' Deal: Dollar Decline and US Grand Strategy after the Crisis," *Review of International Political Economy* (May 8). Accessed June 27, 2013. Available at: http://www.tandfonline.com/doi/abs/10.1080/09692290.2013.779592#.UcyERD54awF.

Stopford, John. (2001) "Multinational Corporations," pp. 72–77 in Robert J. Griffiths (ed.), *Developing World 01/02*. Guilford, CT: Dushkin/McGraw-Hill.

Story, Louise, Landon Thomas Jr., and Nelson Schwartz. (2010) "Wall St. Helped to Mask Debt Fueling Europe's Crisis." *New York Times* (February 13). Available at: http://www.nytimes.com/2010/02/14/business/global/14debt.ntml?pagewanted5all.

Strang, David. (1991) "Global Patterns of Decolonization, 1500–1987," *International Studies Quarterly* 35 (December): 429–545.

Streeten, Paul. (2001) "Human Development Index," pp. 367–68 in Joel Krieger (ed.), *The Oxford Companion to Politics of the World*, 2nd ed. New York: Oxford University Press.

Stross, Randall E. (2002) "The McPeace Dividend," *U.S. News & World Report* (April 1): 36.

Struett, Michael J. 2012. "Why the International Criminal Court Must *Pretend* to Ignore Politics," *Ethics and International Affairs* 26(1): 83–92.

Stuckler, David and Sanjay Basu. (2013) "How Austerity Kills," *The New York Times* (May 12). Accessed June 27, 2013. Available at: http://www.nytimes.com/2013/05/13/opinion/how-austerity-kills.html?pagewanted=all&_r=0.

Suddath, Claire. (2009). "U.S.-Cuba Relations." Time. Accessed on November 22, 2013. Available at: http://content.time.com/time/nation/article/0,8599,1891359,00.html.

Suganami, Hidemi. (1983) "A Normative Enquiry in International Relations," *Review of International Studies* 9: 35–54.

Summers, Lawrence H. (2006) "America Overdrawn," pp. 25–27 in Helen E. Purkitt (ed.), *World Politics 05/06*. Dubuque, IA: McGraw-Hill/Dushkin.

Suominen, Kati. (2013) "RTA Exchange: Resuming WTO's Leadership in a World of Regional Trade Agreements," *International Development Bank* (June). Accessed July 27, 2013. Available at: http://e15initiative.org/wp-content/uploads/2013/06/E15_RTA_Suominen.pdf.

Surowiecki, James. (2007) "The Myth of Inevitable Progress," *Foreign Affairs* 86 (July/August): 132–39.

Sutherland, Peter. (2008) "Transforming Nations: How the WTO Boosts Economies and Opens Societies," *Foreign Affairs* 87 (March): 125–36.

Sylvester, Christine. (2002) *Feminist International Relations*. New York: Cambridge University Press.

Talbott, Strobe, and Nayan Chanda (eds.). (2002) *The Age of Terror*. New York: Basic Books.

Taliaferro, Jeffrey, S. E. Lobell, and N. M. Ripsman. (2009) *Neo-Classical Realism, the State, and Foreign Policy*. Cambridge, UK: Cambridge University Press.

Talmadge, Eric. (2010) "US-Japan Security Pact Turns 50, Faces New Strains," Associated Press (June 22).

Tan, Sor-hoon (ed.). (2005) *Challenging Citizenship: Group Membership and Cultural Identity in a Global Age*. Burlington, VT: Ashgate.

Tarrow, Sidney. (2006) *The New Transnational Activism.* New York: Cambridge University Press.

Tayler, Jeffrey. (2009) "'What Crisis?' Why Europe's Poorest Country Is a Paragon of Financial Stability," *The Atlantic* 304 (1): 28–30.

Taylor, Guy. (2013) "Secretary of State John Kerry Outlines Vision for 'Pacific Dream' Asia," *The Washington Times* (April 15). Accessed May 18, 2013. Available at: http://www.washingtontimes.com.

Tellis, Ashley J. (2005) "A Grand Chessboard," *Foreign Policy* (January/February): 51–54.

Terlinden, Claire and Louise Hilditch. (2003) *Towards Effective Partnership: Untie Aid.* Brussels: Action Aid Alliance.

Teslik, Lee Hudson. (2008) "Council for Foreign Relations Backgrounder: Food Prices," Available at: http://www.cfr.org/publication/16662/price_of_food.html? breadcrumb 5%2 Findex.

Tessman, Brock, and Steve Chan. (2004) "Power Cycles, Risk Propensity and Great Power Deterrence," *Journal of Conflict Resolution* 48 (April): 131–53.

Tetlock, Philip. (2006) *Expert Political Judgment.* Princeton, NJ: Princeton University Press.

Thachuk, Kimberley. (2005) "Corruption and International Security," *SAIS Review* 25 (Winter/Spring): 143–52.

Thakur, Ramesh and Thomas G. Weiss. (2009) "United Nations 'Policy': An Argument with Three Illustrations," *International Studies Perspectives* 10: 18–35.

——— (eds.) (2009) *The United Nations and Global Governance: An Unfinished Journey.* Bloomington: Indiana University Press.

Than, Ker. (2012) "'Shocking' Greenland Ice Melt: Global Warming or Just Heat Wave?" *National Geographic* (July 25). Accessed August 10. Available at: http://news.nationalgeographic.com/news/2012/07/120725-greenland-ice-sheet-melt-satellites-nasa-space-science/.

Thant, U. (1978) *View from the UN.* New York: Doubleday.

The Center for Arms Control and Non-Proliferation. (2013) "Fact Sheet: Global Nuclear Weapons Inventories in 2013." Accessed June 12, 2013. Available at: http://armscontrolcenter.org/issues/nuclearweapons/articles/fact_sheet_global_nuclear_weapons_inventories_in_2012/.

The Hunger Project. (2009) "Bolivia." Available at: http://www.thp.org/where_we_work/latin_america/bolivia?gclid5CP2K7cvIxpwCFVhJ2godk22zKg.

The Institute for Economics and Peace. (2013) *Global Peace Index: 2013* Accessed July 31, 2013. Available at: http://www.visionofhumanity.org/pdf/gpi/2013_Global_Peace_Index_Report.pdf.

Themnér, Lotta and Peter Wallensteen. (2013) "Armed Conflicts, 1946–2012," Journal of Peace Research, 50: 509–521.

Thomas, Ward. (2005) "The New Age of Assassination," *SAIS Review* 25 (Winter/Spring): 27–39.

Thompson, Mark. (2011) "Air Boss: From Her Base in Germany, Major General Maggie Woodward Ruled the Skies over Libya. It was another First for Women in Combat," *Time* (April 18): 37–39.

——— (2007) "Flying Shame," *Time* (October 8): 34–41.

Thomson, James W. (2011) "How the Mighty Are Falling," *USA Today* (March): 14–18.

Thrall, Trevor and Jane Cramer, (eds.) (2009) *American Foreign Policy and the Politics of Fear: Threat Inflation since 9/11.* New York: Routledge.

Thurow, Lester C. (1999) *Building Wealth.* New York: HarperCollins.

——— (1998) "The American Economy in the Next Century," *Harvard International Review* 20 (Winter): 54–59.

Thyne, Clayton L. (2007) *Cheap Signals, Costly Consequences: How International Relations Affect Civil Wars.* Ph.D. Diss., University of Iowa.

——— (2006) "Cheap Signals with Costly Consequences: The Effect of Interstate Relations on Civil War," *Journal of Conflict Resolution* 50 (December): 937–61.

Tickner, J. Ann. (2013) "Men, Women, and War," in *Conflict After the Cold War: Arguments on Causes of War and Peace.* Boston, MA: Pearson. 280–293.

——— (2010) "Searching for the Princess?" pp. 36–41 in Russell Bova (ed.), *Readings on How the World Works.* New York: Pearson.

——— (2005) "What Is Your Research Program? Some Feminist Answers to International Relations Methodological Questions," *International Studies Quarterly* 49 (March): 1–21.

——— (2002) *Gendering World Politics.* New York: Columbia University Press.

——— (1997) "You Just Don't Understand: Troubled Engagements between Feminists and IR Theorists," *International Studies Quarterly* 41 (1997): 611–32.

——— and Laura Sjoberg. (2006) "Feminism," in Tim Dunne, Milya Kurki, and Steve Smith, (eds.) *Theories of International Relations: Discipline and Diversity.* Oxford: Oxford University Press, pp 185–202.

Tiessen, Rebecca. (2010) "Global Actors in Transnational and Virtual Spaces." *International Studies Review* 12: 301–4.

Tilford, Earl H., Jr. (1995) *The Revolution in Military Affairs.* Carlisle Barracks, PA: U.S. Army War College.

Tilly, Charles. (2003) *The Politics of Collective Violence.* Cambridge: Cambridge University Press.

Timmerman, Kenneth. (1991) *The Death Lobby: How the West Armed Iraq.* Boston: Houghton Mifflin.

Tocqueville, Alexis de. (1969 [1835]) *Democracy in America.* New York: Doubleday.

Todd, Emmanuel. (2003) *After the Empire: The Breakdown of the American Order.* Translated by C. Jon Delogu. New York: Columbia University Press.

Toft, Monica Duffy. (2007) "Population Shifts and Civil War: A Test of Power Transition Theory," *International Interactions* 33 (July/September): 243–69.

Toner, Robin. (2002) "FBI Agent Gives Her Blunt Assessment," Columbia, SC, *The State* (June 7): A5.

Tonkiss, Fran. (2012) "Economic Globalization," *Wiley-Blackwell Encyclopedia of Globalization* (February 29). DOI: 10.1002/9780470670590.wbeog163.

Townsend-Bell, Erica. (2007) "Identities Matter: Identity Politics, Coalition Possibilities, and Feminist Organizing," *Iowa Research Online* (May 1). Accessed June 3, 2013. Available at: http://ir.uiowa.edu/cgi/viewcontent.cgi?article=1008&context=polisci_pubs.

Toynbee, Arnold J. (1954) *A Study of History.* London: Oxford University Press.

Trading Economics (2013) "Greece Government Spending," Tradingeconomic.com. Accessed June 27, 2013. Available at: http://www.tradingeconomics.com/greece/government-spending.

Transparency International. (2013) "Corruption Perceptions Index 2012," Transparency International. Accessed May 29, 2013. Available at: http://www.transparency.org/cpi2012/results.

Traub, James. (2005) "The New Hard-Soft Power," *New York Times Magazine* (January 30): 28–29.

Traynor, Ian and John Hooper. (2011) "France and Italy in Call to Close UE Borders in Wake of Arab Protests: Sarkozy and Berlusconi Want Passport-Free Travel within the EU Suspended as North African Migrants Flee North," *The Guardian* (April 27). Available at: http://www.guardian.co.uk/world/2011/apr/26/eu-borders-arab-protests.

Trumbull, Mark and Andrew Downie. (2007) "Great Global Shift to Service Jobs," *The Christian Science Monitor* (September): 1, 10.

Tuchman, Barbara W. (1984) *The March of Folly.* New York: Ballantine.

———— (1962) *The Guns of August.* New York: Dell.

Tures, John A. (2005) "Operation Exporting Freedom," *The Whitehead Journal of Diplomacy and International Relations* 6 (Winter/Spring): 97–111.

UC Atlas of Global Inequality. Created by Ben Crow and Suresh Lodha. (2008) University of California Press. Accessed August 5, 2013. Available at: http://www.ucatlas.ucsc.edu.

UIA (Union of International Associations). (2012/2013) *Yearbook of International Organizations.* Munich: K.G. Saur.

UNAIDS. (2013) "Data and analysis," *United Nations.* Accessed June 22, 2013. Available at: http://www.unaids.org/en/dataanalysis/.

———— (2010) "Global Report." Available at: http://www.unaids.org/globalreport/documents/20101123_ GlobalReport_full_en.pdf.

UNCTAD. (2013) *World Investment Report.* New York: United Nations.

Underhill, Geoffrey R. D. and Xiakoe *Zhang* (eds.). (2003) *International Financial Governance under Stress: Global Structures versus National Imperatives.* Cambridge: Cambridge University Press.

UNDESA. (2013) "DESA News," UNDESA. Accessed June 24, 2013. Available at: http://www.un.org/en/development/desa/newsletter/desanews/2013/05/index.html.

———— (2012) "World Urbanization Prospects, the 2011 Revision," *United Nations.* Accessed June 22, 2013. Available at: http://www.un.org/en/development/desa/publications/world-urbanization-prospects-the-2011-revision.html.

UNDP (United Nations Development Programme). (2013) *Human Development Report 2013.* New York: United Nations.

———— (2011) *Human Development Report 2011.* New York: United Nations.

UNESCO. (2013) UNESCO Institute for Statistics. Accessed May 29, 2013. Available at: http://stats.uis.unesco.org/unesco/ReportFolders/ReportFolders.aspx?IF_ActivePath=P,54&IF_Language=eng.

———— (2010) *UNESCO Science Report 2010: The Current Status of Science around the World.* Paris, France: UNESCO.

Ungerer, Jameson Lee. (2012) "Assessing the Progress of the Democratic Peace Research Program," *International Studies Review* (14) (March): 1–31.

UNHCR. (2013) *Global Appeal 2013 Update.* Geneva: UN High Commissioner for Refugees.

———— (2011) *2010 Global Trends.* Geneva: UN High Commissioner for Refugees.

———— (2009) *2008 Global Trends: Refugees, Asylum-seekers, Returnees, Internally Displaced and Stateless Persons.* Geneva: UN High Commissioner for Refugees.

UNIFEM (UN Women). (2013) "Democratic Governance," *UN Women.* Accessed June 24, 2013. Available at: http://www.unifem.org/gender_issues/democratic_governance/.

———— (2012) "Democratic Governance." Accessed August 8, 2012. Available at: http://www.unifem.org/gender_issues/democratic_governance.

UN (United Nations). (2013) "Scale of assessments to the apportionment of the expenses of the United Nations." Accessed June 3, 2013. Available at: http://www.un.org/ga/search/view_doc.asp?symbol=A/67/693.

———— (2012) "Security Council Fails to Adopt Resolution on Syria," *UN News Centre.* Accessed June 3, 2013. Available at: http://www.un.org/apps/news/story.asp?NewsID=42513#.UazORWR4ZMN.

———— (2012) "Improving the Financial Situation of the United Nations." Available at: http://www.un.org/ga/search/view_doc.asp?symbol=A/66/521/Add.1.

United Nations. (2013a) "Cyberschoolbus," *United Nations.* Accessed June 24, 2013. Available at: http://www.un.org/cyberschoolbus/briefing/soldiers/.

———— (2013b) *Annual Report of the Secretary-General on Children and Armed Conflict.* Accessed June 24, 2013.

Available at: http://childrenandarmedconflict.un.org/annual-report-of-the-secretary-general-on-children-and-armed-conflict/.

——— (2011) "Welcome to the United Nations: It's Your World." Available at: http://un-regionaloffice.org/.

——— (2004) *A More Secure World: Out Shared Responsibility.* United Nations Foundation. Available at: http://www.un.org/secureworld/report2.pdf.

United Nations Department of Economic and Social Affairs. (2009) "World Population Age 80 or Older." Appeared in *Time Health* (February 22, 2010).

United Nations Department of Peacekeeping Operations. (2010) *Fact Sheet: United Nations Peacekeeping* (March). New York: United Nations.

United Nations Environment Programme (UNEP). "Status of Ratification." Available at: http://ozone.unep.org/new_site/en/treaty_ratification_status.php.

UN Office on Drugs and Crime. (2010) "Executive Summary." Available at: http://www.unodc.org/documents/data-and-analysis/tocta/Executive_summary.pdf.

——— (2010) *The Globalization of Crime: A Transnational Organized Crime Threat Assessment.* Vienna: UN Office on Drugs and Crime.

United Nations Peace Operations. (2013) "United Nations Peacekeeping Operations." Accessed August 5, 2013. Available at: http://www.un.org/en/peacekeeping

UNICEF. (2009) *The State of the World's Children 2009.* Available at http://www.unicef.org/sowc09/.

UNIFEM. (2010) "Democratic Governance." Available at http://www.unifem.org/gender_issues/democratic_governance/.

——— (2009) *Who Answers to Women? Gender and Accountability.* Available at: http://www.unifem.org/progress/2008/media/POWW08_Report_Full_Text.pdf.

UNODC. (2010) "The Globalization of Crime: A Transnational Organized Crime Threat Assessment." Available at: http://www.unodc.org/documents/data-and-analysis/tocta/TOCTA_Report_2010_low_res.pdf

Urdal, Henrik. (2011) "A Clash of Generations? Youth Bulges and Political Violence," *United Nations Expert Group Meeting on Adolescents, Youth and Development.* Accessed June 6, 2013. Available at: http://www.un.org/esa/population/meetings/egm-adolescents/p10_urdal.pdf.

Urquhart, Brian. (2010) "Finding the Hidden UN." *The New York Review* (May 27): 26–28.

U.S. Agency for International Development. (2004). *Trafficking in Persons: USAIDs Reponse* [On-line]. Available at: http://www.usaid.gov/our_work/cross-cutting_programs/wid/pubs/trafficking_in_person_usaids_response_march2004.pdf. Accessed August 24, 2009.

U.S. Department of Treasury. (2013a) "U.S. Gross External Debt." Accessed June 27, 2013. Available at: http://www.treasury.gov/resource-center/data-chart-center/tic/Pages/external-debt.aspx.

——— (2013b) "Major Foreign Holders of Treasury Securities." Accessed June 27, 2013. Available at: http://www.treasury.gov/resource-center/data-chart-center/tic/Documents/mfh.txt.

——— (2012) "Major Foreign Holders of Treasury Securities." Available at: http://www.treasury.gov/resource-center/data-chart-center/tic/Documents/mfh.txt.

——— (2010) "Gross External Dept Position." Available at http://www.ustreas.gov/tic/debta310.html.

——— (2009) "Major Holders of Treasury Securities," Available at: http://www.treas.gov/tic/mfh.txt.

U.S. Energy Information Administration. (2013) "How Dependent Are We on Foreign Oil?" *USEIA* (May 10). Accessed June 25, 2013. Available at: http://www.eia.gov/energy_in_brief/article/foreign_oil_dependence.cfm.

U.S. National Counterterrorism Center (NCTC). (2011) *2010 NCTC Report on Terrorism.* Washington, DC: National Counterterrorism Center.

Valentino, Benjamin. (2004) *Final Solutions: Mass Killing and Genocide in the Twentieth Century.* Ithaca, NY Cornell University Press.

Vandersluis, Sarah Owen, and Paris Yeros. (2000a) "Ethics and Poverty in a Global Era," pp. 1–31 in Sarah Owen Vandersluis and Paris Yeros (eds.), *Poverty in World Politics.* New York: St. Martin's.

Van der Ploeg, Frederick and Dominic Rohner. (2012) "War and Natural Resourc Exploitation," *European Economic Review* 56 (8): 1714–1729.

Van Evera, Stephen. (1994) "Hypotheses on Nationalism and War," *International Security* 18 (Spring): 5–39.

——— (1990–91) "Primed for Peace," *International Security* 15 (Winter): 6–56.

Van Riper, Tom. (2009) "The World's Largest Malls," *Forbes* (January 15).

Vasquez, John A. (2009) *War Puzzle Revisited.* Cambridge, UK: Cambridge University Press.

——— (1997) "The Realist Paradigm and Degenerative versus Progressive Research Programs," *American Political Science Review* 91 (December): 899–912.

——— and Marie Henehan. (2010) *Territory, War and Peace.* London: Routledge.

Verba, Sidney. (1969) "Assumptions of Rationality and Nonrationality in Models of the International System," pp. 217–31 in James N. Rosenau (ed.), *International Politics and Foreign Policy.* New York: Free Press.

Verwimp, Philip, Patricia Justino, and Tilman Bruck. (2009) "The Analysis of Conflict: A Micro-Level Perspective," *Journal of Peace Research* 46 (3): 307–314.

Victor, David G., M. Granger Morgan, Fay Apt, John Steinbruner, and Katharine Ricke. (2009). "The Geoengineering Option: A Last Resort against Global Warming," *Foreign Affairs* 88 (March/April): 64–76.

Vidal, Gore. (2004). *Imperial America.* New York: Nation Books.

Vietnamnet. (2012) "Rising Salaries, Amending Law to Reduce Strikes," Vietnamnet.com (January 5). Accessed June 20, 2012. Available at: http://english.vietnamnet.vn/en/special-report/20273/raising-salaries--amending-law-to-reduce-strikes.html.

Vital Signs 2006–2007. New York: Norton, for the Worldwatch Institute.

Voeten, Erik. (2004) "Resisting the Lonely Superpower: Responses of States in the United Nations to U.S. Dominance," *Journal of Politics* 66 (August): 729–54.

Vogel, David. (1995) *Trading Up: Consumer and Environment Regulation in a Global Economy.* Cambridge, MA: Harvard University Press.

Von Drehle, David. (2011) "Don't Bet against the United States." *Time* (March 3).

Vreeland, James Raymond. (2003) *The IMF and Economic Development.* Cambridge: Cambridge University Press.

Wagner, R. Harrison. (2007) *War And The State.* Ann Arbor: Pluto Books, University of Michigan Press.

Walker, Richard. (2010) "Hello Country Number 193: Introducing South Sudan," *The Economist: The World in 2011* (November 22): 82.

Walker, Stephen, Akan Malici, and Mark Schafer. (2011) *Rethinking Foreign Policy Analysis: States, Leaders, and the Microfoundations of Behavioral International Relations.* New York: Routledge.

Wall, Timothy. (2013) "The Economics of Declining Birth Rates," *Futurity* (April 30). Accessed June 19, 2013. Available at: http://www.futurity.org/society-culture/the-economics-of-declining-birth-rates/.

Wallace, Brian. (1978) "True Grit South of the Border," *Osceola* (January 13): 15–16.

Wallerstein, Immanuel. (2005) *World-Systems Analysis.* Durham, N.C.: Duke University Press.

———— (2002) "The Eagle Has Crash Landed," *Foreign Policy* (July/August): 60–68.

———— (1988) *The Modern World-System III.* San Diego: Academic Press.

Walsh, Bryan. (2010) "The Spreading Stain." *Time* (June 21): 51–59.

———— (2006) "The Impact of Asia's Giants," *Time* (April 3): 61–62.

Walt, Stephen M. (2009) "Alliances in a Unipolar World," World Politics 61: 86–120.

———— (2005) *Taming American Power.* New York: Norton.

———— (1998) "International Relations: One World, Many Theories," *Foreign Policy* 110 (Spring): 29-32 + 34-46.

Walter, Barbara F. (2004) "Does Conflict Beget Conflict?" *Journal of Peace Research* 41 (May): 371–88.

Wa.ltz, Kenneth N. (2013) "The Origins of War in Neorealist Theory," *Conflict after the Cold War: Arguments on Causes of War and Peace,* 4th edition. Richard K. Betts, ed. Boston, MA: Pearson. pp. 100–106.

———— (2000) "Structural Realism after the Cold War," *International Security* 25 (Summer): 5–41.

———— (1979) *Theory of International Politics.* Reading, MA: Addison-Wesley.

Walzer, Michael. (2004) *Arguing About War.* New Haven, CT: Yale University Press.

WANGO. (2009) "Worldwide NGO Directory." World Association of Non-Governmental Organizations: New York. Accessed June 8, 2009. Available at http://www.wango.org/resources.aspx?section5ngodir.

Ward, Andrew. (2011) "Finnish Poll Turns on Anti-Euro Feeling." Financial Times (16 April). Available at: http://www.ft.com/intl/cms/s/0/aeed63d4-68d6-11e0-9040-00144fe-ab49a.html#axzz1dvjxCoHr.

Warner, Bernard. (2008) "A Muddy Victory for Downloaders," *Times Online* (January 30).

Waterfield, Bruno. (2011) "Britain and EU Increase Aid to Ethiopia While Ignoring Human Rights Warnings," *The Telegraph* (August 4). Available at: http://www.telegraph. co.uk/news/worldnews/africaandindianocean/ethiopia/8681975/Britain-and-EU-increase-aid-to-Ethiopia-while-ignoring-human-rights--warnings.html.

Watson, Douglas. (1997) "Indigenous Peoples and the Global Economy," *Current History* 96 (November): 389–91.

Watson, Fiona. (2013) "Brazil's Treatment of Its Indigenous People Violates Their Rights," *The Guardian* (May 29). Accessed June 3, 2013. Available at: http://www.guardian.co.uk/commentisfree/2013/may/29/brazil-indigenous-people-violates-rights.

Wattenberg, Ben J. (2005) *Fewer: How the Demography of Depopulation Will Shape Our Future.* Chicago: Ivan R. Dee.

WDI. (2013) *World Development Indicators 2013.* Washington, DC: World Bank.

———— (2012) *World Development Indicators 2012.* Washington, DC: World Bank.

———— (2011) *World Development Indicators 2011.* Washington, DC: World Bank.

———— (2010) *World Development Indicators 2010.* Washington, DC: World Bank.

———— (2007) *World Development Indicators 2007.* Washington, DC: World Bank.

Weber, Cynthia. (2005) *International Relations Theory,* 2nd ed. New York: Routledge.

Weidenbaum, Murray. (2009) "Who Will Guard the Guardians? The Social Responsibility of NGOs," *Journal of Business Ethics* 87: 147–55.

———— (2004) "Surveying the Global Marketplace," *USA Today* (January): 26–27.

Weiner, Tim. (2005) "Robot Warriors Becoming Reality," Columbia, S.C., *The State* (February 18): A17.

Weir, Kimberly A. (2007) "The State Sovereignty Battle in Seattle," *International Politics* 44 (September): 596–622.

Weisbrot, Mark. (2005) "The IMF Has Lost Its Influence," *International Herald Tribune* (September 23): 7.

Weiss, Thomas, Richard Jolly, Louis Emmerij. (2009) *UN Ideas That Changed the World*. Bloomington, IN: Indiana University Press.

Weitsman, Patricia A. (2004) *Dangerous Alliances: Proponents of Peace, Weapons of War*. Stanford, CA: Stanford University Press.

Welch, David A. (2005) *Painful Choices: A Theory of Foreign Policy Change*. Princeton, NJ: Princeton University Press.

Wenar, Leif. (2011) "Clean Trade in Natural Resources," *Ethics & International Affairs* 25(1): 27–39.

Wendt, Alexander. (2013) "Anarchy Is What States Make of It," in Richard K. Betts, (ed.) *Conflict after the Cold War: Arguments on Causes of War and Peace*, 4th ed. Boston, MA: Pearson. pp. 214–235.

——— (1999) *Social Theory of International Politics*. Cambridge, UK: Cambridge University Press.

Wesley, Michael. (2005) "Toward a Realist Ethics of Intervention," *Ethics & International Affairs* 19 (No. 2, Special Issue): 55–72.

Western, Jon. (2006) "Doctrinal Divisions: The Politics of U.S. Military Interventions," pp. 87–90 in Glenn P. Hastedt (ed.), *American Foreign Policy*, 12th ed. Dubuque, IA: McGraw-Hill/Dushkin.

Westing, Arthur H. (2013) "Nuclear War: Its Environmental Impact," *SpringerBriefs of Pioneers in Science and Practice*, Vol. 1. pp. 89–113.

Wheaton, Henry. (1846) *Elements of International Law*. Philadelphia: Lea and Blanchard.

Wheelan, Charles. (2003) *Naked Economics: Undressing the Dismal Science*. New York: Norton.

White, Ralph K. (1990) "Why Aggressors Lose," *Political Psychology* 11 (June): 227–42.

WHO (World Health Organization). (2012a) "World Health Organization." Accessed August 8. Available at: http://www.who.int/en.

——— (2012b). *Global Tuberculosis Report 2012*. Accessed June 22, 2013. Available at: http://apps.who.int/iris/bitstream/10665/75938/1/9789241564502_eng.pdf.

WHO Malaria Report. (2012) *World Malaria Report 2012*. Accessed June 22, 2013. Available at: http://www.who.int/malaria/publications/world_malaria_report_2012/en/index.html.

Widmaier, Wesley W. (2007) "Constructing Foreign Policy Crises: Interpretive Leadership in the Cold War and War on Terrorism," *International Studies Quarterly* 51: 779–94.

Wiegand, Krista E. (2011) "Militarized Territorial Disputes: States' Attempts to Transfer Reputation for Resolve," *Journal of Peace Research* 48(1): 101–13.

Wight, Martin. (2002) *Power Politics*. Continuum International Publishing Group.

Wilkenfeld, Jonathan, Kathleen J. Young, David M. Quinn, and Victor Asal. (2005) *Mediating International Crises*. London: Routledge.

Wilkinson, Paul. (2011) *Terrorism versus Democracy: The Liberal State Response*, 3rd ed. New York: Routledge.

Will, George F. (2005) "Aspects of Europe's Mind," *Newsweek* (May 9): 72.

Williams, Glyn, Paula Meth, and Katie Willis (2009) *New Geographies of the Global South: Developing Areas in a Changing World*. Taylor & Francis.

Williams, Laron K. (2013) "Flexible Election Timing and International Conflict," *International Studies Quarterly* (April 30). DOI: 10.1111/isqu.12054

Wills, Garry. (2004) "What Is a Just War?" *New York Review of Books* (November 18): 32–32.

Wilmer, Franke. (2000) "Women, the State and War: Feminist Incursions into World Politics," pp. 385–95 in Richard W Mansbach and Edward Rhodes (eds.), *Global Politics in a Changing World*. Boston: Houghton Mifflin.

Wilson, James Q. (1993) *The Moral Sense*. New York: Free Press.

Wise, Michael Z. (1993) "Reparations," *Atlantic Monthly* 272 (October): 32–35.

Wittkopf, Eugene R., Christopher M. Jones and Charles W Kegley, Jr. (2008) *American Foreign Policy*, 7th ed. Belmont, CA: Thomson Wadsworth.

Wolfe, Tom. (2005) "The Doctrine That Never Died," *New York Times* (January 30): Section 4, 17.

Wolfensohn, James. (2004) "The Growing Threat of Global Poverty," *International Herald Tribune* (April 24–25): 6.

Wolfers, Arnold. (1962) *Discord and Collaboration*. Baltimore: Johns Hopkins University Press.

Wolfsthal, Jon B. (2005) "The Next Nuclear Wave," *Foreign Affairs* 84 (January/February): 156–61.

Wong, Edward. (2005) "Iraq Dances with Iran, While America Seethes," *New York Times* (July 31): Section 4, 3.

Woodard, Colin. (2007) "Who Resolves Arctic Disputes?," *Christian Science Monitor* (August 20): 1, 6.

Woods, Ngaire. (2008) "Whose Aid? Whose Influence? China, Emerging Donors and the Silent Revolution in Development Assistance," *International Affairs* 84: 1205–21.

Woodward, Bob. (2006) *State of Denial*. New York: Simon and Schuster.

——— (2004) *Plan of Attack*. New York: Simon and Schuster.

Woodward, Susan L. (2009) "Shifts in Global Security Policies: Why They Matter for the South," *IDS Bulletin* 40:121–28.

Woodwell, Douglas. (2008) *Nationalism in International Relations*. London: Palgrave Macmillan.

The World Bank. (2013a) "World Bank Launches Initiative on Migration, Releases New Projections on Remittance Flows." Accessed May 29, 2013. Available at: http://www.worldbank.org/en/news/press-release/2013/04/19/world-bank-launches-initiative-on-migration-releases-new-projections-on-remittance-flows.

——— (2013b) *Migration and Remittances Data*. Accessed May 29, 2013. Available at: http://econ.worldbank.org/WBSITE/EXTERNAL/EXTDEC/EXTDECPROSPECTS/0,,contentMDK:22759429~pagePK:64165401~piPK:64165026~theSitePK:476883,00.html#Remittances.

——— (2013c) "Agreements Library." Accessed May 29, 2013. Available at: http://wits.worldbank.org/gptad/library.aspx.

——— (2013d) "India's Massive I.D. Program Exemplifies 'Science of Delivery,'" *World Bank* (May 2). Accessed June 3, 2013. Available at: http://www.worldbank.org/en/news/feature/2013/05/02/India-8217-s-Massive-I-D-Program-Exemplifies-8216-Science-of-Delivery-8217.

——— (2013e) "People: Population Growth and Transition," *World Bank*. Accessed June 19, 2013. Available at: http://www.app.collinsindicate.com/worldbankatlas-global/en-us.

——— (2013f) *Atlas of Global Development*, 4th ed. Washington, DC: World Bank.

——— (2013g) "South Asia's Greenhouse Gas Footprint," The World Bank. Accessed June 25, 2013. Available at: http://web.worldbank.org/WBSITE/EXTERNAL/COUNTRIES/SOUTHASIAEXT/0,,contentMDK:21641942~pagePK:146736~piPK:146830~theSitePK:223547,00.html.

——— (2013h) "Food Prices Decline but Still High and Close to Historical Peaks," World Bank (March 27). Accessed June 25, 2013. Available at: http://www.worldbank.org/en/news/press-release/2013/03/27/food-prices-decline-still-high-close-historical-peaks.

——— (2013i) "Food Crisis," World Bank (April 15). Accessed June 25, 2013. Available at: http://www.worldbank.org/foodcrisis/bankinitiatives.htm.

——— (2013j) *International Debt Statistics*. Washington, DC: World Bank.

——— (2013k) *Capital for the Future: Saving and Investment in an Interdependent*. Washington, DC: The World Bank.

——— (2013l) *World Development Report 2013: Jobs*. Washington, DC: The World Bank.

——— (2013m) "Social Analysis," Accessed November 2, 2013. Available at: http://web.worldbank.org/WBSITE/EXTERNAL/TOPICS/EXTSOCIALDEV/0,,contentMDK:21154393~menuPK:3291389~pagePK:64168445~piPK:64168309~theSitePK:3177395,00.html

——— (2009) *Atlas of Global Development*, 2nd ed. Washington, DC: World Bank.

World Resources Institute (WRI). (2009) "What Is the State of EcoSystems Today?" Available at: http://archive.wri.org/newsroom/-wrifeatures_text.cfm?ContentID5288.

World Trade Organization (WTO). (2013a) "Trade to Remain Subdued in 2013 after Sluggish Growth in 2012 as European Economies Continue to Struggle," WTO (April 10). Accessed July 27, 2013. Available at: http://www.wto.org/english/news_e/pres13_e/pr688_e.htm.

——— (2013b) "Members and Observers," WTO. Accessed July 28, 2013. Available at: http://www.wto.org/english/thewto_e/whatis_e/tif_e/org6_e.htm.

——— (2013c) "Chronological List of Disputes Cases," WTO. Accessed July 27, 2013. Available at: http://www.wto.org/english/tratop_e/dispu_e/dispu_status_e.htm.

——— (2013d) "Lamy: The World Economy Needs More Trade to Stave Off Recession,'" *WTO*. Accessed July 27, 2013. Available at: http://www.wto.org/english/news_e/news12_e/trdev_28nov12_e.htm.

——— (2013e) "Regional Trade Agreements," WTO. Accessed July 27, 2013. Available at: http://www.wto.org/english/tratop_e/region_e/region_e.htm.

——— (2013f) *World Trade Report 2013: Factors Shaping the Future of World Trade*. Geneva, Switzerland: WTO.

——— (2013g) "Panel Established on Measures Imposed by China on Certain Steel from Japan," WTO (May 24). Accessed July 27, 2013. Available at: http://www.wto.org/english/news_e/news13_e/dsb_24may13_e.htm.

——— (2012a) "Trade Growth to Slow in 2012 after Strong Deceleration in 2011," WTO (April 12). Accessed June 25, 2012. Available at: http://www.wto.org/english/news_e/pres12_e/pr658_e.htm.

——— (2012b) "Statistics Database." Accessed June 22, 2012. Available at: http://stat.wto.org/Home/ WSDBHome.aspx?Language=.

——— (2011) "Briefing Notes: Rules." Available at: http://www.wto.org/english/tratop_e/dda_e/status_e/rules_e.htm.

——— (2010b) *World Trade Report 2010: Trade in Natural Resources*. Geneva: World Trade Organization.

Worldwatch Institute. (2013a) "Food and Agriculture," *Worldwatch Insitute*. Accessed July 4, 2013. Available at: http://www.worldwatch.org/food-agriculture.

——— (2013b) *State of the World 2013: Is Sustainability Still Possible?* New York: Norton.

Wright, Quincy. (1953) "The Outlawry of War and the Law of War," *American Journal of International Law* 47 (July): 365–76.

——— (1942) *A Study of War*. Chicago: University of Chicago Press.

Wroughton, Lesley. (2013a) "Global Finance Officials Endorse World Bank Target to End Poverty," *Reuters* (April 21). Accessed June 3, 2013. Available at: http://www.reuters.com/article/2013/04/21/us-worldbank-idUSBRE93K00E20130421.

——— (2013b) "Global Finance Leaders to Discuss IMF Voting Power Reforms," *Reuters* (April 17). Accessed June 27, 2013. Available at: http://www.reuters.com/article/2013/04/18/us-imf-voting-idUSBRE93H04520130418.

Xinhuanet.org. (2013) "Coca-Cola to Invest Further in China," *Xinhua News Online*. Accessed July 27, 2013. Available at: http://news.xinhuanet.com/english/china/2013-05/09/c_132371245.htm.

Yang, David W. (2005) "In Search of an Effective Democratic Realism," *SAIS Review* 15 (Winter/Spring): 199–205.

Yellin, Jessica and Tom Cohen. (2013) "Obama, Netanyahu Agree of Preventing Nuclear-Armed Iran," *CNN*. Accessed May 6, 2013. Available at: http://www.cnn.com/2013/03/20/politics/israel-obama-visit.

Yergin, Daniel. (2009) "It's Still the One" *Foreign Policy* September/October, pp. 88–95.

——— (2006) "Thirty Years of Petro-Politics," pp. 106–7 in Robert M. Jackson (ed.), *Global Issues 05/06*. Dubuque, IA: McGraw-Hill/Dushkin.

——— (2005) "An Oil Shortage?" Columbia, S.C., *The State* (August 2): A9.

Yetiv, Steve. (2011) "History, International Relations, and Integrated Approaches: Thinking about Greater Interdisciplinarity," *International Studies Perspectives* 12, no. 2 (May): 94–118.

Youde, Jeremy. (2005) "Enter the Fourth Horseman: Health Security and International Relations Theory," *The Whitehead Journal of Diplomacy and International Affairs* 6 (Winter/Spring): 193–208.

Zagare, Frank C. (2004) "Reconciling Rationality with Deterrence," *Journal of Theoretical Politics* 16 (April): 107–41.

——— (1990) "Rationality and Deterrence," *World Politics* 42 (January): 238–60.

Zakaria, Fareed. (2009) *The Post-American World*. New York: W.W.Norton.

Zartner, Dana. (2010) "The Rise of Transnational Crime: International Cooperation, State Contributions, and the Role of the Global Political Economy." *International Studies Review* 12 (2): 316–19.

Zelikow, Philip. (2006) "The Transformation of National Security," pp. 121–27 in Robert M. Jackson (ed.), *Global Issues 05/06*. Dubuque, IA: McGraw-Hill/Dushkin.

Zeigler, Sean, Jan H. Pierskalla, and Sandeep Masumder. (2013) "War and the Reelection Motive: Examining the Effects of Term Limits," *Journal of Conflict Resolution* (March 13). 10.1177/0022002713478561.

Zenko, Micah. (2013a) "To Protect and Defend …" *Foreign Policy* (June 11). Accessed June 17, 2013. Available at: http://www.foreignpolicy.com/articles/2013/06/11/to_protect_and_defend_obama_constitution?wp_login_redirect=0.

——— (2013b) "How Does the Recent Shift in U.S. Drone Policy Impact 'Signature Strikes'? *Council on Foreign Relations* (June 11). Accessed June 17, 2013. Available at: http://www.cfr.org/united-states/does-recent-shift-us-drone-policy-impact-signature-strikes/p30885.

Ziegler, Charles. (2012) "Conceptualizing Sovereignty in Russian Foreign Policy: Realist and Constructivist Perspectives." International Politics 49: 400–17.

Zoellick, Robert B. (2012) "Why We Still Need the World Bank: Looking Beyond Aid," *Foreign Affairs* 91 (2): 66–78.

Zurayk, Rami. (2011) *Food, Farming, and Freedom: Sowing the Arab Spring*. Charlottesville, VA: Just World Books.

NAME INDEX

SUBJECT INDEX

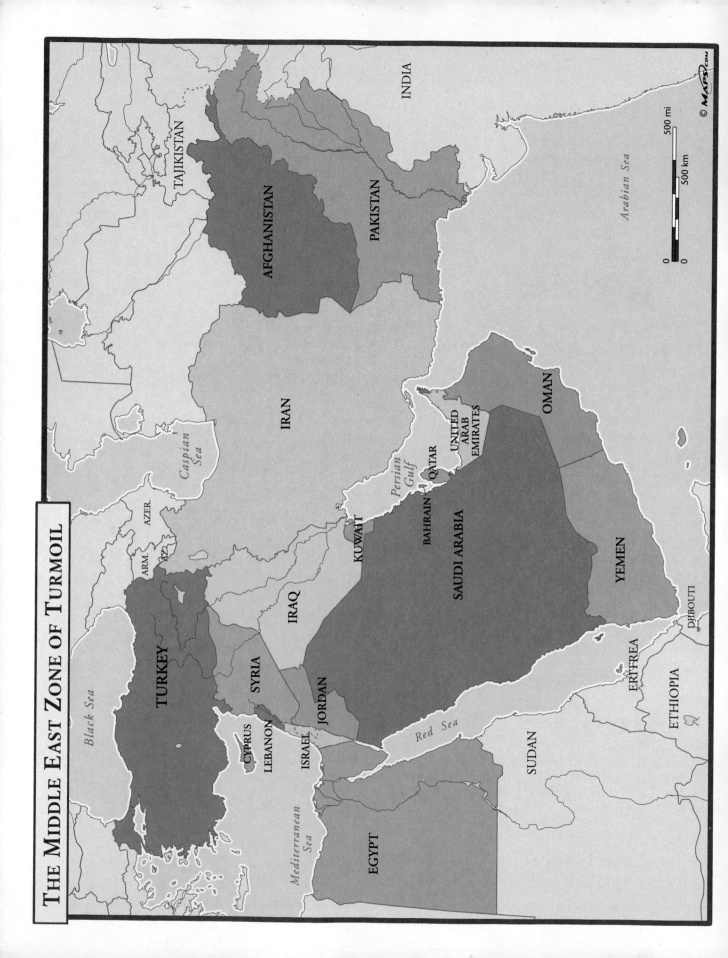

THE MIDDLE EAST ZONE OF TURMOIL